AGAINST

the

GRAIN

Heroic Catholics Through the Centuries

Doug Grane

Preface by
+ Archbishop Carlo Maria Viganò

Against the Grain

Heroic Catholics Through the Centuries

Unless otherwise noted, Scriptural quotations are from the Douay-Rheims Bible.

Cover image: *Presentazione di Gesù al Tempio* (The Presentation of Jesus in the Temple), by Fra Beato Angelico (1450), National Museum of San Marco, Florence.

DEFIANCE PRESS
& PUBLISHING

ISBN-13: 978-1-7372522-9-0 Paperback
ISBN-13: 978-1-955937-01-6 eBook

Published by Defiance Press and Publishing, LLC

Bulk orders of this book may be obtained by contacting Defiance Press and Publishing, LLC.

www.defiancepress.com

Defiance Press & Publishing, LLC
281-581-9300
info@defiancepress.com

Praise for
Against the Grain:
Heroic Catholics Through the Centuries

"God has created men according to His image and likeness. The sin of Adam and Eve and our individual sins have damaged this image and likeness. Jesus Christ, the Incarnated God and Savior of mankind, restored the beauty of that image and only through Him, in Him and with Him man can achieve the likeness of God, which means holiness. The only sure way to heaven is the way of holiness, that means the imitation of the life and the virtues of Christ. Every Christian has the most noble vocation to be like Christ. The imitation of Christ contains necessarily the love for the cross of Christ. God is marvelous in His Saints. The Saints demonstrate to us that holiness is possible in every age, in every circumstance, in every state of life. Even many great sinners became true Saints. This gives hope for everyone.
Doug Grane presents in his masterful work amazing examples of Saints from all periods of time with their main characteristic of a joyful fearlessness and unshakeable trust in God in midst of difficulties and persecutions. May this book be a help to awaken in our time new examples of Saints, whom the Church of our day so urgently needs for her authentic renewal.
I strongly recommend this excellent book. The Catholic Church and our world needs more heroic virtue, it needs more courageous souls, it needs saints!"
+ Athanasius Schneider, Auxiliary Bishop of the archdiocese of Saint Mary in Astana.

"It is said that each of us is the combination of the five people we spend the most time with. Doug Grane, in *Against the Grain,* asks each of us whether we spend time with God's saints? If we want to be a saint, we must learn from them, emulate them, and befriend them! His book offers powerful insights into their lives and virtues that allows us to do just that."
+ Bishop Thomas J. Paprocki

"Dear Family, no matter what storms rage against us, be saints. Stand for the truth. Especially when they call you "divisive and ineffective." At that point double down, be signs of contradiction, go against the grain, and live lives of heroic virtue. Doug Grane's *Against the Grain* is an excellent read - and highly recommended."
- Fr. James Altman

"Many individuals remember records which boasted "Mozart's greatest hits" or "Beethoven's greatest hits," each record just giving a hint of the composers works. Mr. Doug Grane's book *Against the Grain* is a masterful work touching upon some of our Church's greatest "hits" viz, "Our Saints." Selected well known Saints lives of virtue, are presented in a unique way, making them accessible to young and old in a spirit which the world finds threatening. The Saints chosen did go *Against the Grain* while leading so many individuals to heroic lives of virtue. I trust you will find this volume a treasure trove of spiritual insight assisting you, by inspirational writing, to lead a life of greater virtue and dedication to following Christ by "going against today's grain."

- Rev. C. Frank Phillips, C.R.

"Catholics and Orthodox have a relationship with the saints which strikes many non-Catholics as somewhere between idolatrous and extraneous. Why not just honor God? Why all the extra to-do about saints? This book written by Doug Grane gives the basic reason God makes a fuss about saints. To love Him is to love those He loves. To praise them is to praise their God. It's not a zero sum game. Jesus Christ came to make sinners - saints. When an artist works that hard, it's hardly polite to ignore his masterpiece. This book will introduce you to God's masterpieces- God's dream team... Psalm 148:14 (RSV) "...praise for all his saints..." God Love you.

- Jesse Romero - Catholic Lay Evangelist and Radio Host, author of numerous books including, *"The Devil in the City of Angels," "Catholics, Wake Up!" and "Lord, Prepare my Hands for Battle."*

"*Against the Grain* by Doug Grane is not your typical *Lives of the Saints*; neither is it your typical Church history, nor even your typical devotional book. But it does manage in a uniquely fascinating way to combine the best features of all three types of books and gel into one monumental read. What *Against the Grain* does best is situate some of the most unique and powerful (and sometimes little-known) saints in their historical context. And then with a disarming breeziness, bring the text to the present to make contemporary cultural and spiritual applications for the reader. It is a thoroughly enjoyable and engrossing book. The reader will profit well."

- Rev. Anthony J. Brankin

"Not since G.K. Chesterton's *St. Francis of Assisi* and *St. Thomas Aquinas* has a Catholic provided such inspiring insight into the lives of the great, holy heroes of the Catholic Church's history. From an inspiring analysis of Saint Martha and her true friendship with Our Lord to the little known story of Saint Carlo Acutis, Grane gives the tradition minded Catholic a quest: are we humble enough to truly learn the lives of the Saints and attempt to become saintly as a result?; and the ho-hum Catholic a challenge: why have you ignored, indeed avoided the magnificent gift that Christ, through the lives of the Saints have left us and thus the chance to follow them as His friend!? Part hagiography. Part challenge to action. *Against The Grain* is a book I dare Catholics to read."

> *- Mike Church, a.k.a. "The King Dude," is an Author and Host of The Mike Church Show on the Crusade Channel, a Veritas Radio Network Station.*

"Christ calls each of us to perfection (cf. Mt. 5:48), to holiness (cf. 1 Pet. 1:16; Lev. 11:44), which we can attain through the practice of the virtues. But how to practice the virtues poses a challenge. Here we can look to the Saints: their lives of ardent charity, steadfast fortitude, and profound humility provide us with inspiration and offer us models to imitate. In each chapter of *Against the Grain*, Doug Grane offers the reader a concrete vision of Christian perfection, of holiness, through the lens of a particular virtue embodied in the life of a Saint in every century from the first to the present. To this he adds numerous quotes on each virtue from a variety of Saints, insightful commentary on our present cultural crisis, along with sound advice and a firm exhortation ("Virtue Challenge") for the reader himself to practice the virtue exemplified by the saint in that chapter. This book makes for a great read for both young and old."

> **- Fr. Dwight Campbell**

"Doug Grane is the kind of Catholic layman we need nowadays, but have in fact far too few of. He has fought for integrity in Catholic education, the sanctity of marriage, and the safety of unborn children. Now he contributes this book as a guidepost for the perplexed in a time when theological authorities are pumping out lavender smoke, acclaiming globalist idols, and suppressing traditional liturgies. I highly recommend this book for Catholics seeking solid fare, genuine uplift, and sound moral encouragement."

> **- John Zmirak, Senior Editor of *The Stream*, and author of numerous books including *The* Politically Incorrect Guide to Catholicism.**

"You will really enjoy Douglas Grane's book *Against the Grain,* which encompasses solid spiritual food for those seeking to grow more deeply in love with Christ. For those who do not know or understand our Catholic Faith, this is a wonderful book to delve into as a history lesson from the early church describing those saints and heroes who to this day, continue to give us courage, strength, and hope. The saints written of in Mr. Grane's book lead us, through their example, to the witness of both the 'red and white martyrdom' which is a beautiful pathway to eternal life. Isn't that what it is all really about? Enjoy and strengthen your armamentarium as you read *Against the Grain.* For, I believe, the battle is there ahead of us. To all those faith-filled Catholics and other Christians who serve Christ, and not the world, enjoy!"

- Sr. Deirdre "Dede" Byrne, POSC. (Sister, Surgeon and Soldier, who commented during her 2020 Republican National Convention speech, "I'm not just pro-life, I'm pro-eternal life.")

"In every chapter of history, you'll find crowds rushing to do whatever it takes to fit in -- even if it means being casually cruel to innocent people or abandoning vulnerable neighbors in their hour of need. In *Against the Grain,* Doug Grane introduces us to the ones who found a way out of that: The Saints. They're the ones who didn't lose focus, who didn't allow themselves to be deformed by the evils of their times, and who in the end left us with all the lessons we need to follow in their footsteps in our own historical moment. No Catholic should feel lost. Buy this book and start getting to know the role models who got it right."

- Jason Jones, Pro-life Filmmaker/Producer, Host of "The Jason Jones Show" podcast, and author of numerous books including, *"The Race to Save our Century."*

"If the world hates you, realize that it hated me first. If you belonged to the world, the world would love its own; but because you do not belong to the world, and I have chosen you out of the world, the world hates you."
~ Jesus (John 15:18-19)

"Fight, Children of Light, you the few who can see."
~ Our Lady of La Salette

"Think well. Speak well. Do well. These three things, through the mercy of God, will make a man go to Heaven."
~ Saint Camillus

"Only God knows the good that can come about by reading one good Catholic book."
~ Saint John Bosco

"I must be a saint, and a very great one."
~ Saint Maximillian Kolbe

DEDICATION

For my children.

"Do great. Have fun. Be Catholic."
~ Dad

Nathan, Gabi, Charlie and Alex Grane, circa 2012

Also to:
The Immaculate Conception,
Queen of All Saints, our Leader and Co-Redemptrix
who wants to see us fight and implore her victory.

And
Saint Joseph, protector of the Holy Family
Saint Michael the Archangel, Saint Joan of Arc
All the heroic, warrior Angels and Saints
All our heroic, faithful priests

Fighting alongside:
The Mystical Body of Christ

In solidarity with the commissioned officers of:
The Church Militant (the living faithful here on Earth)

In expiation of the temporal punishment of:
The Church Suffering (the holy souls of Purgatory)

In the hopes of uniting one day with:
The Church Triumphant (the angels and saints in heaven)

In Memoriam

John Moorehouse
(1969-2020)

Catholic, Husband, Father
Patriot, Writer, Editor

The genesis of this book originates in the summer of 2020 when Dr. Paul Kengor referred me to John Moorehouse. My friendship with Paul goes back three decades to graduate school at the School of International Service at the American University in Washington, D.C. I mentioned to Paul my interest in writing a book and asked him to recommend an editor. He knew of only one suitable candidate: John Moorehouse.

John and I first spoke on July 7, 2020. From that initial conversation, I could tell John and I would get along great. He possessed an incisive mind and a personality that was calming and supportive. As you'd expect in a great editor, John had an exceptional ability to cut through the clutter so as to identify what was most important. While John was employed full time with TAN books, he offered to assist me with editorial advice, writing, and research on a part-time basis. He was not looking to receive credit, but since his passing I thought it would be proper to acknowledge John's significant contribution as a writer on this book, having produced a first draft for ten of the twenty-one chapters.

From the outset, John counseled that we write the majority of the book before presenting a draft to TAN or other publishers for consideration. In addition to those options, John also raised the possibility of self-publishing. Looking only to serve God and follow John's guidance, I was good with wherever the project went. On August 1, 2020, we officially set sail for open waters writing a book about heroic Catholic saints who went against the grain.

Perhaps John's biggest conceptual contribution to the book came early. As the life and heroic virtue of the saint was being described, John thought the take away would be greatly enhanced if the reader could be encouraged to ask, "Why not me?" From that point forward this literary technique would be infused into each chapter.

My last conversation with John was during his noon lunch break on Dec. 3. We talked for forty-five minutes about where the project stood. Our goal when we set out was to write a chapter a week and have a first draft completed by year's end. As of that call we had collaborated on ten saints and the Introduction. Talking about our collaborative style, I mentioned to John that we were like NFL announcers where he was the "play-by-play" guy and I was the "color" guy. John laughed and said, "I never thought of it that way, but you're right." The last three chapters queued up for John to review were Urban, Lidwina, and Damien. I was expecting to hear back from him that weekend on Urban, but never did.

On the evening of Tuesday, Dec. 8, the feast day of Our Lady's Immaculate Conception, I read a blog post from Dr. Robert Moynihan, Letter #42, "Farewell to a Father." John was editor for Moynihan's recent book, *Finding Viganò*. I was shocked and saddened to read that John passed away suddenly from a heart attack on Saturday night, Dec. 5. My thoughts immediately were for John's soul, for Robin, and their children. I said many prayers for John and his family that night, and for many days thereafter. A Tridentine Requiem Mass was celebrated for John at my parish, St. John Cantius in Chicago.

A couple weeks after his passing I spoke with John's wife, Robin. I asked her permission to include an *"In Memoriam"* page for John along with a photo of him and his family. She graciously agreed. Robin told me one of John's sayings that he applied to writing and editing: "Don't let good become the enemy of good enough." Great advice. One can write and edit without end looking to produce the perfect book. We agreed that if the book had a positive impact on just one soul, it would all be worth the effort. To us, the quality of the book depended in part on how it accorded to the will of God. With John's passing, I hope and pray that his memory is sufficiently honored in these pages.

I am grateful to have known and collaborated with this good man. I will remember John's encouraging nature, his keen intellect, and his joyful soul all my days. He was my conceptual Sherpa and collaborator. His influence will be found on every page. I wish I had the opportunity to complete the book with him, but God, the author of all life, had other plans.

Pictured above is the Moorehouse family.
John is back right, next to his wife, Robin.

My thoughts now turn towards the Moorehouse family. To unexpectedly lose a husband and father is one of life's most difficult tragedies. My heart and prayers continue for the Moorehouse family.

Requiescat in Pace.

Table of Contents

PREFACE

by:

His Excellency
Archbishop Carlo Maria Viganò

This is a book about friendship: the friendship of the Saints with God, the friendship of the Saints with each other, and with us. A friendship based on charity, which is the theological virtue that leads us to love God and our neighbor for love of Him. On the basis of this virtue rooted in the virtue of Faith because it has as its object God himself who "is charity" (1 Jn 4, 8) and Truth (Jn 14, 6), all the baptized are united in a supernatural bond that finds in the Most Holy Trinity its origin, its strength and its goal. For this reason, separating Charity from Faith is a hellish and essentially anti-Trinitarian work.

The Saints that are mentioned in this book, and all the Saints in general, constitute an exemplary model of how we must be, following the commandment of Our Lord: "*Estote ergo vos perfecti, sicut et Pater vester caelestis perfectus est*" [Therefore, be ye perfect, as your Father in heaven is perfect] (Mt 5, 48). Our "having to be" Saints, fighting the evil inclination that we carry within us as a consequence of original sin, and trying to be docile to divine Grace, cannot be considered just a precept, but rather a necessity, a coherent response to our having been redeemed by the sacrifice of Christ, as a consequence of that love he showed for us by sacrificing himself on the Cross. If human love is that natural instinct that moves us towards the good which is divine love, namely, Charity; our soul is led supernaturally towards the Supreme Good which is God, and consequently we are also led towards the saints who participate with us in that attraction towards Him.

We can understand that even human friendship, with the benefit of hindsight, binds us to someone whose talents we admire, and who we think can help us improve, while we are encouraged, in our turn, to behave well in order to be an example to them. If this friendship is established between us and the Saints whom the Church indicates to us as a model to follow, to the point that the New Testament calls the baptized "saints" (Eph 1: 1), we find the perfection to which we are called is fulfilled in them, we draw comfort from them precisely because we feel an affinity for the way they lived, the profession they had, their daily sufferings, their struggle against the world, the flesh and the devil. Prophets, Apostles, Martyrs, Confessors of the Faith, Virgins and Widows are united in showing us how, ultimately, despite our weaknesses, that it is the Lord who makes us saints, and who takes pleasure in pouring out His gifts upon us and making the talents He gives bear fruit. It is for us that the Blessed Virgin sings in the Magnificat: *"Quia fecit mihi magna qui potens est"* [For the Almighty has done great things for me].

We too, even though we are poor sinners, are called to great things: we must not think that the heroism of the virtues that have led our brothers and sisters in the Faith to be celebrated with public honors by Holy Church is the prerogative of just a few, a privilege to which we may not aspire, or even worse, a condition to be deplored because it is no longer in keeping with the mentality of our time. Because it was precisely in having lived for future glory that the saints were able to heroically live in this *vale of tears*; it was their desire to gain the crown that enabled them to try their hand at the race, and to win it. A struggle, or competition, a *"certamen"*, as the Apostle calls it: *"Bonum certamen certavi, cursum consummavi"* [I have run the race, I have completed the course (2Tim 4, 7), such a race is to be undertaken as athletes of Christ who are intent on reaching the finishing line. It is a race against the world, against the flesh, and against the devil: in fact, it is a race in which we literally have to go "against the grain". Against all that since the fall of Adam tempts us to distance ourselves from the destiny to which we have been called, and which we cannot escape unless we want to nullify the redemptive Passion of Our Lord, and be unworthy of joining the company of blessed in heaven.

In this book, Doug Grane chose Saints who are dear to him, drawing from each an example of a particular virtue. We know about the life of the Saints in order to imitate them, knowing that even if we ourselves are not worthy to be raised to the glory of the altars, at least we can have hope, which is a theological virtue, that the Lord will assist us by His Grace in seeing us as He wants us to be: *"ut essemus sancti et immaculati in conspectu ejus in caritate "* [that we might be holy and spotless in charity in his sight] (Eph 1: 4). The first, indispensable virtue of the Saints, and therefore also of those who want to emulate them, is humility: "*deposuit potentes de Sede, et exaltavit humiles*" [He has cast down the mighty from their thrones, and exalted the lowly] (Lk 1, 52).

In this his time of great crisis for the Church, and for the whole of humanity, in which we see the gates of the underworld unleashed for the establishment of the kingdom of the Antichrist, we must see an even greater urgency in the call to holiness, which begins with the life of grace through prayer, the frequent reception of the Sacraments, and the faithful and courageous keeping of the *depositum fidei* [the deposit of the faith], which is today threatened by the very leaders of the Hierarchy. We invoke the Blessed Virgin Mary as *Regina Sanctorum omnium* [Queen of all saints], to make us worthy of the promises of Christ and, under the protection of Her mantle, to accompany us in this earthly pilgrimage to our heavenly home, so that we may meet, in blessed eternity, our friends who intercede for us before the throne of the Lamb.

+Carlo Maria Viganò, *Archbishop.*

28 May 2021

Feria Sexta Quattuor Temporum Pentecostes
(Ember Friday in the Octave of Pentecost)

Introduction

"A Saint is a sinner that keeps trying."
~ Saint Josemaría Escrivá

What is a saint? Derived from the Latin word *sanctus*, meaning "holy," a saint imitates Jesus as best he or she can. A saint evidences heroic suffering, heroic obedience and heroic love. A saint commits his or her life to God in a way that others do not. To be a saint is to detest evil. Conversely, to not detest evil is unsaintly. A saint displays heroic virtue in doing God's will, and is bound toward heaven. In short, a saint is a hero. All are called but few accept. To state this another way, few choose to be a saint. People hold back for many reasons. Some think that by giving all to God they will "miss out" on some other part of life that may, or may not, lead them to heaven. Saints, instead, choose to take that leap of faith, and commit.

What's holding you back from being a saint?

I love the saints. My birthday is May 30, the feast day of the martyred Pope Felix I (274), the brave, wise King Fernando III (1252) and the amazing, courageous Saint Joan of Arc (1431). May 30, 1548 is also the day Saint Juan Diego died (although his feast day was moved to Dec. 9—closer to Dec. 12 and the feast day of Our Lady of Guadalupe). A pope martyr, a crusading king, a warrior general, and humble servant to our Lady, all inspire me greatly.

One of my earliest childhood memories is of my mom driving her Oldsmobile down a tree-lined street, sunlight pouring into the back seat, teaching me the Catholic Faith. The car was big and blue and often had fast food wrappers strewn about the floor. Appropriately, the car was dubbed "The Flying Hamburger." Nothing compared to speeding around town talking about God, His love for us, why Jesus was born, Blessed Mother, the angels and the saints. Hamburgers and heaven—you had me at hello!

In my young mind the Catholic Faith was fascinating. Everything about it made so much sense. Until that day when Mom brought up the rebellion in heaven. Satan vs. God. Evil vs. good. For those old enough to get the reference, cue big record scratch sound here!

If heaven was so great, ordered so perfectly, why would Lucifer—the angel of light, i.e., the smartest angel—rebel against God? What was he thinking?

I was told Lucifer's *Non Serviam!* (I will not serve!) was due to his being bedeviled by one word—pride. In his pride, Satan would not give God that which He was due, i.e., worship. Satan, thus, was damned for his supreme sin of omission. *Non Serviam!* could be the two most consequential words ever uttered in history. Talk about a game changer. How could pride, or anything else, motivate anyone to not serve God? It made no sense. To forsake being close to God for all eternity, enjoying His beatific vision, existing in perfect harmony with the other angels, all because of something called pride? How stupid!

Yet, despite knowing all about good and evil, sin and grace, we sin thanks to the pride of our first parents and the original sin we inherited from them. Saint Augustine has written, "There never can have been, and never can be, and there never shall be any sin without pride." We have moments where we too tell God, *"Non Serviam!"* How stupid. How sad. How reckless. How human. My Jesus, have mercy. Saints of heaven, pray for us.

Shortly after learning of the rebellion in heaven, I was introduced to an equally intriguing drama: when Saint Michael the Archangel drove Lucifer into the abyss—the most epic and consequential battle ever fought. Whoa! Who was this Saint Michael? Tell me more! So began my introduction to, fascination with, and utmost respect for, Saint Michael the Archangel—a veritable hero's hero. Saint Michael's primary role is to serve God by working on missions fighting evil, proclaiming God's truth, and strengthening the faith of the people. Although Saint Michael is called a saint, he is truly an angel. Saint Michael is the leader of God's army, and is above all the holy angels and seven archangels including Gabriel, Raphael, and Uriel. The name Michael means, "Who is like God."

Saint Michael's *Serviam!* (I will serve!), against Lucifer's *Non Serviam!* (I will not serve!)

Either we fight *for* God, or we fight *against* God.

Christ or chaos. Life is just that simple.

Would you be surprised to learn that I chose Saint Michael the Archangel as my Confirmation Saint? Nah, didn't think so.

At my parish, St. John Cantius in Chicago, as you walk across the threshold into the sacred space, you will find a floor medallion in Latin that reads, *"Hinc Humilibus Venia, Hinc Retribuito Superbis,"* which means, "Here forgiveness for the humble, Here retribution for the proud." The inscription is taken from statues of Saint Peter holding the keys to heaven, and Saint Paul holding the sword, on the bridge of the angels (Ponte Sant'Angelo), in front of the Castel Sant'Angel, in Rome. During times of pilgrimage, one would cross via the bridge from profane Rome to sacred Rome. Pope Gregory the Great is said to have had a vision of Saint Michael the Archangel appearing over the Castel on April 25, 590 A.D. returning his sword to its sheath to signify the end of the plague that was at that time ravaging Rome. A huge, impressive, bronze statue of Saint Michael the Archangel would be added atop the Castel in the mid-1700s.

I've walked over the Ponte Sant'Angelo many times and I, along with many other pilgrims, consider it to be one of the most beautiful bridges in the world. First constructed in 134 A.D. by Emperor Hadrian, the bridge connects the left bank of the Tiber with his mausoleum (also known today as the Castel Sant'Angel). Bernini's ten resplendent, angel statues, placed on the bridge in 1670, each holding an instrument of the Passion of Christ, are presented to pilgrims approaching St. Peter's via the ancient jubilar road. The travertine marble, arches, statues, symbolism, and symmetry somehow combine to speak loudly to my soul.

Ponte Sant'Angelo over the Tiber, and Basilica San Pietro, Sunrise. Vatican City
https://www.terragalleria.com/europe/italy/vatican/picture.ital7377.html

What I like best about the Sant'Angelo bridge is the hard-to-describe sense of humility, optimism, and resolve I have while on it. It's a welcome feeling however one might describe it. It's great to see St. Peter's Basilica in the distance, too, but I'm certain that what adds most to this experience for me is the massive statue of Saint Michael the Archangel on Castel Sant'Angel looking out over the bridge. What is the angelic general saying to us?

How does Saint Michael the Archangel's *Serviam* inspire us to be better Catholics? How can we join in his fight against evil, proclaim God's truth, and strengthen the faith of the people? What metaphorical bridges will we cross to serve Christ? How will we advance from the mere profane to the profoundly sacred? Will we do so in humility or pride?

Fast forward to today. As obvious as the choice is between choosing pride and sin over humility and grace, we humans, stained with original sin, sometimes weak in virtue, often make the same mistakes over and over. God does not force us to love and serve Him. Instead, He has given us free will. Fr. John Bartunek, in *The Better Part,* instructs us, "God's omnipotence and omniscience *respects our freedom.*"[1] "And above all, be on your guard not to want to get anything done by force," Saint Angela Merici adds, "because God has given free will to everyone and wants to force no one, but only proposes, invites and counsels."

And with that latitude sometimes we choose to neglect His grace and sin—often venial, sometimes mortal. Some by commission. Some by omission. American author Robert Jordan in *The Great Hunt* describes free will in the following way: "Some men ... choose to seek greatness, while others are forced to it. It is always better to choose than to be forced. A man who is forced is never completely his own master. He must dance on the strings of those who forced him."[2] God never forces. He only invites.

While God gives us free will and the opportunity to choose to love Him, Satan—the name means 'adversary'—lies to us, deceives us, and tempts us. He encourages us to tell God *Non Serviam* just as he did long ago. "My will be done," we tell God, "not yours." At times we are

---

[1] Bartunek, "The Better Part," 591.
[2] Jordan, "The Great Hunt," n.p.

selfish, weak, and, yes, prideful. Satan, who is *princeps huius mundi* (prince of this world), prowls about tempting us to dance on the strings of sin, turn our back to God, and spend eternity with him in perpetual misery and everlasting fire. Talk about the ultimate misery-loves-company scenario.

Archbishop Viganò maintains that the strategy of Baphomet and the children of darkness is "*Solve et Coagula*" (dissolve and coagulate). Scatter and reconvene. Destroy and rebuild. Tear apart existing structures and bring together with secular humanist institutions. Viganò goes on to state, "The strategy and tactics can be deployed to take down an organization, a county (the deep state, globalism, environmentalism, terrorism, pandemics, riots, class warfare, racist warfare, etc.), and even the church (the deep church)."[3] The multi-pronged/tiered deception is infernal—straight from the pit of hell.

Saint Catherine of Siena, another favorite saint of mine, wrote, "I saw the torments of hell and those of purgatory; no words can describe them. Had poor mortals the faintest idea of them, they would suffer a thousand deaths rather than undergo the least of the torments during a single day."

Sometimes we fool ourselves by thinking God would not allow anything bad to happen to us at our final judgment. Many have heard clergy tell us that all men have a "reasonable hope of being saved."[4] Talk about a presumptuous, nasty snare. Instead, we ought to draw upon our healthy fear of the Lord, based on our sincere love of God, and "work out our salvation in fear and trembling." Life was never meant to be easy. Each day we must put on our big boy pants and fight for our salvation!

Each day we have a choice. Do we accept in gratitude all that God has providentially put before us? Or do we rebel with pride against God? Are we on God's team or not? Original sin, alas, does complicate matters. None of us is perfect. Our inclinations, and actions, are not always oriented towards the true, the transcendent. Sometimes we do not conduct ourselves in ways we know we should. We fall. When you fall, hasten to rise again. With effort, and with God's grace, you will get back up. Keep your eyes on the goal—meriting

---

[3] Viganò, "Letter to Trump," June 7, 2020.
[4] Bishop Barron, Word on Fire. https://www.wordonfire.org/hope/

heaven and being with God and the good angels and holy saints for all eternity.

So how do we go about living a life that merits heaven? What's our playbook? Our roadmap? When we plan a week's vacation, we make lots of plans in advance. When we think about our eternal destination, how carefully, diligently, and painstakingly have we made the requisite plans? Saint Vincent de Paul said, "Our business is to attain heaven; everything else is a sheer waste of time." Do we devote sufficient time to the business of attaining heaven? Besides following the way, the truth and the light (i.e., following and imitating Jesus), being Catholic, receiving the Sacraments, and living in a state of grace, where do we look for examples and inspiration to help us obtain heaven?

The saints!

The saints transcend time. The saints changed the course of world history. While on this Earth many of the saints suffered hardship, humiliation, defamation, and some even betrayal because they remained true to God and not man. Some were imprisoned, tortured, and even martyred in painful ways. Others were "dry" martyrs who were attacked in less bloody ways. These saints forgave their enemies. Do we? Suffering hardship has been a part of Catholicism from the beginning. The teachings and example of the saints still speak to us today.

Most who read this book will be familiar with the best-known saints whose examples of holiness and virtue are heroic in magnitude and confirmed by numerous miracles. Names like Saint Joseph, Saint John the Baptist, Saint Peter, Saint Patrick, Saint Francis of Assisi, Saint Thomas Aquinas, Saint Catherine of Sienna, Saint Joan of Arc, Saint Ignatius of Loyola, Saint Thérèse of Lisieux, and Saint Padre Pio. Given how holy they were, and how well they served God, many books have been written about them.

While the more celebrated saints certainly had stories that inspire us to be better Catholics, some eminent saints had qualities that most of us cannot relate to: being the foster father of Jesus, being the first pope, bearing the stigmata, writing the *Summa Theologica*, experiencing ecstasy, advising popes, bilocation, discernment of spirits and reading souls, and hierognosis (the ability to discern holy things from those which are not holy) as with Blessed Anne Catherine Emmerich. To further glorify God, if their lives and deeds weren't enough, some saints have been found to be incorrupt—i.e. not decomposed—upon exhumation many years after their death. All incredible. *Deo gratias* (Thanks be to God).

What about the thousands of other saints who are not well known? How did they live lives of heroic virtue in their times? How can their examples help us to live holier lives in our day? The playbook is there. We need to take another, closer look. Perhaps examining another of their attributes, or virtues, will speak to us—something that beckons us, or reminds us that no matter our state of life, we can live saintly lives. As Catholics, we believe that if these heroically virtuous people were able to live lives that merited heaven, we can too. Hence, we should ask ourselves: "A saint, why not me?"

The United States of America is a relatively young nation with cultural roots going back only a few centuries. Unlike national history, an American Catholic has theological "DNA" that goes back 2,000 years, and beyond. Our past informs to whom we are drawn. As Catholics, we are drawn to Christ and His Saints. Fr. James Altman has written, "That is the beauty of being Catholic. We have 2,000 years of the Bible, 2,000 years of Saints and Martyrs, 2,000 years of the constant teaching of the Catholic Church, 2,000 years of the unchanged and unchangeable Truth."[5] A Catholic walking around today is literally standing on the shoulders of giants with millennia of accumulated heroic faithfulness. Recalling our history gives us confidence in the present and hope in the future.

Yet, Catholics have always been underdogs and always will be. Globally speaking, Catholics have infrequently been the majority in a population or a nation. Catholicism has existed for two millennia, yet we must approach each day as if we are starting from scratch—like an underdog. We can never rest on our laurels. If we are complacent, we will falter, and perhaps even fail. If we trust and cooperate with God, we will achieve a state of grace that will endure with His help. As the secular saying goes, "Nothing is certain except death and taxes." For Catholics, "Nothing is certain except death, taxes, and carrying our crosses."

---

[5] Altman, Let Freedom Ring: "Freedom from Presumption," Day 39, August 14, 2020.

Catholicism is the single greatest force for good in the history of our planet. A Catholic Church is God's house, where His Son is present in the Real Presence that waits for us in the Tabernacle. The Catholic Church is the mystical body of Christ. The Catholic Church alone is the ark of salvation for all. Pope Leo XIII wrote, "Since the Catholic religion is the only true religion, to put the other religions on the same level with it is to treat it with the gravest injustice and offer it the worst form of insult."[6]

Saint John Cantius said, "we look with reverence to the Church, in order that we may have life with the saints." The mystical body of Christ enlightens our individuality and builds up the common good. Nothing else compares to the Church. Nothing else even comes close. Nothing else has the ability to fill heaven with souls like the Catholic Church does. And it does. Father John Hardon declared that,

> We Catholics are in possession of the fullness of truth. The people of our country, and I am using a very weak word, are "starving" for the truth: famished for the truth. They are hungry for the only food that can nourish the human mind, which is the truth... Before God we have a duty to defend the truth and share what we possess, because this is the highest practice of charity. We believe no one can be saved unless they have the true faith. The measure of possession depends on the degree to which those who have the truth share it with others. We shall be judged, judged on our own practice of charity mainly—I repeat— our charity in sharing the truth that Christ gave us, with everyone whom He put into our lives.[7]

While the United States offers us a national heritage, our Catholic faith offers us a magnificent religious heritage. That spiritual heritage, unfortunately, is often times overlooked and left on the shelf gathering the proverbial dust.

Dusting off that spiritual playbook, a central tenet of Catholicism is that we believe in the "Communion of Saints." We have many members, but we are of one mystical body. In other words, we are all linked by a golden Catholic thread. "Every pious desire, every good thought, every charitable work inspired by the love of Jesus," writes

---

[6] Leo XIII, *Humanum genus*, On Freemasonry, n.p.
[7] Hardon, "Convert the Contraceptive Mentality." Audio tape transcript. Catholics Against Contraception. 2001. http://www.catholicsagainstcontraception.com/fr_hardon.htm.

Bl. Anne Catherine Emmerich, "contributes to the perfection of the whole body of the faithful. A person who does nothing more than lovingly pray to God for his brethren, participates in the great work of saving souls."

As Catholics, we are so much more interconnected than we realize. Contemporary Catholics who comprise the Church Militant are not only linked to the Old Testament people of faith, but also all those in purgatory (the Church Suffering), and all those in Heaven (the Church Triumphant). Catholics are *never* alone. They are always connected to the Communion of Saints, the greatest force for good ever assembled. We further believe that everything we do as Catholics either adds to or detracts from the overall strength of the Catholic family.

With the Communion of Saints as a foundational principle, the book will feature a representative saint from each of the twenty-one centuries since Catholicism was founded by Our Lord in 33 A.D. Twenty-one centuries in twenty-one chapters. The saint chosen from each century may not be the most popular, smartest, influential, or consequential saint for their day, but each served God in a way that was highly pleasing to Him. Their qualities were appropriate for their times, and for ours. By applying these traits to our times, we are better able to bolster our resolve to live faithful and heroic lives. This message of heroism was echoed by Fr. Rick Heilman in his 2021 online Lent series:

> Like the heroic first Christians, we go about radiating our love for God and neighbor, while we are willing to die for the TRUTH. This was why the first Christians grew in number so rapidly. They were attractive because they were HEROIC! Now is the time, possibly more than any other time in salvation history, for more and more souls to rise up, as the first Christians did, with that humble and heroic light of truth and love.[8]

Our times could not be calling more emphatically upon Catholics to live lives of heroism. Each saint featured in *Against the Grain* made an inspiring decision to say "yes" to God, and "no" to the guiles of this world. Perhaps you will encounter a saint who was previously

---

[8] Heilman, "Freedom from Pride," Let Freedom Ring, Day 26.

unknown to you, or perhaps you will meet anew a saint you had known but long since forgotten. Each of these featured saints, whether known or unknown, is a genuine Catholic hero. Every one of these great saints is ready to intercede for you as often as you call on him or her. The assistance is there; all you have to do is ask. Reach out you must. (Sounds a bit like Yoda, no?) Or as Saint Thomas More says, "Occupy your mind with good thoughts, or the enemy will fill them with bad ones. Unoccupied, they cannot be."

Our great allies in the next life wish to be close to us in this life. And they are with us in concord and unanimity. Cultivate devotion to the holy saints, patriarchs, prophets, apostles, and martyrs, and petition them to earnestly supplicate the Savior on our behalf so that we may fight and resist temptation, and merit heaven. Call on them saying: "Deliver us for the sake of His Holy Name. Receive our pleas, oh great saints of the heavenly court. Intercede for us! Show us the way! Help us to follow in your footsteps. Help us to be Saints like you!"

What draws humans to inspiring heroes? Feats of strength, bravery, and conquest? Idealized standards? Heightened virtues? From mythical Gilgamesh of ancient Mesopotamia, through figures like Hector, Achilles, Heracles, Sigurd, Beowulf, Lancelot and Fionn mac Cumhaill, mankind has been charmed and captivated by stories of our mythological heroes. Whatever might be the underlying attraction, humans need heroes.

Commenting on how our modern comic book superheroes (i.e., Superman, Batman, Wonder Woman, Spiderman, Aquaman, etc.) are depicted, Sean Fitzpatrick writes, "The concepts of moral consequentialism are slipping with the times…the optimism that shines from an understanding of objective truth, goodness and beauty is getting harder to grasp… When the world is pathetic, desire for the epic will be keen. When vice predominates, men will grope for virtue. When heroism has lost its clarity, there will be a struggle to depict heroes. These issues are to be taken seriously because, after all, the human race still needs to be saved."[9]

Our rational brains inform us that comic book superheroes aren't real, and yet we're fascinated by them nonetheless. Why are humans

---

[9] Fitzpatrick, "'Zack Snyder's Justice League:' The Postmodern Struggle for the Mythic," The Epoch Times, April 7-13, 2021, B9.

are so fascinated by heroes? We love our historical, military, police, firefighters, medical and everyday heroes. Our movies and books are filled with plots about the "heroes journey." Heroes give us solace, energy and hope. As Catholics, we know that those who have lived lives of heroic virtue, our Saints, were real. We look to them to imitate them as they give us true solace, energy and hope.

Catholics distinguish between heroes who are not worth depicting (the godless) and those who are (the god-fearing). Catholics favor godly heroes because they possess supernatural grace while godless heroes are spiritually barren. Single-minded on the supernatural and what it takes for us to attain heaven, Saint Ignatius of Loyola, in his Spiritual Exercises, counsels us to ask "these three questions at the foot of the crucifix: What have I done hitherto for heaven? What ought I to do for heaven? What shall I do henceforward for heaven?"[10]

Speaking to the spiritual challenges facing Catholics, Fr. John Hardon said, "only heroic Catholics will survive."[11] Fr. Hardon believed that only the truly dedicated will not become apostates and thereby lose Heaven. Michael Voris adds:

> If you are not preparing yourself now, and your family now, bracing yourselves spiritually for the darkness into which civilization is descending, you will not survive... People do not suddenly decide to suffer for the Faith. They prepare themselves to suffer great hardships for the Faith, by undergoing little hardships and sacrifices in advance. You could think of it as a kind of dress rehearsal. Our Blessed Lord Himself said conversely: If you cannot be trusted in small matters, you cannot be trusted in larger ones (Luke 16:10). Heroes do not miraculously appear. They have the stuff of heroism inside them all along, cultivated and molded and formed, waiting to emerge publicly if and when the correct circumstances arise.[12]

When considering the great examples of our heroic saints, keep in mind the following spiritual gem from Saint Philip Neri: "Never say, 'What great things the saints do,' but, 'What great things God does in His saints.'" We should adapt his nugget of wisdom as we pursue

---

[10] Ignatius of Loyola, "Spiritual Exercises," 179.
[11] Voris, "Only The Brave Will Survive," *Vortex*, Church Militant, May 28, 2015.
[12] Ibid.

personal sanctity: "What great things God does through His servants." How can we serve God and our neighbors more diligently?

In other words, how does God speak to us through *His* saints? The question is not whether God speaks to us through *the* saints. A subtle yet most important distinction. What does God say to you through His saints? How does God speak to others through you? How saintly are you? How can you improve?

A common theme among saints chosen for this book was that he or she lived an intentional life that went "against the grain." Not going along with the crowd, they did an excellent job resisting the "groupthink" of their day. As we know, the group is often wrong. Very wrong. In Romans 12:2, Saint Paul instructs us, "Be not conformed to this world; but be reformed in the newness of your mind, that you may prove what is the good, and the acceptable, and the perfect will of God." As Catholics, we imitate our Lord Jesus Christ, who divinely and perfectly went "against the grain."

Jesus knew many would reject Him and some would even hate Him. In fact, Jesus declared, "If the world hates you, know that it hated me first." Jesus knew this life was not a popularity contest. Instead, it was all about doing His Father's will. Saint Teresa of Avila reminds us that, "In this life our lot is not to enjoy God, but to do His holy will."

In a sermon, Fr. James Altman preached that Christians "will be hated for speaking the truth." He continued: "Dear Family, what good fruit do we produce that proves we truly are attached to the vine? Right after Jesus spoke about the vine and the branches, he taught, 'because I have chosen you out of the world, the world hates you. They persecuted me—they will also persecute you. Whoever hates me, also hates my Father.' What is the clearest evidence that we are doing the Father's will, that we are producing good fruit? It will be that the world hates us because of our faith."[13] Fr. Altman's fearless sermon concludes with a list of contemporary examples:

> We will know the truth of the matter if we are attached to the vine or not by our enemies. If I am not hated by every Democrat, AOC & her squad, James Martin, Biden/Harris, Black Lives Matter, Planned

[13] Altman, "Hated for Speaking the Truth," YouTube, posted November 29, 2020. https://www.youtube.com/watch?v=TFNJh2trRgg.

Parenthood and every fake Catholic who couldn't argue their way out of a theological paper bag... if I'm not hated by those birds of a feather, then I'm not attached to the vine. If I'm not hated, then I'm not producing good fruit, and that's going to be a problem for me on judgment day.[14]

Pray, dear family, that we do not have any problems on judgment day.

While on earth, Jesus was a maverick. Thus, Catholics *must* be mavericks when they imitate Christ. We must be disruptors and not conform to this world and its anti-God agenda. We must stay close to God if we are to successfully promote virtue and morals. Despite the fact that people naturally want to go along with the crowd, follow the herd, and/or be accepted by the "cool kids," we must resist those impulses and instead listen to that innermost voice that calls us to moral acts and a life of virtue, staying close to God and, if need be, going against the grain in holy boldness and being contradictory.

At the Presentation, when Simeon blessed Joseph and Mary in Luke 2:34, and received Jesus in his arms being the first to publicly recognize Him as the Messiah, he said Jesus was "*signum cui contradicetur*," a sign of contradiction. "Against the grain" is another way of saying "sign of contradiction." We are told to imitate Jesus. How many Catholics know they are called to be a sign of contradiction in their daily lives? If I had chosen a Latin title for this book it would have been, *Signum Cui Contradicetur*. I would have loved a Latin title, but book sales would likely suffer. Instead I chose the title *Against the Grain*. My last name (Grane), moreover, is not a homonym of *Contradicetur*.

There is no avoiding the reality that to follow Jesus involves being contradictory, going against the grain, and, at times, encountering division. In Matthew 10:34-36, Jesus himself says, "Do not think that I have come to bring peace to the earth. I have not come to bring peace, but a sword. For I have come to set a man against his father, and a daughter against her mother, and a daughter-in-law against her mother-in-law. And a person's enemies will be those of his own household." A sword divides. The message of the cross divides. Jesus tells us we will face conflict, and even division in our families as we stand with God, the church, and our faith.

---

14 Ibid.

We will be persecuted for speaking the truth.

While we are signs of contradiction in our outward facing personas, where are our minds regarding those who contradict us? Thomas á Kempis informs us, "… the real test of virtue… is to live at peace with the perverse, or the aggressive, and those who contradict us, for this needs a great grace. … in this mortal life, our peace consists in the humble bearing of suffering and contradictions, not in being free of them, for we cannot live in this world without adversity. Those who can best suffer will enjoy the most peace, for such persons are masters of themselves, lords of the world, with Christ for their friend, and heaven as their reward."[15]

In the end, we know the faithful followers of Christ will be victorious. According to Psalm 68: "God arises, and his enemies will be scattered, and those who hate him will flee before him." In Matthew 10:21-22, we read, "Brother will hand over brother to death, and the father his child; children will rise up against parents and have them put to death. You will be hated by all because of my name, but whoever endures to the end will be saved."

Wherever we are, and whatever is to come, we must stand our ground. We must choose the right team. The faithful who follow the truth versus the unfaithful who oppose the truth. The truth versus the lies. The sheep versus the goats. The few versus the many. Yes, the truth divides. To which team do you belong?

All people should imitate Jesus. He is the fulcrum between the Old Testament and the New Testament and the central figure in world history. Before him, B.C., after him, A.D. How would you characterize someone like Jesus who changed the arc of history? Was He a revolutionary, radical, nonconformist, maverick, or something else? People of goodwill can give different answers to this question. What cannot be debated is the impact of His life, teachings, and death. I consider Him the ultimate freedom fighter. He stood in radical opposition to the evils of the world. Imitating Jesus frees us from sin. How do you hear Jesus's voice? As Our Blessed Lord said, "Anyone who hears the truth, hears My voice." What is His voice saying to you?

---

[15] Kempis, *Imitation of Christ*, 72-73.

Faithful Catholics are often called upon to sacrifice popularity, position, wealth, friends, etc. So be it. Catholics should live by Christian morals and the truth rather than attain worldly pleasures that might jeopardize their salvation. We play the long game. The eternal game. This means there is a contrarian bent to the Catholic approach to life. Deep down we all know our life isn't about this life.

As Catholics, we know that the small and large inconveniences of this life matter little when measured against the everlasting impact of our decisions. Our Lord said to be sober, awake and ready. We are in this life for only a little while. We must be ready for any challenge or difficulty. As Saint Bernard used to say in the midst of trouble, "*Quid hoc ad aeternitatem?*" (What is this to eternity?) Or, as another saying goes, "Life is short, eternity isn't."

As Catholics, it is part of our DNA to go against the grain of this world. A large part of the American collective DNA is also to go against the grain. As such, I write to you as a twenty-first century Catholic American. Do I fully embrace all that it means to go against the grain? I pray and hope so. I have good and bad days. When I am fully living a life that is pleasing to God the Father, I am most intentionally saying "no" to this world—and "yes" to eternity.

We must stand against rather than cooperate with the evil in this world. We must go against the grain. When we compromise with evil, our souls become imperiled. The martyrs said better not to compromise, even if it means losing our lives. For many, faith is a place of safety and comfort. Saint Maximillian Kolbe stands against this illusion. He tells us that death is not the final word. We can die before we die, if we give up our faith. Kolbe steadies us: "Courage, my sons… For Jesus Christ I am prepared to suffer still more…" When sending His disciples out into the world amidst the wolves in sheep's clothing, Jesus counseled his followers to "be wise like serpents and simple as doves." (Matthew 10:16) In other words, don't be gullible and move forward with eyes wide open.

Those advancing the anti-God, secular/naturalist agenda are in full "Beast Mode." Beast Mode means all available weapons are deployed. The Beast could also be a euphemism for the Dragon, or Satan. Insidious. Diabolical. Evil. The anti-God agenda targets the Catholic Church.

The anti-God agenda of Caesar, Mammon, and Sodom has taken over traditional and social media, technology and other corporations, sports leagues, public and private education, government bureaucracies and courts. These predators use Beast Mode to destroy and discard.

The anti-God agenda has even infiltrated all religions—including the Catholic Church. How many bishops and priests embrace anti-God doctrines that were unthinkable only a few decades ago? Modernism is malevolent, malignant, and malicious. It is also omnipresent and perfidious. It's open rebellion and leads to moral collapse. Modernism at its core is pure *"Non-Serviam!"*

In his encyclical *Tametsi* (1900), "On Christ our Redeemer," Pope Leo XIII wrote, "About the 'rights of man' as they are called, the people have heard enough: it is time they should hear of the Rights of God." Amen to that.

To counter Beast Mode, we need "Christ Mode" or "Saint Mode." (Given the heavy lift here, before we start, I vote for some apple pie *à la mode.*) What is the best defense against a metaphorical Medusa, or Hydra, or any opponent in Beast Mode? What would full-on "Christ Mode" look like? The more we practice our Catholic Faith, the more confidence we should have that serving God faithfully is the most effective response. We must stand in the breech between the evil and the souls it seeks to destroy. Jesus, who sacrificed His life for our salvation, tells us, "I am the good shepherd; the good shepherd lays down his life for his sheep" (John 10:11). We must imitate Jesus and live as saints. The victory is in the fight. The outcome is up to God. Let His will be done.

The historical roots of the United States of America are unabashedly Christian. In *U-Turn: Restoring America to the Strength of its Roots*, George Barna and David Barton wrote, "the United States became a unique, prosperous, and admired nation because of its faith in God and the willingness of the people to abide by God's standards and principles." They list early American values: hard work, civic duty, humility, moderation, family, faith, rule of law, respect, frugality, and simplicity. They add, "Over time, however, the people's urge to glorify self rather than God seriously eroded the strength and potential of the nation." In contrast, they list a very different set of modern American values: belonging, choice/control, comfort, entertainment, entitlement, experiences, expression, freedom, happiness, and independence."[16]

Given the cultural and moral deterioration of America, the question then becomes, can the United States sustain its strength if it remains on its current path? What can and should Catholics do? In addition to the classic American values that made the nation great, Catholics can contribute the classic Catholic virtues that have guided us for two millennia. While Catholics were marginalized during periods of American history, they gave thanks to God for this great nation. Many American Catholics recognize, accept and embrace the strong contrarian streak this marginalization gave them. Lest there be any confusion, it is not rebellion *from* God, but rebellion *for* God.

Be edified knowing that you can do what the saints did before you. You too can be a contrarian and go against the grain. In a world where morality is in decline, the culture is in decay, logic is scarce, and confusion reigns in many corners, it is unwise to go along with the crowd. Trying to synchronize with the harmony of this world is unwise. At times, Catholics need to be the discordant note. The one everyone can tell doesn't belong.

Don't be that piece of flotsam that only floats downstream with the current like a dead fish. Only a living thing can swim against the tide. Be Catholic. Be alive. Live a life of intention so that one day you will hear, "'Well done, good and faithful servant. Since you have been faithful over a few things, I will appoint you over many things. Enter into the joy of your Lord.'" (Matthew 25:21) This is what life is all about. It is the reason to have been here.

As we journey together through Church history, each heroic saint will be found in the historical context of their respective century. It is hoped that by reading *Against the Grain* you will gain a greater appreciation of our Catholic heritage. Knowing more about ecclesiastical history will hopefully inspire you to be a better Catholic—someone who lives a heroic life going against the grain. This book is written for a general audience, and specifically to help individuals like you to impact all you meet.

---

[16] Barna, George and Barton, David. *U-Turn: Restoring America to the Strength of its Roots*, (2014), n.p.

17

As you read each chapter of *Against the Grain*, ask yourself, "Why not me?" "Many live like angels in the middle of the world," writes Saint Josemaría Escrivá. "You, ... why not you?" Seriously, why not you? Are you not capable of holiness? Or has the world given you a certificate, or a medal to pin to your chest as a reward for already achieving sainthood? Is now not the opportune time for you? Are you stalling? Whatever your excuse, know it is just that—an excuse. Excuses are unacceptable. We're in a spiritual war. Buckle up buttercup. No more delays. Saint John Vianney encourages us, "The saints did not all begin well. But they all ended well." Begin today, and end well.

If you want a Catholic to perk up, ask these two questions: Who is your confirmation saint? Why did you choose him of her? Many will answer joyfully. The connection they have to their special saint is palpable. Why is that? It's the indelible bond that soul and saint share. Is it also the Communion of Saints coming into play? Regardless, as we have God's natural law written onto our souls, we too, as Catholics, feel the connection to our Confirmation saint in particular and the Communion of Saints in general. It's a Catholic thing. And it's awesome.

It's awesome because the saints lived lives of heroic virtue. But what is virtue? Virtue is a "habitual and firm disposition to do good. The human virtues are stable dispositions of the intellect and the will that govern our acts, order our passions, and guide our conduct in accordance with reason and faith."[17] Saint Agnes said, "Christ made my soul beautiful with the jewels of grace and virtue." In 2 Peter 1:5-8 we read, "For this very reason, make every effort to supplement your faith with virtue, virtue with knowledge, knowledge with self-control, self-control with endurance, endurance with devotion, devotion with mutual affection, mutual affection with love. If these are yours and increase in abundance, they will keep you from being idle or unfruitful in the knowledge of our Lord Jesus Christ."

At the outset it is important to clarify the specific type of virtue that will be referenced throughout *Against the Grain*. "Natural virtue" is virtue originating from good will or a general disposition to do well,

---

[17] Catechism of the Catholic Church, 1833-1884.

but is not sacramental. Natural virtue at times can be tremendous on its own, but as Catholics, we pursue the efficacy of supernatural virtue.

"Supernatural virtue" is infused by God's grace, supplemented by the Holy Sacrifice of the Mass and the sacraments of the Catholic Church, thereby permitting one's soul to be in a state of grace. The gifts of the Holy Ghost perfect the supernatural virtues by enabling us to practice them with greater docility to divine inspiration. As we grow in the knowledge and love of God under the direction of the Holy Ghost, our service becomes more sincere and generous, the practice of virtue more perfect.

Saint Augustine of Hippo coined the phrase "heroic virtue" when he described the virtue of the early Christian martyrs. The term was later applied to other highly virtuous people who perform extraordinarily good works. For beatification (sainthood) in the Church, heroic virtue is a requirement. While natural virtue is good and supernatural virtue is better, we should strive for heroic virtue.

From where does heroic virtue originate? In baptism, we are infused with sacramental grace necessary to live lives of supernatural virtue. Beginning from a base, or foundation, we find foremost among the virtues are the Cardinal Virtues. They are called cardinal because the Latin root *cardo,* means "hinge." All other virtues hinge on these four: prudence, justice, fortitude and temperance. Saint Augustine shares his take on the Cardinal Virtues, or the basic virtues required for a virtuous life: "To live well is nothing other than to love God with all one's heart, with all one's soul and with all one's efforts; from this it comes about that love is kept whole and uncorrupted (through temperance). No misfortune can disturb it (and this is fortitude). It obeys only [God] (and this is justice), and is careful in discerning things, so as not to be surprised by deceit or trickery (and this is prudence)." Given their foundational nature, each of the four Cardinal Virtues will be featured in *Against the Grain.*

To integrate the Cardinal Virtues, we have the Seven Gifts of the Holy Ghost: wisdom, understanding, counsel, fortitude, knowledge, piety, and fear of the Lord. Of the seven, *Against the Grain* will highlight just one, fortitude. The more intellectual associated virtues of wisdom, understanding and counsel were not selected so that other more complimentary virtues to fortitude could be featured such as perseverance, diligence, initiative, and courage. *Against the Grain* seeks to motivate faithful Catholics to stop being silent "couch-potato Catholics" and cooperate more fully with the Holy Ghost to bring the light and message of the Catholic Church more effectively into people's hearts, minds, and souls.

To compliment the Seven Gifts of the Holy Ghost, we have the Twelve Fruits of the Holy Ghost: charity, joy, peace, patience, kindness, goodness, generosity, gentleness, faithfulness, modesty, self-control, and chastity. Of these twelve, *Against the Grain* will feature five fruits: charity, joy, patience, modesty and chastity.

The remaining virtues to be highlighted in *Against the Grain,* not previously mentioned, are: friendship, candor, obedience, humility, longanimity, compassion and hiddenness.

In Saint Louis de Montfort's, *True Devotion to Mary,* he lists the ten principal virtues of the Blessed Mother: deep humility, lively faith, blind obedience, unceasing prayer, constant self-denial, surpassing purity, ardent love, heroic patience, angelic kindness, and heavenly wisdom.[18] Many of these ten primary virtues exhibited by the Blessed Mother will be the focus of discussion in *Against the Grain*. Others will be addressed indirectly. To be sure, as Our Mother Mary is without sin, we know that she excelled with respect to every virtue. Fr. Ed Broom, OMV writes, "May we ardently desire to know, love, and imitate our Blessed Mother Mary, be motivated with a firm decision to meditate frequently and fervently on the virtues of Mary most holy, and then strive to live them out all the days of our lives!"[19]

Dom Lorenzo Scupoli, in *The Spiritual Combat,* counsels us against becoming enamored with the idea of being virtuous, and downplaying the resistance that arises when pursuing virtue. Being virtuous is hard work. Given our individual constitutions, some virtues will be harder to pursue than others. Scupoli writes:

"When we make a good resolution, we merely consider the beauty and excellence of virtue, which attracts even the most vapid minds, but we never consider the difficulties of attaining it. Consequently, cowardly souls are dismayed at the first sign of trouble and they hurriedly abandon their project. For this reason, it would be better for you to

[18] Montfort, *True Devotion to Mary*, 108.
[19] Broom, "Imitate our Lady's Ten Principle Virtues," Catholic Exchange. February 23, 2021.

consider the difficulties which occur in acquiring virtue, rather than the virtues themselves, and to prepare yourself accordingly. You may rest assured that the greater courage you show in conquering yourself or defeating your enemies, the sooner will your difficulties diminish, and they will gradually vanish."[20]

While most everyone would agree that living a highly virtuous life is desirable, making that next step towards this goal can be difficult. Fr. Anthony Rice at St. John Cantius in Chicago breaks it down for us by explaining how intellect and imagination impact the will. He tells us that when we commit to move from idea to action or practice, something inside us often freezes and we resist. Some then abandon their commitment. Fr. Rice adds, "When we think about growing in virtue, we think about muscling our way through it with sheer willpower. But this is to forget a powerful reality of the soul. The imagination is more powerful than reason. The will is drawn to a perceived good. Usually, we attempt to move the will through the intellect alone. The problem is that reason cannot move the will nearly as effectively as the imagination. When it comes to moving the will, the imagination is the most important faculty of the soul. Advertisers understand this principle well."[21] Fr. Rice continues,

[R]eason is safer as imagination can often lead us astray. Sin and vice almost always start in the imagination. If tempered and guided by reason, could not the imagination be a tremendous force for good, and help us to soar toward heaven? Saint Ignatius of Loyola knew the power of the imagination filled with holy desires, and incorporated it into his Spiritual Exercises. Is not also meditating on the mysteries of the Rosary divine assistance to help us train the power of our imaginations directing our will for holy purposes? The spiritual principle is simple, if you contemplate holy things, you will become holy. If we contemplate evil, we will become evil. We have a choice to make.[22]

Against the Grain is intended to be a tool to help us contemplate holy things. The saints and virtues help us focus on how to break the resistance and engage our imagination and, hence, our will, to better

---

[20] Scupoli, "The Spiritual Combat," 94.
[21] Fr. Anthony Rice, Sermon, St. John Cantius, Feb. 13, 2021.
[22] Ibid.

and more fully serve God. Saint Thomas à Kempis in Chapter 1 of his book *The Imitation of Christ*, writes, "In truth, sublime words make not a man holy and just, but a virtuous life maketh him dear to God."[23] Kempis continues, "This is the highest wisdom, by despising the world to tend to heavenly gardens."[24] Be dear to God and tend His garden. Yes. Heart of Jesus, font of all virtues, have mercy on us.

The purpose of *Against the Grain* is to highlight the life and historical significance of a saint to help us better understand and appreciate our Catholic heritage. Our walk through the centuries is also designed to draw attention to a specific virtue that is explicitly, or perhaps implicitly, associated with that particular saint. For instance, take Saint Monica; her heroic patience is known to all. Pretty obvious. Well, what about Saint Thomas Becket? Is obedience the first virtue that comes to mind when you think of him? Maybe. Maybe not. When you think of Saint Etheldreda, do you think of chastity? With Saint Lidwina, longanimity? Decide for yourself if the right virtue is paired with the appropriate saint.

Readers may wonder why *Against the Grain* touches upon politics when this is a book about saints and the Catholic Church? In a public address, Venerable Fulton Sheen helped answer this question: "Patriotism is a virtue that was allied to the old virtue of the Greeks and Romans called *pietas*, meaning love of God, love of neighbor, love of country. And when one goes out, all go out. When we no longer have love of God, we no longer have love of country."[25] Michael Voris of Church Militant went further: "Life is lived at the intersection of politics and religion."[26] And therefore, "God can no more be left out of politics than hydrogen can be left out of water."[27] Pro-life former U.S. Congressman Dan Lipinski (D-IL) applied the principle to practical politics: "If you want to really change the world, you must choose to be Catholic and carry Jesus into the public square."[28]

Many Americans don't understand the recipe of freedom. Os Guinness, English author and social critic, also the great-great-great-

---

[23] Saint Thomas a Kempis, *The Imitation of Christ*, Confraternity of the Precious Blood, 1982, 5.
[24] Ibid, 6.
[25] Sheen, "Patriotism," YouTube posted December 18, 2017. (Original airing date from the 1950's unknown.) https://www.youtube.com/watch?v=2wAF1KiVY_c
[26] Voris, The Vortex, "Theft," January 22, 2021.
[27] Voris, The Vortex, "Get in the Fight," January 21, 2021.
[28] Source unknown.

grandson of Arthur Guinness, the Dublin brewer, distilled freedom into what he referred to as the "The Golden Triangle." Freedom requires virtue, and virtue requires faith, and faith requires Freedom; this process repeats itself over and over. In America, thus, faith and virtue are required for the success of our ongoing experiment in self-government. In his Farewell Address, George Washington declared, "Of all the dispositions and habits which lead to political prosperity, religion and morality are indispensable supports."[29]

The American founders knew very well that a virtuous republic requires a virtuous people. Faith informs virtue, and virtue is a condition of freedom. When faith decreases and virtue deteriorates, mutual respect and civic unity dissipates; thereafter, freedom disintegrates. As John Adams famously said, "Our Constitution was made only for a moral and religious people. It is wholly inadequate to the government of any other." Benjamin Franklin asserted, "Only a virtuous people are capable of freedom. As nations become more corrupt and vicious, they have more need of masters." Alexander Hamilton declared, "The institution of delegated power implies that there is a portion of virtue and honor among mankind which may be a reasonable foundation of confidence." And James Madison warned, "To suppose that any form of government will secure liberty or happiness without any virtue in the people, is a chimerical idea."

Princeton's Robert (Robbie) George adds, "People lacking in virtue could be counted on to trade liberty for protection, for financial or personal security, for comfort… for having their problems solved quickly. And there will always be people occupying or standing for public office who will be happy to offer the deal."[30]

Sam Adams called upon us to, "Set brush fires of liberty." As Catholics we should say, "Set brush fires of liberty and virtuous Catholicism." In the Revolutionary War people put liberty poles in front of their houses as indications of support for America against the British. In our day, we should put out Catholic poles. Or Catholic flags. And statues of Blessed Virgin Mary, and other saints, in our front yards.

---

[29] Washington, "Farewell Address," 1796.
[30] George. *"Ruling to Serve,"* First Things, April 2013.

How are faithful Catholics to respond when our rights are infringed upon? We must always rise up and protect them whether they are in danger from the government, society or the Church. Our rights, given to us by God, are not to be abridged. Our forefathers rebelled against England for far less an infringement on their rights. Pray that we may be as vigilant and courageous while defending our liberties.

We have a Christian duty not just to stick up for ourselves, but to also stick up for our neighbors, community, and country. Silence is not a virtue in the face of moral corruption. If we perceive that America has traded vice for virtue, it is our Christian obligation and our moral and patriotic duty to speak up. As John Hancock, the first signer of the Declaration of Independence, wrote: "Resistance to tyranny becomes the Christian and social duty of each individual. ... Continue steadfast and, with a proper sense of your dependence on God, nobly defend those rights which heaven gave, and no man ought to take from us."[31]

Father John Hardon has a slightly differently take on Adams and Hancock's statements, but arrives at essentially a similar conclusion, "Christianity was instituted by Christ to provide the moral soundness, let's call it 'the soul of society.' As long as Christians remained firm and faithful to their principles, the rest of the world where Christianity was established followed their lead. Once Christians caved in, whole nations fell along with them."[32]

We must appeal to heaven to preserve, protect, and defend our nation. The country is our family. Patriotism is loving your family. If you do not acknowledge God, patriotism, and the reality of sin, you will be more easily deceived by false ideologies—atheistic communism included. Will faithful Catholics stand against the efforts of atheistic communism to enslave the world? Who will oppose the onslaught? Our baptism and confirmation demand that we speak out against the Marxist hatred of God, liberty, and virtue.

The Catholic Church has a great story to tell. Will you have the courage to tell it? You are on the front lines. Be the Catholic rebel speaking truth to a world that is sideways most of the time. Discussing

---

[31] History of the United States of America, Vol. II, 229.
[32] Hardon, "Convert the Contraceptive Mentality," Audio tape transcript, Catholics Against Contraception, 2001. http://www.catholicsagainstcontraception.com/fr_hardon.htm.

upside down, Catholics will differ in their opinion of Joe Biden as America's second Catholic president. I'm all for a *faithful* Catholic being president of the United States. As for the Biden presidency, what will that mean for American Catholics? Will he help them to be better Catholics or will he hurt them? Consider how infuriating and scandalous it is for White House spokeswoman Jen Psaki to pronounce that President Biden "respectfully disagrees" with the U.S. bishops, "who object to the administration using the bodies of aborted children for scientific research."[33] *No*, not acceptable.

If you were to walk one day in the shoes of a saint, what would that look like? What would that mean to you? How would it change your life? What's holding you back? The only thing that perfectly fills the void in our soul is God. For whom will you fight? For whom will you lay down your life? For whom will you speak up?

As Catholics, we know that we must walk through the world differently. "We are Christians," says Saint Augustine, "and strangers on earth. Let none of us be frightened; our native land is not in this world." We must take the path less travelled. If we care enough. Do you want to be counter-cultural? A rebel? Live your life as a faithful Catholic. Start going to church again, or more than once a week. Get married (in the traditional way). Avoid contraception. Have lots of kids. By simply starting a family you will be making quite the religious and political statement. Many in the world will scorn you, but pay no attention. Do not be a "useful idiot" and go along with the propaganda. Be heroic in virtue. Be truly Catholic.

Pixar writer, Andrew Stanton, in his 2012 TED talk, "The Clues to a Great Story," explained that, "People are born problem solvers. We're compelled to deduce and deduct. We can't stop wanting to draw the connection and fill things in. A great story makes the audience put things together." To illustrate, he explained the "Unifying Theory of 2 + 2." A writer does not give the audience "4." He just describes "2 + 2."[34]

Stanton is probably right. In most cases that is how great Hollywood stories are told, about characters with names like Nemo,

---

[33] CV News Feed, "Biden Admin: We "Disagree" With Bishops on Using Aborted Children for Research," *Catholic Vote*, April 28, 2020.
[34] Stanton, "The Clues to a Great Story" TED talk, YouTube posted March 21, 2012. https://www.youtube.com/watch?v=KxDwieKpawg

Dory, Tow Mater, Remy, Woody and Buzz. When someone internalizes "2+2," magic happens as they draw their own conclusion of "4." Many great storytellers use that technique to sell lots of books and movies and become famous. In the same way, Hollywood loves making movies about the "Hero's Journey" wherein someone is living large, encounters a seemingly insurmountable challenge and sinks low, finds a way to overcome the obstacle, and once again lives large. Hooray!

Below is the blueprint for *Against the Grain* covering its general formula, purpose, and hope. Spoiler alert: Saints are heroes. Be one.

On technique, here's the methodology. Over the years many brilliant authors, including some saints, have written amazing books about the lives of saints. Some write in a straightforward, biographical way. Others add texture and unique story-telling techniques. I prefer the latter. To help illustrate my point, if one were to write a book about a healthy lifestyle, they could just focus on eating healthy, and that could make for a great read. What if that book, however, also discussed cardio, exercise routines, vitamins, and mindset? Would the reader be much healthier because of his awareness of a more comprehensive approach? I say yes. As such, in each chapter *Against the Grain* features a saint, a virtue, Catholic history, along with some personal stories and/or commentary on our current culture, country and church.

The chapters will then close with three mini-sections. First up will be "Saints," wherein several saints from that century, along with the year of their death (when available), will be listed in chronological order. Please scan this section to gain additional insight and context as to whom God was utilizing to speak to the world during that particular era.

The penultimate part of each chapter will be "History." In this section you will find a few bullet points of info that are noteworthy as context to further explain our Catholic, or world, history for that century. It may even contain a short story about a saint or two from that century. Defending Catholicism means you should have a better understanding of Catholic history. Note: should you wish to just quickly scan, or review, the "History" section, some of the more important items for that particular century have been put in bold.

Lastly, there will be a section called "Virtue Challenge." Based on the saint and virtue presented in the chapter, this section will highlight key takeaways and ask a few, hopefully evocative, questions to help you further ponder an increase of virtue in your life.

I'd also like to volunteer some contextualization, both theologically and politically, for the era in which this book was written. Theologically, *Against the Grain* was written during what I consider to be the "*Dubia* era of the Catholic Church." A time of: questions about Communion for remarried un-annulled, Pachamama (a South American pagan goddess) on St. Peter's high alter, Vatican financial improprieties, selling out to China permitting them to have say over Catholic bishops, McCarrick sexual abuse scandal, "Who am I to judge?" St. Gallen/Lavender Mafia, Fr. James Martin, S.J., social justice warrior/liberation theology Catholicism, *de facto* collective silence on pro-abortion Catholic politicians receiving Communion, and ecumenical overtures diminishing the primacy of the one true faith. And nobody can question any part of it. Wow!

Politically, the vast majority of the book was written during the dystopian time of the Presidential election of November, 2020, the Inauguration in January 2021, and the bizarre early days of the Biden Presidency where we read memes such as: 'Trump cancelled ISIS. Biden cancelled Dr. Suess and Mr. Potato Head.' Consider *The Blaze* reporter Elijah Schafer's Twitter post on Jan. 15, 2021: "A 78 yr. old man campaigns from his basement, Picks one of the most unpopular VP's, Receives the most votes of any candidate in history at 4am, Confirmed in the middle of the night, An empty inauguration, 20,000 troops to protect him. And nobody can question any part of it, Wow."[35]

Strange parallels between church and state.

What are the faithful to do when faith and flag are in a state of diabolical disorientation? What do people do when they are in a place of spiritual, political, mental or physical discomfort? When uncomfortable, unless utterly despondent, you reach out for that which makes you feel better. That which gives you strength and helps you regain the lost pep in your step. That which allows vitality to return to the blood coursing through your veins. That which puts faith, hope

---

[35] Schafer, Twitter Post, @ElijahSchaffer, January 15, 2021.

and charity into your heart and soul. As Catholics and Americans, we are a can-do people yearning to overcome, accomplish, and achieve greater self-actualization and holiness. We are also called to a higher standard. Lukewarmness must be rooted out.

We are born with the innate desire to please God the Father. Some of us are more aware of this than others. Pleasing God is the itch that we are always trying to scratch. Those who come to this realization truly live.

Against the Grain chronologically tells the story of twenty-one Catholic heroes and saints, who did whatever was necessary to know, love and serve God regardless of what the world threw at them. In their quest to serve God, the audience will be engaged with the hero's struggle, including their inner and outer challenges. What can we learn from each saint's journey?

The saints chosen for *Against the Grain* played an active part in resolving their own internal trials, rather than being rescued by someone else. *Against the Grain* will not simply give an overview of events that happened *to* the hero or heroine. It will take the audience on a journey *with* the hero or heroine.

This book seeks to help the reader locate their place in the world. We wonder about our highest and best purpose. God is wonder. The greatest gift is to help another human being experience wonder. Tapping into wonder is like an affirmation of being alive; it reaches you at a cellular level. Wonder, purpose, joy, and hope are fundamental to us all.

This story isn't just about our Catholic forefathers. It's about each Catholic's personal quest to find the courage to be truly faithful in a world where Catholicism is often unwelcome.

We all love stories. Stories affirm who we are. We all want to believe our lives have meaning. Nothing has greater meaning than when we enrich our lives through stories that cross the barriers of time. They permit us to connect with and learn from others, real and imagined.

Why should you care about being a good Catholic? Too many people focus on things that don't matter. This book is about the only thing that matters.

The heroic stories told in *Against the Grain* are about our precious faith. The book is also about our unbelievable nation. The liberties and freedoms we possess as Americans, coupled with the free will given to us by God, are an unbelievable combination that should not be squandered. How can we as Americans not only help ourselves, but help other nations as well? Yes, it will be hard, but we have been given the great commission by Jesus himself to go out and make disciples of not just our nation, but all nations.

Something must be done. You know it. You feel it. You don't want to merely exist; you want to truly live. You want to serve God in a more meaningful and impactful way. You want to be a better Catholic.

Most everyone recognizes that we are not on the right path. "Unless we recover the zeal and the spirit of the first century Christians," writes Fr. John Hardon, "unless we are willing to do what they did and to pay the price that they paid, the future of our country, the days of America are numbered."[36]

As Pope Saint Pius V said, "All the evil in the world is due to lukewarm Catholics." No more being insipid, or lukewarm. Time to turn up the heat and truly live.

This is not a time for defeatist Catholicism and part-time saints. This is a time for gutsy saints. Live as a true, courageous, and heroic Catholic to one day be among the elect. Contend. Matter. Go against the grain. All you saints of heaven, pray for us!

Live a life of heroic virtue and become a saint. What could be better than that?

On October 3, 1998, the feast day of Sainte Thérèse de Lisieux, Fr. C. Frank Phillips celebrated the Holy Sacrament of Matrimony for Mary and me at St. John Cantius in Chicago. Choosing Sainte Thérèse's feast day was purposeful as we both had a strong devotion to her.

---

[36] Hardon, "Christian Martyrs Our Inspiration," Voccola. October 17, 2012.
https://voccola.blogspot.com/2012/10/christian-martyrs-our-inspiration-st.html

Mary and Doug Grane at Wedding Reception

As a fun surprise, inside my wedding band Mary had inscribed *"aujourd'hui nous commençons."* The French translates as "today we begin." As you and I are about to travel through the centuries meeting some of the Catholic Church's finest saints, it is with grateful appreciation that I say to you, my friends in Jesus and Mary, *aujourd'hui nous commençons.*

CHAPTER 1

Martha

The First Century
Friendship

"Fly from bad companions as from the bite of a poisonous snake. If you keep good companions, I can assure you that you will one day rejoice with the blessed in Heaven; whereas if you keep with those who are bad, you will become bad yourself, and you will be in danger of losing your soul."

~ Saint John Bosco

"The friendship that can cease was never real."

~ Saint Jerome

"A friend is more to be longed for than the light; I speak of a genuine one. And wonder not: for it were better for us that the sun should be extinguished, than that we should be deprived of friends; better to live in darkness, than to be without friends."

~ Saint John Chrysostom

"There is nothing more on this earth to be prized then true friendship."

~ Saint Thomas Aquinas

What must it have been like to be the friend of Jesus?

We read that "Jesus loved Martha, and her sister (Mary) and Lazarus" (John 11:5). After the virtue and confidence of the two holy sisters were put on trial, Christ raised Lazarus. Jesus was friends with all three siblings, and he often stayed at their home. The gospels say that Jesus visited Martha's house in Bethania, about two miles from Jerusalem, on at least three occasions (Luke 10:38-42, John 11:1-53, and John 12:1-9). Who better then to set the table for our book, than Saint Martha?

What experiences did the three siblings share with Jesus to build the bonds of friendship? What qualities did each possess to endear them to Jesus? Was their friendship with Jesus unique compared to the friendship of others who knew Him? Did Jesus feel comfortable enough at their house to "let his guard down" a bit and rest? He did from all accounts. At a friend's house you can really relax, rest, and recharge. "God sends us friends to be our firm support in the whirlpool of struggle," wrote Saint Maximillian Kolbe. "In the company of friends, we will find strength to attain our sublime ideal."[37] This is what friendship is all about. Being yourself, being supported, and being loved no matter where you've been, or what kind of day you've had.

Imagine the following: Jesus, after walking around all day in the hot Judean sun, tired after teaching, feeding thousands, driving out demons, and much else, arrives at Martha's house. Martha, assumed to have been the oldest sibling, in charge of the household, enthusiastically greets Jesus in her courtyard: "Yea, it's Jesus! It's so good to see you my friend! Where have you been? Get over here and give me a hug! Jesus, you look so tired! Come inside and eat some soup. You're so skinny. Skin and bones." Jesus responds, "Seriously Martha? Good to see you, too. Ah, soup, sounds delicious!" That's friendship. Someone saying you don't look your best, but you know they mean well, and you're OK with that. And then there was the part about Martha fussing over Jesus as only friends do. Bet Jesus kind of liked that… just a little. Who doesn't like going over to a friend's house and having them prepare a tasty meal for you? Jesus knew the value of friendship, and he appreciated his good friends.

Of all the great first century saints, of all the heavyweights that could have been selected, why was Martha chosen? Because of her abiding friendship with Jesus. The Latin for abiding is *"maneo"* which means "to remain" or "to stay" or "to endure" (or like the Marine Corps' *semper fi*). The Church Militant Field Manual states:

> Everything in the religious order—sacraments, devotions, teaching, scripture, moral discipline, preaching, etc.— is meant to bring us to this deeper state of being, to this Divine Connection. Jesus calls it "abiding" (Jn 15:4). This Divine Connection, this conformity to love, this participation in the Divine Life of God is the very power of the Holy Spirit and is referred to as being in a state of grace.[38]

---

[37] https://catholic-link.org/quotes/maximilian-kolbe-god-sends-friend-support/
[38] Church Militant Field Manual, excerpt, n.p.

Martha's friendship with Jesus is often overlooked. Some zoom right past the passages in the gospel about Martha like they were no big deal. But they are. Why? Because friendship with Jesus, literally and figuratively, has multiple levels of applicability in our own lives. Friendship with Jesus, i.e., being in the state of grace, is everything.

Despite its spiritual importance, friendship with Jesus is rarely discussed. Ponder for a moment what it must have been like to be His friend. Wouldn't it be thrilling and humbling to welcome Jesus into your home? His very presence brings blessing and comfort.

Jesus's visit to Martha's house is found in Luke 10: 38-42:

> Now it came to pass as they went that he entered into a certain town: and a certain woman named Martha, received him into her house. And she had a sister called Mary, who sitting at the Lord's feet, heard his word. But Martha was busy about much serving. Who stood and said: Lord, has thou no care that my sister hath left me alone to serve? Speak to her therefore, that she help me. And the Lord answering, said to her: Martha, Martha, thou art careful, and art troubled about many things: But one thing is necessary. Mary hath chosen the best part, which shall not be taken away from her.

When the guests are present, Martha faces a choice: be at peace or be distracted. Mary chose peace and listened to Jesus. Mary chose the better portion, the "one thing necessary" (*unum necessarium*). Eternal salvation is our only affair. Martha chose to be anxious, distracted and to listen perhaps only intermittently to Jesus.

Saint Martha was given a gentle rebuke from Jesus to stop her host duties and visit with him and her company. Is it not totally understandable, however, that Martha would like some assistance from her sister? On one level, yes. Looking at this from a different angle, however, Jesus gave Martha feedback because: 1) she asked, and 2) He loved her and gave her fraternal correction (more on that in Chapter 2).

The feedback Jesus gave Martha was a gift. It was an opportunity for personal development. Oftentimes, hearing someone's feedback can be difficult. We feel justified in our course of action and it can be jarring to be challenged by an opposing view. Fortunately, we know that Jesus's positive, specific feedback can be trusted as He is the truth.

Looking at this from another point of view, was Martha prepared to receive His feedback? She may not have expected the answer she received, but a saintly person like Martha is open to divine correction. Furthermore, did Jesus offer his feedback unsolicited? No. He waited until Martha queried Him.

Jesus did not intend to hurt Martha with His gentle rebuke. Many, however, find it difficult to strike the right balance when giving constructive criticism. It's not easy. But it is something followers of Christ must do at times.

Another interesting point to ponder: When Martha received Jesus's feedback, did she argue, defend herself, or even respond to Jesus? No. She remained silent, sat at his feet next to Mary, and listened to his further words. On a path to sainthood, Martha most likely felt nothing but gratitude. Too often we take criticism the wrong way by not receiving it in the spirit in which it was offered. Sometimes we feel bitter or resentful.

Ask yourself what it must have been like for Martha to know that Jesus was coming over for a visit. She most likely thought Jesus, her good friend, was unlike any other friend. Her soul must have been overjoyed to be in His company again. As any good host, she would have wanted her house to be clean, neat and orderly when her special guest arrived. Which then leads to the question, how have we ordered our homes? How welcome would Jesus be if He visited your house this afternoon?

Has your home been blessed by a priest? Is the Epiphany blessing written in chalk over your front door each year? Are Saint Benedict medals hung over your doors? Do you keep and use Holy Water in your home? Would Jesus be disappointed in anything He would see, or find in your house or on your smart phone? Or would He be pleased to see an appropriate and loving display of Catholic pictures and statues in your home? Would Jesus see a Divine Mercy picture in your entrance hallway? Would He see a Sacred Heart statue and/or picture in the family room? How about a statue of His mother, Our Lady of Fatima, in the living room? Would He find several well-used rosaries on a nearby table? Would He see a crucifix on the wall in every bedroom?

In other words, when guests come to visit, do they recognize a Catholic home?

More importantly, do they know you are Catholic even before you speak?

When we attend Mass or say the Rosary, the mind can wander due to mundane distractions. Is that what happened to Martha in the presence of Jesus? Just as Jesus asked Martha to put aside her chores so that she could spend time with Him, so too does He wish us to give Him our focused attention when we pray, attend Mass, or say the Rosary. He knows we have difficulty focusing on what is truly important, but we can focus with His grace and our determined effort.

There are certain moments in the Bible that are more personal and poignant than others. The stories speak differently to our hopes and dreams. One such story is the calling of Saint Matthew. Carravagio's depiction of that event is sublime.

The Calling of Saint Matthew, *Caravaggio*[39]

Imagine Jesus calling Saint Matthew to follow Him. When I look at Carravagio's painting, my soul's imagination is opened wide. In *The Calling of Saint Matthew,* I contemplate and desire the Supreme Good, which is God himself. Out of the many people Jesus could have

---

[39] Wikipedia, https://en.wikipedia.org/wiki/The_Calling_of_St_Matthew_%28Caravaggio%29

chosen, this day He specifically chose Saint Matthew. Similarly, He specifically chooses us. Each of us. He wants us all to hear His voice and follow Him. To know that our God and Savior yearns for each of us to draw near so that we can love and serve Him is the highest and humblest honor and privilege.

The moment when Jesus visits Martha's house is as sublime as the calling of Saint Matthew. Both are a snapshot in time, but so rich in meaning. God visits with us. God calls us. Do we visit with Him? Do we call out to Him? Friendship is a two-way street.

We know that the state of our soul is more important than a physical house. How welcome is Jesus in our souls? Do we frequent the Sacrament of Confession and do our best to live in the state of grace? After Baptism, the Council of Trent called the Sacrament of Penance "the second plank after shipwreck." Are our souls, lives, and homes ordered in a way that says, "Why not me?" with respect to true friendship with Jesus? Or are we busying ourselves with unimportant things?

And, now, a twist. The Bible often explains things through parables. In this instance could it be that Jesus was not speaking to Martha about her physical house? Could it be that He had in mind the state of her soul? Maybe Jesus noticed that in Martha's prayer life she was preoccupied with matters that were keeping her from achieving holiness. Maybe Jesus was pointing out that she was being more of a spiritual "busy body" than a physical "busy body" by attending to household duties when friends came to visit.

And, a possible second twist. Because friendship is a two-way street, do we have the requisite sense of holy awe when we visit Christ's dwelling place each Sunday? We would be elated if Jesus were to visit our house. So, too, should those feelings of elation occur each week when we visit His house—a Catholic church where He is present in the Most Holy Eucharist. As Catholics we are truly blessed to be able to visit with our friend, Lord and Savior every Sunday.

Msgr. Romano Guardini, in "Meditations Before Mass," wrote:

> "When we come into church from the outside our ears are filled with the racket of the city, the words of those who have accompanied us, the laboring and quarreling of our own thoughts, the disquiet of our

hearts' wishes and worries, hurts and joys. How are we possibly to hear what God is saying? That we listen at all is something; not everyone does. It is even better when we pay attention and make a real effort to understand what is being said. But all this is not yet the attentive stillness in which God's word can take root. This must be established before the service begins, if possible, in the silence on the way to church, still better in a brief period of composure the evening before."[40]

Before, during, and after Mass, do we take a few minutes to speak with Jesus present in the Most Holy Eucharist? Do we acknowledge how close we are to Jesus? Do we know how fervently He desires for us to recognize His presence? "Acquire the habit of speaking to God as if you were alone with him," writes Saint Alphonsus Ligouri, "familiarly and with confidence, as to the dearest and most loving of friends." Do we ask God to bless us and send us the many graces we will need that day and the rest of the week until we can visit with Him again next Sunday? He is there in His house. Go. Sit at His feet. Listen. Do not be the "busy body" each week at Mass. Learn from Martha and her holy example.

After Jesus's gentle rebuke at her home, who could deny that Martha was growing in holiness? So, too, it is for us each week when we attend Mass and receive Communion. Jesus gives us the opportunity and graces necessary to increase in sanctity.

Quick side note: The name of the apartment complex next to St. Peter's Church in Vatican City is appropriately Saint Martha. In Italian it is *Casa Santa Marta*. In Latin it is *Domus Sanctae Marthae*. The Old Sancta Marta has rooms for pilgrims. It is a residence for many retired cardinals, archbishops, bishops and monsignors. The New Sancta Marta, during a papal conclave, houses about 120 cardinals.

We may say to ourselves, "If only I were able to meet Jesus and listen to Him first hand, I would be a much holier person." Well, we do have the chance every day to meet, listen to, and get feedback from Jesus. Do we not pray daily? Saint Teresa of Avila instructs us, "For prayer is nothing else than being on terms of friendship with God." We can attend Mass and receive Communion daily. Can we not listen to the Holy Ghost speaking to us when we read Holy Scripture? Jesus also speaks to us through the provision and assistance of our guardian

---

[40] Guardini, "Meditations Before Mass," 17.

angel. Grow closer to your guardian angel. There are so many excuses not to recognize what is right in front of us. We can and must do better.

Jesus is so much closer to us than we think.

When we frequent the Sacrament of Confession, we kneel next to the priest who is acting *in persona Christe* (in the place of Christ). To the priest (Christ) we enunciate our transgressions. Through the priest, Jesus speaks to us. He tells us what we must do to live lives more pleasing to God. We listen to the priest's (Christ's) words. We do not argue nor make excuses. We confess and repent of self-indulgent thoughts or actions with true remorse. We receive Jesus's feedback with gratitude. We accept our penance, and we make a firm pledge of amendment. That is what Jesus our Lord, and friend, desires most for each of us. To be heroic is to receive His counsel, like Martha, and to be more holy in our daily lives.

Our friendship with Jesus will manifest itself in how we treat our neighbors, and especially those most in need. Recall when Jesus said, "And the king will say to them in reply, 'Amen, I say to you, whatever you did for one of these least brothers of mine, you did for me.'" (Matthew 25:40). We can be a good friend to Jesus each day if we so choose.

John 1:7 describes how John the Baptist pointed towards Christ and said, "This man came for a witness, to give testimony of the light, that all men might believe through him." How do we give witness? How do we give testimony to the light? How do we encourage others to believe through him? Our thoughts, actions, and desires must point others to Christ. At times this will require heroic effort. A friend to Christ will follow Him. "Make straight the way of the Lord," (John 1:23).

Do we not see Jesus in those around us? Are we respectful of everyone's dignity, born and unborn, as a child of God? Are we heroic in recognizing that with God there are no coincidences? Each person we encounter and influence by our Catholic example was put before us as an opportunity to bring someone closer to Christ. Your daily interactions matter more than you know. Be heroic and choose to be a friend of Christ. Christ told us in the last verse of Saint Matthew's gospel, "I am with you, always." Can the same be said in reverse? Are we *always* with Christ? Or are we with Him only in good times? Be heroic; and move in the direction you know you must go.

Saint Thomas à Kempis, in *Imitation of Christ*, offers us this splash of cold water with his take on what it means to be a loving friend of Christ:

> "Jesus has many lovers of His heavenly kingdom, but few cross-bearers. Many desire His consolation, but few His tribulation. Many will sit down with Him at table, but few will share His fast. All desire to rejoice with Him, but few will suffer for Him. Many will follow Him to the breaking of the bread, but few will drink the bitter cup of His Passion. Many revere His miracles, but few follow the shame of His cross. Many love Jesus when all goes well with them, and praise Him when He does them a favor; but if Jesus conceals Himself and leaves them for a little while, they fall to complaining or become depressed. They who love Jesus purely for Himself and not for their own sake bless Him in all trouble and anguish as well as in time of consolation. Even if He never sent them consolation, they would still praise Him and give thanks. Oh, how powerful is the pure love of Jesus, when not mixed with self-interest or self-love!"[41]

How do we love Jesus purely for its own sake without expecting something in return? How are we loyal to the God who loves us unceasingly?

Loyalty is a key attribute of friendship. As Proverbs 18:24 says, "One who has unreliable friends soon comes to ruin, but there is a friend who sticks closer than a brother." When your friends are insulted, you come to their defense. It's innate. You jump in no matter the consequences.

I first met Charlie when we were six years old. His family was moving in next door and their house was under construction. Another boy our age, Paul, from down the street showed up and together we did what young boys do on a construction site. We ambled through the dirt and mud, picking up pieces of wood, electrical pipe, wire, and other stuff and threw it at the concrete foundation. Walking around to the back of the house, we noticed that the basement area had accumulated a foot of water. Can't remember how it started, but for

---

[41] Kempis, *Imitation of Christ*, 88-89.

some reason Paul insulted me. Next thing I knew Charlie pushed Paul into the dirty basement water. I don't remember exactly what Charlie said next, but I do remember that Paul wasn't happy, climbed out of the water, and went home. Charlie and I never saw much of Paul after that. As for Charlie and me, we are still close friends to this day—almost fifty years later.

From that moment, I could tell Charlie was the type of friend who would sacrifice for you or show up to help on moving day when others refuse, and he could be relied upon for candid answers. Charlie is a good man, husband, father, and friend. I hope I have been as good a friend to him as he has been to me. Cheers. (Shout out to Erwin and Martin, too. How I met them was not quite as vivid as my first encounter with Charlie. Even so, our friendship over the years has been valued and appreciated by me more than they know. I do love the golf trips, gentlemen. (Where to next?) Loyalty in friendship. It matters.

When people put down our Lord and His Church, do we come to the defense? Or do we slink away in silence thinking *everyone is entitled to their opinion?* Wrong. We must evidence heroic loyalty in friendship to God and His bride. We must not be a fair-weather friend, but instead be an I-got-your back-you-got-mine type of friend. Fierce, loyal, heroic friendship.

Saint Augustine encourages us, "The fruits of charity are joy, peace, and mercy; charity demands beneficence and fraternal correction; it is benevolence; it fosters reciprocity and remains disinterested and generous; it is friendship and communion: Love is itself the fulfillment of all our works. There is the goal; that is why we run: we run toward it, and once we reach it, in it we shall find rest."

In John's Gospel, Jesus tells His disciples: "You are my friends if you do what I command you" (John 15:14). Love demands effort. Let us make a personal commitment to be a better friend to Jesus, a better servant to God the Father, and more charitable to others. "A tree is known by its fruit; a man by his deeds. A good deed is never lost," says Saint Basil the Great. "He who sows courtesy reaps friendship, and he who plants kindness gathers love."

God the Father told Saint Catherine of Siena, "This is why I have put you among your neighbors: so that you can do for them what you cannot do for me—that is, love them without any concern for thanks and without looking for any profit for yourself. And whatever you do for them I will consider done for me." How can we be a friend to our neighbor? Are we kind, gentle, helpful, and forgiving? Or are we at times jealous, envious, bitter, and angry? In other words, how are we meeting our Catholic obligations? How are the saints influencing our behavior?

My favorite movie is *It's a Wonderful Life*. In the closing scene George Bailey opens a Christmas present, a Tom Sawyer book by Mark Twain, and says it is, "a present from a very dear friend of mine." An inscription in the book reads, "Dear George, Remember, <u>no</u> man is a failure who has *friends*. Thanks for the wings! Love, Clarence." Each of us touches the lives of so many people in ways that we may never know. Be grateful for friendship and the opportunity to serve God and others this day and all your days.

In the aftermath of Jesus Christ's Crucifixion, Resurrection, Ascension and the Descent of the Holy Ghost on Pentecost Sunday, the early Christians set out into the world and set it ablaze showing others to love Christ and His bride—the Catholic Church. Early Christian missionaries traveled the world persuading others to accept baptism and follow Christ. Early Christian martyrs bore heroic witness that led to the conversion of nonbelievers to the Catholic faith. Those who preached the "true philosophy" did so against rival pagan beliefs and political powers which maligned and persecuted the Church. Christian persecution was a constant in the first century. Many sought refuge in the catacombs. Many early Christians were ordered to make sacrifices to false gods. If they refused, they were tortured, beheaded, stoned to death, or killed for sport in the Roman Coliseum. Despite numerous challenges, persecutions and martyrdoms, the Christian faith spread quickly in the first century.

According to a medieval legend, Martha, Mary, and Lazarus, along with several other Christians, were seized by Jews, put on a ship with no sails or oars, and set to sea. Miraculously they were guided to Marseilles, France, where they helped to evangelize Provence. Martha's final days were spent in a prayer community of women, marked by her holiness, piety, candor, and prudence. Her body lies in Tarascon, France.[42]

Set the table. Jesus is stopping by for dinner tonight.

Are you ready?

First Century Saints

Saints Joseph, Joachim, Anne, Elizabeth, John the Baptist, Cornelius (the jailer), Simon (the Cyrene), Veronica, Dismas (the Good Thief), Mary Magdalen, John the Beloved, Peter (d. 67), Paul, Andrew, Matthew, James the Greater, James the Lesser, Thomas, Philip, Bartholomew, Simon, Jude Thaddeus, Barnabas, Thecla, Priscilla, Linus, Cletus, Clement, Anacletus, Titus (d. 96) and Timothy (d. 97), pray for us.

Saint Martha is the patron saint of cooks, dietitians, domestic workers, and homemakers.

Saint Martha is often represented with a water pot, a dragon bound with a girdle (symbolizing temptation resisted), torch (symbolizing enlightenment and zeal) and censer (symbolizing prayer and worship).[43]

Saint Martha's traditional feast day is July 29.

Saint Martha, *ora pro nobis* (pray for us).

First Century History

36- **Saint Stephen becomes the first Catholic to be martyred for the faith**.

39- Saint Peter baptizes Cornelius, thus beginning mission to the Gentiles. ("A Timeline of Catholic Church History: 1 - 500 A.D.", Suzanne Fortin, 2003.[44]

---

[42] Catholic Culture,
https://www.catholicculture.org/culture/liturgicalyear/calendar/day.cfm?date=2019-07-29
[43] Ibid.
[44] https://www.catholicbridge.com/catholic/timeline-of-catholic-church.php)

41-54- Roman Emperor Claudius the first to persecute Christians. (From 30 to 311, a period in which fifty-four emperors ruled the Roman Empire, only about a dozen harassed Christians.)[45]

42- The first persecution of Christians in Jerusalem under Herod Agrippa.

44- Martyrdom of Saint James the Great, the first apostle to die for the faith.

67- **Quo Vadis?** When Saint Peter was fleeing danger in Rome via the Appian Way, he encountered Christ heading towards Rome and asked him, *Quo Vadis?* (Where are you going?) Jesus answered, "I am going to Rome to be crucified again." Saint Peter knew that he must return to Rome and would most likely be crucified himself. A Quo Vadis chapel stands today in Rome on the Appian Way.

67 "Saint Peter crucified upside down and buried on the hill of the Vatican where St. Peter's Basilica now stands. It is believed that Saint Paul was beheaded on the via Ostia during the sixties and buried where the Basilica of St. Paul Outside the Walls now stands. "Saints Peter and St. Paul were the foremost founders of the Church in Rome through their apostolic preaching, ministry, and martyrdom in that city. They are the solid rock on which the foundation of the Catholic Church is built. They transformed the capital of the Roman Empire into the heart of the Church, with the mission to radiate the Gospel of Our Lord Jesus Christ throughout the world. Saint Peter and Saint Paul are the patron saints of Rome and they share a feast day on June 29."[46]

64-68 "A great number of Christians perished at the hands of the Roman Emperor Nero during the terrible persecution that lasted about four years. Christianity becomes a capital crime and the holy men and women who first died for the Gospel of Jesus Christ are also called the "Protomartyrs of Rome." Some were burned as living torches in the Emperor's gardens; some were crucified; others were fed to wild animals. Many died even before Saints Peter and Paul, and therefore it is said of them that they are the "Disciples of the Apostles ... whom the Holy Roman Church sent to their Lord before the Apostles' death." God used the sacrifice of these holy men and women, who

---

[45] https://www.christianitytoday.com/history/issues/issue-27/persecution-in-early-church-gallery-of-persecuting-emperors.html
[46] "St. Peter, Saint of the Day," *The Catholic Company*, June 29, 2020.

suffered like their savior Jesus Christ, to lay the indestructible foundation of His Church. Their bold witness for the Christian faith as they endured a brutal death won many converts and caused the Church to grow and spread throughout the world. The feast day of the First Martyrs of the Holy Roman Church is June 30th."[47]

70- **The Destruction of Jerusalem.** Titus sacks Jerusalem and destroys its temple. Three primary ramifications: 1) marked the end of the Jewish state (until State of Israel created again in 1948; 2) ended sacrificial system of the Jews; and 3) the mostly Jewish church to that point quickly became Gentile.

95- Persecution of Christians under Domitian.

All popes in the first century were martyred for the faith (Peter, Linus, Cletus, Clement)

Virtue Challenge #1- Friendship

Like Saint Martha, we have only *unum necessarium* (one necessary affair); that for which alone God created and redeemed us. That is, we are to orient all we do to glorify God, fulfill His will, to be a friend of Christ, to live in a state of grace, and save our souls.

As friendship with Jesus is everything, how will you be a better friend to Jesus today? What steps will you take today to help your soul be in a state of grace? What will you avoid?

How will you bring better bonhomie to all those souls God will place before you in your life?

How will you establish your home to better reflect your friendship with Jesus?

Saint Martha pray for us to accept fraternal correction with the proper heart as you did. Show us the way to be a better friend to Jesus. Help us to be heroic in not only receiving feedback, but in giving it when necessary.

---

[47] "Saint of the Day," *The Catholic Company,* June 30, 2020.

Converse for a moment with the Holy Ghost about friendship. My Lord and my God, how may I serve you more faithfully and completely through the virtue of friendship?

O Great Saint Martha, pray that we may increase in a holy, abiding friendship with Christ.

CHAPTER 2

Polycarp

The Second Century
Candor

"Don't neglect the practice of fraternal correction, which is a clear sign of the supernatural virtue of charity. You may find it hard, for it's easier to be inhibited. It's easier to behave that way, but it's not supernatural. And you will have to render an account to God for such omissions."

~ Saint Josemaría Escrivá

"When you have to make a fraternal correction, do it with great kindness — great charity! —in what you say and in the way you say it, for at that moment, you are God's instrument."

~ Saint Josemaría Escrivá

"Moral principles do not depend on a majority vote. Wrong is wrong, even if everybody is wrong. Right is right, even if nobody is right."

~ Venerable Fulton J Sheen

The 100s

Do you have a family member, or a friend, whom you count on to always tell you the unvarnished truth? Isn't it refreshing to be around that person? Well, most of the time anyway. Who speaks with good old-fashioned candor these days? Over the past few decades, unfortunately, we have been conditioned to filter the truth. We have become afraid to speak our minds in public. All for some lame construct which some label "political correctness."

Communication matters. Candor matters. In recent years, the politically correct have upped the ante with cancel culture and made self-censorship more frequent. As we will discuss later in this chapter, self-censorship is even more insidious than political correctness. On top of political correctness, cancel culture and self-censorship, we will also address compassion (true and false) and fraternal correction in this chapter. Saint Polycarp, and his heroic virtue, punctuated by his unique ability to communicate with candor, will be our focus for the second century.

In the previous chapter, Martha, who walked with, waited on, and welcomed Christ into her home enjoyed the great privilege of being a friend of Jesus while He walked the earth. We read how Martha received a candid rebuke from Jesus and how that interaction positively impacted their friendship. Jesus, most assuredly, did not practice self-censorship.

In the two millennia since, however, the Lord's followers have not had that sublime honor of His physical presence, and yet true friendship with Him remains a possibility, nay a requirement, of discipleship. The stories of all the saints reflect what is possible when that friendship is given priority in one's life. But perhaps few have articulated it as clearly in their words and actions as one of the earliest, Saint Polycarp. That fact is especially fitting given that he was a disciple of Saint John, the Beloved friend and apostle of Christ, and the last of the original twelve to die.

Imagine being a friend of a friend of Jesus Christ. Imagine listening to first-hand stories of time spent with the Lord, little humorous anecdotes, or certain lost parables that were never recorded. Imagine the insights you would glean from such narratives. Our faith rests on two pillars: Scripture and Tradition. Tradition with a capital "T" can be distinguished from tradition or traditions with a small "t" in the following way. Small "t" traditions are practices or ways of doing things that acquire some degree of authority based on their longstanding use and the approbation of the *sensus fidelium*, or the religious sense of the Christian people. But they can be changed as circumstances or customs change.

Capital "T" Tradition, on the other hand, concerns revelation handed down by the apostles to their successors, the bishops in communion with the See of Rome, and safeguarded by the Magisterium, the teaching authority of the Church. And the primary way in which that capital "T" Tradition was handed down in the early Church was not necessarily written and certainly not in anything like a "Bible alone" fashion. There was no Bible! No, Christianity spread based on the oral teaching of its authoritative teachers, those men who based their authority on those who came before them, tracing back to Jesus's original apostles. Polycarp is one of the finest examples.

Many non-Catholic Christians today consider themselves "Bible alone" Christians and feel that by declaring themselves such they are somehow placing themselves closer to the "original" Christians. Nothing could be further from the truth. The books comprising the Bible as we know it today were not definitively determined until the Church Council of Rome in the year 382. That means that for approximately 350 years, the early Christians had no definitive collection of divinely inspired writings to be able to call themselves Bible Christians. To say nothing, of course, of the fact that the majority of the early Christians were illiterate and would have had limited access to the writings outside their celebrations of the Lord's Supper. (And, of course, there is the uncomfortable fact that so-called "Bible alone" Christians today rely upon the decision of the Catholic bishops gathered in council, for the list of books that make up the Bible.)

Again, it is important for Catholic apologists to know that history tells us that the early Church did rely on scripture, but principally on Tradition originating with the Apostles and passed on by ecclesiastical authorities.

And so, the authority of Polycarp, received as it was from the Beloved Disciple himself, was viewed as rock solid by the Christians of his See of Smyrna and elsewhere. So much so that Saint Ignatius of Antioch commented to Polycarp, "your mind is grounded in God as on an immovable rock."

A writing by another early saint and Church Father, Irenaeus, reveals how much the authority of Tradition passed on by Church elders was revered. Here Irenaeus is writing to a friend Florinus who had fallen into heresy:

> These opinions ... Florinus are not of sound judgment ... I saw thee when I was still a boy in Lower Asia in company with Polycarp, while thou wast faring prosperously in the royal court, and endeavouring to stand well with him. For I distinctly remember the incidents of that time better than events of recent occurrence ... I can describe the very place in which the Blessed Polycarp used to sit when he discoursed ... his personal appearance ... and how he would describe his intercourse with John and with the rest who had seen the Lord, and how he would relate their words ... I can testify in the sight of God, that if the blessed and apostolic elder had heard anything of this kind, he would have

cried out, and stopped his ears, and said after his wont, 'O good God, for what times hast thou kept me that I should endure such things?' ... This can be shown from the letters which he wrote to the neighbouring Churches for their confirmation etc.[48]

Just as his disciple, Irenaeus, relied on authority and Tradition handed down, so too did Polycarp. Two stories concerning this great saint reveal how clearly he understood the distinction between capital "T" Tradition and small "t" traditions.

The age during which Polycarp lived was a time of incredible growth of the Church, but also great persecution; it was a time of heresies and the combatting of heresies, which resulted in the clarification or solidifying of certain doctrines, especially those having to do with the God/Man Jesus Christ. When describing the second Christian century, one could very well quote Dickens' classic *A Tale of Two Cities* and say, "It was the best of times; it was the worst of times."

The degree to which Polycarp revered the true teachings of Christ as passed down from the apostles—specifically in this case from Saint John—is evident in the unambiguous language he used when confronting Marcion, a man who taught many errors including that the God of the Old Testament and the God of the New were not one and the same. We learn from Saint Irenaeus that when Marcion demanded that Polycarp recognize him, the saint replied, "Ay, ay, I recognize the first born of Satan!"[49]

That direct speech in the face of heresy, i.e., a break with Traditional teaching, can be contrasted with Polycarp's actions when he visited the pope in Rome to discuss the fact that the churches in the eastern Roman Empire where he lived[50] celebrated Easter on a different day than the churches in the western Empire. According to Irenaeus,

Among these (Victor's predecessors) were the presbyters before Soter. They neither observed it ... [i.e., the same date] ... themselves, nor did they permit those after them to do so. And yet, though not observing it, they were none the less at peace with those who came to them from

---

[48] CATHOLIC ENCYCLOPEDIA: St. Polycarp (newadvent.org)
[49] Ibid.
[50] His diocese of Smyrna is located in what is now Turkey or Asia Minor.

the parishes in which it was observed. . . And when the blessed Polycarp was at Rome in the time of Anicetus, and they disagreed a little about other things, they immediately made peace with one another, not caring to quarrel over this matter. For neither could Anicetus persuade Polycarp ... nor Polycarp Anicetus ... But though matters were in this shape, they communed together, and Anicetus conceded the administration of the Eucharist in the Church to Polycarp, manifestly as a mark of respect. And they parted from each other in peace....[51]

When it came to small "t" traditions, Polycarp and Pope Anicetus anticipated the famous statement of Saint Augustine who lived a few centuries later: "In essential things unity, in non-essential things liberty; in all things charity."

Looking at the narrative between Polycarp and Anicetus in a slightly different, and hopefully instructive, way we observe that while both were firm in their position, the two were cordial, respectful, and fraternal in their disagreement. In other words, they disagreed as true Christians would. In today's anti-God world, on religious and political matters, those with whom we disagree are not afforded liberty but instead are often vilified, and nefarious motives are ascribed to them. It is unfortunate, but it is clear that in these times of diabolical disorientation, the devil is working overtime. As the axiom goes, "God unites, the devil divides."

Twenty-first century Christians can ask themselves how well they live out this statement, how well they follow Polycarp's example of loyalty to his friend, Christ, even at the moment of his martyrdom. He did not seek it out, nor did he run from it. He accepted what God brought his way. Reportedly, as his pursuers closed in upon him, Polycarp even had a vision during prayer in which his pillow was on fire; this told him the manner in which he would die, among the flames.

When he was captured at a farmhouse, he asked for more time to pray and prepared a meal for his captors. "Love those who hate you; pray for those who persecute you." Sounds like someone we know! Polycarp was taken and brought to the arena to be martyred even though he was eighty-six years old.

---

[51] Ibid.

In the arena those close to Polycarp heard what appeared to be a voice from heaven above the crowd, "Be brave, Polycarp, and act like a man." Polycarp displayed his fortitude and loyalty to his friend Christ in dramatic fashion. When asked to say, "Away with the atheists" as a way to condemn his fellow Christians (viewed as atheists by the Romans because of their refusal to worship their multitude of false gods), he instead looked at those calling for his death and said, "Away with the atheists." When he asked Polycarp to swear by Caesar to save himself, Polycarp answered, "If you imagine that I will swear by Caesar, you do not know who I am. Let me tell you plainly, I am a Christian." Finally, when all else failed the proconsul reminded Polycarp that he would be thrown to the wild animals unless he changed his mind. Polycarp answered, "Change of mind from better to worse is not a change allowed to us."[52]

It is also recorded that when asked to curse Christ by the Proconsul, Polycarp replied like a true and faithful friend: "Fourscore and six years have I served Him, and He has done me no harm. How then can I curse my King that saved me?"

That is a steadfast friend, one who is loyal even to the point of death. We can ask ourselves, "Why not me?" Why can I not be that kind of friend to Jesus when confronted by temptation, which is nothing other than being asked by Christ's enemy to deny Him. Perhaps we are not called to be "bloody" martyrs, but maybe we can make Polycarp's final prayer before his martyrdom our own as we begin each day, offering it and all we do, to our Lord and Savior. Consider these powerful words:

O Lord God Almighty, the Father of your beloved and blessed Son Jesus Christ, by whom we have received the knowledge of you, the God of angels, powers and every creature, and of all the righteous who live before you, I give you thanks that you count me worthy to be numbered among your martyrs, sharing the cup of Christ and the resurrection to eternal life, both of soul and body, through the immortality of the Holy Spirit. May I be received this day as an acceptable sacrifice, as you, the true God, have predestined, revealed to me, and now fulfilled. I praise you for all these things, I bless you and glorify you, along with the everlasting Jesus Christ, your beloved

---

[52] https://www.catholic.org/saints/saint.php?saint_id=99

Son. To you, with him, through the Holy Ghost, be glory both now and forever. Amen.[53]

As the pyre was lit to burn the great Polycarp, he said "Amen," and it was seen that God was not done with this holy disciple of His beloved friend John. Rather than being consumed by flames, Polycarp seemed protected by a wall of sorts as the flames formed an arc—some said *sails*—around him. Not to be denied their victim, his captors then proceeded to stab him. Only his blood put out the flames. Miraculous events, to be sure, were occurring at the time of Polycarp's death.

The Roman authorities were afraid of what transpired during the death of Saint Polycarp. So afraid that after his death, they prevented the faithful from retrieving his body as they thought that the Christians would worship Polycarp. Fortunately, some of Polycarp's bones were able to be collected so that others would be edified in advance of their persecution. One of Saint Polycarp's followers said his remains were "more precious to us than the costliest diamonds, and which we esteem more highly than gold."

Polycarp's candor when speaking on matters of faith, when being arrested, and when being put to death, is a model in candor for all time. How often do we hedge when prompted to speak more plainly? Society tells us to "hold your tongue." On other matters we are told to, "Turn a blind eye." Christian candor requires more of us.

How would Polycarp conduct himself in our world of political correctness, cancel-culture and self-censorship? How should we conduct ourselves in this world regarding those realities? Who among us "sticks their neck out" to speak truth to power? Do we 'call 'em like we see 'em'? Or are we merely content to shirk our responsibilities and simply slink away? The world's standard on candor must not be our standard as Catholics. Charity calls us to a higher standard.

About two centuries after Polycarp, Saint Basil the Great would, according to Prof. Plinio Corrêa de Oliveira, "face the totalitarian State in the same way Catholics today will have to act in the face of the new uncrowned neo-pagan emperors, that is, without vacillation or connivance, without concession to error or mutilation of the doctrine

---

[53] Polycarp's Martyrdom | Christian History Institute

of the Church under the pretext of pleasing our enemies."[54] Consider further the story of how Saint Basil spoke with candor and courage when he was summoned by the emperor Valentius to admit the Arians to communion. The prefect in charge, finding that soft words had no effect, said to him, "Are you mad, that you resist the will before which the whole world bows? Do you not dread the wrath of the emperor, nor exile, nor death?" "No," said Basil calmly; "he who has nothing to lose need not dread loss of goods; you cannot exile me, for the whole earth is my home; as for death, it would be the greatest kindness you could bestow upon me; torments cannot harm me; one blow would end both my frail life and my sufferings." The prefect answered, "Never has anyone dared to address me thus." "Perhaps," suggested Basil, "you never before measured your strength with a Christian bishop." The emperor withdrew his commands.[55]

Imagine if our bishops spoke with the authentic strength of true, faithful, Christian bishops. bishops like Saints Polycarp, Basil, and John Fisher. How different would our world be? Instead, we would have had descended into a chasm of false charity where true communication is regulated by woke cancel culture and self-censorship.

In this riven and confused world, we say nothing. We hear error, and say nothing. Instead of effectively engaging anti-Catholics who oppose Christian teachings, we cede to them the media, the town square, our schools and, in some cases, even our parishes. We need strong voices and candor, now more than ever.

Saint Catherine of Sienna commented, "We've had enough exhortations to be silent. Cry out with a thousand tongues—I see the world is rotten because of silence."

In this rotten world people are silent largely because they are afraid. Catholics need to muster the courage to reveal the hard truths. Do not seek the approval of the world and go along with the conformity of the false 'establishment' narrative. The cultural and political establishment is a house built on sand. Seek only the approval of God, who is the truth. Fr. James Altman writes,

---

[54] Corrêa de Oliveira, Traditional Catholic, Facebook post, June 13, 2020. https://sanctoral.com/en/saints/saint_basil_the_great.html.
[55] Ibid.

Speaking the truth is controversial. Speaking the truth is heroic in today's society. Good Catholics do not stay silent when those around us promote intrinsic evil(s). It is grave error to chill the proclamation of the Gospel and the truths of the Church because that is our duty under God. Popes, bishops and priests come and go. But not God. He is and always will be. Therefore, we must always speak God's truth and not those of men who serve an Agenda other than that of God's truth. To squelch the voice of truth, that is diabolical.[56]

Fr. Altman continues,

Love is not demonstrated by playing "doormat." In the face of evil, genuine love is known as "tough love." True love speaks up and speaks out with courage, in the face of grave error that threatens real peace. True love is enshrined in the spiritual works of mercy that teach us to instruct the ignorant and admonish the sinner... In these dark times, let us not fall into the trap of a false mercy, some twisted interpretation of "turning the other cheek." Rather let us be a Light of Christ and an example of genuine love that instructs the ignorant and admonishes the sinner.[57]

Do you choose to remain silent about a known problem? How are you then not complicit? Fr. Altman again commenting on cancel culture references to *Wisdom,* one of the seven books Luther removed from the Bible. "Let us therefore lie in wait for the just, because he is not for our turn, and he is contrary to our doings, and upbraideth us with transgressions of the law, and divulgeth against us the sins of our way of life. He boasteth that he hath the knowledge of God, and calleth himself the son of God. He is become a censurer of our thoughts. He is grievous unto us, even to behold: for his life is not like other men's, and his ways are very different" (Wisdom 2:12-15). In other words, cancel culture advocates silencing alternative views because these views convict them. Says Fr. Altman, "Big tech is trying to cancel the voice of holy people."[58]

Many people are nonplussed by the surge of wokery, the soft totalitarianism of so-called "social justice" ideology and warfare,

---

[56] "Interview with Fr. James Altman," *Church Militant,* October 1, 2020.

[57] Altman, "Freedom from Vengeance" 40-day novena, Day 6 - Let Freedom Ring, Lent, 2021.

[58] Altman, "Why is this Lent more Important Than Others?" Podcast, U.S. Grace Force, February 16, 2021.

intersectionality, cancel culture, critical race theory, white privilege, gender dysphoria, and identity politics that has recently swamped logic. Where did it all come from? How did it all seem to surface at roughly the same time? Who is ultimately behind the agenda? It's rebellion from right and wrong, reason, morality, and God.

Neelay Trivedi took a great dive into cancel culture, conformity, and self-censorship in *The Stanford Review* in October 2020. Mr. Trivedi writes, "Cancel culture is a potent and dangerous force that harms individuals who share contrarian ideas. But while cancellation punishes what has already been said or done, self-censorship preemptively punishes what *isn't* said and constitutes a far more serious challenge to our democratic principles."[59]

Part of the "no" to this world, the going against the grain, must be opposition to the cancel culture, self-censorship, and conformity. The antidote? Contrarianism. Our nation was founded by individuals who fought tyranny and oppression. Today's cancel culture is but the latest tyrannical attempt to deny freedoms and liberties. Cancel culture in its early form suppresses. In its later form it punishes contrarian thoughts, ideas, voices, and persons. Cancel culture has no qualms about targeting, maligning, smearing, and threatening views not in accord with the globalist, anti-God agenda.

Quiz time. What's more sinister, cancellation or self-censorship? Here's my answer: Cancellation focuses on the past. Self-censorship, conversely, focuses on the present and/or future. While cancellation stings, self-censorship suffocates. Thus, self-censorship is more sinister.

Father Rick Heilman, U.S. Grace Force, addressed self-censorship characterizing it as the classic "chilling effect." He writes the chilling effect is, "meant to place fear in anyone who does not stay within the lines of the mob's agenda. 'Chilling effect' is a term in law and communication that describes a situation where speech or conduct is suppressed by fear of penalization at the interests of an individual or group. The problem right now is that this chilling effect is proving to be remarkably effective. Most people are cowering in fear. Even

---

[59] Trivedi, "Repeal the Conformity Tax," *The Stanford Review*, October, 2020.

religious leaders are kowtowing to the mob. Why? Because speaking the truth openly is considered 'divisive.'"[60]

The chilling effect, or self-censorship, has manifested itself in the last century with left wing totalitarian regimes. The enforcer was the state secret police. In Germany, the SS and Stasi. In the USSR, the KGB. In China, the MSS. In Cuba, the CDR. Having visited the latter three communist nations, the omnipresent watching of big brother gave me an icy chill.

The feeling of being a tourist in those unfree nations has me thinking that the path America is on in the 2020s is eerily similar. The leftists and globalists are ratcheting up their intolerance of views that dissent from their worldview. The social media giants have supplanted the state as the *de facto* world secret police. To see corporate America— who owe their existence, growth, and profitability to the citizens of America (and consumers around the world)—turn and bite the hand that feeds it is bizarre in many ways, but not unexpected.

The story of the scorpion and the frog comes to mind. One day the water on the bank of the river starts to rise and the scorpion tells the frog that they must move to higher ground on the other side of the river. The frog says *no* as the scorpion will only sting the frog and he would die. The scorpion says, "Don't be ridiculous, if I sting you while crossing the river, we will both die." Reluctantly, the frog agrees. The scorpion jumps on the back of the frog and they start to cross. About halfway across the scorpion stings the frog and he says, "Hey, why did you do that?" The scorpion says, "It's in my nature."

The moral of the story is that the scorpion (big tech), while telling the frog (USA and world) that it won't sting him, has in their nature the same stinging tendencies. Google when it was founded had a slogan, "Don't be evil." The nature of information search, without being in service to God, can go horribly wrong, horribly fast (banning, shadow banning, censorship, suppression, cancellation, blacklisting, search manipulation, etc.), as we have seen at the outset of the 2020s. Sadly, as we all know, it's in tech's 'nature'…

---

[60] Heilman, "Freedom from Cowardice," Let Freedom Ring: Novena for Our Nation, February 21, 2021.

While America has a proud tradition of fostering innovative ideas and individuals, trailblazers and explorers, society does not always reward those who "rock the boat."

Society imposes, according to Trivedi, what is essentially a "conformity tax" on thinkers who are out of line with prevailing groupthink. "Students pay the conformity tax," according to Trivedi, "when they give up their intellectual freedom to revise essays in hopes of earning a respectable grade. Professionals pay it when they have to choose between their career and sharing their political leanings. Thoughts are suppressed before they have a chance to contribute to the public narrative."[61]

Trivedi continues: "Social networks offer huge rewards for compliance with the norm—likes, follows, and retweets abound. But when an individual refuses to self-censor, they face account restrictions, social media mobs, and outright bans. For young people who grew up online, self-censorship is increasingly becoming a way of life. If practiced for long enough, conformity can become a habit that shifts our culture from one that emphasizes risk-taking and intellectual diversity to one that rewards short-sighted groupthink."[62]

Trivedi concludes, "the conformity tax is extinguishing these intellectual investments and the independent spirit that defines American society. In this way, the conformity tax is far more pernicious than any act of explicit cancellation. It is, at its heart, a form of social credit that attempts to change human thinking and behavior by outlining the price of defiance before any action is ever taken... We must stand up to aggression from conformists and continue to embrace our contrarian streak, no matter how damaging the consequences may seem. If enough of us do so, we will protect American liberty for generations to come."[63]

What is the ultimate target of this chilling effect, self-cancellation and conformity tax? Religious liberty. Each year we observe that religious liberty is ever more squarely in the crosshairs of the leftist, globalist, modernist, Marxist, anti-God intelligentsia. The end game is to cancel not just the Church, not just religion, but God Himself. Don't

---

[61] Trivedi.
[62] Ibid.
[63] Ibid.

let them take our intellect, or our souls. An unrestrained globalist agenda (national sovereignty severely diminished and/or replaced by world government) is pure Luciferian. As Saint Michael, the saints and American patriots did before us, we must embrace the fighting spirit, ingenuity, and the confidence of David as he stepped up to fight and defeat Goliath. Keep fighting. Know that while victory lies in the fight, the outcome ultimately belongs to God. It's time to "David-up."

Saint Francis Xavier instructs us, "It is not the actual physical exertion that counts toward a man's progress, nor the nature of the task, but the spirit of faith with which it is undertaken." Our spirit must be strong. We must resolve to see thing through.

Know that you are alive and doing what you are doing for a reason. Know that you have picked up this book for a reason. Do we conform to the leftist anti-God agenda, or do we resist? Saint Thérèse of Lisieux wrote, "May you trust God that you are exactly where you are meant to be."

About thirty years ago I remember political commentator Pat Buchanan writing about "the visceral recoil of a healthy society wishing to preserve itself." And then when discussing the outcome of the 2020 election and America First, I read Buchanan once again using the "visceral recoil" phrase. I like it. That phrase is most applicable to today's cancel culture and what must be done. As Catholics, how will our "visceral recoil" manifest itself? How does it prescribe we go on the offense? No doubt, we must all be more holy. Pray and fast more. Speak with more charity and more candor.

One of the greatest Catholic communicators of the twentieth century was the Venerable Fulton Sheen. In 1964 he spoke on the topic of "False Compassion." While valuable for those living in the turmoil of the 1960s, Sheen, who was prescient in that his message, speaks to us equally well all these years later in our world of political correctness, cancel culture and self-censorship. Presented below is an extended excerpt from Sheen's talk on "False Compassion":

> Compassion implies there is a distinction between a man destroying himself and being destroyed by others. That's true compassion. What is false compassion? And this is what we are in today. False compassion is a pity shown not to the mugged, but to the mugger. Not

to the family of the murdered, but to the murderer. Not to the woman who was raped, but to the rapist...

There are the social slobberers who insist on compassion being shown to the muggers, to the dope-fiends, to the throat-slashers, to the beatniks, to the prostitutes, to the homosexuals, to the punks so that the decent man today is off the reservation. This is the false compassion.

How did this pity start? It started in literature (Steinbeck, Mendel, James Jones and others) where pity was extended to the good-natured slob, and to every kind of pervert and degenerate. The result is that crime is up and clemency of a false kind is shown to criminals. There is culpability on the part of all those who have participated in false compassion. Why the false compassion? Because we have broken down the standards of right and wrong.

There is latent in our society a grave danger that we may go in for a kind of masochism and cruelty. In the distant future there could be even such a thing as persecution—some social or religious. We need to restore true compassion in our society where we make the distinction between the sin and the sinner. As did the good Lord. Where we will hate the sin, condemn it, and love the sinner.[64]

Hate the sin and love the sinner. So simple. Yet, at times, so difficult. False compassion is often little more than going along with the crowd. Most often it is the easy way out. False compassion is cowardly. Lack of courage, and specifically lack of candor, is one of the keys to understanding what is wrong with the world today. True compassion goes against the grain. True compassion is based on, well, the truth. True compassion is based on true love for another's soul. It is the supreme act of charity to teach someone the truth. Courage, compassion, charity and candor are interrelated. Do we demonstrate compassion and charity, and deploy courage and candor, as often as we should?

Archbishop Sheen also spoke about another current, leftist buzzword: *tolerance.* He said America "is suffering from tolerance.

[64] Sheen, "False Compassion," YouTube post, February 14, 2014.
https://www.youtube.com/watch?v=Sog1oZtt-Q4

Tolerance of right and wrong, truth and error, virtue and evil, Christ and chaos." We should be tolerant of one another's struggles with sin, but never condone that sin. We should not be tolerant of attitudes that give up the fight against sin. Tolerance of anti-God evil is not tolerance; it's cowardice. Christ or chaos.

Sometimes we tell ourselves we should not speak up out of "an abundance of caution." That phrase sounds so defeatist. True, if you don't act, you won't get blamed. At least in this life. God's 'abacus' keeps tally of all the situations He placed you in and you said nothing. To counter "an abundance of caution," think of the situation as calling for "appropriate caution." Notice the difference? The TSA (Transportation Security Administration) phrase comes to mind, "if you see something, say something." If in a crowded space you see a suspected terrorist leaving a backpack and walking away quickly, would you say something to the nearest police officer? Bet you would. If a relatively new acquaintance told you that they were thinking of pursuing a moral wrong like cheating on their spouse or further indulging an addiction, would you say nothing out of an abundance of caution, or with appropriate caution would you use fraternal correction to counsel them to do the right thing?

Former U.S. Secretary of State Mike Pompeo weighed in on the Big Tech censorship at the outset of 2021 calling it "morally wrong." Continuing, the Presbyterian Secretary of State linked Big Tech's censorship to disguised "authoritarianism": "censorship, wokeness, political correctness — it all points in one direction: authoritarianism cloaked as moral righteousness."[65]

A few days before, Pompeo had highlighted the danger of such censorship on social media in a tweet: "Silencing speech is dangerous. It's un-American. Sadly, this isn't a new tactic of the Left. They've worked to silence opposing voices for years. We cannot let them silence 75M Americans. This isn't the CCP."[66]

Governor Ron DeSantis of Florida, echoing Pompeo's comments, has named addressing the censorship of conservatives and conservative viewpoints as a top legislative issue to "get right" moving

[65] Haynes, "Pompeo says Big Tech Censorship is Authoritarianism Disguised As Moral Righteousness," *Life Site News*, January 13, 2021.
[66] Ibid.

forward. He said the country must "really think deeply about if we are a disfavored class based on our principles, based on having conservative views, based on being a Christian, based on whatever you can say that is not favored in Silicon Valley."[67]

Saying what is not favored leads us to fraternal correction, which is closely aligned with true compassion. It is saying what needs to be said out of concern for another's soul. The best piece I saw on this subject was written by Bob Sullivan in 2018. Some extended excerpts:

> Christians are all over the board on how to handle situations where a family member, friend or acquaintance believes something which contradicts the Catholic faith. One extreme is to constantly correct them. This turns people off. The other extreme is to ignore their misunderstanding as we spend our time talking around the truth. In other words, we let them persist in their misunderstanding. After all, who wants to be a thorn in someone's side? Yet Scripture tells us we cannot simply let everything go.

> If I say to the wicked, "O wicked ones, you shall surely die," and you do not speak to warn the wicked to turn from their ways, the wicked shall die in their iniquity, but their blood I will require at your hand. But if you warn the wicked to turn from their ways, and they do not turn from their ways, the wicked shall die in their iniquity, but you will have saved your life. (Ezekiel 33:8-9)

> My brothers and sisters, if anyone among you wanders from the truth and is brought back by another, you should know that whoever brings back a sinner from wandering will save the sinner's soul from death and will cover a multitude of sins." (James 5:19-20)

> Saint Thomas Aquinas taught that all Christians are commanded to speak truth when someone is in error. This is called fraternal correction. Aquinas called it a divine precept which can also be called a law of God. The misunderstanding may be on a theological issue such as the Eucharist, Marian devotion or the divinity of Christ, or it may be on a moral matter such as when someone believes it is okay to steal money from others, or if they claim to be a Christian, yet they

---

[67] Bleau, "Ron DeSantis: Conservative Censorship 'Probably the Most Important Legislative Issue," *Breitbart,* January 15, 2021.

are pro-abortion, or they believe non-marital sex is compatible with the Catholic faith.

Aquinas does not say we must always correct every error immediately. He recognized that there are some situations when the time is just not right. If you immediately offered correction, it would only make matters worse. In that case, we are practicing charity in waiting for a better opportunity which may be a more effective time to talk about it. However, if we avoid offering correction because we fear being called judgmental, or because we do not want to experience emotional discomfort we experience when offering correction, we are not acting with charity, but with our own self-preservation. This is devoid of love and in some cases, this could actually be very hateful.

Fraternal correction is a two-way street. It is important to receive it with as much charity and courtesy as we would hope to see in those to whom we offer it. We never enjoy being corrected, and receiving it with humility is very difficult. But receive it we must. Finally, we should never revel in correcting our brother. While it is wise to consider the timing, it is potentially fatal to avoid it on a regular basis. Mother Angelica once said, "If you are not a thorn in somebody's side, you aren't doing Christianity right."[68]

With fraternal correction on our minds, how are we to think of the current mess in the Catholic Church? What would Saint Polycarp say about current church leadership? Their leadership, candidly, leaves much to be desired. From the abuse scandal to liturgical and doctrinal abuse, to sowing general confusion, to alignment with the globalist and socialist agendas, to not speaking out more courageously and regularly on abortion, traditional marriage and religious liberty, to not condemning Pachamama being placed on Saint Peter's High Altar in the Vatican, it's time to stop the error. And what are the faithful to make of church leaders greenlighting the use of abortion-tainted Wuhan Flu (i.e., COVID) experimental vaccines? In a church led by modernists, moral equivocation is omnipresent. Rationalization and justification can be found for just about anything in today's church.

In an article entitled "We Should Fear Bad Catholics," Msgr. Charles Pope writes:

---

[68] Sullivan, "Fraternal Correction," *Southern Nebraska Register,* June 8, 2018.

Bad Catholics prefer the world and its values to that of Christ and His Kingdom. They will not endure suffering, inconvenience or any difficulty for the Kingdom of God. They will not accept corrections to their worldview, politics, or mindset based on Faith. They are misled and they mislead others. The truth of the Gospel is not their light or compass; it does not provide their marching orders. They will do whatever is expedient to achieve their worldly goals. The cross is not for them. Rather, pleasure, popularity, and possessions are their focus. As Saint Paul says, "For many walk, of whom I often told you, and now tell you even weeping, that they are enemies of the cross of Christ, whose end is destruction, whose god is their appetite, and whose glory is in their shame, who set their minds on earthly things." (Phil. 3:18-19)[69]

Candor, yes. Appeasement, no. Saint Polycarp would no doubt refuse the "extended hand policy" of appeasement favored by so many in the church these days. We need our bishops and priests to be champions of the Faith, defenders of orthodoxy, and guardians of the Church, rather than men of social action, which today is referred to as social justice. To speak to the social justice, or class warfare, Trojan horse narrative for just a moment, when church leaders push the social justice agenda, no matter how much they doll it up, the majority of the faithful's "BS" meter goes off and they reject it outright.

Loyola Academy, the local Jesuit high school near our house—and from what I can tell this is standard operating doctrine for most Jesuits these days—push the social justice agenda and wonder why they are unable to get all the students on board. They also wonder why so many Catholic students abandon their Catholic faith during high school or just after graduation. One answer is simple: Feed Catholics the true and traditional teachings of the church and fruit will result. Push the bad fruit of a twisted leftist and modernist agenda, and there will be little to no fruit.

Case in point: In the spring of 2021, several teachers at Loyola Academy ratcheted up the social justice subversion with the 'soft' launch of the critical race theory curriculum asking students to describe how they have benefitted from white privilege and how they "wield this privilege." Juniors in Peter Jansen's ethics class were required to

---

[69] Pope, "What do Saints Fear?" Blog, December 27, 2015.

answer the following questions: "How do you benefit from white privilege, and how have you held onto that benefit (despite knowing the harm it does)? What have you learned about the ways you have specifically wield[ed] this privilege that do harm (whether you intend to or not)? Dig deep. No sugar coating and no focusing on the good you have done with your privilege. Remember this isn't about being self-congratulatory, it's about pulling out white supremacy. What have you learned about your white privilege that makes you uncomfortable?"[70]

"A second Loyola assignment," according to Fox News, "completed out loud during a lecture in Scott Myslinski's class, gave students a chart with the words 'warmth' on the Y-axis and 'competence' on the X-axis and asked them to rate different groups including Asians, Hispanics, Jews, gay men, transgender people and others. After the graph was completed, the students were asked to use four words (pity, admiration, competence and envy) to describe the groups. A third assignment gave students a list of words paired together (i.e. whites and people of color, women and men, etc.) and asked them to circle which has greater power in American society."[71]

One current Loyola Academy student Hannah Brennan, a student in Jansen's class, told Fox News, "It reminds me of China with the reeducation camps. It feels like they're very much pushing their opinions as facts and teaching opinions as facts. And it's very manipulative."[72] Spot on Hannah. Appreciate your commenting on the record about this fiendish academic theory, along with efforts to bully and silence conservatives at the school. Refuse to accept their leftist lies. Don't be bullied into thinking that you are a racist when you are not. Don't be intimidated by radical liberal, self-destructing, America-hating, anti-reality ideas.

Understandably, many people of faith are disappointed, and some are furious with Loyola. Several are pulling their kids, and bequests, at a rapid pace. Do the Jesuit, leftist, Social Justice Warriors care? Nah, progressivism trumps all. One trusted source told me that Loyola hired David Axelrod's (former Obama advisor) public relations

[70] Garber, "Chicagoland prep school Loyola shames White privilege in student assignment," *Fox News*, March 30, 2021.
[71] Ibid.
[72] Ibid.

firm to help mitigate the fallout from the negative press they had been receiving about the CRT issue. Amidst the fallout, Loyola had the temerity to double down and state that their embrace of critical race theory is consistent with Catholic social teaching. Really? Don't think so. Maybe consistent with radical, liberal, social justice, Jesuit Catholicism. But not authentic Catholic social teaching.

I would like to share one example about my family's experience with Loyola Academy. Because our son attended, we knew about the social justice advocacy issues at the school. As a result, my wife and I were perpetually on guard. During Homecoming Week 2019, I stopped by the school for a meeting. Upon arriving at the main entrance, I was greeted with a gay pride rainbow flag wrapped around the receptionist's desk.

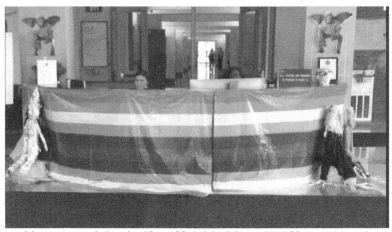

Main reception desk at local Jesuit High School during 2019 Homecoming week.
'Over the Rainbow' Wizard of Oz decoration, or Gay Pride Flag promotion?

Looking at the picture, what first comes to mind for you? For me, it was, "Why is the gay pride flag being displayed so prominently at a supposedly Catholic High School?" My second thought was, *Why have none of the students, teachers, anyone in the administration, or any parents, spoken up and requested that it be taken down?* Flags are displayed by those who have control. Therefore, those in control at the school tacitly approved of the gay pride flag, and by their nature, support those relationships. My meeting that day was with a development person. I did bring it up to him and he said, "Well some of us like to keep a more open mind about things and show everybody they are welcome."

What?

Recognizing that my development contact was part of the problem, I thought about how best to proceed. The next night the president of the school was giving a presentation providentially entitled "Why bother?" at a local parish. So, I bothered to show up to inquire about the flag. Sin has us remain silent when our baptism and confirmation calls us to arms, to stand up and speak out against sin in the world, or, sadly, now even in a Catholic school.

I approached the president at the parish presentation and showed him the picture on my phone. I said displaying the gay pride flag is never appropriate at a Catholic institution, adding it's disappointing that no one else noticed this and had it taken down. His response was, "I'll look into it." I followed up with an email that night to reiterate my point and to facilitate his providing feedback. I heard from him the next day. He wrote, "the display you reference is not nor was it intended to be a display of a 'gay pride flag.' As I mentioned, the theme for homecoming this year is 'There's No Place Like Homecoming' and throughout the week various images or phrases from the Wizard of Oz have been incorporated into the celebration, including 'somewhere over the rainbow'... Nonetheless, given your concern, we did have the display modified today to more closely depict a rainbow and not give the appearance of a flag."

Over the rainbow? By displaying two large gay pride flags? Not buying it. Well, at least a modification was made. That's good. Right? Wrong. I drove over to the school to see the modification first hand. They cut a two-foot arch in the bottom center of the flag believing it was a satisfactory modification. Big whoop. The school was not backing down from their unintentional, or intentional, messaging of support for the gay pride flag. What a shame. Jesuits can be so darn dodgy to deal with at times.

The Catholic Church teaches that a homosexual act is one of the four sins that cry to heaven for justice. The *Catechism of the Catholic Church* states that "basing itself on Sacred Scripture, which presents homosexual acts as acts of grave depravity, tradition has always declared that 'homosexual acts are intrinsically disordered.' They are contrary to the natural law. They close the sexual act to the gift of life. They do not proceed from a genuine affective and sexual complementarity. Under no circumstances can they be approved."[73] In number 2359, the *Catechism* goes on to discuss how Catholic schools should help students who experience same-sex attraction by advising chastity, self-mastery, prayer, and sacramental grace." No dodgy there.

Father Anthony Brankin, former pastor of St. Odilo Parish in Berwyn, Ill, gave a candid sermon discussing the homosexualist agenda. In his 'non-dodgy' homily he, as a Catholic pastor, is atypically blunt on the subject. While charitable in his explanation of the immorality of homosexuality, he is compassionate to those who struggle with this burden. A few excerpts:

> I really do fear that we hardly understand the concept of immorality in general, and of the immorality of homosexual activity in particular, any more. Back in the 19th century, the libertine poets, artistic champions of free and unfettered lust, used to call this particular vice the 'love that dare not speak its name.' Now it can't shut up. It is bombarding us 24 hours a day, seven days a week. Every show has the homosexual component. The propaganda machine is in full active mode; and they are relentless and unyielding in promoting and telling us how good homosexuality is. Modern media life has become all about us accepting homosexual behavior, about how wonderful it is, how it is just two sensitive guys holding hands, how they are a gift to the world, how if we are going to be nice to everyone, we need to embrace their lifestyle.

> I fear the constant barrage in the newspapers, the television, the media and movies has absolutely deadened our sensitivity to the wrongness of homosexuality. And why is it wrong? Because all this propaganda says that that kind of activity is equal to that between men and women—and it isn't. It cannot be—ever—and simply because that activity cannot yield the fruit of children. Life cannot issue forth from that kind of physicality.

> The reason that homosexual activity is so repugnant to healthy societies is because it is a lie. It says that nature doesn't matter; but it does! It says that biology doesn't matter; but it does! It says that God doesn't matter. But He does matter, and most of all.

---

[73] Catechism, 2357.

I hope I recognize that those persons afflicted with this particular temptation have a daily struggle that reaches terrible proportions of anguish and suffering. But the God who loves them does love them. He is there with His grace and help and presence to help them through it all, just as He is there with the rest of us, giving us all the help we need to stay virtuous.[74]

Fast forwarding from 2011 to 2019, Cardinal Raymond Burke and Bishop Athanasius Schneider, along with several other bishops, reiterated the Catholic position on same-sex attraction when they published their "Declaration of Catholic Truths." Compared to Fr. Brankin, their more genteel document states, "Hence, the opinion is contrary to natural law and Divine Revelation that says that, as God the Creator has given to some humans a natural disposition to feel sexual desire for persons of the opposite sex, so also He has given to others a natural disposition to feel sexual desire for persons of the same sex, and that God intends that the latter disposition be acted on in some circumstances."[75]

Despite the clear teachings of the Church, in an apparent attempt to counter the more traditional "Declaration of Catholic Truths" faction, there is a growing movement of dissident clergy and religious in the U.S. who are now openly advocating for confused, and uncharitable, pro-homosexual outreach. Take, for example, Fr. James Martin, the confusion-spreading Jesuit heretic, whose multi-year crusade to bridge Catholic teaching to mortal sin, was at the outset of 2021 joined by a group of twelve U.S. bishops, and the Ursuline Sisters of Louisville, when they told young persons with homosexual inclinations that "God is on your side."[76] Their statement contradicts Church teaching that says homosexuality is not a creation of God.

There is open disagreement (i.e., rebellion) in the Church over homosexuality. It does not appear that the issue will be settled during the Francis pontificate. Therefore, expect the Catholic Church to continue to lose credibility on the matter.

In 2015 at the Synod on the Family, Cardinal Robert Sarah, Prefect of the Congregation for Divine Worship and the Discipline of

---

[74] Brankin, Sermon, Published in "Renew America," June 26, 2011.
[75] Baklinski, "Ursuline Sister Join Growing List," *LifeSite News*, February 8, 2021.
[76] Ibid.

the Sacraments, said, "What Nazi fascism and communism were in the 20th century, Western homosexual and abortion ideologies and Islamic fanaticism are today."[77]

Another example of an organization that has disgraced itself in recent years by drifting to the far left is the "civil rights" group Southern Poverty Law Center (SLPC). Since 1990, the SPLC had published a list of hate groups that started with groups like the Ku Klux Klan and neo-Nazis. By 2020, the center included on its list numerous pro-life and pro-traditional marriage Christian organizations they described as "anti-LGBTQ hate groups."[78]

Many of these groups on the list are "well-respected, such as the Ruth Institute, Alliance Defending Freedom (ADF), Family Research Council, and several smaller Christian churches."[79] Brian Brown, president of the International Organization for the Family rejected the SPLC's hate list classifications. "It is really the SPLC themselves who are motivated by prejudice and bigotry. There is nothing 'hateful' about believing that children deserve a mom and a dad, but it is entirely hateful to persecute organizations and individuals who support this idea."[80]

With the SPLC's logic, who can doubt that one day soon all religions, including the Catholic Church, that espouse pro-life and pro-family moral positions will be listed as hate groups. For that matter, no doubt in coming years we'll see a "ground-breaking blockbuster" report from SPLC condemning the teachings of Jesus Christ. Who ultimately would be behind such a divisive and hateful endeavor like that?

Where some civic leaders desire to take our nation is disgraceful. Sadly, the snowball is only picking up steam, and getting larger as it rolls downhill. Knowing the gates of hell will not prevail against the Catholic Church, however, we know they have a "snowball's chance in hell" of ultimately succeeding. That's not to say that the coming years won't be quite uncomfortable for faithful Catholics in particular, and people of faith in general.

---

[77] Rocca, "Pope Francis Removes Conservative African Cardinal," *Wall Street Journal,* February 20, 2021.
[78] Staff, "SPLC Denounced as 'Thoroughly Disgraced,'" *Catholic News Agency,* February 2, 2021.
[79] Ibid.
[80] Ibid.

With fraternal correction on our minds, how are we to think of what is going on in our country (and the world) with homosexuality and transgenderism? What would Polycarp say about these issues? Discussion of these topics for Catholics, and others of sound morals, was once quite straightforward. In the pre-conciliar Church, catechists and theologians would say this kind of talk is "offensive to pious ears" and anyone engaging in these lifestyles was "living in sin." Respect the sovereignty of God in choosing for you your DNA as male or female. If you have any of the aforementioned proclivities, live chastely. We love you, but sin is sin. Go, repent, and sin no more. We all have our crosses. That's how it would have been approached a generation or two ago. In today's society many have attempted to change the 'rules' for how we may even discuss these subjects. Sadly, even many bishops have been malformed, thus scandalizing and negatively influencing their flocks, and have taken public positions lacking true charity.

The sovereignty of God will not be mocked. When God is evicted, human reason flails. People make decisions that make no sense. How is it that we can do the unthinkable? Often times it is due to the dimming of the intellect. Reason is all but extinguished in some.

Before Vatican II, popes always taught that without the Catholic religion, man's reason will inevitably falter, his understanding of the natural law will subside, and the will weakens. Pope Saint Pius X wrote, "The intellect is a guide ... but if it lacks its companion light, the knowledge of divine things, it will be only an instance of the blind leading the blind."

God the Father said to Saint Catherine of Siena, commemorated in her Dialogues, "Oh, how sweet and pleasant to that soul and to Me is holy prayer, made in the house of knowledge of self and of Me, opening the eye of the intellect to the light of faith, and the affections to the abundance of My charity, which was made visible to you, through My visible Only-begotten Son, who showed it to you with His blood!"[81] "Opening the eye of the intellect to the light of faith" is wisdom—intellectualism infused with reason and faith. Intellectualism without faith is a waste and can often lead to spiritually harmful opinions which are contrary to the teachings of the Church.

---

[81] Catherine of Siena, *Dialogue of Saint Catherine of Siena*, 92.

Continuing in her Dialogues, Saint Catherine wrote about priests who commit homosexual sins appearing before God. The Lord said to her, "like the blind and stupid having dimmed the light of the understanding, they do not recognize the stench and misery in which they find themselves." He continued, "It is not only that this sin stinks before me, who am the Supreme and Eternal Truth, it does indeed displease me so much and I hold it in such abomination that for it alone I buried five cities by a divine judgment, my divine justice being no longer able to endure it."[82]

Due to their angelic nature, Our Lord went on to explain to Saint Catherine that even the demons are repulsed by this sin, "This sin not only displeases me as I have said, but also the devils whom these wretches have made their masters. Not that the evil displeases them because they like anything good, but because their nature was originally angelic, and their angelic nature causes them to loathe the sight of the actual commission of this enormous sin."[83]

Homosexual sin is traditionally one of the four sins that cry to heaven for vengeance. (The other three being willful murder, oppressing the poor, and defrauding the worker of his wages.) God's justice may or may not be served in this life, but His divine justice will most assuredly be served in the next.

Consider the sad fact that the following headline was ever even written, "America's top 10 homosexuality-promoting Catholic bishops." But it was. The list: Cardinal Blaise Cupich (Chicago), Cardinal Wilton Gregory (Washington, D.C.), Cardinal Joseph Tobin (Newark, NJ), Archbishop John C. Wester (Santa Fe, NM), Bishop Robert McElroy (San Diego), Auxiliary Bishop John P. Dolan, (San Diego), Bishop John Stowe (Lexington, KY), Bishop Steven Biegler (Cheyenne, WY), Bishop Edward Weisenburger (Tucson, AZ), Bishop Joseph R. Kopacz (Jackson, MS), retired Cardinal Kevin Farrell (Dallas, TX).[84]

The author, John-Henry Weston, comments on his list: "Knowing this list is actually good news. We can avoid these bishops

---

[82] Baklinski, "Here's how one saintly pope would clean up gay orgies at the Vatican." *LifeSite News*, July 11, 2017.
[83] Ibid.
[84] John-Henry Weston, "America's top 10 homosexuality-promoting Catholic bishops," *LifeSite News*, February 5, 2021.

and we can guard our children, our families, and our friends from their false teaching. But most importantly, we can pray for their conversion... They all believe they are practicing Catholics. It's just that they believe something very different from what the Church has always taught about homosexuality."[85]

Weston continues to explain true Catholic teaching with charity: "Homosexuality is an intrinsically disordered sexual drive. Just like the temptation to any sin, these drives are to be fought against, and giving in to them brings us to sin. The inclination or temptation is not, in itself, a sin. When we give in to the temptation is when we sin, which can deprive us of eternal life. Just like it's a sin for a married man to give in to temptations to be intimate with a woman who is not his wife, or even as Our Lord Himself said, to look at another woman with lust, so, too, do those men and women who give in to the temptations of lustful desires towards people of the same sex harm themselves and those they involve in their behaviors."[86]

Westin concludes with candor: "The Church's stance on this is one of love. Love for God first, and love of neighbor and self. It is not love to offend God, nor to harm your neighbor or yourself. Same-sex sexual behavior harms the body, mind, and soul. To really show love, to really care for those with same-sex attractions is to tell them with kindness and honesty that giving in to such temptations is deadly, and with God's grace those temptations can be overcome. It is a struggle, to be sure, just like it's a struggle to remain pure in this world that is so steeped in sexual temptation. But just remember that Our Lady warned in 1917 that more souls go to hell for sins of the flesh than for any other sin."[87]

Another Catholic commentator who has a decidedly more edgy writing style is John Zmirak. In addition to being the author of *The Politically Incorrect Guide to Catholicism* and editor at *The Stream*, Zmirak is one of the most astute, incisive, witty, and candid Catholic commentators today. In his article, "The Worst Person in America Is a Catholic Bishop. But Which?" Zmirak presents the harm, divisiveness, and confusion caused by three "exceptional" prelates:

---

[85] Ibid.
[86] Ibid.
[87] Ibid.

Cardinal Wilton Gregory (DC), Cardinal Blaise Cupich (Chicago), and Bishop John Stowe (Lexington, KY).

On Gregory: "In violation of canon law, Gregory has offered Holy Communion to anti-Catholic LGBT zealot and infanticide advocate Joe Biden… Gregory winks at Biden's blatantly anti-Christian positions, and praises him for his stances on ecology, big-government spending, and mass immigration… Pontius Pilate never met a Sadducee so eager to collaborate."

On Cupich: "As one acquaintance wrote to me: 'Would [Cupich] ever have criticized Biden as harshly as he is criticizing Gomez and the USCCB?' Well, no, of course not. To ask the question is to laugh at the question."

On Stowe: "This one is my personal favorite. What can you say about a bishop who denounced Nick Sandmann and the other pro-life Covington teens based on thirty seconds of doctored footage? And then refused to back down, retract, or correct himself—even after the *Washington Post* was forced to admit that those boys were framed? That's a special kind of shepherd, one who learned to howl with the wolves."[88]

The sanctity of marriage and even gender itself is under attack. Gender and marriage are instituted by God whose commandments do not change. Marriage is God's faithful union going all the way back to the Garden of Eden. The modern world, however, loves to introduce false and deceptive logic and language in an attempt to distort truth and reality. It's quite evil.

Besides Zmirak, three other leading authors who expose with candor and clarity the deception and depravity of our time are Ryan Anderson, Doug Mainwaring, and Jennifer Bilek. So as to get the highly consequential male/female topic right, I'd like to present to you a few thoughts from Zmirak, Anderson, Mainwaring, and Bilek.

Zmirak leads us off: "the Transgender lobby is the richest racket on earth, funded by a small cabal of white billionaire perverts. These men indulging the fetish of autogynephilia pour their cash into a cause

---

[88] Zmirak, "The Worst Person in America," *American Greatness,* January 31, 2021.

that's destroying women's sports, endangering women worldwide, and aimed at destroying all our mammalian institutions."[89]

Ryan Anderson, named President of the Ethics and Public Policy Center (EPPC) in 2021, is the author of excellent books such as: *When Harry Became Sally: Responding to the Transgender Moment* and *Truth Overruled: The Future of Marriage and Religious Freedom,* and co-authored *What Is Marriage? Man and Woman: A Defense* and *Debating Religious Liberty and Discrimination.* In an article pointing out the contradictions of transgenderism, Ryan observed, "A transgender future is not the 'right side of history,' yet activists have convinced the most powerful sectors of our society to acquiesce to their demands. While the claims they make are manifestly false, it will take real work to prevent the spread of these harmful ideas."[90]

Doug Mainwaring, of *LifeSite News,* commenting in January 2021 around the time the new class of U.S. congressmen was being sworn in, writes, "It's now clear that U.S. House Democrat leadership's descent into depravity is complete. According to newly revealed House rules for the just-begun 117th Congress, terms such as 'father, daughter, mother, and son' as well as gendered pronouns are banned. House Speaker Nancy Pelosi said the new rules reflect 'the views and values of the full range of our historically diverse House Democratic Majority.' And as if to make the depravity of their obsession with gender inclusiveness abundantly clear, during yesterday's first session of the new year Rep. Emanuel Cleaver (D-MO) ended the opening prayer by declaring 'Amen, and Awoman.' ...All this cannot be written off as the silliness of political correctness within the Democratic Party. It's not silly at all; it's diabolical."[91] Mainwaring continues,

> Liberal elites, led by five members of the U.S. Supreme Court, dealt a substantial blow to reality, as well as civil and religious liberty, in 2015 when they altered the immutable definition of marriage to include genderless, anti-complementary "marriage." Something is desperately wrong when the supposed brightest legal minds in the nation determine that sodomy constitutes consummation of marriage and

---

[89] Zmirak, "I Kissed Twitter Goodbye," *The Stream,* January 1, 2021.
[90] Anderson, "Transgender Ideology is Riddled With Contradictions," Heritage Foundation. February 9, 2018.
[91] Mainwaring, "House Dems ban words like 'father' and 'mother,' end prayer with 'Amen and Awoman'" *LifeSite News,* January 4, 2021.

genitalia are no longer indicative of gender. We are witnessing a coup against reality—against science and nature, and, above all, truth—as liberal elites seek to establish and enforce a false construction of reality, an ideological pseudo-reality. "It must be observed that people who accept pseudo-realities as though they are 'real' are no longer normal people," wrote Dr. James Lindsay in "Psychopathy and the Origins of Totalitarianism," presciently published just a few days before the new (2021) Congress began.[92]

Finally, Jennifer Bilek, campaigner for the Rights of Nature in Women and Children, has stated that in a relatively short amount of time, transgenderism has morphed into a global industry. Transactivists, global homosexual non-governmental organizations (e.g., Arcus Foundation, and Gill Foundation) and billionaire philanthropists (e.g., Pritzker) have significant influence on the civic, cultural, and moral debates in the U.S. and other nations through tech platforms and our political infrastructure. The elites have adopted leftist causes with the intent of social engineering and normalizing disordered and perverse transgenderism/body disassociation. Bilek writes,

> The fetish, or mental disorder, was rebranded as transgenderism beginning with a stealth campaign that began in the 1990s. It is the corporatizing of body disassociation. Transgenderism is the colonization of women's bodies for sexual gratification and profit, like porn and prostitution. Whereas porn and prostitution are systems of appropriation of women's sex, transgenderism is the eroticization of the colonization of female sex. Men are going beyond using women's bodies for profit, to taking them over. Why are women being targeted? Without objectification of women, the fetish of transgenderism does not exist.[93]

Catholics must not allow people to continue to be groomed to think of themselves as anything outside of the male/female dynamic. The revolutionaries at work here deeply mistake God. God will not be mocked. Transgenderism is unmoored from God's intentions regarding male and female.

---

92 Ibid.

93 Bilek, "Transhumanism and Autogynephilia," YouTube posted December 17, 2020. https://www.youtube.com/watch?v=9kQ_o0G7D38

The Babylon Bee, a satire website, reported on one of Joe Biden's first executive orders: "Misgendering someone will now be punished with death by firing squad—Deadnaming someone will get you an even worse punishment."[94] Even worse punishment? Ouch. Deadnaming, who knew such a word even existed? (Deadnaming is the use of the birth or other former name [i.e., a name that is "dead"] of a transgender person without their consent. Intentional deadnaming is sometimes used to "aggressively dismiss and reject" a person's gender identity and the name that accompanies it, which they may consider deeply disrespectful.)

Why does our government pay for sex reassignment surgeries? Why do people think they can change their God-given sex without changing their DNA? Why are men allowed to enter women's restrooms and locker rooms, and vice-versa? Why are men allowed to compete in women's sports? Why are single-sex institutions and single gender sports teams fast becoming a thing of the past? Why are the Boy Scouts recruiting girls, and why are the Girl Scouts accepting boys? None of it makes sense. Worse yet, what must God think of it?

It does not make sense because it is anti-God. It is rebellion against God. Those who push for such things are, at their core, anti-God. The intellects have been dimmed due to a lack of faith and grace and it is a full-on attack on the sovereignty of God. Indeed, as Mainwaring said, we are witnessing a coup against reality and a push for power. It's about power, plain and simple.

Those who push this rebellious agenda have been taking aim squarely at our children. The number who self-identify as homosexual was in the low single digits for as long as polls were taken until recently. A 2021 Gallup poll now reports that in Generation Z, those born after 1997, 15.9 percent self-identified as lesbian, gay, bisexual, or transsexual. Among Millennials, or those born from 1981 to 1996, the percentage of those who self-identified as homosexual was 9.1 percent. The percentage in Generation X, born 1965 to 1980, was 3.8 percent, and among Baby Boomers, born from 1946 to 1964, the number was 2.0 percent.[95]

---

94 Staff, "Here is a Terrifying List," *Babylon Bee,* January 21, 2021.
95 Brown, "Number of Young American Who Identify as LGBT Skyrockets," *The Daily Wire,* February 24, 2021.

As government and the law have capitulated on these matters, it appears that only religious doctrine remains to prevent a more virulent attack on gender differences. As Catholics, we know (and even those who mock God most assuredly know) just because man's law permits something does not mean that God's law permits something. The same can be said for *Roe v. Wade*. Abortion is legal. But it has been, and always will be, immoral. Lies. Straight from the Father of Lies. Diabolical madness all. Again, straightforward rebellion against God.

The evil and rebellion extends to depraved slogans promoting the sexual anarchy we see in society on yard signs, bumper stickers, and elsewhere. For instance, "Love is love." Really? Um, no, it's not. Fr. Josiah Trenham spoke on this topic noting the difference between licit and illicit love. He says that the slogan "love is love" was developed by people to tell those who are religious, those who have developed a sense of traditional sexual morality, to "shut up."[96] If "Love is love" is true, when can one person tell another person that whatever they do, or want to do, is wrong? Licit love is love. Illicit love is not love, but self-indulgent, sinful acts that are highly offensive to God. A healthy society abides by a natural and moral code to deter aberrant sexual practices.

While the discussion in this chapter thus far is quite shocking in many ways, it's nothing compared to where the Secular Democrats of America want to take the nation. Several anti-God lawmakers, with strong ties to the Democratic Socialists of America, and membership on the Congressional Progressive Caucus and the Congressional Free Thought Caucus, want to take the rebellion against God in a more aggressive direction. There is an effort afoot to scrub our nation of any mention of God in the public square. The group has published "A Proposal To Legally Silence Christians & Conservatives And To Label Christians As White Supremacists."[97] A name of a proposal like that would have been unthinkable even a decade or two ago. In today's world, it gets published with scant attention or notoriety, let alone condemnation.

---

[96] Trenholm, "Love is Not Love," YouTube posted April 14, 2021 https://www.youtube.com/watch?v=v5NGtA00n7o.
[97] Duclos, "Proposal to Legally Silence Christians and Conservatives," *The Daily Coin*, December 20, 2020.

The atheistic proposal calls for laws and rules to force conservative Christians into silence based on their religious beliefs, to remove 'In God We Trust' from U.S. currency, and to rescind protections of religious liberties, and more. According to *Harbinger's Daily*, the document says the Biden Administration "must 'educate the American public,' particularly those identified as the 'religious right,' on the need to keep their 'religious dogma' to themselves. The document calls for a purge of social conservatives from all levels of government, labeling them as 'white nationalist' and 'conspiracy theorists.'"[98]

Trevor Loudon, author and filmmaker specializing in communist revolutionary movements throughout history, has spent decades studying the speeches, papers, articles, and books put out by radical leftists. He writes that "when the left says they're going to "unbrainwash you," what they're really saying is they want to brainwash you in their way of thinking. This is a document that the communists would be proud of. It is couched in the same sort of manner that I read in the communist press," Loudon said. "They use certain weasel words that you can figure out what it means, and it is very, very scary stuff. The Democratic party is now a Marxist party. This document is aimed at the Marxists' main enemy in this country, which is traditional Christianity. It's very, very clear."[99]

Many deny there is an outright war against Christians right here in the United States of America. They are ostriches with their heads in the sand. They will say that censoring Christian conservatives is just a right-wing talking point. Read the Marxist, Secular Democrats' proposal. Make up your own mind, do the analysis, and decide for yourself.

Catholics need to reclaim the truth. We need to stop the enemies of God from removing Him from society. We need to stop them from championing a false version of truth and advocating immoral policies advocating for homosexuality, transgenderism and gender confusion. Some with an agenda are bastardizing the definition of gender. Some have deified man and humanized God. Many have it backwards and terribly wrong. Some live their lives with a fist in the face of Almighty

---

[98] Hohman, "Dem Document Surfaces Demanding Biden Clamp Down on Religious Conservatives," *Harbingers Daily*, December 16, 2020.
[99] Ibid.

God. God will not be mocked. Catholics must defend God and His complimentary plan for man and woman, traditional marriage, and the traditional family unit. Holding our ground and pushing back, while we are still able—without further cancellation, re-education, persecution, or imprisonment—is what must be done.

So where might all this be headed? What's the end game? For the power hungry, clearly, it's unconditional obeyance. "Do as I say." Whose tactics are to be emulated? Perhaps the atheistic communists of China? Many have heard of China's monitoring campaign, Social Credit system, and re-education camps. "That's communism" you say, "re-education would never happen in the west." Wrong. It's here. The trailblazing western nation is the United Kingdom. Home of the *Magna Carta* and the roots of common law liberty.

In November, 2020, the UK Home Office launched the "Prevent" program, a "re-education program that encourages people to report concerns that loved ones are 'developing extremist views'— which it fails to define—and 'being filled with hate.'" The "thought police" website "gives a few real-life examples of people who have been 'helped' by the Prevent program, which read like a page out of George Orwell's *1984*. Three of the stories describe 'intervention' for people with vaguely defined 'extreme right-wing' views, and three stories describe 'extremist' Muslim views. Conspicuously absent from the list are examples of people with 'extremist left-wing' views."[100]

While the U.K. rolls out the thought police, the Biden Administration's State Department beginning in May, 2021 authorized its embassies to fly the 'LGBT Pride' flag on the same flagpole as the U.S. flag. Pushing the radical homosexual agenda is not only offensive to U.S. citizens of faith and sensibility, it will offend the religious sensitivities of several host nations. To kick off June, the month of the Sacred Heart, the U.S. Embassy to the Holy See sent a message to the world by flying the 'LGBT Pride' rainbow flag at the Vatican.[101] How absolutely disrespectful and offensive to the Sacred Heart of Jesus, the Vatican, and faithful Catholics in the U.S. and around the globe. Talk about unforced errors in diplomacy! Pride, the worst of the seven deadly sins.

---

[100] Mangiaracina, "U.K. Police Launch Program to report 'extremist' friends, relatives for reeducation," *LifeSite News,* December 17, 2020.
[101] "U.S. Embassy Waves Pride Flag at Vatican," Catholic Vote News Feed, June 1, 2021

Who defines extremism, intolerance, and thought crimes? No doubt if anyone holds any beliefs, or takes any positions that are based on the traditional, dogmatic teachings of the Catholic Church, or other religions, the thought police will one day knock on your door to "deprogram" or "reeducate" you, or worse. Manifested as Big Tech, the KGB, Gestapo, and Stasi are on the way.

As parents, how will we properly educate our children and protect them from the false teachings of the world? These are but a few of the most critical issues of our day. Will we tell our children the truth about right and wrong, providing them with accurate history about the fullness and necessity of the one true faith—the Holy Catholic Church? We need to offer "tough love" parenting with truth. There is no excuse for wimpy, dishonest, uncharitable parenting that goes along so as to not rock the boat. We must not abandon Catholic truths that would potentially have us forfeit eternal life. We need to tell them, as Saint Aloysius Gonzaga told us, "It is better to be a child of God than king of the whole world!"

Saint Polycarp lived a life of candor. In the end, when he knew his time was up, what did Polycarp do when the "thought police" knocked on his door? He invited them in, made them a meal, asked them if he could pray, then went cooperatively with them to jail awaiting his execution. Polycarp was a willing martyr for the faith. Pray that we too may be obedient to the will of God and not man's wicked perversion of theological or politically incorrect thinking.

We next turn to the third century and Saint Tarcicius, a young boy who lived a prudent life of love for Christ in the Eucharist.

Second Century Saints

Saints Clement (d. 100), Ignatius (d. 110), Hyginus (d. 142), Pius I (d. 154), Justin (d. 165), Gervase & Protase, and Iraneus, pray for us.

Saint Polycarp is the patron saint of ailments such as earaches and dysentery.

Saint Polycarp is often shown in artwork surrounded by flames and a sword.

Saint Polycarp's feast day is February 23.

Saint Polycarp, *ora pro nobis* (pray for us).

Second Century History

100- Death of Saint John, the last apostle alive.

107-117- Saint Ignatius of Antioch writes and is credited with first having used the term "Catholic" to describe the church, meaning "according to the whole" or "universal."

Ignatius wrote, "See that you follow the bishop, even as Jesus Christ does the Father... Let no man do anything connected with the Church without the bishop... Wherever the bishop shall appear, there let the multitude of the people also be; even as wherever Jesus Christ is, there is the Catholic Church."[102]

138-142- Pope Saint Hyginus combats Gnostic heresy. Institutes practice of godparents at infant baptisms to assist with Christian upbringing; decrees all churches must be consecrated.

155-157- Saint Justin the Martyr writes the Church's "First Apology," or defense of the faith. It focused on atheism, immorality, and disloyalty to the Roman Empire.

156- First recorded instance of devotion to a martyr and the devotion to relics in the *Martyrdom of Polycarp*. Author unknown, but presumed to have been written by the early church fathers.

177- Saint Irenaeus of Lyons writes *Against All Heresies* refuting Gnosticism, which emphasized personal spiritual knowledge over the teachings and authority of the church.

---

[102] Saint Ignatius of Antioch, "Letter the Smyrnaens," Ch. 8.

197- Tertullian, Church father, writes: "The blood of martyrs is the seed of the Church." (Tertullian would later apostatize to the Montanist sect.)

Virtue Challenge #2 - Candor

Saint Polycarp, true friend of Christ, help us to speak with greater candor. Help up to navigate more deftly through the communication minefield of political correctness, cancel culture, and self-censorship. Help us to distinguish between true and false compassion. Help us to not act out of self-preservation, but at all times with true charity. Help us to use fraternal correction as needed and bring others to holiness. Polycarp, pray for us to speak plainly in unambiguous terms on matters where moral clarity is essential. Help us to be wise in our speech.

In the arena on the day of his martyrdom, a voice from heaven was heard, "Be brave, Polycarp, and act like a man." May we too "act like men" all our days. Female Christians, too, should "act like women." In our sideways and sometimes upside-down world, Polycarp, pray for us an increase in true masculinity and true femininity. Help us to accept traditional Church teachings on the complementarity of man and woman and the traditional family unit. Pray for us to respect God's plan in this regard.

Eric Sammons wrote on Twitter on June 12, 2020, "Christians serve the Truth, who is Jesus Christ. As such, to affirm lies—about abortion, homosexual activity, "transgenderism," etc.—is to deny the Lord and cease to be Christian." Do you serve the Truth or do you affirm lies? Do you deny the Lord?

Polycarp, help us to be a true friend of Jesus when we are confronted by temptation, which is nothing other than being asked by Christ's enemy to deny him. Help us not to gamble with eternal happiness by holding our tongue. Purify us of guilt, and make us partakers of a heavenly remedy.

Converse for a moment with the Holy Ghost about candor. My Lord and my God, how may I serve you more faithfully and completely through the virtue of candor?

O Great Saint Polycarp, help us to speak with the candor of saints.

CHAPTER 3

Tarcisius

The Third Century
Prudence

*"The simple believeth every word: but the prudent man
looketh well to his going."*

- Proverbs 14:15

"No arrojemos la soga tras el caldero."
("Let us not throw the rope after the bucket.")

- Miguel de Cervantes, Don Quixote, II. 9

The 200s

The second century candor of Saint Polycarp leads us to the third
century prudence of Saint Tarcisius. During times of significant
persecution for the faith, the virtue of prudence is heightened. The
difference between natural prudence and supernatural prudence was
addressed by Fr. Steven Reuter, "Natural prudence only considers this
life and what's best for me in this life. Supernatural prudence considers
the next life as well. For example, that's why the saints, there were
times when they would hide from persecution and other times when
they would embrace it. What is the best thing to do here and now for
the Church? And Our Lady, we say in the litany, was most prudent.
She really looks at all things considering the whole picture and wanting
God's glory in all things."[103]

Imagine living in the 200s and having to decide, with implications
for your safety or even your life, what is the best thing to do here and
now for the Church? Fast forwarding to today, are your decisions
prudent? Have you factored in God's glory in all things when deciding

---

[103] Reuter, "Comply or Disobey? Priest Explains Just vs. Unjust Laws," *LifeSite News*, January 8,
2021.

whether to do something for yourself, your family, the church, and civil society?

The first centuries after Christ were, as we learned through the life of Saint Ignatius of Antioch, a time of martyrdom for Christians as countless numbers died at the hands of Roman emperors such as Nero and Diocletian. Often the fortunes of the early followers of Christ could change dramatically in an instant, usually from bad to worse. One such flip-flopping emperor was named Valerian; he ruled from 254 to 260.

Valerian's advisors convinced him that the Christians were possessed of great wealth and so the emperor sent his men to the catacombs to claim it by force if necessary, but not before outlawing the celebration of the Mysteries as well as any and all public or private gatherings of Christians. The pope, bishops, priests, and deacons were also obligated to make sacrifices to the Roman gods, or face death, which many did. The pope at the time, Sixtus II, was found celebrating Mass in the catacombs by Valerian's men and executed along with six of the seven deacons who were found with him.

The seventh was the man who is known today as Saint Lawrence, a saint beloved for his constancy under torture, but also for his sense of humor. When pressed by the Romans to reveal the supposed treasures of the Church, he gathered a number of poor people, saying "Here, here are the treasures of the Church." The Romans did not find that funny, nor did they see the truth in it, for Lawrence was condemned to be burned alive and placed on a sort of grill. Famously, he is recorded to have asked his tormentors to turn him over as he was "done on this side," while he was being burned. (Saint Lawrence is the patron saint of many causes including cooks, chefs, comedians, librarians, students, and the poor.) That heroic courage in the face of torture and execution must make us all look at ourselves and ask, "Why not me?" or perhaps "What would I do under such circumstances?"

The heroism of the early Christians was by no means limited to adults. Many were the young people, even children, who displayed great fortitude in dying for Christ. Among the lesser-known martyrs of the age is a twelve-year-old boy named Tarcisius.

Tarcisius is today the patron saint of altar boys which is fitting as he was, according to some accounts, an acolyte who volunteered to bring the Holy Eucharist to relieve the sufferings of his fellow Christian neighbors and friends who were in prison. It was thought that youngsters would be less recognizable as Christians to passersby than adults. When asked by the priest who would volunteer that day, knowing full well the dangers involved, the boy must have asked himself, "Why not me?" and stepped forward in charity and said "Send me."

And so, Tarcisius set out to bring the "Holy Mysteries," concealed within layers of cloth and placed in a case held close to his heart beneath his tunic, to the imprisoned Christians. He had not gone far, however, when he was accosted on the Appian Way by some other youngsters who were playing. They called to him to join them but when he said that he could not, they persisted and asked him why. He tried to move on but seeing that he was hiding something, they pressed him to reveal what it was that he held so close to his heart. He refused and then they turned on him. They began to strike him and throw stones at him, but young Tarcisius would not let go of the Eucharist, so great was his reverence for it.

Accounts as to what happened next differ. Some hold that after he was killed by the other boys, they rolled him over and found nothing. The sacred hosts as well as the linens and the case had miraculously disappeared.

Another version of the story holds that a man was passing by, a soldier in fact, and Tarcisius recognized him as a Christian from their meetings in the catacombs. When the soldier dispersed the boys and picked up a dying Tarcisius, this account holds that the following exchange took place: "I am dying," he said, "but I have kept my God safe from them." And he handed his precious treasure to the soldier, who placed it reverently inside his tunic. "Carry Him to the prison for me," said Tarcisius, and with a gentle sigh he fell back into the soldier's arms.[104]

---

[104] https://www.myfirstholycommunion.com/portfolio-view/st-tarcisius-boy-martyr-of-the-eucharist/

Alexandre Falguiere, Tarcisius, Christian Martyr, 1868, Musée d'Orsay, Paris, France
https://en.wikipedia.org/wiki/Tarcisius

Regardless of which version is closer to the truth, it is stunning to think of the devotion to the Body of Christ that this young boy had, especially when there seems to be so much indifference to our Lord in the Holy Sacrament of the Altar today. Saint Ignatius of Antioch, in words that reflect the deep theology of a mystic, when speaking about the Eucharist, wrote, "Permit me to imitate my suffering God ... I am God's wheat and I shall be ground by the teeth of beasts, that I may become the pure bread of Christ."

But what can you do? What can the example of Tarcisius inspire you to do? How can you ask, "Why not me?" and use Tarcisius as an example when nobody is out there waiting to stone you or attack you at least physically for being a Christian.

There is much you can do. Ask yourself, how much do you revere the Eucharist? Do you ever receive Holy Communion unworthily, that is, in the state of mortal sin? If you do not go to confession with any frequency, the answer to that question is probably *yes*.

When is the last time you said, "Send me" to God in prayer? What would God ask you to do? Does the idea of doing something for God excite you, make you afraid, or something else? If a young boy could step up and say, "Send me," what's your excuse for not doing the same?

The *Catechism of the Catholic Churches* teaches us that "prudence disposes the practical reason to discern, in every circumstance, our true good and to choose the right means for achieving it."[105] Prudence, per Fr. John Hardon in the Modern Catholic Dictionary is, "Correct knowledge about things to be done or, more broadly, the knowledge of things that ought to be done and of things that ought to be avoided."

Prudence, then, is essentially about judgment and making wise decisions governed by both intellect and faith. Prudence often takes time to acquire, but given that it is foundational to the other virtues, it is among the more essential virtues.

Was it prudent for Tarcisius to accept the call for a volunteer to deliver the Holy Eucharist to those Christians in prison? Did he have proper knowledge and regard for that which ought to be done? When he was being attacked, was it prudent for Tarcisius to protect the Holy Eucharist at all costs? The answer is a resounding *yes* to all three questions. Tarcisius was heroic, not just in his bravery to protect the sacred hosts, but also in the holy prudence that guided his thoughts and actions.

Father Hardon continues his explanation of prudence:

"It is the intellectual virtue whereby a human being recognizes in any matter at hand what is good and what is evil. In this sense, it is the moral virtue that enables a person to devise, choose, and prepare suitable means for the attainment of any purpose or the avoidance of any evil. Prudence resides in the practical intellect and is both acquired by one's own acts and infused at the same time as sanctifying grace. It may be said to be natural as developed by us, and supernatural because conferred by God. As an act of virtue, prudence involves three stages of mental operation:

- to take counsel carefully with oneself and from others;

- to judge correctly on the basis of the evidence at hand;

- and to direct the rest of one's activity according to the norms determined after a prudent judgment has been made.

---

[105] Catechism, 1835.

(Etym. Latin *prudentia,* foresight in the practical order; from *providentia,* foresight, directive care, providence.)[106]

In reviewing the story of Tarcisius, it becomes much more meaningful when viewed through the lens of holy prudence. He had keen insight into what was good and necessary and what was evil and to be avoided. Prudence is duty and loyalty. Tarcisius' acts, infused by sanctifying grace, provide us with a most holy example of foresight and directive care.

What foresight do we bring to viewing events occurring in our church and in our world? How do we take directive care of our own souls and those in our family? How can each of us benefit by leaning into the virtue of prudence in our own lives?

When will we step up further in holy, sanctifying grace? What more via duty can we do to assist the pastor and priests at our parish? When is the last time you stepped up and volunteered at your parish? When is the last time someone in your family, or circle of friends, needed fraternal correction? Did you pray about the issue and say, "Send me" to God? Or did you sidestep the issue in the hope the issue would go away, and to date it has not?

The world tells us we can make many moral choices and that the majority of them are perfectly fine. Prudence tells us this is not true. There are correct ways to conduct oneself, and then there are sinful acts that offend God and damage our souls. Repeated bad choices may lead to our becoming "dead in sin" and lost. Are Catholic politicians who publicly support abortion, and receive communion, dead in sin? When their bishops are unable to council them and have them amend their ways, are they lost?

Wisdom is intellect plus faith. Prudence is similar. It is wisdom, intellect, faith and judgment all rolled into one. If someone says you lack wisdom, that can sting a bit. If someone says you lack prudence, that can be a deeper and longer-lasting hurt. Ouch.

Be on guard for an opposite of prudence which is *scrupulosity*. While prudence has us make good decisions based on faith, scrupulosity will have us not act for fear of some negative result. Some

---

[106] Hardon, *Modern Catholic Dictionary,* n.p.

take pride in not making bad decisions. This is not good. God gave us the great commission. We are to love others. Through prudence we do. With scrupulosity, we do not.

So, how about you? How can you exercise greater holy prudence? You, too, can honor the Body of Christ. Honor the Eucharist for which young Tarcisius gave his life by going to confession so that you do not dishonor it when you receive. Honor the Eucharist by defending it against those who do not know any better. You may not be guarding it in your tunic, but you can learn more about it, the Biblical basis for it, and defend that teaching when challenged instead of shrugging your shoulders. In the Bible, John Chapter 6 highlights the truth of this Catholic belief as Jesus himself says, very clearly: "I am the living bread which came down from heaven; if any one eats of this bread, he will live forever; and the bread which I shall give for the life of the world is my flesh."

The Jewish people challenged him when he said this. Jesus did not back down, nor did he say they misunderstood him. Instead, he reiterated: "Truly, truly, I say to you, unless you eat the flesh of the Son of man and drink his blood, you have no life in you, he who eats my flesh and drinks my blood has eternal life, and I will raise him up at the last day."

Defending the faith leads us to another third century saint to whom I have a strong devotion, Saint Sebastien. As Tarcisius died prudently protecting Christ in the Eucharist, Sebastien died prudently protecting Christians from the Romans. Originally from Gaul (today France), Sebastien went to Rome and enlisted in the army to help the Christians. Sebastien was eventually found out, tied to a post, shot with several arrows, but did not die. Saint Irene of Rome attended to him, and miraculously he was healed. Sebastien went to Diocletian to candidly, and prudently, chastise him for his cruelties to Christians, and warn him of his sins. Diocletian's reaction? He had Sebastien beaten and clubbed to death. Thus, Saint Sebastien is known as a twice-martyred saint. (Two other twice-martyred saints are Cecilia and Agatha.)

When in Rome I visit Saint Sebastien at the Basilica San Sebastiano (one of Seven Pilgrimage Churches of Rome), and the catacombs of San Sebastiano, on the *Via Appia Antica* in Rome, just down the street from the *Quo Vadis* Chapel. Relics of Saint Sebastian's martyrdom, like the post he was tied to and some of the arrows that shot him, are on display in the Basilica. The reclining white marble statue of Sebastien pierced with golden arrows is dramatic and moving. Sebastien, buried in the catacombs underneath the Basilica, is the patron saint of soldiers and athletes.

Saint Sebastien at Basilica San Sebastiano, Rome, Italy

The catacombs of San Sebastiano are very close to the catacombs of San Callistos, where Saint Tarcisius is buried. Tarcisius's relics are kept in the church of San Silvestro.

Saint Sebastien was right to go to Rome to do all he could to protect the Christians from Diocletian. Saint Lawrence was right when he showed the poor to his persecutors and called them the treasures of the Church. And Tarcisius was also right when he cherished the Eucharist so very much that he gave his life to protect it. All three saints practiced supernatural prudence in that their actions made due consideration for the next life. We can honor these great third century saints by defending Catholics in the public square, through acts of charity for the poor, and acts of devotion to the Holy Eucharist, most especially through Eucharistic Adoration and through worthy reception of communion.

In closing, while this chapter has been about Tarcisius and the critical virtue of prudence, in the back of my mind I have had the unfortunate ear worm of former President George H.W. Bush (41) saying, "Wouldn't be prudent." On top of that, I have comedian Dana Carvey doing his unforgettable impersonation of Bush saying, "Not

gonna do it. Wouldn't be prudent. Not at this particular juncture." So good. Carvey's hand gestures are priceless, too. If so motivated, check out Carvey on YouTube at "George Bush on Support for the War in Iraq and Bombing – SNL." Or this link:
https://www.youtube.com/watch?v=AMYPvd86R2I

We turn next to the pivotal fourth century for Christians living in the Roman Empire, Saint Monica, and the virtue of patience.

Third Century Saints

Saints Iranaeus of Lyons (d. 203), Perpetua & Felicitas (d. 203), Callistus (d. 222), Cecelia (d. 230), Hippolytus (d. 235), Agatha (d. 250), Victoria (d. 250), Felix of Nola (d. 250), Alexander of Jerusalem (d. 251), Sixtus II (d. 258), Lawrence of Rome (d. 258), Cyprian of Carthage (d. 258), Valentine of Rome (d. 270), Gregory the Wonder Worker (d. 270), Genesius (d. 285), Zoe (d. 286), Regina (d. 286), Sebastian (d. 288), and Victor of Marseilles (d. 290), Anysia of Salonika (d. 298), pray for us.

Saint Tarcisius is the patron saint of acolytes (altar servers) and first communicants.
Saint Tarcisius's feast day is August 15.
Saint Tarcisius, *ora pro nobis* (pray for us).

Third Century History

217- Election of anti-Pope Saint Hippolytus, the first anti-Pope in Church history, and the only one venerated as a saint. He considered Pope Saint Callistus I to be a Monarchian heretic, and he continued his claim through to the reign of Pope Saint Pontian. He reconciled with the Church before being martyred in the mines of Sardinia in 235.

222- Alexander Severus becomes emperor. He lifts many laws against the Christians, essentially permitting them to exist as a religion.

236- Pope Saint Fabian elected Pope, after a dove rested on Fabian's head, as those present considered it to be a divine sign.

250-51- Emperor Decian mandated that all citizens worship the Roman Gods. Christians who refused were imprisoned, tortured, and put to death. Some Christians fabricated certificates saying they had sacrificed. Pope Saint Fabian is martyred during the Decian Persecution.

251- Council of Cartage. Permits lapsed Catholics during the persecution to be readmitted to the Church after a period of penance.

254- Saint Stephen elected pope. He is the first pope to have invoked Matthew 16:18 for authority as to the Chair of Peter.

257-260- Emperor Valerian launches a period of persecution against Christians.

261-303- A period of low Christian persecution.

265- Antioch councils (three).

285- Roman Empire divided into an Eastern half ruled by Diocletian, who had a military mind, and a Western half ruled by Maximian, who had a political mind. Under Maximian's persecutions, anyone who met a Christian could be killed without trial.

Virtue Challenge #3- Prudence

Saint Tarcisius, help us to step up to better serve God through prudential judgment. Help us to make holier decisions. Help us to say, "Send me" in a courageous way. Help us to have initiative when there is risk even though it may cost us everything.

Natural and supernatural prudence are virtues that can be practiced by anyone, old or young. They are virtues that increase the more they are practiced. Learn from your mistakes and learn from others' mistakes. Pray for God to help you become better at judging situations correctly. Pray for divine grace to purify and elevate your virtues. If you think you lack prudence, make a better effort and give it time. It'll be there when it needs to be.

Looking back on a recent issue where greater prudence would have produced a more favorable outcome for you, what did you learn?

What is your takeaway and how might you apply that to future similar, or even dissimilar situations?

Prayer must correspond to action. Be courageous. Have fortitude. Be bold. Be prudent. To better serve Christ and His church, what courageous, prudent action will you soon take?

Saint Joseph most prudent, pray for us.

Converse for a moment with the Holy Ghost about prudence. My Lord and my God, how may I serve you more faithfully and completely through the virtue of prudence?

O Great Saint Tarcisius, help us to have an increase in the virtue of holy prudence.

CHAPTER 4

Monica

The Fourth Century
Patience

"Patience is the root and guardian of all the virtues."
- Pope Saint Gregory I

"The virtue of patience is the one which most assures us of perfection."
- Saint Francis de Sales

*"Be patient, because the weaknesses of the body are given to us in this
world by God for the salvation of the soul. So they are of great merit
when they are borne patiently."*
- Saint Francis of Assisi

*"If there be a true way that leads to the Everlasting Kingdom,
it is most certainly that of suffering, patiently endured."*
- Saint Colette

The 300s

*"And all the roads we have to walk are winding, and all the lights that
lead us there are blinding, There are many things that I would like to
say to you, but I don't know how, I said maybe, you're gonna be the one
that saves me, and after all…"*
- Oasis, "Wonderwall"

Did you marry your high school sweetheart?

Some are blessed by God in meeting their spouse at a young age.
Never wondering. Never having to be patient. For others it takes time.
Sometimes a long time. God's in charge; and if the vocation of
marriage is for us, He will arrange things in accordance with His plan.
Working with God in this regard, many of us learn holy patience. As a
young boy I never envisioned that I would marry somewhat later in life
at the age of thirty-one. (More on this towards the end of the chapter.)

Some, like my wife's Grandma Irene, who lived to 101, didn't get married until she was in her eighties. No matter our age, God has a plan.

Waiting to meet a spouse, have children, find a job, move into a house, switch jobs, overcome a vice or an addiction, overcome an illness, or praying for a child to return to the faith—all require patience. Is being patient easy or difficult for you? If you are a patient, unflappable person, do you emulate anyone in particular, or is it purely innate?

God is patient. Are we patient with God?

Many of the figures profiled in this book led remarkable lives; in some cases the lives were replete with miraculous events or great adventures in far-flung lands. Not so with our saint of the fourth century. Her influence, nonetheless, on the history and development of the Church is incalculable. A case could be made in fact that Monica's influence eclipses that of anyone else in these pages. To some that may seem a strange thing to say about someone who is most famous for being a mother; but perhaps when they consider how important mothers are in the lives of their children, it will seem less strange, and we can hope that when they consider that Monica was the mother of the great Saint Augustine, perhaps the most significant figure in the Church after Christ himself and the apostles, it will not seem strange at all.

Many of us have stories of not fully appreciating the faith that we were introduced to and taught in our youth, wandering a bit and perhaps becoming lost in early adulthood; then, by the grace of God, and a fair amount of our mother's prayers to be sure, we once again discover the eternal truths of the Catholic Church and begin anew our steadfast service to our Lord. The wayward son, Augustine's route, is a fairly common path towards salvation. Sound like any souls you know? Through it all we have the patience of a Monica, and our Blessed Mother, petitioning Jesus that we may get on, and stay on, that path of righteousness, humility and salvation.

An unofficial theme of this book is *Why Not Me?* We look at saints in particular circumstances and speculate that they may have seen a particular situation or perhaps heard a particular call from God and asked themselves, "Why not me?" Why can't I respond to that situation or that call from God with heroic sanctity? But it is hard to think of Monica asking herself that question. She was a wife and mother. Her husband needed her prayers and her patience; her son needed her prayers and her tears; her friends and neighbors needed her kindness, holiness, wisdom, and discretion, and in all of these cases Monica responded as the exemplary, patient Christian she was. She most likely never considered herself; she was too busy thinking of God and others.

When others do not think of us and are not patient with us, how are we to respond? What if they instead come at us with belligerence? Fr. Bill Peckman, in *Let Freedom Ring*, writes:

"We live in a horribly belligerent society right now. So many refer to being "triggered," or easily and frequently offended in such a way that justifies both the tenacity and disproportionate nature of their vengeance. The belligerent see themselves as victims of injustice whose suffering, real or imagined, is sufficient grounds for any destruction and mayhem they may engage in to address the injustice. They wreak havoc in the lives of all who around them. It is as if they look for (even long for) reasons to be angry so that they may act out without regards for consequences.

...our lives will come with burdens, pains, injustices, and sorrows. We will have that temptation to return belligerence for belligerence. Certainly, Christ carried this reality right up the cross. The answer lies in our willingness and ability to show meekness. Meekness has a bad reputation as the quality of being mousy, timid, or weak. Meekness is patience, a virtue that St Paul in Galatians 5:22 reminds us is a fruit of the Holy Spirit. Patience is anything but weakness; patience takes incredible strength. It is the strength that Jesus demonstrated on the cross. He shows His strength in patience and endurance.

Our ability to show meekness in the face of harm neither condones the harm done to us nor allows another to treat us as a doormat. It shows the strength of character that reduces the mocking and ridicule, thus providing a far stronger witness to all. Our war footing should be directed to the devil and his forces... who have no hope of conversion. As for our fellow human beings, if they are on this side of the moment of death, the possibility, however slim, exists for possible conversion.

The Church exists for the salvation of souls. Driving belligerence from our hearts and souls helps us endure the yoke of Christ: the ability to selflessly love and show unswerving obedience to the will of the Father in all things."[107]

Patience is a form of meekness, of suffering. And Monica suffered with endurance for decades. As it says in Luke 21:18, "It is by endurance that you will secure possession of your souls." Father John Hardon, writing in the *Modern Catholic Dictionary*, builds upon our understanding of patience and tells us, "Fruit of Patience: A form of the moral virtue of fortitude. It enables one to endure present evils without sadness or resentment in conformity with the will of God. Patience is mainly concerned with bearing the evils caused by another. The three grades of patience are: Lowest: to bear difficulties without interior complaint, Middle: to use hardships to make progress in virtue, Highest: to desire the cross and afflictions for Christ's love, to have something to offer up, and to accept them with spiritual joy."[108]

Monica is thought to have been born in Tagaste, Algeria. Again, it is worth reminding readers that Algeria is in North Africa, an area that was a major center of Christianity in the 300s . . . until the Muslim conquest a few centuries later. Some of the most significant cities in Christian history, Alexandria, among them, would be overrun, not evangelized but overrun and laid waste by the sword of the "prophet." But in Monica's time at least, that tragedy lay far off in the future.

She was born into a Christian home and early in life struggled with alcoholism, sneaking draughts of wine from the family cellar, before being caught and overcoming the habit. Her parents gave her in marriage to a pagan named Patricius, a man of violent temper and unbridled lust. Happily, his temper never led him to lay a hand in anger on Monica, but sadly his lusts did lead him to be unfaithful to her. In his *Confessions*, Augustine writes of the positive influence Monica's holy demeanor and long-suffering patience had on Patricius, though as with his own conversion, that influence did not bear the desired fruit immediately; the prayers of the wife and mother, would only be answered after many years.

---

[107] Peckman, Bill, "Freedom from Belligerence," *Let Freedom Ring,* Day 10.
[108] Hardon, *Modern Catholic Dictionary,* n.p.

But that is the lesson we learn better from Monica than perhaps any other saint—the power of patience and perseverance in prayer. Her struggles, her crosses, did not concern great empires or great business questions; nor did they concern significant doctrinal questions of the Church; rather they concerned those around her, the people she loved. She bore those crosses in a model fashion and even bore those of her husband, sons, and friends as well. Monica was troubled that Patricius would not allow their three sons to be baptized.

Patricius mocked Monica's devotion and her charitable endeavors among those less fortunate; his mother, her mother-in-law, lived with them and she was, by all accounts, difficult. And yet, Monica would win them both for Christ, not through argument or persuasive speech, but through her kindly, persistent example of how a true Christian acts. Though they mocked it, they must have recognized the beauty in it for both would become Catholics, Patricius the year before he died.

Monica also was a model Catholic in the way she dealt with her friends. Other women would seek her out for her wise counsel and her charitable ways. When they would complain about their husbands, she would not encourage them, nor would she gossip to others about what she heard. She preached love and reconciliation. As a wonderful writer on virtue wrote of her, "Generous with her time to her friends, sensitive to the marital problems suffered by others, and prudent in her conduct and advice, Monica performed many spiritual works of mercy in a quiet, unobtrusive way."[109]

But it is for her influence on her son, the great Saint Augustine, that Saint Monica is best known. Had he not converted, it is likely she would still have been a saint, but she would perhaps have been lost to history, a saint known only to God. As it turned out, she is the patron saint of mothers whose children have lost the faith, and thus, in our time when that situation is all too common, she is becoming among the most famous of female saints, and one who is frequently called upon.

When Augustine was a child, he became very sick, and only after he recovered did Monica's pleas convince her husband to allow the boy to be baptized. That was the answer to a prayer, but as Augustine

---

[109] Kalpakgian, Mitchell, *The Virtues That Build Us Up*, Crossroad, New York, 2016, 154.

grew, he moved further and further away from the practice of his faith. Led by an inquisitive mind and his own lusts, he at one point embraced the doctrine of the Manicheans, a sect which held that "all flesh is evil." The sect believed that there are two equal forces in the world, one good, the spiritual world, and one evil, the physical world, rather than subscribing to the Christian view that God is above all, the Creator of the World, all good and all powerful. And, importantly, they believed that matter, the physical world is not evil. That God became man in Jesus Christ should protect any Christian from holding such a view. But Augustine was not yet a Christian.

Thus, Monica faced the same difficulty as many parents today: How do you deal with a child who has not only abandoned the Faith, but is living an outwardly and obviously immoral life? Monica's first reaction was like that of many; she drove him from her home and wanted nothing to do with him. But she is said to have experienced a vision which convinced her to welcome him back and that it would be easier to "love him home" if she stayed close to him. As Saint Augustine would later say, "Patience is the companion of wisdom."

Monica even followed Augustine to Rome, where he had gone without telling her, and then she followed him to Milan where he was converted, an event predicted by a saintly bishop years earlier. Legend has it that Monica prayed and wept for her son Augustine every night. The bishop is said to have told her that, "The child of those tears shall never perish." And he was right.

In Milan, mother and son came into contact with the great Saint Ambrose who would instruct Augustine and receive him into the Church. The mother's tearful prayers had been answered. Many glorified saints were for a long time in revolt against God's will, and they brought themselves at last into subjection. In Milan, Monica would again become a leader of Christian women, but more of a *servant of the servants* in her son's words. There she would be as she had always been: a devout woman living an exemplary Christian life in the world.

On Saint Monica's deathbed in 387, she said to her son Saint Augustine, "Lay this body wherever it may be. Let no care of it disturb you: this only I ask of you, that you should remember me at the altar of the Lord wherever you may be."[110]

It truly can be said that Monica gave the world Augustine, as every mother gives the world her children. She raises them, prays for them, and hopes they "turn out right." Though she was no theologian, we can see in Augustine, his person and his words, Monica's boy. He recognized as much himself.

> "In describing God's tender, merciful, sensitive love for each person, Augustine- who discovered God's goodness in the loving heart of his mother- describes God's inestimable love for each human being as the most personal of all relationships, as if each person felt like the favorite son or darling daughter of his father: '... O Omnipotent God, you who care for each one of us as though he was your only care and who cares for all of us as through we were all just one person.' Monica's special, unconditional love for her son communicated to Augustine the nature of God's familiar, intimate [love] for each soul."[111]

For parents out there, with or without "wayward" children. Can you not pray for your children in imitation of Saint Monica? And can we all not follow her beautiful example of what it means to be a spouse, a parent, and a friend? Why not all of us?

The Pray More Novenas group sends regular Novenas via email and invites people to pray along for their various intentions. Here are two excerpts from their Saint Monica novena:

> "Today let's pray for all those who feel abandoned by God for whatever reason -- for those waiting for answers to prayer, and for those who are suffering and do not yet see the reasons behind what God is doing in their lives. Let's pray that they will be given the gift of unwavering faith through Saint Monica's intercession, as well as consolation during these difficult times. Saint Monica demonstrated heroic patience during her trials in life. She suffered patiently and with a deep faith in God's goodness. Let's pray today that we may all

---

[110] Tassone, Susan, *Day by Day: For the Holy Souls of Purgatory,* Our Sunday Visitor Publishing, Huntington, IN, 19.

have the faith of Saint Monica- that we will have heroic patience in the face of difficulty."[111]

"Dear Saint Monica, you were once the mournful mother of a prodigal son. Your faithfulness to prayer brought you and your son so close to God that you are now with him in eternity. By your intercession and God's grace, your son Saint Augustine became a great and venerable Saint of the Church. Please take my request to God with the same fervor and persistence with which you prayed for your own son. With your needs, worries and anxieties, you threw yourself on the mercy and providence of God. Through sorrow and pain, you constantly devoted yourself to God. Pray for me, that I might join you in such a deep faith in God's goodness and mercy. Above all, dear Saint Monica, pray for me, that I may, like your son, turn from my sin and become a great saint for the glory of God. Let us pray to bring hope and love into our families. To become holier members of our families."[112]

As Monica was an incredible mother, we now turn to *Mater Admirabilis* ("Mother Most Admirable"), Blessed Mother. At the top of the Spanish Steps in Rome there is the *Trinità dei Monti* convent and church. If you make arrangements you can enter and visit. The *Mater* story is that in 1844 a young French novitiate to the Religious of the Sacred Heart, Pauline Perdreau, painted a large fresco of Blessed Mother. When Mother Superior saw it, she was aghast and said the colors were too bright and had the picture covered and set aside. On October 20, 1846, Pope Pius IX visited the convent and curiously asked what was behind the drape. Mother Superior was embarrassed and tried to dissuade the pope from seeing it. When they uncovered the picture, they found that the colors had been muted to a pinkish, rose color. The pope declared the painting *Mater Admirabilis*, "Mother Most Admirable" and instructed Mother Superior to never cover the beautiful fresco again. Many believe that angels miraculously made the final color adjustments. Since its uncovering, many miracles have been attributed to the icon. October 20 is the feast of *Mater Admirabilis*.

---

[112] John Paul & Annie, "Saint Monica Novena," Day 6. https://www.praymorenovenas.com/st-monica-novena

Mater Admirabilis, *Trinità dei Monti Convent, Rome, Italy*

Saint Thérèse of Lisieux, when she was still discerning her vocation, made a pilgrimage to Rome and prayed before the *Mater Admiribalis* icon. Mary, my wife, and I were married on the feast day of Saint Therese, and she is the patron saint of our marriage. On my first trip to Rome, I was able to pray before the icon saying many prayers for my wife, our marriage, and our children just as Saint Therese had done before the painting over a hundred years before.

Sometimes when one prays to Saint Therese, she arranges to have a rose appear shortly thereafter to acknowledge that she heard your prayer. When I returned to the states a few days later we found an almost six-foot rose waiting for us at our front door. (A neighbor friend who worked as a reporter at *USA Today* dropped the rose off for us to enjoy as the government of Columbia had sent her a box of roses from South America hoping she would write a favorable story about the unbelievable Columbian roses.) I remember it was quite a bit taller than Alex, our eight-year-old son (see picture below). It was the most beautiful rose I had ever seen and all I could do was 'admire' it. Instantly knowing it was from Saint Therese, I said a prayer of thanks to her for the special acknowledgement of my having prayed at a location, and before an icon, that was very special to her.

My Son Alex with Six-Foot Columbian Rose

Guess what? After I had finished writing the aforementioned about *Mater Admiribalis*, Saint Therese, the giant rose, and inserted the above picture of Alex with the rose, I went into our kitchen and there was a single red rose on our counter with the exact same bend to the right as in the above photo. I kid you not. I asked my wife where it came from and she said the seniors at Alex's high school gave roses to the moms today at morning drop off. Uncanny? No. Providential? Yes. Thanks again, Saint Therese!

Sorry to depart from such a rosy discussion, but I'm impatient to get back to our discussion of patience. It's easier to be patient when things are going your way, or coming up roses, but, seriously, how much patience do you have for authors who make bad puns? OK, all done now. Maybe.

Saint Katharine Drexel tell us, "The patient and humble endurance of the cross, whatever nature it may be, is the highest work we have to do." What kind of patience do we show in adversity, or when times get tough? What issues or times have we gone through when we did not show sufficient patience? How can we show more patience in future situations of adversity? How can we bring more grace to situations where we are prone to be impatient? How many opportunities for spiritual growth through patience will we not recognize? To whom can we appeal?

Our best example of patiently staying close to Christ is, of course, Blessed Mother. We realize that most of us are not patient at all times, in all places, and all circumstances. Fr. Ed Broom, OMV writes, "Unlike Mary, who manifested remarkable patience! Consider Mary in her pregnancy, travelling the long trek to Bethlehem and then being rejected—what great patience! Losing the Child Jesus when He was twelve years of age for three long days before finding Him in the Temple—another manifestation of heroic patience! Most especially, in accompanying Jesus in His Passion leading up to His brutal Crucifixion and death, Mary manifested an unequalled patience! When our patience is put to the test, let us call out to Mary for her assistance. She will never fail us!"[113]

Entering my twenties my future was so bright I had to wear the proverbial shades. To that point in time, I had dated a few girls in high school and college, but nothing serious. After graduation, I continued to date with nothing lasting more than a couple months. I wondered when I would meet "the one," my "Mrs. Right." I prayed. I said novenas. I know my mom was praying for me, too. As time went on and I approached thirty, I wondered if my twenties were a lost decade. Did I pass on "the one"? Did I make a mistake? Would I ever get married? I was being patient, but at some point...

Out of the corner of my eye, I saw her walking down the left aisle in the church. Her parents and our families had casually known each other over the years, but for whatever reason up to that point in time Mary was not on my radar. Now she was. I thought more about her that next week and came up with a plan. The next Sunday after Mass I walked up to her mom and asked for Mary's phone number. In retrospect, Mrs. Dowd was actually fairly eager to help me contact her daughter. However, she drew the line and most assuredly did not offer me a dowry at that time. Her brothers observed their mom giving a phone number to some guy at church and told Mary. She was slightly angered. She asked her brothers who I was, and they said, "He's kind of like a 'James Bond' guy." Mary was curious.

I waited to call Mary until after Valentine's Day. It was a great first call. She relayed her brother's James Bond mention and we laughed. Having fun with the 007 reference, for our first date (February 22, 1997) I made a reservation at the Russian Tea Room in Chicago. Did I order a vodka martini, shaken not stirred? No, too predictable. I

---

[113] Broom, Ed, "Imitate our Lady's Ten Principal Virtues," *Catholic Exchange*, February 23, 2021.

ordered the traditional Russian vodka mini-flight, black bread and pickles. In Russia it is customary to break black bread when meeting someone for the first time. (Mary confessed years later that because I ordered the vodka shots on our first date, that the thought of my being an alcoholic did cross her mind that night. Nope. Just partaking in a fun Russian vodka custom.) I proposed to marry the following February on Candlemas, or as most Americans refer to Feb. 02, Groundhog Day. Since that first date we had not been back to the Russian Tea Room until 2021. Returning brought back many fun memories for us. And yes, twenty-four years later, I did order another vodka, bread and pickle. *Za Zdarovje!* ("Cheers!")

In patience I eventually made it through what I thought was a lost decade waiting to meet my wife. Knowing all the roads we have to walk are winding, God let His plan play out for me. With the assistance of Blessed Mother, and the patient prayers of my mom and Mary's mom, I was providentially paired with Mary. But not before clearing one more hurdle.

The first few months of dating were great, until one day we had "the talk" about past relationships and things went a bit wobbly. For a couple of weeks I was uncertain how things would turn out. Would we break up? Or stay together and eventually get married? A lot of soul-searching went on in those days. What did God want? Providentially, Mary and I went to a BoDeans concert at Ravinia, an outdoor venue in Highland Park, IL, and I received a nudge from a song that night called "Good Things." Sitting on the lawn that hot summer night I remember looking up at the stars and the words connected with me in a most reassuring way:

> "… And I say
> No, no, no, don't pass me over
> No, no, no, don't pass me by
> See I can see good things for you and I
> Yeah, good things for you
> Haunted love is all that I see, it's there in your eyes
> See I can see good things for you and I
> Yeah, good things for you…"

Thanks, God. Music is the medium that sometimes is able to get through to me in ways that others do not. Listening to that song, on that night, I knew from that point forward I was all in on marrying

Mary. And just in case I needed some auxiliary backup resolve, a secondary BoDeans lyric from another song that night was, "If I can hold you tonight, I might never let you go." It's been twenty-four years since that concert; we haven't let each other go, and Mary and I have indeed been blessed with many "Good Things."

In wrapping up this chapter about mothers and patience, I would like to take this opportunity to offer a special thanks to my mother-in-law, Marie, for all her love and prayers for her daughter, for me, our marriage, and our children.

A special thank you to my mom, Mary Ellen, for all her prayers, and patience with me, my siblings, our family, and the wise and generous counsel she provides to all. I'm guessing you would not be surprised to learn my mom has many attributes similar to Saint Monica. No matter the situation, I always knew my mom had my back. Textbook definition of Mama Bear. The roles moms play in families, and hence society, in assisting souls getting to heaven should never, ever, be underestimated, but rather only highly appreciated. Thank you Mom, I love you.

And last but not least, to Mary, my wife, watching how you've showered love and patience on me and our four kids has been nothing short of amazing. Every day each of our kids knew that their mom was their greatest champion and advocate for their spiritual, physical and emotional well-being, and hydration. I suppose I could say that "Our kids don't know how blessed they are with you as their mom." But that would not be true. They do know, and they appreciate you, big time. God has blessed us with one outstanding mom as the heart of our family. For all you've done, and continue to do, God Bless. Thank you, Mary. I love you. And kids, do what your mom says, and drink more water. Please. Make her stop reminding you.

Saint Monica and patience were the right saint and virtue to be featured for the fourth century. Let's fly next to Saint Alexius, temperance, and the fifth century.

Fourth Century Saints

Saints Simplicius, Faustinus and Beatrice (d. 302), Genesius of Rome (d. 303), George (d. 303), Elmo (d. 303), Lucy (d. 304), Philomena (d. 304), Agnes (d. 304), Barlam of Antioch (d. 304), Cosmas & Damien (d. 305), Janarius (d. 305), Adrian of Nicomedia (d. 306), Pamphilus (d. 309), Blaise (d. 316), Nicholas (d. 324), Helena (d. 326), Sylvester I (d. 335), Pachomius (d. 348), Abraham of Edessa (d. 360), Hilary of Poitiers (d. 368), Eusebius (d. 371), Athanasius (d. 373), Ephrem (d. 373), Bademus (d. 376), Basil (d. 379), Cyril of Jerusalem (d. 386), Gregory of Nanzianzus (d. 390), Ambrose (d. 397), and Martin de Torres (d. 397), pray for us.

Saint Monica is the patron saint of housewives, difficult marriages, abuse victims, widows, mothers, alcoholics, disappointing children and patience.

Saint Monica's feast day is August 27.

Saint Monica, *ora pro nobis* (pray for us).

Fourth Century History

302-305- "Roman Emperor Diocletian reigns instituting the last and most brutal of the ten persecutions of the early church. Induced to turn persecutor by a subordinate (Galerius), the council of Nicomedia in 302 was used to suppress Christianity. Additional edicts brought about successive stages in the severity of the persecution: the first ordering that the bishops, presbyters, and deacons should be imprisoned; the second that they should be tortured and compelled by every means to sacrifice; the third including the laity as well as the clergy."

312- Constantine defeats Maxentius at the battle of the **Milvian Bridge** on the Tiber River in Rome on Oct. 28, 312. The night before the battle Christ appeared to Constantine and told him that if he would paint the Chi-Rho (the first two letters of Christ's name) on his soldiers' shields and breastplates, he would be victorious the next day. If Maxentius had won the battle of Milvian Bridge, how many more years would the church have had to remain underground?

As such, it was one of the most consequential battles in the history of Catholicism, and the West.

313- Constantine declares religious liberty for Christians with the **Edict of Milan**. The Milvian Bridge victory led to Christianity being freed from Roman persecutions, and eventually becoming the official religion of the Roman Empire. The church emerges from the catacombs.

320- Saint Pachomius founds the first two monasteries, one for males and one for females, in Tabennisi.

324- **St. John Lateran Basilica** (*Basilica di San Giovanni in Laterano*) is consecrated by Pope Sylvester I. It honors Saint John the Baptist and Saint John the Evangelist. St. John Lateran is the oldest Basilica in Europe, and is the most important of the four major basilicas in Rome. St. John Lateran is the seat of popes as the Bishop of Rome. It is considered the mother church of the Roman Catholic faithful. The basilica has survived several fires, and an earthquake in 897, and has been reconstructed many times. All popes were enthroned here up until 1870, when they switched to St. Peters.

325- **Council at Nicea.** Tackled issue of whether Jesus Christ was equal to God the Father. Established the **Nicene Creed**, proclaimed the trinitarian belief in God, and condemned the false doctrine of Arianism that denied the divinity of Christ. The Arian adherents, however, would persist in their errors for quite some time.

326-28- **Saint Helena**, Constantine's Mother, travels to many of the Holy Places in the Middle East. During her trip, she had many churches constructed, including the one at the site of Jesus Christ's birth—the Church of the Nativity, Bethlehem, and another at the site of his ascension—Church of Eleona on the Mount of Olives.

Helena had the temple built over the site of Jesus's death destroyed and excavated leading to the **discovery of three crosses** at Golgotha. Tradition says Helena brought to the cross a woman who was near death. There she had the woman place a hand on all three crosses. Nothing happened when she touched the first two crosses, but when she placed her hand on the third cross, she suddenly recovered. Helena declared the third cross to be the **True Cross**. At this site, Constantine ordered the **Church of the Holy Sepulchre** to be built.[114]

https://www.catholic.org/saints/saint.php?saint_id=123

330- First **St. Peter's Basilica** (*Basilica Papale di San Pietro in Vaticano*) is built in Rome. The High Alter is built over the tomb of the apostle Peter, the first bishop of Rome. It survives until 1506 when it is torn down, rebuilt, and becomes the largest church in the world. St. Peter's is one of Catholicism's holiest shrines.

335- Emperor Constantine builds the original **Church of the Holy Sepulchre** over the place where Jesus was crucified, buried and rose from the dead. (Constantine had the church built over a temple to Jupiter built by Hadrian in 135 A.D.)

337- Sylvester I baptizes Constantine. ("The Baptism of Constantine" is later painted in the Apostolic Palace in the Vatican by Raphael in the early 1500s.)

356- Council at Béziers. The council, convened by Bishop Saturninus of Arles, was another attempt to quash the Arian heresy. Saint Hilary of Poitiers defended orthodoxy and came to known as the "Hammer of Arianism."

360- Council at Constantinople. A partial Council attended by only fifty prelates. (The First Council at Constantinople would occur twenty-one years later.)

361-363- The majority of the bishops were saying Christ was not divine. God permitted wrath. Reign of Julian II the Apostate. He revoked the exiles. He permitted the orthodox, like Saint Athanasius, back in the church.

366-384- During Damasus's reign, Christianity was declared the religion of the Roman state. The worship of the ancient Gods is forbidden.

367- **Saint Athanasius**, as a result of what he believed to be divine inspiration, **compiled the original list of seventy-three books for the Bible.**

381- The First Council of Constantinople proclaims the divinity of the Holy Ghost.

382- Pope Damasus I approves Saint Athanasius's list and it is formally approved at the Church Council of Rome.

390- Saint Ambrose excommunicates Emperor Theodosios I after he massacred 7,000 civilians in Thessalonike, asking him to repent and perform public penance. In doing so, Ambrose asserted church independence from the state, and even its superiority to the state on questions of faith and morals.

393- Councils at Hippo. Ratifies the seventy-three books of the Bible.

397- Council of Carthage. Also, ratifies the seventy-three books of the Bible.

Virtue Challenge #4- Patience

What's that? You're the most patient person you know and a challenge to be more patient is not necessary? Right. Sorry, not into buying bridges in Brooklyn.

Saint Monica is known as a particularly powerful intercessor for the Church Militant here on earth. Let us pray to imitate her heroic patience in accepting the providence of God in all aspects of our lives. Pray that we may repent, like her son Saint Augustine and become great saints ourselves for the glory of God.

Saint Monica, help us to accept long-suffering. No matter how long hardships are with us, pray for us to stay close to Christ. With grace, we will not be defeatists. When others get on our nerves, help us to recall how patient you were in your life. Help us to candidly consider how patient God is with us and all the sins of commission and omission we commit that offend Him.

How will you show greater patience today with your spouse, child, family member, friend, co-worker? How will you show greater patience the next time you are at a restaurant, grocery store or corner drug store?

What good things do you see in your spouse, children, family members and friends? When is the last time in appreciation you pointed out one or more of their good traits?

If you were to be the patient person you know you are called to be, how would your spouse or closest friend characterize that change in you? Is making the change and being that person worth it to you? If so, why? If not, why not?

Consider the temptations of the devil to incite impatience, belligerence and wrath in your soul. Pray to counter these vices with the graces of meekness and patience. Beg God's forgiveness for our rebellion against His command to love our enemies. Pray to the Holy Angels to assist us in fighting the demonic manifestations that oppress us and beckon us to belligerence and rebellion. Pray for the strength, patience and endurance Christ exhibited on the cross.

Blessed be the name of Mary, Mother of God. Mary, *Mater Admiribalis*, pray for your sons and daughters. Let us not only pray the Hail Mary in our Rosary each day, but also the Angelus, and the *Memorare*, to our Mother and Queen of Heaven. Mother most patient, pray for us.

Converse for a moment with the Holy Ghost about patience and meekness. My Lord and my God, how may I serve you more faithfully and completely through the virtue of patience?

O great Saint Monica, through the pain, suffering and frustrations in our lives, pray for us to have increased holy patience.

CHAPTER 5

Alexius

The Fifth Century
Temperance

*"A man who governs his passions is master of the world. We must
either command them, or be enslaved by them. It is better to be a
hammer than the anvil."*
~ *Saint Dominic de Guzman*

*"Join humility to temperance, because without the
former the latter is useless."*
~ *Saint John Climacus*

*"Virtues are formed by prayer. Prayer preserves temperance...
Prayer draws into the soul the Holy Ghost and raises man to heaven."*
~ *Saint Ephram*

*"Temperance is simply a disposition of the mind that
binds the passions."*
~ *Saint Thomas Aquinas*

The 400s

Descending through the intermittent clouds, I remember my Walkman
playing "Cry Little Sister," the theme song from the teen vampire
comedy, *The Lost Boys*, and looking out the window at the English
countryside with its many reddish-hued rooftops for the first time. I
was eager to touch down and set in motion a much-anticipated study
abroad semester in London, I remember focusing on the hauntingly
beautiful chorus, "... Thou Shall Not Fear... Thou Shall Not Fall...
Thou Shall Not Fail..."

The Lost Boys (1987)

The movie title was a reference to J.M. Barrie's stories about Peter Pan and Neverland, who, like vampires, never grow up. It was my junior year of college and I wanted the semester to be a pivotal time, an inflection point if you will, as I charted my next steps into adulthood. Leaving behind the smothering conformity of Purdue University and a more sophomoric view of life, what precisely was I moving towards? My overarching strategy was to be more of my own person and find greater footing with which to take on the world. Part of that process for me was to go out into the world and experience it.

Top of the list? Iconic and cosmopolitan London, with its high street King's Road, Chelsea, home, for a time, to punk counterculture. While my preconceived notions of London invoked thoughts of Lady Diana and the Royal Family, Westminster Palace, Big Ben and Parliament, the English Premier League (soccer), high finance and fashion, Jack the Ripper, Shakespeare, the Magna Carta, red telephone booths, pubs, and fish and chips, I was most attracted to the alternative music scene. Stepping into this world, how would I measure up? Would I fear, fall, and fail? Or would I thrive, ascend and succeed?

That time in London, for me, was largely a blank canvas. I lived on Old Brompton Road near the Earl's Court tube (subway) station. My classes were at 6 Queens Gate Terrace in South Kensington. A primary goal that fall was to search out and experience the British counterculture scene. The soundtrack for that fall was the aptly titled, "Strangeways Here We Come" by The Smiths. My favorite song from the album is, "Stop Me if You've Heard This One Before." I didn't want what I had known before. I had a healthy appetite for *different,* and I had a plan.

First up, alter my appearance. Starting that summer, I grew my hair longer. The plan worked great. When I arrived home just after Christmas my dad took one look at my long hair and in frustration commented, "Oh good, Jesus is home." I then bought me some authentic, UK alternative clothes, the obligatory Doc Martin's boots, and got my ear pierced in Belfast, Northern Ireland. Check, check and check.

Oddly enough, as much as I told myself I eschewed the conformity at Purdue, looking back on it all I just made a trade for the conformity of a slightly alternative look. Youthful folly.

"Lost Boy" Grane

Next up, experiences. Among the more memorable:
- **Chelsea**. I went to a Chelsea football (soccer) game and joined the
hooligan fans singing one crude song involving a "lump of
celery" and another one that goes, "there once was a poor
little fellow, his face was all tattered and torn, he started to
sing, so I hit him with a brick, and now he don't sing
anymore...Chelsea! Chelsea!" (Yikes!);
- **Amsterdam**. Caught an overnight ocean ferry to Holland. Stayed in
a boatel. Rode bikes around Amsterdam. Walked through
the Red Light district seeing, to my surprise, lots of much
older and overweight women (yikes again!),
- **Concerts**. Attended numerous concerts that fall: Billy Bragg, The
Lorries, Into a Circle, Cardiacs, Motorhead, Brian Eno,
Buddy Guy, and Big Audio Dynamite.
- **Rotten**. Slam danced to Johnny Rotten, front man of Public Image
Limited, singing "Rise" ("anger is an energy!") and "Holiday
in the Sun" (a Sex Pistols cover);
- **Edinburgh**. Visited the Edinburgh Castle and Greyfriars Bobby's
Bar (Ay!);
- **Canterbury**. Walked ten hours on the Canterbury Trail (a sixty-mile,
twenty-hour trek), a pilgrimage, for me, to Saint Thomas
Becket's tomb, (only to have the group vote to abandon the
quest midpoint and catch a train to the White Cliffs of
Dover);
- **Ireland**. Visited Dublin, Belfast, and Galway (where I bought a deep
green, traditional Irish wool sweater—which I still own and
wear on occasion).

- **U.S.S.R.** In December I remember throwing snowballs at the Kremlin (causing an angry guard to blow a whistle at me), and after a night at the Bolshoi had shots of vodka at the hotel bar (enjoying spirited conversation with people I was convinced were KGB informants). Leaving Moscow for Leningrad, I walked on the wicked cold, frozen Straights (Gulf) of Finland while in St. Petersburg (then traded, after some deft haggling—a Hard Rock Café Chicago t-shirt for a warm, rabbit hat).

The school portion of the Boston University, South Kensington Communications study abroad program was terrific too. My favorite course was an Advertising/Public Relations course that featured several of Guinness beers' ad campaigns (brilliant!). To me, though, it was the eclectic group of people who, like me, had personalities that that were drawn to London.

Adding to the over-the-top experience of the semester were people like the tri-borough trio of Lisa, Monica, and Anna who brought with them their respective Queens, Brooklyn, and Long Island *joie de vivre*, and my roommates Jon, Pete and Ken, an English major from SUNY-Buffalo, whose pastime was to literally to read the dictionary (first I'd heard of someone doing that). Further included in our group of friends were: Laura, a cheeky redhead who, to her disrepute, would be a *Playboy* playmate the next year, Dana, a future news anchor at superstation WGN, and James, who taught me the Jed Clampett (Beverly Hillbillies) dance, the eventual Director of Photography on the NBC hit show, Chicago P.D.

Romantically, London was... interesting. After a couple brief romances that were ultimately not meant to be, I found someone who rocked my world, or so I thought. At one point I remember thinking to myself that I actually might be deeply in love. When she spoke, I'd've sworn I heard bells, but it turned out just to be a garbage truck backing up.

Politically, I drifted left during my college undergrad years but nothing major. Many college kids have similar experiences given the socialist professors nipping at their ideological heels. I was conservative on some issues and semi-liberal on others. The political point of no return for me would happen about a year later when I voted for the first time. When debating presidential candidates with

Adam, my roommate, he point-blanked me with, "Which candidate would you want to select the next Supreme Court Justice to rule on abortion?" Done and done. From that point forward, I had metaphysical certitude that I would never vote for a pro-abortion candidate over a pro-life candidate.

Despite my quest in London for the alternative, one of my favorite things to do each Sunday morning was to walk through the occasional morning mist and/or London fog to attend Latin Mass at the historic and conservative Brompton Oratory in Knightsbridge. A curious paradox emerged in my consciousness that fall in that the more I searched for the unorthodox outside the Catholic church, the more I ended up on the sure footings of the orthodox inside the Catholic church.

Flashback. In the early 1970s, then Bishop Joseph Bernardin emerged as the nation's leading advocate for communion in the hand. While it appeared that the other bishops agreed to the practice, it would later be revealed that Bernardin rigged the vote and lied about it. Thus, he was responsible for introducing an evil practice that ultimately diminished Catholic belief in the real presence.[115]

To this day, I can still clearly hear Mom telling me when communion in the hand was introduced in our parish that, "only a priests hands have been consecrated, so he is the only one who can touch the host." From what I was taught in grammar school at Saint Joseph's, I responded, "but Fr. Kevin and Sr. Claudia said it was OK." To which Mom replied, "Yes, well, God can see whose hands have had the holy chrism placed on them through their Ordination and Sacrament of Holy Orders." To this day I have never received communion in the hand. Thanks Mom.

Looking back, via providentially oriented eyes, I can now see that while the majority of the Catholic Church continued to go down the ever-evolving path of modernism and the Novus Ordo Mass, I was more comfortable going in a countercultural direction pursuing traditionalism and the Tridentine Mass.

During my London semester I was not looking to flee or escape from truth. Far from it. Mine was a search for greater liberty and

---

[115] Voris, Michael, "Communion and the Crooked Cardinal," *The Vortex*, Church Militant, February 3, 2021.

meaning in life. Up to that point I had a decent moral foundation as to right and wrong, but during that phase I struggled a bit with my current and future role in the world. I remember thinking of myself as a sort of "xenolith." [A xenolith is "piece of rock trapped in another type of rock."[116] In other words is a stone or rock occurring in a rock system to which it does not belong."] At times I felt like I did not belong. Only much later would I better understand that Catholics are indeed not meant to be conformed to this world. We are made for heaven.

I lost my first grandparent, Grandpa Shannon, to Alzheimer's disease that September. He was my Confirmation sponsor. He was always joking, kind, generous, and willing to play catch with me as a boy. He was the best. Our family knew of his deteriorating condition, and his passing shortly after I arrived in London was not unexpected. What did surprise was my Uncle Wally in Boca Raton, Florida, passing away in early December from a stomach embolism. Bracketed by both relative's deaths while abroad, my thoughts were geared toward the eternal a bit more than I was accustomed. It was part of growing up.

At what I felt to be a crossroads moment, I was going through a deeper, somewhat philosophical, process in determining how I would choose to conform my life to truth, the Catholic Church, and to Christ. How would I better channel my thoughts and actions in the pursuit of the good, the true, and the beautiful?

By no means was I a paragon of virtue or on a sure path to sainthood in those days nor now. Nope. I still had the need for frequent confession during that time as I do today. I made my share of mistakes and have my regrets, as we all do. To be cliché for a moment, I can see, looking back on those strange days, that I am who I am today because of the specific experiences I had back then.

In those days, given my outward appearance, I suppose I was a decent case for the truism, "You can't judge a book by its cover." I am curious—how did you judge *this* book by its cover? Alternative on the outside, conservative Catholic on the inside. For some reason, the dichotomy gave me what I needed to become much more aware of the true north compass in my life that was my Catholic faith. In many ways, my alternative phase deserves partial credit for making my eventual

---

[116] "Xenolith," nationalgeographic.org

embrace of the Tridentine Rite within the Church as seamless as it was. To me, the traditionalists were semi-rebels who went against the grain of the Novus Ordo Mass and modernism. I was pleased, and felt (feel) fortunate, to be on board with those who prefer the efficaciousness of the Traditional Latin Mass—the Mass of the Ages—the Mass of the Saints.

After a semester of fun and growth, before returning to the states, there was one last place I wanted to visit, Jerusalem. I had a strong desire to further discover my faith by walking where Jesus walked. I booked my trip to Israel the month the *intifadeh* ("uprising") began. Once I landed in Tel Aviv, I decided that 'since I was in the neighborhood,' I would check out the mystery of the pyramids in Egypt. After a ten-hour bus ride, I checked into a spartan hotel located just off Al-Tahrir Square. I found downtown Cairo to be quite dirty and noisy with car horns honking all the time. I saw the Nile, walked through an Egyptian museum, made my way to the pyramids of Giza, climbed inside for a tour of some of the stuffy and oxygen-challenged rooms and tombs, and then punctuated my visit with a most memorable camel ride in the Saharan Desert.

Camel Ride in the Sahara, Cairo, Egypt

Major Egyptian tourist attractions having been seen, I anxiously returned to Israel to visit the sites that were core to my beliefs as a Catholic, and to think about things that matter most.

The mystery of the Passion is tough to get your mind around. It is somewhat mysterious how the pyramids were made thousands of years ago with brute manual labor and comparatively crude construction implements. Similarly mysterious for many are the reasons why the infinite God would acquiesce to taking the sins of the world upon Himself and subject His mortal body to intense anguish in the Garden of Gethsemane, the scourging at the pillar, wearing a crown of thorns, carrying the cross, being crucified, all as prelude to His suffering an ignominious death upon the Holy Cross.

I remember from my earliest catechism lessons that Jesus died for *my* sins, and for all those who believe in Him. He died to triumph over original sin and to open the gates of heaven. Given that He died for me, what was Christ's Passion asking of me? What insight was I to learn about Him about how to be a better Catholic?

Forgiveness was at the top of my mind. "*... et dimitte nobis debita nostra, sicut et nos dimittimus debitoribus nostris.*" (... and forgive us our trespasses, as we forgive those who trespass against us.) God permits us to participate in His sufferings in various ways. To start my day of contemplation in Jerusalem, God chose for me a special "rock in my shoe." Staying at the youth hostel, just before checking out, I realized that some Bonnie or Clyde had stolen my favorite gray sweatshirt. I figured whoever was bold enough to steal it was smart enough to hide it, but I still did a quick search around the backpacks at the hostel before I left and, as expected, did not find it. While overall petty in the grand scheme of things, I realized that God had permitted that sweatshirt swindle to put on my plate a small taste of bitterness to help me meditate on forgiveness and true suffering.

I started in the Garden of Gethsemane where Christ began His Passion. The garden itself is not in a very large area. In fact, for some reason I remember counting only nine olive trees in the entire garden. I remember looking at each specific tree and asking myself, "Was this the one under which Christ prayed while His disciples fell asleep when they were asked to keep watch?" How many times in my life had I "dozed off," not keeping guard of my soul, and sinned? I envisioned Christ praying so fervently under one of these trees that He sweat blood. How could I ever experience or even comprehend the weight of the world he must have felt? Difficult to do, but I tried.

I then visited the Western Wall and Temple Mount *en route* to Old City and the Church of the Condemnation, the site of the first station on the Via Doloroso, or Stations of the Cross. I remember thinking that some of the stations felt more authentic than others. I realized that not everything was exactly the way it was given, that two thousand years had passed, but symbolically I was able to follow along, pray, and try to place myself in the shoes of one of the observers that day. What would it have been like to stand in the scorching sun with the crowds and observe the innocent *Agnus Dei* (Lamb of God) pass before me? I asked myself if I would have had the courage to help Jesus carry the cross if the Romans had not drafted Simon the Cyrene into service. As the centurion said to Jesus when speaking about the servant in his home, my response that day, too, would have been his humble plea, *Domine, non sum dignus* (Lord, I'm not worthy.)

The highlight of the day was the visit to the twelfth-century Church of the Holy Sepulchre, the site where Jesus's cross was placed atop Calvary, or Golgotha. I remember the ornate room and a large silver medallion being placed toward the back under an altar. I kneeled and reached my right hand towards the medallion. I put my hand into the hole where Jesus's cross was placed. I felt the cool medallion, then the cold "Rock of Calvary." I expected the rock to be jagged, but to my surprise it was somewhat smooth and almost slick. I guess that over the years so many pilgrim's fingers had touched the same area that their natural oils and perspiration had left a residue of humanity wishing for just a moment to be closer to their God, Lord, and Redeemer.

Having been to many of the sites of Jesus's final hours, I had thoughts of going to Bethlehem for Christmas, but was told not to even try as all the rooms had been booked months before. All the rooms in Bethlehem were booked? I recall that happening before. I scrapped my plans for Bethlehem and flew back to London on Christmas Eve. I remember watching *Happy Days* reruns on the tele Christmas Day. The next day I caught a flight back to Chicago, and was greeted by my Dad's pejorative comment about "Jesus" and the long hair.

In the previous chapter we read of Saint Monica's eternal example of heroic patience taking place in the latter half of the 300s. Her son, Saint Augustine, later the bishop of Hippo, would make his mark in the early 400s. Augustine authored two of the greatest theological works in all of Christianity. *Confessions*, written in 400, articulates Augustine's wayward personal path from his simple farm in Algeria to the complex power center of Milan. It chronicles his personal struggle with sexual impurity ("Lord, make me chaste, but not yet"); how he would eschew worldly ambition and marriage, and how he ultimately rediscovered his faith. Written as the Roman Empire was collapsing, *City of God* (426) encourages the reader not to focus so much on this world but on eternal citizenship.

As I was writing my thoughts about the semester abroad, I couldn't help but think of a parallel to Saint Augustine's books. For me, it was a journey from the college cornfields of West Lafayette, Indiana, to the world-class, international city of London, to transferring that next spring to Boston University. In Boston, I would tap into the Revolutionary War roots of the Boston Tea Party, Paul Revere, Bunker Hill, and the Freedom Trail. The quest to be my own person and adopt an alternative veneer permitted me the time and freedom to embrace fully traditional Catholicism a few years later. Since 1991, I've attended Tridentine Rite Masses. And as for *City of God*, after being exposed to more of the world, and more fully appreciating the blessing that is my Catholic faith, I was better able to focus on a path that I believed gave me the best hope of meriting eternal citizenship.

The 400s, while still a time when many Christians would be martyred, was also a time when Christians made great strides in seeking to make disciples of all nations. Besides Augustine, other towering church writers such as Saint John Chrysostom went to Constantinople and Saint Jerome (previously Eusebius Sophronius Hieronymus) traveled to Trier, Gaul, and Antioch.

Mid-century, Saint Patrick was sent to evangelize pagan Ireland. Saint Olivia, through her zeal, converted many pagans in Italy.

Another great fifth-century saint was Alexius of Rome. Alexius, the only son of a rich, distinguished Roman senator, is a complex character who went against the grain avoiding the "distraction of distinction," and instead charted a life course serving God in humility, poverty, and obscurity. From an early age, Alexius's generosity as shown to those in distress demonstrated he was keenly aware of the value of true charity. Being from a family of privilege meant he could have chosen a callous life of indifference to the poor focusing instead on worldly ambition facilitated by his father's political status. Why did Alexius choose austerity over the easier path? Because he had quite the soft spot in his heart for the less fortunate. To identify with the vulnerable, one often becomes vulnerable.

Alexius struggled with his family's position and his future role in the world. Early on he entertained thoughts of renouncing the advantages of his birth. When his parents spoke with him about the marriage they had arranged for him, he knew in his heart he had a higher calling.[117] On his wedding night, with the approval of his fiancé, Alexius broke all ties which held him in the world and fled to Edessa, Syria to live as a hermit in extreme poverty and obscurity.[118]

Disguising himself as a beggar, Alexius lived for seventeen years in great holiness and anonymity in a crude hovel near a church in Edessa dedicated to the Mother of God. "When a statue of Mary spoke to the people of Edessa revealing him to be the Man of God, he returned to Rome to continue his hidden life."[119]

Not recognizing the beggar as his son, Alexius' father gave him a job and a place to live under a staircase in his palace. While alive, his identity was not known by anyone. Alexius lived patiently, humbly, and without complaint in his father's home for another seventeen years. He was friendly to other Christians, shared what he had with the poor, and taught the children of Rome the Christian faith.[120]

Alexius knew that acts of self-denial and mortification, i.e., temperance, would lead to further meekness and humility and enable him to better serve God and others.

How well do we practice the virtue of temperance? Do we have self-control? Do we control our appetites? Do we nourish our bodies with quick junk food or healthy food? Do we exercise as we should? How do we spend our free time? Do we read the right books? When we need to be online, do we fastidiously avoid the click bait? If distracted by nonsense far into the night, do we fail to get proper rest? Or, conversely, do we sleep too much?

Temperance is one of the four cardinal virtues for good reason. The *Catechism* states that temperance is the "moral virtue that moderates the attraction of pleasures and provides balance in the use of created goods."[121] Temperance is closely aligned with fortitude, the

[117] Butler, Alban, Rev., *Butler's Lives of the Saints*, Volume II, The Catholic Press, Chicago, IL, 1959, 801.
[118] Saint of the Day, *The Catholic Company*, July 17, 2020.
[119] Delaney, John, *Dictionary of Saints*, Doubleday, 1980, 42.
[120] Ibid.
[121] Catechism, 1809.

virtue that helps us restrain our fears, both physical and spiritual. Fr. William Saunders writes:

> The exercise of temperance includes two essential parts: a sense of shame and a sense of honor. The sense of shame causes a person to fear feeling the disgrace, confusion or embarrassment from being intemperate in action. The sense of honor causes a person to want to feel the dignity, esteem or love for practicing temperance. On one hand, the sense of shame prevents a person from acting intemperately and, thereby, sinfully; while on the other hand, the sense of honor inspires a person to act temperately and, thereby, meritoriously.
>
> In all, temperance in action is self-preservation, whereas intemperance in action is self-degradation and self-destruction. Virtues aligned with temperance include abstinence, sobriety, chastity, purity, continence, humility, gentleness, clemency, modesty and lack of greed. On the contrary, vices opposed to temperance include gluttony, drunkenness, unchastity, impurity, incontinence, pride, wrath and greed.[122]

Alexius was able to show to those around him that he regarded those recipients of his good works as his greatest benefactors. "If you would rise," Saint John Chrysostom writes, "shun luxury, for luxury lowers and degrades." The more he "enlarged his views of eternity and raised his thoughts and desires to the bright scene of eternal bliss, the more did he daily despise all earthly toys; for, when once the soul is thus upon the wing, and sours upwards, how does the glory of this world lessen in her eye! And how does she contemn the empty pageantry of all the worldlings call great!"[123]

Alexius knew that when we are free from attachments, we are free to pursue God. Saint Augustine has written, "What profit is there in temporal good and in the ties of blood if we willingly spurn the eternal inheritance of Christ?"

How many times do we wish we could hide under the stairs for a few moments for some peace and quiet! If that's your plan, Alexius is your man. Where do you go to recharge and reconnect with God? Is location important or unimportant to you?

---

[122] Saunders, William, Fr., "Justice, Fortitude and Temperance" *Arlington Catholic Herald,* 2002, n.p.
[123] Butler's, *Lives of the Saints,* 801.

Saint Alexius died in the year 400, a confessor due to the 'natural' causes of hunger and neglect. His identity was only revealed after his death when an autobiographical document he carried was found.[124] Alexius' life was "then venerated as a saint, and his father's palace was converted into a church in his honor."[125]

In 1216, Alexius' body was found in the ancient church of Saint Boniface on the Aventine Hill in Rome. The relics of Saint Boniface and Saint Alexius, including the staircase under which he lived and died, were transferred to the new *Basilica Santi Bonifacio e Alessio* with much celebration and pomp by all of Rome. A well-known drama, *The Hidden Gem,* about Saint Alexius was written by Cardinal Wiseman.[126]

With all the great saints of the fifth century, why was this Hidden Gem of a saint chosen over others? I'm not sure. In each century, certain saints are recognized and celebrated for one reason or another. It strikes a certain cord within me that Alexius pleased God by turning down a life of wealth and privilege for a life of temperance that served others. We shall visit another hidden gem of a saint in the nineteenth century.

What similar or even remote choices do we make when choosing God over the fleeting glory, titles, experiences, and possessions of this life? How can we better avoid the distraction of temporal honors? Why do we covet things that serve us in this life so much more than things that will serve us far better in the next life? As Saint Augustine urges us in *City of God*, we must think less about this world and more about eternal citizenship.

Have you heard the saying, "Keeping up with the Joneses"? It refers to comparing yourself to others and doing what needs to be done to match their material wealth, possessions, status, etc. Most often it's a subtle form of brainwashing by society to pressure you into feelings of inadequacy. Most likely your neighbors, colleagues, friends, etc., will have more than you. And who precisely are you comparing yourself to and trying to keep up with? Pursuing parity with them, or exceeding what they possess, is a fool's errand and can be quite harmful to your soul. Covetousness comes to mind. Temperance is the cure.

---

[124] Delaney, *Dictionary of Saints,* 42.
[125] Saint of the Day, *The Catholic Company,* July 17, 2020.
[126] Butler's, *Lives of the Saints,* 801.

Work, study, and do the best you can and be thankful rather than greedily wanting more.

Looking at this from another angle, while God works with each soul and sends them what He deems proper for them to progress spiritually, including even humiliations, how much more appreciative should we be with what God providentially places before us? It's the spirit in which the provisions of God are received. Are you prideful and say, "This material benefit was due solely to my hard work and effort?" Or do you say, "Thanks be to God for these material blessings provided to me." Big difference. Pride almost always remains, even for those who have overcome other vices.

Saint Alexius is the patron saint of beggars. How can we show true charity to our homeless brothers and sisters? How can we better help the effort at the local food pantry? Can we show more charity by supporting our local pregnancy help center(s)?

Perhaps early on Alexius had the understanding, wisdom, and prudence to know his soul would be in peril if he assumed, like his father, a life along the lines of wealth. Maybe Alexius knew that living a life of poverty and prayer was the best way, perhaps the only way, for him to have mastery over the vices with which he contended. As with Augustine who fought for years with the sin of sexual impurity, maybe Alexius chose not to "dance with his own demons" and opted for the ascetic life. Whatever his motivations, he chose wisely. By his holy example, may we also choose wisely, and live a life of heroic temperance.

Did I live a life of temperance during my time in London? Hardly. That fall I had an intemperate and immoderate appetite for new life experiences. But we learn from out past, no? We are the sum of our experiences.

At the outset of this chapter, I described arriving in London and listening to the Lost Boys' song "Cry Little Sister." To bookend the chapter, while landing back home at Chicago O'Hare, I listened to another Lost Boys' song, "I Still Believe" by The Call. The song opens with a tasty bass line, then lyrics that allude to the Jesus trial and temptations while fasting in the Judean Desert, "I've been in a cave for forty days, Only a spark to light my way..." Additional lines from the song sum up my semester, and our chapter on temperance:

I wanna give out, I wanna give in, This is our crime, This is our sin,
But I still believe...
Through the cold, And the heat, Through the pain, And through the
tears, Oh, I still believe...
I'll march this road, I'll climb this hill, Down on my knees if I have to,
I'll wait 'til the end of time, for you like everybody else, Oh, I still
believe...
I'm out on my own walking the streets, Look at the faces that I meet,
I feel like I, like I want to go home, What do I feel? What do I know?
But I still believe...
For people like us, In places like this, We need all the hope, That we
can get, Oh, I still believe...

That strange London semester I wandered a bit, but was not lost.
I've always known who I am called to serve. And, yes, I still wear my
Doc Martins on occasion. And, oh, I still believe.

Fifth Century Saints

Saints Almachius (d. 400), John Chrysostom (d. 407), Euphrasia (d. 410), Jerome (d. 420), Porphyry (d. 420), Benjamin (d. 424), Augustine (d. 430), Celestine (d. 432), Cyril of Alexandria (d. 444), Ursula (d. 451), Patrick (d. 461), Leo the Great (d. 461), Olivia (d. 463), Benignus of Armagh (d. 467), and Hilary (d. 468), pray for us.

Saint Alexius is the patron saint of beggars, pilgrims, nurses, and Alexian Brothers (a community of male religious founded in Belgium in the fifteenth century to care for Black Death victims).

Saint Alexis is depicted in Christian art dressed in ragged attire.

Saint Alexius' feast day is July 17.

Saint Alexius, model of most generous contempt of the world, *ora pro nobis* (pray for us).

Fifth Century History

400- Saint Almachius protests against gladiators fighting to the death for entertainment.

405- **Saint Jerome completes Old Testament translation from Hebrew.**

410- The Visigoths sack Rome. It is the inspiration for Saint Augustine of Hippo's, *The City of God*, (to be written in 426).

411- **Pelagian heresy** introduced. Advocated by a monk named Pelagius, it denied original sin and the necessity of grace, as well as claiming that one could live a life free of sin.

418- Council of Carthage condemns Pelagianism.

418- Saint Augustine of Hippo, considering the moral consequences of war, is one of the first to articulate a philosophical statement on war and justice, known as the *bellum justum*, or **Just War,** doctrine. Saint Augustine wrote: "Peace should be the object of your desire; war should be waged only as a necessity...in order that peace may be obtained.

422- Pope Saint Celestine I elected Supreme Pontiff. "He established the **papal diplomatic service** to send ambassadors, known as *nuncios*, from the Vatican to other governments around the world."[127]

431- Council of Ephesus condemns **Nestorianism**, the belief that Christ is two persons and declared Mary is the Mother of God (theotokos). The council also condemned Pelagianism.

432- **Pope Saint Celestine I sends Saint Patrick to evangelize Ireland.**

450s- "Pope Saint Leo the Great guides the Church through the collapse of the Roman Empire, waves of barbarian invasions, widespread disintegration of morality, and many dangerous heresies including Pelagianism and Manichaeanism. He persuaded Attila the Hun to turn back and forsake his invasion of Italy. One of only two Pope Saints to be called "Great." Pronounced a Doctor of the Church in 1754."[128]

451- **Council of Chalcedon.** This fourth and last of the great ecumenical councils solidified the orthodox view of the person of Christ. Chalcedon affirmed that Christ had two natures—human and divine, and that these two natures existed within one person without being blurred.

491- The Armenian Church breaks away from the Church of Rome and Constantinople.

492- **Apparition of Saint Michael the Archangel on Monte Gargano, Foggia, Apulia, Italy.**

496- "Clovis, king of the Franks (Germanic tribes), converts to Catholicism. When his troops appear to be losing against the Alemanni at Strasbourg, he invokes the God of his Catholic wife Clotilda to give him victory. He is baptized by Saint Remi, and brings the Franks to the Catholic fold, the first barbarian people to adopt Catholicism."[129]

---

[127] "Pope Saint Celestine I- Saint of the Day," *The Catholic Company,* July 27, 2020.
[128] "Pope Saint Leo the Great- Saint of the Day," *The Catholic Company,* Nov. 10, 2020.
[129] "Timeline of Catholic Church," Catholic Bridge,

Virtue Challenge #5- Temperance

Saint Alexius, help us to govern our passions of this world.

When you wake up tomorrow, how will you be more committed to serving God with a temperate heart, mind, and soul? What adjustments, or tweaks, in your thinking do you need to implement? With the help of God, what unruly passion in particular do you need to focus on at this time? Be honest with yourself. Don't choose the minor one you think would be easier to address. Get after the "elephant in the room" that is the primary obstacle to closer union with Christ. Get after it not in pride, but in humility.

One year from now, if your vocation were buttressed by greater temperance, what would that look like for you?

Man possesses a divine spark that reflects God. Through temperance, how will you be a spark that better reflects God?

Converse for a moment with the Holy Ghost about temperance: My Lord and my God, how may I serve you more faithfully and completely through the virtue of temperance?

O Great Saint Alexius, pray for us an increase in the virtue and grace of holy temperance.

CHAPTER 6

Brigid

The Sixth Century
Benignity

*"She opens her mouth with wisdom, and the teaching of
kindness is on her tongue."*

~ Proverbs 31:26

"Be kind to all, and severe to thyself."

~ Saint Teresa of Avila

*"I know now that true charity consists in bearing all our neighbors'
defects, not being surprised at their weakness, but edified
at their smallest virtues."*

~ Saint Thérèse of Lisieux

The 500s

Do you have an Irish friend? Are they from Ireland, or of Irish decent?
What are they like? Are they among your more personable friends?
Most of the Irish people I know are fun, amicable, fiery, and generous.
Our saint from the sixth century, Brigid, is no different. What's with
that Irish DNA? Something in the water? Jameson? Guinness?

The Irish I know love to joke around and make others laugh. My
mom (née Shannon clan, originally from Country Clare) just told me
this one the other day: "Ah, son, as you know, I've always had a double
chin. When God was passing out 'chins,' I thought He said 'gin.' I said,
'Make mine a double.'"

Way back when I was in high school, Mom gave me a small card
with my name on it and a quotation. She found it in an Irish store. I
keep it as a bookmark in my *Imitation of Christ* by Thomas à Kempis.
On the card in the foreground is a man in a small fishing boat with the
Irish countryside in the background. Written over the scene of *Douglas*

(Celtic Origin) Thoughtful, is "I am the good shepherd; I know My own and My own know me." (John 10:14) Each time I look at the card, I wonder about how thoughtful I am concerning knowing Christ. Work in progress.

The Irish the world over are known for their hospitality and warmth. Being twenty-five percent Irish, we have an Irish shamrock-adorned sign at the entrance of our home that reads, *"Céad Míle Fáilte" ("A Hundred Thousand Welcomes.")* Saint Brigid of Ireland, no doubt, would approve.

Ireland, led by Bishop Saint Patrick, and then influenced by several other saints, would eventually welcome Catholicism and the faith in such a way that it would come to be known in the Middle Ages as the "Land of Saints." Later, the missionaries that were to be sent from Ireland to Europe were largely responsible for Christianizing the continent. The Irish, on fire for Christ and the faith, seemed to be one step ahead. Here's one of my favorite popular Irish sayings: "May you be in heaven half an hour before the devil knows your dead." One step ahead, if only.

Saint Brigid (d. 525) was born *Brigit.* Her name means "fiery arrow." There are many spellings of Brigid: Bríg, Brighid, Brigit, Bride, Bride of the Isles, Bridget of Ireland, Brigid of Kildare, Mary of the Gaels. Because Saint Brigid's name was familiar only to those who spoke Gaelic, the English-speaking world knew virtually nothing of her for the longest time.

Brigid shares a name with a Celtic goddess from whom many legends and folk customs are associated. There is much debate over her birthparents, but it is widely believed her mother was Brocca, a Christian baptized by Saint Patrick, and her father was Dubthach, a Leinster chieftain (a big mover and shaker). Brocca was a slave; therefore Brigid was born into slavery.

When Dubthach's wife discovered Brocca was pregnant, she was sold to a druid landowner. It is not clear if Brocca was unable to produce milk or was not present to care for Brigid, but legend states Brigid vomited any food the Druid attempted to feed her, as he was impure, so a white cow with red ears nourished her instead.

Many stories of Brigid's purity followed her childhood. She was unable to keep from feeding the poor and healing them. One story says Brigid once gave her mother's entire store of butter away, only to have it later replenished after she prayed. When Brigid was about ten years old, she was returned to her father's home, as he was her legal master. Her charity did not end when she left her mother, and she donated his possessions to anyone who asked.

Eventually, Dubthach became so tired of her charitable nature he took her to the king of Leinster with the intention of selling her. As he spoke to the king, Brigid gave his jeweled sword to a beggar so he could barter it for food for his family. When the king, who was a Christian, saw this, he recognized her heart and convinced Dubthach to grant her freedom by saying, "Her merit before God is greater than ours."

After being freed, Brigid returned to the druid and her mother Brocca, who was in charge of the druid's dairy. Brigid took over and often gave away milk, but despite her charitable practice, the dairy prospered, and the druid eventually freed Brocca. Brigid then returned to Dubthach, who had arranged for her to marry a bard. She refused and vowed to always be chaste.

Legend has it Brigid prayed that her beauty be taken so no one would want to marry her, and the prayer was granted. It was not until after she made her final vows as Ireland's first nun that her beauty was restored.

Another tale says that when Saint Patrick heard her final vows, he accidentally used the form for ordaining priests. When the error was brought to his attention, he simply replied, "So be it, my son, she is destined for great things."

Little is known about Saint Brigid's life after she entered the Church. She and seven friends, however, organized communal consecrated religious life for women in Ireland, and she founded a double monastic community, one for men and one for women. The Kildare monastery she founded was built above a pagan shrine to the Celtic goddess Brigid, and originally known as *Druim Criaidh*, or the Ridge of Clay. As the monastery was built beside a stately oak tree loved by the future saint, it eventually became known as *Cill-Dara*. In

Gaelic, *cill* means cell or small church, and *dara* means oak. Hence, Church of the Oak, or, in English, Kildare.[130]

Brigid invited a hermit called Conleth, eventually Saint Conleth, to help her in Kildare as a spiritual pastor, and another bishop Saint Nadfraoich she invited to preach and teach the gospel. Her biographer reported that Brigid chose Conleth, also known as Hugh the Wise, as the first bishop of Kildare, "to govern the church along with herself." The major significance of Brigid's establishment at Kildare was that the Abbess ruled over everyone in the community, including Bishop Conleth, who was subordinate in jurisdiction to the Abbess. According to the Saint Brigid Cathedral, Kildare Town website, "This power structure was to continue for centuries and was unique in Europe. It was one of the many features of the early Irish church which distinguished it from continental Christianity, which explains the contemporary association of Brigid with 'Celtic' Christianity."[131]

Brigid later founded a school of art that included metalwork and illumination. Conleth led the school as well. At this school the *Book of Kildare*, which the Gerald of Wales praised as "the work of angelic, and not human skill," was beautifully illuminated, but it was lost three centuries ago. If you are ever in Ireland staying in a castle, be sure to look in the cupboard cabinets, nooks, and crannies for the *Book of Kildare*. You never know…

There is evidence that Brigid was a good friend of Saint Patrick's and that as the *Trias Thaumaturga* claimed, "Between Saint Patrick and Brigid, the pillars of the Irish people, there was so great a friendship of charity that they had but one heart and one mind. Through him and through her Christ performed many great works."

The ancient Celts slowly warmed up to the idea of Christianity due to a fairly common clever practice used by the early Christians. When spreading the Gospel, they would regularly take a pagan feast day that already existed and, whistling innocently to distract attention, insert their own feast day in its place.

Saint Brigid helped many people in her lifetime, but on February 1, 525, she passed away of natural causes. Her body was initially kept to the right of the high altar of Kildare Cathedral, with a tomb

[130] Wikipedia, "Kildare Abbey," https://en.wikipedia.org/wiki/Kildare_Abbey
[131] St. Brigid's Cathedral, Kildare "Heritage," https://www.kildare.ie/heritage/details.asp?GCID=140

"adorned with gems and precious stones and crowns of gold and silver," but in 878, during the Scandinavian raids, her relics were moved to the tomb of Patrick and Columba. In 1185, John de Courcy had her remains relocated in Down Cathedral.

While on a golf trip to the Emerald Isle, after playing what many consider to be the top-rated course in the world, Royal County Down, my friends and I made a pilgrimage to visit the graves of Saints Patrick, Brigid, and Columba, or Columcille. Upon arrival I went straight to the gravesite located on a small hill near the Down Cathedral. I was surprised at the massive stone that had been placed over the grave in 1900. Sadly, although the tomb was for Ireland's patron saints, there were no other visitors while we were there. I had a quiet visit and was able to pray graveside for all my Irish ancestors, my family, friends, the leaders of the Catholic Church... and my golf game.

"In Down, three saints one grave do fill, Patrick, Brigid, and Columcille."

I went inside Down Cathedral and it was a letdown. As Down is in Northern Ireland, the cathedral nearest Ireland's greatest Catholic saints changed hands during the Protestant Reformation and is now owned by the Church of Ireland. Despite the Catholic–Protestant rift rearing its head momentarily, it was a day I will not soon forget. Some days you have to count your blessings twice—Royal County Down *and* a pilgrimage to visit Saints Patrick, Brigid, and Columcille.

Today, most of Saint Brigid's skull can be found in the Church of St. John the Baptist in Lumiar, Portugal. The tomb in which it is kept bears the inscription, "Here in these three tombs lie the three Irish knights who brought the head of Saint Brigid, Virgin, a native of Ireland, whose relic is preserved in this chapel. In memory of which, the officials of the Altar of the same Saint caused this to be done in January AD 1283." Other portions of her skull have been located at Saint Bridget's Church in Killester.

When Brigid died, her sisters kept a holy fire burning for their beloved "fiery arrow" in an enclosure at her Kildare convent. This fire, called *the inextinguishable,* tended by the sisters, burned continuously for almost 700 years until it was put out by order of Henry de Loundres, Archbishop of Dublin, who considered the practice to be superstitious. After a short lapse, the Bishop of Kildare kindled the practice again, and the flame continued for several more centuries until the reign of Elizabeth I, who ordered Brigid's flame to be extinguished, and every other monastic light in Ireland was ordered to be put out due to the perceived threat of a Catholic crusade against heretical England.[132]

Saint Bridget lived a life that was characterized by benignity in the truest sense of the word. In Saint Paul's letters to the Colossians (3:12-15), he writes:

> [12] Put ye on therefore, as the elect of God, holy, and beloved, the bowels of mercy, benignity, humility, modesty, patience: [13] Bearing with one another, and forgiving one another, if any have a complaint against another: even as the Lord hath forgiven you, so do you also. [14] But above all these things have charity, which is the bond of perfection: [15] And let the peace of Christ rejoice in your hearts, wherein also you are called in one body: and be ye thankful.

When you are thankful, it's a bit more difficult to find fault with others. Even at Mass, when we should be most thankful to be in His presence, our thoughts are not always benign regarding others we see there. Have you ever scoffed at how others dress, rather than being thankful that they came to Mass? Do you find fault with how others aren't able to kneel exactly the way you would want them to? Maybe they have a sore knee, and/or a sore back, and they are doing the best they can. Lastly, are you the person who can't help but turn around

[132] Wikipedia, "Kildare Abbey," https://en.wikipedia.org/wiki/Kildare_Abbey

and give a nasty stare to the young parents whose child happens to be a bit unruly that day? Benignity or contemptuousness? You choose.

Benignity is a close cousin to kindness. In 2 Timothy 2:24-26, we read: "A slave of the Lord should not quarrel, but should be gentle with everyone, able to teach, tolerant, correcting opponents with kindness. It may be that God will grant them repentance that leads to knowledge of the truth, and that they may return to their senses out of the devil's snare, where they are entrapped by him, for his will."

Fr. John Hardon writes about the Fruit of Kindness as follows: "One of the fruits of the Holy Spirit; the quality of understanding sympathy and concern for those in trouble or need. It is shown in affability of speech, generosity of conduct, and forgiveness of injuries sustained."[133]

So, starting with your spouse, and/or those in your family, how can your thoughts and actions be more generous, understanding, supportive, and forgiving? More benign?

Speaking of cousins, in the second decade of the Joyful Rosary, we meditate upon the Visitation and the holy example of Mary visiting her cousin Elizabeth. Think of the way that Mary and Joseph must have interacted with their neighbors. We can be sure they were always kind, courteous, and helpful. Hard to imagine more perfect neighbors than the Holy Family. Saint Frances de Sales commented on this virtue: "One can attract more flies with a spoonful of honey then with a barrel full of vinegar." In other words, kindness attracts others to Christ more than being unfriendly or rude.

As you would expect, numerous entertaining stories relate to Saint Brigid. Some are true, and some are a bit exaggerated. Perhaps a little Irish "blarney" as they say. See if you can decide which of the following are true and which are "legend."

⊙ *"Brid agus Muire dhuit,"* (Brigid and Mary be with you) is a common Irish greeting.[134]

---

[133] Hardon, Modern Catholic Dictionary, n.p.
[134] Smith, Tracy Bua, "Here's 31 Things You Probably Didn't Know About St. Brigid of Ireland," *EpicPew*, January 30, 2017.

- The reason for February 1 being the Celtic first day of spring, also known as Imbolc, is due to the pagan goddess named, wait for it, Brigid.[135]
- Brigid is one of Ireland's three patron saints. The other two are: Saint Colmcille and Saint Patrick.
- At age 16, Brigid wanted Jesus Christ to be her spouse and she prayed that He would make her unattractive so no one would want to marry her. Her prayer was answered when she lost an eye and was allowed to enter a monastery. Miraculously, when St. Brigid took the veil, she was healed.[136]
- Brigid drove out demons by simply gesturing the sign of the cross.[137]
- Brigid once fell asleep during Saint Patrick's sermon. He found it humorous and forgave her with a smile.[138]
- Brigid was able to turn bathwater into beer.[139]

Able to discern truth from blarney? Well, all were true—except the last about the bathwater and beer. That's just a fine Irish legend, but one the Irish probably dream about!

Ireland is a nation with many sacred spots and holy wells. By some estimates approximately 3,000 wells are located throughout the Emerald Isle. Several wells are dedicated to Saint Brigid, but the primary one is found in Ballysteen, County Clare (about 235 miles SW of her grave in Down, Northern Ireland). Ancient tradition holds that the well was visited by a fish—the Christian symbol that predates the cross.

Just after my great-grandparents Shannon were married, they visited this Saint Brigid's Well to pray for their marriage and perhaps even their progeny. I'm grateful they did. A couple of days after visiting Saint Brigid's grave in County Down, I was able to visit the same well and pray for them and my family. It was a special day.

We had just left the nearby Cliffs of Moher and set out for pilgrimage to the well. It was a bit hard to find. The GPS was not exact and we drove down the main road a couple of times before realizing we needed to turn down a *side* road to locate the well. After we parked

---

[135] Rogers, Mal, "11 Facts About St. Brigid," *The Irish Post,* February 1, 2017,
[136] Smith, "31 Things."
[137] Ibid.
[138] Ibid.
[139] Rogers, "11 Facts."

and approached the shrine, we were met by an enclosed statue of Saint Brigid. The upper sanctuary (*Ula Uachtarach*) included a cemetery which we read contained many important Celtic kings and clan leaders of Ireland. The lower sanctuary (*Ula íochtarach*), a grotto, certainly had an historic feel to it.

Approaching the well what I noticed first was the sight of hundreds of memorabilia, prayer cards, notes of gratitude, and pictures left on the white walls. Then I noticed the mildly musty smell. The aura of Irish, Catholic warmth I felt at this holy place, however, greatly overshadowed the dampness. To the back of the grotto at its lowest point was the well itself. It was a simple, small area with fresh spring water. I kneeled, touched the water, made the sign of the cross, and prayed for family and friends. Did my great-grandparents ever envision their great-grandson kneeling and praying where they knelt and prayed on their wedding day?

Saint Brigid's Well, Ballysteen, County Clare, Ireland

On December 26, 2020, due to the CCP Wuhan Flu, the Irish republic prohibited public worship throughout the land.[140] While some defied the ban, most Irish endured the hardship of no Mass and sacraments—including confession being illegal. Public worship was reinstated on May 10, 2021. Roughly half a year without the Holy

---

[140] Turley, K.V. "Ireland Returns to Worship After Months Away From the Mass," *National Catholic Reporter*, May 23, 2021.

Sacrifice of the Mass. How could practicing one's faith not have been deemed 'essential'? What must Saint Brigid have thought about this painful and difficult time occurring in her beloved, native land?

Like the Celtic Cross, Saint Brigid's cross has been popularized not just in Ireland but the world over. Often it has been worked into architecture in churches and holy places. In my home parish, Saint John Cantius in Chicago, Saint Brigid's cross has been worked into the wood and tile flooring in several locations. I'm grateful they're there and smile each time I see them. Saint Brigid, pray for us.

Keep an eye out for our great saint's holy cross. It's in more locations than you think. And when you find a Saint Brigid's cross, be of good cheer, smile, make a reverent sign of the cross, and perhaps you too will drive away a demon or two.

Saint Brigid Hearth Keeper Prayer

Brigid of the Mantle, encompass us,
Lady of the Lambs, protect us,
Keeper of the Hearth, kindle us.
Beneath your mantle, gather us,
And restore us to memory.
Mothers of our mother, Foremothers strong.
Guide our hands in yours,
Remind us how to kindle the hearth.
To keep it bright, to preserve the flame.
Your hands upon ours, Our hands within yours,
To kindle the light, Both day and night.
The Mantle of Brigid about us,
The Memory of Brigid within us,
The Protection of Brigid keeping us
From harm, from ignorance, from heartlessness.
This day and night,
From dawn till dark, From dark till dawn.[141]

---

[141] St. Brigid of Ireland, *Catholic Online*, prayer courtesy of *SaintBrigids.org*
https://www.catholic.org/saints/saint.php?saint_id=453

Sixth Century Saints

Saints Eugendus (d. 510), Genevieve (d. 512), Remegius (d. 533), Agapitus (d. 536), Benedict of Nursia (d. 547), Scholastica (d. 547), Cassiodorus (d.583), Fanchea (d. 585), Hermengild (d. 586), and Columba (d. 597), pray for us.

Saint Brigid is the patron saint of Ireland, babies, children whose parents are not married, dairy workers, farmers, midwives, nuns, poets, printers, travelers, and sailors.

Saint Brigid is often depicted holding a reed cross (Saint Brigid's cross), a burning flame, a lamp, a crozier, and a book.

Saint Brigid's feast day is February 1.

Saint Brigid, *ora pro nobis* (pray for us).

Sixth Century History

530- **Rule of Saint Benedict** (of Nursia). Founder of Western Monasticism. (Basil was the found of Eastern Monasticism in 356.) Benedict had a twin sister, Saint Scholastica. They were born in Nursia, Italy and grew up in Rome. According to The Catholic Company, "As a young man [Benedict] found in himself a strong desire to escape the trifling things of the world and serve God. He left his family and wealth and settled in the mountainous region of Subiaco. After three years living in solitude as a cave-dwelling hermit, he was asked to lead a monastery in the place of an abbot who had died. Benedict did as they asked, but his way of life was too extreme for the monks and they tried to poison him. He thwarted their evil designs by blessing the poisoned cup, rendering it ineffective. Benedict returned to his cave, where news of his sanctity and miracles began to spread. Soon a community of men surrounded him wanting to adopt his way of life. To house them Benedict established twelve monasteries, including the world-famous Monte Cassino, and gave them a rule of life to live by, known as the Rule of Saint Benedict. His Rule—still observed by Benedictines today—helped form the civilization and culture of Europe. He is the patron saint of monks, students, farmers, and all of Europe. He is also especially known for his intercession against poison, temptations, and witchcraft."[142]

---

[142] "Saint Benedict, Saint of the Day," *The Catholic Company.*

533- Pope John II becomes the first Pope to adopt a new name as Pope.

537- The **Cathedral of Holy Wisdom** (now the Hagia Sophia) is founded under Emperor Justinian in Constantinople (now Istanbul). At the time of its founding the Cathedral was the largest building in the world, and the largest Christian church. It served as the cathedral of the Patriarch of Constantinople before and after the Great Schism split Western and Eastern Christianity into the Catholic and Eastern Orthodox Churches. Less than 100 years after the Cathedral's founding, Islam would be established in 632. The Cathedral would be converted to a mosque after the Fall of Constantinople by the Ottoman empire in 1453.

590- Saint Gregory the Great institutes **Gregorian Chant**. He also institutes the **Gregorian Masses**, a series of thirty Masses said over thirty consecutive days. Our Lord is said to have appeared to Gregory and said, *"My friend, I want to grant in your favor a privilege that will be unique. All souls in purgatory, for whom thirty Masses are offered in your honor and without interruption, will immediately be saved however great may be their debt to me."*[143]

590- April 25th. Pope Saint Gregory the Great, after leading people of Rome in prayer saw Saint Michael the Archangel with his sword drawn, along with other Angels, descend above the crowd, a heavenly perfume filled the air, and the plague ended on that date. (One of only two times Saint Michael has appeared in public.)

---

[143] Tassone, *"Day by Day- Holy Souls in Purgatory,"* 21.

Virtue Challenge #6- Benignity

Saint Brigid, help us practice greater benignity and kindness to all. Help us to be fiery when it comes to our faith. Not hot-headed or uncharitable with our disposition, but strong and passionate, as you were, about sharing the gospel of Christ and defending our faith as needed. Keep us from heartlessness and harm.

Help us to see the good in others and give them the benefit of the doubt more often than not. Pray for us to do many acts of kindness today for the holy souls of purgatory. Last but not least, pray for us, nudge us to make the sign of the cross more frequently throughout our day.

Saint Brigid, beg Jesus to show us mercy and send us the graces necessary to become saints. To merit heaven would indeed be a great feat. To merit a seat anywhere in the heavenly banquet and spend eternity with God and His saints would be a race well run. Help us to achieve the incorruptible crown.

Everyone loves laughter, even God. You want to make God laugh? Tell him your plans.

Converse for a moment with the Holy Ghost about benignity. My Lord and my God, how may I serve you more faithfully and completely through the virtue of benignity?

O Great Saint Brigid, pray for us an increase in the virtue and grace of holy benignity.

CHAPTER 7

Etheldreda

The Seventh Century
Chastity

"Blessed are the clean of heart, for they shall see God."
- Jesus, Matthew 5:8

"Chastity makes man very similar to God, who is a pure spirit."
- Saint Basil

"More souls go to hell because of sins of the flesh than for any other reason."
- Our Lady of Fatima

"To defend his purity, Saint Francis of Assisi rolled in the snow, Saint Benedict threw himself into a thornbush, Saint Bernard plunged into an icy pond . . . You . . . what have you done?"
- Saint Josemaría Escrivá

The 600s

A major event to impact the seventh century was the founding of Islam in 632 by the prophet Mohammed. The Middle East and Europe would soon face much tumult as Islam competed with Christianity as the various caliphs conquered new territories. Many of the Christian areas brought to submission were conquered by the sword of Islam. (Today, Mohammed's sword is in Topkapi Palace, an Istanbul museum.)

By contrast, Christian missionaries to that point in time preferred to convert by faith, persuasion and grace. In the 600s, missionaries were on the move in northern Europe. As Hilaire Belloc would say, "Europe is the (Catholic) Faith and the Faith is Europe." Examples include: Saint Oswald, a convert to Christianity, focused on reuniting Northumbria and ruled as a saintly and powerful Christian king in justice and humility;[144] Saint Fiacre of Ireland left for France, formed a monastery, and lived a life of great mortification; Saint Kilian, also from Ireland, went to Gaul (present day France and parts of Germany) as a missionary to evangelize the pagans.[145]

The focus of this century, however, is the English princess Etheldreda. Born in 640 in Ermynge, a village in Suffolk, Etheldreda was also known as Ediltrudis, Aethelthryth or, simply,

Audrey. She was the third daughter of Annas, the holy king of East Angles and Saint Hereswyda. Her two older sisters were saints, Saint Sexburga and Saint Ethelburga, as was her younger sister, Saint Withburga.[146]

Five saintly women in one family! Imagine. How blessed King Annas must have been! No fights for mirror time, the hair dryer, who has better hair, who gets to ride shotgun, or who borrowed each other's clothes. No refereeing who was right in that fight from years ago. I'm still not convinced, however, that even though saintly, the four sisters still didn't have 'discussions' (i.e., fights) over who was Daddy's favorite.

Etheldreda loved her dad, and he raised her well in the fear of God. According to the desires of her family and friends, she married Tonbercht, prince of the Southern Girvij, but they lived together in perpetual constancy. Three years after she married, Etheldreda lost her husband. The holy virgin and widow went to the Isle of Ely and lived there for five years. One descriptive passage about Etheldreda during this time it states, "Trampling under her feet whatever attracts the hearts of deluded worldlings, she made poverty and humility her delight and her glory, and to sing the divine praises with the angel's night and day was her most noble ambition and holy employ."[147]

Egfrind, the King of Northumberland and another person with an awesome name from seventh century England, upon hearing of Etheldreda's virtue, asked her to marry him, and she consented. Her vow of virginity, however, was respected by Egfrind. They lived together as brother and sister for twelve years until Egfrind's passing.

[144] Saint Oswalt, "Saint of the Day," *The Catholic Company,* Aug. 5, 2020.
[145] Saint Kilian, "Saint of the Day," *The Catholic Company,* July 7, 2020.
[146] Saint Etheldreda, *Butler's Lives of the Saints,* Volume II, 686.
[147] Ibid.

Etheldreda spoke with her friend, Saint Wilfrid, about serving God as a religious and from him "took the veil" i.e., her vows. Thereafter, she went to the monastery at Coldingham and lived in holy obedience under Saint Ebba.[148]

So many saints! By my count there were at least six saints in Etheldreda's life. They were everywhere she turned. What incredible impact on one's Catholic worldview, character, and virtues that must have been. Imagine if you were able to interact regularly with six saints during your life? Instead, our lives have been blessed with spouses who leave dishes in the sink, the car always on empty, kids who perpetually leave socks, towels and Legos on the floor, who have superpower skills avoiding taking the garbage out, and, by the beard of Zeus, can't remember to flush the toilet.

[Parenting tip. Regarding the unstoppable rebel force that are 'socks on the floor' (feel free to substitute your family's Mt. Everest challenge here), we've tried multiple forms of discipline and enticement with our kids, all to no avail. Sometimes kids have mental blocks regarding a parent's requests and repeated reminders. Sometimes parents lack the will of perpetual follow-up to bring about a desired behavior. No excuses, plenty of fault to go around. Pardon any disrespect taken, but in our house, I have gone spiritual *jiu-jitsu* and now refer to "socks found" as "souls to pray for." In other words, anytime I see a rogue sock on the floor, and before I get frustrated, I say a Hail Mary offering it up for a soul in purgatory. Once said, I then remind Alex or Charlie, for the thousandth time, to pick up their sock(s). As the saying goes, the joy of children is never ending.]

Lord, in your infinite wisdom, you arranged for me to not be surrounded by saints in my life. Instead, it's mouth in motion, brain in neutral; and a healthy dose of Moe, Larry and Curly. Thank you, Jesus. I appreciate the special path you specifically chose just for me. But, seriously, maybe just one saint? Please? Asking for a friend. Some people (Etheldreda!) just get all the saints in their lives. Not complaining. Just observing.

In 672 Etheldreda returned to the Isle of Ely and founded a double monastery on her own estate. As she was the foundress, she governed herself, and was "by her example of a living rule of perfection

---

[148] Ibid.

to her sisters." It was reported that she ate only once a day, except on great festivals or when sick; only wore woolen clothes; and did not go back to bed after matins were sung at midnight but instead prayed in the church until morning.[149]

When a young Etheldreda was at her royal court, she wore rich necklaces with many jewels. With her last sickness she had an enormous and unsightly tumor on her neck, which she gladly accepted as just chastisement for her youthful vanity—wearing fancy necklaces in her early years.

Saint Etheldreda died in 679. When later taken up, her body was found to be uncorrupt. Of note: The physician who had made an incision in her neck during her illness prior to death, was surprised to see the wound had perfectly healed.[150]

Throughout the Middle Ages, a festival, "Saint Audrey's Fair," was held at Ely on her feast day. The exceptional shoddiness of the merchandise, especially the neckerchiefs, contributed to the English language the word "tawdry," a corruption of "Saint Audrey."[151]

In her life Etheldreda placed the highest priority on remaining a virgin. Why? A great explanation is as follows:

> "This great queen and saint set so high a value of the virtue of virginity because she was instructed in the school of Christ how precious a jewel and how bright an ornament that virtue is in his divine eyes, who is the chaste Spouse and Lover of true virgins, who crown their chastity with a spirit of prayer, sincere humility, and charity. These souls are without spot before the throne of God; they are purchased from among men, the first-fruits to God and the Lamb, being the inheritance properly consecrated to God; they sing a new canticle before the throne, which no other can sing, and they follow the Lamb whithersoever he goeth."[152]

---

[149] Ibid, 687.
[150] Ibid.
[151] Saint Etheldreda (Audrey), *Catholic Online,*
https://www.catholic.org/saints/saint.php?saint_id=6
[152] Butler's, 687.

Beautiful. How glorious the holy, true virgins must be in the eyes of God. "The joys of the virgins of Christ are formed of Christ, in Christ, through Christ, and for Christ."[153]

Saint Alphonsus Liguori makes an excellent point when we contemplate the value that Christ puts on virginity, "We would do well to note that Our Lord chose a virgin for His Mother, a virgin for his foster father, Saint Joseph, and a virgin for his precursor, Saint John the Baptist."[154]

In a world of hyper-sexualization, Saint Etheldreda helps us to see that value and virtue of virginity, chastity and abstinence. Many seek sexual gratification outside of the holy bond of marriage and often are met with falsity, emptiness, and treacherousness. Saint Josemaría Escrivá tells us, "When you have sought the company of a sensual satisfaction, what loneliness afterward!" Our world is filled with loneliness and a lack of chastity is a primary cause. Though our culture will almost never explain it that candidly.

According to Saint Thomas Aquinas, the daughters (consequences) of lust are "blindness of mind, thoughtlessness, inconstancy, rashness, self-love, hatred of God, love of this world, and abhorrence or despair of a future world." Pope Pius XII adds, "Mainly thru the sins of impurity do the forces of darkness subjugate souls." Immoral profiteers, influenced by the devil, exploit souls by impurity the world over. Perhaps you've heard of the adage "sex sells." Impure images and discussions dominate the internet, radio, TV, cinema, and many books. Are you in agreement that your virtue is under assault, or have you been numbed and desensitized to it all? Pray that you remain ever vigilant.

While the Confirmed have heard about and received, the Seven Gifts of the Holy Spirit, Holy Mother Church also instructs us on the *fruits* of the Spirit.[155] Of the twelve fruits, while chastity is the last to be listed, it is most assuredly not the least.

Chastity, the virtue that counters the lust of the flesh, is obligatory for single persons and the consecrated religious. For married persons,

---

[153] Ibid.
[154] Saint Alphonsus Liguori, *The 12 Steps to Holiness and Salvation*, TAN Books, Rockford, IL, 1986, 92.
[155] Cathechism, 1832.

a commitment to fidelity, and at times being chaste, are vital. Chastity reminds people in all states of life of the deeper meaning and sacredness of sexuality.

Saint Ephram calls chastity the "life of the spirit." Saint Peter Damien styles it the "queen of the virtues." Saint Alphonsus Liguori writes, "he who conquers the vice opposed to this virtue will easily triumph over the rest. On the contrary, he who permits himself to be ruled by incontinency falls an easy prey to the other vices such as hatred, injustice, etc."[156]

So, what are we to do, or think about, once a bad thought or temptation happens? Once again, we turn to Saint Alphonsus Liguori, who writes, "In temptations against chastity, the spiritual masters advise us, not so much to contend with the bad thought, as to turn the mind to some spiritual, or, at least, indifferent object. It is useful to combat other bad thoughts face to face, but not thoughts of impurity." In other words, when thoughts of impurity occur, run! Do not play with fire, as there is a significant likelihood that you will be burned.

To illustrate the seriousness of consenting to impure thoughts—and this is something that most Catholics have not been taught for generations—consider the following true story:

"A certain woman who was regarded as a saint was tempted one day by an evil thought. Failing to reject it at once, she became guilty of grievous sin. From false shame she neglected to confess the sinful thought she had yielded to, and shortly after, died. Now the bishop of the place had considered her a saint, and accordingly he had her buried in his own chapel. On the following day the unfortunate soul appeared to him and declared that, owing to a sinful thought to which she had consented, she was eternally lost."[157]

How's that for a story? Being damned for a single, consenting sinful thought. To say the least, the road to heaven is narrow. Anyone want to argue that we should not be focused like a laser on working out our salvation in fear and trembling? Stories such as this are not the ones that most homilists or Catholic speakers regularly share with the faithful. And we the faithful are poorer spiritually on account of that.

---

[156] Liguori, 91.
[157] Liguori, 95.

Why are we not routinely reminded of the need for purity of thought? The implications are ominous if we do not heed the message.

Got it. Thoughts of impurity are to be treated differently. Saint Thomas Aquinas chimes in to warn us further, "In the realm of evil thoughts none induces to sin as much as do thoughts that concern the pleasure of the flesh."

Kicking things up a notch, if that's possible, we have Saint Augustine who shared, "lust indulged becomes habit, and habit unresisted became necessity." Caught in a seemingly endless trap, a spiral of sin, what did Saint Augustine do? What did he think about so as to break, or stop, his lustful thoughts and not consent to them? Augustine shares, "there is no remedy so powerful against the heat of concupiscence as the remembrance of our Savior's passion. In all my difficulties I never found anything so efficacious as the wounds of Christ: In them I sleep secure; from them I derive new life." OK, now that was some pretty outstanding saintly advice. Thank you, Saint Augustine!

Fourth century martyrs who surely inspired Etheldreda were Saints Agatha and Agnes. Saint Agatha, a consecrated virgin, was twenty years old when she would not submit to the advances of the evil and sadistic Quintianus. Agatha prayed, "Jesus Christ, Lord of all, you see my heart, you know my desires. Possess all that I am. I am your sheep: make me worthy to overcome the devil."[158] Agatha never lost her confidence in God, even though she suffered a month of assaults and tortures to get her to abandon her vow to God and go against her virtue. She was stretched on a rack to be torn with iron hooks, burned with torches, and whipped. Quintianus then had her stripped naked and rolled over naked over hot coals which were mixed with sharp shards. She died soon thereafter. Agatha endured all the torture with a seeming sense of cheer. Saint Agatha is the patron saint of Sicily, bellfounders, breast cancer patients, rape victims and Palermo.[159]

Saint Agnes, a lovely young woman, maybe twelve or thirteen years old, had consecrated her virginity to Christ, and met a fate similar to Agatha. Agnes's name means 'lamb' or 'chaste.' Agnes, discovered to be a Christian, was brought before the Roman authorities for

---

[158] Saint Agatha, Catholic Online, https://www.catholic.org/saints/saint.php?saint_id=14
[159] Ibid.

sentencing. When the world attempted to win her love, the noble Agnes answered, "Away, away, you seek my love, but I can love none other than my God who has loved me first."[160] Agnes was ordered to be dragged naked through the streets and then forced into a brothel to be sexually abused. Miraculously, Agnes escaped with her virginity preserved, but was ultimately beheaded. Saint Agnes is the patroness of girls, chastity, engaged couples, virgins, rape victims, and Girl Scouts.

Besides the Virgin Mary, Agatha and Agnes are two of the seven women named in the Roman Canon of the Mass. Saints Agatha and Agnes, pray for us. One of Blessed Mary's most sublime virtues is that of her spotless purity. One of her highest titles is the Immaculate Conception. Fr. Ed Broom, OMV adds, "Contemplating a beautiful picture, painting, or statue of Our Lady can instill in us noble aspirations for purity."[161]

When attempting to overcome temptation, know that we always have recourse to fly unto Blessed Mother, the Immaculate Conception, the Virgin of Virgins. Consider The *Memorare*:

> *Remember, O most gracious Virgin Mary, that never was it known that anyone who fled to thy protection, implored thy help, or sought thine intercession was left unaided. Inspired by this confidence, I fly unto thee, O Virgin of virgins, my mother; to thee do I come, before thee I stand, sinful and sorrowful. O Mother of the Word Incarnate, despise not my petitions, but in thy mercy hear and answer me. Amen.*

Fast forward to 1917 when Blessed Mother appeared at Fatima. She said that more sinners go to hell because of sins of impurity than any other. Could Our Lady have been more candid? And she said that over a hundred years ago! How much more impure has our world become since 1917? The sins of the flesh are legion. What people think, how they act, what they do behind closed doors, and how they defile their bodies and those of others, are affronts to human dignity, and greatly offend our Lord.

Blessed Mother also told the three Fatima children that many people go to hell because they have no one to pray and make sacrifices for them. Keeping that in mind, each night, when you perform your

---

[160] Liguori, *12 Steps*, 105.
[161] Broom, Ed, "Imitate Our Lady's Ten Principle Virtues," *Catholic Exchange,* February 23, 2021.

examination of conscience, pray for others and sins against impurity. Ask Christ for forgiveness for yourself, and for others who have no one to pray for them.

The Angel of Fatima, and the other angels, surely knew the value of the virtue of chastity. Chastity brings man closer to not only God, but to angels, too. Saint Francis de Sales, Doctor of the Church, writes, "Chastity is the lily of virtues, and makes men almost equal to Angels. Everything is beautiful in accordance with its purity. Now the purity of man is chastity, which is called honesty, and the observance of it, honor and also integrity; and its contrary is called corruption; in short, it has this peculiar excellence above the other virtues, that it preserves both soul and body fair and unspotted."

"Chastity, or cleanness of heart," writes Saint Augustine, "holds a glorious and distinguished place among the virtues, because she, alone, enables man to see God; hence Truth itself said, 'Blessed are the clean of heart, for they shall see God.'" Seeing God. That's a powerful idea worthy of further contemplation. So worthy it is the quote that I chose to open this chapter. Along similar lines, I have read that angels, from wherever they are, can see the face of God.

Saint John Bosco adds, "Holy Purity, the queen of virtues, the angelic virtue, is a jewel so precious that those who possess it become like the angels of God in heaven, even though clothed in mortal flesh." How beautiful. How well said, Saint John Bosco.

With regard to purity, think of closeness to the angels, and how it honors God's will. Dare not look to society to tell you what is right or wrong, socially acceptable, or even legal. The world gets plenty wrong and glamorizes immorality and impurity almost everywhere you look. Yes, we have general freedoms in society, but those freedoms relate to what you *ought* to do, not to whatever it is you *want* to do. That's license. And there is a big difference. License is freedom without consequences, pleasure without conscience, and laws without morality. License is a big lie, straight from the father of lies. Be on guard for false security from lust and pride.

To counter the two deadly sins of lust and pride, God grants us grace and an increase in the virtues of chastity and humility. The two are inextricably interrelated. Saint Philip Neri tells us, "Humility is the safeguard of chastity. In the matter of purity, there is no greater danger than not fearing the danger. For my part, when I find a man secure of himself and without fear, I give him up for lost I am less alarmed for one who is tempted and who resists by avoiding the occasions, than for one who is not tempted and is not careful to avoid occasions. When a person puts himself in an occasion, saying, I shall not fall, it is an almost infallible sign that he will fall, and with great injury to his soul."[162] We must take care to guard ourselves on multiple fronts.

The primary ways to protect ourselves with purity starts with our mind, how we think; then our eyes; and then perhaps our speech, and even our dress. There are more ways, but these are the foremost means the devil uses towards his end of having us be unchaste.

Impure acts begin with an evil thought or as a temptation in our mind. Do we have the will to dismiss the impure thought as quickly as it entered? Do not be scrupulous. Temptations happen. What matters is whether or not one yields or consents to the temptation. Saint Alphonus Liguoiri warns us, "Therefore an evil thought or desire to which we consent comprises in itself all the wickedness of an evil deed. As sinful actions separate us from God, so wicked thoughts rob us of His grace. 'Perverse thoughts separate us from God,' says the Book of Wisdom 1:3."[163]

Saint Alphonsus Liguori continues by explaining that many sins of impurity start with the eyes. The fall of man began with Eve looking at the tree of life. The eyes occasioned the fall of David, and so too with Solomon. Liguori writes, "We know that the devil tempts man to first look with impure eyes, then to desire, and at last to consent."[164] Saint Jerome says the devil needs only a small opening of consent. It is "enough if we only open the door halfway for him; he will then force it open all the way."[165] As Catholics, we must not look at anything that awakens unclean thoughts within us. In Ecclesiastes 1:8, we read, "The eye is not satisfied with seeing, nor is the ear filled with hearing." The Holy Ghost tells us in Ecclesiastes 9:8-9, "Gaze not upon another's beauty, for hereby lust is enkindled as a fire." We must take note of the example of the saints who did all they could to maintain custody of their eyes.

---

[162] https://americaneedsfatima.blogspot.com/2021/10/no-greater-danger-than-not-fearing.html
[163] Liguori, *12 Steps,* 93.
[164] Ibid, 97.
[165] Ibid.

To protect her virtue, Saint Clare resolved to never look at the face of a man. What have we resolved to do to protect our eyes? We must learn the difference between the glance and the gaze. A first, casual glance noticing the beauty of another is permissible. A second glance, or an intentional gaze, and the line has been crossed. Whom do we gaze upon? When tempted, we should gaze upon the cross to redirect our thoughts toward God. We must petition God to protect us and the purity of our vision. If we deliberately place ourselves in danger, the Lord may abandon us and permit us to fall into sin. Saint Bernard advises, "Downcast eyes direct the heart to heaven."

The commandments are clear prohibiting coveting. I'd like to focus for a quick moment on the ninth commandment, "Thou shall not covet another's wife." Desiring strongly, or concupiscence, is one of the effects of original sin. Saint Paul alludes to this when he writes about the flesh rebelling against the spirit. Thinking about coveting, I recall forensic psychiatrist, turned serial killer, Hannibal Lector in the movie, *The Silence of the Lambs*. Lector, when assisting FBI trainee Clarice with the motive of the criminal she seeks, pronounces, "First principles. Simplicity. He covets, that is his nature. And how do we begin to covet, Clarice? Do we seek out things to covet? No, we begin by coveting what we see every day."[166]

Granted, Lector is a warped, fictional soul, but he was correct when he said, "we covet what we see." The question for you, then, is what do you covet that you see every day? How often do you take a second, or even a third gaze while out and about? What about the second gaze with the click bait on your computer? How can you better protect your virtue of living chastely by guarding your eyes? What comes to mind?

If being vigilant with your eyes is essential, what about your speech? Can speech be impure? Of course. Let us be aware that unchaste conversation is also to be avoided. On impure speech Saint John Vianney doesn't mince the imagery when he tells us, "The man of impure speech is a "person whose lips are but an opening and a supply pipe which hell uses to vomit its impurities upon the earth." Yuck.

---

[166] "Silence of the Lambs... He Covets," YouTube posted October 30, 2015. https://www.youtube.com/watch?v=ZrBxOVX1Hoc

In a similar way, as we mind our speech, we must also be vigilant as to how we dress. Saint Jerome advises us, "Either we must speak as we dress, or dress as we speak. Why do we profess one thing and display another? The tongue talks of chastity, but the whole body reveals impurity." Good point. Modesty in dress matters because it stands as a sentinel over one's interior life. Don't fret about being "old fashioned" when it comes to dressing modestly. You know what is right and what it wrong. Pay attention to your conscience and to your guardian angel.

Thus, great vigilance is necessary on multiple fronts when it comes to chastity. Saint Charles Borromeo counsels us, "It is impossible for you to remain chaste unless you constantly watch over yourself. Negligence in this regard leads almost invariably to the loss of virtue." Purity of intention is key. "God bestows more consideration on the purity of the intention with which our actions are performed," Saint Augustine tells us, "than on the actions themselves."

Increased vigilance, avoiding negligence, and purity of intention. What else do we have in our Catholic arsenal to overcome temptation? Humility. We must continually humble ourselves before God. David fell into serious sin because he was not humble and trusted too much in himself. "Before I was humbled, I offended." (Psalm 118:67)

Are you familiar with Gregorio Allegri's *"Miserere, mei Deus"*? It's based on Psalm 51, King David apologizing to God after he sinned. Clearly inspired by God, it's truly a beautiful song. I, along with many others, consider it the audio pinnacle of songs in the Catholic Church library. I was hooked the first time I heard it. Composed during the1630s during the reign of Pope Urban VIII, it was meant to only be heard in the Sistine Chapel for Tenebrae services during Holy Week. Some of the better YouTube comments I've read about the song are: "one of the highest achievements for humanity." "There is something about this music; it is sad, happy, mysterious, longing, relaxing, all in one. Love it!" and "This music touches the soul. Every time I hear this beauty, I feel the peace of heaven." Superlatives aside, it does touch the soul.

Then, I learned the backstory. It made me appreciate the song that much more.

"This piece of music was proprietary to the Sistine Chapel Choir. The music was not published except to three people; the Holy Roman Emperor, the King of Portugal, and an Italian priest who was one of the leading approved composers of sacred music in his time. This piece was regarded by the Vatican as one of the most "holy", or rather most "useful", musical pieces they possessed in their library. So much so that centuries they guarded the piece and did not allow anyone to copy the manuscript.

(Another version goes 'Miserere, mei Deus' was declared to be too powerful by the pope and locked away. Writing it down or performing it elsewhere were punishable by excommunication.)

In 1770, when he was around 14 years old, Mozart attended a performance of the Choir in which this was the showpiece. When he returned to his room shortly thereafter, he transcribed the complete musical score from memory. Let that sink in for a moment—the libretto, the voices singing each part, and the music for each instrument. He attended an additional performance and made some minor changes from his original work."[167]

Shorter, 5 1/2 minute version:
https://www.youtube.com/watch?v=H3v9unphfi0
- Note the female singer hit the high note at 1:35-1:52, and again later in the song.
One commenter said that this note is called a "Top C." Wow!

Full, 15 minute version:
https://www.youtube.com/watch?v=36Y_ztEW1NE

Imagine David speaking to God, asking him to forgive him, in these lines from Psalm 51:

¹Have mercy on me, O God, according to your unfailing love; according to your great compassion blot out my transgressions.
²Wash away all my iniquity and cleanse me from my sin.
³For I know my transgressions, and my sin is always before me.

---

[167] Wikipedia, "Miserere (Allegri)," https://en.wikipedia.org/wiki/Miserere_(Allegri)

⁴Against you, you only, have I sinned and done what is evil in your sight; so you are right in your verdict and justified when you judge.
⁵Surely I was sinful at birth, sinful from the time my mother conceived me.
⁶You desired faithfulness even in the womb; you taught me wisdom in that secret place.
⁷Cleanse me with hyssop, and I will be clean; wash me, and I will be whiter than snow. 10 Create in me a pure heart, O God, and renew a steadfast spirit within me.
⁸My sacrifice, O God, is a broken spirit; a broken and contrite heart you, God, will not despise.

"Have mercy on me, O God." We know that we must approach God with a pure heart. The Holy Ghost looks for chaste hearts. Saint John Marie Vianney, the Curé of Ars, shares with us, "Like a beautiful white dove rising from the midst of the waters, and coming to shake her wings over the earth, the Holy Spirit issues from the infinite ocean of the Divine perfections, and hovers over pure souls, to pour into them the balm of love. The Holy Spirit reposes in a pure soul as in a bed of roses. There comes forth from a soul in which the Holy Spirit resides a sweet odor, like that of the vine when it is in flower."

With Saint Etheldreda, a pure soul, we have a tremendous example of one who did not complain. Instead, just the opposite. She heroically rejoiced in pains and humiliations. How Catholic. How saintly. Would your family and/or friends say you are a complainer? Guessing that the general response would be mixed. Some complain a lot. Some not at all. Kicking things up a notch, how many of you rejoice in pains and humiliations? Guessing probably very few of you. If that is you, God Bless! Most people in today's world have no conception of the value of willingly and gratefully accepting the pains and humiliations sent to us. Talk about a way to increase virtue and serve God!

To wind down our chapter on the seventh century, Saint Etheldreda, and chastity, let us consider the following enriching thoughts from Saint Peter Eymard, "The state of grace is nothing other than purity, and it gives heaven to those who clothe themselves in it. Holiness, therefore, is simply the state of grace purified, illuminated, beautified by the most perfect purity, exempt not only from mortal sin but also from the smallest faults; purity will make saints of you! Everything lies in this!"

Knowing that everything lies in this, we next turn to the eighth century, Saint Boniface and perseverance. Blessed are they who persevere.

Seventh Century Saints

Saints Gregory the Great (d. 604), Augustine of Canterbury (d. 604), Columbanus (d. 615), Donan (d. 617), Lawrence of Canterbury (d. 619), Isidore of Seville (d. 636), Cronan Mochua (d. 637), Oswald (d. 642), Ethelburga (d. 644), Fiacre (d. 670), Hunna (d. 679), Killian (d. 689), and Sexburga (d. 699), pray for us.

Saint Etheldreda is the patron saint of (N/A).
Saint Etheldreda's feast day is June 23.
Saint Etheldreda, *ora pro nobis* (pray for us).

Seventh Century History

630- Blessed Mother saves Constantinople from siege when she appeared in the sky thereby scaring the Avars and Persians.

632- Islam founded by Mohammed. Islam would expand rapidly throughout the Middle East and North Africa the remainder of the century.

638- Christian Jerusalem and Syria conquered by Muslims.

642- Egypt falls to the Muslims, soon thereafter the rest of North Africa.

680- Third Council of Constantinople ends Monothelitism.

Virtue Challenge #7- Chastity

Saint Etheldreda, help us to be chaste. Pray for our holy purity. Protect us when tempted with even the smallest faults so as to not offend our Beloved Lord. Pray for us to gladly accept, as you did, the pains, humiliations, and any great chastisements that God may send to us.

Help us to avoid the lies of sex without consequences, the hookup culture, co-habitation, adultery, adult and child pornography, human trafficking and sex slavery, homosexual civil unions, and rampant divorce and remarriage. Pray for all the survivors of sexual assault, and protect those women who are in danger.

Saint Etheldreda, help us to accept our state of life, whether it be single, married or religious, and comport our desires and purity accordingly. Vocations are our paths to holiness. While the world scorns chastity, we know that it is highly pleasing to Christ. We know that chastity is a great path to advancing in other virtues.

Saint Joseph, chaste guardian of the Virgin, pray for us.
Saint Joseph most chaste, pray for us.

Help us to guard our minds, eyes, speech and dress. We know that purity will help make saints of us. Help us to choose values that will benefit us forever, and to avoid the false, short-term, indulgences of impurity in this world. Help us to choose chastity!

Converse for a moment with the Holy Ghost about chastity. My Lord and my God, how may I serve you more faithfully and completely through the virtue of chastity?

O Great Saint Etheldreda, pray for us an increase in the virtue and grace of holy chastity.

CHAPTER 8

Boniface

The Eighth Century
Perseverance

"Persevere under discipline. God dealeth with you as his sons; for what son is there, whom the Father doth not correct?"

- Hebrews 12:7

"Blessed is the one who perseveres under trial because, having stood the test, that person will receive the crown of life that the Lord has promised to those who love him"

- James 1:12

"If you learn everything except Christ, you learn nothing. If you learn nothing except Christ, you learn everything.""

- Saint Bonaventure

"Weep for those who die in their wealth and who with all their wealth prepared no consolation for their own souls, who had the power to wash their sins and did not will do it."

- Saint John Chrysostom

The 700s

"Touchdown is confirmed. Perseverance is safely on the surface of Mars."

With those words all those in the NASA control room jumped from their seats, raised their hands high in victory, and cheered loudly for an extended period of time. Many in the world cheered along with the control room.

Flipping the script, what if after you died and were judged by God, the following announcement was made, "Judgement is confirmed. [Suzy Chapstick] is safely in heaven." And all in heaven cheer. Imagine.

The name of the space rover that landed on Mars on Feb. 18, 2021? "Perseverance." Once on Mars, NASA'S tweeted, "I'm safe on Mars. Perseverance will get you anywhere." (A fun play on words, 'perseverance will indeed get you anywhere'… maybe even to heaven.)

A six-wheeled, SUV-size vehicle, Perseverance is the most sophisticated robotic astrobiology lab ever launched, and an experimental aerial drone aboard, is at the heart of the Mars 2020 mission. It blasted off in July on a 293 million-mile journey. After landing, it immediately got to work, taking a photo of its "forever home." The rover is starting its mission, exploring an ancient crater lake bed for signs of past life or in pieces strewn across the Martian landscape. The landing site is Jezero crater, where scientists think a lake was 3.5 billion years ago. Although Perseverance superficially looks a lot like its predecessor, Curiosity, it's carrying a bevy of new scientific instruments. They include a better drill to take surface core samples, higher-resolution cameras, instruments to look at Martian mineralogy and detect organic compounds, ground-penetrating radar, a sort of Mars weather station and even microphones that will let earthlings hear what it sounds like on Mars for the first time.[168]

The $2.7 billion rover, built in NASA's Jet Propulsion Laboratory in Pasadena, Calif., is about 10 feet long, 9 feet wide, seven feet tall and weighs about 2,260 pounds, roughly 278 pounds heavier than its predecessor, Curiosity. *Perseverance*, designed to drive an average of 650 feet per Martian day, is nuclear powered, using a plutonium generator provided by the U.S. Department of Energy. "This landing is one of those pivotal moments for NASA, the United States, and space exploration globally – when we know we are on the cusp of discovery and sharpening our pencils, so to speak, to rewrite the textbooks," acting NASA Administrator Steve Jurczyk said in a press release. "The Mars 2020 Perseverance mission embodies our nation's spirit of persevering even in the most challenging of situations, inspiring, and advancing science and exploration."[169]

All this hoopla, effort, intelligence, skill, time, money, and, yes, perseverance, expended for a space rover. A nice to have, but not a need to have. Our only need to have in this life is the perseverance to

---

[168] Scott Neuman and Vanessa Romo, "'I'm Safe On Mars.' NASA'S New Rover To Scour Ancient Lake Bed For Life Signs," *NPR*, February 18, 2021.
[169] Manfredi, Lucas, "NASA's Perseverance Rover Lands on Mars," *Fox News*, February 18, 2021.

get to, maintain, and die in the state of grace, coupled with the mercy of Jesus. That's it.

Jesus, speaking to Saint Catherine of Sienna, said, "Know, dearest daughter, how, by humble, continual, and faithful prayer, the soul acquires, with time and perseverance, every virtue."[170] Thus the key to an increase in virtue is via prayerful perseverance. In the seventh century we were introduced to Saint Etheldreda and the virtue of chastity. In the eighth century we will discuss Saint Boniface and the virtue of perseverance.

In the 700s, much work was done laying the foundations of Christianity in Europe with missionary figures like Saint Winebald and Saint Adrian of Canterbury. Religious education and learning thrived in many parts of the continent. Islam continued its expansion into the Middle East and into Europe. In 711 the Moors (from Morocco and Algeria) conquered the Iberian Peninsula (Spain and Portugal). In 718, the *Reconquista*, or Reconquest, began. It was the Christian battle campaign to rid their land of the Moors. Eventually, Charlemagne would stop the Moors at the French border later in the century, but the struggle to liberate the Iberian Peninsula would take almost 800 more years, not officially ending until 1492.

Born in Anglo-Saxon England in 675, Winfrith, a leading missionary figure in his day, would eventually be known as Saint Boniface, the "Apostle of Germany." Winfrith was one of the truly outstanding figures to shape the Latin church in Europe. Coming from a respected and successful family, he went against the grain of his father's wishes and pursued the monastic life by training with the Benedictines. He taught at a local abbey school and at the age of thirty became a priest.

Winfreth's first mission was to Friesland (today Netherlands). It did not go well. Upon landing he learned that the ruler had declared war on Christians and he was unable to preach. Winfreth went back to England and regrouped. He then decided he needed to go to Rome to gain the approval of the pope. Eventually, he would get papal approval to be a missionary in Thuringia, Germany, but before he left, the pope gave Winfreth his new name, Boniface, as the previous day was the

---

170 "Dialogue of St. Catherine of Siena," 92.

feast day of the fourth century saint, Boniface of Tarsus. From that point forward, Winfreth was known as Boniface.[171]

Before heading to Germany, Boniface enlisted the missionary training assistance of Willibrord in Friesland. They spent about three years together, and when Willibrord retired, he wanted Boniface to succeed him. Boniface declined and instead went to Hesse, Germany to root out paganism. He was invited by Charles the Hammer (Charlemagne's grandfather). Before heading to Germany, however, Boniface appealed to the pope again for more authority to influence the local chieftains; Boniface received it along with a promotion to bishop.[172]

Boniface began his efforts anew and while finding the people were warming to Christianity, they did not want to give up their old religion as they feared how the old gods would respond. Boniface, confident in the one true God, called the tribes together in northern Hesse and before the giant Donar Oak of Geismar, a sacred tree dedicated to Thor (some say Jupiter), began to chop it down with an axe. Legend says a great wind, as if by miracle, blew the tree over.[173] Boniface, standing unharmed by their old gods, amazed the people, and proceeded to convert Hesse and the region. He used the wood from the tree to build a chapel dedicated to Saint Peter.

After Hesse, Boniface went to Thuringia, and enlisted the assistance of many nuns and monks from England to join him. Working through the difficult issues with the church in Thuringia, Boniface's appealed to the pope for assistance helped to forge a stronger bond between Rome and Germany. This was essential for building the church in Europe.

Boniface, now almost eighty years old, went to Friesland on another mission. His determination to care for the souls of Friesland was abundantly apparent. While there, enemies attacked his group. Many of his companions wanted to fight, but Boniface told them to trust in God saying, "Cease fighting. Lay down your arms, for we are told in Scripture not to render evil for evil but to overcome evil by good." Saint Boniface was martyred in Friesland in 755, along with

---

[171] "Saint Boniface of Mainz," *Catholic Online,*
https://www.catholic.org/saints/saint.php?saint_id=29
[172] Ibid.
[173] "Saint Boniface," Wikipedia, https://en.wikipedia.org/wiki/Saint_Boniface

fifty-two others. An eyewitness says Boniface held up a gospel for spiritual protection during the attack on his life. Boniface is often depicted in art holding a sword piercing a book.

After spending time in Utrecht (Netherlands), his remains were eventually moved to Fulda (Germany) where they are entombed in a shrine under the high altar of Fulda Cathedral.

Saint Boniface wrote, "Let us continue the fight on the day of Lord. If God so wills, let us die for the holy laws of our fathers. So that we may deserve to obtain an eternal inheritance with them." Eternal heritance. Determination. Perseverance. Boniface ventured to Friesland on three separate occasions. He had a mixed record there, but he never gave up. When we think of areas of our life where we have failed, have we taken the proper lessons from those occasions? Have we moved forward with renewed determination and a spirit of perseverance? What was God telling us through our failures? In what ways was God protecting or guiding your soul?

It may be helpful at this point to make the slight distinction between perseverance and steadfastness. Perseverance is the continued effort to do or achieve something despite difficulties, failure, or opposition. Steadfastness means standing strong when it's challenging, difficult and unnerving. Both perseverance and steadfastness require decisions. Both involve endurance, grit, tenacity, tirelessness, resolve, resolution, doggedness, determination, and drive.

If we this day were to dig down and take a metaphorical axe to an idol against which we personally struggle, what would it be? What do you believe God is asking you to fight for, or against, with renewed tenacity? Looking back, in what ways do you think God was helping you to be humble, yet leaving the door open for you to reengage and persevere on something of spiritual benefit to you and or your family? How can we learn from Boniface's example to trust in God and block out what the world wants us to believe?

When you think of 'why not me' and perseverance, what comes first to mind?

What about prayer? Be honest with yourself. Are you truly persistent in prayer?

Bishop Jacques-Benigne Bossuet in *Meditations for Lent*, writes,

"Knock. Persevere in knocking, even to the point of rudeness, if that were possible. There is a way of forcing God and wresting his graces from him, and that way is to ask continually with a firm faith. We must think, with the Gospel: 'Ask, and it will be given to you; seek, and you will find; knock, and it will be opened to you,' which he then repeats by saying, 'Everyone who asks receives, and he who seeks finds, and to him who knocks it will be opened' (Luke 11:9-10).

We must, therefore, pray during the day, pray at night, and pray every time we rise. Even though God seems either not to hear us or even to reject us, we must continually knock, expecting all things from God but nevertheless also acting ourselves. We must not only ask as though God must do everything himself; we must also make our own effort to act according to his will and with the help of his grace, as all things are done with his support. We must never forget that it is always God who provides; to think thus is the very foundation of humility."[174]

Achieving something despite difficulties and opposition can be exceedingly difficult. Most often things worth fighting for are simply that—things that are worth fighting for. It's difficult for a reason. Life is often fraught with challenges, struggles, setbacks and even failures. Knowing what is important, we continue on with new resolve and persevere towards our goal(s). Persevering is often easier when you are well rested and have a full stomach. What about persevering when you are exhausted? That's a different animal (or bird) altogether.

Bitter Winter, A Magazine on Religious Liberty and Human Rights in China, says: "sleep deprivation, commonly used to interrogate religious believers in China, is called 'exhausting an eagle.' The name derives from trainers of falcons and other birds who do not let their birds sleep, eventually, making them obey unconditionally."[175]

The article continues, "Sleep deprivation may sound harmless but is universally recognized as one of the cruelest forms of torture. It is widely used because it does not leave any marks on a victim's body but helps to break down his or her will. Usually, it takes no more than three days for the eagle to become exhausted and turn into an obedient bird.

---

[174] Bishop Jacques-Benigne Bossuet, *Meditations for Lent,* 35.
[175] *Bitter Winter,* April 30, 2020.

The same happens to people that undergo this torture method: they are forced to sit or stand, not allowed to sleep for days. Interrogators would keep a bright light on at all times and make loud sounds by shouting or banging something to prevent a person from falling asleep, beating him or her at the same time."[176]

Amidst the Wuhan CCP Virus shutdown, people felt like they were living through a semi-conscious state of sleep deprivation. The sheltering in place, closing and/or restricting the economy, bolting the doors to churches for a time and/or limiting attendance in churches and discouraging or banning practices like communion on the tongue in some dioceses, is like a bright light perpetually shining on us by someone seeking to find our point of exhaustion. Anyone else feel that government officials and media figures are shouting and banging on about the Chi-Comm 19 Virus is little more than a mass experiment (psy-op) probing for compliance and submission?

We are told the tyrannical actions of sheltering in place, social distancing, wearing largely ineffectual face masks, abiding by edicts about essential/non-essential businesses and professions, etc. are all done in the name of public health and safety. The Nazis allegedly had a phrase which covered all abuses by the state: *"für ihre sicherheit"* --- "It's for your safety."

Decades later, in 1976 to be precise, the Stasi, East Germany's Ministry for State Security, rolled out a nasty program called "Decomposition," from the "Disintegration Directive," that targeted political opponents of communism. Essentially it was used to sabotage/destroy the reputation of a target by negatively manipulating one's family, personal and employment relationships. According to Heywood Floyd, who wrote about this program on March 21, it was a "covert, much more psychological approach to maintaining the Communist monopoly on ideological discourse."[177] Floyd continued, the "parallels with the cancel culture of the modern west are obvious." Sound vaguely familiar to mainstream media in the U.S.? Sound like anything the Democratic Party would advocate for the U.S.? Floyd concluded his article with reason for hope, "To those assisting in leftist disintegrations, I say "Your regime won't last forever." Eventually, the

[176] Ibid.
[177] Floyd, Heywood. "Disintegration Directive," *Thread Reader* post March 21, 2021. https://threadreaderapp.com/thread/1373761707500257280.html

Stasi was dismantled and its records opened. The previously anonymous operatives who carried out the disintegrations became among the most hated people in a united Germany."[178] Karens (a 2020 term for a nosy busybody) of the world, take note.

Back to China and Sun Tzu, *The Art of War* states, "A skilled general must be master of deluding the enemy and concealing his true dispositions and ultimate intent." So, what is the ultimate intent? Fear? Compliance with the unreasonable? Reading the tea leaves, it seems the state wants to muzzle the citizenry who believe in good, old-fashioned American, and even Catholic values.

How soon, you may ask, before the Catholic Church itself is completely muzzled? We hope it would hold out for as long, and as valiantly, as possible. But no. The Catholic Church hierarchy appears to be committing unforced efforts without much prompting from others as they restrict access to what matters most, and jettison various parts of the Magisterium, as they see fit. For all intents and purposes, the highest levels of the Catholic Church hierarchy appear to be on board with the "Great Reset."

Sun Tzu adds, "In planning, never a useless move; in strategy, no step taken in vain." While our collective attention is focused on the "Great Pause" and the coming "Great Reset," where should our focus truly be? On God, Christ, the Catholic Church, and our own souls and those of our loved ones. What about liberty? Yes, to a great extent. We must stand watch and be ever vigilant for both personal and religious liberty. We must persevere.

One other possible outcome of the globalist never-let-a-crisis-go-to-waste crew is the impact on liberty. Most leftists desire ever increasing amount of government control over the citizenry and international bodies who exert greater control over nations. In other words, fully implementing a globalist agenda wherein the state is preeminent. This can be facilitated by general restrictions on fundamental liberties supplemented through mandated vaccines, imbedded chips in humans, global tracking devices, electronic and human snitches, cashless economies, etc. Eventually each nation will have some version of a system to reward and punish through a social credit system, such as the one currently used in China.

---

[178] Ibid.

It's clear that an exhausted eagle is ineffective. Leftist, globalist agenda, step aside. Let the land of the free and home of the brave, the United States of America, shake off its tyrannical torpor and once again be the Liberty Alpha. If at the same time the Catholic Church would once again assume its role as an effective Spiritual Alpha in the world, that would be great, too. We must pray and fast more.

Perseverance is not easy. Following Christ is not easy. As it says in Hebrews, we are to follow Jesus 'outside the walls' and not fear reproach. It is what must be done.

When Rod Dreher published his book *The Benedict Option,* Catholics debated the merits of said strategy. Is it advisable, or desirable, to self-segregate? Can it actually be implemented? Reverend Douglas Wilson, a pastor and theologian at Christ Church in Moscow, Idaho, said while a Benedict Option community has merit, what is called for is something much stronger, a "Boniface Option."[179] While the Benedict Option looks inward and is defensive, the Boniface Option looks outward and is offensive. In essence the Boniface Option is "more confrontational" in that those who want to destroy Christian civilization are engaged with and countered by getting greater numbers of Christians involved with local schools and government to advocate for a more Christian society. The Boniface Option is largely about perseverance.

While the Boniface Option may have merit, it sounds as though it is essentially the "Catholic Option" that Jesus gave us to make disciples of all nations—to get out there and compete against the world seeking success for Christ and His Catholic Church. My conclusion? The Boniface Option is the only option for faithful Catholics.

While contemplating perseverance, endurance, and eagles, I came across a different kind of book, *Can't Hurt Me,* written by ex-Navy SEAL and endurance athlete phenom, David Goggins. He had a brutal childhood, succeeded on an endurance level that few can comprehend. He's completed over sixty ultra-marathons and ultra-triathlons setting multiple course records. Goggins is also a former Guinness World

---

[179] Staff, "Small town in Idaho is a perfect example of the Benedict Option in action." *LifeSite News,* January 27, 2021.

record holder for completing 4,030 pull-ups in seventeen hours. *Outside* magazine named him the "Fittest Man in America."[180]

In *Can't Hurt Me,* Goggins writes about "Taking Souls," a technique he developed during Navy SEAL BUDs training to help him overcome mental and physical obstacles. Essentially, what he meant by the term was to outperform and overdeliver on expectations such that the person you are competing against, or your boss, has no choice but to respect your performance.

A second method is his "40 percent technique." Goggins describes how people only tap into about 40 percent of their mental capacity before their governor kicks in restricting what they are truly capable of. He lays out a path to push past pain, demolish fear, and reach one's full potential. Essentially the 40 percent technique is a form of mental perseverance that helps you go over, around, and through excuses. Whatever self-limiting belief pops into your head, get in front of it, and leave it behind. Goggins claims there is a whole new world on the other side of mastering your mind. It's all a mental game.

While Goggins points were secular, as Catholics, we too are very much in the business of "taking souls." Not that we take them in the way a demon might by causing someone to fall into sin, or that they lose their faith altogether. No. We desire to take souls to heaven. We help people get on—and stay on—the path to salvation. We take souls that are in sin and lead them to grace. We do not 'take souls' as much as we 'save souls.' That is every single Catholic's job every single day. Faithful Catholics are as essential to the spiritual war as the elite forces of our armed forces when it comes to protecting our nation. We persevere when the going gets tough.

Saint Paul says that when you run the race, only one wins the prize, so run to win. Saint Paul also spoke of the need to discipline the body. Goggins admits that he does not compete in his ultra-marathon competitions for the physical challenge alone. He says he does it so that when life gets tough, he knows he can lean into the issue and have the mental toughness to succeed even when others do not have the will to persevere.

---

[180] Goggins, David. *Can't Hurt Me*, Lioncrest Publishing, 2018.

Sounds like excellent advice for Catholics. If someone is in moral peril, we do not leave a soul behind. We are not permitted indifference and inaction. We are more accountable to God than we know. Sometimes we find that taking one step forward results in two steps backward. So be it. Recognize the situation for what it is. When this happens, we must not become discouraged, but get after it and persevere.

Given that we have been discussing perseverance, being steadfast and having endurance when others might give up, let's combine that with a faithful Catholic mindset to the issue of the legalized murder of the soon-to-be born, or as some call it, *abortion.*

With the modern-day massacre of the innocents, there have been at least sixty-two million lost lives in the United through surgical abortion since 1973. The key question then becomes: How must pro-lifers continue to be fearless, tenacious, and tireless in our efforts to protect life?

According to the World Health Organization, there are between forty and fifty million abortions worldwide each year.[181] Extrapolating that number for the past fifty years and the total souls lost to abortion is two billion on the low side, and 2.5 billion on the high side. Think about those numbers for a moment. Over two billion innocent children murdered. And those deaths only take into account surgical abortions. How many more from the multitude of other abortifacients?

Coming at this from a different angle: Consider three additional data points attempting to arrive at a more accurate totality of this issue. First, chemical abortions (the abortion pill, RU-486, injections, IUDs, and "birth control" pills) are estimated to kill up to ten times the number of children murdered by surgical abortion.[182] Second, Human Life International has reported that roughly four times as many preborn children are killed by the birth control pill than by surgical abortion.[183] Third, Dr. Bogomir Kuhar of Pharmacists for Life has estimated that between eight and thirteen million preborn children are killed annually in the United States alone, with a ratio of 90 percent chemical abortions and less than 10 percent surgical abortions.

---

[181] Worldometer. https://www.worldometers.info/abortions/
[182] Staff, "World's Number 1 Killer," *Church Militant,* January 22, 2021.
[183] Ibid.

With a more complete picture of the scale of this issue and how it evidences disregard for life, how do these numbers sit with you? How sad are we? How sad must God, the author of all life, be? How sad must the Sacred Heart of Jesus and the Immaculate Conception be?

How deviously glad must Moloch be? In Leviticus 20:2-3 we read, "If any Israelite ... sacrifices a child of his to the false god Moloch, his life must pay for it ... I will not let him live among my people any longer, once he has outraged my sanctuary, dragged my holy name in the dust, by sacrificing his child to Moloch."

Bishop, later Cardinal Bernardin introduced the scandalous, phony social justice narrative in the Church, termed the "seamless garment," where the slaughter of millions of preborn innocents would be counted as equal to losing your job. What faithful Catholic could ever think that it is morally justifiable and permissible to subsume abortion to the same policy discussion level as immigration, the environment or the death penalty? Abortion is an intrinsic evil; the other three are prudential judgment matters on which Catholics in good conscience may disagree. Seamless-garment Catholic thinking is based on complete falsehood.

One of the pro-life movement's heroic warriors opposing the modern-day version of child sacrifice from the outset was March for Life founder Nellie Gray. Her "life principles," modeled after the Declaration of Independence, asserted that "all human beings are created equal and are endowed by their Creator with certain unalienable rights, among which is the right to life." A key plank of her 'life principles' was: "NO EXCEPTION! NO COMPROMISE!" Nellie said in the Bible you find Christ sayings you are either for or against. There is no compromise. Compromise opened up abortion to all kinds of exceptions—incest, rape, life of the mother, etc.

Consider for a moment the evolution as to how advocates thought of abortion. First, proponents said it was a "necessary evil." While some considered it necessary, they also conceded it was evil. They then supported abortion, but that it should be "safe, legal and rare." Still flawed, but at least they hinted abortions should be performed as infrequently as possible. Then the floodgates were opened fully and advocates even embraced late-term abortion, up to and including just before, or, in some cases, just after birth. A policy of what was once a "necessary evil" is now a policy of "no apology for evil—ever."

If possible, it gets even worse. Many national Democrats (including in the U.S. Senate) embrace infanticide in that they block legislation mandating legal protection and equal care for babies who survive abortions. It is difficult to conceive that there would be opposition to a bill entitled Born Alive Abortion Survivors Protection Act, but, sadly, there is.

Fast forward to the eve of the March for Life 2021. U.S. Senator James Lankford (R-OK) spoke of the uncompromising value of each human life and that "everyone believes that life is precious." He admitted he recently said to his wife, "I can't figure out our culture sometimes." Lankford continued, "A society that is appalled that a baby dies from excessive heat after being left in a car is the same society that is perfectly fine with that same baby being aborted by that same mom just a few months prior. The same people who are furious about the baby left in the car are the same people who argue for "reproductive rights," "reproductive care" or "reproductive freedom." How is it that the only difference in a few months in time is relevant? How could one child be precious and the other not?"[184]

Lankford then went on to make one of the better pro-life arguments I have heard in a long time by laying out a great analogy between the value of gold and the value of children. He began by asking, "Are all babies valuable, or are only some valuable?" He continued, "gold is valuable, it doesn't matter its size… if we found a small amount of gold on the floor it wouldn't matter its shape, size, small or large, we don't discriminate, gold is valuable, everyone recognizes its worth… Gold is around $1800 an ounce now… But we can't seem to agree that all children are valuable… Literally gold is more precious to some people in this room than children are. Children aren't only valuable sometimes, or only certain children. Children are valuable. It can't be that if a Mom and Dad want a child they are valuable, and if they don't want a child they are not valuable, they are disposable. The Mom or Dad get to decide who is precious and who

---

[184] Lankford, James, "Senator Lankford Defends the Value of Life on Senate Floor" YouTube posted January 27, 2021. https://www.youtube.com/watch?v=5kdp2w6FrsY

is medical waste. (Pointing to a 3-D ultrasound of a baby in utero he asks) Is that a baby? Everything else flows from that."[185]

Well said, Senator. Cooperating with the author of all life, God, do we respect his sovereignty at all times regarding life? Who are we to "play God" and decide which defenseless life in the womb is worthy and which is not? We must persevere to protect all innocent life, even when family, friends, neighbors or the culture say otherwise. We must be uncomfortable, if necessary, advocating for life. We must ask: *Why not me?*

Catholics must persevere and continue to lead efforts to end abortion. What are we supposed to do when people who profess to be 'devout Catholics' are pro-abortion? Catholic politicians from the previous generation like Senator Edward Kennedy (D-MA) and Governor Mario Cuomo (D-NY) are two of the immoral and scandalous Catholics who were early leading policy advocates for abortion. Today, we have President Joe Biden (D), Speaker Nancy Pelosi (D-CA) and Mario's son, Governor Andrew Cuomo (D-NY), leading the current crop of scandalous Catholic abortion advocates on the national, and international, stage.

Early on in Pope Francis's tenure, he commented, "it is not necessary to talk about abortion all the time." What a horrible statement. Fortunately Cardinal Burke jumped in and added: "we can never talk enough about abortion." No wonder many Catholic politicians have spines of jello, instead of steel, on the subject of pro-life or pro-abortion. Malformation.

Author Ayn Rand has said, the hardest thing is to explain the obvious to people who refuse to see it. By their positions and actions, pro-Abortion Catholics are "dead in sin." To say this another way, their intellects have been dimmed. As it says in Ephesians 4:18, "They are darkened in their understanding, alienated from the life of God because of the ignorance that is in them, due to their hardness of heart." In Colossians 2:8 we read, "Beware lest any man cheat you by philosophy, and vain deceit; according to the tradition of men, according to the elements of the world, and not according to Christ." We are called to persevere in prayer for their conversions.

---

[185] Ibid.

Pro-life speaker and co-founder of the Canadian Center for Bioethics Reform Stephanie Gray Connors, comes at "dead in sin" from a different angle saying she believes that abortionists are "spiritually blind to the evil they are doing."[186] Engaging against the spiritually blind, Our Lady La Salette implores us, "fight, children of the light, you the few who can see." Connors says that her talks and debates with pro-abortionists are "a sign of the fruits of what you align yourself with if you're on the side of truth and God, or the side of evil and Satan."[187]

Speaking of dead in sin, let's talk about death squads for a moment. Rush Limbaugh on his radio program in 2012 made the following point, "So they say now in the Huffing and Puffington Post that Mitt Romney's Bain Capital—way, way back when it was originally founded—was seeded with money from Latin American death squads [...] Let me ask you a question: What's the difference in that and the Democrats being underwritten by Planned Parenthood and NARAL? If they're not death squads, I don't know what is."[188]

The liberal mainstream media offered a generally favorable review of Biden's faith upon entering office. *The New York Times* called President Biden "perhaps the most religiously observant commander in chief in half a century. A different, more liberal Christianity grounds his life and his policies." CNN professed Biden is "the first publicly churchgoing president in decades" and NBC plugged "Biden's faith on display." Most in the rest of the secular press even refer to Biden as being "devout" in his faith. But when Supreme Court nominee Amy Coney-Barrett was under consideration, she was a "radical" Catholic. Get it? Faithful Catholicism is radical, and modernist/social-justice Catholicism is "devout." As usual, the liberal media has it exactly backwards. As to be expected, the liberal media loves liberal Catholics.

Let's compare and contrast the early secular liberal reviews with those from Catholic commentators like Burch, Royal and Ruse as to what type of Catholicism Biden brings to 1600 Pennsylvania Avenue.

---

[186] Staff, "Abortionists are spiritually blind to the evil they are doing: top pro-life speaker" *LifeSite News*, February 3, 2021.
[187] Ibid.
[188] Limbaugh, Rush, "Obama's Dirty Campaigning Worked" *EIB Network*, August 8, 2012. https://www.rushlimbaugh.com/daily/2012/08/08/obama_s_dirty_campaigning_works/

On January 20, the day of Biden's inauguration, Brian Burch, President of Catholic Vote, commented that Biden's attempt at unity rings hollow as his policies infer, "All white people are racists. Defenders of life are enemies of women's health. Biology is a form of bigotry. Religion is hate. Anyone who voted for Trump is an insurrectionist."[189] Burch added that Biden is a "A Catholic president - - *who supports killing unborn children*. He's got big plans, including restarting the attack on the Little Sisters, gutting core religious freedoms for our Church, penalizing Catholic schools, and shaming those who oppose him as "domestic terrorists." There is no whitewashing this: It's a national scandal to our Church."[190]

Robert Royal, in *The Catholic Thing*, writes, "What's truly unprecedented, then, beyond being an unfaithful Catholic, is that Biden has already shown himself by word and deed to be an anti-Catholic "Catholic." Indeed, he's an equal opportunity religious bigot who, for all the talk of coming together, will ride roughshod over his co-religionists..."[191]

Austin Ruse, president of the Center for Family and Human Rights (C-FAM), commenting on Biden attending Mass at Washington's Cathedral of St. Matthew on the morning of his inauguration: "Joe Biden ate and drank his own spiritual death. That he received the Holy Eucharist from the hands of a Cardinal of the Church adds scandal upon scandal. One radio wag called it a Mass for Planned Parenthood. And so, it was." Ruse continued, "Joe Biden holds himself out as a faithful Catholic, yet he does not believe in the faith's fundamental teachings about the human person or human sexuality. What's more, he advances this unbelief in public policy and will now have the full force of the federal government behind this unbelief... Joe Biden is an enemy of the Catholic faith. This fact must be repeated as often as humanly possible," he added.[192]

Then on his first Sunday in office, Biden attended Mass at the ultra-liberal Jesuit-run Georgetown church, Holy Trinity Parish, where

---

[189] Burch, Brian. "Unity," *Catholic Vote* email, January 20, 2021.
[190] Ibid.
[191] Royal, Robert, "Our First Anti-Catholic Catholic President," *The Catholic Thing*, January 22, 2021.
[192] Ruse, Austin, "Joe Biden Eats and Drinks His Own Spiritual Death," *Crisis Magazine*, January 21, 2021.

a social justice Black Lives Matter banner is displayed near its entrance, but not a pro-life banner.[193]

Sadly, that's an all too accurate description of how Joe Biden entered the office of the presidency and conducted himself during his first week in office. And that's not to mention to numerous anti-Catholic Executive Orders he signed into law. Let us pray for Biden's conversion to be a faithful Catholic. With God all things are possible.

Turning to the *Babylon Bee* for some words of wisdom (i.e., satire). On Jan. 25, 2021 a Bee headline read, Biden: "If You're Not Okay With Women Aborting Their Babies, Then You Ain't Catholic!" A few excerpts from this outstanding satirical article:

> "President Joe Biden doubled-down on his Catholic faith and his pro-abortion policies Sunday. "Let me be clear," he said to reporters as he exited Trinity Catholic Church in Georgetown. 'If you're not okay with women aborting their babies, then you ain't Catholic, Jack!'"

> "Look, the main reason I'm a Catholic is that they're not hung up on things like historical doctrine-- at least that's what I've been told," Biden noted. "There's no single set of core theology that all Catholics are supposed to believe. It's all about freeing yourself from the shackles of organized religion and choosing your own path."

> "Biden then reiterated that pro-life views have no place in the modern Catholic church. 'If you want to honor unwed mothers and little babies, the Catholic church is not the place for you,' he said. 'And I'm sure if the Virgin Marley were still alive, she would tell you the exact same thing.'

> "A Vatican spokesperson refused to comment on Biden's views, stating a long-standing church tradition of not publicly commenting on the theology of Catholic Democrat politicians. "We call it the Kennedy doctrine," the spokesperson said. "It's a policy that has served us quite well for many years."[194]

---

[193] Mainwaring, Doug, "Biden Attends Mass at Ultra-Liberal Jesuit-run Church," *LifeSite News,* January 25, 2021.
[194] *Babylonbee.com*, "Biden: 'If You're Not In Favor of Women Aborting Their Babies Then You Ain't Catholic," January 25, 2021.

Sadly, and this is not said as satire, Biden in his first week in office showed his administration to be the most pro-abortion administration in U.S. history. His conscience is influenced greatly by the demonic and their abortion-related lies. The abortion industry is built on lies. Lies that beget lies which beget lies. Biden, in addition to reversing the Mexico City policy by Executive Order permitting federal funds to be used for abortion outside the United States, stated he also wants a federal law permitting abortion in all fifty states should Roe v. Wade be overturned.

Kansas City Archbishop Joseph F. Naumann remarked the "bishops of the United States have an "obligation" to act when it comes to the country's president identifying himself as a devout Catholic while working to expand abortion. The fact that President Biden identifies himself as a devout Catholic, while working to preserve and expand legalized abortion, even using tax dollars to fund abortion, presents a unique challenge to the bishops of the United States."[195]

Why, Archbishop, is this a unique challenge? As Nellie Gray told us all almost fifty years ago, "No Exceptions! No Compromise!" It remains to be seen how the U.S. bishops will confront Biden on his pro-abortion policies while claiming to be a 'devout Catholic.' Will he be denied communion anywhere in the United States for his pubic support of abortion at any point during his presidency? Biden's advance team should be able to stay in front of any possible declinations and embarrassing situations, but you never know. Only takes one priest, or one bishop...

A "unique challenge" calls for a "unique response." With the stakes as high as they are, a bold response is required. While the U.S. Conference of Catholic Bishops (USCCB) as a collective is not a profile in courage, it would only take a few bold bishops to make a big difference and address this very visible Catholic scandal head-on.

Alternatively, if this challenge, Archbishop Naumann, is as unique as you characterize it, why not, as head of the USCCB's Committee on Pro-Life Activities, call for a public vote of censure, rebuke, or even excommunication, until Biden publicly repents of his

[195] Baklinski, Pete, "Exclusive: Bishop Naumann – US bishops must address scandal of 'Catholic' Biden championing abortion," *LifeSite News,* February 3, 2021.

pro-abortion and anti-God positions? Bringing the matter to a head is, perhaps, the most charitable thing that could be done for 'dead-in-sin' Biden's immortal soul. It would also let the flock see which of the bishops are faithful to the Catholic church's teachings on this matter, and which are not.

In a February 13, 2021 interview with *Catholic World Report*, Archbishop Naumann said, "The president should stop defining himself as a devout Catholic, and acknowledge that his view on abortion is contrary to Catholic moral teaching." He went on to note, "we bishops have the responsibility to correct him" for using the term. Naumann added that Biden "is usurping the role of the bishops and confusing people" by calling himself a "devout Catholic" while opposing the Church's teaching on life issues.[196]

So there you have it. From the minor dustup about Biden's scandalous public positions, we have, thus far, a mild slap on the wrist. How far is Abp. Naumann willing to go in this "game of chicken" (i.e., standoff) with President Biden? Who will 'blink' first? Apparently, Naumann is getting under the skin of some on the left a bit. Faith in Public Life and Faithful America, two progressive groups funded by atheist mega-donor George Soros, have started petitions to have Abp. Naumann fired from his position leading the USCCB Pro-Life Committee.[197]

Abp. Naumann has the opportunity to lead his fellow bishops to standing strong against the highest public figure in the land on a couple key issues. Will he, and they, see it through? The faithful Catholics of America view this for what it is.

Where are the genuine efforts to address the violations to Canon 915? Crickets in the night air. In charity Saint Paul warned the Corinthians that their souls were in peril of damnation for sacrilegious communion. Saints Thomas Becket, Thomas More and John Fisher, pray for us and our current crop of enervated and wispy U.S. bishops.

Two other quick examples of nonsense coming from Catholics on abortion:

---

[196] Staff, "Abp. Nauman: Pres. Biden "should stop defining himself as a devout Catholic," *Catholic World Report,* February 13, 2021.
[197] Wolfe, Raymond, "Soros-backed liberals try to get US bishops' pro-life chair fired for criticizing pro-abortion Biden," *Life Site News,* March 23, 2021.

- Social justice warrior, radical, Modernist, Sister Simone Campbell, of 'Nuns on the Bus' infamy, said Biden has a "developed view of abortion." Sister Campbell then went on to claim that the "political obsession" with the "criminalization of abortion" has broken the Church apart.[198] Abortion is breaking the church apart? A developed view of abortion? How devious and manipulative. Sister, shameful.

- Commenting on the Catholics for Choice group, Jonathan Van Maran created a blog post entitled, "Catholics for Choice makes about as much sense as Vegans for Cannibalism."[199]

Despite all the scandalous Catholic politicians and all the nonsense coming from other Catholics on the pro-life v. pro-abortion issue, why is the life issue important to me? Abortion touches families in many ways. Here's our story.

When my wife was pregnant with our second child, we were at the doctor for a routine ultrasound visit. Lots of chatting about things when all of a sudden the ultrasound technician went quiet. Uh oh. She remained silent for what felt like twenty minutes (it was only a couple minutes) and said she'd be right back and left the room. She came back a few minutes later with a doctor who saw what she saw. The doctor explained that a large pulmonary cyst was pushing on our son's heart. My wife, Mary, began to cry.

The doctor said we had two options. Option one, we leave things alone and hope that as our son grew the cyst would stay the same size, the rest of his body would get bigger, and more space would be created for his heart, and he would be OK. After birth, we could wait a few months and choose to have the cyst removed, or leave it alone and decide what to do years down the road.

The second option was, "the cyst may continue to grow causing the heart to stop. Many people in your similar situation would choose to terminate the pregnancy." More tears from Mary.

Within a nanosecond, Mary answered, *option one.*

---

[198] Scanlon, Kate, "Sister Simone Campbell: Joe Biden Has 'Developed' Approach to Abortion," *National Catholic Register,* January 25, 2021.
[199] Van Maran, Jonathan, "'Catholics for Choice' makes as much sense as 'Vegans for Cannibalism,'" *LifeSite News,* February 1, 2021.

We went home that day greatly concerned about the health of our son. Naturally, we had a thousand questions. What was God's plan? Why would He permit a cyst to grow in a lobe of our son's lungs? Would our son make it? Would he be a healthy child? Would he have ongoing issues? How was it that the doctor was able to mention option two so casually? So cavalierly?

We stormed heaven with prayer. We asked family and friends for prayer. And then we waited. And prayed. And waited some more. It felt like forever until the next ultrasound appointment where we would observe what the cyst was doing. Would it stay the same size or get larger? How was our son's heart? We were nervous, prayerful and hopeful for weeks.

With trepidation we arrived for the follow-up ultrasound. The same technician went right to the trouble area she identified weeks earlier. She gave us the good news, "The cyst stayed the same size and actually moved over a bit giving the heart much more room." Whew. Thank you, God! The doctor came in a short while later and confirmed the tech's initial observation. He said, "There will be continued risk, but given where the cyst was originally, compared to what I'm seeing today, I think he's going to be fine." Again, thank you God!

Our son was born a couple of months later and we named him Nathaniel Michael Vaughan Grane. Nathaniel for "Gift of God" and Michael "Who is Like God," after Saint Michael the Archangel. Other than the cyst, Nathan was born perfectly healthy. We decided when Nathan was three months old to surgically remove the lobe that contained the cyst. Mary and I didn't want any cyst cells to remain in his body and metastasize into a problem at some future point. The doctors said that as the lung lobe was removed so young the remaining four lung lobes would increase in size and he would eventually have normal, 100 percent lung capacity.

Nathan had an otherwise normal, active childhood. He played multiple sports: basketball, baseball, football. Hockey, however, was Nathan's favorite sport. He played defense on many house and travel teams from age five up until his sophomore year in high school. Today, Nathan is a 6'2" 215 lb. serious bodybuilder in college studying to be a commercial airline pilot. Nathan has told me he'd love to compete in high level bodybuilding competitions, but he would not as his left latissimus (lat) dorsi muscle is not perfectly symmetrical due to his surgery as an infant. That having been verbalized, we shared a smile. Nathan accepts his "defect" as a reminder. I said, "If that's the only slight defect keeping you back (pun intended), praise God." While Nathan's lat may not be perfectly symmetrical, him being our "Gift of God" is perfectly symmetrical in every way. God is good.

Saint Michael the Archangel continue to watch over your namesake, Nathaniel Michael Vaughan, all his days. Help him to be a strong Catholic, with great virtue, and to defend God's honor and good name all his days. *Serviam!*

And to that doctor who advised us of "Option Two" … well, God Bless. What can we say? Your advice that "many people in our situation would terminate" was a nonstarter. Aborting Nathaniel would have been the greatest mistake and regret of our lives. We get it. You were just doing your job and giving options. But we're Catholic. We're pro-life. We continue to pray for your conversion to being a 100 percent pro-life doctor.

God permitted the cyst in Nathan most likely for several providential reasons. One of the more apparent is that our family stepped up our support of the pro-life movement and the fight for life in our culture. We began by supporting buses and trips for students to attend the March for Life in D.C. We then donated at the federal level to the National Right to Life organization for several years. Getting more involved each year, we started to attend and host fundraisers for other pro-life organizations such as Live Action. In 2013-14 I had the privilege of working with Lila Rose at Live Action in the Washington, D.C. area as Senior Vice President, Strategic Partnerships focusing on Donor, Policy and Industry Relationships. Eventually, we moved back to Chicago and I transitioned my pro-life activities to serving on the Board at Heartbeat International, the world's largest Pregnancy Help Center Network with 3,000 worldwide affiliates.

In the fall of 2019, I had the privilege of being Co-Executive Producer of the pro-life film, *Divided Hearts of America*. The film is a journey of NFL Super Bowl winner Benjamin Watson's search for the truth about abortion in America. The film was made to address a primary cause of division in our nation—abortion. *Divided Hearts of America's* message is that Americans urgently need to see each other for who we are as brothers and sisters and part of one family made in the image and likeness of God...not members of opposite political party, or as residents of a red or blue state.

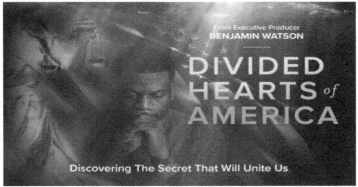

Grateful to Have Been a Co-Executive Producer to Divided Hearts of America

For two days we hosted Ben, Jason Jones (Movie to Movement), and the Production team in our home to film several interviews featured in the film: Rep. Sheila Jackson (D-LA), Obianuju ("Uju" for short) Ekeocha, Yvonne Florczak-Seeman, Dr. Steven Andrew Jacobs, and Lacy and Mary-Logan Miske.

If you watch the film closely, you will see a statue of Our Lady of Fatima (on our kitchen counter), a famed picture of Divine Mercy Jesus, and our King Pelican poster (see Chapter 18 for explanation). It was a blessing to have been a part of the film. Hope you've seen it, or will have the chance to do so soon!

What has God put on your heart regarding defending life? Whose soul(s) will you save today, tomorrow, and in your lifetime? What prayers will you offer for the mom or dad who is considering abortion today or this weekend? Whatever your abortion story is, be it direct or indirect, own it. Move forward the best way you know how. The courage and bravery of those in the pro-life movement who stand up for the millions, and billions, of innocent lives is amazing.

Persevere pro-life warriors. Against the odds, persevere. If you have fear, continue to press forward. To the pro-life generation, keep at it. We're with you. May your convictions be strengthened. May our nation usher in a time of true justice for all. Choose justice. Choose life. Persevere for life. May God bless all those laboring in the pro-life mission. Continue to do great things for God and life. Use your voice for those who have no voice. What has God providentially put before you regarding the pro-life cause? How will you step up to defend life? How will you advocate for life, on behalf of the author of all life, as his hands and feet?

To take a moment to address those moms and dads who are post-abortive, God be with you. I am sorry for what you have been through. I hope you have done all you can to reconcile with God (making a sincere confession and penance, and continuing to offer acts of reparation). I imagine the devil has lied to you, condemned you, and told you the sin of abortion is unforgivable. It is not. Saint Padre Pio of Pietrelcina assists us: "Any mental picture of your life that focuses on past sins is a lie and thus comes from the devil. Jesus loves you and has forgiven you your sins, so there is no room, for having a downcast spirit. Whatever persuades you otherwise is truly a waste of time. It is also something that offends the heart of your tender Lover. On the other hand, if the mental picture of your life consists in what you could be, then it comes from God."[200]

All sins are forgivable by Jesus. As it says in Matthew 15:7, "I say to you, that even so there shall be joy in heaven upon one sinner that doth penance, more than upon ninety-nine just who need not penance." Do not allow yourself to become a prisoner to a moment. If you would like to talk things through with someone, talk with a well-formed, traditional Catholic priest. I have also heard nothing but amazing things about Project Rachel as a ministry for post-abortive women. Please know that post-abortive people have a tremendously strong voice in helping to end abortion. Your voice matters. Use it! Team Life needs you!

This chapter featured the Anglo-Saxon, Winfrith, known as Boniface. With a hat tip to his English roots, we fast forward to 1939, the anticipation of World War II, and the anticipated air strikes on English cities. To shore up the citizenry, the British government produced the motivational poster "Keep Calm and Carry On." The slogan evoked English stoicism to "keep a still upper lip." Citizens were encouraged to have self-discipline, fortitude and to remain calm in adversity. No doubt Saint Boniface would approve.

---

[200] Padre Pio letters, to Maria Gargani, August 26, 1916.

In our culture and in the dark winter that may or may not come, we would do well to remember courage, resolve, and perseverance through it all. Previous cultures and nations have faced down the worst in humanity. As Catholics, through our faith in Christ and through the intercession of his Blessed Mother, we shall remain joyful and steadfast in our optimism.

With respect to perseverance, I'd like to offer a further word of optimism—"yet." I credit author and blogger Seth Godin with introducing me to the concept of *yet*. Appending that simple, yet powerful word to the end of certain sentences motivates us to 'keep calm and carry on.' Think of the following: We haven't ended Abortion in America, *yet*. We haven't properly addressed the scandal of high-ranking Catholic politicians receiving communion, yet. We haven't pushed back enough on the cancel culture and critical race theory, *yet*. I haven't become a saint, *yet*.

Be on guard against your "yet" turning into a "can't." Godin writes, "*Yet* isn't the result of brazen persistence. It's what we earn with learning, insight and generosity."[201] Further assisted by God's grace, may your 'yet' cheerily carry on and persevere.

God has with many of his saints permitted them to go through His version of "yet," long stretches, years even, of spiritual dryness. In His wisdom, God sends grace to us in ways that he knows will permit us to advance in holiness through only a perhaps difficult and significant transition. Through whatever was sent their way, the saints knew to stay close to God and persevere.

Sixteenth-century Spanish poet and mystic, Saint John of the Cross, in *The Dark Night of the Soul*, writes in his introspective masterpiece poem of how God permits necessary purgation on the path to Divine Union. While the *Noche Oscura* (Dark Night) does not refer to difficulties in life in general, it has been used to refer to such trials. Some are providentially permitted to undergo an almost spiritual depression in that they feel abandoned by God. While most all of us may not have the constitution to go through the *Noche Oscura* as the saints before us did, we may still be permitted nonetheless to be perplexed, sad, afflicted, confused and challenged with our own spiritual path. God is permitting us these as an opportunity to grow

---

[201] Godin, Seth, "A Simple Missing Word," Blog. February 4, 2021.

closer to Him. Through perseverance we must not give way to thoughts of despondency and feel forsaken. God does not abandon anyone who does not first abandon him. Persevere on good and bad days. As difficult as it may be, the faithful Christian will embrace what God has purposed for our holy advancement in a spirit of gratitude and joy.

As Catholics, we believe and trust that any obstacle to greater holiness placed before us or others was permitted through God's providence. He is the ultimate drill sergeant in terms of overseeing the ultimate obstacle course. He is rooting for us to persevere like the perfect father he is. He wants us to get spiritually tougher. He wants us to merit heaven, to earn heaven. God will never put us on a customized obstacle course he did not first approve and send along with it the corresponding grace permitting us the opportunity of meeting that particular challenge. We can have 100 percent certainty in this regard. Yes, some pretty bad and awful stuff may be put in our path, but know that God permitted it for the edification of our soul. Let go and let God decide the obstacles there will be. He loves us and so we must focus on being faithful to Him and His church. If you overcome the challenge, praise God. If you fail the challenge, praise God, double down, and try again.

Heaven is for the meritorious. For the would-be and wanna-be citizens of heaven, there are many who believe that because Jesus died for their sins, they are guaranteed heaven. Others think that because they desire heaven that they somehow deserve it. Many approach heaven with an entitlement mindset. When it comes to heaven, it would be helpful for Catholics to adopt the mindset of the ultra-marathoner—the ability to cultivate the mindset of pushing through any and all obstacles singularly focused on finishing the race well. As the saints all finished well, so must we.

In life, is any marathon more ultra than meriting heaven? Regarding the entitled mindset, Goggins would say, "that dead weight thinking needs to be cut loose. Don't focus on what you think you deserve. Take aim on what you are willing to earn!"[202] Don't blame anyone for your failures, your shortcomings, or your sins. When you fall, don't hang your head in shame; get to confession and begin anew

---

[202] Goggins, 323.

asap. Don't let the devil worm his way into your thinking with thoughts of complacency, inadequacy, or despondency. Have hope in Christ and trust in His grace and mercy. As my dad said when I was growing up, "You gotta want it." Do not be derailed on your mission, your goal. Stay humble and sidestep your entitled mind because nothing is guaranteed, up to and including your final hour. Pray for the gift, the grace, of final perseverance. Earn heaven.

To close the century, the pagans of continental Europe had to contend with another formidable figure, Charles, whom the French dubbed *Charles le Magne* (Charles the Great), whose name in English is Charlemagne. Within Charlemagne's Europe, the barbarians perpetually threatened Catholics with impending bondage. All told he would wage approximately fifty military expeditions to defeat his heathen adversaries. By the 790s, Charlemagne was well on his way to becoming the protector of the papacy, including additional victories against the Lombards in northern Italy, greatly assisting the papacy of Leo III.

Eighth Century Saints

Saints Adrian of Canterbury (d. 710), Richard the King (d. 720), Fergus of Scotland (d. 730), Withburga (d. 743), John Damascene (d. 749), Winebald (d. 761), Walburga (d. 779), and Willibald (d. 786), pray for us.

Saint Boniface is the patron saint of Germany and brewers.
Saint Boniface is often portrayed in bishop's robes either holding an axe/sword piercing a book.
Saint Boniface's feast day is June 5.
Saint Boniface, *ora pro nobis* (pray for us).

Eighth Century History

708- Three apparitions of Saint Michael the Archangel at Mont Tombe (later called Mont Saint-Michel) Normandy, France to Saint Aubert, Bishop of Avranches, to ask him to build a church.

711- Moors invade Iberian Peninsula (Spain and Portugal).

718- ***Reconquista***, or reconquest, begins as the Christians engage the Moors in battle.

721- The Moors are temporarily turned away from France at the Battle of Toulouse.

726- Iconoclasm begins in the Eastern Church. Destruction of images continues until 843.

731- The Venerable Bede (a Benedictine Monk) completes his *Ecclesiastical History of the English People.*

732- **Battle of Tours**. Perhaps the most consequential battle in history. Charles the Hammer, founder of the Carolingian dynasty of Frankish kings and grandfather of Charlemagne, defends the Muslims from advancing past Tours. Were they to have done so, they would have had an easy path to advancing to Poland in the northeast and Scotland in the northwest.

756- King Pepin the Short of the Franks grants independent rule of Rome. The **Papal States** are then created.

787- Second Ecumenical Council of Nicaea resolves Iconoclasm.

793- The sacking of the Lindisfarne monastery begins the Viking raids on Christian Europe.

Virtue Challenge #8- Perseverance

Boniface faced challenges and defeat. He had his Friesland. It was a place he had a hard time converting. He regrouped, came up with a new plan, and tried again, and again. He was determined. He was steadfast. He persevered. Saint Boniface, pray for us to approach all our challenges with a holy Catholic perspective and tenacity focused on eternity.

Boniface, help us to learn from our failures. Help us to prepare better and serve God more faithfully.

Boniface, confident in the one true God, help us to take a metaphorical axe to the heathen adversaries who worship the false religion of child sacrifice and the lie that is the abortion industry. Help us to chop down and restrict Big Abortion's impact and access to funding. Help us to convert those who are pro-abortion. Henceforth, how will you persevere and more closely identify with the most vulnerable?

Our Lady of Guadalupe, patroness of unborn children, pray for us.

When God is not answering our prayers in a way that we would like, or a way that we would expect, let us trust His providence that He knows what is best for our souls and soldier on with holy perseverance.

Help us to have the mission mindset of an ultra-marathoner. Pray for us and the grace of final perseverance. Pray for perseverance to get you to heaven.

Converse for a moment with the Holy Ghost about perseverance. My Lord and my God, how may I serve you more faithfully and completely through the virtue of perseverance?

O Great Saint Boniface, pray for us an increase in the virtue and grace of holy perseverance.

CHAPTER 9

Leo

The Ninth Century
Justice

"Charity is no substitute for justice withheld."
- Saint Augustine

*"We shall awaken from our dullness, and rise
vigorously toward justice."*
- Saint Hildegard of Bingen

*"Don't allow the sad sight of human injustice to sadden your soul;
someday you will see the unfailing justice of God triumph over it."*
- Saint Padre Pio

The 800s

Time: Christmas Day, 800
Location: Old St. Peter's, Rome
Scene: Pope Leo III crowns Charlemagne "Holy Roman Emperor"
and thus the world witnesses the genesis of the Holy Roman Empire,
the noblest temporal institution of Christendom.

Before we discuss the coronation, and a most dramatic way to
start a century, I would like to briefly highlight the irreplaceable large,
maroon/purple, marble circle upon which Charlemagne knelt to be
crowned. It is still visible today near the entrance at St. Peter's in Rome
(see picture below). According to Dr. Christopher Longhurst, the
"Operatore Didattico," the teaching operator for the Vatican museums,
the rose porphyry stone is "reserved only for the imperial family. Rose
porphyry is extinct today, it can't be quarried. It's some really tough
marble, unlike the softer marble worn around it through centuries of

visitors." Longhurst continued, "it would take about an hour, using a laser, to cut an *inch* into porphyry."[203]

The term *porphyry* is from Ancient Greek (πορφύρα porphyra) and means "purple." Purple was the color of royalty, and the "imperial porphyry" was a deep purple igneous rock.[204]

Rose porphyry circle where Charlemagne was crowned in 800.
St. Peter's Basilica, Rome, Italy

Porphyry is also the name of a Catholic saint, Porphyry (Porphyrius) of Gaza (347-420). Porphyry was born in Thessalonica, present-day Greece. He went to Egypt as a desert hermit at age twenty-five, was ordained a priest in Jerusalem at the age of forty; then over his protest he was made Bishop of Gaza. As bishop he built a Christian church on the most important pagan temple, converted many through miracles, and successfully spread the faith throughout his diocese.

Many would find it difficult to comprehend what it was like to go to that dark maroon circle in St. Peter's, kneel, touch the marble, close their eyes for just a moment, and try to comprehend this momentous coronation. The crowning of Charlemagne Holy Roman Emperor by Pope Leo in old St. Peter's Basilica over 1200 years ago profoundly changed the ecclesiastical and secular history of Europe.

---

[203] Warga, Jake, "You better watch where you walk the next time you visit the Vatican," The World, September 1, 2014.

[204] "Porphyry," Wikipedia, https://en.wikipedia.org/wiki/Porphyry_%28geology%29

Charlemagne may have been a great military strategist and tactician, but was he a good Catholic? The record is mixed. No one truly knows the state of his soul during his life or at the hour of his death. Detractors might point to the number of battles he waged, or his eighteen children with eight of his ten known wives or concubines. Proponents might point to the fact that although he did not know how to read or write, he possessed great wisdom, intellect, and faith. Reports have him "being present at bishops' councils and after listening to them discuss Church affairs, would take to the floor and delve into theological debates, usually successfully. He was the one who had the right theological formula even though he never went to a seminary."[205]

Despite any personal moral shortcomings, Charlemagne, a son of the Church, was "her rampart, support, and glory. He did not infringe upon her rights but respected her sovereignty and recognized all her power. Accordingly, the Church crowned him."[206] By this act, Leo instituted the legal precedent that only the pope could confer the imperial crown. More importantly for Leo, his coronation of Charlemagne secured his papacy. So, who was Charlemagne?

Charlemagne, the cornerstone of the Middle Ages, would go on to be called *Pater Europae*, the "Father of Europe," unifying most of Western Europe for the first time since the classical era several centuries earlier. Pope Leo III would continue to deftly navigate the politically turbulent times overseeing the expansion of Christianity. So, who was Leo?

Leo was born of humble and moderate means in southern Italy. His parents were Aliguppius and Elizabeth. Not much more is known about his youth. His non-noble background is important as he would never be fully accepted by Rome's aristocrats and papal detractors, even after he became pope. After becoming a priest, Leo fastidiously worked his way up through the ranks of the Church. Eventually Pope Adrian I made Leo the cardinal-priest of Santa Susanna, and then chief of the pontifical treasury.

---

[205] Oliveira, Plinio Corrêa de, "Charlemagne- Cornerstone of the Middle Ages," *Nobility.org*, December 22, 2014.
[206] Ibid.

Leo III was unanimously elected Supreme Pontiff on Dec. 26, 795. His roughly twenty years as pope transpired during a precarious time of tensions between the papacy and Constantinople over rights and responsibilities. Unlike his predecessor, Adrian I, Leo recognized Charlemagne as the protector of the See of Rome. In so doing, he angered the Roman nobility.

In a dramatic series of events that unfolded on April 25, 799, Pope Leo III, leading a procession honoring Saint Mark in Rome through a practice called the Greater Litanies, was suddenly attacked by a mob of Adrian's supporters. The aggressors attempted to cut out Leo's eyes and remove his tongue, so that he could no longer serve in his office. Leo survived the assault, and eventually, some say miraculously, had his eyesight restored while not losing his tongue. He then fled to Charlemagne for protection. Charlemagne escorted Leo back to Rome, and his enemies were put on trial.

To say the least, Leo did not have an easy papacy. If someone attempted to gouge out your eyes and cut out your tongue, would justice not be at the forefront of your mind? How did this event impact Leo's understanding and application of justice?

As Roman pontiff, Pope Saint Leo III was an effective administrator and made many improvements to Roman churches. Leo was adept at diplomatically pursuing a more unified Europe, including steps for the Church to encourage secular Western European nations to maintain their Christian identity.

The Eastern European nations were a different story. Perhaps more significantly, Leo's crowning of Charlemagne greatly angered the Byzantine Church. It contributed to the ongoing disagreements between the Eastern and Western branches of the Catholic Church that would result in a formal schism 250 years later in 1054, a rift that, despite attempts at reconciliation, has continued to this day.

As pontiff, Leo diligently worked for justice and peace as he helped to restore the deposed King Eardwulf of Northumbria. He settled the long-running jurisdictional dispute between the archbishops of Canterbury and York. He reversed the decision of Adrian I to grant the pallium to Bishop Hygebehrt of Lichfield.[207] Pope Leo believed

---

[207] "Pope Leo III," Wikipedia. https://en.wikipedia.org/wiki/Pope_Leo_III

that the injustice occurred as the English episcopate had been misrepresented before Hadrian and that therefore his act was invalid.[208]

Around 809, Leo ordered two heavy silver shields created, containing the original text of the "Nicene–Constantinopolitan Creed" in both Greek and Latin, to be made and placed in St. Peter's Basilica, adding *"Haec Leo posui amore et cautela orthodoxae fidei"* (I, Leo, put these here for love and protection of orthodox faith.)[209]

The dynamic duo of Charlemagne and Leo went to their eternal reward within a couple years of each other. After receiving Holy Communion for the last time, Charlemagne died on leap day, February 29, 814. He was buried "girt with his sword, with a book of the gospels in his hands."[210] Leo died two years later on June 12, 816. Leo, originally buried in his own monument, was later moved into a larger tomb that contained the first four popes named Leo. In the eighteenth century, Pope Leo I (The Great) was removed and entombed in his own chapel. Thus, Pope Saint Leo III rests with his namesakes Leo II and Leo IV in Saint Peter's Basilica in Rome.

The two figures would have a profound effect on European history for centuries to come. Charlemagne as the "Father of Europe" and Pope Saint Leo III for promoting a unified, well-ordered, peaceful Christian world under the supreme authority of the Bishop of Rome, Christ's deputy on earth.

The *Catechism of the Church* defines justice as, "the moral virtue that consists in the constant and firm will to give their due to God and neighbor. Justice toward God is called the 'virtue of religion.' Justice towards men disposes one to respect the rights of each and to establish in human relationships the harmony that promotes equity with regards to persons and common good. The just man, often mentioned in Sacred Scriptures, is distinguished by habitual right thinking and the uprightness of his conduct towards his neighbor. 'You shall not be partial to the poor or defer to the great, but in righteousness shall you judge your neighbor.' (Leviticus 19:15). 'Masters, treat your slaves

[208] "Pope Leo III," Art & Popular Culture, http://artandpopularculture.com/Pope_Leo_III
[209] "Pope Leo III," Wikipedia
[210] Oliveira, "Charlemagne- Cornerstone."

justly and fairly, knowing that you also have a Master in heaven.'" (Colossians 4:1)[211]

Catholics know justice is giving to one what is due. We know that the four last things are death, judgment, heaven, and hell. After our death we will be judged by God's perfect justice and that will decide our eternal fate—heaven or hell. God will not be mocked. God's justice differs quite radically from the world's notion of justice in society, culture, and even our Church these days.

In observing Christ's example, we see that confronting evil, fighting injustice, is doing justice. We know that justice is closely related to charity because charity relates to truth, and Christ is truth. Justice demands that the innocent, who are the most vulnerable, be protected, even at the cost of our own life. Justice may be denied in this life, but perfect justice will surely be done in the next.

In the past several decades, the classical definition of justice has been replaced by radicals who actively subvert justice to advance their leftist interests and agenda. Whatever happened to plain old, simple, straightforward, justice? Justice is justice. You recognize justice when you see it. You know injustice when you see that, too.

What about twisting other words or phrases? The left is masterful at disguising words to advance their causes and candidates to accumulate power. Case in point: rebranding communists as "democratic socialists." Senator Bernie Sanders is not a Democratic Socialist. He is a communist. How many Americans are scared to death of democratic socialists? Not many, or enough. During World War II, murderous sociopath Joseph Satin was rebranded "Uncle Joe." The rebranding may have been necessary for the allies to defeat the Axis, but the softening of Stalin's image was dishonest nonetheless.

Something similar was attempted to disguise the socialist policies of Joe Biden in his campaign for the presidency of the United States. Not that he was dubbed "Uncle Joe," yet, but pretty close. When discussing rioters, he asked, "Do I look like a radical socialist?"[212] About a month before the election on October 6, 2020, Biden quipped, "I look like a socialist? Look, I'm the guy that ran against the socialist."

---

[211] Catechism, 1807.
[212] Scott Detrow, Mara Liasson, Asma Khalid, Joe Biden: 'Do I Look Like A Radical Socialist With A Soft Spot For Rioters?' *NPR*, August 31, 2020.

His leftist mind then delivered this whopper, "I am no more a socialist or a communist than Donald Trump is… Just look at the record. There's not one single syllable that I've ever said that could lead you to believe that I was a socialist or a communist."[213] C'mon man! That's demonstrably false. While Biden has not advocated for *de jure* communist rule, he has continuously throughout his five decades in public office fought for more government control, statist solutions, expanding welfare programs, and social policies (like abortion and same-sex civil unions) that harm the traditional family. Suffice it say, Biden is closer to Bernie Sanders, an avowed socialist, than he thinks he is.

People are easily fooled and duped. Let's further consider manipulation through adjectives. People are adjective happy. Adjectives are great when they describe benign things like tea. Would you rather drink "tea" or "Celestial Seasonings Honey Vanilla Chamomile decaf tea." The former is utilitarian. The latter sounds delicious and tasty. What about adjectives and leftist causes? The record is not so good.

Instead of calling it what it is, the anti-logic, manipulative, wordsmithing left, following Bill Clinton, advocated for abortion in the 1990s by saying they wanted it "safe, legal and rare." Despite the adjectives, it is still abortion, no matter what.

A generation later in the 2020s, the devious left advocates for "reproductive rights," "reproductive care" and "reproductive freedom." Who wants to argue against rights, care and freedom? Nobody. But when one attaches a word like "reproductive" to rights, care and freedom, it means something completely different. It means death. When the left advances euphemisms for their causes that mislead, we are obligated to call them out.

What about adjectives before the word justice? Consider: social justice, racial justice, economic justice, environmental justice, etc. The list goes on and on. (One exception I would make is for *criminal justice*, as in the study of Criminal Law, or the Criminal Justice System.)

How is "classic justice" different than "modern justice"? The chasm between the two is immense. For instance, classical Catholic

---

[213] Arter, Melanie, "Biden: 'I Am No More a Socialist or a Communist Than Donald Trump Is…,'" *CNS News*, October 7, 2020.

social justice is moral and virtuous. Classical racial justice is noble and laudable. However, in the minds of scheming progressives, their notion of social justice, racial justice, and modern justice is unmoored from true, comprehensive, benevolent intent. For leftist masterminds, they understand the ramifications of their twisted, manipulated application of justice. The leftist elites count on the majority of their adherents to support their objectives, but they are largely dupes, not fully understanding the comprehensive, leftist, anti-God agenda.

Catholic "social justice" has been around a while; the modern usage of the term dates back to the 1840s when Jesuit priest Luigi Taparelli first coined it. Classical Catholic social justice looks to protect the dignity of man versus the state. While the Catholic Church has a long history of being unequivocally critical of socialism and communism through the twentieth century, the same cannot be said of many prelates in the twenty-first century Catholic Church.

Two key issues many social justice warriors (SJWs) and faithful Catholics disagree on are abortion and homosexuality.

As for the Jesuits, the 1960s and 1970s saw an acceleration of their orientation towards supporting liberation theology, particularly in Latin America, which was, and continues to be, a socialist Trojan Horse. The anti-Catholic, Marxist, SJW faction in the Church chooses to ignore spiritual truths and distorts doctrine with which they disagree, and they twist morality to justify their predilections for sinful behavior. As much as the SJWs talk about social justice, they actively deny the justice of God, and some Jesuits even go so far as to deny the existence of the devil.

Fr. Arturo Sosa, SJ, Superior General of the Jesuits, declared in August 2019 that the devil "exists as the personification of evil in different structures, but not in persons, because (the devil) is not a person," but is instead "a way of acting evil...It is a way of evil to be present in human life." Sosa went on to say, "Symbols are part of reality, and the devil exists as a symbolic reality, not as a personal reality."[214] So, according to the head Jesuit, the devil is merely a metaphor for evil human acts. The "figure of speech" must be beside

---

[214] Bunting, Deborah, "Head Jesuit Says Devil Just A Symbol Not a Real Being," *CBN News,* August 22, 2019.

himself hooting with pride that the head of the order formerly known as the "Pope's men" thinks he's a fictional construct.

Social justice has since been deployed by modernist, progressive, secular circles as well. Social justice warriors twist and distort traditional Christian teaching on the value of human life, moral progress and social development. The social justice movement has been funded for years by numerous leftist organizations like the Open Society Foundation and the Ford Foundation, as well as many Fortune 500 corporations. Most recently, the social justice elites have been particularly interested in thought control. Hate speech is nothing more than code for speech they want to censor. Collectivists want submission more than anything else. Submission, yes. justice, no.

Communist revolutionaries agitate for "social justice" in this world rather than personal sanctity that is rewarded in the next because they do not believe in the afterlife. As Catholics, we could not disagree more. The whole point of this life is to earn eternal life in heaven. Atheistic and modernist social justice is a mess. What about modern notions of racial justice? Depends on your definition of racial justice. Is it classic racial justice that advocates equality between all races? Or is it modern, Marxist racial justice emphasizing intersectionality and critical race theory?

Let's examine racial justice through the lens of Boston University (B.U.). I'm a graduate of B.U. In the 1960s, east coast radicalism at B.U. paralleled its west-coast counterpart at U.C. Berkeley. Both universities hosted many marches and protests against the multiple leftist causes of that decade. B.U. can be a radical place, but more on that in a bit.

A decade earlier, in 1955, Rev. Dr. Martin Luther King, Jr. received his Doctorate in systematic theology from B.U.'s School of Theology. Six months later MLK led the legendary Montgomery Bus Boycott in Alabama. B.U.'s website states that MLK is "not merely the most celebrated graduate of Boston University; he is its quintessential alumnus, the personification of the vision its founders had in establishing the institution in 1839. In appreciation of his edification and inspiration here, Dr. King donated his papers to Boston University in 1964, the year his stature on the global stage was confirmed in his receipt of the Nobel Peace Prize." Classic anti-racism, the kind espoused by MLK in the 1950s and '60s, spoke of judging one by the content of their character and not the color of their skin. In other words, equal treatment of others, and, hence, moral racial justice.

[Quick aside, speaking of unequal treatment, the racist founder of Planned Parenthood, Margaret Sanger, would be pleased with the statistics on abortion in the black community. While just 13 percent of the U.S. population, Black women account for a tragic 34 percent of all abortions.][215]

When I attended B.U., I took a class with one of the nation's foremost leftists, Howard Zinn, author of *A People's History of the United States*. Zinn was a radical's radical. Understanding and deconstructing communism, socialism and progressivism has always been an intellectual pursuit of mine. (In case you're wondering, I did well in Zinn's class. Out of approximately 300 students that semester, I was told only four received an A, including me.) Simply put, what Zinn taught, and what leftism represents in general, was/is anti-American and anti-God. Leftism, according to commentator John Doyle, "is nothing more than the mass mobilization of the spiritually ill."[216] In another YouTube, Doyle quips to a hypothetical detractor, "You look spiritually unwell, therefore I will not listen to you, though I will pray for you."[217] It is clear that many of the more popular voices at B.U., and elsewhere in academia, media, and other institutions, including the church, are spiritually unwell these days.

B.U. continues its affiliation with radicalism to the present day. One of its infamous socialist alumni poisoning our nation's political discourse and culture is Rep. Alexandria Ocasio-Cortez (D-NY). AOC's embrace of Green New Deal radicalism, and numerous other progressive causes, like re-education camps for political opponents, have gained her national stature. Unwell? Yes. For the record, I did not attend B.U. when Rep. Alexandria Ocasio-Cortez (D-NY) did.

Another B.U. radical is current professor Ibram X. Kendi, author of *How to be an Anti-Racist* and chair of B.U.'s new Center for Antiracist Research. According to Kendi, the modern anti-racism of the 2020s

[215] Kelli, "Four Quotes From Black Leaders Reveal Abortion's Detrimental Impact on Society," *Live Action News,* February 4, 2021.
[217] Doyle, John, "How Porn is Destroying Your Brain," YouTube posted February 18, 2021. https://www.youtube.com/watch?v=Vtp31feyTfM&feature=emb_logo
[217] Doyle, John, "How to Stay Optimistic About the Future of the USA," YouTube posted March 11, 2021. https://www.youtube.com/watch?v=5fXFpi6N9ml

(as opposed to MLK's classical anti-racism of the 1960s), spreads the falsehood that all whites have been racist since the 1600s. In a discussion of anti-racism by Max Eden, Senior Fellow at the Manhattan Institute, for Prager University, he states, "the catch 22 here is that to say you're not racist only proves how racist you are…and if that upsets you, that's proof of your white fragility." Eden continues, "what Kendi is saying is that if you don't voice active agreement with him, you are a racist. If you treat people equally regardless of race, you're also racist. Anti-racists embrace racial discrimination, as long as it's done on their terms. The only remedy to past discrimination is present discrimination."[218]

Dangerous, depraved drivel has come to dominate the racial justice conversation in our nation. MLK said, "Our lives begin to end the day we become silent about the things that matter." James Lindsay at Prager University describes Critical Race Theory (CRT) as, "white Americans no longer judge black Americans by the content of their character, but solely, always unfavorably, consciously or subconsciously, by the color of their skin."[219] Kendi deviously turns MLK's notion of racial equality directly on its head instead embracing an erroneous, angry, and harmful worldview that pits one group against another. In other words, Kendi, and CRT proponents, advocate for the unequal treatment of others, which makes their notion of anti-racism, racist, anti-Christian, and un-American. It also denies and reverses all the civil rights achievements of the past half century. Therefore, the anti-racism/CRT is a counter-American revolution. What's the end game of CRT? Do CRT's proponents desire the destruction of America? Will the USA soon be another failed economy like Zimbabwe?[220] Or perhaps another failed state like South Africa that, during the summer of 2021, imploded after being refounded and governed by identity-based Marxist Critical Race Theory principles?[221]

---

[218] Eden, Max, "There is no Apolitical Classroom," *Prager University*, YouTube posted January 18, 2021. https://www.youtube.com/watch?v=RKcg41vhLmA

[219] Lindsay, James, "What is Critical Race Theory?" *Prager University*, YouTube posted April 26, 2021. https://www.youtube.com/watch?v=8Zy6DQoRYQw

[220] Marawanyika, Godfrey and Sguazzin, Anthony, "Zimbabwe Gives Land Back to White Farmers After Wrecking Economy." *Bloomberg*. May 13, 2020.

[221] Beattie, Darren, "South Africa — The First Country Built on "Critical Race Theory" — Officially Implodes." *Revolver*. July 16, 2021.

What would MLK say about Black Lives Matter (BLM)? According to Will Witt, BLM does not line up with anything MLK says about racial equality and justice on three key metrics:

> First, BLM takes MLK quotes out of context. BLM uses the quote, 'a riot is the language of the unheard,' but they leave out the line just before that when MLK said, 'I will always continue to say, that riots are socially destructive and self-defeating.' Second, BLM wants to disband the western, nuclear family. MLK totally believed in family values... He didn't want to disband the nuclear family, he wanted to strengthen it. Thirdly, BLM loves affirmative action and diversity standards, whereas MLK believes in judging someone on their character... MLK believed in character over color, BLM believes the opposite.[222]

Based on Saint Leo's efforts as pontiff working for justice and peace, what would he say about justice, anti-racism, intersectionality, Critical Race Theory, and Black Lives Matter? He'd most likely start by saying that common sense is not so common anymore. Then, candidly, he would call out the confusion for what it is, telling us that the anti-racism and BLM movement is the emperor that has no clothes. Saint Leo would conclude by comparing Catholic teaching and the positions of Black Lives Matter saying the two are irreconcilable.

African-American journalist Jason Whitlock logically deduced that since BLM was founded as a Marxist organization, and Marxism opposes religion, therefore BLM opposes religion. As such, Whitlock is not on board with BLM. He further decried those race hustlers who demand support for the Democrats and BLM. They say that "if you do, we will protect you. If you don't, we will label you a racist."[223]

Barri Weiss, in an article titled, "Whistleblower at Smith College Resigns Over Racism," discussed how Jodi Shaw, an alum and former employee at Smith, was subjected to a twisted and ever-increasingly hostile, racist, environment grounded in Critical Race Theory. Critical race theory is a radical concept that combines Marxist theories of oppressor versus oppressed viewed through the lens of race. It's a sad, frustrating and bizarre reality at many colleges these days. Weiss writes,

---

[222] Witt, Will, "Martin Luther King Jr. vs. Black Lives Matter," *Prager University,* YouTube posted January 13, 2021. https://www.youtube.com/watch?v=tqzZQZD3UyM
[223] Whitlock, Jason, "Interview: Tucker Carlson Tonight," *Fox News,* January 20, 2021.

"Any ideology that asks people to judge others based on their skin color is wrong. Any ideology that asks us to reduce ourselves and others to racial stereotypes is wrong. Any ideology that treats dissent as evidence of bigotry is wrong. Any ideology that denies our common humanity is wrong."[224] Instead, people stay silent and go along with what is happening because they fear loss of their job or reputation, and for many other reasons. The hour is late, and it calls for more courageous people, like Jodi Shaw.

Saint Martin de Porres, patron saint of mixed race and interracial harmony, intercede for us to end racial division.

At the outset of the Biden Administration, it seems as though "white supremacy" is the catchphrase de jour. The liberal logic is that anyone who voted for Trump is a white supremacist. Will it be a short-lived buzz phrase, or will it have staying power during the Biden years? Time will tell. As Ronald Reagan said in his "A Time for Choosing" speech in 1964, "It's not that our liberal friends are ignorant, it's that they know so much that isn't so."[225] Or that they are spiritually unwell.

What would Saint Leo, or Saint Martin de Porres, say about the topics of white fragility, and, wait for it, "multiracial whiteness?" An associate professor from New York University, Christina Beltrán, wrote an op/ed in the *Washington Post* on January 15, 2021, about the new oxymoronic phenomenon, "multiracial whiteness." Her article begins: "The Trump administration's anti-immigration, anti-civil rights stance has made it easy to classify the president's loyalists as a homogenous mob of white nationalists. But take a look at the FBI's posters showing people wanted in the insurrectionist assault on the U.S. Capitol: Among the many White faces are a few that are clearly Latino or African American."[226] Beltran continued,

> Rooted in America's ugly history of white supremacy, indigenous dispossession and anti-blackness, multiracial whiteness is an ideology invested in the unequal distribution of land, wealth, power and

---

[224] Weiss, Barri, "Whistleblower at Smith College Resigns Over Racism," *Substack,* February 19, 2021.

[225] Reagan, Ronald, "A Time for Choosing," Original speech from October 27, 1964, Ronald Reagan Presidential Library. YouTube posted April 2, 2009. https://www.youtube.com/watch?v=qXBswFfh6AY

[226] Beltrán, Christina, "Opinion: To understand Trump's support, we must think in terms of multiracial Whiteness," *The Washington Post,* January 15, 2021.

privilege—a form of hierarchy in which the standing of one section of the population is premised on the debasement of others. Multiracial whiteness reflects an understanding of whiteness as a political color and not simply a racial identity—a discriminatory worldview in which feelings of freedom and belonging are produced through the persecution and dehumanization of others.[227]

Oh, so Hispanic and black Trump supporters favor "the politics of aggression, exclusion and domination" and therefore suffer from "multiracial whiteness." Personally, I think the Twitter humor of Tatiana McGrath is a suitable response to bizarre liberal claims when she asked, 'what's next "black whiteness?"'[228] Time to stop all the nonsense talk. It does nothing to help bring about a more virtuous nation, but only serves to cultivate, and accelerate, racial division. For some, this appears to be the objective.

Tom Hoopes, in an article titled, "Only the Church Does Anti-Racism Right," states that secularism breeds relativism and relativism is toxic for race relations. Hoopes adds,

If you believe that one God created all people in his image and commands that you love them, you will eventually have to confront your personal feelings, whatever they are, about people of different races. But relativism breeds intolerance. If there is no objective truth that we all have a duty to discover and honor, then whoever has the most power in a given situation determines what is right and wrong—whether it be your schoolteacher, the media or a police officer. You can't teach that racism is wrong *and* that "your truth is as good as my truth... It is no accident that the greatest advances of human rights in the United States have come from religious people, from Sojourner Truth to Rev. Martin Luther King Jr. to the Catholic Church.[229]

Faith is a primary bulwark against the evil of racism. If we love as God loves, the abuse of our neighbor through racism is no longer justifiable. No one is permitted to deny the inherent dignity and comparable worth of any human being created by our sovereign God.

---

[227] Ibid.
[228] McGrath, Tatiana, Twitter post from January 17, 2021, https://twitter.com/TitaniaMcGrath/status/1350905467007102977
[229] Hoopes, Tom, "Only the Church Does Anti-Racism Right," *National Catholic Register,* January 18, 2021.

Each soul has dignity beyond understanding. Each citizen in the world is entitled to equal treatment under the law, human rights and respect. Before God, everyone is born equal and every life matters. Each life is sacred, born and unborn. Catholics see Jesus in everyone. Saint Paul writes in Galatians 3:28 that man-made divisions among people are not of God and are, therefore, inappropriate. The devil loves to stoke racial tensions. Be on guard against his snares. Some Catholics think or act in racist ways and when they do, they should repent to God, and get right with their fellow man.

Blessed Charles de Foucauld said, "We must stand up for the rights of our neighbour who is suffering from injustice; we must defend them all the more vigorously because we see Jesus present in them. Surely this is our duty because of our love for others for his sake. We have no right to be 'sleeping watchmen' or dumb watch-dogs. Whenever we see evil, we must sound the alarm."

In an ideal world, there would be no racism anywhere, but people and nations are flawed. We as a nation must continue to make progress toward authentic racial justice. While racial injustice of any kind should be rejected; false justice, politically or religiously motivated injustice, for the sake of advancing a false narrative or racial division for personal or political gain, should equally be rejected. Don't let the phony, distorters of the truth continue to run roughshod over Lady Justice. She holds two scales. Too much in one direction or the other and there is imbalance. We need a more balanced conversation about true racial justice in America.

The focus of much of this chapter has been on the human notion of justice. What about God's understanding and application of justice? Well, we know that judgments by God are perfect justice in the truest sense of the term. When we die, we will undergo our particular judgment. All the good and bad from our life will be instantaneously presented for God to weigh on His scales of justice. His verdict on our eternal destination will be final. No appeal. Few will merit heaven outright except those who have lived the life of a saint and died in the state of grace. Some, through the mercy of God, will be sent to purgatory to serve God's justice where sins will be expiated to His satisfaction. Once all temporal punishment has been satisfied, the souls will enter heaven for all eternity. For those who did not live their lives in friendship with God and His Church, divine justice will call them to spend eternity in hell. With God there is perfect justice.

Christ was accused and crucified due to the unjust charge of treason. If Christ suffered injustice, what makes us think we can escape the injustice of our enemies? When it comes to those whom you may consider your enemies, let go and let God forgive them. Saint Thomas Becket reassures us of God's protection: "Let it be your consolation, then, that God's enemies, however honourable and exalted they may have been, shall, nevertheless, fade away like the smoke."

On the inevitability of divine justice, Becket adds, "To Him, I look as my judge, to Him, as the avenger of my wrongs, firm in my own good conscience and secure in the sincerity of my devotion, rooted in faith and confident that those who, in the love of justice suffer injury, can never be confounded, nor those, who break the horns of the persecutors of the Church, be deprived of their everlasting reward."

On justice and mercy, Saint Thomas Aquinas reminds us that fraternal correction may also need to be part of the equation. He writes, "mercy without justice is the mother of dissolution; justice without mercy is cruelty. To correct the sinner is a work of mercy."

If you believe that God has not been just with you, or that some great injustice has been perpetrated against you, perhaps a vice in your life needs to be rooted out and that can be done only through tough love that you do not presently understand. God, in His benevolent providence, sometimes acts in ways we do not immediately, or may never understand. We must increase our obedience to His will and trust. As Archbishop Fulton Sheen said, "Sometimes the only way the good Lord can get into some hearts is to break them."

Justice is not always easy to achieve. But it becomes possible as more seek it out. Pope Saint Leo III, help us to champion true justice in this life, so that we may experience eternal justice, in heaven, in the next life.

Ninth Century Saints

Saints Cyril & Methodius (d. 869), and Alfred the Great (d. 899), pray for us.

Saint Leo is the patron saint of (N/A).
Saint Leo's feast day is June 12.
Saint Leo, *ora pro nobis* (pray for us).

Ninth Century History

800- **Charlemagne is crowned forming the Holy Roman Emperor.**

809- The *Filioque* clause, the doctrine that the Holy Ghost proceeds from both the Father and the Son, is introduced into the Nicene Creed.

869- Fourth Ecumenical Council or Constantinople condemns Photius. The Eastern Orthodox Churches denies this council and succeeding general councils.

Virtue Challenge #9- Justice

Saint Leo operated in a world of political and theological jockeying that greatly contributed to his exercise of justice. Leo, pray for us that wherever there is injustice, let us not accept the status quo. Help us to be courageous when others say little or nothing; let us call out error and injustice whenever it occurs. How will you champion justice in your lifetime?

Think about that time in your life when you experienced injustice. How did it make you feel? What recourse did you have?

In what ways may you have been negligent and unjust to those you have encountered in your life?

Let us pray for all those in prison who are innocent. Let us pray for all those guilty who are serving their just punishment that they may one day reenter society as contrite and productive citizens.

What kind of injustice makes you want to ride to the rescue? What suffering are you most sensitized to? What causes fire you up? What cause gets you angry, passionate, determined or excited? What charitable groups allow you to make an unusual impact?

Create a list of those individuals, groups, causes, needs and injustices that draw you to serve and give for the greater good. Then for each on the list, ask yourself: Why am I drawn to this? What do I bring to this? Why not me?

Converse for a moment with the Holy Ghost about justice. My Lord and my God, how may I serve you more faithfully and completely through the virtue of justice?

O Great Saint Leo, pray for us an increase in the virtue and grace of holy justice.

CHAPTER 10

Wolfgang

The Tenth Century
Diligence

"Be sober and watch: because your adversary the devil, as a roaring lion, goeth about seeking whom he may devour."

~ I Peter 5:8

"Go to the ant, o sluggard, observe her ways and be wise."

~ Proverbs 6:6

"Here is the call for the endurance of the saints, those who keep the commandments of God and the faith of Jesus."

~ Revelations 14:12

"You cannot be half a saint, you must be a whole saint, or none at all."

~ Saint Thérèse of Lisieux

The 900s

"Chickens in the bread pan pickin' out dough. Granny does your dog bite? No child no."[230]

It was 1979 and our family was cruising around town listening to the Charlie Daniels Band's "The Devil Went Down to Georgia." The up-tempo, bluegrass song described the devil's failure to gain a young man's soul through a fiddle-playing contest. It was a catchy tune and a line in the song prompted me to ask, "Mom, can the Devil steal your soul?" I remember her response like it was yesterday, "No, not unless you let him." She then added, "but sometimes people do sell their soul to the Devil." Wait, what?

---

[230] Charlie Daniels Band, "The Devil Went Down to Georgia." *Million Mile Reflections*, Epic Records. 1979.

She continued, "Some singers might be very popular and have lots of money, but some of them got there because they made the bad decision to sell their soul to the devil." Being young, I didn't fully grasp what Mom meant, but I knew it wasn't good. Did the devil show up like a lawyer offering a contract to sign waving a pen saying, "In exchange for your soul I will make you rich and famous?" Imagined transactions of that nature haunted my youth for years.

Oddly enough, from time to time when older I would read reports of musicians making deals with the devil. When it comes to music it is said that Lucifer has a special affinity for stringed instruments, particularly the violin and the guitar. I found a listing of musicians on Listverse who many suspect of having sold their souls to Satan.[231] A few entries from the list:

- Niccolo Paganini. Many considered him to be the greatest violin virtuoso of all time. He was so much better than his peers that a rumor circulated, and persisted, that he must have sold his soul in exchange for his virtuosity (though not his virtue). He was a great womanizer and was said to trap the souls of young women inside his violin.
- Giuseppe Tartini. Said not only to have sold his soul to the devil, but also to have composed a song with him. *Trillo del Diavolo*, or The Devil's Trill, came to Tartini in a dream, after his dream-self had also sold his soul.
- Robert Johnson. A 'terrible guitarist,' Johnson took his guitar to Clarksdale Crossroads where the devil gave him lessons over a couple weeks. When he returned, his terrible guitar technique was now described as 'formidable' and 'masterful.' Robert Johnson died in 1938, at the age of 27, and is now known officially as the Devil's Bluesman.
- Jimmy Page. Legendary Led Zeppelin guitarist was a student of occultism. Many claimed that to play the guitar so well, Page sold his sold to the devil to get such fast fingers. Buried deep, indeed backwards, within "Stairway to Heaven," arguably the quartet's biggest song is the message *"There's no escaping it. It's*

---

[231] Ward, Hazell, "Top 10 Musicians Who Sold Their Soul To The Devil," *Listverse,* September 24, 2020.

my sweet Satan. The one will be the path who makes me sad; whose power is Satan."[232] Blimey!

- John Lennon. Famous for saying, "The Beatles were bigger than Jesus." Lennon allegedly signed his pact with Lucifer in December 1960 and was promised twenty years of success before the devil would claim his soul on December 7, 1980. Mark David Chapman, Lennon's murderer, said he was told by demons to kill Lennon.[233]
- Bob Dylan. Once said, "It's a destiny thing. I made a devil's bargain and I'm holding up my end."
- The Rolling Stones. Since their 1968 hit, "Sympathy for the Devil," The Stones were dogged by rumors of devil worshiping.
- Snoop Dogg. Snoop freely admits that at the time he wrote one of his albums, he was in a dark place, and he heard a voice say, "Bring your lifestyle to me I'll make it better." Mr. Dogg asked how long he would live, and the voice cried back, "Eternal and forever."

Here are a couple other bands whose songs aroused suspicions as to deals with the devil:

- AC/DC, whose name means bi-sexual, had a mega hit with, "Highway to Hell." How many people, Catholics included, the world over have joined in singing along to this nihilistic anthem, "I'm on a highway to hell"? With the 'promised land' in the song referring to hell, the domain over which Satan presides?
- Van Halen. "Running with the Devil," perhaps VH's most popular song, is their *magnum opus* to rebellion. Some have commented the song offers a benediction to Satan. Eddie Van Halen, one of the world's greatest guitarists, grew up Roman Catholic as did his brother Alex, the band's drummer. While touring in their later years, Eddie's son Wolfgang joined the band.[234]

[232] Brannigan, Paul, "Why Your Favorite Rock Band is a Tool of Satan & Must Be Stopped," *Louder*, May 19, 2016.
[233] "Lennon, Luther and Schonborn," *Tradition In Action*, https://www.traditioninaction.org/Questions/B240_Lennon.html
[234] Stewart, David, "Van Halen's Dead End in the Lake of Fire," *Jesusisprecious.org*, August, 2013.

So why start a chapter on Saint Wolfgang and the tenth century with talk of musicians and how they sold their souls to the devil? Diligence. Or, to be more precise, a lack thereof. In "Wrapped Around Your Finger," The Police sang, "Mephistopheles is not your name. I know what you're up to just the same." Do we really know what the devil is up to? *Against the Grain's* chapters are geared primarily toward presenting a saint and discussing a virtue in light of that saint. While emulating a saint and virtue is laudable, what about being more aware of the strategies and tactics of the adversary? How diligent are we in our awareness of and resistance to Beelzebub (a name that means "The Lord of the Flies") and his temptations, who looks to lead us away from Christ and to spiritually destroy us? Not to be too unnerving about this, but I know you get it, "every breath you take, every step you take, you know who is watching you." The devil is the ultimate predator.

The above examples of individuals and bands are from an industry notorious for 'running with the devil.' To date myself a bit, musicians from Black Sabbath, Deep Purple, Megadeath, Iron Maiden, KISS, Alice Copper, Santana, The Eagles, Queen, to Madonna regularly invoked blasphemy, cursed the name of Jesus, and glorified all types of immorality in the pursuit of music sales and stardom.

What about current music stars? Persistent demonic rumors are associated with: Marilyn Manson, Nikki Minaj, Taylor Swift, Miley Cyrus, Rihanna, Ke$ha, Eminem, DMX, Jay-Z, Beyonce, Katy Perry, and Lady Gaga. Listening to their filth and having it negatively impact your will is precisely the opposite of diligence and protecting one's soul.

Rapper Lil Nas X teamed up in March 2021 with shoe maker MSCHF to release Nike demon-themed red and black "Satan's Shoes" that had a bronze pentagram, the numbers 666, and one real drop of human blood. Advertising for the $1,018 shoes states it is "better to reign in hell than serve in heaven."[235] Can it get any more nasty and overtly demonic than that?

Many musicians have short-term thinking about fame and money. They are not concerned with the long-term that is eternity.

[235] McLoone, David, "Custom footwear retailer MSCHF sells 'Satan Shoes' containing human blood." *LifeSite News*, March 30, 2021.

Some have not been taught the one, true faith. Others have. Some Catholics compromise, or jettison altogether, their faith for money, fame and power. The list of persons partnering with the devil for fame and influence is not limited to musicians. We can expand the list to Hollywood, Media, Sports, Tech, Business, Politics, Religion, and more.

Sometimes we can look at the over-the-top lifestyle of a rock star and conclude that since we didn't release a song entitled, "Highway to Hell" that we're not so bad, and comparatively speaking, we are pretty good so we must be in God's good graces. Surely, we are not like them. Right? How many times have you compromised your values, morals, and your faith to indulge a desire. Never? Few and far between? Or frequently?

With what we've pursued in this life, the question needs to be asked: Have we, too, sold our souls to the devil in some, or any, regard? What about harboring certain sinful behaviors that we know are offensive to God but in our weakness, we persist in ways that continue to offend God? Our consciences and guardian angels tell us to stop these acts or behaviors, and promptly go to confession. Do we? Do we repent and make firm purpose of amendment? Are we truly diligent in caring for our souls getting to and remaining in the state of grace? Or are we more concerned with being of this world? Our version of 'running with the devil'?

To their credit, in their 1984 song "Shout," Tears for Fears sang "… you shouldn't have to sell your soul..." Are we diligent in the music we listen to, movies we watch, media and technology we consume, sports we watch, and businesses we support? What about the priests and parishes we support? In all we do, do we support the good and morally virtuous? Or do we go with the flow, who is popular, regardless of the impact on our soul? Are we diligent in guarding not just our souls, but those of family members and friends?

Do we run with (i.e., vote for) pro-abortion politicians?

Have you made any 'deals' with the devil?

Most would stipulate that some musicians and other mega-wealthy individuals have sold their souls to the devil. Some say that anti-family (pro-abortion and pro-homosexual civil union) politicians have sold their souls to the Democratic Party and to the prince of liars.

Have you ever heard of a saint making a deal with the devil? Hold my beer. Let me introduce you to Wolfgang of Regensburg. More on his deal with the devil a bit later.

Wolfgang, also known as the Great Almoner (being a great distributor of alms), was born in Swabia, Germany, into the noble class, and received a great education at the abbey of Reichenau school. While at the abbey he met Henry of Babenburg, who would one day become the Archbishop of Trier. Through the years Wolfgang remained in contact with the archbishop who taught at his cathedral school. Upon the death of the archbishop in 964, Wolfgang chose to become a Benedictine monk and he moved to the abbey of Maria Einsiedeln, now part of Switzerland. He was ordained a priest by Saint Ulrich in 968, and soon after was appointed the director of the Einsiedeln monastery school.[236]

On Christmas Day 972, Emperor Otto II appointed Wolfgang Bishop of Regensburg, near Munich. Wolfgang deserved credit for the disciplinary activities in his diocese including initiating reform of the clergy, religious life and the monasteries under his jurisdiction. Wolfgang's services in this new position were of the highest importance, not only for the diocese, but also for the cause of civilization as he would tutor the future Emperor Saint Henry II, as well as Poppe, son of Margrave Luitpold, Archbishop of Trier (1018), and Tagino, Archbishop of Magdeburg (1004–1012). As prince of the empire, Wolfgang performed his duties towards the emperor and the empire with the utmost diligence, and, like Saint Ulrich, was one of the mainstays of the Ottonian policies.[237] Wolfgang preached with much passion, always demonstrating special concern for the poor. Wolfgang was integral in the missionary efforts to evangelize the Magyars in what is today modern Hungary.

When Wolfgang was approaching his final years, he went to what is now called Saint Wolfgang's Lake in Austria. Before he chose the serene location on which to build a church and hermitage, he prayed, and then threw his axe into the thicket. On the spot where it landed,

---

[236] St. Wolfgang, *New Advent*, https://www.newadvent.org/cathen/15682b.htm
[237] Wolfgang of Regensburg, Wikipedia, https://en.wikipedia.org/wiki/Wolfgang_of_Regensburg

he built his cell. According to local legend, Saint Wolfgang tricked the devil into helping him build the church by promising the devil the first soul that came through the church doors. After the church was completed, a wolf was the first to cross its threshold, thus tricking the devil.

Wolfgang became ill while on a journey and died on October 31, 994 in Puppingen near Linz, Austria. He was canonized in 1052 by Pope Leo IX. His feast day is celebrated widely in Bavaria and Austria. Wolfgang is regarded as one of the three great German saints of the tenth century, the other two being Saint Ulrich of Augsburg and Saint Conrad of Constance. Many miracles have occurred at Wolfgang's tomb, especially those related to stomach ailments. His axe can be viewed in the small town of Saint Wolfgang near his old cell and church.[238]

Wolfgang could be depicted as a man with rolled-up sleeves, embodying the strong, German work ethic. On several occasions he tried to retire to solitary prayer, but his sense of responsibility kept calling him back to serve his diocese. Doing what had to be done, or diligence, was his path to holiness.

In the Garden of Eden God said that man would work. Genesis 2:15 "And the Lord God took man, and put him into the paradise of pleasure, to dress it, and to keep it." To 'dress it' means to tend to it, to work it. Saint Vincent de Paul tells us, "Let us love God, but with the strength of our arms, in the sweat of our brow." Let us work to serve the Lord as Wolfgang did.

Diligence is defined as, "steady, earnest, and energetic effort: devoted and painstaking work and application to accomplish an undertaking: assiduity." Are we as assiduous as we should be in caring for our souls? Diligence is effort, work and application. Do we put enough effort into tending our souls? Do we work at it? Do we apply ourselves to becoming holier? In other words, are we diligent in serving God? How exactly are we working for God, his kingdom, and for others? Saint Clare of Assisi said, "*Love God, serve God; everything is in that.*"

---

[238] St. Wolfgang, *New Advent*, n.p.

Do we serve the church? If so, how? Do we defend the errors being lobbed at her? Or are we indifferent to her defense? Saint Augustine, in *Augustine Day by Day,* writes, "Scattered about the entire earth, your mother the Church is tormented by the assaults of error. She is also afflicted by the laziness and indifference of so many of the children she carries around in her bosom as well as by the sight of so many of her members growing cold, while she becomes less able to help her little ones. Who then will give her the necessary help she cries for if not her children and other members to whose number you belong?"[239]

To what extent are we lazy and indifferent about our faith?

With regard to defending and leading our families as Catholics, what's our plan? Given the state of the world, is our plan sufficient? What are the deeds by which an objective person could look at and say, this is a practicing Catholic family as evidenced by the following ways? How often would we prefer to watch tv instead of leading the family in a Rosary? How often do we compromise our values and leave a tv program on or leave a song on the radio that has an inappropriate scene or phrase?

In the opinion of the world, do we subject ourselves to "not being cool" and instead stand for our faith? Saint Athanasius of Alexandria said, "...and He endured insults from men that we might inherit incorruption."

While we must recognize the need for diligence all our days, what about procrastination? The devil loves procrastination. It is one of his favorite snares. "Don't say your rosary now, you are much too busy, too tired. Say it later today." And then we get busy later and forget to say our daily Rosary. Recognizing his pattern of persuading us to procrastinate, we no longer put off tending to the spiritually important. When our guardian angel nudges us to say our Morning Prayer, our daily Rosary, the Noon Angelus, our evening prayers, we must do them at that time. Lest we move on to other matters and shirk our Catholic responsibilities.

Saint Philip Neri encourages us in the face of temptations. He writes, "Do not grieve over the temptations you suffer. When the Lord

---

[239] Saint Augustine, *Augustine Day by Day,* 90.

intends to bestow a particular virtue on us, He often permits us to be tempted by the opposite vice." If we are diligent and work on our virtue, with God's help we will be successful. Only, however, if we remain diligent and steadfast.

The Germans have a fabulous word to describe diligence— *sitzfleisch*. With a literal meaning of "sitting meat," or "butt flesh," *sitzfleisch* refers to the "chair-glue mindset" needed to sit down, carry on with the task at hand (especially if it is difficult), and see it through to completion, even if it requires doing so for an extended period of time. In another word, *stamina*. A good example of *sitzfleisch* is the difference between a writer and an aspiring writer. Directed towards one's particular judgment, *sitzfleisch* is the difference between being directed to heaven or to purgatory. Regarding your faith, what do you need to do to better cultivate *sitzfleisch*?

The comedian, Larry the Cable Guy, is known for his phrase, "Get 'er done." I envision that Wolfgang, with his German work ethic, would no doubt identify with the sentiment behind Larry's maxim. When it comes to saying our prayers, doing what needs to be done to live a holier life, do we "get 'er done"? Do we work for our faith? Do we make a genuine effort? Do we make excuses, or do we 'get 'er done'?

Closely aligned with diligence is patience. To be sure, one must not confuse patience with procrastination. When God wants a breakthrough, it will happen. We can do everything in our power to provide good soil, sunlight and water for a seed, but it is only God who will permit the seed to grow. (*Sitzfleisch* can also refer to the patience needed for any given task.)

A similar take can be applied to gold. Gold does not first appear in the jewelry store as a finished product. Gold starts as a rock in the dirt. It must be found, shaped, and polished. Through a diligent process the value of the gold becomes apparent. So too is there a process with our souls. Diligence takes effort and time.

In much that same way that Boniface persevered, Wolfgang was diligent. In the chapter on Boniface we discussed Navy Seal David Goggin's technique of "taking souls" as a mental technique to persevere and to overcome obstacles. In a similar way we have another Navy Seal, Jocko Willink, and his approach to mental toughness. Jocko

Willink is another popular author on the topic of self-mastery and motivation. One of my favorite Jocko YouTube videos is a two-minute clip called "Good." It's about how to deal with failure and bad situations.

Jocko narrates, "When something is going wrong, there is going to be some good to come from it. Didn't get the new high-speed gear we wanted? Good. Didn't get promoted? Good. More time to get better. Didn't get funded? Got injured? Got beat? Good. You learned. Unexpected problems? Good. We have the opportunity to figure out a solution. That's it. When things are going bad, don't get all bummed out, startled, frustrated. If you can say the word "good" it means you're still alive and breathing. If you're still breathing, well now, you've still got some fight left in you. So get up, dust off, reload, recalibrate, reengage. Go out on the attack. Get after it."[240]

Our daughter Gabrielle attends The Citadel, The Military College of South Carolina. During Senior year they have The Ring Ceremony where Seniors are presented with class rings. Many choose to have an inscription engraved inside their band of gold. Gabi's inscription? "Good." Get after it Gabi (Class of '22). Dad's proud of you.

While Jocko's message was meant primarily for a military/secular audience, can you see the applicability in our spiritual battles? Gave in to temptation? Don't get bummed out. You've still got fight left in you. Get to confession and reengage. Be diligent.

On matters of faith, get 'er done, and get after it.

Rush Limbaugh, conservative talk show radio host *par excellence*, a while back spoke about diligence. He said that 80 percent of the formula for success in life is sticking with it. There is no substitute for desire. Mental toughness is needed to overcome adversity. There are countless ways to do what you want to do. The pressure on everyone is to conform. Be a non-conformist. Some people are made for conformity. Be honest with yourself about your passions. What motivates you? Apply that to anything in life that you want. Well, Rush, I'd like to take your comments and apply them to my faith. How 'bout you? Rush, passed away in February 2021; to the mercy of God, may he *requiescat in pace* (rest in peace).

[240] Willink, Jocko, "Good" YouTube posted January 25, 2016.
https://www.youtube.com/watch?v=IdTMDpizis8

Saint Thérèse of Lisieux encourages us, "Yes, my heart's dear one, Jesus, is here with His cross. Since you are one of His favorites, he wants to make you into His likeness; why be afraid that you will not have the strength to carry this cross without a struggle? On the way to Calvary, Jesus did indeed fall three times and you, poor little child, would like to be different from your spouse, would rather not fall a hundred times if necessary, to prove your love to Him by getting back up with even more strength than before your fall!"[241]

Can you envision the Navy SEALs pushing through pain, staying mentally tough, and getting back up quickly after they have fallen? Of course, you can. As a Catholic making the effort to be a saint, how quickly, resolutely, and diligently will you push through pain (offer it up), stay mentally tough (in your prayer life) and get back up after you have fallen (into sin)? With all the crosses, trials and tribulations that Christ will send to you, will you accept them with gratitude no matter how light or heavy the cross(es) may be? Will you have the mindset of a saint and say, "Good, more opportunity to develop virtue." Will you tap into the warrior ethos and say, "Why not me?"

Why two chapters on essentially the same topic (perseverance and diligence)? Because in our culture, Catholics need a double dose of techniques and encouragement that we can do it. That we can answer Christ's call to imitate him in this life. Some days, we can continue to operate in the normal rut. Other days, we need to step up our game quite a bit by thinking like an elite Navy SEAL. Or in our case, as a true friend of Christ, as a faithful Catholic. Whatever, whoever, or wherever the obstacle, we need to muster the resolve to succeed for Christ. Satanist Aleister Crowley said: "Do what thou wilt shall be the whole of the law." We need to be diligent in doing God's will and not our own. As Catholics we must be ever vigilant and avoid the pitfalls, traps, guiles and temptations of the devil.

In the state of grace, we can increase our holiness and merit heaven. We must not think it is good enough to shoot for purgatory. No. Heaven it is. We can do it as no other religion offers what the Catholic Church does. Jesus Christ, God and man, founded our church. Through the Magisterium and the Sacraments, we are brought closer to Christ. All other Christian religions were founded by flawed

---

[241] White, Joseph, "Saint Thérèse of Lisieux: Meditations with the Little Flower," 87.

men impacted by original sin. Non-Christian religions do not have Christ at the center. The Church has traditionally taught that there is no salvation outside the Catholic Church.

Regarding leaning into our faith, one holy example rises to the top to encourage us when the situation appears difficult, or perhaps even bleak, Saint Joseph, Jesus's foster-father. Saint Joseph, a role model for us for many of his virtues, had holy diligence. Do we ever read that Saint Joseph gave up when he faced hardship? When he needed a room at the inn in Bethlehem for Mary, did he stop looking when all the rooms were occupied, or did he press on and find the best possible solution? Did he give up looking for Jesus when they could not find him for three days? Or did he tirelessly keep at it and eventually find Him? Where there is a will, there is a way. Saint Joseph, model of workmen, pray for us.

In the Litany of Saint Joseph, he is given the title, "Terror of demons." Exorcists know that the mention of his name makes demons tremble and flee. Why? Because of Saint Joseph's steadfast faith, holy chastity, assiduous perseverance, and exceptional humility. Furthermore, he was diligent in watching over the early church, the Holy Family, which was the church in its infancy. Saint Joseph guarded Blessed Mother and Jesus. He was their protector. He can be our protector too. With any temptation, go to Saint Joseph.

Michael R. Heinlein, editor of *Simply Catholic,* wrote "Advent is the Perfect Time to Ponder the Witness of Saint Joseph." Heinlein touches upon Joseph's diligence:

"I often find myself imagining I was in Saint Joseph's shoes. So many situations of life present similar circumstances like he faced. The qualities of his life should be those appropriated by anyone who wants to follow Jesus more closely. When life's darkest moments hover around us — akin to the dark days of December's Advent season — we can ask Saint Joseph to help us. We can turn to his example for strength to persevere. We should desire and seek to emulate his faith, hope and love. In meditating on the life and witness of Saint Joseph we can learn a fundamental truth described by Saint Paul:

217

"We know that all things work for good for those who love God, who are called according to his purpose" (Rom. 8: 28).[242]

The virtue of diligence is doing whatever it takes, for as long as it takes, to reach your objective. The Church knows the importance of diligence because the Bible reminds us on more than one occasion. A few examples:

- Proverbs 21:5 *"The plans of the diligent lead surely to abundance, but everyone who is hasty comes only to poverty."*
- 2 John 1:8 says, *"Watch out that you do not lose what we have worked so hard to achieve. Be diligent so that you receive your full reward."*
- I Timothy 4:15 says, *"Be diligent in these matters, give yourself wholly to them, so that everyone may see your progress. Watch your life and doctrine closely."*

As parents we have the opportunity to read Deuteronomy and the couple of references it makes on diligently raising our children. "...you shall teach them diligently to your children, and shall talk of them when you sit in your house, and when you walk by the way, and when you lie down, and when you rise."[243] "Only take care, and keep your soul diligently, lest you forget the things that your eyes have seen, and lest they depart from your heart all the days of your life. Make them known to your children and your children's children..."[244]

Failure can be a key part of diligence. We all fail at times. How do we deal with failure? How do others see us deal with failure? Are we humble? As a supervisor, manager or leader of an organization, do you encourage diligence? As a dad, mom, or even as an older sibling, how do we encourage diligence? How do we help kids after they fail? In general, people fear failure. People don't try sometimes because they fear failing. Parents can help kids cover their failure. Let them fail and learn. We have misconceptions about success and failure. We get trophies today just for being on the team. It's OK to be distraught. Talent is only part of the equation. Diligence, patience and courage are

---

242 Heinlein, Michael, "Advent is the Perfect Time to Ponder the Witness of Saint Joseph," Simply Catholic, https://simplycatholic.com/advent-the-perfect-time-to-ponder-the-witness-of-st-joseph/
[243] Deuteronomy 6:7
244 Deuteronomy 4:9

key. So many of the virtues discussed in *Against the Grain* are interrelated.

An unknown author once said, "the best strategy in life is diligence." Is that true? If it were revised a bit to say, "The best strategy in life is holy diligence" I might consider it. Well, in order to be holy, it certainly helps if one is diligent. I get that. Conversely, Jesus told Saint Faustina, "the greatest obstacles to holiness are discouragement and anxiety." If Jesus tells us to watch out for discouragement and anxiety, He knows full well that those thoughts could provide an opening that could be exploited by the devil and lead one to sin, or worse, abandon their faith altogether. Diligence via faith, hope and charity are thus key.

What have your pursued that has caused you discouragement or anxiety? Did that pursuit lead you to compromise your faith? In retrospect, do you see how that worldly pursuit caused you to crucify our Lord all over again?

As Catholics sometimes it crosses our mind that because God has not destined for us to win the mega-million lottery, he has not blessed us abundantly. Although a simplistic and erroneous example, it does help illustrate the point that we Catholics have won in so many ways we might not take a step back often enough to realize exactly what we have. For example, if you are a cradle Catholic, jackpot! If you are a convert to Catholicism, jackpot! If you keep the commandments, attend Mass weekly, receive communion, go to confession regularly, and are in the state of grace, live with faith, hope and charity in your heart, are humble, etc., you are among the few who have hit the spiritual jackpot. If you've picked up this book and made it to this point, I think it's fairly safe to say you value your faith. You know the value of your Catholic faith, and you wouldn't trade your faith for all the money, fame, or power in the world. Blessed be God in His Angels and in His Saints!

From this point forward, how will you diligently protect your soul? Attaining and permitting your soul to remain in the state of grace? "There is still time for endurance," writes Saint Basil the Great, "time for patience, time for healing, time for change. Have you slipped? Rise up. Have you sinned? Cease. Do not stand among sinners, but leap aside." How will you diligently guard against the sin of presumption?

As Saint John Vianney said, *"The saints did not all begin well. But they all ended well."*

It may be fair to say that we, too, most likely did not start well, but we know now that must end well. We know we must persevere to the end. Up to and including the hour of our death. We pray that Blessed Mother be with us now, and at the hour our death. We pray that Saint Joseph, powerful in his example of perseverance, will also be with us at the hour of our death. Saint Wolfgang, pray for us to have your diligence. Help us to have your determination to worthily serve God in a way that is pleasing to Him.

Once we are on our way, being diligent is one thing. But before something is in motion and we can call on diligence to see it through, we must have initiative. How is it we are motivated to start to do something holy? Let us proceed to the eleventh century and learn about Blessed Urban.

Tenth Century Saints

Saints Wenceslaus (d. 936), Matilda of Saxony (d. 968), and Ulric (d. 973), pray for us.

Saint Wolfgang is the patron saint of carpenters, stroke victims, and the paralyzed.
Saint Wolfgang is often depicted with a crozier in the left hand and an axe in the right.
Saint Wolfgang's feast day is October 31st.
Saint Wolfgang, *ora pro nobis* (pray for us).

Tenth Century History

910- The Great Benedictine monastery of Cluny rejuvenates western monasticism. Monasteries soon spread throughout isolated regions of Western Europe.

962- King Otto the Great of East Francia (Germany) was crowned Holy Roman Emperor by Pope John XII at St. Peter's Basilica.

966- Mieszko of Poland converts to Catholicism, beginning the Baptism of Poland.

988- Vladimir the Great is baptized; becomes the first Christian Grand Duke of Kiev, Ukraine.

993- Pope John XV canonizes Ulric of Germany in the first recorded canonization by a pope.[245]

Virtue Challenge #10- Diligence

Saint Wolfgang, thank you for your holy example of being diligent with your faith. Pray to the Lord for us that he may loosen from us the chains of our sins and keep us from all adversity.

Pray for us to be more aware of our vices and the corresponding virtues necessary to increase in holiness. Help us to bring a moral sense to even the darkest places.

Saint Wolfgang, we know the devil schemes for us to be separated from our shepherd through despair and desolation. He wants us to turn to the emptiness of the flesh and the world rather than focus on the spirt and eternal life. Consider the additional steps will you take to protect yourself, and your loved ones, from the lies of the devil. How will you not simply go through the motions, the basic obligations of being a Catholic, by "phoning it in" or "mailing it in"? With today's culture being what it is, what's your plan to step up and draw closer to Christ?

Being objective with yourself, perform an examination of conscience to discern any way that you may have compromised with the devil. How will you guard your soul and address this issue going forward so that it does not happen again? If there is an issue, big or small, where you believe you have sold your soul to the devil, literally or figuratively, what's your next move? How will you make things right with God? Our faith and salvation require effort. In what key area of your spiritual life are you not making sufficient effort?

In what one aspect of your faith will you no longer procrastinate? What holy book have you been meaning to read? What Novena have

---

[245] Delaney, *Dictionary of Saints*, 563.

you put off starting? How will you roll up your sleeves and get to work on your faith today?

In the spirit of being expansive (and not limiting) with your faith:
- List three holy things you will do today to 'get 'er done.'
- List three holy things you will do tomorrow to 'get after it.'

Leaning into Christ, His grace and His mercy, proceed henceforth with Catholic verve, excellence, humility and diligence.

Saint Joseph, Model of workmen, pray for us.
Saint Joseph, Glory of domestic life, pray for us.
Saint Joseph, Pillar of families, pray for us.

Converse for a moment with the Holy Ghost about diligence. My Lord and my God, how may I serve you more faithfully and completely through the virtue of diligence?

O Great Saint Wolfgang, pray that we may live well, and end well, through an increase in holy diligence.

CHAPTER 11

Urban

The Eleventh Century
Initiative

"To convert somebody, go and take them by the hand and guide them."
~ Saint Thomas Aquinas

"When eagles are silent, parrots begin to chatter."
~ Winston Churchill

"The mark of man is initiative..."
~ Ven. Abp. Fulton J. Sheen

"Unless you are willing to do the ridiculous,
God will not do the miraculous."
~ Mother Angelica

The 1000s

When you have an itch, how long does it take to scratch it? When a small rock gets in your shoe, how long does it take to remove it? When you have a room in your home that needs painting, how long is it before that task is completed? When you need to get in shape, how long is it before you commit to a fitness and nutrition program? When your current employment isn't working out for you, how long is it before you start a new job?

In all of the aforementioned examples, there is something that must be done to address a situation. Some are easy. Some are difficult. Some things can be taken care of with little effort and the issue goes away. Some things require additional thought and effort to get to the goal.

Everything that is done, however, begins with initiative. The desire to begin. To instigate due to the belief that the outcome is worthwhile. To commence and then see things through to completion. Making the first move, taking the first step, takes guts. Initiative is when 'when' is now.

In our country, we know that taxes are too high; the United States is involved in "forever wars" with no end in sight; the federal debt continues to expand; illegal aliens continue to come into our nation; abortions continue to happen in America and around the world. In our church we know there is corruption in the clergy that manifests itself through Modernism, and there is the sexual abuse scandal, homosexuality in the clergy, pilfering of Vatican funds, and general lack of Catholic leadership. Numerous consequential issues in the country and in the church need to be addressed. So, what to do? Say it's not my problem, and go about your day like there is nothing you *can* do?

In the twenty-first century, many of us think the cultural rot has never been as bad as it is now. Let's go back in time a thousand years or so to the mid-eleventh century, a time of great ecclesiastical corruption and moral scandal in the church (sound familiar?). Then, as now, those in positions of authority chose not to call out their fellow clergy and put an end to the malfeasance and immoral conduct. The hierarchy "looked the other way." Disgusted by the immoral crises of his day, few in the history of the church have spoken with the mettle of Saint Peter Damien. Asking himself, "Why not me?" he got to work speaking against simony that bought and sold ecclesiastical offices, including the episcopy, the concubinage and marriage common among the clergy, and the "cancer of sodomy," perversion, and pedophilia at the monasteries. Saint Peter Damian fearlessly denounced these evils, threatened the punishments of hell, and petitioned the pope to purify the church with disciplinary measures.

In the *Book of Gomorrah*, Saint Peter Damian writes, "A certain and most abominable and exceedingly disgraceful vice [sodomitic impurity and other unnatural sexual practices] has grown in our region… Alas, it is shameful to speak of it! It is shameful to relate such a disgusting scandal to sacred ears! But if the doctor fears the virus of the plague, who will apply the cauterization? If he is nauseated by those whom he is to cure, who will lead sick souls back to the state of health?… The skilled machination of the devil thus contrives these grades of corruption so that… the more deeply the souls many be plunged into the depths of hell."[246]

Saint Peter Damian was an influential figure who took the initiative and crusaded both for ecclesiastical reform and ending unnatural sexual practices. He was a friend and adviser to both popes and emperors, and was made a bishop, a cardinal, and eventually for his clear and cogent writings, Pope Leo XII in 1823 awarded him the title, "Doctor of the Catholic Church." While the mid-eleventh century had a host of issues with which the church was forced to contend, the initiative shown in the last decade of the century is the focus of this chapter.

Imagine what Pope Urban must have been thinking in the mid-1090s when he considered what to do about the fact that the Seljuk-led Turks were occupying Jerusalem and the Holy Land. The Muslims, moreover, had been occupying the Holy Land since the early 700s—meaning that this was an issue that had been around for centuries and would soon be approaching 400 years. (It is interesting to note that when Augustus Caesar came to power as Roman Emperor, the prophets of Israel too had been silent for 400 years.) Is the 400 years mere coincidence or is there biblical significance behind it? (40 x 10?) I have no idea. Regardless, given the four centuries, would it not have been logical for Urban to say, "This is something that has been around my whole life. Who am I to think I can change the situation?" Or he could have said, "If I proceed with plans to reclaim the Holy Land for Christ, it will result in thousands of men dying; who am I to ask them to lay down their lives for Christ?"

The number of questions going through Urban's mind and the minds of his trusted advisors were surely overwhelming and probably both mentally and physically exhausting. The moral aspects to consider waging war must have been daunting. Yet, even given the long odds, Pope Urban marshalled the initiative and the will to see things through. Urban asked God, "Why not me?" He believed that with the help of God, the Christians would reconquer the Holy Land for Christ. Urban's initiative to reclaim the sacred, now nearly a thousand years later, is indeed an inspiration for us all.

---

[246] Saint Peter Damian, *"The Book of Gomorrah,"* Ite Ad Thoman Books and Media, New Braunfels, TX, 2015, 81-3.

Born to a knightly family in France in 1042, Pope Blessed Urban II, otherwise known as Otto, Odo of Châtillon, or Otho de Lagery, was best known for launching the Crusades. Otto studied under Saint Bruno in Reims. (Bruno is perhaps best known for his quote, "While the world changes, the cross stands firm.") In the 1070s he assisted Pope Gregory VII with reforms in the church. In 1078 he became Cardinal Bishop of Ostia and was Gregory's chief advisor. Urban served as pope from 1088 until his death in 1099.

Urban had to contend with the antipope, Clement III, during his entire pontificate. Clement's antipope tenure spanned a total of four successive popes, with Urban being the third. Pope Gregory VII was the first of the four to butt heads with Clement. The primary issue of disagreement was that Gregory led a movement in the church which opposed the traditional claim of European monarchs to control ecclesiastical appointments. This led to the conflict known as the Investiture Controversy.

The first half of Urban's pontificate was spent in exile, in southern Italy and in France. In late 1093 Urban gained a foothold in Rome, and gradually expanded his power in *Urbs Aeterna,* or "Eternal City," with each successive year. While Urban managed Clement's presence and influence as best he could, he also had the will and initiative to launch the Crusades while facing long odds.

In 1095 Pope Urban II launched the First Crusade or "Holy War" with the primary goal of Christian to re-conquer lands (the sacred city of Jerusalem and the Holy Land) that were taken by the Muslims in the 700s. In March, 1095 Byzantine Emperor, Alexios I Komnenos, requested military support to fight the Turks at the Council of Piacenza. Later that year, at the Council or Clermont, France, Urban agreed to support the effort. His speech, one that would change history, has had several different versions associated with it.[247] The version below is from Robert the Monk. (Note: I omitted a few passages to condense the text.)

"Oh, race of Franks, race from across the mountains, race chosen and beloved by God as shines forth in very many of your works set apart from all nations by the situation of your country, as well as by

---

[247] CBN.com "Calling for the First Crusade," https://www1.cbn.com/spirituallife/calling-for-the-first-crusade

your Catholic faith and the honor of the Holy Church! To you our discourse is addressed and for you our exhortation is intended. We wish you to know what a grievous cause has led us to Your country, what peril threatening you and all the faithful has brought us.

From the confines of Jerusalem and the city of Constantinople a horrible tale has gone forth and very frequently has been brought to our ears, namely, that a race from the kingdom of the Persians, an accursed race, a race utterly alienated from God, a generation forsooth which has not directed its heart and has not entrusted its spirit to God, has invaded the lands of those Christians and has depopulated them by the sword, pillage and fire; it has led away a part of the captives into its own country, and a part it has destroyed by cruel tortures; it has either entirely destroyed the churches of God or appropriated them for the rites of its own religion. They destroy the altars, after having defiled them with their uncleanness. [Urban next lists many of the gruesome, physical atrocities committed against the Christians (not listed here).]

On whom therefore is the labor of avenging these wrongs and of recovering this territory incumbent, if not upon you? You, upon whom above other nations God has conferred remarkable glory in arms, great courage, bodily activity, and strength to humble the hairy scalp of those who resist you.

Let the deeds of your ancestors move you and incite your minds to manly achievements; the glory and greatness of king Charles the Great (Charlemagne), and of his son Louis, and of your other kings, who have destroyed the kingdoms of the pagans, and have extended in these lands the territory of the holy church. Let the holy sepulcher of the Lord our Savior, which is possessed by unclean nations, especially incite you, and the holy places which are now treated with ignominy and irreverently polluted with their filthiness. Oh, most valiant soldiers and descendants of invincible ancestors, be not degenerate, but recall the valor of your progenitors.

But if you are hindered by love of children, parents and wives, remember what the Lord says in the Gospel, "He that loveth father or mother more than me, is not worthy of me." "Every one that hath forsaken houses, or brethren, or sisters, or father, or mother, or wife, or children, or lands for my name's sake shall receive a hundredfold and shall inherit everlasting life." Let none of your possessions detain you, no solicitude for your family affairs... Let therefore hatred depart from among you, let your quarrels end, let wars cease, and let all dissensions and controversies slumber. Enter upon the road to the Holy Sepulcher; wrest that land from the wicked race, and subject it to yourselves. That land which as the Scripture says "floweth with milk and honey," was given by God into the possession of the children of Israel Jerusalem is the navel of the world; the land is fruitful above others, like another paradise of delights. This the Redeemer of the human race has made illustrious by His advent, has beautified by residence, has consecrated by suffering, has redeemed by death, has glorified by burial. This royal city, therefore, situated at the centre of the world, is now held captive by His enemies, and is in subjection to those who do not know God, to the worship of the heathens. She seeks therefore and desires to be liberated, and does not cease to implore you to come to her aid. From you especially she asks succor, because, as we have already said, God has conferred upon you above all nations great glory in arms. Accordingly undertake this journey for the remission of your sins, with the assurance of the imperishable glory of the kingdom of heaven."

When Pope Urban had said these and very many similar things in his urbane discourse, he so influenced to one purpose the desires of all who were present, that they cried out, "Deus Vult! Deus Vult!" "It is the will of God! It is the will of God!" *When the venerable Roman pontiff heard that, with eyes uplifted to heaven he gave thanks to God and, with his hand commanding silence, said:*

"Most beloved brethren, today is manifest in you what the Lord says in the Gospel, "Where two or three are gathered together in my name there am I in the midst of them." Unless the Lord God had been present in your spirits, all of you would not have uttered the same cry. For, although the cry issued from numerous mouths, yet the origin of the cry was one. Therefore, I say to you that God, who implanted this in your breasts, has drawn it forth from you. Let this then be your war-cry in combats, because this word is given to you by God. When an armed attack is made upon the enemy, let this one cry be raised by all the soldiers of God: *"Deus Vult! Deus Vult!"* (It is the will of God! It is the will of God!)

And we do not command or advise that the old or feeble, or those unfit for bearing arms, undertake this journey; nor ought women

228

to set out at all, without their husbands or brothers or legal guardians. For such are more of a hindrance than aid, more of a burden than advantage. Let the rich aid the needy; and according to their wealth, let them take with them experienced soldiers. The priests and clerks of any order are not to go without the consent of their bishop; for this journey would profit them nothing if they went without permission of these. Also, it is not fitting that laymen should enter upon the pilgrimage without the blessing of their priests.

Whoever, therefore, shall determine upon this holy pilgrimage and shall make his vow to God to that effect and shall offer himself to Him as a, living sacrifice, holy, acceptable unto God, shall wear the sign of the cross of the Lord on his forehead or on his breast. When,' truly',' having fulfilled his vow be wishes to return, let him place the cross on his back between his shoulders. Such, indeed, by the twofold action will fulfill the precept of the Lord, as He commands in the Gospel, 'He that taketh not his cross and followeth after me, is not worthy of me.'[248]

Urban's speech in Clermont on that day, where he raised the level of war from *bellum justum* (just war), to *bellum sacrum* (holy war), was so great that the crowd went forth that day with a battle cry, a barbaric yawp, that would be bellowed by the noble nights as they sought to recover the holy ground: "*Deus Vult! Deus Vult!*" (It is the will of God! It is the will of God!).

Urban's speech and call to arms was met with an enthusiastic popular response across all social classes in western Europe. Multitudes of predominantly poor Christians numbering in the thousands, led by Peter the Hermit, a French priest, were the first to respond. In what has become known as the Princes' Crusade, members of the high nobility and their followers embarked in late summer 1096 and arrived at Constantinople between November and April the following year. In total, including noncombatants, the army is estimated to have numbered as many as 100,000.[249]

The crusaders marched into Anatolia, Turkey, while the Seljuk Sultan of Rûm, Kilij Arslan, was away resolving a dispute. The Frankish

[248] Munro, Dana, "Urban and the Crusaders", Translations and Reprints from the Original Sources of European History, Vol 1:2, (Philadelphia: University of Pennsylvania, 1895), 5-8.
[249] "First Crusade," Wikipedia, https://en.wikipedia.org/wiki/First_Crusade

siege and Byzantine naval assault captured Nicea in June 1097. Marching through Anatolia, the crusaders suffered starvation, thirst, and disease before encountering the Turkish lightly armored mounted archers at the Battle of Dorylaeum. The first Crusader state established was the County of Edessa. Antioch was captured in June 1098. Jerusalem was reached in June 1099, and taken by assault from July 7-15, 1099. After this the majority of the crusaders returned home. Four Crusader states were established: the Country of Edessa, the Principality of Antioch, the Kingdom of Jerusalem and the County of Tripoli. The Crusaders stayed in the region in some form until the city of Acre fell almost 200 years later in 1291, leading to the rapid loss of all remaining territory in the area. There were no further substantive attempts to recover the Holy Land after this.[250]

Pope Urban II died on July 29, 1099 A.D., fourteen days after the soldiers of the First Crusade captured Jerusalem. The military campaign was in many ways miraculous, so much so that historians have a difficult time explaining it. One of the keys that confounded the Muslims at the time, and analysts after, was that the Catholics, being in the state of grace and grounded in their faith, fought differently, as if they had no fear of death. Do we live our lives the same way? Do we fear death? Do we cower over a virus?

The Crusaders took Jerusalem because Urban called them, promised victory, and it was in accordance with the will of God. The First Crusade would be followed by nine others. The crusades changed Europe as they championed Christ's message and defended the rights of Christians against the pagan barbarians. For this reason, while Urban is "the most hated pope by enemies inside and outside the Church, he should be the most beloved by all who truly love the true God."[251]

What in our lives are we not doing that we know must be done? Which soul, or souls, in our care or circle need extra attention, charity and love? To which effort should we "stick our neck out" and get involved? No matter if the promptings are small, medium or large, God appreciates those who show some "fire in the belly" to lean into what is difficult and make the effort. Whatever we do in the spirit of

---

[250] Ibid.
[251] Bugnolo, Br. Alexis. "Bl. Urban, Patron of Popes Who Courageously Oppose Anti-popes," *From Rome*, February 6, 2020.

service for Him, God will assist us as much as our success is in accordance with His will.

There are virtually limitless opportunities to leave the safety of our harbor, what we consider to be safe and comfortable, and set sail on voyages for far-away lands. There are virtually limitless battles in which you can choose to engage. There are innumerable ways you can look to modify and adapt how you approach your faith to slay your personal dragons. Whatever your destinations, battles, and dragons may be, show the initiative to begin. Choose your battles wisely, but begin. Don't wait. Don't leave it to someone else to handle. God has motivated you to pick up this cross, at this time, on this issue. Embrace your cross.

Our nation's culture is one of the bigger issues with which we must contend. Culture is in many ways a mirror that reflects *who we are*. The globalist, anti-Christian, secular forces have occupied the primary means of shaping our culture for decades. The media, schools, businesses, etc. have been infiltrated by those pushing a Marxist, anti-God Agenda. While many faithful Catholics despair, know that before Pope Blessed Urban II launched the Crusades, much of southern Europe and the Middle East was occupied by Muslims for hundreds of years. Our nation is not even 300 years old. As Catholics we must understand that a few decades of fighting occupying forces is a comparatively short amount of time given the scope of Catholic history. We must be of firm resolve to never give in to any perceived or actual occupying force. As Catholics we are to be resolute.

The key question for this chapter then is, "What's your Crusade?" You most likely are not in a position to be able to assemble a multi-nation fighting force to right a geopolitical wrong in a foreign land. But what can you do that is right in front of you? Will you encourage a family member who has not gone to Mass, confession and communion in years to once again return to the church, the sacraments, and a state of grace? Will you finally have that candid and charitable conversation with your friends who left the Catholic Church long ago and are now Protestants about returning to the Catholic Church? Will you pick up the phone and call an estranged family member and say, "It's been too long, I'm sorry for what was said. Please forgive me. I don't know what to say next, or where this will all go, but life is short and I love you. You are important to me."

When it comes to a crusade, how will you answer, "Why not me?"

Confront, while being a potentially intimidating word, can also be, potentially, a truly charitable word. Many years ago, I read a quote from Saint Augustine, "true charity must sometimes offend." I have tried many times since to find the origin of the quote, but have been unsuccessful. I am not sure if I wrote the quote down wrong, or if somehow someone paraphrased a longer explanation by the Saint and that's what I recall. Nonetheless, I like how it speaks to charity. The corresponding example is at the top of my mind: When the doctor disinfects a wound, sometimes that act of charity stings initially. But it is needed to heal.

As out Lord said to Saint Faustina, "I am giving you three ways of exercising mercy toward your neighbor: the first - by deed, the second - by word, the third - by prayer. In these three degrees is contained the fullness of mercy, and it is an unquestionable proof of love of me."[252] Is your Crusade in deed, word or prayer? How do we avoid temptation? Regarding those who trespass against us, do we freely and willingly forgive them, or is it more half-heartedly and begrudgingly? How do the Seven Deadly Sins (Pride, Envy, Gluttony, Greed, Lust, Sloth and Wrath) impact your soul? How do you judge yourself in this regard? Which sins in particular are holding you back from being a more holy person? What does your conscience say about your being a trustworthy steward of the Catholic Faith and a member in good standing of the Catholic Church? Where, in your life, is there room for improvement?

How do you show initiative to address the Seven Deadly Sins? How do you shut down the deadly thoughts when they arise? To highlight one deadly sin that relates to initiative, do you suffer in any way from sloth? How can you better spend your free time? Watching more television, or getting off your keister and helping out at the local food pantry? Do you sleep in every Saturday morning instead of regularly showing up to pray and peacefully protest in front of your local abortion facilities? When did you last donate time or supplies to your local Pregnancy Help Center? How many months, or years, has it taken you to start reading that religious book you were so enthused about when you made the original purchase?

---

[252] Kowalska, Saint Maria Faustina, *Dairy*, 742.

God appreciates initiative. In the Bible one can find ninety-two references to initiative.[253] Here are a few:

- *"So, whoever knows the right thing to do and fails to do it, for him it is sin."* James 4:17
- *"All Scripture is breathed out by God and profitable for teaching, for reproof, for correction, and for training in righteousness."* II Timothy 3:16
- *"As it was written in the book of the sayings of Isaias the prophet: A voice of one crying in the wilderness: Prepare ye the way of the Lord, make straight his paths."* Luke 3:4

Do we take the initiative by knowing what is right and doing it? Do we take the initiative to teach, reprove, correct and train in righteousness? Do we make ready the way of the Lord? Do we make straight his path? Do you make the crooked ways straight? Do you make the rough ways smooth? In other words, do we take the initiative to be the Catholics we are called to be?

Sometimes it can feel herculean to take the initiative to encourage a family member, talk with a friend about a critical topic, or phone someone whom you haven't spoken to in a very long time. Such a task can seem harder than launching a multi-nation crusade. We all have our personal Mt. Everest of things we'd rather not do. We kid ourselves that we should let inactive problems remain so, and let the "sleeping dog lie." Deep down you know what must be done. You just presently lack the initiative and will to see things through.

Keep in mind that God has not put anything on your plate, or in your path, that He knows you cannot handle. Your promptings for wanting to reach out, reconcile and right wrongs are coming from a good place. Your fears about reaching out are most likely obstacles, excuses and lies being put in your path by your infernal adversary. Fr. Jacques Philippe explains this further, "The experience of the Church and the saints demonstrates a general law: what comes from the Spirit of God brings with it joy, peace, tranquility of spirit, gentleness, simplicity, and light. On the other hand, what comes from the spirit of evil brings sadness, trouble, agitation, worry, confusion, and darkness. These marks of the good and the evil spirit are unmistakable signs in

---

[253] "Initiative," *Open Bible,* https://www.openbible.info/topics/initiative

themselves."[254] What is agitating, worrying and confusing you at this time? Once you address this or that issue, do you perceive that you would experience joy, peace and light? If so, move forward in faith.

It should be noted that when Catholics make heroic decisions to assemble in His name, the Holy Ghost is present. The need to show initiative to "reclaim the sacred" is once again before us. It is our time to launch the next Crusade. What, in your opinion, needs to be reclaimed? Start in your own soul, with your own dignity, in your own home, with your immediate and extended family, in your circle of friends, in the workplace, in your parish, etc. What must be done? Begin where you are motivated to act upon the initiative that has been inside you for some time. Get underway.

Benjamin Franklin commented, "Never leave till tomorrow that which you can do today." He was right. No amount of genius, talent or good looks can hold a candle to those who operate with initiative, perseverance and diligence. But wait, there's more.

To kick it up a notch, as a Catholic, you have the additional benefit of grace within you. You know the holy spark is inside you. Man is nothing more than a human spark that reflects God. Be a spark that better reflects God in you. Enkindle that spark into a flame and a larger fire. As Saint Catherine of Siena said, "Be who God meant you to be and you will set the world on fire." NOTE: I'm not talking about an ANTIFA urban-riot type of fire. Just the good, old-fashioned, time tested, 'love God and love your neighbor,' type of fire. Show some spark and initiative. Do what you can to conscript all to serving Christ and reclaiming the sacred.

While Urban crusaded against the Seljuk Turks, who occupied the Holy Land in his day, how are we to get along with our Muslim brothers and sisters in the world today? While some associate Muslims with Islamic extremist terrorism, the overwhelming majority of Muslims in the world are not ideological extremists. Do Catholics hold different views about our faith, sin and salvation than Muslims? Of course. Do we wish for them to be converted to Christianity like all non-Catholic faiths? Of course. As Catholics, we do not agree with *sharia* (Islamic law) superseding a nation's civil law. As Catholics, we have issues with *taqiyya* (the Islamic principle of lying to protect or

---

[254] Philippe, Fr. Jacques, *In the School of Holy Spirit,* 51.

advance Islam). As Catholics, we have issues with *hijrah* (the Islamic doctrine of conquest by emigration). As Catholics we know that in over fifty nations, due to *sharia* law, to publicly proclaim the divinity of Jesus Christ is a capital offense and you could be executed or imprisoned. As Catholics, we understand that religious freedom and *sharia* law are incompatible. While we disagree with Muslims on these and several other key regards, we know that each person is created in the image and likeness of God. Therefore, in charity, we pray that our Islamic brothers and sisters may one day know Our Lord and Savior, Jesus Christ and the Catholic faith.

Today, 1.5 billion Muslims make up 22 percent of the world's population. Given the demographic trends in Europe (where many nations now have between 5-10 percent Muslim populations), we can get a look as to what the future may hold for America with regard to Muslim majority towns, counties and states. With Islam, the religious, legal, political, economic, social, and military components make democratic societies particularly vulnerable to Muslim demands for religious privileges. In America, critical Muslim population levels will be reached by 2040-2050. By the end of the century, Muslims are projected to exceed 50 percent of the world population.[255]

Changing demographics will have significant implications for the world's Catholics, and all other religions, in coming decades. How will further threats to religious freedom and persecution manifest themselves going forward? Will it be easier or more difficult to be a faithful Catholic in the United States and around the world in future years? Change is guaranteed. Are we ready?

Speaking of change, what are we to make of the "ecumenical" outreach of the church since Vatican II? More recently, what about Pope Francis' Islamic outreach to the "children of Abraham" with the support of the interfaith Abraham Family House compound in Abu Dhabi, and his visit to the pagan Ziggurat in the ancient Mesopotamian site of Plain of Ur in Iraq? Sure seems the Pope is cozying up to, and indirectly paying homage to, the Tower of Babel. No thank you. The Pope should be preaching the gospel of Jesus Christ and not interfaith nonsense. Instead of visiting a pagan, Muslim shrine, the Pope should be advocating conversion, the suppression of idols, and the destruction

---

[255] Ellis, Mark, "How Islam Progressively Takes Over Countries," *God Reports*, September 23, 2015.

of non-Christian shrines similar to what Pope Saint Gregory the Great advised to King Ethelbert of Kent in 601. Dr. Taylor Marshall asks, "Imagine if Pope Francis would write a letter like that to President Biden?"[256]

In closing, we have before us the opportunity to go on whatever crusade we desire. A crusade, with its basis in religion, is distinct from a cause, something nonreligious. With finite time, resources, and overall bandwidth, to address the confusion in the world, to eliminate the chaos, we must be prudent to put aside the cause and focus primarily on the crusade that we are called to embark upon. May Blessed Urban II help us discern the necessary from the nonessential.

Pope Urban II was beatified a Blessed almost 800 years after his death by Leo XIII on July 14, 1881. The church, 140 years later, has not yet made him a Saint. Given the continued outreach of the church to various leaders of Islam, it is not anticipated that Urban will be declared a saint at any point in the near future.

We turn next to the twelfth century, to England, and the obedience of Thomas Becket.

Eleventh Century Saints

Saints Bernard of Montjoux (d. 1008), Aquilinus of Milan, aka Aquilinus of Cologne (d. 1015), Henry II (d. 1024), Stephen of Hungary (d. 1024), Odilo (d. 1048), Edward (d. 1066), Peter Damian (d. 1072), John Gaulbert (d. 1073), and Canute IV of Denmark (d. 1086), pray for us.

> Blessed Urban is the patron of Popes who oppose anti-Popes.
> Blessed Urban's feast day is to be January 29.
> Blesses Urban, *ora pro nobis* (pray for us).

Eleventh Century History

1000- Stephen I of Hungary become King of Hungary. He would later convert to Roman Catholicism becoming the founder of the Catholic Church of Hungary.

---

[256] Marshal, Dr. Taylor, "Pope Francis' Tower of Babel Ecumenism," Podcast 639. February 25, 2021.

1054- July 16. **Formal schism between the Western and Eastern branches of Catholicism.** The schism would be known as the "East-West Schism." Three legates entered the Cathedral of the Hagia Sophia during Mass on a Saturday afternoon and placed a papal Bull of Excommunication on the altar against the Patriarch Michael I Cerularius. The legates left for Rome leaving behind a city near riots.

Two factors stand out as reasons for the "Great Schism." First, the Western Church asserted that the pope's authority extended over the entire church, including the East. The Eastern Church, however, rejected papal authority. Second, the Western church argued that the Holy Spirit proceeded from both the Father and the Son. The East said that the Holy Spirit proceeded only from the Father.[257]

1091- Blessed Mother in invoked as Our Lady of the Militia in Sicily, Italy appeared in the clouds, driving away the Saracens.

1094- in the ongoing Christian-Moor war on the Iberian Peninsula, El Cid, the national hero of Spain, wins a victory at Valencia.

1095- November 27. Pope Urban II at the Council of Clermont (France) launches the **First Crusade** to retake the Holy Land.

1099- The Crusaders retake Jerusalem, establish Crusader kingdoms, and Latin bishops are appointed to the largely Orthodox dioceses.

Virtue Challenge #11- Initiative

What's your crusade? What's your mountain? Pope Blessed Urban II help us to have the initiative, and courage, necessary to serve Christ in whatever way we are called.

What big undertaking came to mind for you as you read this chapter? Where will the motivation to begin come from? How will you hold yourself accountable as you begin to address that issue? How will you show greater initiative each day in your routine? What's your strategy to pair grace with initiative?

---

[257] "The 10 Most Important Dates in Church History," *Journey Online,*
https://journeyonline.org/the-10-most-important-dates-in-church-history/

Initiative has multiple benefits. For instance, while you can't control everything that happens around you, or to you, you can control how you respond. How will you respond differently to events around you going forward? Being proactive nips problems in the bud. Fear is a trap that prevents you from moving forward. What irrational fears will you address through initiative?

God wants to partner with you as you step out with holy initiative. Given the talents He has given you, what do you believe He is calling you to do? How will you be a role model to others and courageously take that first step towards your goal? *Quo Vadis?* (Where are you going?)

What issue in society urgently needs your taking initiative and getting involved asap? Fighting pornography, drug addition, alcohol abuse, sex trafficking, socialism, corruption in your parish or the larger church? Take your pick. Pray and fight where motivated. Apathy and indifference have no business being associated with faithful Catholics. Choose your crusade, launch, and don't look back.

If you were to be known as the guy/gal who gets things done for the faith, where would you start?

One way to learn about yourself is to take risks. Sometimes making mistakes is an indication that you are stretching and growing. If you don't have the initiative to leap and learn, how will you ever determine your capabilities? Do not hide your light under a bushel. On what issue, or issues, will you be a light in the darkness?

Blessed Urban, pray for us to have the initiative and the discipline to get things done even when we don't feel like engaging let alone completing certain tasks.

Converse for a moment with the Holy Ghost about initiative. My Lord and my God, how may I serve you more faithfully and completely through the virtue of initiative?

O Great Blessed Urban, pray for us an increase in the virtue and grace of holy initiative.

CHAPTER 12

Becket

The Twelfth Century
Obedience

"Obedience is better than sacrifices."

~ The Holy Ghost (1 Kings 15:22)

"You are my friends, if you do the things that I command you."

~ John 15:14

*"Never is the will of God more perfectly fulfilled than
when we obey our superiors."*

~ Saint Vincent de Paul

*"God is the supreme ruler, above Kings.
We ought to obey God rather than men."*

~ Saint Thomas Becket

The 1100s

What was the original, original sin?

God created mankind in His image—in the image of God. Male and female He created them. God blessed them and said: "Be fertile and multiply; fill the earth and subdue it" (Genesis 1:27-28). In the Garden of Eden, man and woman had dominion over the earth. They were given one rule, do not eat of the fruit of this tree. Adam and Eve could have lived in paradise, in harmony with God, if they were obedient and abstained from one thing, but they blew it. They were disobedient and ate the apple. From that point forward man would work, woman would bring forth children in pain, and all their posterity would be forced to contend with original sin. God knows the importance of—and loves in a special way—those who practice faithful obedience.

In the twelfth century alone, there were eleven antipopes. It is amidst this confusion in the church that we make the acquaintance of Saint Thomas Becket, or, Thomas à Becket as he is sometimes called, one of the best-known saints in the English-speaking world. But perhaps knowledge of this man of God, who opposed his friend and King, Henry II over the rights and prerogatives of the Church, is lessening today, and some of what is thought to be true is not true.

The story of Becket and his King, Henry II, was made famous to the modern world through the 1964 film titled *Becket*. Though there are a fair number of historical inaccuracies in the movie, the essential point of conflict is well depicted. It is between King Henry, who thought he had selected an archbishop of Canterbury he could control, and Becket, who upon assuming the office seems to have asked, "Why Not Me?" and taken his episcopal duties seriously.

Becket was born in 1120. After his schooling and sometime in the employ of a relative, he secured a position with the Archbishop of Canterbury Theobold. He was such an effective worker and emissary for the archbishop, going on diplomatic missions for him to France, Rome and elsewhere, that Theobold recommended him to the young King Henry for the position of chancellor.

The two became close, and Becket dedicated his energies to serving his king. He did so ably, even on the battlefield as Becket displayed courage in combat during the king's war in France. Henry loved and trusted him so much that he even sent his son to live in Becket's household.

Becket was not yet a priest. The Church at the time did not function quite like it does today, and the king had the prerogative to name, or nominate at least, whomever he wanted for bishoprics. And so, when Theobold died, the King chose his favorite Thomas Becket to be Archbishop of Canterbury. Becket's nomination was approved by a council of bishops and nobles in May of 1162, and he was ordained a priest on June 2 and consecrated archbishop the following day, June 3.

In the life of a Catholic, the sacraments are among the ordinary means of receiving God's grace. That does not mean there is anything about grace that can be said to be "ordinary." It means that the sacraments convey grace, and we Catholics who lead a sacramental life can receive those graces regularly, in the ordinary course of things. God, however, can bestow his grace in any way he likes, and grace, of course, is a remarkable thing, a miracle in fact. *The Catechism of the Catholic Church* tells us that, "Grace is favor, the free and undeserved help that God gives us to respond to his call to become children of God, adoptive sons, partakers of the divine nature and of eternal life."

In that definition, we see our great opportunity. God gives us help to respond to his call to become His children. Too few of us, however, respond properly to God's grace, and often we see little evidence in day-to-day life of this miracle that occurs within us. Not so with Thomas Becket when he was ordained. For him, the graces of that sacrament changed everything. Thomas truly asked God, "Why not me?" He had been a lover of pleasure, a companion to the king, but now he was a man of God and the change was dramatic. Perhaps few men in history have demonstrated such an abrupt and obvious change upon receiving holy orders. Becket proved the truth of the words of Saint Paul to the Corinthians. "Therefore, if anyone is in Christ, he is a new creation; the old has passed away, behold, the new has come. All this is from God, who through Christ reconciled us to himself." (2 Cor 5:17-18)

But, just as Jesus warned his followers that the world will hate them the more they love and follow him, Henry's love for Becket turned to hate, as his friend and confidante began to place the prerogatives of the Church above those of his king. Becket, for his part, recognized he could not serve two masters and so resigned his chancellorship.

Today, the particular issues on which they clashed can seem difficult to understand. A major point of contention was the right of the State to try clergy in its own courts as opposed to those of the Church. King Henry convened the bishops to a hunting lodge in Clarendon where the sixteen clauses of what became known as the Constitutions of Clarendon were agreed to . . . by all the bishops with one exception. Thomas a Becket.

Becket stood on the principle of benefit of clergy, which held that members of the clergy could only be tried in ecclesiastical courts. The extent to which the barbaric physical punishments meted out by the king's courts versus the comparatively lenient ones administered by the Church, at least physically, may have influenced Becket's thinking on the matter. It is not clear. What is clear is that he stood over and against the power of the State to defend the rights of the Church. When one considers the spiritual measures by which the Church could and did punish or correct her wayward sons, they don't seem so lenient after all, and quite likely were more effective in calling a lost child of God back to him.

Among the other causes Becket opposed for attacking the independence of the Church were the following:

- that no election for vacant bishoprics could occur without the king's permission
- that during the vacancy of those sees, all the revenues attached to them should go to the royal purse
- that no archbishop, bishop or other high churchman should leave the realm without the king's permission
- that no one should be allowed to appeal to Rome with the king's consent
- that all disputes concerning ecclesiastical offices should be decided in the king's court.

In any case, Becket's intransigence on the question infuriated the King, and finally the archbishop offered his consent and took an oath, but refused to sign the documents. Upon returning to Canterbury, Becket repented of his acquiescence and sent the king a recantation of his oath, incurring the wrath of his former friend.

Becket was persecuted the remainder of the year through various charges against him and levees of fines he would be expected to pay. Ultimately, in 1164, Henry had him tried as a traitor. Becket, however, was able to escape to France where he was protected for a time by King Louis VII. In one account of his escape he is said to have lifted his archbishop's cross and made his way through the bishops and others gathered in the king's presence, and, amid the confusion, donned a disguise and sailed away.

He then went to see Pope Alexander III, who refused his resignation. After that Becket sought refuge in the peace of a Cistercian monastery in France. But during this time, Henry continued his persecution of Becket, reaching him by banishing his relatives and confiscating his property. Next, he threatened the Cistercian Order if they continued to harbor the archbishop in exile.

The dispute raged on for a few more years. Papal diplomacy played a role in making it possible for Becket to return to England, but he would soon find himself again faced with a question of principle that would pit him against his king.

Becket, ever vigilant for the rights of the Church, excommunicated three prelates who usurped his own authority by crowning the young heir to the throne, the next Henry. Henry, the king, was at the time at his castle in Burgundy, France. As dramatically depicted in film and books, Henry is reported to have said aloud there, "Will no one rid me of this meddlesome priest?"

Four knights (Reginald Fitzurse, William de Tracy, Hugh de Morville, and Richard le Bret) set out for Canterbury and on December 29, 1170, they set upon Archbishop Thomas Becket in his cathedral and committed one of the most famous and consequential murders in English history. Reportedly, Becket told his fellow clergymen, who were terrified and so tried to bar the door, "It is not right to make a fortress out of a house of prayer," and ordered them to unbolt the doors, allowing his murderers inside.

But Becket was ready. He had defended the rights of the Church and his conscience was clear. When accused by the four men of being a traitor, the saintly archbishop said, "For the name of Jesus, and the protection of the church, I am no traitor, and I am ready to embrace death." The narrative of Becket's murder continues:

'Fitzurse flung down his axe and drew his sword. You pander, you owe me fealty and submission!' exclaimed the archbishop. Fitzurse shouted back, 'I owe no fealty contrary to the King!' and knocked off Thomas' cap. At this, Thomas covered his face and called aloud on God and the saints. Tracy struck a blow, which Grim intercepted with his own arm, but it grazed Thomas' skull and blood ran down into his eyes. He wiped the stain away and cried, 'Into Thy hands, O Lord, I commend my spirit!' Another blow from Tracy beat him to his knees, and he pitched forward onto his face, murmuring, 'For the name of Jesus and in defense of the Church I am willing to die.' With a vigorous thrust Le Bret struck deep into his head, breaking his sword against the pavement, and Hugh of Horsea added a blow, although the archbishop was now dying.[258]

While a thunderstorm took place outside the cathedral, the people inside were trying to process the sacrilege that had just happened. Becket's body lay lifeless and for a time no one approached it. When King Henry heard of the murder, he self-isolated (self-quarantined?) and fasted for forty days. He later offered public penance in the Canterbury Cathedral.

It was discovered that Becket wore a hair shirt under his ecclesiastical garb, a penance he is thought to have begun upon receiving the grace of the sacrament of holy orders. There is evidence of other austerities.

The reaction to the martyrdom of Thomas Becket was swift. Miracles were reported and Canterbury soon became one of the preeminent sites of pilgrimage in not just England, but in all of Christendom. It would serve as the inspiration, too, for one of the greatest works of English literature, Chaucer's *Canterbury Tales*. Thomas Becket was canonized a little over two years after his death and remains an inspiration for all Catholics who stand for their rights in the public square.

Thomas Becket's martyrdom changed the course of history with numerous constitutional limitations being instituted regarding the power of the state over the Church. Forty-five years after Becket's death, the Magna Carta of 1215 would declare: "[T]he English church shall be free, and shall have its rights undiminished and its liberties unimpaired." Just over 600 years after Becket's death, America's first President George Washington would proclaim, "All possess alike liberty of conscience and immunities of citizenship" and that "it is now no more that toleration is spoken of, as if it was by the indulgence of one class of people, that another enjoyed the exercise of their inherent natural rights."

While Saint Thomas Becket is one of the higher profile saints to be discussed in *Against the Grain*, he was selected not because he was an advisor to kings; nor that he was a bishop, or a great statesman, though all true and impressive. Instead, he was chosen primarily as the

---

258 "Saint Thomas Becket," *Catholic Online*, https://www.catholic.org/saints/saint.php?saint_id=12

saint for this century solely for his unwavering obedience to God. Obedience amidst the crushing pressures of the state. Becket no doubt could have continued with a life of position and had a very comfy existence if he would have betrayed his conscience and simply given in. Why did he not deliver to the king what he wanted? Why would Becket choose to defy Henry? For the simple, yet profound, rationale "God is the supreme ruler, above Kings" and "we ought to obey God rather than men."

What are we to make of obedience to those in authority, especially to those with whom we disagree? If they ask you to do something immoral and betray your conscience, resist. If what they ask is not immoral, obey. Saint Francis de Sales has said, "Saint Paul commands us to obey all superiors, even those who are bad. Our Blessed Saviour, His Virgin Mother, and Saint Joseph have taught us this kind of obedience in the journey they took from Nazareth to Bethlehem, when Caesar published an edict that his subjects should repair to the place of their nativity to be enrolled. They complied with this order with obedience, though the Emperor was a pagan and an idolator, so desirous was Our Lord of showing us that we should never regard the persons of those who command, provided they be invested with sufficient authority."

Saint John Bosco informs us, "Many people [in authority] oppose us, persecute us, and would like even to destroy us, but we must be patient. As long as their commands are not against our conscience, let us obey them, but when the case is otherwise, let us uphold the rights of God and of the Church, for those are superior to all earthly authority."

Pope Saint Gregory the Great, Doctor of the Church, adds, "By the other virtues, we offer God what we possess; but by obedience, we offer ourselves to Him. They who obey are conquerors, because by submitting themselves to obedience they triumph over the Angels, who fell through disobedience."

We all, through original sin, have issues to one degree or another, with pride and subsequently with obedience. Fighting pride and practicing greater obedience, play key roles in our spiritual development. A truism is that the fruit of disobedience never advances us spiritually. Obedience, properly practiced, counters pride of life.

Contrary to what the world tells us and tempts us with, obedience is a gateway that allows us greater freedom.

In our own lives, how were we disobedient today? What about yesterday? To look at this from another direction, each day do we do what we ought? As Catholics, do we go against the grain of the world as necessary? Or do we push God to the side, neglecting His holy promptings, and obey our own whims or those of other people? It's hard most of the time to obey God. Most often obeying God somehow involves sacrifice. We humans have a hard time with sacrifice. The instantaneous gratification offered by society is at war with sacrifice. Obeying men is much easier, right? A simplistic example is that indulging our thoughts and wants is akin to eating sugar. It provides a momentary rush, but the sugar crash afterwards is not so much fun.

Two quick tweets for you. First, @EricRSammons, "A false understanding of obedience is a far greater problem in the Church today than disobedience."[259] @EdLatimore, "Most people don't want freedom. They want security. They don't want choices. They want directions."[260] Most people want *easy*. Hard is *difficult*. Have no regrets. Regrets last a lifetime. Failure hurts for a short while. Seek a true understanding of obedience. Remember Catholics, we are stronger, much stronger, than the world gives us credit for.

How often do we simply give in and go along with the crowd? How often do we compromise our values to be accepted? How often do we let stand an inappropriate joke or look the other way when someone has acted unethically at work? When on the internet, how often do we pursue a click-bait trail that offends God? How often do we vote for a pro-abortion candidate because we tell ourselves he or she is pretty good with their other policy positions? How often do we give in to the unjust, immoral dictates of the state?

How often do we accept and do nothing about our flawed and enervated church leadership and their feeble attempts to address sexual abuse, doctrinal abuse, or financial impropriety in the church? What do we do when they close or restrict our churches amidst flu season? What do we do when they instruct us to violate our consciences and

---

[259] @EricRSammons, Twitter post April 26, 2021,
https://twitter.com/EricRSammons/status/1386691726442733573
[260] @EdLatimore, Twitter post December 29, 2020,
https://twitter.com/EdLatimore/status/1343950217213829121

receive communion in the hand rather than on the tongue? Obedience or disobedience?

Do we pray enough for our priests and bishops? Do we provide respectful, fraternal correction regarding issues on which they have erroneously spoken and taken positions? The Catholic Church is not a democracy. Understood. Saint Athanasius taught us that obedience to disobedience is wrong. Obedience to error is error, no? Violation of conscience comes in many shapes, sizes and circumstances. We must be vigilant.

The state loves compliant, malleable bishops. Saint Thomas Becket epitomizes a bishop, and, hence, the church, standing up to a tyrant. On a scale of 1-10, with 1 being no resistance and 10 being maximum resistance, when warranted, what is your perception of how the bishops in the USA stand up to the federal and state governments? How outspoken are our bishops on the issues that matter most to Catholics? Concerning policy proposals that are contrary to church teaching, do our shepherds instruct their flocks on issues of grave moral matters? Or are they largely silent and ineffective? Of the roughly 450 active and retired bishops in the USA, how many would Saint Thomas Becket speak approvingly of with regard to their taking stands against the state on abortion, homosexual civil union, or religious liberty? Out of the 450 bishops, do even 1 percent of American bishops lead their diocese in the tradition of Saint Thomas Becket? If not, why not? The overwhelming lot of bishops today are nothing short of spiritual criminals.

With our culture crumbling and society falling apart, with sixty-five million surgical abortions and counting, crime rates skyrocketing, prisons overflowing, cohabitation at record levels, illegitimacy soaring, marriages down, etc., who among the American bishops would our elected leaders point at and say, "Will no one rid me of this meddlesome priest?" Who's making a ruckus? In an ideal world 100 percent of the bishops would present a united front in defense of God and the Catholic faith. But sadly, are even 2 or 3 percent of the bishops in the U.S. outspoken, yet alone effective? Who is the most effective bishop representing Catholic values at the national level? Regional level? State level? Does anyone come to mind?

What about obedience from the bishops to Rome? In 2004, one year before Cardinal Ratzinger became pope, when he was the Prefect of the Sacred Congregation for the Doctrine of the Faith, Fr. James Altman shares that, "Ratzinger issued specific instructions to the U.S. bishops that they shall not distribute communion to pro-abort politicians. Cardinal McCarrick hid that from the USCCB, and said it was up to each individual Bishop what he would do in his own diocese. That was not the truth."[261] It was not obedience, and look at the fallout since.

Coming at obedience from a different angle, what are the obligations of the lay faithful to be obedient to a pope or bishop when what they say or write (not *ex cathedra*) is not in accordance with Church tradition? How are we to respond? Are we to obey the pope over God? Are we to obey a pope over Church Tradition, or truth? There is a hierarchy of obedience. As Venerable Fulton Sheen has spoken, "a chemical cannot tell a plant what to do, a plant cannot tell an animal what to do, an animal cannot tell a person what to do, and a person does not tell God what do to. There is a divine order to life. A lower being cannot tell a superior being how to act."[262] When there is conflict on who to obey, we go to the higher source. God, Tradition (Magisterium), pope, bishop, priest.

Archbishop Carlo Maria Viganò is clear on the issue of obedience commenting, "Let us not forget that as Catholics we have a very great responsibility, both towards our pastors as well as towards those who govern us. Our obedience can and must cease in the moment in which we are asked to obey sinful laws or laws contrary to the unchanging Magisterium of the Church."[263]

When discussing Thomas Becket, we can fast forward several centuries to draw parallels to the time of Henry VIII. As Henry II had his "meddlesome priest," so too did Henry VIII. The thorns in his side? Saint John Fisher and Saint Thomas More. Of all the nonsense proposed by Henry VIII, no bishops in the British Isles spoke out against him, save Fisher and More. Saint Thomas More famously said, "I do not care if I have against me all the bishops, I have with me all

[261] "Fr. Altman Shares the Path Forward After 2020." *Alpha News*. You Tube posted January 14, 2021. https://www.youtube.com/watch?v=MSmnqYcrO0A&t=2118s

[262] Sheen, Archbishop Fulton, "The True Meaning of Christmas," Original Airing 1956. YouTube posted June 23, 2014. https://www.youtube.com/watch?v=sOvlFDqOusE

[263] Viganò, Archbishop Carlo Maria, "COVID agenda aims to destroy national sovereignties and the divine mission of the Church," *LifeSite News*, Original interview in *Deutsche Wirtschaftsnachrichten*, March 28, 2021.

the Saints and the doctors of the Church." Where are today's Beckets, Fishers and Mores? Who speaks with great clarity and candor to secular leadership? Who defends God and the Magisterium?

Where are the bishops who fought vocally and vociferously to keep the churches in their diocese open during the Wuhan Virus? Or did they all quickly cave to the state and lock the churches? Did the bishops follow the magnificent, supreme law of the church, or the pedestrian law of the state? Which bishop(s) permitted the faithful to receive the sacraments? Confession? Communion? Anointing of the Sick? If it is safe for people to be in big box retailers, then it OK for people to be church in proportionately acceptable numbers. The bishops will be accountable to God.

The world will tell you that speaking the truth is "divisive." The implication being that because the truth is divisive, don't speak it. Keep in mind, however, that not speaking the truth is dividing people from a closer union with God. Hence, the rub. Our obedience to make disciples of all nations is more important than the number of "likes" one may accumulate on social media. Dr. Taylor Marshall stated on his podcast ("Evil Bishops Make Evil Rules: Label as Divisive Rule (LAD Rule)"), that priests can say what they want about the gospels, and make other questionable statements, but if a Traditional Priest steps out of line he is censured with Canon Law, and will perhaps be suspended. He is then LAD- "Labelled as Divisive..."[264]

Marshall continues, "there are moral, doctrinal, sexual and financial scandals in the church, as well as heresy and confusion. If a priest of lay person points to the immorality and scandal in the church, the Bishops 'label as divisive' (LAD). They say, 'You are divisive. You are a bad person. We are pastoral. They LAD people to destroy their enemies. The LAD playbook is their plan, their strategy, and they do it over and over. People are labelled rigid, extremist, or see things too black and white. The church says it has progressed. Doctrine has evolved. God is more merciful. You are a conspiracy theorist. You are a traditionalist- a rad trad (radical traditionalist). You can never make them happy. So, what's the answer to all this? The Bishops are most likely embarrassed and scared of what they know about all the scandal in the church. Being effeminate is failing to do the hard things- you

---

[264] Marshall, Dr. Taylor, "Evil Bishops Make Evil Rules: Label as Divisive Rule (LAD Rule)," Podcast 572, December 1, 2020.

don't want to do the difficult thing. So, you don't. You do the easy thing. They label those pointing out mess and scandal as divisive, and say we are pastoral."[265]

We live in a time of choosing between pro-God and anti-God, between patriots and anti-patriots. Life and anti-life. Stand with America. Or fall with globalism. And soon perhaps even between human dignity and no human dignity. Be a witness to our faith. What hardship are you prepared to face? What are you prepared to do to enter heaven? Use the small tests of faith that are put before us each day, permitted by God, as training for the larger sacrifices and tests you may encounter down the road.

Where most would be hesitant to name names, in the spirit of Becket, Fisher and More, I present an abbreviated list of the few in the church these days that are on my radar:

- Tier 1- Archbishop Carlo Maria Viganò; Bishop Athanasius Schneider; Fr. James Altman (LaCrosse, WI)
- Tier 2- Cardinal Raymond Leo Burke, Cardinal Gerhard Ludwig Müller; Bishop Strickland; Fr. Chad Ripperger, Fr. John Zuhlsdorf "Fr. Z"
- Tier 3- Cardinal Sarah; Archbishop Cordileone; Bishop Paprocki; Monsignor Charles Pope; Fr. Frank Pavone (speaking on pro-life matters), Fr. Richard Heilman (Madison, WI)

On the other hand, who among church leadership confuse the most? Pope Francis; Uncle "Ted's (McCarrick) nephews" like Cardinals Cupich and Tobin; Cardinals Dolan and Gregory; and Fr. James Martin, SJ.

We are awash in an ocean of rationalization and justification for being obedient to the world and not to God. Do we disengage from the fight due to its enormity? Or do we fight because it is our duty to be obedient to God? Who among us will step up? Who among us would our government or church hierarchy say is meddlesome (but in a good way)?

In the American Revolution it is said that just 3 percent of the citizenry took up arms to fight for freedom. In most parishes less than

---

[265] Ibid.

3 percent of congregants are involved in helping the parish function at a basic level. In August 2019, it was reported that less than 20 percent of baptized Catholics attend Mass regularly, and that approximately 70 percent of Catholics do not believe in the real presence of Jesus Christ in the Eucharist.[266] What is going on with these percentages? Why the malformation, indifference, and apathy? Saint Maximilian Kolbe has said, "The most deadly poison of our times is indifference." Who's to blame? More importantly, who will do what to address the issue?

Catholics, like most people, choose comfort, complacency and non-challenging behavior over obedience and consequence. That dynamic needs to change. To state the obvious, people are not obedient. We do not respect authority. We lack moral fortitude to do what is right—what is, or may be, difficult. People fold with not much prompting. We are soft. As long as we can pick up a family meal chicken bucket on the way home from work and watch vapid TV shows and play vacuous video games, we're good. Most of us do what we can to avoid taking responsibility for our nation and for our church. We are complacent.

Where does moral courage come from? Tracing courage back to its roots, we follow the vine back to God, our maker. Obedience to God permits us to stay connected to him, the true vine, and gain nourishment in the form of moral strength and courage. The decision that must be made is one of obedience. Yes or no? Do we serve God, or the world? Do we stand with God, or man? Do we kneel before God in humility and filial devotion to his will, or do we kneel at the altar of more friends on social media, a bigger paycheck, a bigger home, a bigger bucket of chicken?

In other words, do we live lives of integrity in service to God or are we merely content to be compromised by consumerism, vices, or other distractions that mean nothing toward our eternal salvation?

Life is short, eternity isn't. We must choose better. Let us make a firm purpose of amendment to be more obedient to God and not to man. It's OK that we will be in the minority. Be OK with that. It's OK that some of our relationships and worldly ambitions will be negatively impacted. Think not of what you will be losing but that which you will

---

[266] Pattison, Mark. "Pew survey shows majority of Catholics don't believe in 'Real Presence,'" *National Catholic Reporter,* August 8, 2019.

be gaining. Do not continue to give in to the world telling you how you must conform and sell out to fit in, get along and be accepted. Think more about the freedom you will gain by your steadfast obedience to the Holy Trinity. Think about the true freedom to be found in Christ rather than the false freedom found away from Christ. Be the son or daughter of God you are called to be. Draw upon the heroic virtue that has been dormant inside you for far too long. Tap into your Catholic heritage and fully act like the baptized and confirmed Catholic you are. Live more fully. Be alive to God.

Let us embrace these gems of wisdom from our friends, the saints, about obedience:

> "Oh! how sweet and glorious is the virtue of obedience, by which all other virtues exist, because it is the offspring of charity! On it is founded the rock of faith; it is a queen, whom he that espouses is rich in every kind of good and whom no evil can assail."
>
> - Saint Catherine of Siena, Doctor of the Church

> "Obedience unites us so closely to God that in a way transforms us into Him, so that we have no other will but His. If obedience is lacking, even prayer cannot be pleasing to God."
>
> - Saint Thomas Aquinas

> "Without a doubt, obedience is more meritorious than any other penance. And what greater penance can there be than keeping one's will continually submissive and obedient?"
>
> - Saint Catherine of Bologna

> "One of the greatest graces for which I feel myself indebted to Our Lord is, that His Divine Majesty has given me the desire to be obedient; for in this virtue I find most consolation and contentment, it being that which Our Lord recommended by His own example more than any other, and on this account I desire to possess it more than anything else in the world."
>
> - Saint Teresa of Avila, Doctor of the Church

> "I often thought my constitution would never endure the work I had to do, (but) the Lord said to me: 'Daughter, obedience gives strength.'"

"On each occasion I say: 'Lord, thy will be done! It's not what this or that one wants, but what You want me to do.' This is my fortress, this is my firm rock, this is my sure support."

- Saint John Chrysostom

"It is not hard to obey when we love the one whom we obey."

- Saint Ignatius

"Obedience is a virtue of so excellent a nature, that Our Lord was pleased to mark its observance upon the whole course of His life; thus, He often says, He did not come to do His Own will, but that of His Heavenly Father."

- Saint Francis of Sales, Doctor of the Church

"Naturally, we all have an inclination to command, and a great aversion to obey; and yet it is certain that it is more for our good to obey than to command; hence perfect souls have always had a great affection for obedience, and have found all their joy and comfort in it."

- Saint Francis of Sales, Doctor of the Church

"I know the power obedience has of making things easy which seem impossible."

- Saint Teresa

"The power of obedience! The lake of Gennesareth had denied its fishes to Peter's nets. A whole night in vain. Then, obedient, he lowered his net again to the water and they caught 'a huge number of fish.' Believe me: the miracle is repeated each day."

- Saint Josemaría Escrivá

"Obedience is mission: "I have come into this world to do the will of my Father, who has sent me." Where there is no obedience, there is no virtue; where there is no virtue there is no good; where good is wanting, there is no love, there is no God; where God is not, there is no Heaven."

- Saint Padre Pio

The devil in his pride is rightfully fearful of those who have humility. He understands all too well that humility is a gateway to obedience which is a superhighway to trust in the Lord. Fr. Richard Heilman from Wisconsin talks about, "Going Weapons H.O.T." The H.O.T. being an acronym for Humility, Obedience and Trust. Humility before God. Obedience to God. And Trust in God. When engaging in spiritual combat, going weapons H.O.T. is essential.

Besides Jesus, when we think of humility, whom do we next think of for her example? Blessed Mother. Her humility, obedience, and trust were all front and center the moment she gave her consent at the Annunciation, "Behold, I am the handmaid of the Lord; be it done to me according to your word." (Lk 1: 38) Fr. Ed Broom, OMV writes, "Mary displayed an admirable attitude of obedience to the Word of God and trust in His holy will. When we are tempted to rebel and turn against God, let us, through Mary's prayers and example, obey God like Mary, and like Jesus who 'was obedient to death, even death on the cross.'"(Phil 2: 8)[267]

Be less concerned about what the world thinks of you and more concerned with what God thinks of you via holy obedience. In the end, being candid with yourself, you know that accumulating and coveting is worthless. Serving God is priceless. Throughout the day, be more aware of the promptings of your Holy Guardian Angel. Say the Angelus faithfully. Each evening before you retire, perform an Examination of Conscience and then say a good Act of Contrition. All in a spirit of obedience to God the Father. In the *12 Steps to Holiness and Salvation*, Saint Alphonsus discusses obedience by writing that it is "more meritorious to pick up straw from the ground, out of obedience, than from self-will to make a long meditation or scourge ourselves to blood."[268]

The first step, or couple of steps, towards a more obedient life may be difficult. But you know the reward is so worth it. Let go of whatever is holding you back. Take that first step. Then the next step. Be a stronger link in the Communion of Saints, assent to Dogma, be united to the Deposit of Faith. It's time to step up. No more excuses. We need you. Our team (country and church) needs a better effort from all. In case you haven't looked outside lately, the world is kicking

---

[267] Broom, Fr. Ed, "Imitate Our Lady's Ten Principal Virtues," *Catholic Exchange,* February 23, 2021.
[268] Liguoiri, 12 Steps, 109.

our butt. Godlessness is on the rise. Heretical and confused Catholics are everywhere. Socialism is on the march in most nations. Immorality in media is omnipresent. In sum, the anti-God forces are brazened in their strategy and tactics. Time for faithful Catholics to stand up and step out in obedience to God and fight. Fight for our faith. Fight to be holy. Fight to serve God.

A key to fighting is learning to say *no*. No to temptation, giving in, weakness, lust, anger, bitterness, laziness, sloth, and in general just being soft. Quit it. We live in a time that is ripe for faithful Catholics to more fittingly engage in the spiritual battle of our day. The time for cowardice and retreating is long gone. The saints in heaven are rooting for us and will cheer us on every step of the way. Reclaim the sacred. Deus vult! (God wills it!)

As Saint Thomas Becket was so integral to religious liberty in multiple nations throughout the world, and in particular to the American experiment, President Trump, on the 850th anniversary of the martyrdom of Saint Thomas Becket, issued a Presidential Proclamation.

Here are a few excerpts:

NOW, THEREFORE, I, DONALD J. TRUMP, President of the United States of America, by virtue of the authority vested in me by the Constitution and the laws of the United States, do hereby proclaim December 29, 2020, as the 850th anniversary of the martyrdom of Saint Thomas Becket. I invite the people of the United States to observe the day in schools and churches and customary places of meeting with appropriate ceremonies in commemoration of the life and legacy of Thomas Becket.

… As Americans, we were first united by our belief that "rebellion to tyrants is obedience to God" and that defending liberty is more important than life itself. If we are to continue to be the land of the free, no government official, no governor, no bureaucrat, no judge, and no legislator must be allowed to decree what is orthodox in matters of religion or to require religious believers to violate their consciences. No right is more fundamental to a peaceful, prosperous, and virtuous society than the right to follow one's religious convictions.

… On this day, we celebrate and revere Thomas Becket's courageous stand for religious liberty and we reaffirm our call to end religious persecution worldwide… We pray for religious believers everywhere who suffer persecution for their faith. We

especially pray for their brave and inspiring shepherds, like Cardinal Joseph Zen of Hong Kong and Pastor Wang Yi of Chengdu, who are tireless witnesses to hope.

To honor Thomas Becket's memory, the crimes against people of faith must stop, prisoners of conscience must be released, laws restricting freedom of religion and belief must be repealed, and the vulnerable, the defenseless, and the oppressed must be protected. The tyranny and murder that shocked the conscience of the Middle Ages must never be allowed to happen again. As long as America stands, we will always defend religious liberty. A society without religion cannot prosper. A nation without faith cannot endure — because justice, goodness, and peace cannot prevail without the grace of God.[269]

"A nation without faith cannot endure." Whether Republican, Democrat or Independent, America's social fabric, and our collective success, is more intertwined with faith and religious liberty than most realize. The Obama administration went after people of conscience, including the Little Sisters of the Poor and Hobby Lobby for objectionable coverages in the health care mandates. The Biden administration has suggested they will go after people of conscience. Despite Saint Thomas Becket's martyrdom and the significant progress made over the centuries regarding religious liberty, the threat to religious liberty in twenty-first century America and elsewhere around the world remains all too real.

In a widely circulated homily touching on Saint Thomas Becket, Fr. Jeffrey Kirby of Our Lady of Grace Parish in Lancaster, South Carolina, warned Americans who believe in God of the "dark" four years they have before them under a Biden administration. Fr. Kirby stated he believed an assault on religious freedom will especially target Christians, resulting in persecution. "We have a dark four years coming as a Church, and we need to get ready," said Fr. Kirby. "Some of you, I know, voted for someone who is now going to suffer (hurt) and persecute the Church for the next four years. That on top of the fact that he supports the utter slaughter of the unborn!" he said. Then raising his voice Fr. Kirby asks, "What have you done? What have you done to your Church?"[270]

---

[269] Trump, Donald. "Proclamation on 850th Anniversary of the Martyrdom of Saint Thomas Becket," *The White House*, December 28, 2020.
[270] Baklinski, Pete. "Catholic priest in inspiring message of hope tells Christians how to survive 'evil' Biden administration," *LifeSite News*, January 7, 2021.

Fr. Kirby called Saint Becket a "providential figure" for Christians regarding "what we are called to do" during the Biden administration. "It is now time for us to find our voice. It is once again important that we see the heroism of this martyr and find in our hearts the strength and the grace to speak the truth and to find that fortitude in ourselves," he said. "Never forget that the only thing evil needs to succeed is for good people to remain quiet. The only thing that evil needs to conquer is for holy people to remain quiet. So, find your voice. Say a few prayers to Saint Thomas Becket. And then begin to speak the truth."[271]

Saint Thomas Becket spoke the truth in obedience to God. He paid the ultimate price of martyrdom. In our time we too need to speak the truth in obedience to God. Only God knows our fate, but we can rely on the holy example of the saints who blazed a trail before us. Often times obedience to God, conforming our will to Him, and not the world, requires significant courage. With God's grace, may we be faithful in holy obedience to Him.

Let us next enter the "Dark Ages" and the unique courage for the faith exhibited by the "not born" Mercedarian, Saint Peter Nonnatus, in the thirteenth century.

Twelfth Century Saints

Saints Bruno (d. 1101), Anselm (d. 1109), Isidore (d. 1130), Norbert (d. 1134), and Bernard of Clairvaux (d. 1153), pray for us.

Saint Thomas Becket is the patron saint of priests.
Saint Thomas Becket is often depicted with a sword through a mitre.
Saint Thomas Becket's feast day is December 29.
Saint Thomas Becket, *ora pro nobis* (pray for us).

---

[271] Ibid.

Twelfth Century History

1119- "The Poor Fellow-Soldiers of Christ and of the Temple of Solomon, also known as the **Knights Templar,** were a Catholic military order founded in 1119, headquartered in Jerusalem. The Templars became a favored charity throughout Christendom, growing rapidly in membership and power. Templar knights, in their distinctive white mantles with a red cross, were among the most skilled fighting units of the Crusades. Non-combatant members of the order, estimated at 9 percent of membership managed a large economic infrastructure throughout Christendom, developing financial techniques that were an early form of banking. Building a network of nearly 1,000 commanderies (administrative properties) and fortifications across Europe and the Holy Land they arguably forming the world's first multinational corporation.[272]

1147-49- Second Crusade.

1150- Publication of *Decretum Gratiani,* a guide to canon law for centuries, until 1918.

1163- **Council of Tours** names the Albigneses, a neo-Manichaean sect, that began in Southern France, The Albigensian Heresy. It was not one heresy, but many. The primary heresy advocated that a good deity created the spirit world, and an evil deity created the material world, including the human body itself.

1184- The **first formal Inquisition** established in France to combat religious dissent, particularly among the Cathars and Waldensians. The inquisitorial courts from this time until the mid-fifteenth century are together known as the Medieval Inquisition.

1187- October 2. The Siege of Jerusalem prompts the Third Crusade.

1189/92- Third Crusade.

1189/90- The **Teutonic Knights**, formally House of the Hospitalers of Saint Mary of the Teutons in Jerusalem are formed. The Germanic order originally was created to nurse the sick and provide hospital care to Christians in the Middle East, then Eastern Europe in

---

[272] "Knights Templar," Wikipedia, https://en.wikipedia.org/wiki/Knights_Templar

1211, and then Prussia in 1225. The Teutonic Order's rule in Prussia would come to an end in 1525, when the territory became under Protestant influence. In 1809 under Emperor Napoleon, who was at war with Austria, declared the order to be dissolved and distributed most of its remaining lands among other principalities. In 1834 the Austrian emperor reestablished the order in Vienna, as an ecclesiastical institution. Today, headquarters of the order are in Vienna, where it maintains a church and archives. Branch houses also exist in Bavaria, Hesse, and the Italian Tyrol.[273]

1198- Pope Innocent III elected pope. His pontificate is often considered the height of the temporal power of the papacy.

Virtue Challenge #12- Obedience

Be obedient. Whatever the fallout from saying no to man and yes to God, do it. Commit more resolutely to your faith. In all likelihood, you will be called arrogant, inflexible, and combative. So be it. Be watchful; if by being obedient and you happen to become prideful, reverse course. Become once again tethered to God in humility so that you may become as honey and not vinegar in your social circles. In a spirit of humility, petition Blessed Mother by saying the Angelus morning, noon and night. Her "fiat," was a turning point in world history. Her being obedient and "letting it be unto me" was a game changer in our salvation. By being obedient to God, what will be your turning point? What will be your game changer?

Blessed Mother, most obedient, pray for us.

Do you have the guts to order your soul in true preparation for eternity? If yes, God bless. If no, making excuses or blaming God, the church, or your specific situation isn't going to help anyone. Dig deep. Draw upon the graces infused into your soul through the Sacraments of Baptism, Confirmation, Holy Communion and Confession. The ember is there. The grace is there. Serve God more faithfully my brother or sister in Christ. Resolve today to be the Catholic you know you want and are called to be.

---

[273] "Teutonic Order," *Britannica*, https://www.britannica.com/topic/Teutonic-Order

How will your life and your family be positively impacted if you buckle down and be more obedient to God? What bad habit(s) or misdirected instinct(s) do you need to reexamine and or jettison altogether?

To whom, to what or where in your life do you need to say, "No" rather than taking the easier, perhaps indulgent, path? What aspect of your life deserves greater loyalty to God?

By being more obedient to God, how will you amplify the better angel of your nature? As you are more obedient to the holy prompting of your guardian angel, how will your day, or life, change for the better?

God the Father dwells in your heart, memory, intellect, and even your imagination. Imagine the state of your soul, one year from today, if you were to live a life that was consistently obedient to the grace that God infuses into your heart, mind and soul. Do you not feel the calling to live as a more faithful Catholic? Imagine.

Where will you lower your net today? Tomorrow? What small (or large) miracle will you experience in your life each day as a result of your saying *Serviam* (I will serve) to God?

Saint Joseph, most obedient, pray for us.

Heart of Jesus, made obedient unto death, have mercy on us

Pray today that we may be more like Saint Michael the Archangel in our obedience to God and defend Christ's teachings.

Converse for a moment with the Holy Ghost about obedience. My Lord and my God, how may I serve you more faithfully and completely through the virtue of obedience?

O Great Saint Thomas Becket, pray for us an increase in the virtue and grace of holy obedience.

CHAPTER 13

Nonnatus

The Thirteenth Century
Courage

"Have I not commanded you? Be strong and of good courage; be not frightened, neither be dismayed; for the Lord your God is with you wherever you go."

~ Joshua 1:9

"… whoever wishes to be great among you will be your servant; whoever wishes to be first among you will be the slave of all. For the Son of Man did not come to be served but to serve and to give his life as a ransom for many."

~ Mark 10: 44-45

"We shall steer safely through every storm, so long as our heart is right, our intention fervent, our courage steadfast, and our trust fixed on God."

~ Saint Francis de Sales

"Though a person shall have bestowed an immense treasure in alms, he has done nothing equal to him who has contributed to the salvation of a soul. This is greater alms than ten thousand talents; than this whole world, how great soever it appears to the eye; for a man is more precious than the whole world."

~ Saint John Chrysostom

The 1200s

Set in Chicago, the 1991 movie *Backdraft* starred William Baldwin, Kurt Russell, Robert DeNiro and Donald Sutherland. It portrayed the bravery, courage and sacrifice of firefighters in a way that resonated in an odd way with me—including the scene at the end of the film with the massive fire fighter funeral complete with bagpipes, hundreds of marchers in uniform, and heavy emotion. Little did I know that I, too, would march in a firefighter funeral paying tribute to a fallen colleague a decade later.

261

About two years after Mary and I moved to Western Springs, an otherwise quiet, almost Mayberryish suburb of Chicago, I enrolled as a probationary firefighter in the village's all-volunteer fire department. Our class of a dozen recruits would meet once a week to learn safe fire fighter procedures and protocols. At the end of the course we were to take an exam to be certified "Fire Fighter II" and cleared to respond to fire calls in the village. Towards the end of our training, we had the opportunity to practice in a "tear down" house in the Village. I remember my heart rate escalating as I went into that house. It was filled with fake smoke to simulate conditions for us as we searched the bedrooms utilizing the leg sweep technique searching for the department dummy. After each search team had their turn, we were allowed back in the house to practice mule kicks in the drywall. So fun.

Firefighter Grane with daughter Gabi

On Monday, May 14, 2001, I was at work and not feeling all that well. I went home a bit early, decided I was not up for the fire training that night, and called in sick. Tuesday morning I awoke to find messages that Willard, a fellow recruit, had passed away Monday night after a tragic training accident. Each recruit was to walk up the 105-foot aerial ladder (elevated at 65 degrees) and then come back down the ladder. From what I was told, Willard made it to the top of the ladder, started to descend, and then for some reason at the 65-foot level, he inexplicably turned, and fell backwards never reaching out, nor making a sound. The fall caused multiple injuries from which Willard would not recover.

Although Willard did not die while on a fire call, he did die during a training exercise, so, technically, it was in the line of duty. Accordingly, he was afforded the honor of a full firefighter funeral. Two days later our probationary class was fitted at the station for firefighter funeral suits, caps, white gloves, and shiny shoes. On the day of the public service, our recruiting class marched directly behind the fire engine, draped in funeral bunting, carrying Willard's coffin throughout Western Springs. Firefighters and fire trucks from almost every town in the Chicago area were sent to honor their fallen brother. The hundreds of procession vehicles seemed to extend for at least a mile.

The most difficult, and unforgettable, part of the tribute procession that day culminated in our marching past the Fire Department Station, saluting a pair of lone fire boots placed in the main driveway of the station, listening to the fire station siren wail in the air all around us for several minutes. It was truly a lump-in-the-throat, almost surreal, once-in-a-lifetime moment as I marched in formation saluting Willard via those empty boots. More importantly, of course, was how Willard's wife Lucy, and their two children, must have felt that tragic and sorrowful day. My only recourse was to offer near continual prayers that day for Firefighter Willard Christoffer. May he rest in peace. Saint Florian, patron saint of firefighters, pray for us.

With our family growing we moved a few months later to Elmhurst, a nearby suburb. Although Elmhurst did not have a volunteer fire department, they did have a Citizens Police Academy which I joined and from which I graduated. I've never thought of myself as a firefighter, or policeman, or pro-life warrior, let alone a hero in any way, shape or form, because I'm not. It seems that others make deeper commitments on those fronts in ways that heretofore I have not. To all those who do serve others, I salute, admire, and appreciate you. I believe my instincts are good to want to serve and protect others, but for whatever reason I have not done so on a sustained basis. I wonder if God somehow providentially had me training for some future utility for which I may be of service to Him. Who knows? All I can say is may His will be done. If ever I am called to serve in a more substantial way, I pray to have the courage to do so.

Over the years I've had occasion to drive past the Western Springs Fire Department. When I do, it's always melancholy. I remember Willard being a soft-spoken soul. Ten years later a memorial plaque remembering Willard would be placed on a large rock on the Fire Station property. On the twentieth anniversary of his passing, they had a Memorial Ceremony on May 10, 2021, the Monday training night closest to his passing. I was unable to attend, but I stopped by the Fire House that afternoon, touched the memorial plaque commemorating Willard, and said a couple of prayers for him and his family. I also left a note with the chief to hand to Willard's widowed wife Lucy that night letting her know I was in Willard's probationary class, that I continued to pray for their family, and that Willard is remembered.

Less than four months after Willard's passing, I would watch, along with the rest of America and the world, scores of firefighters ascend into the World Trade Center buildings on September 11, 2001 only to never make it our alive when the buildings came crashing down. Courage runs deep in those who valiantly serve God and others.

Entering the 1200s, what kind of century must it have been for Blessed Mother to have appeared on Earth to give us both the Rosary (1214) and the Brown Scapular (1251)? History would refer to this era as the apex of the "Dark Ages." The term *Dark Ages* actually represents the 1,000-year period after the fall of the Roman Empire in the fifth century continuing until the fifteenth century and the beginning of the Italian Renaissance and Age of Exploration. Catholic professor and author Anthony Esolen has suggested that this time period should be called "The Brilliant Ages" as it was a time of great progress made with science, architecture, music, art, and the establishment of universities.[274]

In other words, the Dark Ages were anything but *dark*, and were instead a period of great enlightenment. Of note are the timeless works of the "Seraphic Doctor," Saint Bonaventure, as well as Saint Albertus Magnus, a teacher of Saint Thomas Aquinas, and their combined contributions to science, philosophy and theology. The 1200s also were witness to the tremendous contributions to Catholicism by Saints Felix of Valais, John Matha, Dominic, Francis of Assisi, Anthony of Padua, Elizabeth of Hungary, King Ferdinand, Clare of Assisi, Simon Stock, King Louis of France, Peter Nolasco and Raymond of Peñafort.

---

[274] Esolen, Anthony, "Were the Middle Ages Dark?" *Catholic Education Resource Center.* https://www.catholiceducation.org/en/controversy/common-misconceptions/were-the-middle-ages-dark.html

In sum, the Dark Ages of the thirteenth century would be better referred to as a radiant time of epic contributions from several of the greatest saints of our faith.

While there was momentous progress on many fronts, not everything everywhere was trending favorable for Christians. Islam had arisen in the eighth century and soon had conquered the once Christian Middle East. It was very much a brutal military conquest, not a spiritual one as much of the Christian "conquest" of the world had been. Certainly, the sword was employed by various Christian rulers at times, but in terms of the conversion of great swathes of peoples, it was the appeal of the Good News of the Gospel, the evident holiness of so many religious men and women who led lives devoted to God and neighbor, and, of course, the influence of the Holy Spirit that predominated.

In contrast to this great "spiritual conquest," that of Islam was achieved exclusively by the sword, terror tactics, and discrimination. Common images in the terrorized imaginations of Christians from areas that interacted with Islam included rape, pillage, long trains of slaves being marched eastward; the young boys were marched to slavery or perhaps a future as a Janissary in the Sultan's armies, while the young women disappeared into harems or other degrading situations.[275]

In those places where Muslims ruled over Christian populations, the Christian was always and everywhere a second- if not third- or fourth-class citizen with many extra taxes to pay and other legal, civil, and religious impediments. Islamic belief teaches that Muslims should rule non-Muslims. That is why for centuries both Christian and Jewish communities in the Middle East would be subject to the humiliating *dhimmi* status.

The very real horror of knowing that their fellow Christians were falling into the hands of Muslims as slaves shocked the consciences of many. And, as always happens, when certain historical situations present themselves, some Christians felt a particular call from God to do something about it, in this case something rather dramatic. Groups of men formed orders with the express purpose of either raising money to ransom captives out of slavery, or, in the extreme case, they placed

---

[275] "Janissary," *Britannica*, https://www.britannica.com/topic/Janissary

themselves in slavery for the people that they sought to free. The two most famous of these orders were the Trinitarians and the Mercedarians.

The Trinitarians were founded in Rome at the end of the twelfth century by Saint John Matha and Saint Felix of Valois, an elderly hermit. The distinctive mark of their rule was that a third of their revenues should be set aside for the specific purpose of being spent in ransoming captives.

The story of the Mercedarian founding is fascinating as it involves two saints, a king and a dream or vision. The Iberian Peninsula at that time was largely under Islamic domination. The young king of Aragon, named James, had a tutor, a layman named Peter Nolasco. Nolasco was noted for his piety as well as his learning. However, he would soon become best known for his charity. He ransomed certain captives of the Moors, giving away all of his money. He was from a wealthy family, but that would not be enough for the holy man's zeal. In a dream on August 1, 1218, he heard the Blessed Virgin say to him, "Find me men like yourself, an army of brave, generous, unselfish men and send them into these lands where the children of the faith are suffering."

Reportedly he went to his confessor, the saintly scholar Raymond of Peñafort who had also miraculously had a similar dream; the two inspired men then went to Nolasco's former student, King James, and found that he, too, had had the dream. Blessed Mother's apparition and message soon spread throughout the entire kingdom. And so began the Order of Our Lady of Mercy for the Ransom of Captives (or Mercedarians), eventually receiving approval of Pope Gregory IX. Peter was the first superior and also had the title of *ransomer*, a title given to the monk sent into the Muslim-controlled lands to arrange for the redemption of captives.

One of the most well-known and holy saints produced by the Mercedarian order has the curious name of Saint Raymond Nonnatus. *Non natus* means "not born" and the future saint did not enter the world in the usual fashion. Tragically, his mother died, and the baby was taken from her womb afterward. God seemed to have chosen that child for some special task or tasks, and the life of young Raymond would bear witness to the truth of that expectation, and even go beyond it.

In his youth, Raymond had great piety and was drawn to the religious life, but his father wanted him to serve in the royal court of the King of Aragon. To distract Raymond from a religious vocation, his father had him work the family fields. This only permitted Raymond more time to grow in virtue through obedience to his father, and the opportunity to pray in the country chapel. His father eventually relented and acceded to him joining the Mercedarians.

Raymond's extraordinary fervor and sanctity were immediately recognized upon his entrance into the Mercedarians. He had perfect disengagement from the world, was humble, and had a great affection for mortification and penance. The swiftness of his spiritual progress was surprising to all. Within a couple years of joining the order, he was chosen to be Ransomer, or Master General, the office which the founder Peter Nolasco had held. And, so, Raymond set off for Algiers in the north of Africa where he ransomed many, many Christian slaves from their Islamic masters.

Though in Muslim lands, he fulfilled his vows exquisitely, offering himself as a slave in exchange for others once the money he had brought for the purpose ran out. Caring more for their souls than for his own body, Saint Raymond preached the Gospel of Jesus Christ to Christian and Muslim alike. He would pay a heavy price for doing so.

He was tortured, made to run the gauntlet (passing through rows of people who would thrash, beat, and cudgel the individual) and sentenced to death by impalement. Thinking that he was worth more dead to them than alive, as they expected he would fetch an impressive ransom, his captors spared his life. They would send him back to Spain but only after piercing his lips with a red-hot spear and "locking" them together with a padlock. Why did they do that? So that the great man of God would no longer be able to preach the gospel. Little did they know, however, that the "blood of the martyrs is the seed of the Church" and that even if his mouth was silenced, his brutalized state—evidence of what he had done for his suffering Christian brothers and sisters—would serve as perhaps the most effective sermon he could give. As Saint Francis of Assisi said, "Preach the gospel at all times; only using words when necessary."

After Raymond returned to Spain Pope Gregory IX made him a cardinal. Raymond downplayed the honor and did not change one thing about where he stayed or how he dressed. Material indulgence was not something Raymond did. Shortly thereafter the pope called the holy Raymond to Rome. Just outside Barcelona and six miles into his trek to Rome, Raymond contracted a fever, and died on August 31, 1240.

After his death there was debate about where he should be buried. It was decided to place Raymond's body on a donkey and see where the animal went. The donkey went to the chapel where Raymond prayed as a youth when attending his family's fields. Raymond is buried in the chapel of Saint Nicholas.

We can ask ourselves what inspired these holy men to give up everything, up to and including their freedom, to free their neighbors from captivity. But by this point in the book, we surely know the answer. Men like Saint Peter Nolasco and his companions, men like Saint Raymond Nonnatus led lives of deep piety and prayer; they looked around them at the world and that deep prayer life inspired action…first they may have asked themselves, "Lord, what would you have me do?" And upon receiving the answer, whether in a dream or not, they acted upon it. They said yes. They asked, "Why not me?" I, too, can be a saint. I, too, can be a hero of God. The church, under Our Lady of Ransom, instituted a feast day on September 24, to ask for heaven's assistance with this scourge. Our Lady of Ransom, pray for us.

One of the first things that comes to mind concerning ransoming yourself for another is what unbelievable courage that must have taken. To gather the resiliency necessary for ransoming work is almost unimaginable. As a parent, I would like to think that if one of my children were in peril I would, without hesitation, change places with them so they could be ransomed, and be free. But for someone I have never met? For someone, after learning more about them, I may even conclude that I dislike? My ability to grasp what the ransomers did and the mindset they deployed to approach their mission, is, at best, limited.

Turning for guidance to Saint Thomas Aquinas: "When a man suffers for another for charity's sake, the satisfaction on the penance that he offers is more pleasing to God than if he offered it for himself."

Substitution. Exchange. Ransom. Starting to understand a bit more now. What else? What about mortification and self-denial? Yep, them too.

Speaking of self-denial, permit me to briefly discuss my appreciation for the game of golf. Visiting different local courses and playing a round with family or friends is truly enjoyable. Travelling for a golf trip, and visiting Catholic holy sites on pilgrimage, is perhaps, for me, one of life's finer pleasures and sweeter indulgences. Applying what I have come to learn in this chapter about the courageous, selfless souls who ransomed themselves for others, my thoughts, for some bizarre reason, turned to golf.

Would I give up an invitation to play a round of golf, purely as a form of self-denial, for the conversion of sinners? Yes. Would I pass on a trip to play a few rounds with good friends? Sure. Would I skip a trip to play Pebble Beach? Probably. Would I decline an invitation to play a round at Augusta National? Um, no. Sadly, I would draw the line there. Sorry to let you down folks, I have to be realistic. I am sure that I could think of a thousand other sacrifices to make before I would pass on a round at Augusta.

But then again, I ponder this: What if my passing on playing Augusta resulted in one mom choosing life for her child instead of abortion? No brainer. Done. What about ransoming one person from human sex trafficking? Done. What about helping free one soul from purgatory? Done, done and done! I will probably never receive an invitation to play Augusta, so it most likely is a moot point. (However, if anyone reading this book knows a member at Augusta and can help arrange a round, I hereby gladly offer a signed copy of this book.) One can dream, no?

What about you? When it comes to self-denial, what's your heroic act? As the opportunity to ransom your life for someone in captivity may not be as readily available these days, what can you do? Along the lines of giving up something in lent, what could you give up as acts of reparation for sins committed against the Sacred Heart of Jesus and the Immaculate Heart of Mary? What comes to mind for you? Chocolate, alcohol, certain foods, television, gossip, etc.? No one is asking you to push a boulder up a mountain. Do what you can. Where you can. When you can. It all matters. Saying one Hail Mary for a poor soul in purgatory is for them akin to your drinking a cool glass of water on a scorching hot summer day. I've read that offering prayers for the souls in purgatory quenches the flames of purification more than you could ever imagine.

Is ransoming the captive a corporal work of mercy? Yes, it is. Perhaps ransoming captives is a bit off our radar in the twenty-first century, but ransoming the captive is indeed one of the seven corporal works of mercy paired with 'visit the prisoner.' Does being pro-life fit in with ransoming the captive? What about pro-life sidewalk counseling? I believe that, yes, saving a baby from execution while in the womb is a form of ransoming the captive. Those who work at Pregnancy Help Centers, pro-life supporters, and sidewalk counselors, are all courageous.

Speaking of Pregnancy Help Centers (PHC), I'd like to take a moment to say how essential, charitable and admirable are all the local PHCs. Think about, and appreciate, the roles that PHC staffers and volunteers play in reaching, rescuing and renewing the moms and dads who feel there are no alternatives to abortion. Please help spread the word about options to abortion.

Full Disclosure: At the time of this writing (2021) I am serving my second term on the Board at Heartbeat International, the world's largest PHC network with 3,000 affiliates. In 2021, Heartbeat is celebrating fifty years of providing hope to both clients and those on the front lines of the fight against abortion. Congrats Heartbeat!

What about those women who have started a chemical abortion through pills and now regret their decision to start the abortion protocol? Is there hope? Is it possible to ransom a preborn baby in this situation? Yes! The Abortion Pill Reversal Network (APRN), now run by Heartbeat International, has rescued over 2,500 children since its inception and continues to expand each year. Check it out at: _https://www.heartbeatinternational.org/our-work/apr_ Another Heartbeat service is Option Line where calls for help are taken twenty-four hours a day, 365 days a year, connecting women to pregnancy help every ninety seconds. Option Line assists well over 300,000 persons each year.

Thank you PHC community for all you do! And a big thank you to all those who prayerfully and financially support your local PHC affiliate or national PHC organization.

Knowing that abortion has killed hundreds of millions in the world over the past several decades, what would you do to ransom one baby in the womb of one mother who plans to abort the child in the next few days? When did you last pray for abortion-minded women and men? When did you last make a donation to a pro-life non-profit? When did you last pray outside an abortion clinic? Confronting the feeling of evil that shrouds an abortion location is not pleasant or easy. Kudos to all those sidewalk warriors who regularly pray to ransom the souls of the preborn. Keep up the great work. We appreciate you more than you know. God bless.

Aristotle called courage the most important human quality. Courage is not the absence of fear; rather it is taking action despite being fearful; it is a decision. Pray for those who are hostage to long-term debilitating medical issues. Help us bring hope to those who have no hope. Most often we associate courage solely with physical courage. What about spiritual courage? Jesus knew we would need spiritual courage. He told us, "Be not afraid" and "In the world you will have tribulations, but fear not, I have overcome the world."

Jesus reiterated the importance of courage to Saint Catherine of Siena when he said, "Therefore bear yourselves with manly courage, for, unless you do so, you will not prove yourselves to be spouses of My Truth, and faithful children, nor of the company of those who relish the taste of My honor, and the salvation of souls."[276] Saint John Vianney tells us, "You must accept your cross; if you bear it courageously it will carry you to Heaven." In Psalms 30:3-4 we read, "Be my rock of refuge, O God, a stronghold to give me safety. You are my rock and my fortress; for Your name's sake You will lead and guide me."

Speaking of courage, are you an 'open Catholic' or a 'secret Catholic?' Are you open about letting others know you are Catholic? Are you hesitant, or even afraid, to tell new friends, co-workers, or the world that you love Jesus and His Blessed Mother? That you love the Catholic Church and all its tradition? That you love the angels and the saints? Do you go along with the culture most of the time, or do you not? Do you allow others to silence you through pressure to conform to the world? Do you boldly defend Jesus and Holy Mother Church,

---

[276] "The Dialogue of St. Catherine of Siena," TAN Books, 10.

or are you largely silent? Do you say grace before your meals in public, starting and ending with the sign of the cross, or do you not? Faithful Catholicism requires courage.

Let us turn our attention for a moment to the twentieth century and consider the courageous and magnificent example of World War II ransomer, Oscar Schindler, a German industrialist and member of the Nazi Party, who protected many Jewish lives during the holocaust. Schindler did so primarily by bribing Nazi SS officials to avert the execution of his factory workers during the war. By May 1945 he had spent millions and was penniless. He is credited with saving 1,200 souls and earned the everlasting gratitude of the 'Schindlerjews.' His actions were, simply, heroic. As the Jewish proverb states, "if you save one life you save the world over." Schindler did what his conscience told him to do in his time with what God had providentially placed before him. What do you see before you that requires your courage to act upon in this twenty-first century?

Saint John Eudes encourages us to courageously embrace serving God:

> "Undertake courageously great tasks for God's glory, to the extent that He'll give you power and grace for this purpose. Even though you can do nothing on your own, you can do all things in Him. His help will never fail you if you have confidence in his goodness.
>
> Place your entire physical and spiritual welfare in his hands. Abandon to the fatherly concern of his divine providence every care for your health, reputation, property, and business; for those near to you; for your past sins; for your soul's progress in virtue and love of Him; for your life, death, and especially your salvation and eternity—in a word, all your cares. Rest in the assurance that in His pure goodness, He'll watch with particular tenderness over all your responsibilities and cares, arranging all things for the greatest good."[277]

Wouldn't it be miraculous if the U.S. bishops for the greatest good courageously told the U.S. government that they would no longer support or partner with a government that supported abortion? Dialogue has not worked. Time to get tough. Taxpayer funding of abortion needs to end. When I think about rescuing one soul from

---

[277] "A Year With The Saints" 363.

abortion, or rescuing one person from human trafficking, it is obvious that so much more must be done. What examples come to mind of others who risked much, or everything, for the sake of saving others? Whatever first comes to mind, maybe that is the Holy Ghost asking you to participate, to cooperate, in what must be done to add to the Communion of Saints. Nobody needs to know what you will undertake to be of service to God the Father. Whatever contribution you decide to make, please, don't become glum about it. Be sure to tackle it with a courageous and joyful disposition.

Fr. James Altman asked during the Wuhan Virus of 2020/2021 pandemic how many priests have said, "God first. God last. God always in the middle. God and God alone. Where is the courage of the shepherds in our day from something that you have a 99.92% of recovering from?"[278] Fr. Altman continued, "We look to the example of great saints who fearlessly tended to their congregations during plague and disease. Saints like Saint Charles Borromeo who climbed a pile of dead corpses to anoint one who had not yet died. Saint Aloysius Gonzaga, who died at the age of 23, after serving in a hospital during the plague of 1597 in Milan (receiving last rites from Saint Robert Bellarmine)."[279] And, of course, Saint Damien of Molokai, who will be featured in Chapter 19, who was spiritually charitable and physically courageous to administer to the lepers of Kaluapapa. Fearless heroes all.

Which should Christians fear more, a viral, or a moral, pandemic? More importantly, from God's perspective, is He more concerned with a viral pandemic or a moral pandemic? To mention a few viral pandemics: Spanish Flu, German Flu, Chinese Flu, Bird Flu, Swine Flu, etc. What about the "moral pandemics"? What does the phrase 'moral pandemic' even mean? To mention a few things that I would consider to be moral pandemics: abortion, contraception, pornography, homosexuality, transgenderism, etc. And what about the capital vices, or seven deadly sins? pride, envy, lust, anger, gluttony, greed and sloth. While the world has been significantly impacted by a viral pandemic and burns. What about the implications of all those souls being damned to suffer eternal flames? Good and justice can come from any pandemic. For many it is a wake-up call. Just how 'spiritually woke' are

[278] Fr. James Altman, "Fr. Altman Shares the Path Forward After 2020." *Alpha News.* You Tube posted January 14, 2021. https://www.youtube.com/watch?v=MSmnqYcrO0A&t=2120s
[279] Ibid.

you? What in your life is displeasing to God? In what ways should you amend your life? Hereinafter what will you prioritize?

The media and government have held up medical personnel as heroes. What about our priests? Are they not even greater heroes? Where are their commercials with grateful souls clapping for them? As Catholics we 'clap' for all our priests via our prayers. They are the true heroes who will help us live a life that is judged by God to merit heaven. Viral pandemics can be quantified via numbers of those infected and deaths. How are moral pandemics quantified? How many souls alive are not in the state of grace? How many people die in the state of mortal sin and are damned for all eternity?

Archbishop Charles Chaput said that "evil preaches tolerance until it is dominant, then it seeks to silences good." So, what's it like being a Christian in today's world? Surely, in our advanced times and modern societies there is plenty of liberty and freedom everywhere such that oppression of Christians and human slavery are no longer issues. Right? Wrong. According to the U.S.-based Christian advocacy group Open Doors' "2021 World Watch List," one in eight Christians around the world are fighting for their faith and life.[280] One in eight! The list contains fifty countries who systematically repress their citizens. The top three most oppressive? North Korea, Afghanistan and Somalia. If found to be a Christian in any of those countries prison, and perhaps killing, occurs. Some cultures even permit "honor killings."

We also know that we must pray much more for our fellow Catholics in China, where the atheistic Communists are increasing Christian persecution. Sadly, Pope Francis and the bishops remain largely *de facto* silent as the flock is imprisoned, tortured and martyred. Why? Exiled Chinese dissident Guo Wengui has alleged that the Chinese Communist Party (CCP) allocates $2 billion a year to pay off the Vatican to gain influence over the Vatican's internal policy making and to pay for its silence on the CCP's repression of religious freedom and human rights atrocities.[281] For silence? For cooperation? If true, two billion, or whatever the amount, sure sounds a lot like thirty pieces of silver. Again, if true, the Vatican must make amends—asap.

[280] Moyski, Martina, "Christians Under Fire Worldwide," *Church Militant,* January 26, 2021.
[281] Williams, Thomas D., "Whistleblower Claims Chinese Communists Pay Vatican $2 Billion in Bribes." *Breitbart,* June 23, 2020.

To add insult to injury, Bishop Marcelo Sanchez Sorondo, chancellor of the Pontifical Academy of Social Sciences, has offered jaw-dropping praise for China going on the record stating that atheistic, communist China has created the "best model for living out Catholic social teaching today."[282] We must continue to pray for oppressed Christians of our day. Through the Communion of Saints, we Catholics know, as it says in 1 Corinthians 12:26: "If one part [of the Body of Christ] suffers, every part suffers with it." What self-denial can we offer today for the persecuted Catholics alive during our time?

If you listen to your mind, it may tell you not to act, to be afraid. If you listen to you heart, your heart will tell you to be brave. If you listen to your soul, your soul will tell you to have faith, to trust in God. When times get tough and courage is required, listen not as much to your mind, but more to your heart and your soul. Criticism will likely arise from those around you who lack the courage, guts and stamina to do what is right. Block those voices out. Achieving worthwhile change for God and country is often accompanied by a chorus of naysayers. When faith is put into action, what imprint will you leave for your posterity, nation and church?

While we are considering ransoming those from slavery, let's wade further into the waters of modern-day evils and have a candid discussion about modern-day slavery and perhaps the most pervasive form of slavery in existence today, pornography. The proverbial "elephant in the room" that most would focus on first would be pornography, with modern-day slavery, the "800 lb. gorilla in the room," being discussed secondarily. But this is *Against the Grain*, so we will focus on modern-day slavery first, with pornography secondarily. Once these two have been discussed, we'll turn our attention to another form of slavery in the world that may surprise some.

According to Human Trafficking Search, modern-day slavery is "an umbrella term—often used interchangeably with human trafficking—that refers to the exploitation of individuals through threat or use of force, coercion, abduction, fraud, and/or deception. It includes the practices of forced labor, debt bondage, domestic servitude, forced marriage, sex trafficking, and the recruitment and use

---

[282] Williams, Thomas D., "Top Vatican Official Proposes Communist China as 'Best' Model of Catholic Social Teaching Today," *Breitbart,* February 7, 2018.

of child soldiers, among others. The most common forms of exploitation are forced labor, which, according to the International Labor Organization, impacts 24.9 million people a year."[283]

The countries with the highest percentage of their population in modern-day slavery, according to the Global Slavery Index, are North Korea (4.37 percent), Uzbekistan (3.97 percent), Cambodia (1.64 percent), India (1.40 percent), and Qatar (1.35 percent).[284] While percentages of population are informative, the country with perhaps the greatest number of modern-day slaves is China.

Are you familiar with the plight of the Uyghurs in Chinese-occupied East Turkistan?

Vox reports the Uyghur ethnic-religious mass internment (slavery) is the "largest of its kind since World War II. The Chinese Communist Party has detained between "1 and 3 million Uyghurs in 380 re-education camps and prisons in Xinjiang and forced them to undergo psychological indoctrination programs, such as studying communist propaganda and giving thanks to Chinese President Xi Jinping, while being forbidden from participating in religious observances. Chinese have also used waterboarding and other forms of torture, including sexual abuse, as part of the indoctrination process."[285]

The Australian Strategic Policy Institute writes that it's not just the Chinese government who benefits by having Uyghur slave labor pick cotton in Chinese fields, but multiple reports link forced Uyghur labor to U.S. Corporations such as Apple supplier Lens Technology, Gap, Abercrombie & Fitch, Calvin Klein, H&M, L.L.Bean, Lacoste, Nike, and many other brands.[286]

At this point everyone should be crystal clear what Saint Raymond would say, and do, about modern-day slavery. And you? In Romans 8:15-17 we read, "For you did not receive a spirit of slavery to fall back into fear, but you received a spirit of adoption, through which

---

[283] Akannksha, "Top Countries for Modern Day Slavery," *Human Trafficking Search,* December 18, 2017.
[284] Ibid.
[285] Kirby, Jen, "Concentration Camps And Forced Labor: China's Repression of the Uighurs, Explained," *Vox,* September 25, 2020.
[286] Olohan, Mary Margaret, "Here Are the Companies Linked to Forced Uighur Labor," *The Daily Caller,* December 30, 2020.

we cry, "Abba, Father!" The Spirit itself bears witness with our spirit that we are children of God, and if children, then heirs, heirs of God and joint heirs with Christ, if only we suffer with him so that we may also be glorified with him."

One Sudanese daughter of the church that went from being a victim of human trafficking to being a Catholic saint was Saint Josephine Bakhita. Bakhita, whose name means "fortunate" in Arabic, was kidnapped at age nine and sold into slavery. She was sold and resold, beaten, tortured and abused until she was purchased by an Italian who cared for her and took her to Italy to work as a nanny. Soon thereafter the Italian courts declared her to be a free woman. She was introduced to the Catholic faith and remained in Italy. Bakhita was baptized in 1890 and received her First Holy Communion from the future Pope Saint Pius X. She took the Christian name of Josephine, and in 1896 entered the Institute of Canossian Daughters of Charity. She served in religious life for fifty years and was known for her charity and joy. Patron of Sudan, Saint Josephine Bakhita had her feast day, February 8th, designated as the International Day of Prayer to Stop Human Trafficking.[287]

In the United States, January 11 is National Human Trafficking Awareness Day; it is held in January, which is National Slavery and Human Trafficking Prevention Month. With all these times to highlight the scourge of human trafficking, is any true progress being made? Human trafficking is most likely a bigger issue than you think. In 2019 there were more than forty million estimated victims of trafficking worldwide—twenty-five million of them trapped in labor or sex trafficking, and fifteen million people in forced marriages. Human trafficking has been calculated to be a $150 billion industry. Right here in America in 2019 there were 11,500 cases of reported human trafficking.[288] The Federal Human Trafficking Report indicates that 76 percent of the victims under the ten years old were trafficked by a family member.[289]

---

[287] Saint Bakhita, "Saint of the Day," *The Catholic Company*, February 8.
[288] https://humantraffickinghotline.org/states
[289] Feehs, Kyleigh and Currier, Alyssa, "2019 Federal Human Trafficking Report," *The Human Trafficking Institute*.
https://www.traffickinginstitute.org/wp-content/uploads/2020/05/2019-Federal-Human-Trafficking-Report_Low-Res.pdf?mc_cid=f165715951&mc_eid=f8bab6998c

Is the Catholic church 100 percent committed to eradicating human trafficking? With the staggering numbers of victims in the U.S. and our world, how can, and should, we do more? Catholic leaders continue to speak on the issue. "It is shocking to consider the size and scope of the tragedy of human trafficking that exists in our world in 2021," stated Bishop Robert Deeley of Portland, Maine. He called human trafficking "a horrific crime against the basic dignity and rights of the human person." Trafficking victims are everywhere, but hiding in plain sight, said a Catholic Relief Services (CRS) advisor. "They are hidden from view. You don't recognize them in the back kitchens, shops, gas stations and in hospitality. They are also tucked away in fields," said Dr. Lucy Steinitz, Catholic Relief Services senior technical advisor for protection.[290]

These forms of "modern-day slavery" look quite different from those of centuries past, she added. "They [victims] are not in shackles or on farms," Steinitz said. "People are coerced into harsh employment under horrible conditions, and then have no freedom to leave." The problem of trafficking, Bishop Deeley said, runs so deep that it requires action at all levels of government. He called on Congress to pass comprehensive immigration reform to encourage legal immigration and reduce the risk of refugees and child migrants being trafficked. (Ibid)

Thinking about this topic, is modern-day slavery even on your radar? The people behind this malevolent operation are 100 percent evil and need to be brought to justice. The victims deserve dignity, assistance and support. Many people have dedicated their lives to not stopping until every human trafficker has ceased operations, and every survivor has been liberated. Those who know have many sleepless nights fretting about doing something to rescue others. Let us pray for those who courageously wake up every day to fight this modern-day scourge. Ending human trafficking is worth the noble fight.

The horrors related to child abduction are too numerous to list. A movie on this topic yet to be released is the *Sound of Freedom* starring Jim Caviezel. It is the story of Tim Ballard (Caviezel), a former CIA operative, who quits his job with Homeland Security Investigations (HSI), in order to devote his life to rescuing children from cartels and

---

[290] CAN, "National Human Trafficking Awareness Day," *National Catholic Register*, January 11, 2021.

global sex traffickers. Caviezel has stated that this was the second most important film he has ever done, ranking only behind *The Passion.*[291] Keep an eye out for the film when it is released. In the interim, check out the trailer here: *https://www.imdb.com/title/tt7599146/*

What would Jesus say about those who are actively involved in ending human and child trafficking? What would he say about those brave individuals on the ground who actually identity a human trafficking ring, find their location, break into that secure area, and find several souls awaiting rescue? How pleasing it must be to God the Father to send extra blessings and graces to those who courageously commit to rescuing others, and restoring their dignity. Those who work and fight to end human trafficking do not swim downstream. They do not take the easy path. No, they go against the grain and fight for the vulnerable. They are modern-day warriors fighting modern-day slavery. Their mental, physical and spiritual strength is to be commended. They are most deserving of our prayers and our support.

Stop for a moment and hear the cries of the victims. Now that you know more about this issue, how does "Why Not Me?" apply? It's decidedly one of the most evil and heartbreaking things that occur every day in this world of ours. What can you do to ransom or save those who wish to break free from the slavery of human trafficking? Have you, or will you, contact your representatives to support further government initiatives to disrupt and end large-scale organizations that profit from human trafficking?

While you may or may not decide you want to ransom yourself for those who have been trafficked, you can decide to support the nonprofits who are dedicated to ending this scourge. Support those silent warriors dedicated to bringing a new dawn of hope to those despondent souls trapped in human trafficking. Among the many groups who are doing great work in this regard, I'd like to highlight two here, Operation Underground Railroad (O.U.R.), Tim Ballard's group who "Exists to Rescue Children from Sex Trafficking and Sexual Exploitation." Another great group in this field is the Guardian Group. One of Guardian's taglines is, "Bringing the full fight to sex trafficking in the United States." Guardian's efforts are most admirable and worthy of your support. Check them out at guardiangroup.org.

---

[291] "Sound of Freedom," Wikipedia, https://en.wikipedia.org/wiki/Sound_of_Freedom_(film)

The National Center on Sexual Exploitation (NCOSE) defends human dignity and is dedicated to addressing the full spectrum of social harms that emerge from the production, distribution, and consumption of pornography, including human trafficking. NCOSE's website is: *https://endsexualexploitation.org/*

The evil of human trafficking for adult or child sexual slavery is more in front of us than we realize. If we knew what to look for, we would see human trafficking all around us. To learn more about this the U.S. Department of Health and Human Services has published a "10 Ways You Can Help End Trafficking" guide. It includes items such as: know the signs, report a tip, spread the word, volunteer locally, stay informed and raise your voice. Check out the link at: *https://www.acf.hhs.gov/otip/about/ways-endtrafficking*

In the post-Trump era we can all be thankful we have a "devout Catholic" in the White House to address this troubling topic and further champion protecting the vulnerable. Right? Wrong. On Feb. 24, 2021, 'Catholic' Biden cancelled the Trump program to remove convicted sex offenders living in the United States illegally. As reported in *Human Events*, "South Carolina Attorney General Alan Wilson joined a coalition of 18 state attorneys general to urge Biden to reverse the cancellation, 'We're working hard to fight human trafficking and sex crimes in South Carolina and allowing convicted sex offenders who are here illegally to remain in our country makes absolutely no sense,' Wilson said. 'These trafficking and sex crimes are repugnant to human decency generally and to children specifically,' he added."[292] The article said the attorneys general argued that "canceling Operation Talon could encourage sexual predators to attack" and concluded with the question, "If the United States will not remove even convicted sex offenders, whom will it remove?"[293] Great question. Why would Biden protect pedophiles and rapists here in the U.S. illegally? Thanks for nothing on this issue "devout Catholic" Biden. Sex offenders rejoice! (sarcasm)

While human and sex trafficking is a massive financial operation, it is but a fraction compared to the much larger worldwide specter of pornography. The word pornography comes from the Greek words

---

[292] Human Events Staff, "Biden Cancels Trumps 'Operation Talon' Program That Targeted Sex Offenders Living In U.S. Illegally," *Human Events,* February 26, 2021.
[293] Ibid.

porne (prostitute) and *graphos* (to write). Pornography is pernicious, rampant, and only accelerating. Pornography today is estimated to be a $100 billion dollar business that fuels human trafficking. The numbers who access porn regularly, or semi-regularly, are heartrending. Most studies of men under the age of thirty conclude that roughly four out of five have accessed it in the past week, with 98 percent viewing porn in the past six months; 50 percent of boys by the age eleven will have viewed porn, with that percentage sadly increasing each successive year. The numbers are not going in the right direction. One commentator makes the argument that, "Pornography breeds mental illness. Mental illness breeds leftism. It's unavoidable."[294]

Priests will tell you that there are fewer more potent cancers in our society today than pornography. Porn is one of the most frequently confessed sins. Porn is a total rejection of God's plan for human sexuality. It eviscerates the will, and eventually the soul, of anyone who indulges this temptation and proclivity. It can be as addictive as some of the more hard-core drugs like heroin or methamphetamines as it alters one's brain chemistry. Brain desensitization and dopamine signaling are often manifested through depression, hostility, social anxiety and loss of focus. Be honest with yourself. One's purpose is greater than porn. Get help. Return to a state of grace. Time to ban porn to help improve our culture and society.

One great resource to help stop porn addiction and live with confidence is the Christian accountability software organization, Covenant Eyes. (*https://www.covenanteyes.com*) Covenant Eyes has graciously partnered with a sister blog: Clean Heart Online! managed by a Catholic Content Specialist. The Clean Heart Online blog offers support and resources for Catholics seeking purity and freedom from pornography. (https://cleanheart.online/)

Are Catholics as resolute as we need to be in the face of sexual exploitation, human trafficking, and pornography? Are we more committed to ending these practices than our enemies are in perpetuating them and enslaving more souls? To be determined. Perhaps like Esther, however, maybe we were born "for such a time as this." Despite the in-your-face evil, troubles and challenges, we must have increased courage to stand for purity, morality, the one, true faith,

---

[294] Doyle, John. "How Porn Is Destroying You and Our Country," YouTube posted February 18, 2021. https://www.youtube.com/watch?v=Vtp31feyTfM&feature=emb_logo)

and Christ. John 16:33 tells us, "I have told you this so that you might have peace in me. In the world you will have trouble, but take courage, I have conquered the world." If interested in getting involved in the fight to end sexual exploitation, human trafficking, and pornography, pray, research the issues, check out some of the links provided, pray some more, ask, "Why Not Me?" and see where God leads you.

Against the Grain would like to address one last aspect of slavery with a leading question. What is the ultimate goal of anti-God, Big Tech? I pray I'm wrong, but all indications point to enslaving us in a world where there is no freedom of religion, no religious liberty, only conformity under threat of persecution and imprisonment to support immoral practices and autocratic, progressive government control. All Big Tech's power comes from content filters that manipulate thought and behavior. Individual quality scores, like Communist China's Social Credit Rating System, are ready to be fully activated, further calibrated, and aimed squarely at suppressing (enslaving via digital serfdom) anyone who opposes the anti-God, Marxist worldview. Americans, and all persons of goodwill, should be protesting these unjust and immoral tech strategies, tactics and goals. Critical numbers will not be aware all this is occurring until well past the point of no return. Will lawmakers regulate this malevolent behavior before it is apparently too late? Again, praying, but not holding my breath while doing so.

Saint Raymond Nonnatus led a remarkable life in service to God by liberating the slave.

The thirteenth century witnessed many other incredible saints: The Lord's Dog (Saint Dominic), The Astonishing (Saint Christina), The Hammer of Heretics (Saint Anthony of Padua), a Magnanimous King who spoke with Christ (Saint Fernando III), O Good Fortune (Saint Bonaventure) and the Dumb Ox (Saint Thomas Aquinas). Each of them could have easily been the subject of the 1200s, but, alas, it was Saint Raymond and his courage that won out. Next up? Saint Roch and his humility.

Thirteenth Century Saints

Saints William of Rochester (1201), Felix of Valais (d. 1212), John Matha (d. 1213), Dominic (d. 1221), Christina the Astonishing (d. 1224), Francis of Assisi (d. 1226), Anthony of Padua (d. 1231), Elizabeth of Hungary (d. 1231), Ferdinand – King (d. 1252), Clare of Assisi (d. 1253), Peter Nolasco (d. 1256), Simon Stock (d. 1265), Louis (France) (d. 1270), Margaret of Hungary (d. 1271), Zita (d. 1271), Bonaventure (d. 1274), Thomas Aquinas (d. 1274), Raymond of Peñafort (d. 1275), and Albert Magnus (Albert the Great, d. 1280), pray for us.

Saint Raymond Nonnatus is the patron saint of children, childbirth, pregnant women, infants, midwives, and priests defending the confidentiality of confession (no doubt due to Raymond having had a padlock placed through his lips by his captors so he couldn't speak).

Saint Raymond Nonnatus' feast day is August 31.
Saint Raymond Nonnatus, *ora pro nobis* (pray for us).

Thirteenth Century History

1202-1204. Fourth Crusade. On April 13, 1204, Crusaders sack Constantinople, beginning the Latin Empire of Constantinople.

1205- Saint Francis of Assisi becomes a hermit and founds the Franciscan order.

1214- **Saint Dominic**, a great debater of the Albigensian heretics, during a period of prayer, **receives the Rosary from an apparition of the Blessed Virgin Mary** at the abbey in Prouille, France. It is believed the Blessed Mother gave the Holy Rosary to Saint Dominic to initially combat the Albigensian heresy then wreaking havoc in the church.

1215- Fourth Ecumenical Lateran Council is closed by Pope Innocent III. Seventy decrees were approved, including the pre-Thomistic definition of transubstantiation.

1215- Cardinal Stephen Langton, an early Catholic English cardinal, becomes an important player in the dispute between King John and Pope Innocent III. The tense situation led to the signing of the *Magna Carta Libertatum* (Latin for "Great Charter of Freedoms"), commonly called *Magna Carta* ("Great Charter").

1216- The Order of Preachers (Dominican Order) is founded by Saint Dominic.

1217-1229- Fifth Crusade.

1230- King Saint Fernando III permanently combines the Kingdoms of Leon and Castile, thus conquering more Islamic territory than any other Christian, and inflicting on medieval Islam its greatest defeat up until that time.

1236- Half of the Iberian Peninsula has been liberated from Moorish occupiers. "The Almogavars were soldiers from Christian Iberia (what is now Spain and Portugal) who fought the Muslims during the Reconquista. Before and during battle, the Almogavars would shout *"Desperta Ferro!"* —meaning "Awaken Iron!"—while striking their swords and lances on stones to create a cascade of sparks."[295]

1251- July 16. Blessed Mother appears to Saint Simon Stock at Cambridge, England and instructs him to create a sacramental, the **Brown Scapular**, for people to wear saying, 'Take, beloved son, this scapular of thy order as a badge of my confraternity and for thee and all Carmelites a special sign of grace; **whoever dies in this garment, will not suffer everlasting fire.**"

1252- King Saint Fernando III dies. One of history's most gifted and formidable warriors, while being at the same time one of the greatest Catholic monarchs to have served God, the Church, and his country, Spain. His incorrupt body, enclosed in a marvelous gold and crystal casket worthy of the Castilian king, lies in the Cathedral of Seville. King Saint Fernando is the only king whose earthly crown has never been taken away, for his golden crown still encircles his head as

---

[295] McKay, Brett and Kate, "Sound Your Barbaric Yawp! 20 Battle Cries Through the Ages," *Art of Manliness.com*,
June 8, 2015.

he reclines beneath the statue of the Virgin of the Kings, awaiting the day of resurrection.

1269- Saint Thomas Aquinas, when he was working on Part II of the *Summa Theologica,* has dinner with Saint Louis of France (perhaps the greatest Catholic monarch to have served God, the Church, and his country, France). Nothing major to report here, other than two awesome saints having dinner, which, to me, is really cool.

1274- **Saint Thomas Aquinas**, while in Salerno, Italy working on finishing the third part of the Summa, had Jesus appear to him. "One night shortly after he had composed the treatise on the Eucharist, was praying in his chapel and heard a locution for the crucifix on the wall. **Christ spoke to him saying, 'Thomas, my son, you have written well of me. What will you have as your reward.' The saint answered, *'Non nisi te, Domine.'* ("Only yourself, Lord.")**[296] At that point Saint Thomas Aquinas went into ecstasy, levitated, and was found suspended there in his chapel by his brothers. Shortly thereafter, one day while Aquinas was celebrating Mass, he was granted a profound grace of mystical union, which so transfixed him that he declared he could no longer continue his writing. When his brother friars begged him to explain himself, Thomas told them "Compared with what has been revealed to me, all that I have written seems like so much straw."[297]

1298- Saint Gregory the Great, Saint Ambrose, Saint Augustine and Saint Jerome are made Doctors of the Church.

Virtue Challenge #13- Courage

Saint Raymond Nonnatus, pray for us to have the courage to conquer our wills with resignation to do the will of God. Help us to have courage to align our souls with Christ. Pray for us to have an increase in the virtues of mortification, love of our enemies, patience in adversity, and humility. Pray for us to have courage when those around

---

[296] Lord, Bob, "Jesus Speaks to Saint Thomas Aquinas," *ezine articles.com,* January 6, 2010.
[297] Freyaldenhoven, Joseph, "Jesus speaks to Saint Thomas Aquinas from the Crucifix," *Catholic365.com,* February 3, 2020.

us do not. Help us to be magnanimous and take the road less travelled. Pray for us to be sacrificial in all we do in imitation of our Lord.

Turn to Christ, in sorrow and guilt, and beg forgiveness for your fear and timidity. Pray to have the courage to stand out in our culture. Blood of Christ, courage of martyrs, save us.

For all those "dads" who say it is a "woman's choice" when deciding to abort your baby or not, do not be a coward. If you do not stand for life, you are a coward. There is no other way to say it. Do not permit cowardice. Be a man.

For all those moms who say it's a "woman's choice," it's not a choice. It's a child. Have courage. It may be difficult. Cooperate with God, the author of all life.

Pray for all those souls trapped by either modern-day slavery or pornography. May the chains be broken through the mercy of God. Help Catholics step up to fight these scourges.

Pray to stand with Mary at the foot of the cross in courage. Do not flee for fear of the Romans or the wolves, secularists, progressives, Communists or modernists. How will you stand with Mary?

Converse for a moment with the Holy Ghost about courage. My Lord and my God, how may I serve you more faithfully and completely through the virtue of courage?

O Great Saint Raymond Nonnatus, pray for us an increase in the virtue and grace of holy perseverance.

CHAPTER 14

Roch

The Fourteenth Century
Humility

"Humility is the foundation of all the other virtues hence, in the soul in which this virtue does not exist there cannot be any other virtue except in mere appearance."

~ Saint Augustine

"The spirit of humility is sweeter than honey, and those who nourish themselves with this honey produce sweet fruit."

~ Saint Anthony of Padua

"Often, actually very often, God allows his greatest servants, those who are far advanced in grace, to make the most humiliating mistakes. This humbles them in their own eyes and in the eyes of their fellow men."

~ Saint Louis de Montfort

"The most powerful weapon to conquer the devil is humility. For, as he does not know at all how to employ it, neither does he know how to defend himself from it."

~ Saint Vincent de Paul

"There is more value in a little study of humility and in a single act of it than in all the knowledge in the world."

~ Saint Teresa of Avila

The 1300s

The late 1200s and early 1300s was the time of the legendary Scottish freedom fighter, William Wallace (1270-1305). As featured in the Mel Gibson film, *Braveheart*, Wallace led his countrymen against the English in the First War of Scottish Independence. He valiantly fought to live free and not as a subject of an occupying country. His bravery, including his last unforgettable shout of "Freedom" in the movie's

287

closing scene still resonates more than 700 years after his death. The message of the gospel is freedom. Freedom from the oppression of sin. What occupying ideology and/or force will you courageously fight against in your lifetime? What's your 'England?'

Just as our saint from the 1200s, Raymond Nonnatus, lived a dramatic, and courageous, life filled with signs and wonders, so too did our Saint Roch of the 1300s. And, yet, what is most inspiring about both men is their love for God and neighbor, as opposed to the miracles that blessed them and those with whom they came in contact. Our lives most likely will not be marked by such dramatic signs and wonders, but we can imitate Christ, we can imitate his saints in that which makes them saintly, their love for God and neighbor, and their humility. Why not you?

Roch was born in what is now France, near the end of the thirteenth century and died around thirty years later. But in his short life, he did so much to inspire his fellow Christians that he became one of the most loved medieval saints, such that numerous confraternities and other religious foundations took his name.

Roch seemed marked for distinction as a special Christian from birth. He was born with a bright red birthmark in the shape of a cross on his chest. It was believed that the red cross was a sign from Virgin Mary, that she had answered his mother's prayer to heal her barrenness. This birthmark, however, unlike others, grew as he grew.

Roch was born to well-off parents, his father being governor of Montpellier. They instilled in their son a love for God and the poor that he took to heart, so much so that he felt a call to follow Christ and responded to that call in a way similar to Saint Francis of Assisi. At the age of twenty, Roch's parents died, and rather than come into his inheritance, he distributed it to the poor and entered upon the life of a mendicant pilgrim bound for Italy as a third-order Franciscan. Roch would no doubt have been in agreement with another fourteenth century saint, Catherine of Siena, when she said, "He will provide the way and the means, such as you could never have imagined. Leave it all to Him, let go of yourself, lose yourself on the Cross, and you will find yourself entirely."

It is, perhaps, not surprising that he did so for the example set by his parents in both word and deed was that of exemplary Christians.

Though fully engaged in the activities of the world, in a position of great responsibility, Roch's father, as he lay dying, told his son what was truly important in life:

Before all things, devote yourself to the service of God, and meditate diligently on the sufferings of our Divine Lord. Be the stay of the widow, the orphan, and all those in misfortune. Above all, keep yourself from avarice, the source of very many sins. Be eyes to the blind, and feet to the lame, be a father to the poor, and know that by employing the property which I leave you in works of mercy, you will be blessed by God and man.[298]

All of us who are parents should leave such a legacy of Christian thought to our children and grandchildren. There is no reason we cannot repeat the words if we imitate the life so that they do not seem like the words of a hypocrite to our offspring. Let us try to at least imitate Roch's father if we remain in the world, and his saintly son if God calls us to a more radical following of Him and his Gospel.

Roch's travels were accompanied by the above-mentioned signs as wonders. This was a time of the Plague, but Roch, free of fear, devoted his time to serving and ministering to the suffering, and it is said that he cured many by simply making the sign of the cross on their foreheads. Among the cities he passed through, curing people as he went were: Aquapendente, Cesena, Rome, Mantua, Modena, Parma, and finally Piacenza. It was there that he contracted the plague that he had been healing others of throughout his travels.

The saintly Roch, not wanting to place others in danger, removed himself from the town and went into the forest where he lived in a small, abandoned hut. As he had ministered to so many plague-sufferers, he was ministered to by a man named Gothard who discovered the future saint's place of hiding in a miraculous way.

Roch was nearly at the point of death when miraculously a dog discovered him in his hut. Some might ask what was so miraculous about that. Well, the dog did not come empty-pawed so to speak but had in its mouth a loaf of bread which the dying holy man of God

---

[298] Who is St. Roch? | St Roch Catholic Church, Flat Rock Archdiocese of Detroit - Michigan (strochflatrock.com)
Quoted from the website of the Parish of St. Roch in the Archdiocese of Detroit.

received and ate. He blessed the dog who had saved him, and the dog licked the wounds caused by the plague, healing them.

The dog belonged to Gothard, a wealthy nobleman in the area. After seeing the dog leave numerous times with a loaf of bread in its mouth, Gothard decided one day to follow him. Discovering the now-recovering Roch, Gothard took him back to his home and nursed him back to health. The two then became partners in works of charity, humility, prayers, and penance.

Upon fully recovering, Roch returned to the city of Piacenza where he resumed healing the sick and this time also reportedly extended his healing ministry to animals. He, like his model in Christ, Saint Francis, is known for his love for animals and is usually depicted in art with a dog holding a loaf of bread in its mouth.

After some time, Roch felt called by God to return to his home, Montpellier. And so, he promptly responded to this latest call and did so.

The south of France at the time was embroiled in strife and war. Roch was not recognized upon his return, thought to be a spy, and was thrown into prison. Accepting this latest misfortune as the will of God, Roch was content to remain unknown and languished in prison for five years even though he could have revealed himself to be the then governor's nephew.

Perhaps Roch, imprisoned and abandoned, felt most closely then to his Lord, who like him could have put an end to his suffering at any moment he wanted. Can we do the same when we are in difficult circumstances? Roch embraced his suffering as Christ did, as Francis did. Why not me? Why not you? Why must we complain at our sufferings when our Lord and Savior told us to pick up our cross and follow him?

Eventually, Roch could tell he was going to die and so he sent for a priest. The following account of Roch's last moments reflects more of the signs and wonders with which the life of this holy, humble man of God was marked:

> Upon entering the room, the priest beheld a supernatural light noting that the poor captive was radiant. After having given Roch the Last Rites the priest quickly informed the governor of what he had seen.

While Roch slumbered he saw in his dream a heavenly messenger that said to him, *"Roch, the time is come for you to receive the reward for your labors and sufferings, and for your soul to repose in Heaven. God is pleased with you."* He awoke, with his soul bathed in holy joy. Addressing God, Roch asked that whosoever is attacked by the plague, or in the danger of being so attacked, shall implore my protection with faith and may be delivered from the sickness or preserved from his scourge. These words were barely out of his mouth when Roch expired, whilst raising his eyes to Heaven and pressing his crucifix to his heart.

As soon as he died the angels sang sweet melodies and the prison shone with celestial light. By his side was found a tablet on which an angel had written in letters of gold the name of Roch and the words: *"I announce protection and deliverance to all those who being endangered by the plague, shall have recourse to my intercession."*

When the governor came to see the deceased, he was amazed to find that it was his nephew! His family was summoned and uncovering the chest of Roch once again saw the wondrous, red cross with which he had been marked from birth.[299]

Saint Roch died in 1327.

In pursuing humility, we often encounter peace. Without life's material encumbrances, we are free from the attachments that take us away from God. Christ is the only one to whom we should turn. When we are free from materialism, we are freer to pursue God.

Another fourteenth century saint, Peregrine Laziosi (1265-1345), has a story similar to Roch in that he contracted a serious leg illness, and he too was miraculously healed. Peregrine in his youth joined those who opposed Pope Martin IV for placing his hometown, Forli, Italy under spiritual interdict (closing the churches in the town) to get them to modify their beliefs and practices to fall into line with Rome. Peregrine, a ringleader of rebels, confronted the pope's legate, Philip Benizi, and physically struck him in the face during a dispute. Realizing what he had done, Peregrine cast himself at the feet of the wounded priest, and asked for forgiveness. Benize granted it, and Peregrine's life would change from that moment forward.

---

[299] Who is St. Roch? | St Roch Catholic Church, Flat Rock Archdiocese of Detroit - Michigan (strochflatrock.com).

Sometime later when kneeling in prayer, Blessed Mother appeared to Peregrine and said, "Go to Siena. There you will find devout men who call themselves my servants. Attach yourself to them."[300] Peregrine would join the Order of Servites (Servants of Mary), and lead a holy life atoning for past youthful transgressions with harsh penances. He grew in holiness, gave great spiritual advice, and was soon called the "Angel of Good Counsel." (More from Siena later in this chapter.)

A few years later a diseased growth appeared on his right foot. After meeting with a doctor, it was decided to amputate. The night before the surgery, Peregrine prayed intensely. Dozing off, he dreamed that Jesus touched his foot and healed it. When he awoke the foot was wholly healed. Word spread of the miraculous cure, and many began to visit Peregrine asking for their maladies to be cured. For some, when Peregrine would say the name, "Jesus" to them, they too would receive a miraculous cure. Peregrine is a patron saint of persons with cancer, foot ailments and incurable diseases.[301]

What ails you? Cancer, weak heart, sore back, bad knees, poor sight, chronic halitosis, or maybe even a diseased right foot? Whatever the condition, with the assistance of Saint Peregrine, say the name of "Jesus" with confidence for healing, or being better able to accept the illness and/or disease. Know that holiness, like that which Saint Peregrine and Saint Roch possessed, is more important than a life free of suffering. Pray for closeness to Our Lord. An excellent novena to Saint Peregrine, as well as many others, can be found at: https://www.praymorenovenas.com

Besides Christ, Blessed Mother, without original sin, was the humblest. Fr. Ed Broom, OMV writes, "A humble person recognizes that all the good they have done, and can do, is a result of the Presence of God in their life. Mary was most humble calling herself the servant or the handmaid of the Lord. Also, in her magnificent canticle of praise that we call The Magnificat (Lk 1: 46-55), Mary states that God has looked with favor upon the humility of His handmaid. Let us beg Mary for a meek and humble heart so that like her, we will attribute our

---

[300] "The Story of St. Peregrine: The Rebel Who Became a Saint," Franciscan Mission Associates, https://franciscanmissionassoc.org/prayer-requests/devotional-saints/st-peregrine/the-story-of-st-peregrine/
[301] Ibid.

successes to God and our failures to ourselves."[302] To commemorate Mary's humility, and to act as a counter to our fallen, prideful nature, we should faithfully say the Angelus three times a day.

Saint Catherine of Siena is one of my favorite saints. My daughter and I were in Italy and planned a day trip from Rome to Siena to visit the hometown of her confirmation saint.

On the way there we enjoyed the morning train ride through the Tuscan countryside. When in Siena we toured the Basilica San Domenico that displayed Saint Catherine's partially incorrupt head (see below) and her right thumb. We were blessed to be able to pray near our beloved Saint Catherine's incorrupt relics.

Saint Catherine of Siena's Incorrupt Head (1347-1380)
Basilica San Domenico, Siena, Italy
https://www.atlasobscura.com/places/st-dominics-basilica

After the cathedral we were able to visit Catherine's home. The highlight was her cell, or room, the exact place where she prayed and united her heart so well to serving Christ. Outside her cell is an area containing a couple of large paintings. Jesus appeared to Saint Catherine of Siena and said he was pleased with her devotion. He asked her if she would like a crown of gold and jewels, but in his other hand he had a crown of thorns. Saint Catherine replied, "My Lord, as you

---

[302] Broom, "Imitate,"

chose a crown of thorns, how could I not choose the same." Humility.
There it is. Here is the scene:

Painting Outside Saint Catherine's Cell
Siena, Italy

If you were offered the same choice by Christ today, which crown would you choose? The question is not as hypothetical as you might imagine. Christ each day offers us the opportunity to unite ourselves more closely to him, or we can choose to indulge ourselves with instant gratification, simple pleasures, and perhaps even luxuries, via one, or many, choices throughout our day. How much self-denial, mortification, and humility do we consciously deploy, with the right spirit of service to God, each day? For most of us, the answer is clearly, I can do more. In practicing humility, we would do well to listen to Saint Thomas More, "The ordinary acts we practice every day at home are of more importance to the soul than their simplicity might suggest."

In the chapter on Saint Etheldreda, we read how pleasing to God are virginity and chastity. In terms of which virtues to pursue, obviously an all-of-the-above approach would be the best, but what about comparing say, humility and virginity? Is there one that is more beneficial to the soul? Fortunately, we have the answer to that from Saint Thomas who said, "Speaking absolutely, humility excels virginity." To impress this point upon you, let us consider two additional quotes. The "Doctor of Light," Saint Bernadine of Clairvaux (1090-1153), wrote, "The three most important virtues are: humility, humility, humility." The "Mistress of Theologians," Saint Angela of Foligno adds, "Without humility of heart all the other virtues by which one runs toward God seem, and are, absolutely worthless."

As pride is the worst sin, its corresponding virtue, humility, must then be the best quality. A case could be made, therefore, that, while tangentially oxymoronic, humility is the best virtue. If I were to bring up humility to my friend Martin, his standard joke right about now would be, "I'm the humblest person I know."

Wondering which virtue most appealed to Christ, we turn to Saint Alphonsus Maria de Liguori, "Humility and meekness were the favorite virtues of Jesus Christ; so that he bade His disciples: 'Learn of Me: for I am meek and humble of heart.'" Picking up where Jesus left off, Saint Francis De Sales follows up with, "Humility makes our lives acceptable to God, meekness makes us acceptable to men."

In one of the leading books on humility in all church history, Padre Gaetano Maria de Bergamo, in "Humility of Heart," writes:

"He who is humble, even though he fall through frailty, soon repents with sorrow and implores the divine assistance to help him to amend; nor is he astonished at having fallen, because he knows that of himself, he is only capable of evil and would do far worse if God did not protect him with His grace. After having sinned, it is good to humble oneself before God, and without losing courage, to remain in humility in order not to fall again... But to afflict ourselves without measure and to give way to a certain pusillanimous melancholy, which brings us to the verge of despair, is a temptation of pride, insinuated by the devil... However upright we may be, we must never be scandalized nor amazed at the conduct of evildoers, nor consider ourselves better than they, because we do not know what is ordained for them or for us in the supreme dispositions of God."[303]

It may not be apparent at first, but humility does indeed require courage. Sometimes tremendous courage to recognize how dependent we are upon God. As Fr. Ignatius of the Side of Jesus has written, "There is nothing more dangerous than to confide in our own strength,

[303] de Bergamo, Padre Gaetano Maria, "Humility of Heart," Founding Fathers Films Publishing, Mandeville, LA, 2017, 56-57.

and trust to feelings of fervor. We are full of malice, and capable of committing the most enormous crimes, unless God supports us."[304] Humility is an absolute necessity for us to advance in holiness.

Saint Thomas of Villanova writes, "Humility is the mother of many virtues because from it obedience, fear, reverence, patience, modesty, meekness and peace are born. He who is humble easily obeys everyone, fears to offend anyone, is at peace with everyone, is kind with all."

As humility, the mother of many virtues, is perhaps one of the most important and least understood virtues, below is a sample flight of some additional excellent quotes about humility:

"By reason of His immensity, God is present everywhere; but there are two places where He dwells in a particular manner. One is in the highest heavens, where He is present by that glory which He communicates to the blessed; the other is on earth- within the humble soul that loves Him."
- Saint Alphonsus Maria de Liguori

"There is something in humility which strangely exalts the heart."
- Saint Augustine

"It was pride that changed angels into devils; it is humility that makes men as angels."
- Saint Augustine

"Do you wish to be great? Then begin by being. Do you desire to construct a vast and lofty fabric? Think first about the foundations of humility. The higher your structure is to be, the deeper must be its foundation."
- Saint Augustine

"If humble souls are contradicted, they remain calm; if they are calumniated, they suffer with patience; if they are little esteemed, neglected, or forgotten, they consider that their due; if they are weighed down with occupations, they perform them cheerfully."
- Saint Vincent de Paul

---

[304] Fr. Ignatius of the Side of Jesus, "The School of Jesus Crucified" 85-6.

"The life of our flesh is the delight of sensuality; its death is to take from it all sensible delight. The life of our judgment and our will is to dispose of ourselves and what is ours, according to our own views and wishes; their death, then, is to submit ourselves in all things to the judgment and will of others. The life of the desire for esteem and respect is to be well thought of by everyone; its death, therefore, is to hide ourselves so as not to be known, by means of continual acts of humility and self-abasement. Until one succeeds in dying in this manner, he will never be a servant of God, nor will God ever perfectly live in him."
- Saint Mary Magdalene de Pazzi, ("Cultivating Virtue: Self-Mastery With the Saints," p. 126)

"It is no great thing to be humble when you are brought low; but to be humble when you are praised is a great and rare attainment."
- Saint Bernard

"No one reaches the kingdom of Heaven except by humility"
- Saint Augustine

"Nothing is more powerful than meekness. For as fire is extinguished by water, so a mind inflated by anger is subdued by meekness. By meekness we practice and make known our virtue, and also cause the indignation of our brother to cease, and deliver his mind from perturbation."
- Saint John Chrysostom

Recognizing that humility is essential to our salvation, I am motivated to keep our discussion about this virtue short and sweet. Similarly, in the spirit of the virtue, I will forego regaling you with some of my many, many, many heroic examples of humility. Instead, let us close with the Litany of Humility:

Litany of Humility

O Jesus, meek and humble of heart, *Hear me.*
From the desire of being esteemed, *Deliver me, O Jesus.*
From the desire of being loved, *Deliver me, O Jesus.*
From the desire of being extolled, etc.

From the desire of being honored,
From the desire of being praised,
From the desire of being preferred to others,
From the desire of being consulted,
From the desire of being approved,
From the fear of being humiliated,
From the fear of being despised,
From the fear of suffering rebukes,
From the fear of being calumniated,
From the fear of being forgotten,
From the fear of being ridiculed,
From the fear of being wronged,
From the fear of being suspected,

That others may be loved more than I, *Jesus, grant me the grace to desire it.*
That others may be esteemed more than I, *etc.*
That, in the opinion of the world, others may increase and I may decrease,
That others may be chosen and I set aside,
That others may be praised and I go unnoticed,
That others may be preferred to me in everything,
That others may become holier than I, provided that I may become as holy as I should,

Fourteenth Century Saints

Saints Gertrude (d. 1302), Nicholas of Tentina (d. 1306), Clare of Montefalco (d. 1308), Bl. Margaret of Castello (d. 1320), Elizabeth of Portugal (d. 1336), Juliana Falconeri (d. 1341), Peregrine (d. 1345), Bridget of Sweden (d. 1373), and Catherine of Siena (d. 1380), pray for us.

Saint Roch is the patron saint of dogs, surgeons, invalids, bachelors, and against plague and pestilence.
Saint Roch's feast day is August 16th.
Saint Roch, *ora pro nobis* (pray for us).

Fourteenth Century History

1300s- Bl. Ramon Llull, mystic, philosopher, and <u>Doctor</u> Illuminatus "Enlightened Doctor," is believed to have first used the phrase, "Immaculate Conception."

1300s- The Ottoman Empire begins its expansion taking land from the Byzantine Empire.

1305- French influence causes the pope to move from Rome to Avignon.

1320- Dante Alighieri writes the *Divine Comedy*, one of the greatest works of world literature.

1347-1351- The black death plague arrives from the east. It was the most fatal pandemic in human history causing the deaths of 75-200 million people in Europe, Asia and North Africa.

1370- Saint Catherine of Siena calls on the pope to return to Rome.

1378-1417- The Western Schism, also called Great Schism or *Great Western Schism*, was a period when there were two, and later three rival popes, each with his own following, his own Sacred College of Cardinals, and his own administrative offices.

1387- Lithuanians accept the Catholic faith, becoming the last in Europe to do so.

1389- Battle of Kosovo. Ottomans defeat Serbians gaining entry into Europe.

Virtue Challenge #14- Humility

Saint Roch, we are humbled by our physical ailments, maladies, aches and pains. Saint Roch help us to work with God's grace as he molds us. Pray for us to better understand the Father's will and love for us. Help us to be, like you, humble.

Lord Jesus, help us to be meek and humble like you. You are the King of Kings, yet you chose to humble yourself, be born of man, live a hidden life for thirty years, then humbly minister for three years, culminating in your Passion and ignominious death on the cross. You did it all for my sins, and for those of all mankind. In humility, we know we can never repay the debt you satisfied for us. We are grateful, even when we don't always show it and we sin. Pray for us to increase in meekness and humility. Show us the way.

In *Humility of Heart,* Rev. Cajetan da Bergamo, writes, "Christ Himself taught humility of heart, and the heart must not remain idle, nor fail to product the necessary acts." (p .138-140)

Bergamo then asks some great questions for us to answer, "And what acts of humility do you make before God? How often do you make them? When have you made them? How long is it since you made them?" (Ibid)

Immaculate Mary, meek and humble of heart, make our hearts like unto the Heart of Jesus.
Blessed Mother most humble, intercede for us.
Saint Joseph most humble, pray for us.
Saint Michael the Archangel, help us to not be overcome with pride but remain steadfast in humility.

In humility, pray for the freedom and exultation of Holy Mother Church.

Converse for a moment with the Holy Ghost about humility. My Lord and my God, how may I serve you more faithfully and completely through the virtue of humility?

O Great Saint Roch, pray for us an increase in the virtue and grace of holy humility.

CHAPTER 15

Lidwina

The Fifteenth Century
Longanimity

"Blessed be He, who came into the world for no other purpose than to suffer."

~ Saint Teresa of Avila

"All the science of the Saints is included in these two things: To do, and to suffer. And whoever had done these two things best, has made himself most saintly."

~ Saint Francis de Sales

"The more the wicked abound, so much the more must we suffer with them in patience; for on the threshing floor few are the grains carried into the barns, but high are the piles of chaff burned with fire."

~ Pope Saint Gregory the Great

"Nothing afflicts the heart of Jesus so much as to see all His sufferings of no avail to so many."

~ Saint John Mary Vianney

"If God sends you many sufferings, it is a sign that He has great plans for you, and certainly wants to make you a saint."

~ Saint Ignatius Loyola

The 1400s

Why does God allow suffering?

To personalize this, what's been your greatest suffering? Loss of a loved one? Divorce? Abuse? Cancer? Bankruptcy? Trump losing to Biden? I know. All bad.

While many of us have gone through much pain, living in the United States of America has afforded us, overall, lives of comparative comfort. Some of us, to a smaller or larger extent, have even grown complacent, wimpy and soft. We bellyache over minor aches, whine when the TSA line at the airport is too long, and complain when they are out of decaf coffee in the waiting room at the car repair shop. Life sure can be rough! Given what's on the horizon, Catholics need to get tough. Are we a weak, or strong, link in the Communion of Saints? What are some ways that God helps us to build virtue and spiritual toughness? Suffering. Longanimity (defined as, "extraordinary patience under provocation or trial"). Following his footsteps in the Passion. Embracing each of the crosses he sends to us in love.

With original sin there comes suffering. How do we handle our suffering, pain and hurt? Do we accept or reject the reality of suffering? How do we pursue God, perfect love, despite the crosses he permits? The wood of the manger and the wood of the cross point to the same reality. Similarly, Blessed Mother always points us to Christ. Longanimity can unite us with Christ.

Saint Lidwina, whose Flemish name "Lyden" means "suffering," (others explain her name means "great patience" in German) was born in 1380 into a poor family in the town of Schiedam, County of Holland, part of the Holy Roman Empire. Today, Schiedam is a suburb of Rotterdam in the Netherlands. Lidwina's parents were exemplary Catholics and attended well to their religious duties. Unbeknownst she would soon deliver, Lidwina's mother was attending High Mass on Palm Sunday, when she began her labor pains. She rushed home and it is said she was born as the Passion of Our Savior was being read in church. Her biographers, and contemporaries, including Thomas a Kempis, attest that her name and moment of the day she was born were prophetic as her life was one of sufferings in union with the Passion of Our Savior.[305]

The only girl among nine children, from a young age Lidwina prayed, sometimes the whole night, before the miraculous statue of Our Lady of Schiedam. Blessed Mother shared with Lidwina that Christ would ask her to endure great sufferings, and if she accepted his offering, Mary would help her through her intercessory power and additional graces.

---

[305] Cruz, Joan Carrol, "Secular Saints," TAN Books and Publishers, Rockford, II 1989. 432.

When Lidwina was fifeen years old, she was invited ice skating with friends, and had a hard fall breaking a rib on her right side. This was to be the beginning of her long-suffering. Despite seeing many doctors, the rib would not heal. Eventually, gangrene would appear and spread over her body. She was unable to recover and for years she endured great pain that only grew worse each day. Lidwina suffered from nausea, headaches, and dehydration. It is reported that she became paralyzed except for her left hand, parts of her body fell off, and blood came regularly from her mouth, nose and ears. Some say she was the first recorded case of multiple sclerosis.[306]

Her pain was so intense she could find no relief whether she was sitting, standing or lying down. Lidwina had the urge to constantly change her position and began to move herself around on her knees— she did this for three years. When she could do this no longer, she was confined to bed for the rest of her life.[307]

Many thought Lidwina's severe illnesses were nothing more than her faking. Others thought she was perhaps under demonic influence. One incident of note was when her pastor, Andries, brought Lidwina an unconsecrated host. She knew right away that it was not the true Eucharist.[308]

The list of ailments affecting Lidwina were numerous. Here is a partial list: her forehead became cleft from her hairline to her nose; her chin dropped under the lower lip; she became blind in her right eye; she became extremely sensitive to light; she had violent neuralgic pains; a pounding noise in her head; she suffered violent toothaches with some lasting for weeks; severe inflammation of the throat; her lungs and liver decayed, and a cancer consumed her flesh. And to all that add dropsy, which became so bad that her stomach had to be held together with wrappings.[309]

Saint John Baptist de la Salle said, "You can do more with the grace of God than you think." Lidwina's extreme maladies were unbearable but for the grace of God who supported her as a victim soul. It is said when Lidwina's pains began, she complained a bit, but she eventually came to realize that her sufferings were expiation for

[306] "Lidwina," Wikipedia, https://en.wikipedia.org/wiki/Lidwina
[307] Cruz, 433.
[308] "St. Lidwina," New Advent, https://www.newadvent.org/cathen/09233a.htm
[309] Cruz, 434.

not just the sins of others, but for the benefit of the entire church. After that realization she accepted her physical challenges willingly and patiently. Lidwina even said that if a single Hail Mary would end her suffering, she would not say it.[310] Talk about embracing the spirit of longanimity! Perhaps Saint Vincent de Paul was thinking of Lidwina when he commented, "If we only knew the precious treasure hidden in infirmities, we would receive them with the joy with we receive the greatest benefits, and we would bear them without complaining or showing signs of weariness."

For the last nineteen years of her life, Lidwina ate nothing but the Holy Eucharist. During the eleven years prior to that she had the equivalent of what one person would eat in three days. For the last seven she suffered perpetual insomnia. The twenty-three years prior to the seven-year period, the saint slept the equivalent of only three good nights.[311]

Due to her physical condition and her lack of nourishment and sleep, Lidwina became an oddity and was visited by innumerable people, which only added to her sufferings. Fortunately, her family recognized her sanctity and assisted her as best they could. Despite all the infirmities and conditions, a sweet perfume emanated from the sickened areas.

Despite Lidwina's longanimity, God favored Lidwina with the gift of prayer, visions and mystical phenomena. It is said that several miracles occurred next to her bed, such as healing the sick. Lidwina could see events from a great distance, and she could give details of places that she had never visited. She then began to prophesy, bilocate and read hearts. In the year 1407, Lidwina was blessed with visions of angels, Blessed Mother, the Holy Child, saints (including Saint Paul and Saint Francis of Assisi), and our suffering Lord. She then received the stigmata and they remained with her until her last breath.

In one of Lidwina's visions she was shown a rose bush with the words, "When this shall be in bloom, your suffering will be at an end."[312] In the spring of 1433, Lidwina called out, "I see the rose-bush in full bloom!" From the day of her skating injury at age fifteen, until

---

[310] Ibid.
[311] Ibid, 438.
[312] Ibid.

her death thirty-eight years later, every day was a day of pain and longanimity for Lidwina. On Easter Tuesday, she had a vision of Christ administering the Sacrament of Extreme Unction, and died later that day.[313]

After her death Lidwina's body miraculously transformed. All of her wounds were healed, the cleft forehead disappeared, and Lidwina seemed to be a lovely girl of approximately seventeen years of age smiling in her sleep. Many who came by to pay their respects noticed that a strong sweet odor of sanctity emanated from her body.[314] Placed in a marble tomb, her grave quickly grew into a place of pilgrimage. Today, her relics remain in the Basilica of Lidwina in Schiedam.[315]

Lidwina is described as a prodigy of human misery and heroic patience. In Catholic homilies, the virtue of longanimity is not discussed very often. For the most part suffering, whenever it is discussed, is the proverbial skunk at the garden party. Talks on charity, hope and mercy are much more palatable to the majority. Who, if anyone, is attracted to talks on long-suffering? It's tough stuff. In our fast-food society, how is it that any of us have forbearance and the disposition to bear injuries patiently? Who among us can say we are calm in the face of suffering and adversity? As Catholics, no matter what physical, mental, societal, professional, familial hardships we go through, God is with us.

Do you fear suffering? Hunger? Cold? Job insecurity? Loneliness? Sin? What exactly do you fear most? How can you better accept what you fear as a means to help you grow closer to Christ? Besides the model of the saints in general, let us look to the excellent example of Jesus's parents, Blessed Mother and Saint Joseph. Neither feared suffering. From the beginning, they knew hardship. The holy parents bore patient, silent, invisible pleas wishing only to care for their son, and serve God the Father.

Fr. Jacques Philippe, writing in *Interior Freedom* tells us, "What really hurts is not so much suffering as the fear of suffering. If welcomed trustingly and peacefully, suffering makes us grow. It matures and trains us, purifies us, teaches us to love unselfishly, makes

---

[313] New Advent, https://www.newadvent.org/cathen/09233a.htm
[314] Cruz, 435.
[315] "Lidwina," Wikipedia, https://en.wikipedia.org/wiki/Lidwina

us poor in heart, humble, gentle, and compassionate toward our neighbor. Fear of suffering, on the other hand, hardens us in self-protective, defensive attitudes, and often leads us to make irrational choices with disastrous consequences."[316]

Understandably, very few people wish suffering to come their way. If someone seeks suffering, that's considered saintlike. But most mere mortals do all they can to avoid discomfort, let alone pain itself. How can you find purpose in suffering? For some, their purpose in life came through suffering. Think about all the post abortive women who began pregnancy help centers. Think about all those who suffered injustice in the criminal justice system, who started prison reform and inmate placement services. Think about those who suffered from illness or cancer, were made well, and now volunteer at a local hospital. Much good can come from suffering. In a way it is using the leverage of the hardship to go on the offense, in a jiujitsu sort of way. Saint Cyprian has said, "This, in short, is the difference between us and others who know not God, that in misfortune they complain and murmur, while the adversity does not call us away from the truth of virtue and faith, but strengthens us by its suffering."

In his book *The Mystery of Suffering*, Dom Hubert van Zeller explains, "The saints flinch as instinctively as others when the cross comes along, but they do not allow their flinching to upset their perspectives. As soon as it becomes clear to them that this particular suffering is what God evidently wants suffered, they stop flinching. Their habitual state of surrender to God's will has a steadying effect: they do not get stampeded into panic or despair or rebellion or defeat."[317]

What value can there be in suffering? Well, physically it allows us to get tougher to be better able to face greater pain down the road. It builds up tolerance and the ability to gut something out. "As iron is fashioned by fire and on the anvil," Saint Madeline Sophie Barat explains, "so in the fire of suffering and under the weight of trials, our souls receive that form which our Lord desires them to have."

Saint John Vianney tells us, "There is no doubt about it: a person who loves pleasure, who seeks comfort, who flies from anything that

---

[316] Phillipe, *Interior Freedom*, 47.
[317] van Zeller, Dom Hubert, *The Mystery of Suffering*, n.p.

might spell suffering, who is over-anxious, who complains, who blames, and who becomes impatient at the least little thing which does not go his way - a person like that is a Christian only in name; he is only a dishonor to his religion, for Jesus Christ has said so: 'Anyone who wishes to come after Me, let him deny himself and take up his cross every day of his life, and follow Me.'"

Fr. John Hardon in the Modern Catholic Dictionary describes the Fruit of Longanimity as "Extraordinary patience under provocation or trial. Also called long suffering. It is one of the fruits of the Holy Spirit. It includes forbearance, which adds to long suffering the implication of restraint in expressing one's feelings or in demanding punishment or one's due. Longanimity suggests toleration, moved by love and the desire for peace, of something painful that deserves to be rejected or opposed."[318]

A passage in "Interior Life" by Fr. Jacques Philippe states, "By accepting the sufferings 'offered' by life and allowed by God for our progress and purification, we spare ourselves much harder ones. We need to develop this kind of realism and, once and for all, stop dreaming of a life without suffering or conflict. That is the life of heaven, not earth. We must take up our cross and follow Christ courageously every day; the bitterness of that cross will sooner or later be transformed into sweetness."[319]

Suffering is part of the human condition. Fr. Ed Broom, OMV, adds this clever maxim: "Suffering either makes you better or bitter." Bitter, if one suffers for the mere sake of suffering! Better, sanctified and growing in holiness, only when our suffering is united with the suffering of Jesus on the cross in Holy Mass."[320] Do we view suffering as making us better or bitter?

What about the other side of the coin? For those who are in good health, is there proper perspective and appreciation for your blessing of good health? Being aware of all the maladies that affect others, how aware are people that health is fragile? Are we as compassionate as we should be regarding others who are in poor health?

---

[318] Hardon, Fr. John. *Modern Catholic Dictionary*, n.p.
[319] Phillipe, *Interior Life*, 49.
[320] Broom, Fr. Ed, "We Can Offer Up Our Sacrifices & Sufferings," *Catholic Exchange*, February 9, 2021.

Suffering benefits the Church and the Communion of Saints in numerous beautiful and mysterious ways. A benefit for our individual souls is the salvific value of making reparation for past sins. Saint Augustine of Hippo instructs us, "Trials and tribulations offer us a chance to make reparation for our past faults and sins. On such occasions the Lord comes to us like a physician to heal the wounds left by our sins. Tribulation is the divine medicine." Suffering can be a potential source of conversion of sinners.

Suffering is also a means to alleviate the suffering of souls in purgatory. When you were young, your mom evidenced great spiritual wisdom when you complained about eating your vegetables and she simply said, "Offer it up." When you whined after your brother took the last piece of pizza, she said, "Offer it up." And, lastly, when you scraped your knee after falling off your bike, and just before the Bactine disinfectant went on, she said … "Offer it up!" Indeed, any hardship that comes your way or sacrifice you make, *Offer it up*. You can do so for family members, friends, or anyone you can think of. You can also offer it up for the soul in purgatory who has no one to pray for them.

When others are in pain, do we empathize with them? Do we care for those in our family with a bit more charity when they are unwell? When others are shut in with a long-term illness, do we visit them? As we know, visiting the sick is a corporal work of mercy. The Venerable Archbishop Sheen had the right take on suffering in hospitals when he said, "Much suffering in hospitals is wasted."

It's somewhat easy and understandable to fall into the rut of "poor me" when discussing longanimity. What about others? How tuned in to others are we when it comes to their corporeal suffering? A charitable heart focuses on assisting and comforting others in need, not just when they are sick, but also when they are hungry or thirsty, in need of clothes or shelter, and when it is time to bury the dead.

What are we to think of the incarnation of Jesus in terms of him agreeing to suffer and die for us? How can we sympathize with the sufferings of our Creator and the Fruits of Christ's Passion? What sorrow do we have when we contemplate this? The Son of God atoned for our sin. To offer to the Father full abandonment and satisfaction. We deny Christ by our sinful actions. When we do deny him, we crucify Christ again. The bitter chalice and agonizing torture of Christ's passion. His whole body was covered with painful tortures. Judas betrayed Him. Peter denied Him. His other disciples abandoned Him, save John the Beloved. Saint Paul writes, "I enjoy my sufferings for you."

Regarding seeking pleasures versus accepting the pains of this life, consider this Diary entry from Saint Maria Faustina Kowalska, "One day, I saw two roads. One was broad, covered with sand and flowers, full of joy, music and all sorts of pleasures. People walked along it, dancing and enjoying themselves. They reached the end of the road without realizing it. And at the end of the road there was a horrible precipice; that is, the abyss of hell. The souls fell blindly into it; as they walked, so they fell. And there, numbers were so great that it was impossible to count them. And I saw the other road, or rather, a path, for it was narrow and strewn with thorns and rocks; and the people who walked along it had tears in their eyes, and all kinds of suffering befell them. Some fell down upon the rocks, but stood up immediately and went on. At the end of the road there was a magnificent garden filled with all sorts of happiness, and all these souls entered there. At the very first instant they forgot all their sufferings."[321]

Saint Francis de Sales writes, "All the science of the Saints is included in these two things: To do, and to suffer. And whoever has done these two things best, has made himself most saintly." As the Corporeal Works of Mercy assists physical suffering and needs, the Spiritual Works of Mercy assist spiritual suffering. We are to: instruct the ignorant, counsel the doubtful, admonish the sinners, bear patiently those who wrong us, forgive offenses, comfort the afflicted, and pray for the living and the dead.

Saint Paul knew the value of suffering in that it allowed us to unite our sufferings to the Passion and to the Cross. Saint Paul writes that we suffer "to make us rely, not on ourselves but on God who raises the dead." (2 Corinthians 1:9) Saint Paul was speaking of redemptive suffering. Saint James also addresses redemptive suffering at the beginning of his letter, "My brethren, count it all joy, when you shall fall into diverse temptations; Knowing that the trying of your faith

---

[321] Kowalska, Saint Maria Faustina, *Dairy*, n.p.

worketh patience. And patience hath a perfect work; that you may be perfect and entire, failing in nothing." (James 1:2-4)

Both Saint Paul and James realized the revolutionary element of the gospel and redemptive suffering. They understood that Jesus conquered evil with good. We can imitate Jesus and participate in redemptive suffering too when we unite our heart to his in all we do, hardships and all. Saint Aloysius Gonzaga tells us, "He who wishes to love God does not truly love Him if he has not an ardent and constant desire to suffer for His sake."

The mystery of the cross is the most fervent way of uniting ourselves to Christ. Saint John Vianney explains, "A cross carried simply, and without those returns of self-love which exaggerate troubles, is no longer a cross. Peaceable suffering is no longer suffering. We complain of suffering! We should have much more reason to complain of not suffering, since nothing makes us more like Our Lord than carrying His Cross. Oh, what a beautiful union of the soul with Our Lord Jesus Christ by the love and the virtue of His Cross!"

The Venerable Fulton Sheen encourages us to consider long suffering from a slightly altered perspective, that of God's time being different than ours, "God's delays are mysterious; sorrow is sometimes prolonged for the same reason for which it is sent. God may abstain for the moment from healing, not because Love does not love, but because Love never stops loving, and a greater good is to come from the woe. Heaven's clock is different from ours."[322]

Saint Albert the Great encourages us to accept our cross in whatever temptations come our way, "Now there's no one who approaches God with a true and upright heart who isn't tested by hardships and temptations. So in all these temptations see to it that even if you feel them, you don't consent to them. Instead, bear them patiently and calmly with humility and longsuffering."[323]

With original sin comes suffering. On suffering, Saint Josemaría Escrivá shares, "Suffering overwhelms you because you take it like a coward. Meet it bravely, with a Christian spirit: and you will regard it as a treasure." How do we choose to handle the suffering, pain and

---

[322] Sheen, Ven. Fulton, *Life of Christ,* 357.
[323] St. Albert the Great, *Manual for Spiritual Warfare,* 164.

hurt? Do we accept or reject the reality of suffering? How do we pursue God, perfect love, despite the crosses he sends to us. The wood of the manger and the wood of the cross point to the same reality. Our Blessed Mother always points us to Christ. Saint Joseph is the man who understands our difficulties and brokenness. Go to Joseph. Blessed Mother and Saint Joseph did not fear suffering. Go to Bethlehem and the Holy Family with your suffering, hurts and pains.

Blessed Anne Catherine Emmerich writes of their trip to Bethlehem for the birth of Jesus. On the way into town they were quite hungry and Joseph knew of a fig tree. They stopped to eat, yet the tree had been picked over due to the many travelers. Emmerich describes how Jesus visited that same fig tree thirty plus year later when he was active in ministry and cursed the tree and said it would never again bear fruit. Jesus, our God, knew which tree would not give fruit to his parents when they were hungry the day he was to be born. Not that He held a grudge against the tree; it is, however, interesting that Emmerich pointed out that it was the same tree from three decades prior. Hungry, they pressed on.

When they began the journey, Joseph was confident he could secure a place to stay in Bethlehem as he had family and contacts in town. Yet when they arrived in Bethlehem, he went from place to place and found no room at the inn. Blessed Mother consoled Joseph as he wept in frustration knowing Mary's hour was close. Joseph thought of shelter on the outskirts of town where the animals were kept in caves. A dirty cave was the best he could do. When they arrived, they cleaned out an area that would work for them. And Jesus was born and placed in a manger. The wood of the manger to start his life. The wood of the cross at the end of his life. Go to Bethlehem and the Holy Family with your suffering, hurts and pains.

Speaking of wood and pain, across the street from Saint John Lateran in Rome one can find the *Scala Sancta*, the Holy Stairs, in the Lateran Palace. They are the twenty-eight white marble steps that Christ ascended to meet Pontius Pilate and accept his fate. Saint Monica brought them back to Rome from her travels to Jerusalem in the fourth century. To protect the marble stairs, they are currently covered with walnut wood. As such, pilgrims ascend the walnut stairs on their knees. About halfway up the stairs, one realizes that walnut is quite the hardwood, but you endure.

Praying on each stair, occasionally noticing a brass plate with an opening to see down to the marble itself where it is believed to be some blood from Christ that is still visible. To spend fifteen to twenty minutes ascending the stairs is a minor form of suffering. Suffering to be united with Christ in his physical tortures and pains. Suffering of heart to be united with Christ in him being crucified and dying for the sins of the world. To think, Lidwina willingly accepted intense pain for thirty-eight years, and I grumble a bit about minor pain ascending stairs for twenty minutes. A plenary indulgence is granted to the believers who climb the stairs on the knees.

Scala Sancta, *the Holy Stairs, Lateran Palace, Rome, Italy*

At the bottom of the stairs is a statue of Judas betraying Christ with a kiss. The statue disturbs me whenever I look, or think, about it. I replay in my mind the scene of Jesus asking Judas, "are you betraying the Son of Man with a kiss?" (Luke 22:48). How many times have I through sin betrayed Jesus? With this in mind, I get on my knees and ascend the *Scala Sancta.*

Judas Betraying Christ, Lateran Palace, Rome, Italy

At the top of the *Scala Sancta* is a room, the *Sancta Sanctorum,* or "Holiest of Holies" as the chapel contains numerous holy relics. The Sancta Sanctorum is where Pope Leo XIII had a remarkable vision exactly thirty-three years to the day prior to the great Miracle of the Sun in Fatima, that is, on October 13, 1884. When the pontiff had finished celebrating Mass in his private Vatican Chapel, he suddenly stopped at the foot of the altar. The account continues, "He stood there for about 10 minutes, as if in a trance, his face ashen white. Then, going immediately from the Chapel to his office, he composed the above prayer to Saint Michael, with instructions it be said after all Low Masses everywhere."[324]

When asked what happened, the pontiff said he "heard voices - two voices, one kind and gentle, the other guttural and harsh. They seemed to come from near the tabernacle. As he listened, he heard the following conversation:

The guttural voice, the voice of Satan in his pride, boasted to Our Lord: "I can destroy your Church."

The gentle voice of Our Lord: "You can? Then go ahead and do so."

Satan: "To do so, I need more time and more power."

Our Lord: "How much time? How much power?

Satan: "75 to 100 years, and a greater power over those who will give themselves over to my service."

[324] "The Vision of Leo XIII," *Michael Journal,* https://www.michaeljournal.org/articles/roman-catholic-church/item/the-vision-of-pope-leo-xiii

Our Lord: "You have the time; you will have the power. Do with them what you will."[325]

In 1886, Pope Leo XIII decreed that the Saint Michael Prayer be said at the end of "low" Mass throughout the universal Church, along with the Salve Regina (Hail, Holy Queen). These prayers continued until about 1970, with the introduction of new rite of the Mass.[326]

With longanimity we think primarily about what sufferings the individual undergoes for Christ. In a similar way, we can look at the longanimity experienced by the Bride of Christ herself. The church has suffered increasingly from attacks from inside her ranks with each successive generation since Leo XIII's 1884 vision. The modernist efforts to reform the church have been unrelenting and by virtually every major metric the modernist impact on the church has been disastrous. To name just a few, vocations, church attendance, Catholic school's attendance, and belief in the True Presence in the Holy Eucharist are all down precipitously. Has the Catholic Church been destroyed? Not completely. But no one can deny the church is considerably less strong compared to three, four and five generations ago.

Individuals, families, communities, nations and the church itself undergo longanimity. The enemy has the time and the power. We courageously stand with Christ and defend His bride. Saint Maximilian Kolbe said, "For Jesus Christ I am prepared to suffer still more." Saint Thérèse of Lisieux encouraged her novices, "I always want to see you behaving like a brave soldier who does not complain about his own suffering but takes his comrades' wounds seriously and treats his own as nothing but scratches."

With longanimity we treat wounds as scratches, and being steadfast we press on to the high drama of the sixteenth century with Martin Luther, the Protestant Reformation (Revolt), Henry VIII, the Council of Trent, the Counter-Reformation, the Battle of Lepanto, and Saint Nicholas Owen and the virtue of fortitude and the forty Martyrs of England and Wales.

---

[325] Ibid.
[326] Ibid.

Fifteenth Century Saints

Saints Vincent Ferrer (d. 1419), Joan of Arc (d. 1431), Frances of Rome (d. 1440), Bernadine of Sienna (d. 1444), Colette (d. 1447), Bl. Fra Angelico (d. 1455), Rita of Cascia (d. 1456), John Capistrano (d. 1456), Thomas à Kempis (d. 1471), John of Kęty (Cantius) (d. 1473), Casimir (d. 1484), Nicholas of Flue (d. 1487), and John of God (d. 1495), pray for us.

Saint Lidwina is the patron saint of ice skaters and chronically ill.

Saint Lidwina is often represented receiving a branch of roses and a flowering rod from an angel.

Saint Lidwina's feast day is April 14.

Saint Lidwina, *ora pro nobis* (pray for us). (In Dutch, *Sint Liduina, bid voor ons.*)

Fifteenth Century History

1400- Geoffrey Chaucer completes *The Canterbury Tales*, stories told by pilgrims on a journey to visit the shrine of Saint Thomas Becket of Canterbury.

1431- **Saint Joan of Arc**, after success in battle against the English, is captured, condemned as a heretic, and burned at the stake. She was nineteen. A later investigation concluded she was innocent and proclaimed her a martyr.

1442- Council of Florence. Biblical canon definitively reaffirmed.

1453- **Fall of Constantinople.** After a siege of fifty-five days, and accompanying cannon barrage, of Constantinople, Sultan Mehmed II of the Ottoman Empire, conquers the city thus marking an end to the 1500-year-old Byzantine Empire. Constantinople's fall removed what was once a powerful defense for Christian Europe against Muslim invasion, thereby allowing for uninterrupted Ottoman expansion into eastern Europe.[327]

1455- **Gutenberg Bible.** Johann Gutenberg, inventor of the printing press, produces the first mass-produced Bible.

---

[327] "Fall of Constantinople," Britannica, https://www.britannica.com/event/Fall-of-Constantinople-1453

1468- Ferdinand II of Aragon and Isabella of Castille, known as "The Catholic Monarchs," join their kingdoms to form a unified Spain.

1478- The Tribunal of the Holy Office of the Inquisition, commonly known as the **Spanish Inquisition**, was a tribunal established by Ferdinand and Isabella to end the Medieval Inquisition begun almost 300 years prior. The Inquisition was intended to maintain Catholic orthodoxy in their kingdoms, root out heresy, and ordered Jews and Muslims to convert or leave Spain. Over the next three centuries, around 150,000 were prosecuted for various offenses, out of which between 3,000 and 5,000 were executed.[328]

1492- The *Reconquista* is complete after the Moors are defeated in Granada, Spain. The Alhambra Decree edicts forces additional conversion or expulsion of Jews and Muslims from Spain. Isabella appoints Tomás de Torquemada as the first Inquisitor General of the Inquisition.

1492- Ferdinand and Isabella commission the expedition of Christopher Columbus. Reaching the Americas, one of his exploration goals is to bring Christianity to other lands and peoples.

1497- John Cabot lands in Newfoundland, Canada to claim land for King Henry VII, and to recognize the religious tradition of the Catholic Church.

1495- Leonardo da Vinci completes "The Last Supper."

Virtue Challenge #15- Longanimity

Saint Lidwina, thank you for your heroic example as a victim soul. While few reading this wish to become victim souls, help us to accept a sliver of our current suffering for the conversion of sinners and the overall church. Help us to pick up our cross daily.

Tap into the history of the church and consider all those who were martyred for the faith, who endured hardship for you to have the faith and the church you have today. How will you sidestep your

---

[328] "Spanish Inquisition," Wikipedia, https://en.wikipedia.org/wiki/Spanish_Inquisition

inclination for comfort and embrace a portion of the church's historical suffering essential to spiritual growth?

When the lure of the world and it's shiny pursuits are omnipresent, how will you silence the noise for attention and focus on serving God?

How will you discern from among the pull of false doctrine coming from the church and certain bishops and priests? How will you cut through the pain of confusion in the most charitable way possible? In what ways will you guard against the drift and lure of progressive, modernist Catholicism?

Last but not least, what's your game plan to be joyful amidst life's travails, suffering, and even long suffering? In pain to come, how can joy be used to share the cross and better serve God? Deprivation and suffering help our faith to grow. Contemplate how grace, patiently and joyfully endured, outweighs pain associated with suffering.

Converse for a moment with the Holy Ghost about longanimity. My Lord and my God, how may I serve you more faithfully and completely through the virtue of longanimity?

O Great Saint Lidwina, pray for us an increase in the virtue and grace of holy longanimity.

CHAPTER 16

Owen

The Sixteenth Century
Fortitude

"I am not afraid; I was born for this!"
~ Saint Joan of Arc

"I do not care very much what men say of me, provided that God approves of me."
~ Saint Thomas More

"All the evil in the world is due to lukewarm Catholics."
~ Pope Saint Pius V

The 1500s

"A hero is a man who does what he can."
~ Romain Rolland, 9/11 boat captain

In the wake of the Islamic extremist attack on 9/11, Tom Hanks narrated "Boatlift- An Untold Tale of 9/11 Resilience" about America's Dunkirk. Recounting a dramatic day of fortitude, Hanks begins:

"On 9/11 every mode of transportation out of Manhattan shut down. Cars, buses, subways, bridges. Boats, usually an afterthought in New Yorkers minds, were for the first time in a century the only way in or out of Manhattan. Just a few boats. So many people on each boat. 10 people deep in certain areas. The Coast Guard said this needs to be better organized. So, they made the call on the radio, "All available boats, this is the United States Coast Guard, anyone willing to help with the evacuation of lower Manhattan, report to Governor's Island."

"When that call came on the radio, they were coming. About 15-20 minutes later there were boats all across the horizon. A flotilla of ferries, tugboats, private boats, party boats. They were all coming. And they were coming fast. Moving towards danger. Towards the dark, black smoke and dust. Once the boats got close from out of nowhere people were appearing. They looked like zombies. They were helpless. It is the worst feeling in the world when you feel helpless. They were humans and they needed to be saved. The boats went back and forth all day long. Average people stepped up. "I've gotta do something. I have to do what I have to do." A hero is a man who does what he can."

"The boat evacuation of 9/11 became the greatest sea evacuation in history. In the Evacuation of Dunkirk in WWII, 339,000 people were evacuated over 9 days. On 9/11, nearly 500,000 evacuated in less than 9 hours. "Everybody has a little hero in them. It will come out if need be." Never go through life saying "I should have."[329]

If you try and fail, so be it. If you succeed, praise God. A hero is a man who does what he can. Everyone has a little hero in them. What hero do you have in you? God chose you to be alive for this specific time, for this specific fight. This is a call out for faithful Catholics. "All available American faithful Catholics, report for duty." What kind of calls could our U.S. bishops put out to mobilize faithful Catholics to change our nation, to change our world? Imagine.

What if all U.S. bishops, effective immediately, ended communion for any pro-abortion Catholic politician? What if the U.S. bishops spoke out clearly and mobilized the faithful on matters of religious liberty? What if the U.S. bishops were united and led with no confusion on the immorality regarding homosexuality, same-sex civil unions, and gender dysphoria? Imagine how the faithful would respond. This can be a Catholic moment. Who will lead? And who will answer the call?

In crisis mode, people act and think differently. They act with urgency, resolve and fortitude that otherwise may not be there. On September 11, 2001, 2,977 innocent people, plus 16 Islamic terrorists, died. NYC, DC and America responded heroically to the tragedy of that day. In America, approximately 3,000 abortions murder the innocent preborn each day. It is nothing less than a crisis of the first order of magnitude. Averaging over one million surgical abortions

329 "Boatlift- An Untold Tale of 9/11 Resilience (HD Version)" YouTube posted September 7, 2011. https://www.youtube.com/watch?v=18lsxFcDrjo

each year for the past fifty years, many have unfortunately lost their fervor to treat abortion as the crisis it is, and act with utmost urgency.

Saints are heroically less weary and grow less tired of the battle than us mere mortals. With supernatural grace they remain steadfast and persist. God works through His saints infusing them with fortitude, a gift of the Holy Ghost, denoted as a "firmness of mind in doing good and in avoiding evil, particularly when it is difficult or dangerous to do so, and the confidence to overcome all obstacles, even deadly ones, by virtue of the assurance of everlasting life."[330]

Before we delve into a discussion of dangerous sixteenth-century England and how Saint Nicholas Owen served his God, his Catholic faith, and his country by overcoming the obstacles of his day through fortitude and ingenuity, let us quickly survey the political and religious landscape of the larger world to better appreciate the times in which Owen lived.

On October 31, 1517 the church would experience perhaps its biggest earthquake and fissure when priest and moral theologian Martin Luther posted his 95 Theses (critiques of the church) on the door of All Saints (Castle) Church in Wittenberg, Germany. His revolt would come to be known as the Protestant Reformation. Shortly thereafter England would experience its own rupture with the Catholic Church. While the second half of the century will be the focus of this chapter, it is the first half of the century that gave us the great English Saints Thomas More and John Fisher and their confrontations with Henry VIII.

When in England a few years back we were blessed to be able to visit the prison cell in Bell Tower in the Tower of London where Saint Thomas More, after refusing to swear the Oath of Succession, was held from 17 April 1534 until his execution on 6 July 1535. To walk in the prison cell where More walked, knelt, prayed and wrote was an incredibly humbling experience. We were told that Saint John Fisher's cell was directly above More's cell.

---

[330] Blissard, Frank, "The Seven Gifts of the Holy Spirit," *Catholic.com*, June 10, 2019.

Saint Thomas More's Cell, Tower of London

After the cell we were able to visit St. Peter ad Vincula (St. Peter in Chains) within the Tower of London. Beneath the Church is the crypt where the headless body of Saint Thomas More lies. (Saint Thomas More's skull—once impaled on a spike on London Bridge—lies in a family vault in a church in Canterbury.) Also in the crypt are the remains of Saint John Fisher.

At the Tower of London one can view the Crown Jewels. Thousands of people queue each day to see a room full of the worlds costliest and most valuable jewels. A hundred feet away are the cells and crypts of Saint Thomas More and Saint John Fisher which are infinitely more valuable than the nearby room of costliest diamonds and jewels. No lines for the saints. Special access only. What a statement it makes on our times that the people standing in queue for the Crown Jewels and the cells/crypt aren't reversed! Blessed be God's jewels in his saints! Saint John Fischer, pray for us. Saint Thomas More, "Henry's loyal servant, but God's first," pray for us.

Most all of us are familiar with Christopher Columbus sailing the ocean blue in 1492. In the successive decades thereafter, multiple other sailing expeditions brought the gospel of Christ to new lands. For instance, in 1516 Blessed Bartholomew of Olmedo, a Spanish

Mercedarian priest, was the first priest to arrive on Mexican soil. He was chaplain for the expedition of Fernando Cortés, who began the Spanish colonization of the Americas and the downfall of the Aztec empire. Bartholomew, teaching the Christian faith, pleaded with the Aztecs to end their brutal practice of human sacrifice. Bartholomew alone baptized 2,500 Aztecs.

A few years later in December, 1531, to assist further with the conversion of the indigenous peoples, Blessed Virgin Mary would appear five times to Juan Diego, now Saint Juan Diego, in Mexico City as *Nuestra Señora de Guadalupe,* or "Our Lady of Guadalupe." To help convince Archbishop Zumárraga that the apparitions were authentic, he asked Juan Diego to ask Blessed Mother for a truly acceptable, miraculous sign to prove her identity. The next day Blessed Mother revealed to him a cloak with her image on it. The miraculous cloak, rich in Catholic symbolism, is enshrined today within the Basilica of Our Lady of Guadalupe in Mexico City. The basilica is the most-visited Catholic shrine in the world, and the world's third most-visited sacred site.[331]

Our Lady of Guadalupe would go on to become the Patroness of the Americas and the patroness of the pro-life movement. Providentially, when we face hardship or tumult, we know we can turn to Our Lady, who consoled Saint Juan Diego (and to all her sons and daughters): "Let not your heart be disturbed... Am I not here, who is your Mother? Are you not under my protection? Am I not your health? Are you not happily within my fold? What else do you wish? Do not grieve, nor be disturbed, by anything."

With Christianity spreading in the new world, back in old world Europe, it took the Catholic Church almost thirty years to begin to seriously address Luther's revolt. In 1545, Pope Paul III convened the Council of Trent. The undertaking was massive as nearly all major church doctrines had been challenged by Luther, including the Real Presence of Christ in the Eucharist, and the validity of the sacraments. The Council of Trent would not conclude until eighteen years later in 1563. However, it took three more years—only after Pius V was elected pope—that among his first acts as pontiff he would enact Trent's pronouncements with the seal of doctrinal law.

---

[331] "Our Lady of Guadalupe," Wikipedia, https://en.wikipedia.org/wiki/Our_Lady_of_Guadalupe

Sticking with Pope Saint Pius V for one other major sixteenth century incident, we have the Battle of Lepanto. A battle that literally saved Christendom and western civilization. Ascending to the papacy, Pius V not only had to deal with the continued theological fallout from the Protestant revolt and implement the pronouncements of the Council of Trent, he had to deal with the greatest geopolitical challenge to the Catholic Church at that time, the ever-advancing Ottoman Empire. Pius V understood the Muslim Turks' desire to conquer the Mediterranean and the potential of the *jihad*, or holy war, to be waged.

At the beginning of our chapter, after the Islamic extremist attack on 9/11, we read how the Coast Guard put out the call for boats to assist with the evacuation of lower Manhattan. Four hundred and thirty years earlier, facing the Islamic aggressors at Europe's doorstep, Pope Saint Pius V put out a similar call for his day, "All available Christians, this is the pope, anyone willing to help defend Europe and Christendom, report to the Mediterranean and Lepanto." When the pope put out that call, the Catholics were coming.

Pope Pius V assembled the Holy League from the Christian nations of Europe to fight the Ottoman Turks. When the battle commenced in the Gulf of Patras in southwestern Greece on October 7, 1571, Pius V asked Catholics everywhere to pray the Rosary asking for our Lady's intercession. Under the military leadership of Don Juan of Austria, the Christian fleet won a surprising victory over the much more numerous Ottoman Turkish fleet. Pope Saint Pius V declared that from that day on, October 7 would be Our Lady of Victory. Today, we call that day Our Lady of the Rosary.[332]

What is it about boats being used to respond to Islamic aggression? I'm not entirely sure. Perhaps it is just a strange coincidence. What was not a coincidence was that both heroic maritime efforts, comprised of the forces of good taking on the forces of evil, required considerable fortitude and prayers to see things through. In all actuality, from start to finish, the entire sixteenth century would require faithful Catholics to press on with elevated levels of fortitude to contend with formidable foes. Fortunately, nay providentially, souls like Saint Nicholas Owen stepped to the fore in defense of the faith.

---

[332] Peterson, Larry, "The Pope That Saved the Church and Christendom... The Story of St. Pius V," *Catholic365.com*, October 10, 2017.

Confession time. Saint Nicholas Owen while born in 1550, died a few years into the seventeenth century (1606). He made, however, his greatest contributions during the sixteenth century (1580-1599) and so was chosen as the sixteenth century's saint. Please permit my "literary license" in this regard. Owen's story is fascinating, and delving into it will permit us the opportunity to better understand the courageous, virtuous era filled with fortitude that gave us the Forty Martyrs of England and Wales.

"I verily think no man can be said to have done more good of all those who laboured in the English vineyard. He was the immediate occasion of saving the lives of many hundreds of persons, both ecclesiastical and secular." So said John Gerard, Jesuit priest in England in the sixteenth and seventeenth centuries, of the subject of this story, Saint Nicholas Owen. And Gerard, author of the thrilling account of his own life *Autobiography of a Hunted Priest,* would know, as you will come to learn.

The Saxon Kingdom had been Catholic since the time of Augustine; no, not that more famous Saint Augustine, author of the classics *Confessions* and *City of God,* but rather Saint Augustine of Kent who was sent by the pope to evangelize that isle that would one day be known as England, and even "Merrie England." (Augustine would convert and baptize Ethelbert, King of Kent, in 596.)

The term Merrie England refers to a time, generally considered to extend from the mid-1350s to 1520 or so, when Catholic sacramental life and the various feast days and celebrations throughout the liturgical year were so deeply ingrained in and a part of English culture that it could be said that the national life was lived Catholicism.

That England, Merrie England, however, was destroyed because a Catholic king asked, "Why me?" rather than "Why not me?" Why should he, Henry VIII, have to remain married to his wife Catherine of Aragon when she was unable to give him a male heir? Why should he, Henry VIII, have to remain married to his wife when he lusted after another woman, Anne Boleyn? Why indeed? Why should any of us have to obey the laws of God? To ask that question is to answer it. We are not God; God is God and we were made to know him, love him, and serve him in this life and be happy with him in the next.

The situation was even perhaps more tragic for Henry personally because he had been such a devout Catholic that he had earned the title "Defender of the Faith" from Pope Leo X on Oct. 17, 1521 for a treatise he had written against Luther's new doctrines. Few people have made such dramatic, public, and consequential shipwrecks of the faith as did Henry Tudor. Contrariwise, few people in history give us such an example of steadfast faith amid incredibly trying circumstances and physical challenges, as Saint Nicholas Owen. Upon hearing of his story, we should ask ourselves, "Why not me?" and "How can I do what I can?"

Nicholas Owen was born in Oxford to a devout family during the time of the Penal Laws of England. Owen was trained as a master builder, skilled in carpentry and masonry. His skill in these areas came despite his very short stature, such that in some accounts, he is described as being nearly a dwarf. Owen had a crippled leg from a horse falling on him. What is more, he suffered from a hernia and is, again in some accounts, described as being a hunchback. These challenges notwithstanding, Nicholas Owen stands tall as a true hero of Catholic history. His firmness of mind to doing good under difficult and dangerous circumstances was heroic.

The Catholic-Protestant dispute over the head of the church in England was exacerbated significantly on April 27, 1570 when Pope Pius V issued the bull *Regnans in Excelsis* excommunicating Elizabeth I, Queen of England. Pius V claimed that there was no salvation outside the Roman Church, and that the pope alone was successor to Peter. The text reads, "...we do out of the fullness of our apostolic power declare the foresaid Elizabeth to be a heretic and favorer of heretics, and her adherents in the matters aforesaid to have incurred the sentence of excommunication and to be cut off from the unity of the body of Christ... And moreover (we declare) her to be deprived of her pretended title to the aforesaid crown and of all lordship, dignity and privilege whatsoever."[333]

The pope forbade "all nobles, subjects and people to obey Elizabeth on pain of excommunication. This, of course, placed England's Catholics in a trying position. While most were loyal to the throne, some used the papal statement as an excuse to plot against

---

[333] Scarisbrick, Jack, "Was Pius V Right to Excommunicate Elizabeth I?," *Catholic Herald (UK)*, February 20, 2021.

Elizabeth for the purpose of replacing her with a Catholic. Elizabeth cracked down on these opponents with vigor. Innocent Catholics suffered alongside the guilty."[334]

The situation in England after 1585 under Queen Elizabeth was truly precarious for Catholics as the faith was outlawed; hence priests were hunted and arrested, and often executed when found, as were laypeople at times. A significant fine was the least price one could expect to pay. It was in this situation that Nicholas Owen found himself, as the saying goes, right in the thick of things.

The reason that Owen was so placed was that he gave his life entirely to the protection of God's priests and in so doing attached himself to some of the most hunted men in England, including that most famous of the many Jesuit martyrs of Elizabethan England, Saint Edmund Campion.

When Campion was arrested, Owen protested his innocence and was imprisoned. Campion died a gruesome martyr's death as would many of his Jesuit brothers during that time. Once released, rather than devote himself to making money through his exceptional skill, Nicholas Owen had the inner fortitude and will to return to his work protecting God's priests. The year 1588 would begin an eighteen-year span during which he dedicated himself to building "priest-holes" or "hides" as they were called, hiding places for priests in the large homes of wealthy Catholics.

By one account it was recorded that "every time Nicholas was about to design a hiding place, he began the work by receiving the Holy Eucharist, accompanied the project by continuous prayer and offered the completion of the work to God alone. No wonder his hiding places were nearly impossible to discover."[335]

The "hides" could be under staircases, behind false walls, or even a further extension beyond another priest hole built as more of a decoy. In other words, Owen was clever enough to build an easily discovered outer hiding place, which concealed an inner hiding place. Examples of Owen's work survive at Sawston Hall in Cambridgeshire, Oxburgh Hall in Norfolk, Huddington Court in Worcestershire and Coughton

---

[334] Graves, Dan, "Pius V Excommunicated Queen Elizabeth I," *Christianity.com*, May, 2007.
[335] "St. Nicholas Owen," *America Needs Fatima*, https://americaneedsfatima.org/Saints-Heroes/st-nicholas-owen.html

Court in Warwickshire.[336] Due to the ingenuity of his craftsmanship, some of Owen's "hides" may still be undiscovered.

There is a lesson in that fact, too, especially for wealthy Catholics. Think of what your Elizabethan era ancestors in the faith risked, not just money but death, in order to "live Catholic."

As in any time of persecution and resulting "underground" activity, great discretion and prudence was required. And Owen was up to this task. To preserve the secret locations of the holes, he would often work at night and alone and would only reveal the location of the hiding place to the head of the household.

The Jesuits were the Catholic heroes of Elizabethan England. Men such as Saint Edmund Campion, the poet priest Robert Southwell, and the already mentioned John Gerard, risked all to provide the sacraments to the persecuted faithful and, they hoped, to bring once Merrie England back to the Faith which had created it. The leader of the Jesuits for many of these tragic years was Father Henry Garnet. It was to his service (and Gerard's) that Owen would dedicate the rest of his life, and it would be in his service that he would be captured, tortured, and killed in 1606. But Owen himself was a Jesuit as well; he was a lay brother and is an example for all of us laity to put our talents to work for God, from whom they come.

Some sources say that Owen was the mastermind behind the dramatic escape by Father Gerard from the Tower of London. With help from other members of the Catholic underground, Gerard escaped on a rope strung across the tower moat the night of 4 October 1597. Despite the fact that his hands were still mangled from the tortures he had undergone, Gerard succeeded in climbing down by rope to a waiting boat. Gerard even arranged for the escape of his gaoler (jailer), with whom he had become friendly, and who he knew would be held responsible for the jailbreak.[337]

Soon after the failure of the Gunpowder Plot in 1605, which was blamed on the Jesuits, a furious, elevated search for the Catholics ensued. Owen's work as a builder of "hides" would make his own final capture, when it happened, cause for much rejoicing by his captors,

---

[336] Hollingsworth, Gerelyn, "Mar. 22, St. Nicholas Owen, S.J., Martyr," *National Catholic Reporter*, March 22, 2010.
[337] "John Gerard," Wikipedia, https://en.wikipedia.org/wiki/John_Gerard_%28Jesuit%29

including a horrible man named Richard Topcliffe, a leading pursuivant (or hunter of priests, particularly Jesuits) and a sadist to boot who would be the one to torture the great man of God.

After hiding for eight days in a small space in which he could not stand or stretch his legs, on January 27, 1606 Owen sacrificed himself voluntarily at Hindlip Hall in Worcestershire in the hopes of protecting his master, Father Henry Garnet, who was hiding nearby along with another priest. His hiding place was not discovered as it was so well designed. Capturing Owen was a prize the pursuivants had long sought and, knowing him to be a "keeper of secrets" as well as a "builder of holes," after being transferred to the Tower of London, he was subjected to the most brutal of tortures designed to get him to reveal what he knew.

But Nicholas Owen, who was sometimes referred to as Little John, and Little Michael and used the aliases of Andrews and Draper, remained steadfast and said nothing even though he was subjected to what was known as Topcliffe's Rack, named for the man earlier described. His wrists manacled, he was raised from the floor with his arms over his head and made to hang for hours on end for a number of days in a row. For a man such as him, of already compromised physical condition (remember his hernia?), the pain must have been even more excruciating than it would have been for more healthy individuals. And still Nicholas Owen had the intestinal fortitude to say nothing. "For those few grim days in February, writes a historian, as the Government tried to break him, the fate of almost every English Catholic lay in Owen's hands."[338] Another would add, "In life he had saved them, in death he would too: not a single name escaped him."[339] He was true to the end which came in dramatic and painful fashion.

On Owen's final hours it was written, "In frustration the torturers kept adding weight to his feet but went beyond all limits. On March 1 it is believed a cut to his hernia caused his abdomen to burst open and his intestines then spilled out. Owen lingered on for one painful day before dying in the early hours of March 2. He had persevered to the end, never betraying any soul he was committed to protect. The rack-master tried to cover his behavior, excessive even

[338]https://web.archive.org/web/20140811074825/http://www.stnicholasowen.co.uk/articles.php?action=fullnews&id=6
[339] Ibid.

under the harsh standards of the day, by saying that the Jesuit had committed suicide."[340] While short of stature, Owen had the virtue of a Catholic giant- of a saint.

Owen was one of the Forty Martyrs of England and Wales. May the blood of these brave martyrs help one day to heal the separation of the Anglican Church from the Catholic Church. May the sacrifice of the martyrs inspire us to forge ahead in our defense of the faith, whatever hardships, difficulties and dangers present themselves.

As Catholics, we know the Seven Gifts of Holy Ghost to be: Wisdom, Understanding, Counsel, Fortitude, Knowledge, Piety, Fear of God. While each could, and perhaps should, have been featured as a core value associated with a saint over the twenty-one centuries in *Against the Grain*, only fortitude was chosen to speak to our culture and times. Faithfully serving God during a dreadful time in anti-Catholic England, from the first time I read about Nicholas Owen, fortitude was blinking at me in large neon lights.

In the *Modern Catholic Dictionary*, Fr. John Hardon writes, "The Gift of Fortitude: One of the seven gifts of the Holy Spirit; it gives a person a special strength of will. This gift confers an extraordinary readiness to undergo trials for love of God or in fulfillment of the divine will; unusual courage to bear difficulties even for many years; firmness in carrying arduous tasks to their completion; perseverance in a lifetime fidelity to one's vocation in spite of heavy trials or disappointments sent by God; and gladness in being privileged to suffer persecution or humiliation in union with Christ and for the sake of his name." Fr. Hardon's explanation of fortitude could very well have been written specifically for Owen.

The decision to do what is right in difficult circumstances can be examined from several angles. We can of course point the finger at ourselves and ask, "Why not me?" With that route we would have much to ponder and act upon. Of Owen, Butler's *Lives of the Saints* says: "Perhaps no single person contributed more to the preservation of Catholic religion in England in penal times."[341] Courage. Steadfast. What can the single person do?

[340] Hollingsworth. "March 22."
https://web.archive.org/web/20140531010405/http://stnicholasowen.co.uk/LifeofNichOwen.htm

Owen lived a couple generations after Saint Thomas Becket and Saint John Fisher, Bishops who spoke to Henry VIII and defended the faith. The dialogue between bishops and heads of state has been both a source of accord and discord over the centuries. An added dynamic then could be what can a single bishop do? Who among today's bishops in the U.S. are willing to take on society and persuasively, resolutely and effectively address the scandal over communion for politicians who support abortion, same-sex unions, gender rebellion, and the threats and restrictions on religious liberty?

When thinking of the U.S. bishops, the analogy that comes to mind is crabs in a bucket. I've lost count of how many times my dad has brought up that analogy to describe how when one crab wants to climb out, the other crabs pull it back down. "It's the nature of crabs" he would say. So, too, we see that with the bishops. As soon as one steps out to defend a moral teaching, another bishop will attempt to counter them, or pull them back into the bucket. Is it "the nature of bishops?"

A salty example of this phenomenon was on display for the world the see January 20, 2021, the day of Joe Biden's inauguration. The two crabs? Archbishop Gomez of Los Angeles and Cardinal Cupich of Chicago. The USCCB President's Statement on Biden's Inauguration, written by Gomez, set for release at 9 a.m., was, according to media reports, held by Cardinal Cupich of Chicago and Cardinal Tobin of Newark after they "called the Vatican to intervene."[342] The reason? Gomez's Statement, "warned Biden's agenda 'would advance moral evils on several fronts – from abortion to transgender ideology to attacks on religious freedom.' Here are two of the paragraphs that most likely caused the Statement to be held back:

"[A]s pastors, the nation's bishops are given the duty of proclaiming the Gospel in all its truth and power, in season and out of season, even when that teaching is inconvenient or when the Gospel's truths run contrary to the directions of the wider society and culture.

"So, I must point out that our new President has pledged to pursue certain policies that would advance moral evils and threaten human life and dignity, most seriously in the areas of abortion, contraception, marriage, and gender.

---

[342] Catholic Vote, "Unity" email, January 20, 2021.

Of deep concern is the liberty of the Church and the freedom of believers to live according to their consciences."

Cupich took to Twitter to issue a scathing criticism of the USCCB's official statement on Biden's inauguration. In his four-part Twitter thread, Cupich tweeted, "the U.S. Conference of Catholic bishops issued an ill-considered statement on the day of President Biden's inauguration. Aside from the fact that there is seemingly no precedent for doing so, the statement, critical of President Biden, came as a surprise to many bishops, who received it just hours before it was released."[343]

Later on Inauguration Day, the full statement, perhaps due to pressure, the USCCB released the full statement. Statement notwithstanding, how will the U.S. bishops work with Biden on issues of morality? Will they advocate for the authentic teachings of the Church, or will they acquiesce to the Biden agenda through their silence?

The public disagreement aired by Cupich was pathetic, but not unexpected. It's standard operating procedure for the modernist, progressive factions in the church. It's almost as if some bishops seek to impose a cancel culture on other bishops. It's maddening.

Some called Gomez' statement brave and heroic. Heroic? Gomez did not confront the candidacy of Biden when he had the chance months earlier. Doing so then would have had greater impact. He missed his opportunity and, thus, shirked his responsibility. His indifference during the campaign to speak out forcefully and fully use his bully pulpit, and that of the USCCB, speaks volumes. Instead, he waited until the proverbial 'horse had left the barn' and his comments were of little value. His statement is akin to wanting to add yeast to bread that has just been taken out of the oven. Respectfully, Archbishop, you missed your moment. Some essential ingredients need to be added to the recipe prior to baking. Yeesh. Once the election happens, you cannot affect the outcome. In other words, too little, too late.

To state this another way, politicians know the difference in casting votes for impact or for show. Gomez's statement has all the

---

[343] CNA Staff, "In unprecedented move, Cardinal Cupich criticizes USCCB statement on Biden," *Catholic News Agency,* January 20, 2021.

appearances of a 'show vote.' Maybe he and fellow pro-lifers can go into their dioceses now and say, "Did you see my pro-life statement?" Yes, we saw it, and it was about six months too late. Big whoop.

Coming at this from another angle, the bishops have the ongoing responsibility to correct the impenitent sinner. So how many have made public pronouncements about denying Biden communion for his scandalous positions? Seems to me like the opportunity for the bishops to instruct before and after are not materializing. Bishop Saint Ambrose correcting Theodosios this was not.

Out of the 450 active and retired bishops in the U.S., just a dozen bishops publicly came out in support of the USCCB's statement warning about Joe Biden's pledge to pursue anti-life and anti-family policies that would advance moral evils in the areas of abortion, contraception, marriage, and gender. Here is a list of the fourteen bishops who initially spoke out publicly in support of Gomez Jan. 20 statement on Biden's inauguration:

Archbishop Samuel Aquila of Denver, Archbishop Salvatore Cordileone of San Francisco, Archbishop Allen Vigneron of Detroit, Bishop James Conley of Lincoln, Bishop Donald Hying of Madison, Bishop Thomas Paprocki of Springfield, Bishop Steven Raica of Birmingham, Bishop Kevin Rhoades of Fort Wayne-South Bend, Bishop Thomas Tobin of Providence, Bishop James Wall of Gallup, Bishop Rick Stika of Knoxville, Archbishop Alexander Sample of Portland, Bishop Thomas Olmsted of Phoenix, Bishop Joseph Strickland of Tyler, TX. [344]

To be charitable, better late than never, but again this really is a case of too little, too late. The statement should have been made immediately after Biden received the Democratic nomination. It should have then been recirculated at the time of the Democratic Convention, during the debates, once voting began in the states and then read from the pulpits the weekend before the November election. If that was done, it would have been a good start. Anything short of that is weak. The weak, waffling bishops are not protecting the flock, but leaving us exposed to the scheming wolves in sheep's clothing. Crabs in a bucket.

---

344 Baklinski, Pete, "Over dozen bishops publicly back USCCB's statement condemning Biden's plan to pursue 'evil' abortion, gender policies," LifeSite News, January 21, 2021.

As it was from the beginning, and as it will most likely be until the end of time, there will be bishops who are essentially eunuchs and view getting along with the State a higher priority than the salvation of souls. It cannot be stated more emphatically that our bishops, priests, and other church leadership is in dire need of our prayers to remain faithful to their vows in leading souls to heaven. It reminds me of a story about Saint Margaret Mary Alacoque, who on one New Year's Day was praying for three persons who had recently died, two religious and one secular. Jesus appeared to her and asked, "Which one do you wish to give to me?" In humility she answered, "Lord, you make the choice in accordance with your greater glory and good pleasure." Jesus chose the soul of the secular, saying he had less compassion for the religious, because even though they had more means of meriting and expiating their sins during life, they had been unfaithful to the practice of their rule.[345]

We must increase our prayers for our bishops and priests to be faithful to the practice of their rule.

Which leads us to Matthew 7:3, "And why seest thou the mote that is in thy brother's eye; and seest not the beam that is in thy own eye?" Fussing about what the bishops do, or don't do, should not be the focus of as much of the laity's collective attention as it is. More often than not finding fault with the weak, ineffective bishops is a distraction from us focusing on our souls and those within our own circle of influence.

Returning to our crabs in a bucket analogy, who among the Traditional Catholic circles would deny that there is an over-abundance of opinions about who attends what Mass, with what priest, with what order, reading what Bible, down to who wears a mantilla, or chapel veil, and who doesn't, etc.? While Traditionalists find fault with the Novus Ordo Mass and the Modernist church, many spend an inordinate amount of time criticizing other traditional Catholics for operating in a way that they might not approve of 100 percent. It's as if the devil masterfully assembles the Traditionalists in a circular firing squad and gives the command to "fire" whenever he wants. I've also heard Traditionalists that chomp on other Traditionalists being frequently referred to as "alligators." Beware of alligators! While some

---

[345] Tassone, "Fidelity to Grace," *Day by Day*, 32.

Traditionalists may be right with what they think, say, or do, very few are 100 percent correct in all they think, say or do. Hence, more mercy, forgiveness, charity and humility are warranted in Traditionalist families, parishes and media circles.

As faithful, Traditional Catholics, without additional charity and humility, are not our souls in danger of abusing the grace of the New Testament? Are we not at times complacent, presumptuous, and prideful? Do we fool ourselves that we are in good favor with the Lord? As it says in Hebrews 12: 28-29, "Therefore receiving an immovable kingdom, we have grace; whereby let us serve, pleasing God, with fear and reverence. For our God is a consuming fire."

As Traditionalists, are we playing with fire? Let us pray that we have an increase of the flame of the gift of holy fortitude as sent to us from the Holy Ghost. Let us trust in God that He will provide and keep us on the correct path moving towards eternal salvation in His kingdom. Let us pray for an increase in the grace of fortitude and being steadfast all our days, especially on those days when it is not so easy. In considering fortitude, we see it being closely aligned with its virtuous cousin, *steadfast*. In researching what it means to be steadfast or having courage and making and keeping a commitment, I found the following:

"Steadfast doesn't mean when it's easy; the term has no meaning when things are working according to our own convenient interests. Steadfast means standing strong when it's challenging, difficult and unnerving. Just as courage is not the absence of fear, rather it is taking action despite being fearful; so too is steadfast a decision. Often when things are disconcerting, we retreat to the place where we are comfortable. However, *steadfast* is unwavering despite the obstacles and difficulties. When we don't hold the words to comfort the grieved, yet we show up and sit quietly just to eliminate loneliness, that is a steadfast commitment. When we see adversity on the face of another, and we choose to engage with our time and comfort, that is a steadfast decision."[346]

The vast majority of Catholics have retreated to a comfortable place. The world and the church beat us down and we go to a place to self-protect. In so doing, how often do we choose to not engage when

---

[346] Sundance, "Steadfast Doesn't Mean When It's Easy," *The Conservative Treehouse,* December 29, 2020.

we see adversity in the face of another? Sadly, the vast majority of Catholics, bishops, and even many traditionalists, fear the media, groupthink, and going against the grain, more than we fear God.

The devil loves complacent Catholics, those without commitment, the lukewarm. The devil loves when we think everyone makes it to heaven with little or no effort. All we have to do is be is a good person and we are in, right? Not so fast. Getting into heaven is not easy. The path is straightforward, but the execution part is difficult. The devil would also like for us to believe that the souls in purgatory are not in need of our prayers. He is always setting traps and snares for us. Catholics cannot afford to be complacent in the least. We must have fortitude to see that we do not give the devil an opening he is able to manipulate and place our souls in peril.

Stephen Kokx writes, "When men rebelled against Christendom and the Catholic world order during the 1500s, society began to decay. Grace began flowing to fewer and fewer souls due to Protestantism ensnaring more and more men in its theological falsehoods… Many so-called 'nationalists' and populists are rising up across the U.S. and Europe to fight the globalist, one-world agenda. That's all well and good. But what is nationalism without God? What is populism without Christianity? Didn't Christ himself say, "Without me, you can do nothing? The best message a politician can give right now is one that includes not only Jesus Christ, but, more specifically, the Catholic faith."[347]

Earlier in the chapter we discussed how Pope Pius V summoned the Holy League to fight the Ottomans at the Battle of Lepanto. He rose up for God. He did it with God. What if Pius V had been complacent about his response to Muslim aggression? What if he had been lukewarm? For Catholics, lukewarm is not a place we ever want to be. Perhaps a better way to understand a concept like fortitude is to study its opposite. In the case of fortitude, its antonyms are: apathy, cowardice, timidity, tepidity, laziness, lethargy. To this we can add, lukewarmness.

Remember Pius V's quote about all the evil in the world and the lukewarm referenced in the Introduction, and featured again at the

[347] Kokx, Stephen, "Only The Catholic Faith Can Ward Off Leftist Attacks On Us," *LifeSite News*, July 7, 2020.

start of this chapter? It's so true. Whenever I think about being a lukewarm Catholic, it freaks me out a bit. Pointing the finger directly at me I ask, "How lukewarm am I?" Let's submerge ourselves with a mini-deep dive on 'lukewarm' with the assistance of Fr. Rick Heilman. In his email, "Freedom from Lukewarmness" he writes:

"In the Book of Revelation, we see the Lord has some rather severe words about the lukewarm: *"I know your works; I know that you are neither cold nor hot. I wish you were either cold or hot. So, because you are lukewarm, neither hot nor cold, I will spit you out of my mouth."* Pope Saint Pius V went so far as to say, *"All the evil in the world is due to lukewarm Catholics."* Pope Saint Pius X showed no less disdain with, *"All the strength of Satan's reign is due to the easygoing weakness of Catholics."* Wow! All the evil in the world? All the strength of Satan's reign? Spit you out of my mouth? The level of fury toward the lukewarm is alarming. Why?"

"… Because the lukewarm do the most damage. They are very effective in modeling for others how to be a very poor, or even a "fake" Catholic. While "cold souls" openly disavow any claim to be a faithful Catholic, lukewarm souls make that claim, while they betray the Lord at every turn… Lukewarm souls will often "use" their Catholic faith to build their own personal brand. So, you'll often see politicians make the claim of being a devout Catholic, while they advocate for a plethora of evil policies that horrify God. Or, there are those lukewarm Catholics who see no problem voting these evil politicians into power. This is A-Okay for the lukewarm, as they have convinced themselves that God's 'mercy' extends to allowing every kind of sin."

"Lukewarm souls are like a dangerous virus that spreads throughout the Church. On issues of human life, sex, marriage and family, faith, and morality, many within the Catholic Church have absolutely no problem advocating laws and policies, and the politicians who support them, that clearly oppose the will of God. This "lukewarm virus" has spread so far that as much as 40% of Catholics favor abortion; 61% of Catholics support gay marriage. Now, you can see why our Lord, Pope Saint Pius V and Pope Saint Pius X, are so outraged by the lukewarm."

"In order to combat the demonic viral spread of lukewarmness, we must cultivate in ourselves the Holy Spirit gift of "Fear of the Lord," also known as "Awe and Wonder." "Fear of the Lord" is the gateway gift to all of the Gifts of the Holy Spirit. If your local parish is cultivating a watered-down, lukewarm version of Catholicism that avoids Church teaching on any "hot button" issues, "GET OUT!" Or, if possible, work with the pastor to cultivate reverent liturgies, frequent Confession, ample Adoration of the Blessed Sacrament, and the practice of many devotions. This gives the soul immunity to the virus of lukewarmness."[348]

It is clear that as Catholics we must not be content with merely being "a good person." With fortitude, through what we may consider to be any less than desirable circumstances, we must make the extra effort to serve God. Know that the devil will distract us with comforts and attempt to lull us into tepidity. Yes, the devil will also make many promises, not so that he may give them to us, but so that he may take away from us. (Sounds a bit like the Democratic Party and all their empty promises and policies that deprive people of their dignity and rot citizen's souls.) We must rebel against the prince of this world and serve God first and foremost.

In the Divine Mercy Novena, Christ said to Saint Faustina on the ninth day about the lukewarm souls, "These souls wound My Heart most painfully. My soul suffered the most dreadful loathing in the Garden of Olives because of lukewarm souls. They were the reason I cried out: 'Father, take this cup away from Me, if it be Your will.' For them, the last hope of salvation is to run to My mercy." Pray to bring the lukewarm souls into the abode of Jesus's most compassionate heart. Pray that the fire of Jesus's pure love will allow these tepid souls, who, like corpses, filled Him with such deep loathing, be once again set aflame.

Lukewarm Catholics pain Christ and hurt the church. They are weak links in the Communion of Saints and most likely will not assent 100 percent to the Deposit of Faith. We all have to be more courageous in prayer and deed. I'm not sure where I first came across this statement, but it has stuck with me for more than a decade, "If you lack apostolic zeal you will become insipid." In this day in age, insipid Catholicism will not do. Fearing lukewarm, I also fear being insipid. How about you? My hope quickly rebounds when I think of Our Lady of La Salette saying to Maximin Giraud and Melanie Calvat in France in 1846, "Fight, children of light, you, the few who can see." A true

[348] Heilman, Fr. Richard, "Freedom from Lukewarmness" email, July 23, 2020.

Catholic cannot fail to see. The good understand. The wicked deny. Do you see? I want to see and fight as a child of the light. With fortitude, will you fight for God?

While reading through this chapter you might have thought to yourself, "If I lived during the time of Lepanto and I heard the pope call for people to serve in the Holy League, I would definitely have been there johnny-on-the-spot, ready, willing, and able to serve God." Oh, really? God did not choose to have you live during the time of Lepanto and fight in that battle. He chose you for this time and our cultural battles. Dr. Helen Alvare at the National Catholic Prayer Breakfast on May 9, 2013, spoke about the Good Samaritan in a way that has stuck with me ever since—in a good way. To paraphrase, "We do not get to pick our issues or choose who we help. We are where we are. We live where we live. We must embrace who and what is before us. We mustn't squander this period of the world's history that God has entrusted to each one of us." In other words, Dr. Alvare tells us, today's issues are the equivalent of the Good Samaritan.

OK, so advancing globalism and socialism, some of the key issues of our day are tyrannical political leadership in the U.S., continued modernism in the church, weak Catholic leadership, pro-life, traditional marriage, religious liberty, gender dysphoria. And there are others. With a litany of ills, what should we focus on first and foremost as Catholics? Considering Our Lady of Fatima told Sr. Lucia that the final battle would be between Our Lord and Satan over marriage and family, perhaps that is the highest and best direction for our individual and collective efforts?

God did not place you in the 1500s to fight at Lepanto, but he did place you in the 2000s to fight, with His grace and your virtue, for life (anti-abortion), marriage, family, and any other evils plaguing our country and world. How's that fight going for you? When you see the man on the side of the road who needs assistance do you keep walking by pretending you don't see him? Yes, there are still people in need of assistance (homeless, the hungry, the poor, etc.) They need our *physical* assistance. We must never forget the literal symbolism of what the parable of the Good Samaritan teaches us. However, a twenty-first century figurative version of the Good Samaritan very well could also apply to the five non-negotiables of Catholic morality (abortion, human cloning, euthanasia (assisted suicide), stem cell research, homosexual "marriage")? Are you active on the cultural battlefield, or are you complacent, walking on by, leaving the heavy lifting to others?

Remember, all the evil in the world is due to what? Lukewarm Catholics. If you're on it, God bless. If you need to step up, pray; then get after it. All hands on deck. What can you do?

God expects us to give it all and not hold back. Saint Francis of Assisi said, "All the darkness in the world cannot extinguish the light of a single candle." You can most likely find others in the fight for our faith and freedom. If so, great. If not, be the single candle. When we decide for God, we lose nothing and gain everything. In fighting against being lukewarm, know that God does not lose battles. In fact, God never loses. Keep this in mind, "God and one person is a majority." Isaiah 6:8 says, "And I heard the voice of the Lord, saying: Whom shall I send? and who shall go for us? And I said: Lo, here am I, send me."

Mustering fortitude, will you ask God to send you? Or, will you choose to remain lukewarm, complacent, insipid, without fervor? Matter. Or, better yet, matter more. Our families, culture and church need a better effort from all Catholics. Do what you can.

To open the century, we read about Catholic explorers travelling west to the new world. To close the century, heading in the opposite direction, we see Saint Francis Xavier doing what he could to bring Catholicism to the far east in India and Japan. At first Christianity was permitted in Japan. Things changed quickly, however, when the Japanese government waged a brutal war to suppress the nascent new religion on the island. Twenty-six martyrs were marched 600 miles and offered freedom if they renounced their faith. None did. All twenty-six would be crucified for the faith in 1597. Their witness motivated many Japanese to convert to Catholicism.

As the 9/11 boat captain launched our chapter with, "a hero is a man who does what he can," we see Saint Nicholas Owen as a hero who did all he could to protect Catholics during a time of immense persecution in England. Saint Thomas More, Saint John Fisher and Saint Francis Xavier were not complacent and advocated with fortitude for the faith in good times and bad. The steadfast saints of the sixteenth century lived in a time of tremendous turbulence in the church and the world. We would witness God at work in the century through many other spiritual heavyweights, His saints, such as: Thomas of Villanova, Stanislaus Kostka, John of Avila, Teresa of Avila, Charles Borromeo, Aloysius Gonzaga, John of the Cross and Philip Neri.

While this chapter could have been focused on any one of these great saints, it was Saint Nicholas Owen, with his unique story, talents, and fortitude who was selected to speak to our times. Do what you can. We set sail in our next chapter across the Atlantic and head to South America, Saint Rose of Lima, and her holy example of modesty.

Sixteenth Century Saints

Saints Jane of Valois (d. 1505), Catherine of Geneo (d. 1510), John Fisher (d. 1535), Thomas More (d. 1535), Angela Merici (d. 1540), Juan Diego (d. 1548), Francis Xavier (d. 1552), Thomas of Villanova (d. 1555), Ignatius of Loyola (d. 1556), Stanislaus Kostka (d. 1568), John of Avila (d. 1569), Francis Borgia (d. 1572), Pius V (d. 1572), Edmund Campion (d. 1581), Teresa of Avila (d. 1582), Charles Borromeo (d. 1584), Felix of Cantalice (d. 1587), Catherine del Ricci (d. 1590), Aloysius Gonzaga (d. 1591), John of the Cross (d. 1591), Philip Neri (d. 1595), Peter Canisius (d. 1597), and Paul Miki and his twenty-five companions, known as the Martyrs of Nagasaki (d. 1597)

Saint Nicholas Owen is the patron saint of escapologists and illusionists.
Saint Nicholas Owen's feast day is March 22.
Saint Nicholas Owen, *ora pro nobis* (pray for us).

Sixteenth Century History

1506- Founding of the **Swiss Guard,** as Kaspar von Silenen and first contingent of Swiss mercenaries enter the Vatican during the reign of Pope Julius II. From that time, until today, the Swiss Guard functions as the pope's security detail.

1506- Construction on the new St. Peter's Basilica in Rome begins. (Construction ends in 1626.)

1512- Michelangelo completes painting ceiling of Sistine Chapel.

1516- Saint Sir Thomas More publishes *Utopia* in Latin.

1517- Oct. 31. **Martin Luther** posts his **95 Theses** to the All Saints (Castle) Church in Wittenberg, Germany, protesting, among other things, the sale of indulgences. With Luther's split from Catholic Church, Protestant denominations begin. Dr. Taylor Marshall adds,
"Luther rejects Catholic teachings, Transubstantiation, Apostolic succession, and removed books from the Bible. Martin Luther was not a reformer; he was a revolutionary."[349]

1517- After defeating the Mamluks and conquering much of the Middle East, the Ottomans hold the Muslim Caliphate. The Ottomans then brought most of the relics of the Prophet Mohammed from Cairo to Istanbul and, since then, they have been kept in the Chamber of the Holy Relics inside the Privy Room, the sultans' living quarters for centuries, in Topkapi Palace, the Ottoman empire's headquarters.

1521- Pope Leo X formally excommunicates Luther from the Catholic Church. That same year, Luther again refused to recant his writings before the Holy Roman Emperor Charles V of Germany, who issued the famous Edict of Worms declaring Luther an outlaw and a heretic and giving permission for anyone to kill him without consequence. Protected by Prince Frederick, Luther began working on a German translation of the Bible that took ten years to complete.

1521- First Baptism of Catholics in the Philippines, the first Christian nation in Southeast Asia.

1526- Eighty-one years before the coming of the English to Jamestown in 1607, a settlement was made in Virginia by Spaniards from San Domingo, under the leadership of Lucas Vázquez de Ayllón. The expedition set sail in three vessels from Puerto de la Plata, in June 1526. The severity of the winter, the rebellion of the settlers, and the hostility of the natives caused the abandonment of the settlement in the spring of 1527.[350]

---

[349] Marshall, Taylor, "Evil Bishops Make Evil Rules Label As Divisive," podcast 572. https://taylormarshall.com/2020/12/572-evil-bishops-make-evil-rules-label-divisive-rule-lad-rule-podcast.html?ct=t(Regular_Blog_Updates_Campaign)
[350] "Catholic Church in the 13 Colonies," Wikipedia, https://en.wikipedia.org/wiki/Catholic_Church_in_the_Thirteen_Colonies

1531- Blessed Virgin Mary appears to Juan Diego in Mexico City as *Nuestra Señora de Guadalupe* (**"Our Lady of Guadalupe"**). The miraculous cloak, rich in Catholic symbolism, is today enshrined within the Basilica of Our Lady of Guadalupe in Mexico City.

1534- August 15. Saint Ignatius of Loyola and six others, including Saint Francis Xavier, meet in Montmartre, near Paris to form the non-monastic religious order, the Society of Jesus, later commonly known as the Jesuits.

1534- The Diocese of Goa is created by Portuguese missionaries to serve the West Coast of India.

1534- October 30. The English Parliament passes Act of Supremacy recognizing the King of England as the Supreme Head of the Church of England. By so doing the national church was canonically alienated from the Bishop of Rome, the pope.

1535- After spending his life serving under King Henry VIII of England, Saint Thomas More was sentenced to death after condemning the King's divorce.

1541- After five years, Michelangelo completes the *Last Judgement* painting in the Sistine Chapel.

1541- The Archdiocese of Lima is founded in Lima, Peru.

1546- **Council of Trent** meets to address the Protestant Reformation. It codifies the Tridentine Rite as the Mass of all time; in full conformity and faithfulness to the Church's liturgical tradition. The Mass is to be in Latin to avoid the abuses that occur in local vernacular. The Protestant doctrines of "scripture alone" and "justification by faith alone" were condemned and curses were pronounced on those who believed these doctrines. Affirms that the sacraments are necessary for salvation. Bans indulgences and curtails clergy corruption. Reaffirms Saint Athanasius's original list of seventy-three books to be included in the Bible. The Council of Trent, relying heavily on the teachings of Thomas Aquinas, would characterize Roman Catholicism until the 1960s, when Vatican II would disrupt many church practices.

1549- August 15. Saint Francis Xavier, S.J., reaches Kagosima, Japan.

1551- The first diocese of Brazil is created. One year later a Portuguese appointed bishop reaches Bahia, Brazil.

1568- Saint John Chrysostom, Saint Basil, Saint Gregory Nazianzus, Saint Athanasius and Saint Thomas Aquinas are made Doctors of the Church.

1570- Pope Pius V on July 14, 1570, through the apostolic constitution *Quo Primum* that promulgates the **Tridentine Liturgy** as the **"Mass of all Time,"** writing, "it shall be unlawful henceforth and forever throughout the Christian world to sing or to read Masses according to any formula other than this Missal published by us. This present constitution can never be revoked or modified, but shall forever remain valid and have the force of Law, and if, nevertheless anyone would ever dare attempt any action contrary to this Order of ours, handed down for all times, let him know that he has incurred the wrath of Almighty God, and the blessed Apostles Peter and Paul."

1571- On October 7, 1571, in the Gulf of Patras at the **Battle of Lepanto,** the Ottoman Empire fleet is defeated and Islam is expelled from Europe.

1577- Saint Teresa of Ávila writes *The Interior Castle*, a classic work of Catholic mysticism.

1578- Saint John of the Cross writes *Dark Night of the Soul*, a classic work of Catholic mysticism.

1582- Matteo Ricci, S.J., arrives in Macau to begin his missionary work in China.

1586- September 28. Domenico Fontana successfully finishes re-erecting the Vatican Obelisk at its present site in St. Peter's Square. Hailed as a great technical achievement of its time.

1597- Paulo Miki and the Twenty-Six Martyrs of Japan were a group of Catholics who were executed by crucifixion on February 5, 1597, in Nagasaki, Japan. As the first martyrs of Japan, they are especially significant in the history of the Catholic Church in Japan.

Virtue Challenge #16- Fortitude

Saint Nicholas Owen, pray for our religious that they may be faithful to the practice of their rule.

We ask you to intercede for us that we may intercede as necessary to assist and support our faithful priests and nuns. Pray that we use well the grace of the New Testament. Pray for us that we may have an increase in the virtue of fortitude.

Pray for our bishops to have greater faithfulness, fortitude, and strength in the tradition of Saints Thomas More and John Fisher. Pray for them to protect their flocks from the ravenous wolves. Pray for them to have more fidelity to grace and concern for souls versus the temptation to be on amicable, worldly terms with sinful, secular leaders—even if they be Catholic.

What aspect of your life could be considered a shipwreck? Is it well in the past, or something with which you currently contend? If you were to bring greater fortitude and forgiveness, courage, meekness, humility or charity to the situation, how would things change for the better?

If you could change it all, and were to be steadfast in seeking to do only God's will henceforth, how would the situation improve?

What challenges has God permitted to surface in your life so that you may increase in the holy virtue of fortitude? How have you responded at all times with grace to these gifts from above?

Think of your Elizabethan era ancestors and what they risked to live the faith. Not just money, but persecution and death in order to "live Catholic." What do you risk to live Catholic?

Saint Nicholas Owen, pray for us to use, as you did, our unique skills to serve the church and God's glory. Help us to find new ways to put our talents to use for God. Help us to spot the unlikely places to assist God and serve our neighbors. Help us to serve God with fear and reverence. Help us to be steadfast in serving God's greater glory and good pleasure.

Pray for the lukewarm to amend their lives to be Catholics of fortitude. Let us pray to overcome our hesitation to serve, our lukewarmness. (Opposite of lukewarmness—fervor and fortitude.) Say this prayer to overcome lukewarmness: *"Since you, O my Jesus, have been so liberal with your graces toward me and have deigned to give your Blood and your life for me, I am sorry for having acted with so little generosity towards you, who are worthy of all honor and love. But, O my Jesus, you know my weakness; help me with your powerful grace. In you I confide, O Immaculate Virgin Mary, help me to overcome myself and become a saint. Amen."*[351]

Is it easy for the devil to "find" you? In other words, are you careless at times in protecting your soul? To look at this from another angle, when you are under attack from the devil and his minions, and things go deep or dark, to what "hide" do you retreat for safety in Christ or under Mary's mantle? Rosary? Holy Water? Sign of the cross? Appeal to your guardian angel? Think through and consider what other Catholic "hides" could you better utilize in times of temptation, frustration or weakness.

How much fortitude do you have in keeping your baptismal vows and Lenten resolutions? Yes, it can be hard to fast and enter into deeper prayer and be charitable to others and turn away from sin, habitual sin. Difficulty does not mean impossibility. What is your intention? Do you only consider the difficulty and give in? People do difficult things all the time. The soldier on the battlefield carries on and accepts the difficulty of the situation. As Catholics, we must accept the difficulty in any situation and not lose heart. There is too much at stake. Let us not complain about weak bishops. Let us do what we can do. Recommit yourself to serving God. Keep the goal in mind. You can avoid sin. You can be more charitable. You can seek closeness in prayer with God. With fortitude and with the grace of Almighty God, you can become a saint.

Each Catholic alive today has a hero or heroine inside of him or her. When the time is right, and led by the grace of God, the hero will come out. Is your time now?

In the movie *The Passion of the Christ*, a poignant scene is when after Jesus had fallen under the weight of the cross; Blessed Mother, unsure of her ability to go to Jesus, flashes back to how as a young boy when He fell, she without hesitation went to comfort Him. Then having mustered the holy fortitude to do the difficult, Blessed Mother, with resolve and empathy, picked herself up and went to Jesus. With

---

[351] Tassone, Day by Day, October 23.

fortitude, resolve, and empathy, how will you go to Jesus today and say, "I'm here"?

Converse for a moment with the Holy Ghost about fortitude. My Lord and my God, how may I serve you more faithfully and completely through the virtue of fortitude?

O Great Saint Nicholas Owen, pray for us an increase in the virtue and grace of holy fortitude.

CHAPTER 17

Rose

The Seventeenth Century
Modesty

*"In all your movements, let nothing be evident that would
offend the eyes of another."*

~ Saint Augustine

"Where Christ is, there modesty is found."

~ Saint Gregory

*"Another weapon the devil employs is immodesty, or more frankly,
impurity. My dear children, be on your guard. The devil will tempt you
with bad books, bad thoughts, or the foul conversation of a companion.
When any such fellow approaches you, say to yourself, This is a minister
of Satan. And let these wretches who indulge in foul conversation say to
himself, I am a minister of Satan because I help him ruin souls!"*

~ Saint John Bosco

*"By the virtue of modesty, the devout person governs all his exterior acts.
With good reason, then, does Saint Paul recommend this virtue to all
and declare how necessary it is and as if this were not enough, he
considers that this virtue should be obvious to all."*

~ Saint Padre Pio

The 1600s

It would be difficult to find a life more filled with adventure and
derring-do than that of Saint Nicholas Owen, who is profiled in the
previous chapter. Yet, to open this century, we begin with Pope
Clement VIII. His daring feat of heroism? Having a cup of coffee. In
the year 1600, a petition was underway to ban the Muslim pick-me-up
beverage as "the devil's drink." After the pope sipped a cup, he
declared it "so delicious that it would be a pity to let the infidels have
exclusive use of it. We shall cheat Satan by baptizing it."[352] Clever

---

[352] Myers, Hannah, "Suave Molecules of Mocha: Coffee, Chemistry, and Civilization," *New Partisan/
Wayback Machine*, March 7, 2005.

Catholic. And thus, coffee was endorsed for consumption by Catholics.

After the massive tumult of the 1500s, the jolt of caffeine would prove to be helpful with what was on the horizon in the 1600s. In England, and elsewhere in Europe, the Protestant revolt against the church continued to spread like a wildfire across the previously majority Catholic continent. God gave rise to many Catholic saints to act as counter-measures to the Protestant Reformation. Saints like Saint Francis de Sales, who, while bishop of Geneva, Switzerland, "returned thousands of obstinate heretics to the true Faith," through his "gentleness, preaching skill, zeal for the faith, and his clear explanations of Catholic doctrine."[353]

While seventeenth-century Europe would remain a focal point in the Catholic-Protestant division, brave missionaries continued to sail off to the "New World" of North America to share the gospel of Christ and the Catholic faith. The missionaries no doubt kept in mind Jesus's own words to his disciples when they set out, "And Jesus coming, spoke to them, saying: All power is given to me in heaven and in earth. Going therefore, teach ye all nations; baptizing them in the name of the Father, and of the Son, and of the Holy Ghost." (Matthew 28:18-19)

Saint Boniface offers us a nautical metaphor, "In her voyage across the ocean of this world, the Church is like a great ship being pounded by the waves of life's different stresses. Our duty is not to abandon ship but to keep her on her course." A primary focus of the 1600s would be on the "New France," which we now know as the Canadian province of Quebec. Saints like Isaac Jogues, Jean de Brébeuf, and Gabrielle Lalemont wanted to instruct and tend to the souls of the colonists and Native Americans. The three aforementioned saints were among the original eight Canadian martyrs killed by the Amerinds. Canada's first female saint, Marguerite Bourgeoys, was the foundress of the Congregation of Notre Dame in Montreal. Hearty, courageous, frontier persons all.

To the south, in the British colonies, or "New England," the situation of the Catholic Church in the Thirteen Colonies was characterized by an extensive religious persecution, originating from

---

[353] St. Francis de Sales, "Saint of the Day," *Catholic Company*, January 24, 2021.

Protestant sects' past experience with the English Reformation, which would barely allow religious toleration to Catholics living on American territory.[354] British colonists, opposed not only the Catholic Church but also the Church of England, which they believed perpetuated some Catholic doctrine and practices, and for that reason deemed it to be insufficiently Reformed. Monsignor John Tracy Ellis wrote that a "universal anti-Catholic bias was brought to Jamestown in 1607 and vigorously cultivated in all the thirteen colonies from Massachusetts to Georgia."[355]

Catholicism was formally introduced to the English colonies in 1634 with the founding of the Province of Maryland by Cecil Calvert, 2nd Baron Baltimore, based on a charter granted to his father George Calver, 1st Baron Baltimore. The first settlers were accompanied by two Jesuit missionaries travelling as gentlemen adventurers. George Calvert, 1st Baron Baltimore (1580-1632), was an English politician serving as a member of parliament and later Secretary of State under King James I. In 1625, he declared his Catholicism publicly and resigned his offices. He was created Baron Baltimore in the Peerage of Ireland and located Baltimore Manor in County Longford, Ireland. Calvert became interested in the British colonization of America, originally for commercial reasons and then as a refuge for persecuted Irish and English Catholics. Moving his commercial operation from Newfoundland, he sought a royal charter to settle the region in what would be become Maryland. Lord Baltimore would die five weeks before the new Charter was sealed, leaving the settlement of the Maryland colony to his son Cecil Calvert.[356]

Cecil Calvert, 2nd Baron Baltimore (1605-1675), was an English nobleman who was the first Proprietor of the Province of Maryland. His title was "First Lord Proprietary, Earl Palatine of the Provinces of Maryland and Avalon in America." He received the proprietorship after the death of his father. Cecil, Lord Baltimore, established and managed the Province of Maryland from his home, Kiplin Hall, in North Yorkshire, England. As an English Roman Catholic, he continued the legacy of his father by promoting religious tolerance in

[354] "Catholic Church in the Thirteen Colonies," Wikipedia, https://en.wikipedia.org/wiki/Catholic_Church_in_the_Thirteen_Colonies
[355] Ibid.
[356] "George Calvert" Wikipedia, https://en.wikipedia.org/wiki/George_Calvert,_1st_Baron_Baltimore

the colony. Maryland became a haven for Catholics in the New World, particularly important at a time of religious persecution in England. Lord Baltimore governed Maryland for forty-two years.[357]

Elsewhere in the colonies mid-century we find the unique Native American soul of Saint Kateri Tekakwitha (1656-1680). Kateri, born in present-day New York, had an Algonquin mother who was converted by Jesuit missionaries. Her family died from small pox when she was four, and eventually at the age of twenty she was introduced to new missionaries who converted her. Taking the baptism name Catherine, after Saint Catherine of Sienna, it translated into Indian as Kateri. Due to harsh treatment on account of her Christian faith, Kateri fled 200 miles on foot to a French Jesuit mission in Montreal, Canada. Kateri, known for her love of Christ, was as a miracle-worker who lived a life of prayer, penance, sanctity, and virtue. She died of illness at the age of twenty-four. (The Catholic Company. Saint of the day, July 14, 2020)

The life we shall now present certainly offers little to nothing of daring exploits and life-risking travails to the New France, the "New England," or other locations when viewed in the most obvious way. Representative of the spread of Catholicism in Latin America, and building upon the example of the modest servant Juan Diego and the apparition of Our Lady of Guadalupe in 1531, Saint Rose of Lima was something of a recluse during the years in which her sanctity became known. But viewed in another way, hers, too, was a life filled with adventure, the adventure of the interior life, and a life lived wholly and entirely for God. And what is more, it was a life marked by the miraculous on numerous occasions.

Isabel Flores de Oliva, one of ten children, was born in Lima, Peru in the year 1586. Her father was a Spanish immigrant and her mother was Inca Indian. It is said that a servant of the family saw her face change into or assume the aspect of a rose, and so young Isabel began to be called Rose. She made it "official" when she took that as her confirmation name. Incidentally, this future saint was confirmed by another, the archbishop of Lima, the future Saint Toribio de Mogrovejo. In English we know him as Saint Turibius.

It is interesting when studying the saints to see how one influences the other and the connections between them. This saint

---

[357] "Cecil Calvert," Wikipedia, https://en.wikipedia.org/wiki/Cecil_Calvert,_2nd_Baron_Baltimore

knew that one, or that saint confirmed these three saints. Or that one inspired this one. The best-selling book of all time after the Holy Bible is said to be *The Imitation of Christ* by Thomas a Kempis. It was and remains today a pre-eminent "saint-maker" of a book for it teaches its readers how to be more like Christ. Similarly, if you want to be holy, find a saint to whom you are attracted and imitate them.

That is exactly what Rose did. In imitation of the great Saint Catherine of Siena, Rose fasted three times per week and secretly underwent severe penances out of love for Christ. She gave up meat altogether. What she did not abstain from, however, was the Blessed Sacrament; it is said she received communion daily, which was exceedingly rare at that time.

But Rose's life was not without difficulty; many obstacles were put in her way on the path to holiness, or strife. From the very beginning, her parents opposed her desire to be a nun and to live solely for God and his poor. In fact, they did forbid her from entering the convent. But they must have known that their daughter was a most unusual young lady and was determined to let nothing stop her quest. A further obstacle in a sense between her and her desired union with God was her appearance; because she was beautiful, she caught the eye of many young men. Not wanting such attention from them, she cut her beautiful hair very short and even went so far as to mar her face, some say by burning it, others by applying pepper and lye to it...which would serve to in a sense burn it.

Though extreme, Rose clearly felt called to give her life to God and would let nothing stand in the way. But even though she was determined to give her life to God, she was also an obedient daughter. And so, when her father forbade her from entering the convent, she consented and lived a life of holiness under his roof. He gave her a room for herself, cut off from the others, and she began to live the life of a holy recluse, leaving only to go to church or to carry out some good work. Rose perpetually looked for opportunities to convert those she met. She wrote, "Know that the greatest service that man can offer to God is to help convert souls."

Rose took her talents and, rather than burying them like the unfaithful steward of scripture, used them to help her family and God's poor, even from her little hermitage within the home. She would bring the poor into her room to help them; she produced exquisite needlework, lacework, and embroidery which she sold to raise money for her family and the people who needed help. Saint Rose of Lima said, "When we serve the poor and the sick, we serve Jesus. We must not fail to help our neighbors, because in them we serve Jesus."

Though she was active in that sense, Rose was truly removed from the world and "cloistered" in a very real sense. Since she could not become a Dominican nun, she became a member of their third order, a tertiary, a form of Dominican life for laypeople in the world. (Just like the mystic, writer, activist and stigmatist example provided her by the tertiary Dominican, Saint Catherine of Siena.) Truly Rose could be said to have been "in the world, but not of it."

And though it was mentioned above that her life may have lacked some of the outward qualities of an adventurous life, limited as she was to her native city and even her family home for the most part, her spiritual life was marked by extraordinary occurrences. She is said to have experienced many apparitions, inner locutions, and conversations with our Lady. She once saw Mary appear to her as the Queen of the Most Holy Rosary, dressed in a Dominican habit, a reaffirmation that she was called to live the life of a Dominican tertiary.[358]

The miracles which abounded in the life of Rose were not of the interior variety alone. Even during her life, she was credited with saving the city of Lima through the force of her prayers alone when a powerful earthquake struck. Additionally, many cures of sick people were attributed to her. Because she had received so many visions and mystical gifts, a commission of churchmen was delegated to investigate her; they did so and found that, in their opinion, Rose's gifts were indeed of supernatural origin.

Contemplating the path to heaven, Saint Rose of Lima wrote, "Our Lord and Savior lifted up his voice and said with incomparable majesty: 'Let all men know that grace comes after tribulation. Let them know that without the burden of afflictions it is impossible to reach the height of grace. Let them know that the gifts of grace increase as the struggles increase. Let men take care not to stray and be deceived. This is the only true stairway to paradise, and without the cross they can find no road to climb to heaven.'" (Yeah. Maybe Led Zeppelin

---

[358] Much of the accounts of the miraculous occurrences in Rose's life come from *Compendium of the Miraculous* by Deacon Albert E. Graham, published by TAN Books. p. 332-3.

should have read Saint Rose of Lima's quote from Jesus before they strayed, made a deal with the devil, and composed "Stairway to Heaven" with its Satanic references. Just sayin'.)

Previously mentioned was how interesting it can be to study the relationships between the saints. Our parents taught us when we were young that you are the company you keep. If so, Rose was wise in her choice of companions for she also worked with the great apostle of the African slaves Saint Martin de Porres. Her deep prayer in her solitude was the "soul" of her apostolate.

Such privileged souls as Rose are often attacked by the devil more than the rest of us. She experienced the *noche oscura*, or "dark night," of the soul for many years suffering the slings and arrows of Satan. In those moments, Rose, as we all should, had recourse to her guardian angel, and she was blessed one time to have a vision of her guardian angel before the throne of God begging him to help Rose in her difficulties and struggles with Satan.

Despite the many attacks by the devil, and spiritual dryness at times, Saint Rose kept great perspective commenting thus, "If only mortals would learn how great it is to possess divine grace, how beautiful, how noble, how precious. How many riches it hides within itself, how many joys and delights! No one would complain about his cross or about troubles that may happen to him, if he would come to know the scales on which they are weighed when they are distributed to men."

God listened and gifted Rose with a deeper experience of his Son's cross by imprinting the Stigmata, the five Sacred Wounds of Jesus in her heart. She may also have supernaturally received the crown of thorns wounds as well, but one of her penances was to fashion a crown with inward spikes which she would wear in imitation of that part of Our Lord's Passion.

Though she was only thirty-one, Rose of Lima died in the odor of sanctity. It is said that she was granted to know the date of her death and even the manner of it, during a vision of the Sacred Heart. The first native-born saint from the Americas to be canonized, after her death, many miracles have been attributed to Rose of Lima's intercession.

Rose of Lima was called to imitate Christ and the saints she admired in a way perhaps few of us will be. Saint Rose of Lima said, "Apart from the cross, there is no other ladder by which we may get to heaven." Certainly, though she did not travel far or serve in the missions in the middle of the jungle, we can learn from Rose and imitate her in those things, like living modestly, which we are able to do. Be devoted to God and live a life for him and our neighbor. And if, in His Providence, God does call any one of us to the heights of spirituality and mysticism to which he called Rose, God willing, we will be ready to respond, "Here I am, Lord. Why not me?"

When discussing modesty, the *Catechism of the Catholic Church* states at the very outset that purity can be a battle. It goes on to explain that the baptized must continue to "struggle against concupiscence of the flesh and disordered desires. With God's grace he will prevail."[359]

It continues, "purity requires modesty, an integral part of temperance. Modesty protects the intimate center of the person. It means refusing to unveil what should remain hidden. It is ordered to chastity to whose sensitivity it bears witness. It guides how one looks at others and behaves towards them in conformity with the dignity of persons and their solidarity."[360]

The CCC further counsels that modesty requires patience, moderation, and purity of intention. Modesty is decent and discreet. It avoids situations where curiosity may lead to heightened risk. Modesty informs the choice of clothing. Modesty resists improper fashion and focuses on respect for the human person. The aim of modesty is to achieve purity of heart, which will then enable one to see God.

An article, "What is Modesty?" by the Archdiocese of Minneapolis-St. Paul states, "Modesty is a virtue necessary for purity. It flows out of the virtues of temperance, chastity, and self-control. A modest person dresses, speaks, and acts in a manner that supports and encourages purity and chastity, and not in a manner that would tempt or encourage sinful sexual behavior... Growth in modesty requires loving support from family and friends as well as wise counsel and the

---

[359] Catechism, 2520.
[360] Catechism, 2521.

practice of virtues… The Church calls us to be signs of contradiction in an overly sexualized society."[361]

Father John Hardon, S.J. defined modesty as: "The virtue that moderates all the internal and external movements and appearance of a person according to his or her endowments, possessions, and station of life. Four virtues are commonly included under modesty: humility, studiousness, and two kinds of external modesty, namely in dress and general behavior."[362]

Fr. Hardon continues his discussion of modesty beginning with humility, writing, "…humility is a virtue by which one recognizes his talents and attributes, and appreciates them as gifts from God to be used wisely and for His glory. In humility a person, as creature, walks humbly with His God. Humility also counteracts the vice of pride."[363]

Pride. There it is. They are putting Christ on the cross again this time for human pride. With something as pleasing to God as modesty, the anti-God forces embrace the vice of pride and push their twisted agenda. No better example can be found than the Democratic Party's so-called "Equality Act." While the Catechism is clear about the "definitive giving and commitment of man and woman to one another be fulfilled," the anti-God left seeks to blur the lines of gender confusing our young, influencing the immature, and perverting adult thinking.

In declaring war on Christians in America, the proponents of the legislation desire that "sexual orientation" and "gender identity" be a protected class added to race, color, religion, sex, and national origin, protected forms of discrimination under the 1964 Civil Rights Act.

Despite the Supreme Court's misguided Bostock decision that already codified these new categories, the radical left wants to take things further in that they want to redefine any religious expression in support of traditional morality as "discrimination."

---

[361] "What is modesty? Why is it important? How is it relevant to me?," Archdiocese of Minneapolis and St. Paul,
https://www.archspm.org/faith-and-discipleship/catholic-faith/what-is-modesty-why-is-it-important-how-is-it-relevant-to-me/
[362] Hardon, *The Pocket Catholic Dictionary*, 1985.
[363] Ibid.

Standing up for morality, modesty, and common sense in America could soon be labelled discrimination. That's the left being led by the father of lies. The "Equality Act" is the single most dangerous bill ever proposed to the freedom of speech and the freedom of religion. Professor Robert Gagnon has written of the "Equality Act" using particularly arresting language, "You will be made to conform. If you resist, you will be fined, fired and ultimately threatened with imprisonment. Under certain circumstances even your children can be taken away. It is police-state ideological enforcement of radical, biology-denying fake science. Kiss goodbye the liberties you hold so dear and for which countless fought and died."[364]

The U.S. House of Representatives passed similar legislation in 2019, but it was not taken up and debated in the Republican-led U.S. Senate. Now in 2021 with the Marxist Democrats in charge of the House, Senate and White House, it's possible the inequality advocated in the "Equality Act" could soon become federal law. The showdown will be in the U.S. Senate where it would have to pass the filibuster with sixty votes. Will ten Republicans join with their Democratic colleagues? By the time this book is published, perhaps we will have our answer. Regardless of whether the legislation passes or not, how is it that our culture and nation have gone so far down this road as to not seriously consider this insanity and rebellion against God?

The "Equality Act" is a full-out assault on women. Brian Burch of Catholic Vote writes, "the proposed legislation would deny the very real physiological differences between men and women. These differences led to the creation of separate men's and women's sports teams. But soon this natural division will be considered 'hateful' or 'bigoted.' The Equality Act will be a bulldozer against girls' sports. Any child born a boy can simply change his identity and compete on the girls' basketball or track teams. In fact, it's already happening. And many states are considering legislation to protect girls' sports. The Equality Act would end these protections."[365]

Burch adds, "The so-called 'Equality' Act would also be a direct assault on the family. That's because puberty-blocking hormonal treatments on young children, along with surgical procedures would be deemed 'necessary' and standard health care. Our U.S. bishops have

[364] Gomes, Jules, "Equality Act: Most Dangerous Bill Ever," *Church Militant,* March 1, 2021.
[365] Burch, Brian, "Equality Act Declaration of War" email, *Catholic Vote,* Feb. 25, 2021.

warned: 'Under the Equality Act, refusing this type of treatment could be used by states to take children away from their parents, as has already occurred in certain places such as Cincinnati in 2018.'"[366]

A leading voice denouncing the pro-abortion, anti-religious freedom "Equality Act," is Georgia Republican Rep. Marjorie Taylor Greene. In a scorching speech she derided the act as "a completely evil, disgusting, immoral bill." She lamented, "It's not about stopping discrimination, it's creating it. It's creating discrimination against every single woman and girl in this country." Greene criticized the 'woke' Democrats as "defying science, defying God's creation, and only care about governing over people's feelings… But now we find ourselves in a time where Democrats are running, indeed, a tyrannical Congress and federal government."[367]

David McLoone, writing in *LifeSite News,* covered Green's speech writing, "The effects of the bill are far-reaching, writing transgenderism into federal civil rights law, compelling medical professionals to commit abortions and transgender surgeries, and expanding taxpayer-funded abortion on demand."[368]

Green warned, "Every single person should be outraged at this bill. You should be angered, you should be concerned for the safety of all the little girls that are going to go into a bathroom, not knowing if there is a man in there that calls himself a woman." She continued, "Over the past century, our great grandmothers, our grandmothers, our mothers fought for women's rights, and the Equality Act, with a single vote, wipes it out."[369]

McLoone's article continued, "Greene made headlines recently after a spat between herself and her Democrat Rep. Marie Newman. Newman, who favored the Equality Act, erected a transgender pride flag outside her office to taunt Greene, whose office is across the hall. In response, Greene displayed a sign outside her own door that reads: "There are TWO genders: MALE & FEMALE 'Trust the Science!'"[370]

---

[366] Ibid.
[367] McLoone, David, "Marjorie Taylor Greene calls Equality Act 'disgusting' in epic rant against it," *LifeSite News,* February 26, 2021.
[368] Ibid.
[369] Ibid.
[370] Ibid.

During Greene's speech, she noted the many consequences of the bill, fearing especially for children who are exposed to new risks. "Boys that want to call themselves girls do not belong in my daughter's bathrooms, in my daughter's locker rooms, on my daughter's playing field, traveling with her team where she is forced to share a hotel room with him. No. They don't belong." Green added that biological males, even when they are confused about their gender, should "compete with the rest of the biological males, which is what they are."[371]

Women's rights, too, were at the top of Greene's list, which she stated will be grossly violated by the Equality Act. "I'm sorry, it's not about their feelings. We have to govern in what's right and wrong, not about people's feelings. This is what is wrong with America today," she said. "You see, no one's talking about all of the consequences that come with the Equality Act," she noted, "but they are very real. All you have to do is read the text to the bill, which the Democrats lie (about) and tell you that it won't destroy religious freedoms, and it won't destroy women's rights."[372]

Rep. Marjorie Taylor Greene, or "MTG" as some have dubbed her, packed a lot of truth into her speech critiquing the "Equality Act." She was joined, to their credit, by several other members of the House Freedom Caucus. What about other national political and religious leaders? On Feb. 23, 2021 a letter was written by five USCCB committee chairs to members of Congress stating that they are opposed to the legislation as it upholds gender ideology and the redefinition of marriage and frames gender as simply a "social construct."[373] The letter was a first step. What about the next steps? What about aggressively voicing their opposition from every pulpit in America for the next several weeks until this religious freedom crushing bill is defeated? Either the bill is crushed, or our religious liberties as Catholics will be.

On the floor of the U.S. House of Representatives, Rep. Greg Steube (R-FL) raised a religious concern that the act would allow men to dress as women in public. "It's not clothing or personal style that offends God," he said, "but rather the use of one's appearance to act

---

[371] Ibid.
[372] Ibid.
[373] Hadro, Matt, "House passes Equality Act, which bishops warned would 'punish' religious groups," *Catholic News Agency,* February 25, 2021.

out or take on a sexual identity different from the one biologically assigned by God at birth." To which Rep. Jerry Nadler (D-NY) responded: "… what any religious tradition describes as God's will is no concern of this Congress."[374] Really, Rep. Nadler? Not a moment too soon to walk that one back.

The anti-God opposition in the United States is as emboldened as never before.

Who reading *Against the Grain* thinks men identifying as women is a good idea? What do you think of the law that mandates that men have access to areas previously designated as being for women only? What are your thoughts about adult male perverts having access to female restrooms with not just adult females, but young girls? How do female teens in high school feel about teen boys (identifying as women) having access to previously female-only locker rooms? Decision-making adults have tremendous culpability for shattering, or at least profoundly diminishing, modesty in our youth. How will that negatively impact our nation years down the road? How do females truly feel about men competing against them in sports? What recourse do our Marxist-led school administrations and faculties offer? Nothing but contempt and derision for modest and moral people.

Who will do what about this egregious and massive invasion of privacy and all-out affront, assault and attack on modesty? And consider what will transpire on a larger scale when a 300 lb. convicted male rapist, who says in court he identifies as a woman, is sent to a women's prison and shares a cell with a 100 lb. woman. What are the chances she makes it one week with her dignity preserved? Who will protect her? Anyone? Our nation, and our church, must do better. What culpability do we have for not doing all we can to address this issue? This gender identification sickness is a scourge.

Patriotic, Catholic men protect your wives, sisters and daughters! Again, one can only draw the conclusion that the ruling class has utter contempt for the citizens of America. Mike Church from Crusade Channel radio mused, "The Guess Who did a song "American Woman" in the 1970s. According to the gender police, thought control, perverts making laws, can that song be played anymore

---

[374] Orsi, Fr. Michael, "Nero, Rep. Jerry Nadler, and the victory of the Nazarene," *LifeSite News,* March 2, 2021.

without someone being fined?"[375] Sadly, that's now a relevant question in 2021 America. How mortifying.

In attempting to be modest, some may find it useful to draw upon the spiritual tool of mortification. One contemporary seventeenth century saint of Saint Rose of Lima, who was quite focused on mortification, was Saint Joseph of Cupertino (1603-1663). Cupertino was:

"an intellectually dull child who constantly found himself the worse off in every situation. He was awkward, absent-minded, and difficult to be around. Many people thought he was good for nothing—including his own mother, who treated him harshly and considered him a burden. Added to the scorn he received from everyone, at the age of eight he began receiving ecstatic visions for which he was also ridiculed. At the age of seventeen Joseph found work with the Capuchin Franciscan friars, eventually joining their order once they recognized his holiness beneath his irritating demeanor. His ecstasies became more pronounced, and he would often levitate or float as they happened. These ecstasies could be triggered easily through the mention of anything heavenly, or by any mortification. These occurrences became a spectacle and disturbance to others and caused Joseph much suffering; they were a cross he would bear his whole life. For example, as a priest he could not celebrate Mass publicly due to his distracting ecstasies. He was even reported to the Inquisition for fear he was involved in witchcraft. Yet Saint Joseph lived a life of deep prayer and severe penance through continual fasting, subjecting himself every year to seven Lents of forty days each. Sometimes called "The Flying Saint," Saint Joseph of Cupertino is also the patron of air crews and aviators."[376]

Through mortification, we can greatly assist our souls to increase in holiness. Self-denial, not self-indulgence, is a hallmark to those seeking greater virtue in service to God. Unfortunately, self-denial is not as celebrated in our culture that would much rather monetize self-indulgence and instant gratification through consumerism. Immodesty is not just exhibited in our clothing choices; it is also be found in the

---

[375] Church, Mike, "Daily Show," *The Crusade Channel*, January 22, 2021.
[376] St. Joseph Cupertino, "Saint of the Day," *The Catholic Company*, September 18, 2020

movies and TV we watch, the songs we listen to, the books and magazines we read, the social networks we visit, and the conversations we have. Society tells us modesty and mortification are uncool, and immodesty and indulgence are cool. As Catholics, we know the world has it backwards.

There are plenty of things we see driving around in our PG-13 rated world that we observe as being immodest. Life can be R rated. What are we to do when we encounter R rated, or worse, material? Though it should be a source of mortification, exposing oneself to viewing pornography or taking naked pictures of yourself and texting (sexting) are most certainly immodest and sinful. While pornography was discussed earlier in Chapter 13 with Saint Raymond Nonnatus and the virtue of courage, modesty as it relates to pornography is worth addressing briefly again here.

Fr. Bill Peckman in "Freedom from Pornography" discusses how accessing pornography can be a gateway to other sinful thoughts and behaviors. He writes,

"Porn reduces sex to something outside of the marital bond and objectifies others for physical gratification. The human body should not be unveiled... Jesus is clear in his teaching that sexual immorality is not only a matter of one's actions, but also a matter of one's heart: " You have heard that it was said to them of old: Thou shalt not commit adultery. But I say to you, that whosoever shall look on a woman to lust after her, hath already committed adultery with her in his heart." (Matthew 5:27-28). Pornography in its variety of forms (print, movie, virtual, TV, music) must be purged from a faithful Catholic's home. It must be treated as the voracious cancer it is."377

In today's world people don't like to think about immodest and impure thoughts as being offensive to God, but they truly are. A first line of defense is always prayer and the sacraments. A pure and modest mindset is the second line of defense against immodesty. A third line of defense is dressing modestly. We don't have to dress in an unfashionable way, but at the same time we do not want to call attention to our body parts. At a minimum, a good starting point would

---

377 Peckman, Fr. Bill, Novena, Day 13 - Let Freedom Ring, March 1, 2021.

be for all Catholics to do a better job of dressing more appropriately for Mass. Modesty matters. G. K. Chesterton wrote, "Modesty is always beautiful."

Back in England in the second half of the seventeenth century, the monarchy persecuted and martyred scores of Catholic priests and laypersons when Catholicism was outlawed. In the infamous "Popish Plot" of 1678, the Protestant government fabricated yet another conspiracy accusing Catholics of subversion of the nation's Protestant religion, and created anti-Catholic hysteria throughout England. The crackdown was especially violent for Catholic priests such as Blesseds John Fenwick and John Gavan, and Saints John Kemble and Oliver Plunkett.

With pilgrims emigrating to America from England and other European nations throughout the 1600s, Catholics would not find the colonies all that welcoming to their faith. Despite the best endeavors of Catholics like Lord Baltimore in the 1630s, efforts to have Catholics and Protestants live together amicably found infertile soil on the east coast. Toiling to have Catholicism take root in the colonies, and finally be accepted in America, would unfortunately continue into the 1900s. If the "Equality Act" of 2021 is made into law at the federal level in the U.S., Catholics once again would be unwelcome, suppressed and persecuted in America.

Bastardized thinking such as that found in the Equality Act can be traced directly back to the so-called "Age of Enlightenment" that took root in the seventeenth century. First voiced in 1637, some attribute René Descartes's philosophy of *Cogito, ergo sum* ("I think, therefore I am") as the beginning of the intellectual and philosophical movement. Other Enlightenment philosophers would include Francis Bacon, David Hume, Immanuel Kant, John Locke, Montesquieu, Jean-Jacques Rousseau, Adam Smith, Hugo Grotius and Voltaire. Focusing on the pursuit of happiness and the sovereignty of reason, the 'Enlightenment' promoted/promotes secular ideals such as liberty, fraternity, constitutional government, religious toleration, and the separation of church and state. Methodically building advocates and adherents with each successive decade, the Enlightenment would eventually undermine the authority of the monarchy, and the Catholic

Church, leading to the political revolutions of the eighteenth and nineteenth centuries.[378]

Several intellectual and political figures of the American Revolution in the next century would draw inspiration from the Enlightenment. Thomas Jefferson incorporated several Enlightenment ideals into The Declaration of Independence in 1776, as would James Madison with the United States Constitution in 1787. The Enlightenment would also greatly influence the French Revolution in 1789.[379]

Heading into an uncertain environment and undefined frontier, that is what our saint from the eighteenth century, Saint Junípero Serra, would encounter. Serra would trek from Veracruz to Mexico City, then on to Sierra Gorda, Baja Mexico, and Alta Mexico, eventually known as California, and establish the California mission system bringing faith, hope and charity to all he encountered.

Seventeenth Century Saints

Saints Robert Bellarmine (d. 1621), Francis de Sales (d. 1622), Martin de Porres (d. 1639), Jane Francis de Chantal (d. 1641), Peter Claver (d. 1654), Andrew Bobola (d. 1657), Louise de Marillac (d. 1660), Vincent de Paul (d. 1660), Joseph Cuppertino (d. 1663), John Eudes (d. 1680), Bl. John Fenwick (d. 1679), Bl. John Gavan (d. 1679), John Kemble (d. 1679), and Katerina Tekakwitha (d. 1680), pray for us.

Saint Rose of Lima is the patron saint of gardeners, florists, needle-workers, and against vanity. Saint Rose of Lima is the patroness of Peru, the Americas, the Philippines, and India.
Saint Rose of Lima's feast day is August 23rd.
Saint Rose of Lima, *ora pro nobis* (pray for us)

---

[378] "Age of Enlightenment," Wikipedia, https://en.wikipedia.org/wiki/Age_of_Enlightenment
[379] Ibid.

Seventeenth Century History

1600s- **Catholics not welcome in USA.** Restrictions placed on Catholics by various colonies, including Maryland.

1606- Franciscans opened a school in what is now St. Augustine, Florida.

1610- Apparition of Our Lady of Manaoag, in Manaoag, Philippines.

1626- Construction ends on the new St. Peter's Basilica in Rome. (Construction began in 1506.) It is the largest Catholic church in the world.

1631- April 25. Saint Michael the Archangel appears in Tlaxcala, Mexico to signify the end of the plague. (One of only two times Saint Michael has appeared in public.)

1634- Catholicism formally introduced to the English colonies with the founding of the Province of Maryland by Cecil Calvert, 2nd Baron Baltimore.

1638- Shimabara Rebellion leads to a further repression of Catholics in Japan.

1643- **Jansenism** heresy introduced. Primarily active in France. It focused on original sin, human depravity, the necessity of divine grace and predestination. Dr. Taylor Marshall has referred to it as sort of a "Calvinism for Catholics." The movement originated in 1643 from the posthumously published work of the Dutch theologian Cornelius Jansen, who died in 1638. Jansenism was opposed by many in the Catholic hierarchy, especially the Jesuits. The apostolic constitution *Cum occasione*, promulgated by Pope Innocent X in 1653, condemned the five cardinal doctrines of Jansenism as heresy.[380]

1649- Maryland passed the **Toleration Act**, America's first law on Religious Liberty.

1674- Quebec City, Canada is elevated to a diocese with its own bishop.

---

[380] "Janesenism," Wikipedia, https://en.wikipedia.org/wiki/Jansenism

1677- Jesuits establish preparatory school in Newtown, Maryland.

1683- Following up her intercession at the Battle of Lepanto against the Muslims, Blessed Mother is invoked as the **Queen of Victories in Vienna** and grants victory to the Christian army of the Holy League against the Turks. The Turks do not threaten Western Europe militarily again.

Virtue Challenge #17- Modesty

Saint Rose of Lima, help us to increase in the virtue of modesty and recognize the sacred dignity of women. Pray for women to cease seeking degrading forms of attention and accepting it as compatible with their dignity. Pray for men to cease treating women as mere objects of pleasure.

Saint Rose of Lima, to be more modest, you cut your hair to better serve our Lord. What will we do to better serve our Lord?

Saint Rose of Lima, help us to guard against vanity. Pray for us to be modest in all we do.

Help us to stand for the defense of chastity and human dignity in our world. That others may be praised and I go unnoticed, Jesus, grant me the grace to desire it.

Social media is often an insatiable trap for many to gloat about themselves. To show the places they visit, to evidence the fine restaurants they visit, to show off their new clothes, hairstyle, etc. Saint Rose of Lima, help us not to use social media as a platform to be vain.

If outwardly attractive, do we dress and live humbly? How can we better combat vanity? Do we properly counsel our children against vanity? What can we do to better guard our eyes against the impurities in the world? Do we guard our eyes against the filth on the internet, in magazines, on television and in cinema? Blessed Mother, Virgin most modest, pray for us.

Converse for a moment with the Holy Ghost about modesty. My Lord and my God, how may I serve you more faithfully and completely through the virtue of modesty?

O Great Saint Rose of Lima, pray for us an increase in the virtue and grace of holy modesty.

CHAPTER 18

Junipero

The Eighteenth Century
Charity

*"But above all these things have charity, which is
the bond of perfection…"*

~ Colossians 3:14

"You cannot attain to charity except through humility."

~ Saint Augustine

"No act is charitable if it is not just."

~ Saint Bruno

"A judicious silence is always better than truth spoken without charity."

~ Saint Francis De Sales

The 1700s

"Too melancholy, pass." "No, not that one." "What about this one?" It was Saturday afternoon and my wife and I were at the local mall after a recent move. All the furniture was in place and we were trying to find a new, large picture for a wall in the corner of our family room. Then we found it. "Hey, look at this one. It's kinda cool. What do you think?" We were sizing up a large, vintage (c. 1920s), framed advertising poster of a fruit crate label of the California company, King Pelican Lettuce.

King Pelican Brand Lettuce Poster (c. 1920's)

The green bird feathers looked like lettuce leaves. The pelican was wearing a red, bejeweled crown. There was something about the picture that drew my wife and me to make the purchase. Perhaps not everyone's taste for their family room, but for our family, budget, and decorating scheme, it would work perfectly.

Only years later did we learn that in Christian symbology, for a long time Christ was represented by a pelican. Why? A pelican mother, in time of famine, will pierce her own flesh to feed her young in order to keep them alive. Christ, through his sacrifice in the Holy Eucharist, gives us his own flesh to eat and blood to drink, in order to keep us alive. Ergo, Christ is the ultimate King Pelican. Only years later would I learn that at my parish, Saint John Cantius in Chicago, and most likely many other parishes, there is a golden pelican just above the tabernacle. Sometimes symbolism is so sublime. Providential that we were to have a King Pelican image in our home? My wife and I think so.

Saint Thomas Aquinas in his great hymn to the Holy Eucharist, *Adoro Te Devote*, wrote, *"Pie pellicáne, Jesu Dómine, me immúndum munda tuo sanguine."* ("Lord Jesus, Good Pelican, wash me clean with your blood.") In his Summa, Aquinas writes, the Eucharist "is perfective of all the other sacraments, in which Christ's virtue is participated... Hence, this sacrament is the sign of supreme charity, and the uplifter of our hope, from such familiar union of Christ with us."[381]

Interesting to note, the King Pelican Lettuce company was based in California, just like our saint for this century, Saint Junipero Serra. In many ways, Father Serra was sacrificial like Christ, the King Pelican. Through his illnesses, he pressed on wishing to bring eternal life to all those he encountered in both Baja and Alta, or Nueva, California. How are we sacrificial to those in our family and among our friends, our parish, community and nation?

While many virtues discussed in this book are efficacious, none is as essential as charity. Christ himself places the highest value on charity. We do not gain heaven without it. It's difficult to find a better summation of charity than I Corinthians 13:1-13:

[1]If I speak with the tongues of men, and of angels, and have not charity, I am become as sounding brass, or a tinkling cymbal.[2] And if I

---

[381] Aquinas, Summa, III, 75, 1, c

should have prophecy and should know all mysteries, and all knowledge, and if I should have all faith, so that I could remove mountains, and have not charity, I am nothing [3]And if I should distribute all my goods to feed the poor, and if I should deliver my body to be burned, and have not charity, it profiteth me nothing.

[4]Charity is patient, is kind: charity envieth not, dealeth not perversely; is not puffed up [5]Is not ambitious, seeketh not her own, is not provoked to anger, thinketh no evil;

[6]Rejoiceth not in iniquity, but rejoiceth with the truth: [7]Beareth all things, believeth all things, hopeth all things, endureth all things. [8]Charity never falleth away: whether prophecies shall be made void, or tongues shall cease, or knowledge shall be destroyed.[9]For we know in part, and we prophesy in part.

[10]But when that which is perfect is come, that which is in part shall be done away.

[11]When I was a child, I spoke as a child, I understood as a child, I thought as a child. But, when I became a man, I put away the things of a child. [12]We see now through a glass in a dark manner; but then face to face. Now I know I part; but then I shall know even as I am known. [13]And now there remain faith, hope, and charity, these three: but the greatest of these is charity.

The greatest of these is charity. We need to put away the things of a child. Charity beareth, believeth, hopeth and endureth all things. In other words, charity isn't always easy or obvious. It becomes more apparent, however, the more we view others with the dignity they deserve. Serving others through unselfish charity often has a multiplying effect. A great case could be made for saying that one of the most charitable people of the eighteenth century was Father Junípero Serra.

Junípero Serra was born into a farming family on November 24, 1713 in Petra, on the island of Mallorca off the coast of Spain. He was baptized the same day he was born as he was sickly and it was believed he did not have long to live. Though little known or thought of today, that island and others off the coast of Spain, have produced more than their fair share of saints. Serra was educated by the Franciscans, and in 1730 he joined the Franciscans being ordained a priest.

The future saint had been born into an exciting era in the Spanish empire...it was the time of great adventures overseas in the Americas, and many men sought their fortunes in those far-flung lands while many others sought their eternal salvation and that of others by attempting to bring the gospel of Jesus Christ to the native peoples. Saint Serra was among the greatest of the latter type of "'adventurer."

He did not start off as a great missionary. Considered brilliant by his peers, Serra was a scholar, a doctor of theology and a teacher of philosophy at the university when he felt the call to evangelize in the missions in the Americas. He asked himself that dramatic question: "Why not me?"

Landing in the city of Veracruz on the east coast of Mexico in 1750, he proceeded to walk all the way to the capital of Mexico City in the center of the country. During this arduous trip, he injured his leg, and that injury would trouble him throughout his life. Despite that, he would continue to travel great distances on foot, undoubtedly offering up his sufferings and uniting them to those of Jesus on the cross.

Though known today in the United States and around the world mainly as the apostle of California, his first missionary forays were into the Sierra Gorda, a mountainous area in what is now the state of Queretaro north of Mexico City. Those missions are little known outside of Mexico, but they are in some ways as exciting a story as those in California. During his time there, he is said by some to have learned the language of the natives and translated the catechism the better to evangelize them. Other accounts are not so sure of this, but what is sure is that he dedicated his life to the spiritual and material betterment of the Pame people. *Pame* was the name of the local tribe.

One way he did this was by leading them in moving Catholic devotions and processions, such as the Stations of the Cross. Serra himself would carry a heavy cross as they reenacted Jesus's painful journey to Calvary and the crucifixion. Serra, maligned by those who tore down his statues and set fire to his California missions, would actually wash the feet of the natives on Holy Thursday. He was no oppressor of his flock; he loved them and dedicated his life to them.

The great missionaries built a Christian culture among the natives and in their efforts to save souls, they also built beautiful churches, and Serra was no different. In the Sierra Gorda, he helped to construct the church at Jalpan. Today those churches constitute a touristic and spiritual circuit of travel and pilgrimage. The mission churches are: the one Serra built at Santiago de Japan, Nuestra Senora de la Luz in Tancoyol, Santa Maria del Agua de Landa, San Francisco del Valle de Tilaco, and San Miguel Conca in Arroyo Seco. They are beautiful churches and the native influence is easy to discern.

Rather than oppressing the natives, Serra and the Franciscans like him were the truest friends they had. When conflict arose between Spanish settlers and the natives, due to the Spaniards encroaching on native and mission lands, Serra advocated courageously and effectively for the Indians. Their persistence was rewarded, and the Crown recognized the claims of the natives and the Franciscans and the settlers had to move out.

After nine years of apostolic labors in the Sierra Gorda, he spent time preaching in the capital and was then, in 1767, he was named the superior of a Franciscan delegation sent to the west coast, the fabled land of California. We Americans don't necessarily think of it, but there are two places called *California*, one in the United States and another, called Baja California, which is part of Mexico. Baja means lower in this case, and the California of the U.S. was, during Serra's time, known as Alta California.

Serra's next mission was to Baja California, from which the Jesuits, who had founded numerous missions on that arid peninsula, had been expelled by the King of Spain. (That is another story, but the Jesuits were expelled from the entire Spanish empire by the king at the time.) Serra did not spend much time in Lower California. His efforts there were not as successful as they had been in the Sierra Gorda, partly due to the harsh conditions of the land and partly to the more complicated relations with the military governor.

After a relatively short time in Baja, Serra would make the arduous journey north to San Diego. His friends, especially fellow famed missionary Francisco Palou, tried to dissuade him from making the journey due to his leg wound which continued to bother him and did so throughout his life. But the saint would not be discouraged; he was no stranger to pain and penance as he had frequently practiced rather severe self-mortification. Many thought he went too far. We modern Catholics often find it difficult to offer the smallest sacrifice for our sins. We are likely not called to the extremes of mortification

371

that men such as Serra inflicted on themselves, but can we not ask ourselves, "What sacrifice can I make for God?" every day of our lives?

On July 1, 1769, after journeying 900 terribly difficult miles from Loreto in Baja California, Serra and his fellows finally arrived in San Diego, a more hospitable natural environment than the lands further south from which they had come. Their reception was not so hospitable (as the plush and swanky Hotel del Coronado had not yet been built). Instead, however, they were attacked by the natives and there were injuries and deaths on both sides.

After that rocky start, the work of bringing the gospel of Jesus Christ and salvation to the natives would begin in earnest. It is true it went hand in hand with the Spanish colonization effort, but the popular narrative that the missionaries were mere tools of the Spanish crown to oppress the natives is simply not true. In the first case, there were abuses of the native peoples, but the Spanish crown sought to mitigate such abuses and did far more than their English and other European counterparts to protect the Indians that their explorers and missionaries encountered.

But conflicts between settlers and natives would inevitably arise and when they did, Serra and his fellow Franciscans could be counted on to be the best advocates and friends the natives could have. Andrew A. Galvan, the curator at Mission Dolores in San Francisco, who also served on the board of directors of Serra's cause for canonization, wrote the following in the September 2020 issue of *Columbia Magazine,* the journal of the Knights of Columbus: "To get a true sense of Father Serra, I always tell people to go back to his writings and see how he described the Indians. He was in love with the native peoples; there's no other way to put it. And he saw the faith as the greatest good he could give them." And that love was reciprocated for as Galvan relates, "At the time of Serra's death, the Carmel Indians were weeping because they knew they were losing their protector, and he was remembered as "el santo" –the saint."

On August 28, 1784, Serra died at the age of seventy from tuberculosis at Mission San Carlos Borromeo del río Carmelo, one of the missions he founded. Pilgrims from all over world visit his grave at Mission San Carlos. Serra was beatified in 1988, and the first canonization Mass to take place on American soil occurred for Saint Junípero Serra in 2015. As a result of Serra's tireless missionary efforts, he is largely responsible for the spread of Catholicism along the western coast of the United States, as evidenced by the Spanish Christian names of so many Californian cities. Serra founded the first nine of twenty-one Catholic missions that spread along the California coast. The saint-to-be converted thousands of Native Americans to the Christian faith baptizing over 6,000 people and confirming 5,000.[382] Through it all his unquenchable zeal was fed by prayer each night, often from midnight till dawn. Padre Serra was an animated man of heroic charity who gave his life for his neighbor, the native peoples, for the love of God and the church.

From the *Catechism of the Catholic Church* we understand the three theological virtues of faith, hope and charity as being the "foundation of Christian moral activity; they animate it and give it its special character. They inform and give life to all the moral virtues. They are infused by God into the souls of the faithful to make them capable of acting as his children and of meriting eternal life. They are the pledge of the presence and action of the Holy Ghost in the faculties of the human being."[383]

With specific focus on charity, the CCC states that charity is the "theological virtue by which we love God above all things for his own sake, and our neighbor as ourselves for the love of God.[384] Jesus makes charity the new commandment. By loving his own "to the end," he makes manifest the Father's love which he receives. By loving one another, the disciples imitate the love of Jesus which they themselves receive. Whence Jesus says: "As the Father has loved me, so have I loved you; abide in my love." And again: "This is my commandment, that you love one another as I have loved you."[385]

The CCC continues:

"Christ died out of love for us, while we were still 'enemies.' The Lord asks us to love as he does, even our enemies, to make ourselves the

---

[382] "Saint Junipero Serra- Saint of the Day," *Franciscan Media,* July 1, 2020. https://www.franciscanmedia.org/saint-of-the-day/saint-junipero-serra
[383] Catechism, 1813.
[384] Ibid, 1822.
[385] Ibid, 1823.

neighbor of those farthest away, and to love children and the poor as Christ himself."[386]

"The practice of all the virtues is animated and inspired by charity, which "binds everything together in perfect harmony"; it is the form of the virtues; it articulates and orders them among themselves; it is the source and the goal of their Christian practice. Charity upholds and purifies our human ability to love, and raises it to the supernatural perfection of divine love."[387]

"The practice of the moral life animated by charity gives to the Christian the spiritual freedom of the children of God. He no longer stands before God as a slave, in servile fear, or as a mercenary looking for wages, but as a son responding to the love of him who 'first loved us': If we turn away from evil out of fear of punishment, we are in the position of slaves. If we pursue the enticement of wages... we resemble mercenaries. Finally, if we obey for the sake of the good itself and out of love for him who commands... we are in the position of children."[388]

The CCC concludes with the "fruits of charity are joy, peace, and mercy; charity demands beneficence and fraternal correction; it is benevolence; it fosters reciprocity and remains disinterested and generous; it is friendship and communion: Love is itself the fulfillment of all our works. There is the goal; that is why we run: we run toward it, and once we reach it, in it we shall find rest."[389]

Rest sounds great, but rest is not a word usually associated with Saint Francis of Assisi. Saint Francis, one of the best examples of charity in the church, offers us these profound words on charity:

"Furthermore, let us produce worthy fruits of penance. Let us also love our neighbors as ourselves. Let us have charity and humility. Let us give alms because this cleanse our souls from the stains of sin. Men lose all the material things they leave behind them in this world, but they carry with them the reward of their charity and the alms they give. For these they will receive from the Lord the reward and recompense they deserve. We must not be wise and prudent according

---

[386] Ibid, 1825.
[387] Ibid, 1827.
[388] Ibid, 1828.
[389] Ibid, 1829.

to the flesh. Rather we must be simple, humble and pure. We should never desire to be over others. Instead, we ought to be servants who are submissive to every human being for God's sake. The Spirit of the Lord will rest on all who live in this way and persevere in it to the end. He will permanently dwell in them. They will be the Father's children who do his work. They are the spouses, brothers and mothers of our Lord Jesus Christ."[390]

Saint Vincent Ferrer advises us about maximizing charity in our hearts. "If you truly want to help the soul of your neighbor," he writes, "you should approach God first with all your heart. Ask him simply to fill you with charity, the greatest of all virtues; with it you can accomplish what you desire."

"Raised to the altars and declared a saint in 2015, but thrown to the ground a mere five years later." That is one thing that you could say about Saint Junipero Serra, justly known as the "Apostle of California" and the "Father of California," who was frequently in the news in 2020. He is the 'Apostle' due to the missions he established serving as centers of civilization, but also in the paternal sense in that he was, as all priests are called to be, a 'Father' in the truest sense of the word to everyone he encountered.

We say "thrown to the ground" because in 2020, a year in which mobs of uneducated vandals rioted and destroyed property in various cities and states for many months, they toppled (pulled down) statues of Padre Junípero Serra in San Francisco, Sacramento, and Los Angeles.

We say "uneducated" specifically with regard to the indiscriminate fashion in which they go about tearing things down, for if they knew anything at all about this devoted follower of Saint Francis, they would know he was among the best friends the natives had during the Spanish colonial era. Regardless of Padre Serra's contribution, the assailants claim the statues erected to him paid homage to white privilege and indigenous exploitation. The ignorant, ideological protestors did not know, or dismissed, Saint Serra's numerous accounts showing him as a great defender of the local indigenous peoples. Serra was vilified in much the same way that Jesus was calumniated against.

---

[390] Walsh, Milton, "Witness of the Saints: Patristic Readings in the Liturgy of the Hours," 333.

The calumny of those who seek to destroy the Catholic faith know no limits; travelling back to the closing years of the eighteenth century we encounter the French Revolution (1789). Many historians ascribe blame for the revolt to the *Ancien Regime* and its failure to respond to social and economic inequality. As Catholics, we view the Revolution differently. We consider it to epitomize the depth of the time immemorial struggle between God (religious tradition/Catholic Royalists) and anti-God (secular/naturalist revolutionary democracy inspired by masonic ideals). In total, over 40,000 French citizens were executed for their Catholic Faith and objecting to the ironically named "Committee of Public Safety." Two events in particular from this time stand out: War in the Vendée, and the Blessed Carmelite sisters of Compiegne.

The War in the Vendée was waged between 1793-96 as a counter-revolution in the coastal Vendée region in western France during the French Revolution. The peasant uprising was considered by the Jacobin government in Paris to be Royalist. The uprising was headed by the newly formed Catholic and Royal Army. Tens of thousands of civilians, royalists, and religious were massacred. The war has been characterized by many as genocide.[391]

Shortly after the French Revolution began, the Catholic Church was targeted and contemplative religious communities were required by law to disband. Many of them continued in hiding. Among them the Carmelite nuns of Compiegne. The Sisters made an act of consecration by which the community would offer itself as a sacrifice to appease the anger of God. On the way to their execution, they sang the *"Miserere," "Salve Regina,"* and *"Te Deum."* Seeing the nuns, a complete silence fell on the raucous, brutal crowd. At the foot of the guillotine, their eyes raised to heaven, the sisters sang *"Veni Creator Spiritus."* One by one, they renewed their religious vows. One by one, they pardoned their executioners. Sister Teresa, their prioress, requested and obtained permission to go last under the blade.[392]

It is reported that each of the sisters, in obedience to the end, asked their prioress for "permission to die." Sister Teresa answered each, "permission granted." One observer cried out: "Look at them

---

[391] "War in the Vendée," Wikipedia. https://en.wikipedia.org/wiki/War_in_the_Vendée
[392] Pio, Joseph, "The Sixteen Carmelite Martyrs of Compiegne," *Catholic Restoration,* July 17, 2017.

and see if they do not have the air of angels! By my faith, if these women did not all go straight to Paradise, then no one is there!"[393] On July 17, 1794, 16 Carmelite sisters of Compiegne heroically died for our faith. Blessed Carmelites of Compiegne, pray for us!

Saint Junípero Serra's motto was "always forward, never back." With your permission, we now turn forward to the nineteenth century, and the holy compassion of Saint Damien of Molokai.

Eighteenth Century Saints

Saints Joseph Mary Tomasi (d. 1713), Louis de Montfort (d. 1716), Francis de Girolamo (d. 1716), J. Baptist de la Salle (d. 1719), Paul of the Cross (d. 1775), Alphonsus de Liguoiri (d. 1787) and the martyrs of the War in Vendee (d. 1793-1796), and the Sixteen Bl. Carmelite Sisters of Compiegne (d. 1794), pray for us.

Saint Junípero Serra is the patron saint of (N/A).
Saint Junípero Serra's feast day is July 1.
Saint Junípero Serra, *ora pro nobis* (pray for us).

Eighteenth Century History

1700s- Catholics not welcome and/or oppressed in the USA.

1700- Maryland recorded fewer than 3,000 Catholics out of a population of 34,000 (around 9 percent of the population).[394]

1712- At this time, the Quebec diocese (Canada) covered most of the American continent (French, English and Native American territories/colonies) to the Gulf of Mexico. No other Christian community, Catholic or otherwise, had a bishop in those territories at the time.

---

[393] Ibid.
[394] "Catholic Church in the 13 Colonies," Wikipedia, https://en.wikipedia.org/wiki/Catholic_Church_in_the_Thirteen_Colonies

1717- Freemasonry. **"Permanent Instruction of the Alta Vendita"** (Latin for "High Marketplace"), subtitled 'A Masonic Blueprint for the Subversion of the Catholic Church.'

1718- The Franciscans open a school for boys in New Orleans, LA.

1721- Kangxi Emperor bans Christian missions in China.

1727- Ursuline sisters arrive from France in New Orleans and open the first formal Catholic charity in the United States. It was an orphanage, school for street girls and health facility.

1738- April 28. Pope Clement XII publishes the Bull *In Eminenti* forbidding Catholics from joining, aiding, socializing or otherwise directly or indirectly helping Freemasons under pain of excommunication. Membership to any secret society would also incur the penalty of excommunication.

1760 and 1770s- Leading up to the Revolutionary War, Maryland's Catholics were once again oppressed and the Church of England was made the official religion. Catholics were denied the right to vote and were prohibited from holding public office.

1773- Suppression of the Jesuits by Pope Clement XIV, already excluded from many states. Only in the Russian Empire are they able to remain.

1776- July 4. The United States **Declaration of Independence** is adopted by the Second Continental Congress meeting in Philadelphia, PA, on July 4, 1776. The Declaration explained why the Thirteen Colonies at war with the Kingdom of Great Britain regarded themselves as thirteen independent sovereign states, no longer under British rule.

1776- Despite being able to hold elected office, **Charles Carroll of Carrolton** was selected as a Delegate from Maryland to represent his state at the Continental Congress and is the only Catholic to sign Declaration of Independence. John Carroll, the first Catholic bishop in the U.S., founded Georgetown University. Charles Carroll of Carrolton was the last Signer of the Declaration of Independence to die.

1782- Catholics in Philadelphia opened St. Mary's School, considered the first parochial school in the United States.

1784: Baptism of the first Catholic in Korea.

1789- French Revolution erupts. Priests forced into hiding and every day they heroically risked their lives to give the sacraments. God would work through a great many Catholic saints to reestablish the church in France in the next century.

1789- John Carroll, Charles's cousin, the first American Catholic bishop (from Baltimore), establishes Georgetown University in Washington, D.C., the nation's first Catholic and Jesuit University.

1790- When the newly founded United States counted almost four million people, there were fewer than 65,000 Catholics (about 1.6 percent of the population). There were only twenty-five priests.[395]

1793-96 **War in the Vendée** Counter-revolution in the Vendée region of France during the French Revolution.

1794- Carmelite sisters of Compiegne. "Permission to die. Permission granted." Blessed Carmelites of Compiegne, pray for us!

1798: Pope Pius VI is taken prisoner by Napoleon I and dies in captivity in France.

Virtue Challenge #18- Charity

Saint Junípero Serra, help us to be sacrificial and charitable, like you. Help us to imitate Christ, the true King Pelican, to bring others to heaven.
Padre Serra, help us to move "always forward, never back" in charity.

When it comes to charity, have you sufficiently 'put away the things of a child?' In maturity, what more can you bring to your daily life with respect to charity?

---

[395] "Catholic Church in the 13 Colonies," Wikipedia,
https://en.wikipedia.org/wiki/Catholic_Church_in_the_Thirteen_Colonies

While founding twenty-one missions and naming many towns in a state may not be in your future, how can you serve as a missionary in your family, workplace or community to bring souls to Christ in charity?

In what ways will you make time today to serve those who are most in need of encouragement or assistance?

Knowing that charity demands beneficence and fraternal correction, how will you reach out to your friends in charity who have left the Catholic faith and who now practice as Protestants or another religion?

Drawing inspiration from the martyrs of the French Revolution, how will you stand strong for the faith in charity when called upon to do so?

Jesus multiplied the barley (grain) loaves to nourish us. How will you go against the grain in our culture and country to multiply Christ's message in charity so that others may be nourished?

Lord, grant us permission to serve you more faithfully all our days.

Converse for a moment with the Holy Ghost about charity. My Lord and my God, how may I serve you more faithfully and completely through the virtue of charity?

O Great Saint Junípero Serra, pray for us an increase in the virtue and grace of holy charity.

CHAPTER 19

Damien

The Nineteenth Century
Compassion

"He who closes his ear to the cry of the poor will himself cry out and not be heard."
~ Proverbs 21:13

"Clothe yourselves with compassion, kindness, humility, gentleness, and patience."
~ Corinthians 3:12

"I have never seen a compassionate and charitable man die a bad death."
~ Saint Augustine

"I make myself a leper with the lepers, to gain all to Jesus Christ."
~ Saint Damien of Molokai

The 1800s

"Are there any truly unselfish acts?" So began a fun college conversation with friends. After going 'round and 'round with "but what about" statements and other interesting scenarios, we realized that we could not come to a consensus that evening. So, what say you? Do any truly unselfish acts come to mind for you? What about in times of war? Medicine? The Faith?

As referenced at the end of the last chapter, the French Revolution attempted to strangle, if not snuff out, the influence of the Catholic Church. From the blood of martyrs, the 1800s was a century in which God would work through numerous French speaking saints to minister to the spiritual carnage left in souls by the revolution. Many French soon became indifferent to, or ignorant of, the Faith. Some of the French saints who sought to reverse this trend include: Julie Billart,

Rose Phillipe Duschene, Emily de Vialar, John Vianney, Madeline Sophie Borat, Catherine Laboure, Bernadette Soubirous and Thérèse of Lisieux.

Another saint to be from a neighboring country to France, Belgium, is the focus of this chapter—Damien of Molokai. Father Damian compassionately and selflessly served those with leprosy (Hansen's Disease) in Hawaii. He responded heroically to Saint Paul's summon: "He who sows sparingly, shall reap sparingly" (2 Cor. 9:6). Damien sowed unselfishly; saying "yes" when others said "no."

Before we discuss Damian arriving in Hawaii in 1864, let us briefly discuss two other major events transpiring that decade. First, the U.S. Civil War, or as they say in the South the "War of Northern Aggression," which took place from 1861-1865. Although the battles would occur far from the Kingdom of Hawaii, (the islands would not become a U.S. state until August 21,1959), it is worth noting that the Civil War was raging at the time Damian decided to go to Hawaii.

The second event was Vatican I (1869-1870), the twentieth ecumenical council in Church history, and the first to be held since the Council of Trent three centuries earlier. Unlike the previous five councils that were held in the Lateran Basilica, this council met in the Vatican Basilica, hence its name. With planning beginning in 1864, and convoked by Pope Pius IX in 1868, the council opened on December 8, 1869. After months of discussion the bishops were permitted to return home for a few months. Before they reassembled, Piedmontese troops occupied Rome causing the pope to adjourn and suspend indefinitely, the council on October 20, 1870. (Vatican I would only be officially declared closed much later in 1960).[396]

The First Vatican Council was convoked to deal with contemporary ideologies and their influence such as rationalism, materialism, anarchism, communism, socialism, liberalism, naturalism, and pantheism. Besides combatting these ideologies, the council's purpose was to define Catholic doctrine. Two constitutions were approved: the Dogmatic Constitution on the Catholic Faith *(Dei Filius)* and the First Dogmatic Constitution on the Church of Christ *(Pastor*

---

[396] "First Vatican Council," Wikipedia, https://en.wikipedia.org/wiki/First_Vatican_Council

Aeternus), the latter addressing the primacy and infallibility of the pope (Bishop of Rome).[397]

As Saint Paul reminds us, "Jesus Christ is the same yesterday, today, and forever" (Heb. 13:8). As such, doctrine is unchanging. That is why Chapter 4 of *Dei Filius* clearly speaks to those who would want to replace Church teaching with modern preferences, "The doctrine of the faith which God has revealed, is put forward not as some philosophical discovery capable of being perfected by human intelligence, but as a divine deposit committed to the spouse of Christ to be faithfully protected and infallibly promulgated." (The modernists undeterred with this temporary setback would regroup and strike again with more success following Vatican II in the 1960s.)

The political ramifications of the doctrine of infallibility quickly drew responses from many secular states. Among them, Austria annulled the *Concordat* arranged with the Vatican curia in 1855. Ultramonatism (an emphasis on the powers of the pope) would eventually cause the anti-clerical Republican regime in France in 1905 to revoke the *Concordat* of 1801 and completely separate Church from the State. In Prussia, the anti-Catholic *Kulturekampf* broke out immediately afterwards as Otto von Bismarck attempted to consolidate recently acquired Catholic lands (mainly Bavaria and some Polish territory) into the Prussian empire. In July 1870, the Franco-Prussian war would ignite between Napoleon III and Bismarck. (More on that later in the chapter with Saint Bernadette Soubirous.)

Who among us today volunteers to serve those who have contagious diseases? Medical and first responders who assist others are indeed brave, compassionate souls. We appreciate their service to others. During the CCP Wuhan flu we observed many donning protective gear and ministering to the physical and spiritual needs of others. Wonder how many Catholic healthcare workers have said prayers to Saint Damian before their shift?

Let us return to the philosophical question of whether there are any truly unselfish acts. Who among us would accept a death sentence for the sake of someone in our family? What about non-family members? We know we will all die eventually. To accelerate, however,

---

[397] Ibid.

the process of your own death not for yourself but for the sake of strangers is truly heroic.

In that regard, Saint Damien of Molokai is a prototypical saint who went against the grain by living heroic compassion with a disregard for self-preservation. He asked, and definitely answered, "Why not me?" He put his physical health at risk, having a lower regard for himself, so he could maximize regard for others. In short, he was very Christ-like.

Jozef De Veuster was born January 3, 1840, in Tremelo, a village in the Flemish part of Belgium. He was the youngest of seven children. His parents were Joannes Franciscus ("Frans") De Veuster, a Flemish corn merchant, and his wife Anne-Catherine ("Cato") Wouters. Two of his sisters became nuns, and one of his brothers became a priest. Jozef decided to become a religious at the age of eighteen, and entered the novitiate of the Fathers of the Sacred Heart of Jesus and Mary at Louvain. Jozef took the religious name of Damien, presumably after the fourth century saints Cosmas and Damien. During seminary, Damien prayed each day before a picture of Saint Francis Xavier, the patron saint of missionaries, to be selected to serve on a mission. When Father Pamphile (Auguste) was unable to travel to Hawaii as a missionary because of illness, Damien was permitted to take his place.[398]

Damien arrived in Honolulu, Oahu in March, 1864 and was ordained a priest soon thereafter on May 21, 1864. He served the locals and sailors on the island by celebrating Mass, administering the sacraments, and converting souls to Christ. The native Hawaiians were highly susceptible to infectious diseases like smallpox, cholera, influenza, and whooping cough. In the 1830s and 1840 it is thought that Chinese workers brought leprosy to Hawaii.[399]

Fearing leprosy, Hawaiian King Kamehameha V and the Hawaiian Legislature passed the "Act to Prevent the Spread of Leprosy." The law said the lepers would be quarantined at Kaluapapa on Moloka'i. Between 1866 through 1969, about 8,000 Hawaiians were sent to Kaluapapa for quarantine.[400]

---

[398] "Father Damien," Wikipedia, https://en.wikipedia.org/wiki/Father_Damien
[399] Ibid.
[400] Ibid.

In 1873, the local bishop announced that Kaluapapa needed a chaplain. All those who considered the assignment knew that leprosy once contracted was incurable. In effect, accepting the call to serve the lepers on Molokai was a death sentence. While his physical health surely would have been a big concern for Father Damien, he placed greater importance on serving their spiritual needs.

Upon arriving at Kaluapapa, Father Damian was taken aback at the distressing situation he found. Physically, the conditions were horrible. Spiritually, morality was largely absent. Father Damian first went to work repairing the chapel, Saint Philomena. Second, he visited each leper. It was difficult work cleaning and bandaging their ulcers. Early on he wrote, "Many a time in fulfilling my priestly duties at the lepers' homes, I have been obliged, not only to close my nostrils, but to remain outside to breathe fresh air. To counteract the bad smell, I got myself accustomed to the use of tobacco. The smell of the pipe preserved me somewhat from carrying in my clothes the obnoxious odor of our lepers."[401]

The lepers had come to think of themselves, reinforced by the outside world, as outcasts from society, worthy of little respect. Father Damian knew that each of the souls now in his care had incomparable dignity as children of God. At first the lepers considered Damien's words to be insincere. Eventually, through his compassionate actions and selfless works, the lepers began to trust and accept Damian. In addition to caring for the individual's physical health, Damian also helped create greater general order in the colony through planting crops, raising animals, and repairing and constructing buildings.

Of the many edifying stories of Father Damian's heroic virtue, I consider with empathy the isolation he must have felt not having the comradery of fellow religious. On the issue of confession alone, the opportunities for Damian occurred only every few years. Once when an archbishop attempted to visit Moloka'i, he grew afraid and stayed off shore requiring Damien to make his confession shouting from the beach. The ease of most of us being able to make confession, weekly if we so desire, should never be taken for granted.

Physically, Father Damian was blessed by God with not contracting leprosy until 1884, eleven years after his arrival in

---

[401] Gedney, Albert, "Saint Damien of Molokai," *Catholic365.com*, October 11, 2014.

Kaluapapa. Another confession-related story: In October, 1885, he wrote to his superior in Hawaii, Father Leonor Fouesnel, "I am a leper. Blessed be the good God. I only ask one favor of you. Send someone to this tomb to be my confessor." It would be almost four years before the next priest was to visit the leper colony.[402]

In the last years of his life, Damian's body deteriorated precipitously. He bore large sores on his chest and back; his nose, mouth, and throat were greatly affected; his cheeks, lips, forehead, and chin were excessively swollen. His body became emaciated.[403] He accepted his suffering as only a saint could do.

In another letter to his superiors in Rome, Damian wrote, "I have been decorated by the royal Cross of Kalakaua and now the heavier and less honorable cross of leprosy. Our Lord has willed that I be stigmatized with it.... I am still up and taking care of myself a little. I will keep on working...."[404]

Shortly before Damian's death, a priest was sent to hear his confession and give him viaticum. Franciscan sisters also arrived at that time, led by Marianne Cope, to run the colony and the orphanages. Father Damian died on April 15, 1889. Through his life of compassion, patience, and suffering, he served God exceptionally well, drawing many souls to Christ. Saint Damian of Moloka'i was an inspiration for countless souls around the world.

Mahatma Gandhi commented that Father Damien's work inspired his own social campaigns, leading to Indian independence, as well as obtaining aid for the needy. Gandhi was quoted in a 1965 publication, *Mahatma Gandhi Answers the Challenge of Leprosy*, as saying,

The political and journalistic world can boast of very few heroes who compare with Father Damien of Molokai. The Catholic Church, on the contrary, counts by the thousands those who after the example of Fr. Damien have devoted themselves to the victims of leprosy. It is worthwhile to look for the sources of such heroism.[405]

---

[402] Ibid.
[403] Ibid.
[404] Ibid.
[405] "Father Damien," Wikipedia, https://en.wikipedia.org/wiki/Father_Damien

In 2005, Damien was honored with the title of "De Grootse Belg," (The Greatest Belgian) throughout the nation's history by the Flemish public broadcasting service, VRT.[406]

Father Damian, a martyr of compassion and charity, has always held a special place in my conception of a saint. John 15:13 tell us, "Greater love than this no man hath, that a man lay down his life for his friends." His selfless love and over-the-top heroic, saintly behavior has always inspired me.

In 2016, I was blessed to make a pilgrimage to the island of Molokai and visit shrines dedicated to Saint Damien of Molokai and Saint Marianne Cope. We visited Father Damien's church, Saint Philomena, and his old burial site next to the church. His body was transferred to Leuven, his hometown in Belgium, in 1936. His right hand, however, was returned to Hawaii in 1995 to be reburied in his original grave at Kaluapapa.

Saint Damien's Grave Next to Saint Philomena Church, Kaluapapa, Moloka'i

I was also fortunate to visit a grave monument of Saint Marianne, who helped with the lepers for a short while when Fr. Damien was alive, and then she became a primary caregiver for the colony upon Fr.

---

[406] Ibid.

Damien's death. Saint Marianne is buried at Cathedral Basilica of Our Lady of Peace in Honolulu.

After visiting the religious sites and praying, we went to the bookstore in Kaluapapa. There I met Boogie, a "patient" (how they refer to those affected by Hanson's disease today) who worked in the bookstore. I was told that Boogie previously had Hanson's disease, but through medication, the progress of the disease was arrested decades earlier. His hand was slightly disfigured, but it was tough to discern unless one was close to him. I bought a couple of books and had a brief conversation with Boogie. I had no idea if arrested Hanson's disease was a threat in any way to my health. I'm guessing the two people I was with would have counseled me not to get too close if there was a threat, but the strange thing is I didn't think to ask. All I saw was a man working in a bookstore, doing his job. I'd like to think for just a few minutes I was acting as Fr. Damien would, just interacting with people going about their day.

With Boogie at the Kaluapapa Bookstore.
My T-shirt is of Miguel Pro, Mexican Christero and Martyr. "Be a Hero."

I do not for one second think that my interaction with Boogie was heroic because it wasn't. But for a few moments I was able to spend some time with one of the native Hawaiian descendants of those who perhaps may have been served by Fr. Damian and Sr. Marianne roughly 130-150 years prior.

Observing the vast Moloka'i sky that day, the cerulean ocean, the verdant mountains, and the towering palm trees, it did feel as though I were walking in the footsteps of Catholic giants, of Catholic heroes, of Catholic saints. It was awe-inspiring, and humbling. It was a great day.

Some today do not look to Damian for inspiration. Advocates of cancel culture look to denigrate his memory and tear him down. In particular, Rep. Alexandria Ocasio-Cortez (D-NY) denounced the presence of a statue honoring Father Damien in Statuary Hall in the U.S. Capitol, as a remnant of "white supremacist culture."[407] Christian compassion and charity is white supremacy? For the spiritually disoriented, right-side up is upside down. Saint Anthony the Great summarized well today's progressive politicians: "A time is coming when men will go mad, and when they see someone who is not mad, they will attack him, saying, 'You are mad; you are not like us.'" AOC, we don't want to be like you.

Regardless of the occasional detractors, Damian is a beloved hero in Hawaii and around the world. In showing compassion, Damian also gave us a great example of suffering. Through him we see there is dignity in suffering. Many saints freely accepted redemptive suffering as a way to become more closely united to Christ. In today's world we complain about the smallest hardships or minor aches and pains. We would be well served to consider what Damian accepted and endured for love of Christ and neighbor. Saint Vincent de Paul tells us, "We should strive to keep our hearts open to the sufferings and wretchedness of other people, and pray continually that God may grant us that spirit of compassion which is truly the spirit of God."

What does Jesus's compassionate interactions with lepers tell us? Similar to the plan for lepers at Molokai, lepers during Jesus's time were to be cut off from human contact. If they ventured into town, they were to give notice by wearing bells and shouting, "Unclean! Unclean!" wherever they went. Being abandoned and cut off from others brought considerable loneliness. The rabbis considered leprosy to be chastisement from God due to morality. So, with lepers, in addition to the physical dimension, there was also a spiritual dimension.

---

[407] Berry, Susan, "AOC Refers to Canonized Saint Fr. Damien Who Served Lepers As Part of 'White Supremacist Culture,'" *Breitbart,* July 31, 2020.

We read about Jesus healing the ten lepers in Luke 17:11-19:

> Now on his way to Jerusalem, Jesus travelled along the border between Samaria and Galilee. As he was going into a village, ten men who had leprosy met him. They stood at a distance and called out in a loud voice, "Jesus, Master, have pity on us!" When he saw them, he said, "Go, show yourselves to the priests." And as they went, they were cleansed. One of them, when he saw he was healed, came back, praising God in a loud voice. He threw himself at Jesus' feet and thanked him—and he was a Samaritan. Jesus asked, "Were not all ten cleansed? Where are the other nine? Has no one returned to give praise to God except this foreigner?" Then he said to him, "Rise and go; your faith has made you well."

Where are the other nine? Nine of the ten healed by Jesus most likely ran off combating disbelief that they had just been healed, forgetting the person who healed them. How many times has Jesus through compassion and mercy forgiven us, or sent us graces, and we have not returned to throw ourselves at Jesus's feet and properly express our gratitude to Him? In what other ways does this story of nine of ten not showing proper thanks to Christ the healer speak to us?

In Luke 5:12-13 we read of Jesus's interaction with a single leper, "And it came to pass, when he was in a certain city, behold a man full of leprosy, who seeing Jesus, and falling on his face, besought him, saying: Lord, if thou wilt, thou canst make me clean. And stretching forth his hand, he touched him, saying: I will. Be thou cleansed. And immediately the leprosy departed from him." The Kyrios, Jesus, took note of the man's faith and agreed to heal him. Jesus reaches out, touches him, and he is healed. You can feel the compassion Jesus had for this unclean man. It was a big deal for Jesus to touch the leper. No one was permitted to touch the unclean as it was believed the person who touched would instantly become unclean. But Jesus is Jesus. He goes against the grain. What did God look for in the leper? Faith. What does God look for in us? Faith.

The lepers in both passages are models of faith. What is your disease? What brokenness afflicts you? What faith does He find in your heart? Jesus heals all who have faith. Jesus heals the contrite. Jesus reaches out to us too in our uncleanness, to heal us through the touch of confession. Jesus loves those who approach Him in confident faith. Ask, seek, knock, in faith, and you will be heard; and possibly physically healed if it is in accordance with the will of God.

In an article entitled, "Leprosy is a Perfect Metaphor For Sin," Father Dwight Longenecker writes, "It starts as an invisible infection and then slowly dominates one's life. It is invisible to start with, but eventually the person becomes deformed and ugly. Furthermore, the body becomes numb. Sin makes us numb to the abundance of life and we become dull and unfeeling. Sin also isolates us from others."[408]

Speaking of being isolated from others, when walking around outside during the CCP Wuhan Flu, and as others approach you on the sidewalk, it's fairly common for some of them to cross the street so as to avoid you. It's weird behavior to observe. In some ways it's the twenty-first century version of treating others as lepers, minus the bells and people announcing, "Unclean, Unclean." Some do not see people as people, but only as germ/pathogen carriers to be avoided. Soon after, people started betraying their neighbors for not adhering to government social distancing and mask mandates. It's dehumanizing.

What about the psychological harm of "facelessness?" Fear, not charity, can ramp up virtually overnight and reign in people minds, hearts, souls... and that of states and nations, too. Thank goodness for Texas being the first state, on March 2, 2021, to revoke the mask mandate and permit the state to open up 100 percent.[409] Texas forever!

Speaking of fear, what about false charity? A great portion of this chapter is devoted to physical charity, specifically the care of those with leprosy. Charity also occurs through our spoken words. Are we charitable in our thought and speech? In Chapter 2 on Polycarp, we spoke of false compassion. False compassion is a close cousin to false charity. I see bumper stickers, often on Subarus, about "hate." "End Hate." "Resist Hate." While a hate bumper sticker on the surface is hard to disagree with (who is really for hate?), once you dig a little deeper, the hate-related bumper stickers do not hold up to. After all, is all hate bad? What does the Bible say about hate? We read in Saint

---

[408] Longenecker, Fr. Dwight, "Leprosy is a Perfect Metaphor For Sin," *National Catholic Register,* October 4, 2017.
[409] Sabawi, Fares, "'It is now time to open Texas 100%': Texas Gov. Greg Abbott reverses statewide pandemic orders," *KSAT.com,* March 2, 2021.

Paul's letter to the Romans 12:9, "Let love be without dissimulation. Hating that which is evil, cleaving to that which is good."

Hate evil. Love good. Straightforward enough. A pro-abortion person might say that anyone who objects to their sinful choices is hateful. In contrast, Catholics believe hating evil is true charity. Yes, feathers will be ruffled in the short term, and some progressives may become apoplectic, but hopefully the person will one day realize the one speaking truth to them was being charitable and had great concern for their soul, and will choose to repent. Back to the bumper stickers. Should we end hatred of human trafficking? Should we resist hatred of genocide? Pedophilia? The list goes on. There is evil in the world. We must oppose the acceptance of evil. We must hate sin and love good.

Given original sin, you can't remove hate or evil. They're not going anywhere. What about instead of the "End Hate" and "Resist Hate" bumper stickers, we had "End Evil" and "Resist Evil" bumper stickers? But to all progressive/socialists driving their Subarus, the virtue signaling wouldn't be nearly as meaningful.

As heroic and inspirational as Saint Damian is, for a short while I debated between using him and Saint Bernadette Soubirous for this chapter. Saint Damian and his heroic compassion won out. Still, two particular aspects of Saint Bernadette's life drew my attention. First, it would have been wonderful to write about the Immaculate Conception appearing to Bernadette at Lourdes and delve into the healing waters of Lourdes. Second, her, "I fear only bad Catholics" story grabbed me by the lapels the first time I heard it and has not yet let go. As countless others have written on Lourdes, I'd like to present the "bad Catholics" exchange here. With the state of our world being what it is, I think of this story fairly often. Here is a condensed version:

Soon after Napoleon III had surrendered to the Prussians, they looked to invade France. On the evening of October 24, 1870, the following discussion occurred between Saint Bernadette Soubirous (SBS) and another member of her community:

Sister: *"The Prussians are at our gates. Don't they inspire you with terror?"*
SBS: *"No"*
Sister: *"So, there is nothing to fear then."*
SBS: *"I fear only bad Catholics."*
Sister: *"Do you fear nothing else?*

392

SBS: *"No, nothing."*[410]

Let those profound words sink in for just a moment.

To many, if reading such words with a secular worldview, they can be taken the wrong way. To faithful Catholics, the succinct exchange speaks volumes. The Catholic confidence and clarity captured align perfectly with *Against the Grain*. Fear nothing in this world—war, sickness, bad politicians, suppression of liberties, communism, etc.

Instead, be good Catholics. That is all.

Monsignor Charles Pope wrote about the Saint Bernadette exchange and provides additional brilliant commentary for us, "to the spiritually minded, bad Catholics *are* something to fear, indeed something more to fear than even suffering and death… Bad Catholics prefer the world and its values to that of Christ and His Kingdom. They will not endure suffering, inconvenience, or any difficulty for the Kingdom of God. They will not accept corrections to their worldview, politics, or mindset based on the Faith... Bad Catholics are at extreme risk of losing their eternal salvation. Further, due to their poor example, others are also put at serious risk."[411]

Monsignor Pope continues, "To some degree, we all suffer the tendency to be bad Catholics. We all sin, fall short, and have some bad priorities. But today there are increasing numbers of bad Catholics who are stubbornly unrepentant about this, instead insisting that the Church and Scriptures should be changed. This is a lamentable and fearful situation both for them and for those they influence."[412]

Saint Gregory of Nazianzen, the fourth-century archbishop of Constantinople, spoke specifically on the existence of bad bishops who reject church teaching, "Now of the lion one need have no fear; the leopard is a gentle creature and even the snake you are terrified by is likely to turn in flight; but there is one thing you must beware of, I assure you: bad bishops."[413]

[410] Larentin, Fr. Rene, "Bernadette Speaks. A Life of Saint Bernadette Soubirous in Her Own Words," Pauline Books, 415-416.
[411] Pope, Msgr. Charles, "What do Saints Fear?" December 27, 2015. http://blog.adw.org/2015/12/what-do-saints-fear/
[412] Ibid.
[413] "Most Dangerous," Vortex, Church Militant, June 23, 2021.

It is reasonable to conclude that all saints feared bad Catholics. A saint wants no soul to steer other souls away from God. A saint wants no soul to be lost for all eternity.

Do you fear bad Catholics? Do you fear bad leadership in the Catholic Church? Do you fear bad Catholic elected officials? Do you fear bad Catholics in your family? Do you fear being a bad Catholic yourself? Is eternal salvation your true priority? It was the priority of the saints. It needs to be ours, too. But for the grace of God go we.

What did Father Damian fear? Was it disease, suffering, bad Catholics? No. It was souls not being brought to Christ. He had the right priorities; he had the priorities of a saint. Saint Damian wrote, "Jesus in the Blessed Sacrament is the most tender of friends with souls who seek to please Him. His goodness knows how to proportion itself to the smallest of His creatures as to the greatest of them. Be not afraid then in your solitary conversations, to tell Him of your miseries, fears, worries, of those who are dear to you, of your projects, and of your hopes. Do so with confidence and with an open heart."

Fr. Damian is a breathtaking example of heroic compassion, selflessness, and fearlessness. Back in Europe to close the nineteenth century, we find a French saint, one of the most beloved saints in all the Church, The Little Flower, Saint Thérèse of Lisieux. While Damien was called to minister to the sick in a big way, Saint Thérèse was called to serve others through her "Little Way" found in the tasks and people she would encounter on a daily basis. Her heroism was to embrace the little things with a spirit oriented towards God. Saint Thérèse's powerful, simple, and often times hidden way to achieve union with God is an ideal bridge to have us turn our thoughts next to the twentieth century, and the hiddenness of Franz Jägerstätter.

Nineteenth Century Saints

Saints Augustine Zhao Rong (d. 1815), Julie Billart (d. 1816), Elizabeth Ann Seton (d. 1821), Bl. Anna Katharina Emmerick (d. 1824), Rose Phillipe Duschene (d. 1852), Emily de Vialar (d. 1856), John Vianney (d. 1859), John Neumann (d. 1860), Gabriel Possenti (d. 1862), Madeline Sophie Borat (d. 1865), Catherine Laboure (d. 1876), Bernadette Soubirous (d. 1879), John Bosco (d. 1888), Charles Lwanga and Companions (d. 1885-87), Thérèse of Lisieux (d. 1897), and Gregory Grassi and companions (d. 1900), pray for us.

Saint Damien of Moloka'i is the patron saint of people suffering from leprosy and outcasts.

Saint Damien of Moloka'i's feast day is May 10.

Saint Damien of Moloka'i, *ora pro nobis* (pray for us).

Nineteenth Century History

1804- December 2. Napoleon crowns himself Emperor of the French in the Notre Dame Cathedral in Paris in the presence of Pope Pius VII.

1806- August 6. Dissolution of the Holy Roman Empire.

1834- In Spain the practices of the Inquisition are finally outlawed.

1842- The University of Notre Dame is founded in South Bend, Indiana by French-speaking priests led by Father Edward Sorin of the Congregation of the Holy Cross

1844- Anti-Catholic riots where churches were attacked. These were called "The Bible Riots." One famous church in Philadelphia was burned. During this time the archbishop of New York actually had armed guards protect St. Patrick's Cathedral.

1854- The dogma of the Immaculate Conception is proclaimed by Pope Pius IX.

1858- On February 11, 1858, the Blessed Virgin Mary appeared to fourteen-year-old Bernadette Soubirous at **Lourdes,** in the hollow rock of Massabielle in southern France. Bernadette would report eighteen total apparitions that year. Our Lady revealed herself as the "Immaculate Conception." She told Bernadette to drink from a spring at the grotto. The stream has since had multitudes of medically documented miraculous healings. Lourdes is one of the most visited pilgrimage sites in the world.

1861-1865- **U.S. Civil War**

1865-1899- In post-Civil War America, many immigrant Catholics arrive from Germany, Italy and Ireland. The Irish are met with NINA signs, ("No Irish Need Apply").

1868-1869- **First Vatican Council.** (The twentieth ecumenical council and the first held since the Council of Trent three centuries earlier.) The best-known decision of Vatican I is its definition of **papal infallibility.**

1870- Saint Bernadette Soubirous- **"I only fear bad Catholics."**

1871- Infamous cartoon mocking Catholic priests as alligators.[414]

1873- "American Catholic intellectual Orestes Brownson spoke of the desperate need for the United States to convert to Catholicism. His words are prophetic. "Let the American people become truly Catholic ... and their Republic is safe," he wrote in an article for his *Brownson Quarterly Review* of that year. "Let them refuse and seek safety for the secular order in sectarianism or secularism, and nothing can save it from destruction."[415]

1875- Blaine Amendments. Anti-Catholic bigotry that permitted state governments to discriminate against Catholic schools. (Finally ruled against in 2020 in the Supreme Court decision Espinoza v. Montana.)

1887- **Football at the University of Notre Dame, South Bend, IN, begins.**

1891- Leo XIII- *Rerum Novarum.* Encyclical on Catholic social teaching focused on the rights and duties of capital and labor.

---

[414] https://www.msn.com/en-us/news/us/justice-alito-cites-1871-anti-catholic-political-cartoon-of-priests-as-crocodiles-in-religious-liberty-opinion/ar-BB16abJq
[415] Kokx, Stephen, "Only the Catholic faith can ward off leftist assaults on US," *LifeSite News,* July 7, 2020.

Virtue Challenge #19- Compassion

Saint Damian of Moloka'i pray for us for an increase in the virtue of compassion. Help us to serve those in need. Help us to defend others who are unable to defend themselves, especially the preborn and the terminally ill. Pray that we may step up our charitable works.

What is your disease? What brokenness do you carry? What faith does Jesus find in your heart?

Show us how to be more selfless in serving God and His Church. How can you participate a little, or perhaps a lot, in redemptive suffering? Pray for us to accept all trials as a means of fulfilling our debts to God.

How many of us can say that those in our lives believe we are heroes for them? If we have not begun heroic love in earnest, what about taking the first step today to show greater compassion and understanding to those with whom we interact on a consistent basis? What kind of sacrificial life can we lead in service of those to whom God has entrusted us?

To whom can you show compassion today? What about tomorrow? This weekend can you visit someone cut off from human contact and show compassion? In humility, whom do you know that is in need of love, forgiveness, acceptance, and charity?

Do you fear bad Catholics? What can you do to ensure that you are not a bad Catholic? Do you fear that souls in your circle of influence will be lost for all eternity? If so, what will you do about that?

Saint Damien, help us to care for and bring souls to Christ, as you did.

Converse for a moment with the Holy Ghost about compassion: My Lord and my God, how may I serve you more faithfully and completely through the virtue of compassion?

O Great Saint Damien of Molokai, pray for us an increase in the virtue and grace of holy compassion.

CHAPTER 20

Franz

The Twentieth Century
Hiddenness

"For the growing good of the world...
the number who have lived a hidden life..."
~ George Elliot

"Behold, I am with you all days, until the end of the world."
~ Matthew 28:20

"O my God, how sweet it is to suffer for You, suffer in the most secret
recesses of the heart, in the greatest hiddenness."
~ Saint Faustina Kowalska

"O my God, fill my soul with holy joy, courage, and strength to serve
You. Enkindle Your love in me and then walk with me along
the next stretch of road before me."
~ Saint Benedicta of the Cross (Edith Stein)

"Evil may have its hour, but God will have His day."
~ Ven. Archbishop Fulton Sheen

The 1900s

"Brothers, what we do in life, echoes in eternity."
~ **Maximus Decimus Meridius**, Gladiator

When we think of the seminal moments in history, we often consider men who exhibited courage: the warrior leader, the trailblazer, the one who went against the grain, and especially those who fought, and persevered, despite long odds. Most who are remembered were good, some bad. This includes men like Noah, Abraham, Moses, King David, Leonidas, Spartacus, Alexander the Great, Sun Tzu, Julius Caesar, Attila the Hun, Charlemagne, Genghis Khan and William Wallace. In the U.S., we think of generals like George Washington,

Ulysses S. Grant, Robert E. Lee, Dwight D. Eisenhower, George Patton and Douglas McArthur. (Named "Douglas" after MacArthur. I'm grateful my parents didn't go with "Genghis" Grane!)

When we think of the twentieth century, our minds are quickly drawn to war, despotism, cultural upheaval, along with a few uplifting stories of prominent individuals and events. To mention a few: First World War, Fatima, Communism, Great Depression, Second World War, Hitler, Mussolini, Fascism, Roosevelt, Hiroshima and Nagasaki, Stalin, Mao, the Cold War, Korean War, Pornography (magazines), Vatican II, Contraception, Vietnam War, Landing on the Moon, No Fault Divorce, communion in the hand, Roe v. Wade, USA Men's Hockey Team defeating the U.S.S.R. at the 1980 Olympics ("Do you believe in miracles?"), Reagan, Chicago Bears win Superbowl XX, the fall of the Berlin Wall, Tiananmen Square, the Internet, and Pornography (digital).

All momentous events and figures to be sure. How is it then that the person chosen for this chapter is not even a saint, but a blessed? Well, because amidst the whirlwind, chaos, monumental change, and all the wars, one man chose to live a simple, hidden life of faithfulness to God. A tremendous example for our times.

Perhaps no horrific event, atrocity, or demonstration of man's capacity for evil, has so dominated the emotional and intellectual landscape of the twentieth century as the Holocaust, the attempted genocide of the Jewish people, and other persecuted groups by Adolph Hitler's Third Reich. The Holocaust bestows upon the last century a certain uniqueness in the annals of history; there have been other attempted genocides based on race or religion, but none have so discomfited the world as what occurred during World War II.

As it haunted the world, so, too, has it haunted the memories of individual Germans and Jews as well as the descendants of victims or perpetrators. Many studies have been conducted and books written on the various psychologies at play among both the victims and villains, and everyone in between. How could such a thing have occurred in a country which had a glorious Christian heritage? Where were the Christians? Where were the Catholics? Great heroes did emerge who spoke up against what they saw going on, men of the Church like Blessed Clemens von Galen, the "Lion of Munster," who raged against Hitler's policies. But, still, one wonders how could it have happened?

Perhaps it is simplistic, but is the answer that not enough German Christians asked themselves, "Why not me?" "Why should I not lay down my life for my neighbors who are being unjustly persecuted? Why should I not stand up to this vicious atheistic regime?"

One who dared to do was Franz Jägerstätter, now Blessed Franz. This is his story. As Saint Alexius from the fifth century was known as a "Man of God" and the "Hidden Gem," so too we have a gem of a hidden soul from the twentieth century. Let us say, *Grüß Gott!* ("Greet God!"), the traditional Austrian greeting, to Franz.

Franz Jägerstätter was born in Sankt Radegund, Austria in 1907. His father, Franz Bachmeier, was killed in the first world war, and young Franz took the surname of his stepfather when his mother married Heinrich Jägerstätter. Growing up, he was a bit wild and fathered a daughter out of wedlock. However, on Holy Thursday, 1936 he married a woman named Franziska, who took her Catholic faith seriously, and together they lived a Catholic life; Franz became a sacristan and began the practice of attending daily Mass at the St. Radegund parish church built in 1422.[416]

Franz and Franziska began praying together and he began studying the Bible, taking a particular interest in the lives of the saints. Bl. Franz later wrote that the Bible became the couple's guide for everyday life, saying, "We helped one another go forward in faith."[417]

Franz on His Motorcycle, the First in St. Radegund
(Image- Dr. Erna Putz, "Against the Stream" published by: Pax Christi.
http://www.c3.hu/~bocs/jager-a.htm)

---

[416] Several excerpts, with edits, of Jägerstätter's bio are taken from John Moorehouse's "Manual for Men."
[417] Warde, Samuel, "Franz Jägerstätter Chose The Guillotine Over Pledging Loyalty To Hitler," *allthatsinteresting.com,* December 24, 2019.

This was also the time of Hitler's rise to power, and Franz thought deeply about what his faith demanded of him in the context of the troubling developments of the time. He displayed the courage of his convictions by being the only person in his village to vote no on April 10, 1938 to the *"Anschluss,"* Germany's proposed annexation of Austria. Nevertheless, the local authorities suppressed Franz's dissent and announced unanimous approval. He was dismayed to observe that so many Catholics in his town supported the Nazis, writing, "I believe there could scarcely be a sadder hour for the true Christian faith in our country."[418]

On December 8, 1940, Franz joined the Third Order of Saint Francis. On June 17, 1940, Jägerstätter, aged thirty-three, was drafted for the first time and in October he reported to the German Wehrmacht completing his training at the Enns garrison. Franz refused to take the Hitler Oath, but was permitted to return home in 1941 under an exemption as a farmer. Faced with his experiences in military service, the suppression of the church, as well as reports on the Nazi *Aktion T4* (short for *Tiergartenstraße 4*, a street address of the Chancellery department set up in early 1940 to recruit and pay doctors for the "mercy deaths" of hospital's sickest patients), Franz began to examine the morality of the war.[419]

Jägerstätter understood that bishops and priests would be arrested by the Gestapo if they said anything other than that which the government permitted. Franz nevertheless asked, "If the Church stays silent in the face of what is happening, what difference would it make if no church were ever opened again?"[420] In fact eight of twelve priests in the Deanery of Ostermiething, to which St. Radegund belonged, were arrested.

Franz traveled to Linz to visit with Bishop Fliesser to discuss these issues. The bishop was unsure whether Jägerstätter was a spy, so he answered Franz's questions carefully, primarily referencing biblical obligations to the Fatherland. Franz left the conversation disappointed and saddened that the episcopate appeared afraid to address his concerns. In 1946, Bishop Fliesser wrote of his conversation with

[418] "Franz Jägerstätter," Wikipedia, https://en.wikipedia.org/wiki/Franz_Jägerstätter
[419] Ibid.
[420] Dr. Erna Putz, *"Against the Stream"* published by: Pax Christi. http://www.c3.hu/~bocs/jager-a.htm

Jägerstätter: "I explained in vain to him the moral principles on the degree of responsibility that the private citizen has for the actions of the authorities, and reminded him of the much higher responsibility he had for those around him and particularly his family."[421]

Blessed Franz remained openly anti-Nazi and vowed to not wear the Nazi uniform. It soon became clear to all those around him that the positions he held as a conscientious objector would cost Franz his life. Franziska too tried to counsel him at the start, but soon abandoned her efforts saying, "If I had not stood by him, he would have had no one."[422] Franz knew he could "change nothing in world affairs" but he wished "to be at least a sign that not everyone let themselves be carried away with the tide."[423] He and his family had hoped the war would end before he was called into service again. Jägerstätter reported to Enns on March 1, 1943, announced that he was refusing to fight, and was kept in prison in Linz through April. In early May, 1943, he was transferred to the Berlin-Tegel, one of Germany's largest prisons.

Criticized at the time for his willingness to go to prison and be executed for his principles when he had a wife and family (three daughters with Franziska), Franz noted from his cell, "I cannot believe that just because one has a wife and children, a man is free to offend God."

Franz also wrote, "Everyone tells me, of course, that I should not do what I am doing because of the danger of death. I believe it is better to sacrifice one's life right away than to place oneself in the grave danger of committing sin and then dying."[424]

Writing to his family from prison Bl. Franz wrote: "These few words are being set down here as they come from my mind and heart. And if I must write them with my hands in chains, I find that much better than if my will were in chains. Neither prison nor chains nor sentence of death can rob a man of the Faith and his free will. God gives so much strength that it is possible to bear any suffering, a strength far stronger than any might of the world."[425]

---

[421] Ibid.
[422] Ibid.
[423] Ibid.
[424] "Bl. Franz Jägerstätter: Martyr & Dad," *yourbibleversesdaily.com*, May, 2020. https://yourbibleversedaily.com/2020/05/bl-franz-jagerstatter-martyr-dad/
[425] "Franz Jägerstätter," *findagrave.com*, https://www.findagrave.com/memorial/69747837/franz-jägerstätter

Standing for one's principles in a vacuum is one thing, but how does one approach decisions that impact a spouse, family, or others in a profound way? Through his process of discernment, Franz had spoken with Church leaders and prayed. On the website "Your Bible Verses Daily," in a post entitled, "Bl. Franz Jägerstätter, Martyr and Dad," it states:

"Martyrdom is inimical to human fatherhood—or, at least, it seriously goes against the grain. When men of character sign up for marriage and children, they know they're committing themselves to provide and protect, and to be there for the long haul... With specific reference to his duties as a father, Jägerstätter saw himself fulfilling his paternal responsibilities by modeling for his children what Dietrich Bonhoeffer called the 'cost of discipleship.' Here's how Bl. Franz expressed it: 'I have faith that God will still give me a sign if some other course would be better... Christ, too, prayed on the Mount of Olives that the Heavenly Father might permit the chalice of sorrow to pass from His lips—but we must never forget this part of his prayer: 'Lord, not my will be done but rather Thine.'"[426]

The post continues, "To change his mind just because he was going to be executed would've been an object lesson in extreme cowardice and faithlessness that Jägerstätter was unwilling to display to his children. Yet, Franz Jägerstätter had no illusions regarding the ultimate cost to his three young daughters: They would be deprived of the security and safety his fatherly presence represented. Even so, the conscientious Jägerstätter thought ahead: 'I greet you, my dear little girls,' he wrote. 'May the child Jesus and the dear Mother of Heaven protect you until we see one another again.' His solicitude for his family even extended beyond their temporal needs, writing from prison that 'I will surely beg the dear God, if I am permitted to enter heaven soon, that he may also set aside a little place in heaven for all of you.'"[427]

---

[426] "Bl. Franz Jägerstätter: Martyr & Dad," *yourbibleversesdaily.com*, May, 2020. https://yourbibleversedaily.com/2020/05/bl-franz-jagerstatter-martyr-dad/
[427] Ibid.

Franz Jägerstätter received this picture of his girls in the Berlin prison:
it brought him joy and "damp eyes". The message reads "Dear Father, come soon!"[428]
(Image - Dr. Erna Putz, "Against the Stream" published by: Pax Christi.
http://www.c3.hu/~bocs/jager-a.htm)

The main trial of Franz Jägerstätter occurred July 6, 1943 before the second panel of the *Reichskriegsgericht*, national court martial, in Berlin-Charlottenburg. Led by Werner Lueven, Bl. Franz was condemned to death for *Wehrkraftzersetzung* (undermining of military morale).[429] In the judgment, made available to view at the military archive in Prague in 1990, the reasons given for Jägerstätter's death sentence are thus:

"In February 1943 the accused was again called up, by written command, for active service with motorised replacement unit 17 in Enns from 25 February 1943. At first, he ignored the call-up, because he rejects National Socialism and therefore does not wish to do military service. Under pressure from relatives and the persuasion of his local priest, he finally reported on 1 March 1943 to the permanent company at motorised replacement unit 17 in Enns, but immediately announced that because of his religious views he refused to do armed military service. During questioning by the court officer, despite detailed instruction and advice as to the consequences of his conduct, he maintained his negative attitude. He explained that if he fought for the

---

[428] Dr. Erna Putz, *"Against the Stream"* published by: Pax Christi. http://www.c3.hu/~bocs/jager-a.htm

[429] "Franz Jägerstätter," Wikipedia, https://en.wikipedia.org/wiki/Franz_Jägerstätter

National Socialist state, he would be acting against his religious conscience.

"… However, he declared himself willing to serve as a medical orderly as an act of Christian charity. At the main trial he repeated his statements and added that it was only during the last year he had reached the conviction that as a believing Catholic he could not perform military service, he could not simultaneously be a National Socialist and a Catholic: that was impossible. If he had obeyed the earlier call-up papers, he had done so because at that time he had regarded it as sinful not to obey the commands of the state: now God had made him think that it was not a sin to reject armed service: there were things over which one should obey God more than man: because of the command 'Love thy neighbour as thyself' he could not fight with weapons. He was however prepared to serve as a medical orderly…"

"Nevertheless, despite being told about the consequences of his conduct, he stubbornly refuses for personal reasons to fulfil his patriotic duty in Germany's hard struggle for survival. Accordingly, the death sentence is pronounced."[430]

The court did not respond to Jägerstätter's request to be allowed to do medical service.

Picture Source (historic): geocities.com/ingrile/images[431]

---

[430] Ibid.
[431] Dr. Erna Putz, *"Against the Stream"* published by: Pax Christi. http://www.c3.hu/~bocs/jager-a.htm

On the morning of August 9, 1943, Franz Jägerstätter was taken from Berlin to the nearby Brandenburg-Görden Prison. Franz was told that his death sentence would be carried out that afternoon. Fr. Jochmann from Brandenburg spent time with him and was impressed with Bl. Franz's calmness and composure.[432]

Bl. Franz's last recorded words before his death were, "I am completely bound in inner union with the Lord."[433]

On August 9, 1943, at 4 p.m., Franz Jägerstätter was beheaded by guillotine by the Nazis, the first of sixteen victims.

Later that night Fr. Jochmann told Austrian nuns that Franz Jägerstätter was the only saint he had ever met.[434] Fr. Jochmann learned from the cemetery superintendent where Jägerstätter's urn was buried and told the nuns. After the war, the nuns brought the urn containing Bl. Franz's ashes to his homeland. On August 9, 1946 Franz Jägerstätter's remains were buried at his parish cemetery near the church wall in Sankt Radegund.[435]

On May 7, 1997, Jägerstätter's original death sentence was officially overturned by the *Landgericht Berlin*, Berlin's District Court.[436]

The procedure to beatify Jägerstätter officially began in 1997, after the Austrian Bishop's Conference unanimously voted in support. The Vatican, issuing an apostolic exhortation on June 1, 2007, officially confirmed Jägerstätter's martyrdom. His wife and three daughters gathered at the New Cathedral in Linz on October 26, 2007 to observe his official beatification held by Cardinal José Saraiva Martins.[437]

Many people visit St. Radegund and Bl. Franz's grave throughout the year, and particularly for the annual services commemorating his death on August 9. In Franz Jägerstätter they find strength, consolation, and direction.[438] His wife, Franziska Schwaniger Jägerstätter, born in 1913, passed away in 2013.

---

[432] Ibid.
[433] "Franz Jägerstätter," Wikipedia, https://en.wikipedia.org/wiki/Franz_Jägerstätter
[434] Ibid.
[435] Ibid.
[436] Warde, Samuel, "Franz Jägerstätter Chose The Guillotine Over Pledging Loyalty To Hitler," *allthatsinteresting.com*, December 24, 2019
[437] "Franz Jägerstätter," Wikipedia, https://en.wikipedia.org/wiki/Franz_Jägerstätter
[438] Ibid.

From Bl. Franz Jägerstätter, Catholics can learn that you must form your conscience through study, prayer, fasting, and reception of the sacraments. Formed properly in the Faith, Blessed Franz gives us an example of the power of the statement, "No, that I will not do." Franz believed that to pick up arms in the furtherance of the Nazi cause would be sinful. He was not an out and out pacifist; he simply believed that fighting on behalf of Hitler and his regime was unjust. He sought permission to serve as a paramedic, which indicates he did not seek death. But when his request was denied, he did not compromise his principles to avoid it.

At the time, his neighbors, and even some priests and bishops, argued with him. Franz was surrounded by Catholics who said "yes" in easygoing weakness, and went along with the crowd. Pope Saint Pius X would prophetically declare a few decades before Franz, "All the strength of Satan's reign is due to the easygoing weakness of Catholics." Franz looked to the Bible for guidance and to the example of figures such as Thomas More who stood with God against the state. Looking back, one can wonder how the world would have been different had more Catholic men joined with Franz saying, "No, that we will not do."

Consider how often you have the chance to stand strong and say no to temptations of the flesh, to gossiping, to mistreating others, to defrauding your boss through shirking your responsibilities. And then consider how often you yield and say, "Yes." You are not facing death, but you betray your principles perhaps out of fear of ridicule or a blow to your pride or a missed chance to be thought clever. Perhaps it is simply sloth, greed, envy, or anger. So often men are measured by their willingness to fight physically, but Bl. Franz Jägerstätter fought the spiritual battle and won the crown of martyrdom and heaven through his fidelity to God and the still, small voice of conscience that God had placed in him. Listen to your conscience and learn to say, "No" when you should.

One of the factors weighed when considering the saint to select for the twentieth century was fellow Illinois native Terrence Malick's 2019 film *A Hidden Life*. Malick's storytelling talents and cinematography skills are formidable. *A Hidden Life* excels in this regard with character development, dialogue, and lengthy outdoor scenes featuring the sound of thunderstorms and wind passing through the Austrian Alps, babbling streams, and serene shots of the lush, green farmland. The numerous Catholic religious images in the Jägerstätter home speak to their family's priorities, loyalties, and hopes.

The beautiful and profound film has ensconced its place firmly among my top five films of all time. Owen Gleiberman, in *Variety*, described the film as, "Cinema at its mightiest and holiest, a movie you enter, like a cathedral of the senses."

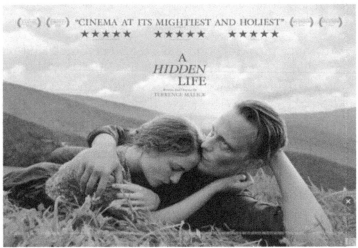

Poster for A Hidden Life

James Newton Howard's musical score for *A Hidden Life* is equally masterful. To listen to the moving main theme, with its emotion laden, searing violin, is an intense yet delicate endeavor. In its layered notes you feel the unforgettable sadness in Franz's heart as he stands with God and his conscience against his village, his quiescent church, and the Third Reich. In its melodies you experience the unbreakable bond of love, and the respect and admiration shared between husband and wife. In its beat you sense God encouraging one to stand resolute in Him.

Truly, with Him all things are possible. Called a traitor by many, Franz was one of the outstanding figures of Christian resistance to National Socialism. Gleiberman observes that, "the quietest acts of resistance are part of what save civilization."[439]

---

[439] "A Hidden Life: Movie Trailer," https://www.youtube.com/watch?v=X6dL2AmPBo8)

Some of the thought-provoking lines of dialogue from the film:

"If our leaders are evil, what does one do?"

"If God gives us free will, we are responsible for what we do, and what we fail to do."

"We have to stand up to evil."

"I can't do what I believe is wrong."

While the movie is packed with such moral assertions, without a doubt the most poignant scene in the film is when Franziska visits Franz in prison for the last time. Sitting across a table from one another, his execution imminent if he does not sign papers and forego his conscientious objection, a haunting chorus playing in the background, Franziska, in a tender voice not much greater than that of a whisper, resolutely states to Franz, "… Whatever you do… I'm with you … always." Upon hearing those words, a heartrending anguish washes over Franz. Soon thereafter, with conscience mollified one last time, Franz has been liberated. His resolve strengthens, and his spine stiffens. Hearing those words, what man wouldn't be deeply motivated to endure any hardship for his God, church, wife, family, and country? A wife's support is incalculable.

What is more, Franziska's line hits Franz, and Christians everywhere, in a most specific way in that it is essentially the last line of Matthew's gospel where Jesus resolutely states, "…and behold I am with you all days, even to the consummation of the world" (Matt. 28:20). Having Jesus, one's spouse, a family member, a friend "with you" means the world to us. In times of trouble, frustration, or sadness, has anyone ever said to you, "I'm with you"? Did it not validate and support the emotions you were experiencing? When we hear those empathetic words, our souls, united to Christ, can endure anything. Even the words, "Learn now to die to the world that then you may begin to live with Christ" (Rom. 6:8).

Through Franz, how do we begin to live with Christ? In some respects, I was unsure as to which virtue to feature for Franz and the tumultuous twentieth century. Was it steadfastness, meekness, courage, or something different altogether? In the end, the film's use of the word "hidden" was beyond intriguing to me. Compared to the heavyweight virtues of faith, hope, and charity, the Cardinal Virtues of prudence, justice, fortitude, and temperance, the many virtues associated with the Seven Gifts and Twelve Fruits of the Holy Ghost, hiddenness is a real lightweight. Or is it?

In a world so full of pride, hidden, and hence, hiddenness, is so countercultural. *Ergo,* hiddenness is an ideal fit for *Against the Grain.*

Pro-life warrior, filmmaker, author, and friend, Jason Jones, a huge Malick fan, when interviewed by John-Henry Weston about raising kids strong in the faith referenced Jägerstätter and *A Hidden Life* commented, "Franz would not take the loyalty oath to Hitler. Even Franz' Bishop encouraged him to say the oath to the regime, but he would not, he could not. Franz was encouraged to just say the oath, but don't mean it when you say it, so that you can go home to your wife and daughters." Jones continued, "Another Catholic Nazi officer begged Franz, 'you think you have the right not to say this oath?' Franz responded, 'you think I have the right to say it?' So powerful."[440]

Channeling his inner Catholic philosopher, and Malick, Jones closed with, "Even in the midst of this violent, cruel, viscous ideology, that had captured his country and was piercing in on his home, their home was filled with beautiful art, beautiful music, flowers. We should not allow the world to puncture the moral imagination of our children."[441]

In a world full of war, confusion, pain, and sin, how do we as Catholics transform our homes into domestic sanctuaries welcoming Christ, His Blessed Mother, the angels and saints to be with us throughout our day? Away from the world, how do we live hidden lives of service to God? When we go out and about, do we bring virtuous joy, meekness, and humility to all those we encounter? What exactly do we model for our children?

Only to the humble does God reveal himself—like the children of Fatima. God is not always found in the thunder and lightning, but more often He is in the gentle breeze. The still, small voice in the breeze. With Christ inside us, our consciences are in perpetual communication with our Lord. We know the voice of Jesus, the Good Shepherd. And He knows our voice.

---

[440] Westen, John-Henry, "How to Prevent Your Kids From Abandoning The Faith- With Film Producer Jason Jones," *LifeSite News,* February 12, 2021.
[441] Ibid.

To help the faithful through the pain and sorrow of the twentieth century, God did great things through His saints like Lucia, Francisco and Jacincta Marto, Maximillian Kolbe, and Edith Stein. When Saint Maximillian Kolbe was asked how to become a saint, he wrote the following formula: "w = W." Translation: You become a saint when you conform you will (small "w") to God's will (big "W").

Michael Matt, from *The Remnant*, said,

God will not be mocked. Never ever count out the children of light. The lesson is to never count God out. Let's not forget how those deemed "losers" by the Nazi's are now household names. Yes, people remember the evil names of the Third Reich's high command, but the world also remembers the heroic names: Fr. Maximillian Kolbe, Edith Stein, Sophie Scholl, Klaus von Stauffenberg, Blessed Mary Stella and her 10 companions (Sisters of the Holy Family of Nazareth) and Franz Jägerstätter. All "cancelled" by the Thousand Year Reich at the time, but immortal in the pages of history as saints.[442]

We must be strong no matter how hidden, or how visible, our cooperation with God is in serving Him and His holy will. And, of course, not just strong in the eyes of the world, but strong in the eyes of God. Persecuted strong. Martyr strong. Saint strong. Catholic strong. We know there's only one way. To pick up our cross and follow Him. *Viva Christo Rey!* And now, let's get after it.

War was a near constant in the twentieth century, during Franz's life in the late 1920s, on the other side of the Atlantic in Mexico; the situation with the *Cristeros* was proving to have many similarities to the famous rising of the Vendée during the French Revolution. The Cristero rebellion is epitomized in Mexico by the martyrdoms of the firing squad execution of Bl. Miguel Pro and the government murder of fourteen-year-old Saint "Joselito" (José Luis Sánchez del Río). The two famed Catholic resistance efforts share the following points in common: religious persecution; priests refusing to take an oath of loyalty to the state; a schismatic church created by the state; bishops who show indifference to a suffering flock; and a poor, unequipped, courageous citizenry willing to do all they can to oppose government anti-Catholic policy.

---

[442] Matt, Michael, "Video Post," *RemnantTV.com*, November 12, 2020.

Catholics and Christians in Europe had been killing each other for centuries. There is a direct connection between weak or bad faith and war. Monsignor Charles Pope writes, "War is but the cumulative effect of sin, the collective rejection of God's commandments and of the call to love God, our neighbor, and our enemy. At times, wars of defense have been and are sadly necessary. But wars among Christians are an especially poignant reminder of the failure to live the faith on innumerable levels."[443]

In asking the question "How do we otherwise well-intentioned people fail to live the faith and so quickly get consumed and conformed into the *zeitgeist* of the age?" George Orwell's 1940 essay "Inside the Whale" tackles the issue. While Orwell focuses his attention on the western intelligentsia's attitude toward communist ideology, it could have also been written about Fascism or any other extremist creed that dominated his century or ours.

"So, after all, the 'Communism' of the English intellectual is something explicable enough. It is the patriotism of the deracinated. But there is one other thing that undoubtedly contributed to the cult of Russia among the English intelligentsia during these years, and that is the softness and security of life in England itself. With all its injustices, England is still the land of habeas corpus, and the over-whelming majority of English people have no experience of violence or illegality. If you have grown up in that sort of atmosphere it is not at all easy to imagine what a despotic régime is like. Nearly all the dominant writers of the thirties belonged to the soft-boiled emancipated middle class and were too young to have effective memories of the Great War. To people of that kind such things as purges, secret police, summary executions, imprisonment without trial etc., etc., are too remote to be terrifying. They can swallow totalitarianism because they have no experience of anything except liberalism."[444]

At the end of the movie, *A Hidden Life*, a quote from George Eliot appears, "The growing good of the world is partly dependent on unhistoric acts; and that things are not so ill with you and me as they

---

[443] Pope, Msgr. Charles, "We Should Fear Bad Catholics" December 28, 2015.
https://abitadeacon.blogspot.com/2015/12/we-should-fear-bad-catholics-by-msgr.html
[444] Orwell, George, "Inside the Whale," *The Orwell Foundation*, 1940.
https://www.orwellfoundation.com/the-orwell-foundation/orwell/essays-and-other-works/inside-the-whale/

might have been, is half owing to the number who lived faithfully a hidden life." What unhistoric acts will you make today as you live out your hidden life?

Saint Theresa of Avila wrote of *Deus Absconditas*, or the Hidden God. If God can be hidden, so too can man. Some may have an *Anima Absconditas*, or Hidden Soul. And some may live a *Vitae Absconditas*, or Hidden Life.

The Catholic feast day of the Holy Family draws attention to the hidden life. For his first thirty years, Jesus spent time in the quiet happiness of domestic life with his mother and father. This sacred time is known as the "hidden life." This hidden life of Jesus is one we know very little about from sacred scripture. But it happened. And we can infer that these years lived by Jesus contain great value. Time with family is indeed sacred time. The Church saw the bigger picture here long ago drawing the connection between family time, sacred time, and the hidden life.

Imagine how Franz, as husband and father, must have had a strong devotion to one of the most hidden saints in all the Church, Saint Joseph. Saint Joseph, earthly guardian, protector, and foster father of Jesus, understands our difficulties and brokenness. In Joseph's hiddenness and silence, we find a prime example of courage, faith, and love. Remind me, how many quotes of Saint Joseph are there in the Bible?

Saint Joseph, the silent saint, knew that he was the least in importance in the Holy Family, and he was OK with that. He put his wife and child first. Due to Saint Joseph's leadership of the Holy Family, he has been declared the protector and patron of the universal Catholic Church. The model of Saint Joseph as leader of the Holy Family is often overlooked. In a world that has declared war on the family and depicts fathers, the head of the household, as buffoons and weak, Saint Joseph was anything but buffoonish and weak. He exhibited quiet calm, hiddenness, graciousness, and strength. As Franz most likely did, we too can go to Joseph. As husbands in need of strength for our wives and children, go to Joseph. As wives, praying for your husbands and children, go to Joseph. In our hiddenness, we can go to Joseph. *Ite ad Joseph* (Go to Joseph).

413

Our lives are filled with so much noise. God speaks to us in silence. How can we ruthlessly eliminate hurry and better enjoy and grow from silent time with God? We should not be afraid of hiddenness nor silence. Seek the silence. Enjoy it. British band Depeche Mode even wrote a song about it, "Enjoy the Silence." "All I ever wanted, All I ever needed, is here in my arms, Words are very unnecessary, they can only do harm."[445] Not that "Enjoy the Silence" was a Christian song, but it did have an uber catchy beat and refrain.

If there were more silence in the world, that would be a great thing. Why? Because holy hiddenness and silence together point us to the peace, joy, and strength found in Christ Jesus in the Holy Eucharist. The bread of life. The purpose of life. Saint Charles Borromeo encourages us to stay quiet with God: "If a tiny spark of God's love already burns within you, do not expose it to the wind, for it may get blown out... Stay quiet with God. Do not spend your time in useless chatter... Do not give yourself to others so completely that you have nothing left for yourself."

Author Vinny Flynn writes, "A spiritual Communion acts on the soul as blowing does on a cinder-covered fire which was about to go out. Whenever you feel your love of God growing cold, quickly make a spiritual Communion. Quickly! There's a sense of urgency here. The saints are trying to tell us that we should not limit our union with Christ in the Eucharist to sacramental communion once a week, or even once a day."[446]

Thinking about silence, two additional pop culture references come to mind. First, "Hello darkness my old friend" the opening line of Simon and Garfunkel's 1964 groovy tune "The Sound of Silence." What does silence sound like? Second, the 2016 Martin Scorsese film *Silence*, about Christianity, Jesuit missionaries, and seventeenth-century Japan. Based on the 1966 novel of the same name by Shūsaku Endō, *Silence* takes place during the Shimbara Rebellion (1637-1638) against the Tokugawa shogunate when Japanese Catholics resisted government persecutors. These faithful today are called the *kakure kirishitan*, or "hidden Christians."[447] *Silence* was a controversial film

---

[445] DePeche Mode, "Enjoy the Silence," https://www.youtube.com/watch?v=aWGzr-kOoQY&feature=emb_rel_pause
[446] Flynn, Vinny, "7 Secrets of the Eucharist," 98-9.
[447] "Silence (2016 Film)" Wikipedia, https://en.wikipedia.org/wiki/Silence_(2016_film)

when released since it dealt with one's obligation to remain faithful to God in the face of seemingly unbearable adversity. It is one of those films you need to steel yourself to watch as it asks whether it is ever OK to apostatize. For us, the answer is, "No." Our traditional faith teaches us that apostasy leads to damnation.

The film also prompted discussions of God's silence. For instance, is the message of God the silence of God? Is the silence of God actually an accompaniment for the forsaken and suffering? Is the silence of Jesus best portrayed as kenosis (self-emptying)? In *Silence* the statement, "It's only a formality" is used to induce the lead character (Fr. Sebastião Rodrigues) to step on a *fume-i*, an icon of Jesus or Blessed Mother to apostatize. In *A Hidden Life* the question "Who will know?" is used to try to induce Franz Jägerstätter to apostatize. The former was successful. The latter was not. Scorsese chooses to show man's inner struggle with, and the eventual abandonment of, his faith. Malick chooses to show man remaining faithful to the end.

In our imitation of Christ, should we pursue heroism (i.e., saintliness) by taking on another's weakness, or should it be a heroism of triumphant resolve? *Against the Grain* certainly relates more to the latter. However, as we know with victimized souls and those who identify with the vulnerable, the former also has tremendous merit.

In his review of *Silence*, Deacon Steven D. Greydanus observes that the Japanese inquisitors are portrayed as having figured out that they could deny Christians their triumph associated with visible martyrdoms, like what occurred in the early centuries with the bread and circus of the Colosseum martyrdoms.[448] Instead, the Japanese isolated the Christians and had them suffer their ignominious persecutions, tortures, and deaths away from the public gaze. Public and private martyrdom affects the faithful differently. Public martyrdom spreads the faith faster than private martyrdoms. Whether public or private, God sends His signal graces to each soul. May His will be done.

In Hollywood, heroes are often portrayed as over-the-top, super-human characters capable of unbelievable act of bravery or valor that few are capable of emulating or experiencing. While some actions or

---

[448] Greydanus, Deacon Steven D, "SDG Reviews 'Silence,'" *National Catholic Register,* December 21, 2016.

undertakings are indeed monumental in scope, other heroic acts can be small and even go unnoticed. Heroism can be an everyday type of thing. It can be done simply by orienting all that you do for the service of God and for others. Saint Thérèse of Lisieux and her book, "Little Way" is an excellent example.

For instance, what about all those pro-life warriors who live "A Hidden Life for Life" working to end the greatest destroyer of peace in our times, abortion? For all those strong, hidden, and silent pro-life warriors, *thank you.* Thank you for all you do to positively impact the fight against abortion with efforts that are not known to others. Thank you to all who pray without fail for our Church, political, and pro-life leaders. Thank you to all those who stand across from abortion facilities and pray at times when no one knows they are there. Thank you to all those who quietly send in monthly donations to pro-life apostolates. For all those who give a voice to the voiceless, for all those who defend life and stand with the vulnerable, thank you.

In the twentieth century, humanity witnessed world and regional wars. Add to this list of violent conflict insurgencies and terrorist movements. On a geopolitical scale, well over a hundred million lives were lost to war and totalitarian persecution. How many hundreds of millions, perhaps even over a billion, lives in the century were murdered by the ghastly reality of abortion? War and abortion are but mere tragic symptoms of the larger disregard and loss of respect for human life. To this we note that the contraceptive mindset only added fuel to the deterioration of values toward vice in Western culture.

In the 1960s, with the availability of oral contraception, the insidious war against morality accelerated. With contraception, people pursued the unitive and denied the procreative element present in the marital act. With abortion, life can be terminated. With contraception, life can be prevented. In not being open to life in marital relations, man denies his essential role as co-creator of life with God.

Father John Hardon, S.J., has written extensively on the moral conflict over contraception. Two titles speak volumes in and of themselves, "Contraception: Fatal to the Faith" and "Contraception Feeds Social Decline." From his essay "Contraception: Fatal to the Faith," Father Hardon writes:

416

All the evidence indicates that the core issue at stake is contraception. If contraception is not a grave sin, well then what is? And why go to confession if I am still in God's friendship although practicing contraception. What is the new conclusion? That the single, principal cause for the breakdown of the Catholic faith in materially overdeveloped countries like ours has been contraception. Saint James tells us that faith without good works is dead. What good is it to give verbal profession of the Catholic faith, and then behave like a pagan in marital morality?

What followed was as inevitable as night follows day. Once firmly believing Catholics became confused, or bewildered, or simply uncertain about the grave moral evil of contraception. The spectacle of broken families, broken homes, divorce and annulments, abortion and the mania of homosexuality—all of this has its roots in the acceptance of contraception on a wide scale in what only two generations ago was a professed Catholic population.

The Catholic Church teaches infallible doctrine, both in faith and morals... The grave sinfulness of contraception is taught infallibly by the Church's ordinary universal teaching authority. Therefore, those who defend contraception forfeit their claim to being professed Catholics.[449]

In "Contraception Feeds Social Decline," Fr. Hardon writes, "People who practice contraception become habitually selfish. Experience shows that their selfishness will not even exclude killing the unborn child that was unwillingly conceived. There is only one solution. Re-evangelize, in order to re-Christianize, in order to revitalize a decadent human society."[450]

The negative ramifications of this "Contraceptive War," saying *Non-Serviam* ("I will not serve") to God, are inestimable. How many priests have spoken, let alone effectively, on the immorality of contraception from the pulpit? How many priests teach that the deliberate use of contraceptives between husband and wife is objectively a mortal sin? How many priests have given penitents

---

[449] Banet, Kevin, "Contraception: Fatal to the Faith," *Fr. John Hardon, SJ, Archive and Guild,* March 30, 2014. https://hardonsj.org/contraception-fatal-to-the-faith/
[450] Hardon, Fr. John, "Contraception Feeds Social Decline," *Online Musings,* posted March 19, 2011. https://prachion1.wordpress.com/2011/03/19/hello-world/

permission to use contraceptives? How many Catholic moral theologians openly defend contraception? How many bishops claim that contraception is really a matter of conscience? How many bishops, priests, and theologians actually believe contraception is immoral?

Time indeed to re-evangelize, re-Christianize, and revitalize both church and society. As the twentieth century opened the floodgates to the widespread acceptance of the contraceptive mindset, I thought it important to address briefly its ramifications for marriage, our faith, and our culture.

Speaking of events with massive ramifications for our faith and culture, consider Vatican II. To give you an idea of my thoughts on Vatican II, a quote from St. John Henry Newman: "I thank God that I live in a day when the enemy is outside the Church, and I know where he is, and what he is up to. But, I foresee a day when the enemy will be both outside and inside the Church ... and, I pray for the poor faithful who will be caught in the crossfire."

In his 1947 "Signs of the Times" sermon, commenting on the anti-Christ and the crisis in the Church and society, then Monsignor Fulton Sheen, preached the uncompromising truth: "He will set up a counter-Church, which will be the ape of the Church because, he the devil, is the ape of God. It will be the mystical body of the anti-Christ... It will have all the notes and characteristics of the Church, but in reverse and emptied of its divine content... We may see the future as a time of trial... We must recognize the world is summoning us to heroic efforts at spiritualization."[451] Seems to me like Sheen was spot on in describing the post-Vatican II Church. Do we know the signs of our times?

Fr. Gabriele Amorth was mired in the diabolical crossfire like few others in his role as eventual Vatican Chief Exorcist. A contemporary of Saint Padre Pio, Fr. Amorth gave an interview in 2011 under the condition that it only be published after his death. Describing a conversation from 1960, Fr. Amorth said that Padre Pio knew the Third Secret of Fatima and was concerned about entering, "the great apostasy within the church." He added, "One day Padre Pio said to me very sorrowfully: 'You know, Gabriele? It is Satan who has been

---

[451] Sheen, "Signs of the Times," Original radio broadcast January 27, 1947. YouTube posted October 10, 2016. https://www.youtube.com/watch?v=LhaCjUGamjk.

introduced into the bosom of the Church and within a very short time will come to rule a false Church."'[452]

Since so much has been written by others about Vatican II and the false church, we will limit our discussion of it here. However, given Vatican II's tremendous impact on the Church, our faith, and the world, a few words are appropriate. Judging a tree by its fruit, objectively speaking, Vatican II was a fabulous disaster. A total dumpster fire. To pretend otherwise is to delude oneself and is insanity defined.

The Modernists, ascendant in the Church hierarchy during the 1950s made their definitive move with the election of Angelo Roncalli (Pope John XXIII). As anti-Catholic forces worked to corrupt and weaken the Church from the outside, John XXIII sided with Modernists, anticlerical liberals and revolutionary socialists on the inside to introduce major changes, especially regarding interreligious dialogue and worship.[453] John XXIII used his charisma to introduce moral relativism, socialism and secular humanism "reforms" that sought to replace the Deposit of Faith not with minor alteration, but through radical change.[454]

John XIII opened the council on October 11, 1962. Less than a year later, in June 1963, he died from stomach cancer. Fr. Radecki writes, "On January 16, 2001, examiners exhumed his body for the recognition of his future canonization. John XXIII's body had literally turned over in its grave and was facing downward.[455] If true, how is one to process and reconcile this striking and shocking occurrence?

Where John XXIII opened a window to modernism, his successor and fellow modernist, Giovanni Battista Montini (Paul VI), opened wide the front door. Paul VI would oversee the council that would set in motion the *Novus Ordo Missae* (New Mass) and ratify and promulgate decrees that would radically change the way Catholics would practice their faith. Vatican II was closed by Pope Paul VI on December 8, 1965.

---

[452] Hickson, Dr. Maike, "Chief Exorcist Father Amorth: Padre Pio Knew The Third Secret," *One Peter Five*, May 23, 2017.
[453] Fr. Francisco Radecki, CMRI, *Vatican II Exposed as Counterfeit Catholicism*, St. Joseph's Media, 2019. 183.
[454] Ibid. 184.
[455] Ibid. 232.

Addressing modernism in his characteristic pithy wisdom, the Venerable Archbishop Fulton J. Sheen quipped, "If the church marries the mood of the current age, it will become a widow in the next."[456]

The difference between the pre- and post-conciliar Church are day and night. Dr. Taylor Marshall lists some of the changes in his, "Who Created the Pre and Post Conciliar Distinction" podcast: "The ordination for deacon, priest and bishop was changed. The Baptism and Confirmation rites were changed. [In particular, the Oath Against Modernism was no longer required to be said by new ordinates.] The Holy Sacrifice of the Mass was dramatically changed. The prayers at the foot of the altar, the offertory, and the Last Gospel were all removed. Latin and Gregorian Chant were removed." Marshall continued, "what happened was a bunch of 'experts,' like Karl Rahner and Annibale Bugnini, said they wanted to modernize the liturgy. That Freemasons and Protestants had input into Vatican II and the *Novus Ordo* Mass cannot be disputed. Why were persons not in communion with the Church permitted to have input into how we worshipped God?"[457] The answer, we know, is indefensible.

Changes made after Vatican II include the following: the dramatic stripping of the Latin rite Mass of its liturgical moorings with the approval of vernacular languages during worship and the celebration of the Mass *versus populum* (facing the people) from *ad orientem* (facing east and the crucifix); ecumenical outreach to other religions; a modified liturgical calendar; and introducing modern aesthetic changes focused on contemporary religious rather than sacred liturgical music and artwork. Wikipedia closes its discussion of the Vatican II changes with this understatement, "Many of these changes remain divisive among the Catholic faithful."[458]

So what were the fruits of Vatican II? In addition to a widespread loss of faith, according to the Index of Leading Catholic Indicators, the following key metrics are all down: Mass attendance, priests and priestly ordinations, brothers and women religious, students at Catholic high schools and grade schools, baptisms and marriages.[459]

---

[456] Fulton J. Sheen, "Ways of Killing Freedom," *The Ottawa Citizen*, August 22, 1959, 16.
[457] Marshall, Dr. Taylor, ""Who Created the Pre and Post Conciliar Distinction?" podcast, YouTube posted March 14, 2021. https://www.youtube.com/watch?v=TYj0tIWIfVY
[458] "Second Vatican Council," Wikipedia, https://en.wikipedia.org/wiki/Second_Vatican_Council
[459] "Statistical Decline of the Catholic Church Since Vatican II," *These Last Days Ministries*, https://www.tldm.org/news6/statistics.htm

With so many things down, is anything up? Sure. The following key metrics are all up: number of clergy sex abuse cases, homosexual priests and bishops, priestless parishes, financial mismanagement, church closures, general disrespect at Mass (including communion in the hand and immodest attire), and divorces.[460] Also, as mentioned in Chapter 12, a 2019 study found that 70 percent of Catholics no longer believe in the true presence of Christ in the Eucharist—an all-time high. Given the extensive malformation of Catholics in the post-Vatican II Church, is anyone surprised that today more Catholics believe in same-sex unions than they do in the true presence of Christ in the Blessed Sacrament?

As I'm solely a casual observer of Vatican II, the aforementioned items are not meant to be an exhaustive list. Professional theologians, scholars, and critics can, and have, written extensively about the failures and the negative impacts of Vatican II. Suffice it to say, by any objective measure, more damage than grace came out of the council. By a tree's fruit you shall know it. One can only conclude that Satan played a major role during Vatican II and its subsequent post conciliar twisted implementation.

Let's look to Pope Paul VI and his words on the role the devil played. In his homily delivered June 29, 1972, Pope Paul VI states that something deep and negative was increasingly afflicting the Church. He goes on to state, "… through some mysterious crack—no, it's not mysterious; through some fissure, the smoke of Satan has entered the Church of God… There is doubt, uncertainty, problems, unrest, dissatisfaction, confrontation. The Church is no longer trusted."[461]

Despite Paul VI's laments, he was largely responsible for the post–conciliar crisis. We all want better, but our bishops and priests force the inferior *Novus Ordo* faith and Mass on us. Why?

On July 16, 2021, a day that will live in infamy, Pope Francis issued his Moto Proprio ironically titled *"Traditionis Custodes,"* "Guardians of Tradition."[462] It is a document that suffocates

---

[460] Ibid.

[461] del Guercio, Gelsomino, "What did Paul VI mean by saying "the smoke of Satan has entered the Church"?" *Aleteia*, July 6, 2018.

[462] https://www.vatican.va/content/francesco/en/motu_proprio/documents/20210716-motu-proprio-traditionis-custodes.html

Benedict's 2007 Latin-Mass Decree, *Summorum Pontificum*. For what it's worth, recall that Benedict said, "What earlier generations held as sacred, remains sacred and great for us too, and it cannot be all of a sudden entirely forbidden or even considered harmful."[463]

Eric Sammons, editor of Crisis Magazine commented on *Traditionis*, "One of my first thoughts when reading the Pope's decree was our Lord's words, "What father among you, if his son asks for a fish, will instead of a fish give him a serpent?" (Luke 11:11) Sammons added, "I think also of those Catholics who are tired of being vilified by the pope and will now be tempted to leave the Church, to go to Eastern Orthodoxy, or fall into sedevacantism (the belief that there is no reigning pope), or look to some other "independent" Catholic chapel."[464]

Lamenting the "divergences, disagreements and divisions" that the Tridentine Rite has allegedly caused in the church, and the opposition to the Second Vatican Council (and Bugnini's Novus Ordo Mass), Pope Francis reasoned that righting these perceived wrongs would be best accomplished by imposing restrictions that essentially "throw a wet blanket" on the increasing fire that was burning among the faithful attending the Traditional Latin Mass. Will it work? Time will tell. Early indications are that many who exclusively attend the Novus Ordo are now more curious than ever about the benefits of the bulwark of the Tridentine Rite.

Kennedy Hall commented, "Thank God for the TLM restrictions: You wanna corral trad-leaning Catholics into a traditional parish? *Good.* You may as well say, "We want to suppress the military by getting them to train with the SEALS." Get ready for a hoard of Tridentine super-soldiers. Deus Vult."[465]

What does not make sense is that while the church is "on fire" in terms of its liturgical, financial, and sexual abuse scandals, the rogue German bishops (considering blessing same-sex relationships and the ordination of women), abandonment of the church in China and lack of standing in solidarity with the Uyghurs, Pachamama idols, Pope Francis, instead, chooses to stand with the modernists, globalists,

---

[463] Biorseth, Vic, "Letter to Bishops on Summorum Pontificum,"
https://www.catholicamericanthinker.com/Letter-to-Bishops-on-Summorum-Pontificum.html
[464] Sammons, Eric, *Traditionis Custodes*: Serpents Over Fish," *Crisis*, July 16, 2021.
[465] Kennedy Hall, Twitter post, July 19, 2021.

transhumanists and environmentalists, conduct Islamic outreach to the "children of Abraham" and sends handwritten notes of support of Fr. James Martin, S.J. and his homosexual advocacy efforts. In terms of the immutable Catholic Magisterium and being a 'Guardian of Tradition,' who here is being divisive?

The battle lines have been drawn. Let us pursue increased unity to God, Christ, Blessed Mother, the Magisterium, and the Mass of All Ages. We stand in faith with *Quo Primum*, which Pope St. Pius V said the Tridentine Rite "cannot be revoked or modified, but remain always valid and retain its full force. No one whosoever is permitted to alter this notice... Would anyone, however, presume to commit such an act, he should know that he will incur the wrath of Almighty God and of the Blessed Apostles Peter and Paul."[466]

Returning to solitude, silence and simple, Saint Thomas à Kempis in *The Imitation of Christ* writes, "The greatest saints avoided the company of men as much as they could and chose to live to God in secret."[467] Kempis continues, "Shut thy door upon thee, and call to Jesus thy beloved. Stay with Him in thy cell, for thou shall not find such great peace anywhere else."[468]

Human happiness comes in living a simple, peaceful, and virtuous life. Pondering this further, I obviously thought of Lynyrd Skynyrd's "Simple Man." A power ballad in which a Mom counsels a young boy on the keys to a life well lived:

Troubles will come and they will pass. You'll find a woman and you'll find love.
And don't forget, son, there is someone up above. Baby, be a simple kind of man.
Forget your lust for the rich man's gold. All that you need is in your soul.
And be a simple kind of man.
Boy, don't you worry, you'll find yourself. Follow your heart and nothing else.
And you can do this. And, be a simple kind of man.[469]

[466]Staff, "LifeSite journalists react to 'cruel,' 'hateful' new motu proprio restricting Latin Mass." *LifeSite News.com*, July 19, 2021.
[467] Kempis, "The Love of Solitude and Silence," *Imitation of Christ*, Book I, Chapter 20, 65.
[468] Kempis, "The Love of Solitude and Silence," *Imitation of Christ*, Book I, Chapter 20, 69.
[469] "Simple Man - Lynyrd Skynyrd - Lyrics HD," YouTube posted September 29, 2011. https://www.youtube.com/watch?v=sMmTkKz60W8

Franz was a simple kind of man. His mom would have been proud. He followed heart and soul, and had deep moral courage. When he needed to be an army of one, he was. Franz stood as one, as an army that said, "No." He knew when to say "beyond this point I cannot and will not consent."

Tucker Carlson, speaking at the Turning Point USA Conference in December 2020, made the following statement,

> None of it is worth it if you betray your principles. That is essential. If the world hates you and your values, ignore the world's standards. The system is a joke. Don't be shallow, banal, and ordinary. Don't play along. Act like it's a free country. Be true to yourself, your conscience, your faith, and your God. Opt out of popular society. To make a difference you don't need to be loud, be a jerk, or get in people's faces. What it takes is small acts of personal courage and conviction. "No, sorry, I don't believe that and I'm not going to pretend that I do." Some of the most powerful examples through history... have been quiet people who just refused to obey at a certain point because it was too much... It's always been true... The people with deep moral courage don't need to call too much attention to themselves they just need to stop obeying. I would recommend that to everybody, but I also recognize the costs are very real.[470]

Franz knew the costs. In the movie he was asked, "who will notice what you are doing?" For Franz, this question cut to the quick of his soul. God, of course, would know what he was doing. To the non-believer, the question means little. To the Catholic, the question means everything.

While the positive attributes of hiddenness, silence and simplicity have been highlighted in this chapter, it is important to address an elephant in the room—the negative consequences of complicity via silence that afflicts our church and world today. In our comfortable Catholicism, we have been conditioned (supplemented by a healthy dose of our own cowardice) to remain silent when we ought not. How often do we choose to avoid uncomfortable, candid conversations with family members and friends on matters of importance to our church,

---

[470] Krayden, David, "Tucker Carlson: You're Actual Enemy is the Person Whose Funding ... Some Crazed Ideologue Wearing Black." *The Daily Caller*, December 30, 2020.

country or culture? How will we be judged to have been complicit with the evils around us by our silence?

In our times, most all of us know the costs of "sticking our neck out" and saying what needs to be said. Do we nonetheless speak out in charity? Do we speak uncompromising truth to power? Do we not question church hierarchy as Saint Paul questioned Saint Peter? As with Saint Polycarp in our second chapter, we are called to speak with holy candor. We must set aside our comfort and add our voices to the pressing matters in our church, country and culture. Clear, strong voices are needed now more than ever.

Integrity in Christ, living virtuously, is diminished, mocked, and belittled in today's world.

As society encourages people to apostatize, to go along with the crowd, and social media encourages people to be prideful, outrageous and noteworthy, being Catholic sometimes means going in the opposite direction. In a fleeting man-centered world of self-promotion, notoriety, and outrageousness, pride is promoted. In a God-centered and grounded world of virtue, consistency of character, resoluteness, an apostolic nature, holiness is always rewarded. Not rewarded by this world but by God. And that is all that matters. Being a simple kind of man matters. A simple man of virtue matters.

Virtue is the big importance of little things.

What little things have big importance to you? Are you a simple man of God? Or are you a complex man of the world? Saint John Vianney states, "You either belong entirely to the world, or entirely to God." Have you chosen this day whom you will serve? The advice of Saint John of the Cross is also important to keep in mind, "Whenever anything disagreeable or displeasing happens to you, remember Christ crucified, and be silent." How countercultural. How Catholic. Talk about going against the grain. If we are slighted in the least, society tells us to speak up quickly and sometimes loudly. Do not be afraid of the silence. The hiddenness and silence will point us to peace and joy found in Christ Jesus and the Holy Eucharist.

Speaking of joy, here is a fun twentieth-century story. On a hot summer day in 1941, Blessed Solanus Casey (from Michigan), was receiving people at his door seeking his blessing and counsel. One visitor came to thank him for his help and brought ice cream cones to celebrate. Called to another matter, Blessed Solanus put the ice cream in his desk drawer. Another who stopped in was a fellow Capuchin friar on his way to have emergency dental work; he asked for a blessing due to the serious nature of the dental surgery. He was instantly healed when Solanus blessed him. Returning later the friar reported that the dentist had found his tooth perfectly healthy. "This calls for a celebration!" said Fr. Solanus. Opening his desk drawer they had the ice cream cones that were given to him an hour earlier. Despite the heat, they hadn't melted! Saints, miracles, and ice cream. More reasons why I love being Catholic!

Let us put the wars, revolutions, and the general heaviness of the twentieth century behind us, and turn next to the joy of Carlo Acutis, our twenty-first century saint.

Twentieth Century Saints

Saints Maria Goretti (d. 1902), Gemma Galgani (d. 1903), Francis Xavier Cabrini (d. 1917), Marianne Cope (d. 1918), Francisco (d. 1919), Jacinta Marto (d. 1920), Pier Giorgio Frassati (d. 1925), Joseph Moscoti (d. 1927), Fr. Miguel Pro (d. 1927), the Cristeros (d. 1926-28), Faustina Kowalksa (d. 1938), Maximillian Kolbe (d. 1941), Benedicta of the Cross/Edith Stein (d. 1942), Josephine Bakhita (d. 1947), Katherine Drexel (d. 1955), Bl. Solanus Casey (d. 1957), Padre Pio (d. 1968), and Ven. Fulton Sheen (d. 1979), pray for us.

Bl. Franz Jägerstätter is the patron saint of (N/A).
Bl. Franz Jägerstätter's feast day is May 21 (the day of his baptism). August 9 (day of death).
Bl. Franz Jägerstätter, *ora pro nobis* (pray for us).
A final Austrian phrase, *Gott behüte Dich* ("May God protect you").

Twentieth Century History

1908- Pope Saint Pius X writes **Modernism** is the "synthesis of all heresies."

1910-Saint Pope Pius X's institutes "Oath against Modernism." (Rescinded in 1967.)

1914-1918- **World War I.** Pope Benedict XV declares neutrality. His peace initiatives are rejected by both sides as favoring the other. Massive papal charity in Europe during war.

1916-Racist Margaret Sanger opens first birth control facility in the U.S.

1917- **Our Lady of Fatima.** A series of apparitions ending with the Miracle of the Sun. Blessed Mother shares three secrets and implores us to pray the Rosary. Convert Russia to her Sacred Heart.

1917- Communist revolution in Russia.

1917- U.S. bishops form the National Catholic War Council (NCWC) to enable American Catholics to support servicemen during World War I.

1918- Persecution of the Roman Catholic Church, and especially the Eastern Catholic Churches, in the Soviet Union (until 1985).

1921-Racist Margaret Sanger founds the American Birth Control League, which later becomes the Planned Parenthood Federation of America. She dies on Sept. 6, 1966. (Yes, an evil 666.)

The iniquitous Sanger wrote, among other things, "The most merciful thing that the large family does to one of its infant members is to kill it."[471]

1922- G.K. Chesterton, philosopher, poet, and writer, converts to Catholicism.

1926-40- *Cristeros* **in Mexico.** Religious persecution by Mexican government led by Mason Elias Calles. Brave witnesses of the Mexican clergy-martyrs, like Bl. Miguel Pro, or the incomprehensibly brave fourteen-year-old boy, Saint José Sánchez del Río.

1929- February 11. The Lateran Treaty is signed by Benito Mussolini and Cardinal Gasparri establishing Vatican City as an independent State.

---

[471] Sanger, Margaret, *The Pivot of Civilization,* Echo Library, April, 1922, n.p.

1931- Pope Pius XI declared, "Religious socialism and Christian socialism are contradictory terms, for no one can be, at the same time, a good Catholic and a true socialist."

1931-36- Persecution of the Church in Spain. During the Red Terror, it is estimated that 7,000 members of the Catholic clergy were killed.

1939-45- World War II. The Vatican declares neutrality and conducts massive Vatican relief intervention for displaced persons, prisoners of war and needy civilians in Europe. During World War II: Convents, monasteries, and the Vatican are used to hide Jews and others targeted by the Nazis for extermination. The Nazis imprison and at times execute Catholic clergy, monks and nuns who criticize Nazi ideology.
- 1944. The German Army occupies Rome. Hitler claims he will respect Vatican neutrality; however several incidents, such as giving aid to downed Allied airmen, nearly cause Germany to invade the Vatican. Rome is liberated by the Allies after only a few weeks of occupation.

1949- Pope Pius XII's "Decree Against Communism" excommunicates all Catholics collaborating with or voting for communist organizations.

1950- The Assumption of Mary is defined as dogma by Pius XII.

1953- Hugh Hefner mainstreams pornography (print).

1954- J.R.R. Tolkien publishes *The Lord of the Rings*, filled with Catholic themes.

Late 1950s- Sr. Lucia says that Communism would be in all nations, including the USA.

1959- Vatican II called.

1960- John F. Kennedy becomes first Catholic elected president of the United States.

1962-65. **Vatican II.**

1962- U.S. Supreme Court in Engel v. Vitale declares school-sponsored prayers unconstitutional.

1965- U.S. Supreme Court in Griswold v. Connecticut strikes down state laws prohibiting contraception.

1966- The National Conference of Catholic Bishops (NCCB) and the United States Catholic Conference (USCC) were established out of the National Catholic Welfare Council (NCWC). (The NCCB and USCC would become the USCCB in 2001.)

1969- Vatican II introduces radical reform of the rite of Mass including protestantizing elements of offertory prayers, freestyle moments, and focus on celebration (not sacrifice). First Novus Ordo Masses said on first Sunday in Advent, 1969.

1969- Communion in the hand introduced. "The praxis of Communion in the hand over the past fifty years," Bishop A. Schneider would write in May, 2020, "has led to an unintentional and intentional desecration of the Eucharistic Body of Christ on an unprecedented scale."[472]

1970- No Fault Divorce. California first state to pass law. Signed by Gov. Ronald Reagan.

1972- June 29, Pope Paul VI states, "the smoke of Satan has entered the Church of God."

1973- Abortion legalized in Roe v. Wade.

1980s- Tridentine Mass permitted with approval of local bishop.

1980s- Ecumenism accelerated.

1988- June 30. Archbishop Marcel Lefebvre of the Society of St. Pius X (SSPX) consecrates four men as bishops at Écône, Switzerland, without the express permission of the pope.

1989- November 9. The Berlin Wall falls.

1990s- Pornography (digital) ascendant when internet expands.

1991- December 31. The Soviet Union is officially dissolved. Persecuted Catholic Church re-emerges from hiding, especially in the Ukraine and the Baltic States.

---

[472] Smeaton, Paul, "Bishop Schneider: Bishops who banned sacraments during pandemic behaved as 'fake shepherds,'" *LifeSite News*, May 22, 2020.

1992- Oct. 3, On Saturday Night Live, singer Sinéad O'Connor tears up picture of pope to protest child abuse crisis in the Catholic Church... ten years ahead of the 2002 *Boston Globe* "Spotlight Investigation" series that exposed widespread clergy child abuse.

Virtue Challenge #20 - Hiddenness

Blessed Franz, help us to be silent like Christ was at times. To all of those out there who say, "I'm a nobody. I'm not a politician, a priest, or a poet. I'm not a business person, or any one important. I'm just a normal person, with a very normal boring life. I'm Catholic and nobody cares what I think." Not true. Consider Franz. A "normal, boring farmer" from a small Austrian village. Generations later we admire his virtue and resolve to stand with God and his conscience against the Third Reich. How will you guard against becoming despondent? How will you develop greater resolve? What are you called to do as an army of one? Are you ready? If not, why not?

Can our defiance change the course of things? Perhaps. If not in that moment, perhaps God will use our example to help inspire others for another time. How will you inspire others today?

If you have not seen the movie *A Hidden Life,* rent it and watch with your spouse or family. Due to its content I'd hold off showing it to anyone not yet in high school. (Viewer's tip: Pay particular attention to the cinematography, music, and sounds of nature in the film. Enjoy!)

If going through a tough time where hard choices need to be made, or perhaps you find yourself going against popular opinion, perhaps also pick up a copy of Gordon Zahn's book, *In Solitary Witness: The Witness of Franz Jägerstätter.* May Bl. Franz's story inspire you to serve God.

When are we to defy state directives? What does your moral compass say? When the government compels us to say *yes* to immorality, Blessed Franz help us to follow your example and say, "No."

Are we ever to defy our Church? What if the Church tells us that this or that moral taboo is now OK? Are we obliged to accept modern opinions that contradict the traditional Magisterium? When the world, or even the Church, scorns us for our faith, pray that we remain faithful to Christ alone.

When in the course of discussing immoral choices of others, do you apostatize in small or large ways, choosing to not defend the teachings of the Church and, hence, God? Pray for increased moral courage to better serve God faithfully amidst our dazed and confused culture.

Saint John tells us that where there is love, there is no fear. What issue(s) or person(s) do you need to approach with greater love (and by so doing are not stymied by fear)?

Saint Joseph, help us to be strong in our silence and hiddenness. Pray for us to be attentive to pursuing the quiet happiness of domestic life. Blessed Franz, in hiddenness, help us to be holy.

How can you be a more effective voice for the voiceless among us?

How can you do a better job of being present with others in their hurt by being with them in silence? Whom can you call today and say, "I'm with you"?

Each Catholic alive today has a hero or heroine inside. When the time is right, and led by the grace of God, the hero will come out. Is this your time? If not, why not?

Are you a simple man in Christ, or are you a complex man of the world? Which master do you serve? Blessed Franz, pray for us to be simple men.

Pray for the grace not to express yourself on every subject. Pray to mute your desire to straighten out other's affairs. Pray for the grace to be helpful, but not bossy.

Converse for a moment with the Holy Ghost about hiddenness. My Lord and my God, how may I serve you more faithfully and completely through the virtue of hiddenness?

O Blessed Franz, pray for us an increase in the virtue and grace of holy hiddenness.

CHAPTER 21

Carlo

The Twenty-First Century
Joy

"God mounts his throne to shouts of joy: a blare of trumpets for the Lord."
~ Psalm 47:2

"Looking on Jesus, the author and finisher of faith, who having joy set before him, endured the cross, despising the shame, and now sitteth on the right hand of the throne of God."
~ Hebrews 12:2

"A spiritual joy is the greatest sign of the divine grace dwelling in a soul."
~ Saint Bonaventure

"Be humble, be simple, and bring joy to others."
~ Saint Madeline Sophie Borat

"Serve the Lord with laughter."
~ Saint Padre Pio

The 2000s

Are you part of the "frozen chosen"? When our family lived in McLean, VA, we attended St. John the Beloved parish and school. Fr. Paul Scalia was the pastor, and one Sunday in his homily he asked the "frozen chosen" question. Arrested by the phrase, I leaned in to decipher where he was going with this. Some Catholics get so caught up with putting on a pious Catholic demeanor, he explained, they act in a "very off-putting way... they are dour and smug"- i.e., they lose their joy. Do we have a truly joyful demeanor at all times? As children of God, do we possess childlike joy? Do we embrace joy even in hard times and in suffering? When forgiving others, are we joyful? Are we examples of living joyfully during challenging times with laugher and a

432

smile? The "joyful chosen" or the "frozen chosen," we get to choose each day.

Reminds me of a CatholicConnect "You know you're Catholic when…" Instagram post. When at a downhill ski resort, while on a chair lift and passing a support tower, someone takes his ski pole and clinks the tower, making a sound that is akin to the timbre you'd hear while in church. A Catholic, riding up in the chair directly in back of the 'clinker,' upon hearing the reverberation, breaks into chant, *"In Nomine Patris, et Filii, et Spiritus Sancti."* Catholic joy!

I share this chair lift vignette as a lead in to a comment made by Christine Silveira about this simple, yet merry, scene. She wrote, "The best argument for Christianity is Christians; their joy, their certainty, their completeness. But the strongest argument against Christianity is also Christians—when they are somber and joyless, when they are self-righteous and smug in complacent consecration, when they are narrow and repressive, then Christianity dies a thousand deaths." Bravo. Well said Christine.

The person we highlighted for the 1900s was Bl. Franz Jägerstätter. He lived a Catholic life of principle in hidden service of God. His life and death confirmed for us that sanctity is possible in the modern world. He figured out how to be courageous and joyful amidst the brutality and heartache of war. Where there is a will oriented toward God, there is a way.

In the twenty-first century, two saints were considered: Saint Leonella Sgorbati, who, in 2006, was martyred when she was shot in the back by a Muslim while working in Mogadishu, Somalia; and Carlo Acutis, who spread devotion to Eucharist Miracles via the internet and died when just a teenager. While the battle for souls among Catholics and Islam will continue until the Son of Man comes again, the concluding saint chosen for our tour through the centuries focuses on Christ's presence in the Eucharist, and Carlo's joy for life, as he shared his Eucharistic Miracle apostolate.

Born in London on May 3, 1991, Carlo was baptized at Our Lady of Dolours, Chelsea, on May 18, 1991. When still a baby, his family moved back to Milan. When we look at Carlo's life, what strikes us is that it was so truly and thoroughly Catholic. Catholicism is a "both/and" religion, and Carlo embodied that way of living. The

Church knows that we humans are composed of body and soul, but that the soul has priority. The spiritual life, that life which depends upon God's grace to thrive, is the engine which allows us to carry out the works of mercy, both corporal and spiritual. We must nourish our souls, and to do so we don't need to reinvent the wheel, as we can quickly learn by looking at the fruit produced by Carlo Acutis in his short fifteen years of earthly life. We just have to make use of the tools provided for us by God through his Church.

Saint Carlo Acutis[473]

Carlo lived a "normal" modern life; he just lived it as a saint. He prioritized the right things. Consider his spiritual life. When we say he lived a thoroughly Catholic life, we mean he lived a sacramental life; the sacraments were foundational parts of his very existence. He attended Mass daily, before or after which he would spend time in adoration of the Eucharist in the Tabernacle. He also prayed a daily Rosary and read the scriptures daily. He went to confession weekly and met with a spiritual guide once a month.

All that sounds so normal when we read about it, but we know that it is not normal today. Why not? Carlo was a normal modern teenager in a bustling city, Milan, Italy. Surely, he, like so many of us, could have been "too busy," for all that, but he chose not to be. *Why not me? Why not you?*

---

[473] https://www.catholicworldreport.com/2018/07/06/venerable-carlo-acutis-a-patron-of-computer-programmers/

Instead of asking, "Why not me?" and reaching out to others in Christian joy, we often make excuses for ourselves. We may say things like: "Oh, the saints lived in another time." "Life is too busy." "Living with virtue is too difficult." "The poor are taken care of by the government." But if we examine our lives, what would we see? More importantly, what does God see? How much time do we waste either online or watching TV? There is nothing wrong with either activity, of course, but too often hours, days, weeks, months, and years of one's life can be frittered away and, in the process, we forget why God made us: To know him, love him, and serve him in this life—to be happy with him in the next.

When we stop and remind ourselves of why God made us, it makes the question even more pressing. *Why not me?* What was special about Carlo? Perhaps his secret was that he actually took it seriously; not that we don't (although maybe deep down we actually don't), but perhaps we don't put that seriousness into action by devoting more time to prayer, to Mass, to the Rosary, to reading the Bible, to going to confession, to becoming holy. On confession Carlo said, "Our soul is like a hot air balloon. If by chance there is a mortal sin, the soul falls to the ground. Confession is like the fire underneath the balloon enabling the soul to rise again. . . It is important to go to confession often." Maybe we want to say we are serious about our souls, but are we? God has given us all the tools. Carlo used them. Do we?

Carlo's life embodied Ecclesiastes 11:9-10, "Rejoice therefore, O young man, in thy youth, and let thy heart be in that which is good in the days of thy youth, and walk in the ways of thy heart, and in the sight of thy eyes: and know that for all these God will bring thee into judgment. Remove anger from thy heart, and put away evil from thy flesh. For youth and pleasure are vain."

His sacramental and prayer life fueled his works of mercy, both spiritual and corporal. Carlo prayed for others, but he is best remembered for being the "cyber-apostle of the Eucharist." He devoted time to studying computers, and he was thought by many to be especially gifted in that field, perhaps even a genius. And yet he studied diligently in order to make the most of the talents God gave him. Carlo, though a boy, was like the "faithful and wise steward" in Luke 12:42. Online he created websites designed to interest people in and educate them about the Catholic faith. In that sense, he was a

435

global apostle, from his home. He seems to have asked God, "How can I serve you?" . . . and then acted on the answer.

His apostolate did not end at the seven spiritual works of mercy: (1) Admonish sinners, 2) Instruct the uninformed, 3) Counsel the doubtful, 4) Comfort the sorrowful, 5) Be patient with those in error, 6) Forgive offenses, and 7) Pray for the living and the dead). However, Carlo had a heart for those less fortunate. He took food to the homeless and on at least one occasion actually brought a sleeping bag to a man who lived on the streets near his home. In his personal relationships, he was much loved, perhaps because he loved much. He loved spending time with his friends, but would also reach out to those on the margins, who perhaps did not have many friends. There was a certain joyfulness and generosity of soul in the boy that manifested itself in a genuine interest in everyone he met. Carlo took to heart the words of Saint Philip Neri, "A servant of God ought always to be happy."

Though he was in the right sense attached to his family and friends and his apostolic activities, it is said that his guardian angel was his best friend. Carlo would say, "Continuously ask your Guardian for help. Your Guardian Angel has to become your best friend."[474] How many Catholics today, especially young ones, have the type of lively relationship with their own guardian angel that this Italian teenager had? Carlo lived the Catholic concept of detachment from material things. It is said that he would feel uncomfortable when he was given things that he did not feel he needed. This was a boy of the late twentieth and early twenty-first century? It was.

Carlo used to say to his mother, "I want to be a saint." He liked movies, comic editing and PlayStation video games. The message to young people is unmistakable; they see in Carlo a saint that is close to them. He was ordinary and yet extraordinary. Not different and yet so different. What was different about Carlo?

Carlo, the first millennial to be beatified, was a twenty-first century original. Many are content to go with the flow of cultures that degrade rather than elevate our minds and souls. With all the nonsense and distractions of modern life, Carlo found, and spread the word about what mattered most. Carlo said, "All people are born as originals,

---

[474] "Blessed Carlo Acutis: An Example to be Emulated." *Catholic Journal.* Nov. 12, 2020.

but many live as photocopies." Let us not be photocopies of our secular culture, but go against the grain and be the originals God created us to be.

Saint Carlo Acutis[475]

What was different must be that he seems to have, from an early age, resolved to be holy, and unlike so many of us and our own resolutions, he succeeded. The life of his soul, holiness, happiness, was important to him; it was a priority. "The only thing we have to ask God for, in prayer," said Carlo, "is the desire to be holy." As he grew into his teen years and his friends began dating, girls for Carlo were not a priority. Carlo one day commented, "The Virgin Mary is the only woman in my life." How many parents of teenage boys have heard their sons say that?

And so, Carlo set out not to reinvent the wheel, but to do what Catholics have been doing for two millennia. There really is no secret knowledge, special handshakes or hidden codes. We must want to be saints, and we must not just say it, we must do it. He lived Catholicism. That was Carlo Acutis's plan of life. In fact, Carlo could not have been more clear when he said, "To always be close to Jesus, that is my life plan."

Carlo knew one of the keys to his advancing spiritually was to avoid sadness. As Saint Padre Pio said, "Don't allow any sadness to

---

[475] https://en.wikipedia.org/wiki/Carlo_Acutis

dwell in your soul, for sadness prevents the Holy Spirit from acting freely." Carlo knew this, internalized it, and once commented, "Sadness is looking at ourselves, happiness is looking towards God."

The saints are those who have lived the life of faith and virtue that we are called to live, and so the Church offers them to us as models. Any Catholic who desires to emulate the saints naturally has a favorite or two, or ten, who hold a special attraction. For Carlo, he loved reading about Tarcisius, Anthony of Padua, Francisco and Jacinta Marto, and Bernadette Soubirous. He also had a strong devotion to the Little Poor Man of Assisi, Francis, *Il Povorello*. Assisi would become one of Carlo's favorite places to visit.

We see similarities between Carlo Acutis and Blessed Pier Giorgio Frasatti (1901-1925) from the previous century. Both died relatively quickly after falling ill, and both spoke of their impending deaths like, well, like one would expect saints to speak. Pier Giorgio said, "The day of my death will be the happiest day of my life." Carlo said, "I am happy to die because I have lived my life without wasting a minute on those things that do not please God." And added, "Our goal must be infinite, not the finite. The infinite is our homeland. Heaven has been waiting for us forever." Pier Giorgio would often pass whole nights in Eucharistic adoration. Little wonder he was described by friends as "an explosion of joy." Remember Bl. Pier Giorgio's motto, *verso l'alto* ("to the heights").

Carlo, too, knew the importance of Christ in the Eucharist, as did all the saints who came before him. Three quotes from Carlo:

"I don't need to go to Jerusalem to find Jesus, I find him in the church."

"The more Eucharist we receive, the more we will become like Jesus, so that on earth we will have a foretaste of heaven."

"The Eucharist is the highway to heaven."

Indeed, the Eucharist would be a superhighway of holiness for Carlo whose apostolate had a foundational base of devotion to the Holy Eucharist. It included websites and newsletters, and he orchestrated fundraisers as needed to support his mission. Carlo's book about Eucharistic Miracles is titled, *The Eucharistic Miracles of the World*. Carlo used his passion for computers to evangelize. Here are a few of the website's Carlo created:

Eucharistic miracles:
http://www.miracolieucaristici.org/
Marian apparitions:
http://www.apparizionimadonna.org/it/avm/
Hell, Purgatory, and Heaven:
http://www.carloacutis.net/InfernoPurgatorioParadiso/
Apparitions of angels and demons:
http://www.carloacutis.net/AngeliDemoni/

As Catholics, we know there is joy, and glory, even in suffering. Hard for many to believe, yet alone accept, but true. In bearing the faults of others, joy. In being falsely accused, joy. The list goes on. The enemies of Catholicism are confounded that we muster joy when they deliver confusion, insults, lies, pain and suffering. They do not know that deep inside us we seek to imitate Christ. They do not understand how we do not fear death. They cannot conceive that we, should we be martyred for our faith, after achieving the sweet release of death, will soon stand before God, the angels, and the saints.

The Greek word for joy is *charan*, with root word *charis*, or "grace." When life is joyful and moving along like a gravy train with biscuit wheels, grace is a bit easier to comprehend. When life takes a turn for the worse and presents minor or major trials, do we approach our day with the same joy? Do we consider our crosses as occasions for joy, and grace because God is permitting us to sanctify our souls?

As Catholics, we don't pursue pain, sickness and hardship for their own sake. No, we accept them in that each permits us to pick up our cross and follow Christ pursuing holiness with joy. Michael Voris from Church Militant said, "Do not let the world get you down. Be it the leftist church hierarchy, political parties and their leaders, the Luciferian media, leftist family members or friends, do not let them steal your joy. If there's one thing the secular, radical left hates (besides anyone saying the name "Jesus"!) it's the joy of Christians. Be joyful as you serve the Lord!"[476] Saint Thérèse of Lisieux reminds us, "A word or a smile is often enough to put fresh life in a despondent soul."

We, the everyday people of the church, are blessed to be called to engage in joyful battle to fight for God, the church, and morality in

---

[476] Vortex episode unable to be identified.

society. Austin Ruse of C-FAM, author of *"No Finer Time to Be a Catholic,"* stated in a *LifeSite News* interview, "We must have joy in our heart, and a fighting spirit."[477] Fighting for the church, we know that life is not chaotic; manning our respective battle stations is all part of working God's plan. Cardinal Saint John Henry Newman said, "He has an end for each of us; we are all equal in His sight, and we are placed in our different ranks and stations... As Christ has His work, we too have ours; as He rejoiced to do His work, we must rejoice in ours also."

Whatever negativity society may send our way, Saint Peter Damien encourages us to press on with a joyful, radiant countenance, "Therefore, my brother, scorned as you are by men, lashed as it were by God, do not despair. Do not be depressed. Do not let your weakness make you impatient. Instead, let the serenity of your spirit shine through your face. Let the joy of your mind burst forth. Let words of thanks break from your lips."

Speaking on joy and a fighting spirit, during the 2021 Super Bowl, Michelob beer ran an ad featuring various sports mega-stars. The ad asks, "We're wrong to think that joy only happens at the end; after the sacrifice, after the commitment, and after the win. What if happiness has always been there, fueling the run toward greatness? What if joy is the whole game? Not just the end game? Are you happy because you win, or do you win because you're happy?"[478] While the ad was made for a decidedly secular audience, please reread the ad copy thinking specifically about Catholic joy in this life. As Catholics, we know happiness is fleeting, but holiness is eternal.

Circus promoter PT Barnum once said, "The noblest art is that of making others happy." Not quite. As Catholics, we know that, "The noblest pursuit is that of helping others be holy." Or as Saint Rose of Lima said, "Know that the greatest service that man can offer to God is to help convert souls."

Which reminds me of something similar from a secular perspective I once read from John Lennon of Beatles fame, "When I was five my mother always told me happiness was the key to life. When I went to school, they asked me what I wanted to be when I grew up.

---

[477] Staff, "'We should be fearless': Catholic leader on how Christians can survive 'cancel culture,'" *LifeSite News*, January 14, 2021.
[478] "Michelob ULTRA | "Happy" Super Bowl," YouTube posted January 25, 2021. https://www.youtube.com/watch?v=6nzZW8BN-WY

I wrote down "happy." They told me I didn't understand the assignment. I told them they didn't understand life." Clever, like the Michelob ad, but incomplete.

If we were to substitute "holy" for "happy," we have the Catholic version of the Lennon yarn, "When I was five my mother always told me holiness was the key to life. When I went to school, they asked me what I wanted to be when I grew up. I wrote down "holy." They told me I didn't understand the assignment. I told them they didn't understand life." Ah, much better.

The distinction between happiness and holiness is essential. In our family, to distinguish among the two I bought a small hinged picture frame that holds left and right photos. In the left frame I placed the secular Lennon quote about "happy." In the right frame I placed the virtuous Catholic quote about "holy." I'm not sure how often people look at, or think about, that small attempt at a life lesson sitting on our family room shelf, but no matter how small your attempt to advance the faith, do it. Do what you can do, and leave the rest up to God.

Happiness and holiness are not the same objectives. How many times have you heard of someone struggling with one of life's challenges and the concluding counsel imparted by a fellow Catholic is, "I just want them to be happy." Lame. Consider the following examples:

- When someone is considering divorce, "I just want them to be happy."
- When someone is considering abortion, "I just want them to be happy."
- When someone is struggling with homosexuality, "I just want them to be happy."
- When someone is struggling with gender issues, "I just want them to be happy."
- [Insert almost any moral issue here]… "I just want them to be happy."

You get the point. No, happiness is not the be all end all goal. Holiness is. Revisit the above couple of statements with your Catholic worldview and substitute the word holy at the end of each line. It appreciably changes the dynamic of the advice being offered. Advice focused on happiness can be superficial. For some it is the easy way out to go with what society would tell them to do rather than what a moral person would suggest they do. It's non-confrontational and can be false charity as was previously discussed in Chapter 2 with Polycarp and Candor. At all times, we need to encourage others to make holy choices whatever situation, challenge, or struggle they find themselves in. Morality matters. Virtue matters. Holiness matters. True happiness is dependent upon morality, virtue, and holiness.

How do you find true joy and bring that joy to others? True joy consists of finding God's will in all things. True joy consists in imitating Christ in all things. Forget following the demonic lynch mob of society. Do you go along with the crowd, or do you march to the beat of your own drum? How do you make music in society by expressing your opinion on moral matters? Are you the melody, the beat, or do you avoid confrontation due to fear of offending, being labeled or canceled? Do you go along to get along? Or do you "go Catholic" to help get yourself and others to heaven? How do you impart the gift of true, Catholic joy to others?

While Catholics find joyful merit in suffering, we also find joy in plain-old-simple, joyful and fun situations too. Saint Thomas Aquinas affirmed, "It is requisite for the relaxation of the mind that we make use, from time to time, of playful deeds and jokes."

When I think of the word joy, my mind immediately drums up Christmas. Advent is a time of prayerful, joyful anticipation. My favorite Christmas song? The Little Drummer Boy. As a child, the imagery of a young, poor boy offering newborn baby Jesus the only gift he could, a song played on his drum, appealed to me a great deal. I, of course, realize the song is fictitious, but going with the narrative for a joyful minute, what must Blessed Mother have thought when the little drummer boy showed up? Resting after giving birth, and perhaps soon after she had just gotten baby Jesus to sleep, the holy family was approached by a young man who thought to himself, *What this family needs is a drum solo!* Joy. Love it!

As an adult, the words to the Little Drummer Boy maintain equal appeal to me, but for different reasons. Thinking about what present you could possibly bring Jesus is joyful to ponder. What gifts do we have, as children or adults, that are fit to give the King of Kings? What shall we give the babe in the manger? Is anything less than everything we have acceptable? What about making a big financial contribution to the church, a pro-life group, or a charity that assists the poor? Or what about donating a bit more than we can really afford? Can we play an orchestra-caliber Christmas song? Or does God smile a bit when we try our best, but sing slightly out of tune, to honor Him in Church? In other words, what's our drum? What do we offer to God as our highest and best?

The crescendo line, for me, in the Little Drummer Boy is "... then he smiled at me ... me and my drum." Imagine that—you offering God your very best, and then He smiles at you! Wow! How would that make you feel? What more out of life could we want than that?

As Jesus smiled at the Little Drummer Boy, he most assuredly smiled at Carlo, a young man who found his drum bringing his love of the Blessed Sacrament to the world via the internet. It was his highest and best. Carlo wanted everyone to know Christ in the Blessed Sacrament, the way that he knew Christ as a daily communicant.

Find your drum. Offer your best to the Lord. And one day, may Jesus smile at you, too.

The Venerable Archbishop Fulton J. Sheen, in his 1956 broadcast, "The True Meaning of Christmas," tells us:

"... Suppose any of us who are creatures, who are just men, began to take on a more divine nature, and suddenly began to be children of God, so that the divine nature began to pulsate within us, so that we were lifted up by offering our human nature, as Mary offered the first human nature, so that we could be united with the divine person, so that his truth, with all that great wisdom, would begin to flood our minds, and his will and love would begin to possess us, and would impregnate and suffuse itself over every single love that we have. Oh it that ever came to pass. And it does come to pass. That would be the meaning of Christmas. That's why the Son of God came to this earth- to make us other sons of God. To make us more than just human beings. It's not easy. It's very hard. You say, "oh, I'm a beast, I'm foul, I cannot be lifted up." Remember, that he was laid in a manger and his companions were beasts. That is our hope, our joy, our peace, our Merry Christmas."[479]

Saint Francis of Assisi and Saint Anthony of Padua were strong inspirations for Carlo. Why? Their intense love for the poor. When we make donations to the poor, do we do so out of abundance or when we can feel the pinch? We know the difference, and, of course, so too does God. Let us be more generous with the poor. How we treat our poor neighbors is a key factor in whether we have a highway, a side road, or a walking path, to heaven. The saints knew the spiritual benefits of devotion to the poor. We would be wise to learn from them and imitate them in this regard.

In Carlo we find a young boy who speaks to the world because he fell in love with Jesus. He only lived to be fifteen years, but they were an intense fifteen years. Carlo was first diagnosed with the mumps, but that was soon changed to one of galloping leukemia, which meant a short time to live. Carlo was joyful to the end commenting, "I know that there are others who are suffering much more, much more." And, "I would like to leave this hospital, but I know I will not do so alive."

Carlo Acutis died on October 12, 2006 in the odor of sanctity. His manner of death confirmed for many the sanctity of his life.

Carlo and his life of heroic virtue was declared Venerable on July 5, 2018. He was declared a Blessed a few years thereafter, and Beatified in Assisi on Oct. 10, 2020 in the Basilica of Saint Francis of Assisi. Saint Carlo's body is not incorrupt; however his relics can be visited today in the church of Santa Maria Maggiore in Assisi.

Being a teen Carlo loved the company of his friends. Through the witness of Carlo's life and his love of his Catholic faith, Carlo converted a Muslim friend. Circling back to where we began in Chapter 1 with Martha, we return to the virtue of friendship. More importantly, we once again have the opportunity to ponder our friendship with Jesus. As Jesus told us, "These things I have spoken to you, that in me you may have peace. In the world you shall have distress: but have confidence, I have overcome the world." (John 16:33) We have

---

[479] Sheen, Archbishop Fulton, "The True Meaning of Christmas," Original Airing 1956. YouTube posted June 23, 2014. https://www.youtube.com/watch?v=sOvlFDqOusE

confidence in the joy in friendship, candor, patience, chastity, obedience, humility, modesty, and, of course, charity.

Thus, we conclude our tour of twenty-one saints and twenty-one virtues through twenty-one centuries. What was the greatest Catholic century? Which was your favorite saint? Favorite virtue? Why?

In the end, you start thinking about the beginning. Saint Gregory of Nissa stated, "He who climbs never stops going from beginning to beginning, through beginnings that have no end." The band Semisonic shared a similar sentiment when they sang, "Every new beginning comes from some other beginning's end." How is this ending your beginning? What will you let go of to move forward? A life of virtue well lived, what does this make possible?

To all the saints in heaven metaphorically wearing "Wish You Were Here" T-shirts, thanks for the encouragement. We're trying. If you would, a little more help, please. Much obliged for any additional intercession on our behalf. As you know, some days down here can be pretty rough contending with original sin and the nasty, unrelenting powers and principalities. Saints of heaven, help us to live holy lives, so that one day we may hear from God the Father, like you did, "Enter into the joy of your eternal reward."

In reading *Against the Grain*, what insight into your soul was sparked? Perusing the heroes of past centuries, how did you see yourself in them? If you are motivated to be a better Catholic, the hero is you. If you are ready to do whatever it takes to gain heaven, and bring many others along with you, the hero is you. My dear brothers and sisters in Christ, this book was never really about the saints, the virtues, our faith, or our nation. All along, this book has been about you. You are the hero of your life, of your own salvation. Catholics being good Catholics in the world is the key to making your life, and that of everyone else, a better life. Serving God and others via virtue, you must be the hero.

As Catholic Americans, we the faithful are part of the greatest religion in the history of the world. As Catholic Americans, we the citizens are part of the greatest country in the history of the world. As Catholic Americans, we willingly undertake sharing our faith and our freedom as our greatest responsibility. In our souls, we hold the future;

the destiny of our American Republic, our Catholic Church, and our eternal citizenship.

Saints, Patriots, in joy, let's roll.

Quo vadis? Serviam! Fiat! Deus Vult!
(Where are you going? I will serve! Let it be done! God wills it!)

Twenty-First Century Saints

Saint Leonella Sgorbati (d. 2006)- shot in the back in Mogadishu, Somalia.

Saint Carlo Acutis is the patron saint of (N/A). (Some have suggested that Saint Carlo Acutis be the patron saint of the internet, but Saint Isidore of Seville (636) is already the patron saint of computers and the internet. Who knows if and when the Church will decide?)
Saint Carlo Acutis' feast day is October 12.
Saint Carlo Acutis, *ora pro nobis* (pray for us).

Twenty-First Century History

2002- *Boston Globe* "Spotlight Investigation: Abuse in the Catholic Church" series breaks focusing on the sex abuse scandal in the Archdiocese of Boston, and throughout America.

2003- In Lawrence v. Texas the U.S. Supreme Court rules to constitutionally protect homosexual sodomy.

2006- Hi-speed internet implemented. Online pornography begins vast year-over-year expansion.

2007- July 7. **Summorum Pontificum** allows all priests to celebrate the Tridentine Latin Mass in private and to hold public Masses when requested by the faithful, not needing approval of the local bishop.

2010- March 23. Affordable Care Act (Obamacare). Mandates objectionable coverages for persons of faith (contraception, sterilization, gender reassignment surgery, abortion, etc.) Religious Liberty challenges to persons of faith.

2013- March 13. Pope Francis elected.

2015- June 26. Obergefell v. Hodges. Same-sex marriage legalized in America. Majority opinion written by Justice Anthony Kennedy (Catholic).

2016- Transgenderism gains traction with advocates in the U.S. Homosexual lobby targets persons, businesses of faith legally and financially. Restrictions increase on thought, speech, gender characterization, etc.

2020- Suppression of the Sacraments from the Faithful. Inability to attend Mass in person. Even during the first 300 years of the Catholic Church when Christians were routinely executed for their Faith, people still attended Holy Mass in the catacombs. Even during the French Revolution and the Bolshevik revolutions, the Mass was never closed to the public.

2020- Supreme Court rules that the Blaine Amendments were laws "born of bigotry" and cannot be used to discriminate against religious groups. (Believe it or not, thirty-seven state constitutions around the country contained anti-Catholic provisions into the 1990s.)[480]

2021- July 16. Pope Francis issues his Moto Proprio oxymoronically titled *"Traditionis Custodes,"* "Guardians of Tradition."[481] The document suffocates Benedict's 2007 Latin-Mass Decree, *Summorum Pontificum.*

Virtue Challenge #21- Joy

Are you part of the "frozen chosen" or the "joyful chosen?" If you have been playing more for the frozen chosen team, what will it take

---

480 Becket Group email, "Espinoza v. Montana case marks the end of the Blaine Amendments – an ugly historical legacy of religious bigotry deployed nowadays for all-around religious persecution." No date.
481 https://www.vatican.va/content/francesco/en/motu_proprio/documents/20210716-motu-proprio-traditionis-custodes.html

for you to join team "joyful chosen?" Is it necessary for you to overcome any early formation, or current bad habits, that would enable you to arrive at a place of joy in your countenance and soul?

Carlo said "Not me, but God." His short life was a testament to that short, yet profound, statement. All for God. Do we live lives that say the same? Saint Carlo Acutis, help us to also say "Not me, but God." When we say the Joyful Mysteries of the Rosary, let us pray for increase in a joyful heart and countenance.

Saint Carlo Acutis, help us to make good and holy use of the internet. May it not be wasted time or sinful time for us. Protect us to have modesty and guard our eyes from the filth that is a click or two away. Help us to make holy use of computers in a way that recognizes the dignity of all.

What does the phrase, "You can't take it with you" mean to you?

How can you be less stingy, miserly and selfish with your time, money or the gifts that God has given to you? How can you be less inward in your focus, and instead be generous and outward focused on charity and bringing joy to others?

Do you keep well the joy of the Christmas season? What will you do differently next Christmas to bring more joy to others? What about doing something year round to bring joy to others?

Pray to be joyful and grateful for all that God has given you, not unhappy for what you do not have.

Pray for us to increase in our devotion to Christ in the Eucharist and the practice of making regular Eucharistic Adoration.

What's your Holy Ghost inspired action plan to go joyfully against the grain? Whatever your plan is, execute it heroically.

Converse for a moment with the Holy Ghost about joy. My Lord and my God, how may I serve you more faithfully and completely through the virtue of joy?

O Great Saint Carlo Acutis, pray for us an increase in the virtue and grace of holy joy.

AFTERWORD

Twenty-First Century Heroic Catholicism

I live a block away from where the actor Bill Murray grew up in Wilmette, IL. Murray starred in blockbuster films such as *Caddyshack, Stripes, Ghostbusters, What About Bob?, Groundhog Day*, and many others. My favorite Murray film? *St. Vincent*. Why? Because the 2014 film is an honest, hometown, love-thy-neighbor story. It portrays how anyone, even an uncouth, flawed misanthrope, can have the impact of a saint on another person's life.

St. Vincent Movie Poster

In wanting to learn a bit more about the film, I came across a St. Vincent Q&A session from Oct. 24, 2014 where the director, Theodore Melfi, shares that the genesis of the script is based on true events in his life. Melfi explained, "My oldest brother passed away in 2006 leaving behind an 11-year-old daughter. My wife and I adopted her and moved her from Tennessee to [California]. She attended Notre Dame H.S. in Sherman Oaks, during her sophomore year, she was given a homework assignment- find a Catholic Saint that inspires you, and find someone in your life that mimics the qualities of that saint. She picked Saint William of Rochester, and she picked me."[482]

In the emotive closing scene (spoiler alert), young Oliver makes a presentation at his school nominating Murray's character, Vincent, as his Modern Day Saint. Enjoy the YouTube clip: "Touching final scene from the movie 'St. Vincent,' starring Bill Murray,"[483]

Here is the transcript of Oliver's moving speech about Vincent:

"Saints are human beings we celebrate for the commitment and dedication to other human beings." - Brother Garrity, circa, around March.

For my Modern Day Saint, I chose a man who shares many of the same qualities as Saint William of Rochester. On the surface one might think my saint is the least likely candidate for sainthood. He's not a happy person. He doesn't like people and not many people like him. He's grumpy, angry, not of the world, and I'm sure full of regrets.

He drinks too much, smokes, he gambles, curses, lies and cheats and he spends a lot of time with the lady of the night. That's what you see at first glance. But if you dig deeper you see a man beyond his walls.

Mr. Vincent McKenna was born in 1946 in Sheepshead Bay. The son of first-generation Irish immigrants. Growing up poor on the streets of Brooklyn, Vincent learned all the things that kids shouldn't need to know: fighting, cursing and gambling.

In 1965 as a member of the United States Army's 5th Regiment, Vincent was among the 450 soldiers dropped into the Ia Drang Valley and immediately ambushed by 2,000 enemy troops. He heroically saved the lives of two wounded officers pinned down by enemy fire and carried them to safety. He was awarded the Bronze Star for his bravery.

I imagine the best way to tell you who Mr. Vincent McKenna is, is to tell you what he's done for me. When me and my Mom first moved here, we knew no one and Mr. McKenna took me in when he didn't

[482] "St. Vincent Q&A (2014) - Bill Murray, Melissa McCarthy Comedy HD," YouTube posted October 24, 2014. https://www.youtube.com/watch?v=EA2zq3vVzUU
[483] "Touching final scene from the movie 'St. Vincent,' starring Bill Murray," YouTube posted February 7, 2015. https://www.youtube.com/watch?v=r6pvNP_RRMA

have to and most likely didn't want to. But he did it anyhow, 'cuz that's what saints do.

We visited his wife Sandy of forty years who recently passed away. Vince has done her laundry every week for the past eight years long after she no longer recognized him. 'Cuz saints never give up.

He taught me how to fight, to stand my ground, and BE BRAVE. How to speak up and BE BOLD, because saints fight for themselves and others so that they might be heard.

He taught me how to gamble, horse racing, Keno, the over and under- which is a big reason why I am grounded until I am eighteen. But in that I learned how to take risks and go for broke because in life the odds can be stacked against you. This is Vince's cat Felix who gets gourmet cat food while he eats sardines. 'Cuz saints make sacrifices.

Yes, Mr. Vincent McKenna is flawed- seriously flawed- but just like all the other saints we studied. Because after all saints are human beings, very human beings.

Courage. Sacrifice. Compassion. Humanity. These are the markings of a saint and what makes Mr. Vincent McKenna not so far removed from Saint William of Rochester.

And with that I'd like to present my friend and babysitter, Mr. Vincent McKenna, for Sainthood, and hereby proclaim him Saint Vincent of Sheepshead Bay.[484]

Homework assignment: Find a Catholic saint that inspires you and then find someone in your life that mimics the qualities of that saint. Who would that saint be, and who would you nominate? When is the last time you expressed to that person you hold them in high regard and that you appreciate their presence in your life? Would you be willing to write a letter to that person, along the lines of the above movie transcript, and mail it? How would that person feel reading the letter from you? What's holding you back from writing that letter in the next couple of days? If there are obstacles to writing that letter, how will you overcome them? Do it in the next couple of days, because if you wait much beyond that, we both know it will most likely never be done. Be bold. Write the letter. Mail it.

---

[484] Ibid.

Looking at this from another angle, is there anyone who would nominate you as their Modern Day Saint? If yes, keep doing what you are doing, and then maybe do a little more. If no, what do you need to amend in your life to show up better for other people?

What an interesting exercise to think about people in your life, or yourself, as potential saints. Why else are we here?

How can you give other people the benefit of the doubt more often? Do you have any idea as to the full load of crosses Christ has given others to carry in this life? What would it be like to "walk a mile in their shoes?" What particular crosses, burdens and temptations are they struggling with, and hopefully through, at this time? How can you charitably support them in their efforts to be more holy? How can you step up for them?

God is asking for volunteers. Are you raising your hand and saying, like young Saint Tarcisius, "send me"? *Why not me?*

What steps can you take today to be more saintlike? If you haven't already started, commit to being a saint. Don't wait. Yes, many saints began in earnest when they were older. No matter your age, why not start today? Everyone is capable of being a saint. The excuses we have are just that, excuses. Excuses are nothing more than lies. Is not God, the Communion of Saints, the world, our culture, our nation, your family and your own soul worthy of a more saint-like effort today? Indeed, they all are.

For the record, yes, I have also seen the 1997 movie *The Saint* starring Val Kilmer. It's mildly interesting that Val's character chooses saints names as cover for his espionage work, but otherwise it's just a mildly satisfactory popcorn movie. Meh.

God has called you to be a saint; a real saint, not a fake Hollywood saint only when the cameras are on and others are around. Be a saint 24/7. Fulfill his desire for you. You have no idea what you with God can do. "If we do not risk anything for God," writes Saint Louis De Montfort, "we will never do anything great for Him." Be encouraged. Live as virtuous a life as possible. Saint Anthony of the Desert said, "One should not say that it is impossible to reach a virtuous life; but one should say that it is not easy. Nor do those who have reached it find it easy to maintain." Claim your space in heaven by making the heroic effort of which you know, as a Catholic, you are capable.

If you have any hesitation about where to begin, start exactly from where you are. Whom do you need to forgive? Whom do you need to 'get complete with' in your life? To whom should you write a 'make amends' letter? To whom should you place a 'make amends' phone call? If that person were to pass away and suddenly no longer be with us, would you have regrets about not having reached out to them? Benjamin Franklin once said, "Don't put off until tomorrow what you can do today." It's great advice for us all.

You can be a good person, but if you have not a loving heart, a charitable heart, all is in vain. As it says in I Corinthians 13:1-2, "If I speak with the tongues of men and of angels, but have not love, I am become sounding brass or a clanging cymbal. And if I should have prophecy and should know all mysteries, and all knowledge, and if I should have all faith, so that I could remove mountains, and have not charity, I am nothing."

How are we dedicating a part, or parts, of our day to being more charitable and, hence, being better Catholics? From wherever you are spiritually, start afresh. From this point forward, approach your next tasks with a newfound spirit of service to God, and to others. Increase your level of devotion to God. Ask for God's assistance. Get closer to Jesus. Ask for Blessed Mother's intercession. Have hope. Make small sacrifices throughout the day. Offer up a few more prayers. Desire heaven. Seek to avoid time in purgatory. Pursue plenary indulgences. Help the poor. Ask for additional assistance from your confirmation saint, your guardian angel, and all the saints in heaven. You will never be alone in your pursuit of sainthood. You can do it.

Your path to increased virtue will not be easy. God will send you, however, additional graces to advance in the faith. The devil, conversely, may also be permitted to increase his attacks against you. Be aware of these dynamics, and trust in Jesus, Blessed Mother, the saints, and your guardian angel to guide, preserve and protect you. Move forward in virtue, never backward. Saint Teresa of Avila provides us with further insight, "Do not suppose that after advancing the soul to such a state God abandons it so easily that it is light work for the devil to regain it. When His Majesty sees it leaving Him, He feels the loss so keenly that He gives it in many a way a thousand secret

453

warnings which reveal to it the hidden danger. In conclusion, let us strive to make constant progress: we ought to feel great alarm if we do not find ourselves advancing, for without doubt the evil one must be planning to injure us in some way; it is impossible for a soul that has come to this state not to go still farther, for love is never idle. Therefore it is a very bad sign when one comes to a standstill in virtue."[485]

We all know how noisy the world is. The 24/7/365 war for our attention through TV, radio, marketing, advertising, social media, and just plain noise (I would know. I'm from 'Illinoise'.) Makes it harder to find the quiet and subtle and listen to God. Think about it for a moment; how precisely are we searching for God and seeking His direction? How would your spiritual life change for the better if you took a few minutes each day to sit in silence and listen to God? What would He tell you? Listen for God's voice. He will show you the way.

With God, nothing is impossible. But faith is required. Jesus tells us in Matthew 17:20, "For, amen I say to you, if you have faith as a grain of mustard seed, you shall say to this mountain, remove from hence hither, and it shall remove; and nothing shall be impossible to you." Faith without fear. Don't just be Catholic. Be a Catholic's Catholic.

In the gospel about the infidel centurion who asks Jesus to heal his servant, faith is instrumental to the exchange. He says, "Lord, Kyrie, my servant is paralyzed. I am not worthy for you to enter under my roof. So, say the words and my servant shall be healed." And the Kyrios, having compassion for human mystery, heals. Jesus comments, "As you have believed, so it is done. I have not found faith like this in all of Israel." What a statement.

What if our secular leaders, or more to the point, all our Catholic leaders, had the true faith? One can dream, no? Who will stand up to save the hundreds of thousands, the millions, who otherwise will fall into despair and sin due to a false sense of spirituality? Who will speak truth to power? Which bishop will publicly excommunicate the heretical Catholic politician? Do we believe? Truly believe? Does Jesus find faith in us? In our family? Do we have faith on par with that of the centurion? Have our hearts grown cold, insipid or lukewarm? How do we approach the Kyrios? Do we have faith? The true faith?

---

[485] Saint Teresa of Avila, *Interior Castle*, 99.

Fr. James Altman commented, "With Jesus in our boat (or us staying in his boat- the Catholic Church) we have nothing to fear. When the storm raged on the lake, Jesus wasn't worried, he took a nap. When we see the storm clouds of life all around us, we should not fret, because we are in the boat with Jesus. In Sacred scripture 365 times it says 'Be not afraid.' One for each day of the year. Saint John said, 'Perfect love drives away fear.'"[486]

How much do we truly care about getting to heaven? When Jesus asks you on the day of your particular judgment, "Did you love others as I loved you?" "Did you have faith?" How will you respond?

Scottish novelist Robert Louis Stevenson, author of the *Strange Case of Dr. Jekyll and Mr. Hyde*, wrote, "Sooner or later we all sit down to a banquet of consequences." Standing before God, unobstructed by any façade, who will God judge us to be? Saint or damned? Will God tell us, "Well done good and faithful servant? Enter into your eternal reward." Or, will he say, "Begone wicked and slothful servant. I know ye not. Be cast into everlasting fire."

The purpose of our life on earth is simple. To live a life that merits heaven. Eternal happiness. How? Follow Jesus. Carry your cross. Get to and stay in a state of sanctifying grace. Remain inside the Catholic Church, Noah's ark, the barque of Peter. Be Catholic!

You only have one life. This is not a dress rehearsal. When the music stops, will it be the up or down elevator? Heaven or Hell? As musician Johnny Cash once remarked, "I have learned that there is no fence to sit on between heaven and hell."

The world is binary. You either serve God, or you don't. Hilaire Belloc commented, "There are only two alternatives for society- Christ or chaos." In 1957, Sr. Lucia, "we are either for God or for the devil, there is no other possibility." Saint Thomas Aquinas describes the binary choice as one between the Kingdom of Christ and the Kingdom of Satan. We are either children of the light, or we are children of the darkness. We choose heaven or hell.

---

[486] Fr. James Altman, "Fr. Altman Shares the Path Forward After 2020." *Alpha News*. You Tube posted January 14, 2021. https://www.youtube.com/watch?v=MSmnqYcrO0A&t=2120s

And then at some future point on the day of the general judgment we, as members of the Communion of Saints, will see how our lives impacted everyone else, and how their lives impacted us. Nothing unnoticed. Nothing unimportant. Will we have made an overall positive or negative contribution? Cutting through all the excuses, did you give or did you take? Were you generous or selfish with your time, talents and treasure? With Jesus as your example, how will you have done?

Will you one day be a saint?

Work while it is still day. Fight while you still have breath in your lungs. Today is the day the Lord has made; rejoice, and be glad. Nothing you do in a spirit of service to God is done in vain. All your good works are noted by God.

Please, plead on behalf of the souls of purgatory. From the Offertory in the Holy Sacrifice of the Mass on 11/27/20 we read, "O Lord, Jesus Christ, King of Glory, deliver the souls of all the faithful departed from the pains of hell and the deep pit; deliver them from the lion's mouth, that hell engulf them not." "He who offers a prayer for the souls of purgatory," writes Saint Louis Guanella, "obtains a treasure for his own soul."

Now that we are more aware of some of the Catholics who have come before us, and especially more aware of those who have suffered for the faith and carried their crosses, it is hoped that we will all choose to be better Catholics. Better citizens. Better family members. Not just marginally better, but *much* better. As in the, "Be a saint today as there may be no tomorrow" kind of saint.

The more we nurture an understanding of our faith, the more we will pay attention to it. As Catholics we know the four last things are death, judgment, heaven and hell. Now that you know, or have been reminded, to what will you pay more attention? Things that matter? Or things that do not matter?

We need to ready our souls for what is on the horizon. If you have been paying attention in the least, you see that additional storm clouds are gathering. American Catholics could be the last bulwark against the dam getting ready to burst through and unleash a torrent of hellish Modernist, progressive, socialist, Marxist, globalist, secular, naturalistic, masonic pain on the USA and the world.

We must go into battle serving God. The warnings from the popes against Modernism started almost two centuries ago. In the 1999 TAN book, *The Popes Against Modern Errors,* Anthony Mioni, Jr., editor, presents 16 Papal Documents from Pope Gregory XVI (1832) - Pope Pius XII (1950). Each pope saw it coming from a different perspective; yet they all concluded that Modernism was a formidable foe, and each sounded the alarms as best they could.

Saint Pius X, over a hundred years ago, was perhaps the most vocal pope calling out the Modernists for who they were, and what their false conscience and false doctrine represented. Upon ordination, he required all priests to take the "Oath Against Modernism." It's a short oath. If interested, look it up and have a read. The oath stayed in effect through Vatican II, then jettisoned when the Modernists had sufficient numbers to do so.

In what the world is now facing, how seriously have we considered the link between modernism and socialism/communism/atheism/humanism? Specifically, in *Pascendi Dominici Gregis,* written by Pius X in 1907, he states in the two closing sentences of Section 39, "Modernism, Synthesis of All Heresies," that, "These reasons suffice to show superabundantly by how many roads Modernism leads to atheism and to the annihilation of all religion. The error of Protestantism made the first step on this path; that of Modernism makes the second; atheism makes the next."[487] Prescient.

The Catholic Church has been attacked from the inside for almost two centuries now by Modernism. For the past one hundred years or so, from the outside, by communism (economic, social and sexual). A formidable 1-2 punch. From the outset, the Catholic Church did a fair job of speaking against the communists. It dropped the ball, however, keeping the Modernists at bay. The tide significantly turned with the election of John XXIII when the majority of Cardinals voted Modernist. Since then, we've lived through/witnessed sixty years of Modernist impact on the church. Judge a tree by its fruit, modernism by all objective measures is a corrosive, metastasizing cancer. To conclude otherwise one would have to be ignorant and or dead in sin.

---

[487] Pius X, *Pascendi Dominici Gregis,* Section 39, "Modernism, Synthesis of All Heresies," 1907.

Why is modernism so bad? Simply put, it is the bastardization of the faith that has the ultimate goal of neutering, then destroying, the faith. Modernism is all about a brotherhood without the fatherhood of God. Modernist prelates and advocates, truth be told, have a visceral hatred for anything sacred. To the unsuspecting, Modernism is no big deal. Modernism and its toxic heresy, however, is akin to rat poison. Little known fact: Rat poison itself is 99 percent nutritious. It is the highly toxic one percent strychnine that does in the rat. So it is with modernism. A portion of what Modernists present is acceptable. Most Catholics, though, are unable to distinguish the good from the small amount of Modernist poison slipped in. In time one's soul is denied otherwise available graces and slowly atrophies. Despite the toxicity some are able to hang on while others fall away from the faith altogether. Modernism is nasty stuff.

Saint Fidelis of Sigmaringen, preaching in counter-reformation Germany, said of heresy, "I came to extirpate heresy, not to embrace it." With Modernism, the synthesis of all heresies, we must indeed extirpate it and never embrace it.

The rat poison analogy is one way to explain Modernism. Another analogy I like is if there are one hundred M&M'S in a bowl, and two or three are revealed to you to be poison, are you willing to grab a handful and eat them? You'd take a pass altogether, right? Yeah, me too.

A third analogy about Modernism is to compare it to pornography. When looking at art and if there is a sculpture or painting of someone in an otherwise benign state of undress, most Catholics are able to maintain custody of their eyes and it is not a sinful situation. Much art in this category would not be considered pornography, but nonetheless we avoid taking a second look and do not consent to impure thoughts. So how do you know if something is pornography or not? Well, there the adage of, "You know it when you see it." As faithful Catholics, therefore, we know it's best not to even get anywhere near pornography as it is highly corrosive to grace. The same can be said of Modernism. Most faithful souls in the state of grace "know Modernism when you see it." Best to stay far away, or avoid is altogether.

What to do facing the specter of Modernism at work in our church? Writing about the crisis in the Church today, Eric Sammons wrote there are three different ways to respond:

✗ Abandon the Church.

✗ Bury your head in the sand.

✅ Become a Saint.[488]

As the Venerable Fulton Sheen has said, "the greatest freedom in the world is the freedom to become a saint." (source unknown)

We are going through a crucible of history. Don't be frustrated, be determined. How you respond from this day forward will have eternal consequences...for you and those around you. You may be on the verge of giving up. Never give up. Don't ever give up. You can change history. With God's strength and help, your descendants will call you blessed.

In recent decades we have been forced to contend with a third key adversary, Islam. Communism killed how many in the last century? One to two hundred million? Muslim critical population mass in multiple regions, states and nations will be achieved in the next generation or two. And then? Who knows? As Islam conquers by the sword, we must pray that losses will be nothing like the loss of life suffered under the communists.

A nasty combo are the Islamic principles of *Sharia* and *Taqiya*. *Sharia* law is Muslim law superseding civil law. *Taqiya* means that Muslims are encouraged, under Sharia law, to lie to advance Islam. Lenin's speeches in the late 1910s and early 1920s advanced denials to the unsuspecting citizenry (i.e., dupes) to help advance the communist conspiracy. There are interesting parallels to the 'justified' denials of *taqiya* advancing Islam. Lies to advance an agenda. The Father of Lies would approve.

Putting the pieces together concerning the various malevolent forces at work against the Catholic Church should be of great interest to all. The Catholic Church is truly the last citadel standing in the way of greater spiritual, social/cultural and economic anarchy.

---

[488] @EricSammons, Twitter, October 12, 2020.

Unfortunately, the church is showing great strains under the pressure. More prayers and more fasting (and less feasting) are needed.

As was mentioned in Chapter 15, Pope Leo XIII's Oct. 13, 1884 vision and him composing the Prayer to Saint Michael is another piece to the puzzle. Chilling. The timing is crazy too. Seventy-five years puts it at 1959. Blessed Mother's message from Fatima also weighs heavily in this. She warned us and told us what to do. Per Sister Lucia, Blessed Mother wanted the Third Secret revealed by 1960 at the latest. What are the implications for Modernism and communism and the smoke of Satan infiltrating the spirit of Vatican II? Heaven help us. We're waist deep in it now.

Modernism, communism and Islamism. The adversarial, ideological trident against which traditional Catholicism now fights.

One such force for good in Catholicism that continues to be ascendant is Traditionalism. Catholics who prefer the efficacy of the Tridentine Rite have been standing in the gap since the 1970s. While the wake of the post Vatican II reforms were implemented, the modernist majority in the church sought to cancel its traditional moorings (liturgical, doctrinal, historical and formative). We who recognize the rupture of Catholic tradition these past two generations, who stand today for Traditional Catholicism, who fight for Our Lord and his Blessed Mother, it is indeed an humble privilege to be alive in this time to do all we can to restore honor, fidelity and the heroism characteristic of the Catholic faithful found throughout the centuries. Try as they may, the Modernists in the Church will never be able to cancel the Traditionalists. May all who participate in this effort receive an increase of religious integrity in our church and religious liberty in our nation. Let us take up our Rosaries and defend Holy Mother Church. *Deus vult! ("God wills it!")*

The Catholic Church has been in de facto schism for decades. Most adhere to the tenets of Modernism and the Novus Ordo eucharistic celebration. Some adhere to Traditionalism and the Tridentine Rite. Many Modernists follow the world and their own consciences. For all intents and purposes, a significant number of them are cultural Catholics, or CINOs (Catholics In Name Only.) Conversely, the Traditionalists follow scripture and the Magisterium. As Saint Peter Canisius counseled: "Better that only a few Catholics should be left, staunch and sincere in their religion, than that they should, remaining many, desire as it were to be in collusion with the Church's enemies and in conformity with the open foes of our faith."

When Jesus gave the Apostles the Great Commission, he said "Go and make disciples of all nations." The disciples understanding that to be a big ask, responded by asking how are we to act as sheep among wolves? Jesus said, "Be as cunning as the serpent and as peaceful as the dove." In other words, Jesus expects his followers to be prudent and wise when engaging. (I've heard it said, jokingly, that in today's culture, Catholics, "Need to be as cunning as serpents and as peaceful as serpents.")

We have to decide to care and fight back in this war of confusion and apathy. As my dad says, "You gotta wanna." The Venerable Fulton Sheen adds, "Strong passions are the precious raw material of sanctity."[489] How will you amend your weak tendencies and turn towards God asking, begging, for His redirection? Saint Alphonsus Liguori cheers us on, "Let us make up for lost time. Let us give to God the time that remains to us." What do you care about? How will you push back against the noise of distraction and temptation? How will you remain steadfast and diligent? Will you commit to daily doing differently to be more holy and a better Catholic?

As Catholics, throughout our history, as our Lord who was crucified for our sins, many saints heroically gave their lives are martyrs. From the first martyr, Saint Steven (36 AD), Catholics on down through the centuries have been martyred in horrifying ways for the faith: crucified upside down (Saint Peter, 64), thrown to the lions in the Coliseum (Saint Ignatius of Antioch, 68), stoned to death (Saint Timothy, 97 and Saint Telemachus, 404), burned at the stake (Saint Polycarp, 155 and Saint Joan of Arc, 1431), grilled (Saint Lawrence, 258), boiled in oil (Juliana of Nicomedia, 270), shot by arrows and clubbed to death (Saint Sebastien, 288), beheaded (Saint Valentine, 270, and Saint Agnes, 304), torn with wool combs then beheaded (Saint Blaise, 316), hanged, drawn and quartered (Saint Edward Campion, 1581), crushed to death (Saint Margaret Clitherow, 1586), scimitar blow to split his head in two (Bl. Dennis of the nativity, 1638), guillotined (Sisters of Compiègne, 1794, and Bl. Franz Jägerstätter, 1943), executed by firing squad (Bl. Miguel Pro, 1927), concentration

---

[489] Sheen, Fulton. *Peace of Soul*. 185.

camp execution (Saint Maximillian Kolbe, 1941, and Saint Benedicta of the Cross/Edith Stein, 1942), and shot by Islamic extremists (Saint Leonella Sgorbati, 2006).

And that is just a partial list of the many ugly, horrific ways that Catholics have died for the faith through the centuries. The glorious mystery to it all is that wherever Catholics have been put to death for their faith, the church was made stronger. On being stronger, Bl. Solanus Casey said, "Do not pray for easy lives. Pray to be stronger. Do not pray for tasks equal to your powers. Pray for powers equal to your tasks." Catholicism truly is, as Tertullian said, "built from the blood of martyrs." *Deo Gratias* ("Thanks be to God.")

Whatever is to come, Catholics will assuredly remain high on the list of persons to be disrespected, mocked, marginalized, persecuted, tortured and even put to death. Catholics must continue to go against the grain, be signs of contradiction, be counter-cultural, and be true to Jesus Christ and his bride the Catholic Church. We will not dismiss the reality of our past, the challenges of our present, or the potential persecutions in the future. We are ready. We are Catholic.

Anti-Catholicism is taught throughout most other religions. Disdain for vigorous religious convictions, especially the Catholic kind, is a virus that's going around. U.S. Archbishop Thomas Wenski from Miami, the USCCB religious liberty chair as of 2020, has warned of a "soft despotism of religious intolerance in the U.S." and that "new Jacobins are driving Catholics from the public square for their beliefs. We're not second-class citizens because we are people of faith."[490]

Two Twitter posts about anti-Catholicism: @JerryDunleavy wrote, "People like Catholics just fine so long as we don't believe in any of that icky Catholicism."[491] @marykinva tweeted, "it's okay to be #Catholic as long as you're a Cafeteria Catholic and your tray is empty."[492]

What does the near-term future look like for the direction inside the church and the faith overall? Most likely, more Modernism. In his article "Preparing Now for the What the Future May Hold," the skillful

---

[490] Hadro, Matt, "'Soft despotism' of anti-Catholicism on the rise." *Catholic News Agency,* July 1, 2020.
[491] @JerryDunleavy, Twitter post September 23, 2020.
[492] @marykinva Twitter post September 23, 2020.

Peter Kwasniewski states that we are most likely looking at a Francis II, Francis III and Francis IV. He goes on to say, "They will continue to foster violations of the Ten Commandments, the rejection of established dogmas, and the sacredness of the liturgy, using the tools of ambiguity, winks and nudges, speeches and documents of minimal authority, committees and conferences, and lower-level appointees who will do the heavy lifting. They will attempt to abolish the traditional Latin Mass, eradicate religious communities that use it, suspend priests who continue to say it, and close hitherto flourishing churches and chapels."[493]

It may not all be fun, but what a great time to be alive. We look to the past for inspiration from previous Catholic heroes, our saints. By doing so we are better able to understand that to be holy is to do the will of God in the present moment. It is up to each of us to conform our wills to doing what must be done in this present moment to serve God. The future will be what it will be. We don't know what challenges to our faith and families that God will permit, but we have today to heroically focus on this moment, this one moment, to do the holy will of God. Find holiness in not just the herculean challenges and big tasks of life that you currently have or that may come; find holiness in the smaller responsibilities and quiet thoughts of each day.

Saint Gabriel Possenti reminds us that, "Our perfection does not consist of doing extraordinary things, but to do the ordinary well." Go. Take on the day. Merit your halo today and all your days.

In a mad world that seems to be changing at a pace we may be unfamiliar, and perhaps uncomfortable with, what is our best response? To know that we have God. To be grateful to be able to serve His holy will and be as resilient as He needs us to be. Saint Theresa of Avila encourages us, "Whoever has God lacks nothing, God alone is enough." Things in the world will most likely not turn out the way we expect. Relying on the grace of God and focusing on living lives of virtue, heroic virtue when need be, is our path. To be Catholic is to live this path. It always has been and always will be.

Heart of Jesus, abyss of all virtues, have mercy on us. Marshal diligence, fortitude, and perseverance for our faith when things don't

---

[493] Kwasniewski, Peter, "Preparing Now For What the Future May Hold," *One Peter Five*, January 27, 2021.

turn out the way we planned. Especially then. If our best case scenario doesn't come to fruition—*fine*. Come what may, we pray to be ready. Sailors know that fixing to a point on the horizon is a good way to survive a storm. If we doubt our course at all, go to Saint Joseph, the patron saint against doubt, the dying and a happy and holy death. If Blessed Mother and Jesus relied on him for direction and protection, so too can we. As Catholics, we know that serving God, heroically if need be, is how we will survive any storm that presents. That's the best path forward.

We are blessed, and what a gift it is, to be alive at this time. What a great opportunity to choose to be saints and saint makers. It is said that the final battle will bring about the greatest saints the world has ever seen. Knowing a bit more about the amazing saints of the past, our church history, and about the heroic virtue that lies inside us, gives us inextinguishable hope for our future. The darker the night, the brighter the light from the candle of our faith. Do not hide your light under a bushel basket. Display it for all to see from near and far. Let the confusion, chaos, and division dissipate when you bring your Catholic worldview to the fore. Stand firm with your faith, logic, and morals. Stand up and say "I am Catholic. Your ways are not the way of the Lord. Repent. Go. And sin no more."

Know that God does not ask us to do the impossible. We may be busier than a one-armed wallpaper hanger, but He will help us when the task is too great. He sends sufficient grace to avoid all temptations and weather all storms. Not some, but all. Many saints said they would rather die than commit a sin. Can we say the same? Will we defend our soul at any price? Your faith has prepared you for this moment. Are you ready to fight as a child of the light? Are you ready to deploy the invincible weapons of your faith? Are you ready to be God's battle axe and a weapon of holy war? Are you ready for the crusade of our time? Archbishop Viganò astutely sums up our current situation:

> "This is a war without quarter, in which *Satan has been unchained* and *the gates of hell* are trying in every way to prevail over the Church herself. Such a contradiction must be faced above all with prayer, with the invincible weapon of the Holy Rosary.

"Biden reveals himself as a marionette maneuvered by the elites, a puppet in the hands of people thirsting for power and ready to do anything to expand it.

"We would find ourselves facing an Orwellian dictatorship desired by both the "Deep State" and "Deep Church," in which the rights that today are considered fundamental and inalienable would be trampled with the complicity of mainstream media.

"They are opposing the Mystical Body of Christ, which is mankind's only ark of salvation, with the mystical body of the Antichrist. [everything outside the barque of Peter is in peril of no salvation.]

"Ecumenism, Malthusian environmentalism, pan-sexualism, and immigrationism are the new dogmas of this universal religion, whose ministers are preparing the advent of the Antichrist prior to the final persecution and the definitive victory of Our Lord."[494]

Those advancing the Agenda, the children or darkness, have dumbed down the people of God to such a degree that the victims have become complicit—a sort of Catholics' Stockholm syndrome. Most Catholic laity in the Novus Ordo church are now suffering from a kind of battered wife syndrome: A belief that things are really fine, except for the frequent liturgical abuse, ever-increasing heresy, and general disrespect and rebellion shown to God.

Returning once again to the perspective of Archbishop Viganò, "… I am referring to all the times when Satan has been unleashed against the Church of Christ, from the persecutions of the first Christians to the war of Khosrow of Persia against Byzantium, from the iconoclastic fury of the Mohammedans to the Sack of Rome at the hands of the German *Landsknechte*, and later the French Revolution, the anticlericalism of the 19th century, atheistic communism, the *Cristeros* in Mexico and the Spanish Civil War, up to the heinous crimes of the communist partisans during and after the Second World War and the forms of *christianophobia* that we see today all over the world. Each time, invariably, the Revolution – in all of its various forms – confirms its own Luciferian essence, allowing the Biblical enmity between the offspring of the Serpent and the offspring of the Woman

---

[494] Viganò, Archbishop Carlo Maria, Open Letter, October 1, 2020.

to emerge, between the children of Satan and the children of the Most Holy Virgin. There is no other explanation for this ferocity against the Blessed Mother and her children."[495]

We must stay close to Blessed Mother as her children via the Rosary. What a great time to be alive. A time to consciously and purposely go against the grain. To say "no" to the crowd. To say "no" to the great reset. (Jesus was our great reset; we're not in need of any other, thank you Klaus Barbie, er, Schwab.) To say "no" to the world. Fortunately for us, as Catholics, we can say "yes" to Christ, his message, and his church. To say "yes" to Christ is to say "yes" to true freedom and liberty. When we fully say "yes" to Christ, we say "yes" to eternal salvation.

Japanese Catholics went underground for two hundred years; English Catholics, during the penal times, went underground for almost three hundred years. More recently in Mexico in the 1920s and 1930s, when Catholic worship was outlawed and Christian speech restricted, the church was driven underground. Leaders, however, did rise up. Catholic Vote.org posted a video about this saying, "One of those leaders of the *Christeros* resistance was Blessed Miguel Pro. Executed by firing squad he declined the blindfold, raised his arms in imitation of Christ on the cross, held a Rosary in one hand and a crucifix in the other, and before he was executed shouted, *Viva Christo Rey!* (Long live Christ the King!) Martyred for the faith, may Miguel Pro's willingness to stand against a government that suppressed religious worship be an example for us all."[496]

Who are we to think that the Good Lord does not wish for us to go underground for some time too? Or perhaps our turncoat, traitorous, marionette Catholic leadership, among others, in America will permit further white (unbloody) martyrdom in the public square. Perhaps the martyrdom will turn bloody. We don't know. When you are thrown in the fire, figuratively or literally, how will you respond? Remember Saint Joan of Arc, "I fear nothing, for God is with me." Luke 12:4-5 tells us, "I tell you, my friends, do not fear those who kill the body, and after that can do nothing more. But I will warn you

---

[495] Hickson, Maike, "Abp. Viganò: We're witnessing 'general rehearsal for the establishment of the kingdom of the Antichrist,'" *LifeSite News*, December 23, 2020.
[496] "Blessed Miguel Pro: How to Rescue Religious Freedom," *Catholic Vote,* YouTube posted November 20, 2020.
https://www.youtube.com/watch?v=xKgMU7aPUOk

whom to fear: fear him who, after he has killed, has authority to cast into hell. Yes, I tell you, fear him!"

Saint Jerome tells us, "You are deceived if you think that a Christian can live without persecution. He suffers the greatest persecution of all who lives under none. A storm puts a man on guard and obliges him to exert his utmost efforts to avoid shipwreck." Focus your point solely on God to survive the storm. Make no mistake about it that Christians in general, and Catholics in particular, will be considered enemies of the state. Serve the state and man, or serve God? We will soon have no choice but to stand with God, consequences be what they will. "Be on your guard; stand firm in the faith; be men of courage; be strong." (1 Corinthians 16:13) Just as the early Christians opposed the Roman gods, so too will Catholics soon oppose the state and their ever-increasing implementation of diabolical policies. Rogue Catholics may be ascendant, but so are true Catholics. Where the peril is greatest, the closest one to us is God. "And if you be unwilling to serve the Lord, choose this day whom you will serve...but as for me and my house, we will serve the Lord." (Joshua 24:15)

The scriptures say that, "You will take the seal of God or the mark of the beast." Which will you choose? We don't know when that time will be, but it may be prudent to prepare. The trends and recent developments do not look promising. If and when it does happen, you will have to make difficult decisions. One of the key decisions will be to apostatize or not. Pray for the Holy Ghost to guide you. Whatever the short-term pain, remember life is short, eternity isn't. Saint Francis of Paola counsels us, "I earnestly admonish you, therefore, my brothers, to look after your spiritual well-being with judicious concern. Death is certain; life is short and vanishes like smoke." Take heart, however, as I Corinthians 10:12-13 tells us, "God is faithful and will not let you be tried beyond your strength; but with the trial he will also provide a way out, so that you may be able to bear it."

You woke up this morning for one reason. What is it? At this point in the book, if you've read this far, made it to this page, most likely you know what your reason is. And, yes, you are ready. You are ready to align yourself, your life, your reason for being, more fully in alignment with serving God. You are ready for what's next. For today's, and tomorrow's, challenges to living more fully as a Catholic.

And not as an average or nominal Catholic. And not just as a good Catholic. You know that you were called to be, in all humility, a great Catholic. A heroic Catholic. A saintly Catholic. And then at some point the adjectives dissipate. There is no heroic Catholicism, or living as a saintly Catholic. There is only Catholic.

Living as a Catholic, and all it implies, calling us toward the light, the way, and the truth. Living for only one reason. To align with who God has created you. To say yes to serving God and being a Catholic of conviction. In 2012, Peoria Bishop Daniel Jenky said, "We can no longer be Catholics by accident, but instead be Catholics by conviction. In our own families, in our parishes, where we live, study and work… we must be bold witnesses to the Lordship of Jesus Christ. We must be a fearless army of Catholics, ready to give everything we have for the lord, who gave everything for our salvation." To loving Him, your neighbor as yourself, and one another as Jesus loved us. To being a hero and a saint. To being Catholic.

While Catholicism draws on its tradition and saints, it is not a religion of yesterday. Catholicism has always been about today and tomorrow. *Quo vadis?* Where are you going? This is a moment for you to decide. Will you leave your comfort and embrace the uncomfortable? Will you imitate Jesus and be a *signum cui contradicetur*, a sign of contradiction, in the world? Or will you sell out to the world, to Baphomet and *"Solve et Coagula."* (Dissolve and coagulate.) Will you be among the children of the light, or the children of the darkness? Will you serve Christ or will you not? *Serviam* or *Non Serviam?* We can live like saints and suffer, at times, in imitation of Christ, or we will not. How we proceed from this point forward is up to each of us. How will you live a life of heroic virtue? How will you go against the grain?

Fellow Catholics, keep in mind that we are never alone in our quest to serve God. Through the Communion of Saints we have more allies praying for us, rooting for us, that you could ever possibly imagine. Saint Michael the Archangel, Saint Joan of Arc, and all the angels and saints, are on our side. The martyrs of the Coliseum, the English martyrs, the Japanese martyrs, the Vendéens, and the *Christeros* are on our side. Pray for your soul, for the souls of your family and friends, the soul of our nation, and the souls of the nations of the earth. Repent. Be holy.

Everything of value comes with a price. Passion costs. What price would you be willing to pay for your God, your church, your family, and your country? As Christ told the disciples (and us), "When you have done all that has been commanded say, 'We are unworthy servants, we have only done what was our duty.'" (Luke 17:10) Whether it be the jackboots of tyranny, the dogs of war, or the hounds of hell, we will resist and stand with Christ and His Church.

Patrick McGuigan, in *Ninth Justice: The Fight for Bork* wrote, "That for which we exist, is upon us." Embrace this fight. If it is not knocking on your door yet. It soon will. Do not fear the fight ahead. Christ had his fight. The Catholic Church has had its share of fights, and continues to do so. Every century has had its fight. Every generation has had its fight. Every person has their own unique and individual fight. Each and every fight is permitted by God in His infinite wisdom. Whether big or small, embrace your fight. The foil of suffering leads us to true, authentic happiness. Be humble and grateful to God for your particular struggle and simply say, *"Deo Gratias."* (Thanks be to God.)

Pope Leo XIII once pronounced, "Catholics were born for combat." We are in a war that must be won. To all who oppose Christ and our sacred duty, the traditional Catholic Church and all it teaches, and the United States of America, with its traditional American values, please consider the following slogans the courageous faithful may draw upon as appropriate for inspiration:

- As Leonidas said to Xerxes at the Battle of Thermopolye, *"Molon Labe"* (Come and Take Them)
- As they said during the first Crusade, *"Deus Vult!"* (God wills it!)
- As the Almogavars would shout, *"Desperta Ferro!"* (Awaken Iron!)
- As Patrick Henry said, "Give me liberty, or give me death."
- As Nathaniel Hale said, "I regret that I have but one life to offer for my country."
- As they said in the Revolutionary War: "Appeal to Heaven" and "Don't Tread on Me."
- As they said in the Christero War: *"Viva Christo Rey"* (Long live Christ the King)
- As they say in Vermont, "Live free or die."

- As rocker Pat Benatar sang, "Hit me with your best shot..." (... Fire away!)
- And finally, as G. K. Chesterton said, "I believe in getting into hot water; it keeps you clean."

In other words, if something is worth fighting for, FIGHT! Our church's tradition, our nation's tradition, is to fight for what is right. Guard the Faith from assault. The Catholic version of Nathan Hale's pronouncement would be, "I regret that I have but one life to lose for my God and His church."

"Let us be filled with confidence," Saint John Chrysostom spurs us on, "and let us discard everything so as to be able to meet this onslaught. Christ has equipped us with weapons more splendid than gold, more resistant than steel, weapons more fiery than any flame and lighter than the slightest breeze ... These are weapons of a totally new kind, for they have been forged for a previously unheard-of type of combat. I, who am a mere man, find myself called upon to deal blows to demons; I, who am clothed in flesh, find myself at war with incorporeal powers."

As Romans 8:31 says, *"si Deus pro nobis, qui contra nos?"* (If God be for us, who is against us?) 2 Timothy 1:7 tells us, "For God did not give us a spirit of cowardice but rather of power and love and self-control. So do not be ashamed of your testimony to our Lord, nor of me, a prisoner for his sake; but bear your share of hardship for the gospel with the strength that comes from God." How will you defend the true faith under attack by its enemies? We must summon our common DNA of Catholic tradition, our cultural heritage spanning many centuries, to better serve our faith, family and flag.

Thomas Paine wrote on 19 December, 1776, in "The American Crisis, No. I" a timeless piece that applies to today's world as much as it applied during the Revolutionary War:

THESE are the times that try men's souls. The summer soldier and the sunshine patriot will, in this crisis, shrink from the service of their country; but he that stands it now, deserves the love and thanks of man and woman. Tyranny, like hell, is not easily conquered; yet we have this consolation with us, that the harder the conflict, the more glorious the triumph. What we obtain too cheap, we esteem too lightly: it is dearness only that gives everything its value. Heaven knows how to put a proper price upon its goods; and it would be strange indeed if so celestial an article as FREEDOM should not be highly rated.

Our souls will indeed be tried with greater frequency and consequence in coming days and years. Let us not be summer Catholic soldiers and sunshine patriots, but this day petition God for additional graces to be year-round Catholic soldiers and all-weather patriots for our church and our country. Remember, the harder the conflict, the more glorious the triumph. Let us put our free will and our freedom to the best possible use in the service of our God, church and country. Be not afraid fellow Catholics and citizens.

Hailing from Illinois, due largely to its poor leadership and horrible fiscal management, the pride in our state is comparatively low. Growing up near Chicago, the pride of the big city is a bit higher. Traveling the world, when I would tell someone I was from Chicago they would often say "Ah, Chicago- bang, bang! Michael Jordan!" Right, Al Capone and the Chicago Bulls.

What would it be like to be from Texas? There they say "Texas forever." That resonates. In 1835 at the Battle of Gonzales during the Texas war for independence, they said, "Come and Take it." (First used in 480 BC by King Leonidas as a defiant answer to the Persian Army.) Another recent state tag line was, "Don't Mess with Texas." Texas, they got it going on with their slogans.

What about Catholicism? I'm sure the church has numerous slogans that resonate. What about "Catholic forever"? What does that even mean? It means everything. It means if a life is lived well, eternal life. Stand firm. Hold your position. Be Catholic. Be a Saint.

When commenting about the bishops in the U.S. pushing back on secular leaders and the Wuhan (aka, ChiComm-19) Virus church closures, Matthew Archbold wrote, "Catholicism must be heroic, brave, and countercultural. Or it is nothing."[497] He continued:

"But I plead with all of them right now. Catholics need a hero. The faithful are calling out to the clergy for one perhaps ridiculous and fruitless effort to show how important the eucharist truly is. The American Church is desperate for some action.

---

[497] Archbold, Matthew, "No Abp. Cordileone, These People Wish Catholics III," *Creative Minority Report,* November 24, 2020.

Archbold goes on, "There's a time for lawyers and press conferences and petitions. This is not that time. Now is the time Catholics must be willing to draw a line in the sand and say *here*, and no further. Open the churches. Don't allow them to be closed. Let's be willing to go to jail. Let's be fools for Christ. Take a stand. Imagine the impact of seeing a priest put in jail for celebrating Mass. Yes, the media would ridicule that priest. Perhaps many in the Church would as well. But it would inspire millions to understand that ours is not a passive faith. We are different because we believe. Think of all the young men who might see that and be inspired."

Archbold concludes, "Force the secularists to put a priest, bishop, or cardinal in jail or rescind their anti-Catholic mandates. Force them to unmask themselves. Show the world who they really are. And let's show the world who we are. I'm reminded of these lines from Animal House:

> Otter: *I think this situation absolutely requires a really futile and stupid gesture be done on somebody's part.*
> Bluto: *And we're just the guys to do it.*
> D-Day: *Let's Do It!*
> Bluto: *LET'S DO IT!*[98]

OK, so maybe we skip the "really futile and stupid gesture" part. I propose we amend that to a "really Catholic and heroically virtuous gesture" part. Or at least something along the lines of, "We are fools for Christ's sake, but you are wise in Christ." (I Corinthians 4:10).

But, as far as motivational speeches go, we *are* just the guys to do it. We're Catholic! We were born to be heroic, brave, countercultural, and to go against the grain. The only way into heaven is to be heroic. God placed something in each of us that would be ignited at the right time.

In the *Chronicles of Narnia* by C.S. Lewis, we know the lion, Aslan, represents Christ. Through our faith we know that *Agnus Dei*, the lamb of God, also represents Christ. So do we view Christ as a lion or a lamb? Maybe the question is unfair. Of course He could be both. Saint Francis de Girolamo (1642-1716) was a renowned public preacher due to his distinguished and eloquent voice. He was described as "a lamb

---

[498] Ibid.

when he talks, and a lion when he preaches."[499] When we speak with others and are called upon to defend the faith, are we lions or sheep? When we speak with others and are called upon to defend the faith, are we lions or sheep? When you think of the Ven. Abp. Fulton Sheen, do you think of him as a lion or a sheep? As Alexander the Great said, "I am not afraid of an army of lions led by a sheep; I am afraid of an army of sheep led by a lion." Catholics are to be meek and humble, but, when need be, lions for the faith, and in particular in defense of God. Society tells Catholics to perpetually act as sheep and, sadly, we listen to them. It is as if we have the body of a lion, yet think of ourselves only as a sheep. A Catholic paradox.

The world tells us that there is a crisis of "toxic masculinity." No. We are suffering from a deficit of genuine masculinity. What gentleman today is agreeable to the violence of abortion, sinful same sex civil unions, and gender dysphoria in society? No true gentleman.

American author, Norman Mailer, wrote, "Masculinity is not something given to you, but something you gain. And you gain it by winning small battles with honor." Adapting that to Catholicism and sainthood, one might say, "Sainthood is not something given to you, but something you gain. And you gain it by winning small battles with humility."

Will you hold to all your principles every time you are challenged? Hoping yes, but probably no. Most likely you will fail on several occasions. Just as before when you have sinned soon after thinking you were strong (i.e., prideful). It is OK to fully accept and understand that you are not, yet, a saint. But you know what must be done. You know which direction you must go. You know that you must persevere and never give up. If need be, return again, and again, to petition God for his mercy, grace and favor. That you may be true to Him, and only Him, on those coming days and interactions that really matter. For this we pray. To be strong, to have fortitude, be steadfast, and muster longanimity, for Christ.

Don't wait for someone to step in and be the hero. Don't pass the buck to someone else. Be the hero. Not a zero. Pray to be a saint today. Appreciate that tomorrow may be too late. Saint Augustine exhorts each of us to, "Take care of your body as if you were going to

---

[499] "Your Morning Offering, Saint of the Day," *The Catholic Company*, May 11, 2021.

live forever. Take care of your soul as if you were going to die tomorrow."

Along similar lines General George Patton once said, "A good plan violently executed now, is better than a perfect plan next week." In other words, don't wait for conditions to be exactly right before you begin. The perfect time to begin may be a mythical construct in your mind that may in fact never realistically materialize. Therefore, begin today even if things are imperfect. With an eye towards eternity, let us live today in the service of our Lord and our neighbor. With God's grace, you've got this.

Here be dragons. If you are hesitant to live as a saint, what do you fear? Examine what you fear to lose, and let it go. Even if it be your life, do what the martyrs did before us. The martyrs were anything but fools. "But wait," you might say, "you're a good person. No reason to risk it all now. Better to be patient, manage the decline, and wait until your time finally comes—that's when you can do the greatest good." Right? Wrong. Whatever is holding you back, let it go. As the band The Smiths pose, in one of my favorite songs, "How soon is now?"

"Faith means battles," Saint Ambrose writes, "if there are no contests, it is because there are none who desire to contend." Go boldly towards the battle and stand shoulder to shoulder with your fellow Catholics. And, if God wills it, your fellow saints. Contend.

Are we saints in the making or not? When our families, our nation, and our church is on fire, why do we avert our eyes like a bunch of cowards? Where is *matria*, love of the Catholic Church, our holy mother? Where is our *patria*, love of America, our fatherland? *Matri* and *Patria* cannot be thrown out of the heart. Are we so complacent and comfortable that we do not see the fast-approaching abyss of a possible totalitarian society? If we do not step up right quick, how will the world change for the worse? Blessed Pier Giorgio Frassati wrote, 'To live life without faith, without a patrimony to defend, without a struggle for truth, that is not living, but existing."

Catholics were created by our sovereign God not to merely exist. Our story is much more.

"In a time of Universal deceit," George Orwell wrote, "telling the truth becomes a revolutionary act." Well, then, get on with it. Who can deny we are living in a truly Orwellian and dangerous time of soft-totalitarian punctuated by information suppression and self-censorship? Don't envision many hands being raised. So, what can we do about it? Be revolutionary by pursuing the truth, telling the truth, and defending the truth. For God is truth.

Abp. Fulton Sheen commented on revolution, "We started our country with a revolution. Revolution is in the air today. In fact, the arguments, today, are that we started that way, why not continue it? We do live in America with a revolutionary tradition. But the question is, what kind of revolution should we have?... Now, what's the revolution of today? *Violence!* Violence just for the sake of violence... the new type of revolt, which involves the destruction of everything in the past. And these people who are actuating violence today, claim they are in line with the American Revolution. *They Are Not!* Their revolution rejects God, in favor of man."[500]

Casey Chalk in *The Federalist* takes the discussion of virtue in a most practical direction in a wise article where he suggests that Catholics should be counter-cultural focusing on virtue aimed at the welfare of one's actual, flesh-and-blood neighbors rather than an online, abstract community.[501] Chalk encourages us to eschew "digital communities" and the fleeting glory of picture-perfect social media posts, and instead "do mundane things for one's neighbors, helping local businesses stay in business, or in performing community service."[502]

Another particularly powerful voice who went against the grain in his day was Ronald Reagan. In his "A Time for Choosing" address on behalf of the Goldwater Presidential Campaign on October 27, 1964, it was so effective it become known simply as "The Speech."

In it Reagan stated:

"You and I have a rendezvous with destiny. We'll preserve for our children this the last, best hope of man on earth or we will sentence

---

[500] Sheen, Fulton. "Revolution." You Tube. https://www.youtube.com/watch?v=gy6VtXVcGFw
[501] Casey Chalk, "Americans Need To Tend Our Actual Communities, Not Virtual Ones" The Federalist, June 2, 2021.
[502] Ibid.

them to take the last step into a thousand years of darkness. We are at war with the most dangerous enemy that has ever faced mankind. It has long climbed from the swamp to the stars. And it has been said, If we lose this war, and in so doing, lose this great way of freedom or ours, history with report with greatest astonishment, that those who had the most to lose, did the least to prevent it from happening. Well, I think it's high time now that we ask ourselves if we still even know that the freedoms that were intended for us by our founding fathers."[503]

Another actor, Jim Caviezel, who portrayed Jesus in *The Passion*, said the following to a FOCUS conference on March 4, 2018. Caviezel, reiterating Reagan's above words, added:

"This message is for you. A great man once said, 'Evil is powerless if the good are unafraid... Every generation of Americans needs to know that freedom exists not to do what you like, but having the right to do what you ought. You weren't made to fit in, my brothers and sisters. You were born to stand out. Set yourself apart from this corrupt generation.' Be saints. God bless you."[504]

Set yourself apart and follow our Lord's instructions to: love God with your whole heart, mind and soul; love your neighbor as you love yourself (which was superseded later by love your neighbor as I [Jesus] loved you). That is God's will. We know He will provide for us as He provides for the birds of the air. In Matthew 5:11-12, Jesus says: "Blessed are you when they insult you and persecute you and utter every kind of evil against you (falsely) because of me. Rejoice and be glad, for your reward will be great in heaven. Thus, they persecuted the prophets who were before you."

Saint Maximilian Kolbe wrote in 1922, "Daily experience, in fact, teaches us that the Church's enemies have more abundant natural means, and often, as Christ has told us, they are wiser in their own ways than the children of light. Further, to obtain the conversion and sanctification of souls, grace is needed, whereas corrupt nature tends

---

[503] Reagan, "A Time for Choosing," YouTube, posted Oct. 27, 1964. Ronald Reagan Presidential Library.
[504] FOCUS video no longer available. Similar speech available at The Thinking Conservative. September 19, 2020 https://www.thethinkingconservative.com/jim-caviezel-on-reagan-and-freedom/

by its own inclination towards sin. Consequently, we can count solely on help from on high."[505]

The atheistic agenda is diabolical. What right do people have to corrupt content, flout moral bounds, and attempt to make perverts of us all? Communists manipulate sensitive souls by playing upon the evil in our midst. They are given examples of discrimination, racism, injustice, social justice, income disparity, environmentalism, etc. They want to destroy the country rather than work to make things better. We need to apply our Catholic ethic to solve problems the Catholic way. Old fashioned Catholic values will save us from this anti-God terror. The crusade to restore the sacred must begin ASAP. The inner and outward manifestations to stand with and for God are primed and ready. Are we ready to initiate, or perpetuate, with firmer resolve? A greater level of arming yourself with an increased prayer life, living more holy, confronting evil, defending the church, and serving God, is every Catholic's playbook now. "For God has not given us a spirit of fear and timidity, but of power, love, and self-discipline." (2 Timothy 1:7)

As it says in 2 Timothy 4: 2 "be persistent whether it is convenient or inconvenient; convince, reprimand, encourage through all patience and teaching." Persistence when convenient most can do. But when inconvenient—that is when it shifts into the realm of doing the heroic and being saintly. However small or large the task, if done in a spirit of serving God—that is what matters. There's purpose in you. Your destiny is to be determined by saying *yes* or *no* to God. "There is no fear in love. But perfect love drives out fear, because fear has to do with punishment. The one who fears is not made perfect in love." (1 John 4:18)

Come what may, will you have the resolve to see it through? Will you "end well"? Only the good Lord knows. But whatever you do, whoever you meet, wherever you go, pray to face it courageously with the testimony of the saints firmly ensconced on your heart, mind and soul.

When writing from behind the relative safety of a keyboard, it is easier to speak candidly. I pray that when the time comes that I too may be bold, move forward and stand with resolve and a firm purpose.

---

[505] Kolbe, Maximilian. "The First Condition." May, 1922.

When the time comes will I "man up?" "There is one rule, above all others, for being a man," writes James Oliver Rigney Jr., better known by his pen name as Robert Jordan, in *The Great Hunt*, "Whatever comes, face it on your feet."

As a Catholic, whenever we are called upon to do so, we hope and pray for the courage to stand for God, Holy Mother Church, and our faith. Before we do stand, however, we know we must kneel. As Archbishop Fulton J. Sheen said, "it's impossible to lose your footing on your knees." Kneel to petition God for additional graces corresponding to the Cardinal Virtues, and gifts and fruits of the Holy Ghost. With God, all things are possible. Without him, good luck.

Saint Alphonsus Liguori counsels, "He who trusts himself is lost. He who trusts in God can do all things."

As we read in *The Soul of the Apostolate* by Dom Jean-Baptiste Chautard, O.C.S.O, "When one is involved in works of spiritual or corporal charity, his works can only be truly efficacious when he anchors his Interior Life in Christ. Without Christ we can do nothing."[506] Dom Chautard continues, "Our Lord categorically demands that those whom He associates with his apostolate should not only *persevere* in their virtue, but *make progress* in it."[507]

I'm a natural optimist. To state that another way, I'm Catholic. Part of being Catholic implies optimism. To say one is an "optimistic Catholic" is redundant. We know God wins, and we are blessed to be on His team. As optimistic, or as Catholic, as we are, we do see that storm clouds are on the horizon. We see the dark winter. With darkness in our vista, Catholics focus on the light (Christ). We must persevere and make progress in our faith.

The pressure to ideologically conform to the cultural, political, and religious *zeitgeist* (spirit of the age) does not seem that it will relent any time soon. In fact, we can fully expect in this epoch in world history the pressures to conform will metastasize in stifling, and perhaps even crushing, new ways. In other words, there is an excellent chance we will be presented with numerous small, medium and perhaps even large ways to be martyred for faith, family and flag.

---

[506] Chautard, Dom Jean-Baptiste, *Soul of the Apostolate*, n.p.
[507] Ibid, 71.

The opportunities to jettison traditional western Judeo-Christian beliefs (what the radical left pejoratively nowadays refers to as "white privilege") for ideological conformity will be omnipresent via: social interactions, social media, at work, in the marketplace, in the town square, in the country, and even within the Modernist church. The Agenda of the world has an insatiable appetite to denigrate and attempt to eliminate those who hold traditional moral views. It always has and always will—until the second coming of the Son of Man, The King of Kings.

From this day forward, whatever we choose to do, we must never give in to fear and betray our faith, our heritage, our beliefs, and our hopes. Instead, we must lean into our foundational principles and our aspirational desires with the heroic confidence in Christ shared by all the saints.

As Catholics, we see things differently. Our spirits are oriented towards God serving Him in virtuous and heroic ways. We do not just possess a Biblical worldview, or a Christian worldview; no, we possess a Catholic worldview.

And an American worldview. In several of his 2020 Presidential campaign speeches, Donald Trump said: "We will not bend. We will not break. We will not yield. We will never give up. We will never back down. We will never, ever, surrender. Because we are Americans, and our hearts bleed red, white and blue." His words are most applicable to being Catholic in today's increasingly secular and anti-God America. In his farewell address President Trump described Americans thusly, "our spirits are oriented towards daring and defiance, excellence and adventure, courage and confidence, loyalty and love."[508] What great appreciation of, and belief in, the can-do spirit of America.

In this chaotic time, we need truth. In this confused world, we realize that those pursuing the anti-God agenda hold people like me in low regard on multiple fronts. I am a white, heterosexual, married, Traditional Catholic, America-first patriot. I am aware that many persons and constituencies rationalize that many, if not all, of my demographic markers may be held against me in contempt. In fact, many factions feel they have justification to flat-out hate me. Many leftists and progressives have had their minds and souls corrupted by

---

[508] Trump, Donald J., "Farewell Address," January 19, 2021.

their desires. Rationalization and justification can be an extremely slippery slope to error and sin.

In speaking the truth about the faith, I recall the incident where Jesus confronted the guard at his trial before the Sanhedrin, saying, "If I speak the truth, then why do you strike Me?" People sometimes lash out against the truth. If Jesus himself was subjected to injustice, we must ask, "Why not me?" If talking about the saints, virtue, our church and nation, and relaying a few personal stories and anecdotes through the lens of Catholic truth opens the door to others thinking negatively of me, hating or persecuting me for doing good, I will be joyful and march on. Saint Ignatius of Antioch, commenting on the church being hated wrote, "Our task is not one of producing persuasive propaganda; Christianity shows its greatness when it is hated by the world."[509]

Utilizing hate to make a point, the Venerable Fulton J. Sheen commented, "If I were not a Catholic, and were looking for the true church in the world today... I would look for the church the world hates." Brilliant. Sheen's logic is impeccable. Extrapolating his logic, consider the following:

True, the Catholic faith goes against the ways of the world.
True, the world hates the Catholic Mass.
True, most of the Catholic hierarchy dislikes the Tridentine Mass.
Ergo, go to the Tridentine Mass.

Yes, there are the ever-present effects of original sin and my own personal shortcomings that result in me offending God through my own faults. Nonetheless, I am not too proud to go to confession regularly to beg for God's mercy and forgiveness to return to a state of grace. "O God, punish me in this life" prayed Saint Augustine, "just so long as you need not punish me in the next."

I am fully aware that I will struggle against sin all my days, just as the Catholic saints did before me. As Saint Louis de Montfort said, "Often, actually very often, God allows his greatest servants, those who are far advanced in grace, to make the most humiliating mistakes. This humbles them in their own eyes and in the eyes of their fellow men." So be it. God is good.

---

[509] Saint Ignatius of Antioch, *Witness of the Saints,* 194.

It is said that in the final days the greatest number of saints ever will rise up and defend Christ and his church. There will be saints. There will always be, God willing, saints among us. Be one of them.

Heart of Jesus, delight of saints, have mercy on us.

Winding things down and completing this section, a song popped into my head. I'm not a big sing-along type of guy, but on this one, I do appreciate the lyrics and music whenever I hear them. It's such a can-do type of tune. Join me, if you will:

"Oh, when the saints, go marching in,
Oh, when the saints go marching in,
Oh Lord, I want to be in that number,
When the saints go marching in."

God would like nothing better than for each of us to march straight into heaven as saints. He chose each of us out of nothingness and has given us the opportunity to be alive for precisely a time such as this. For the freedom and exultation of Holy Mother Church. For this day. For this fight. For His service. For His glory. Saint Louis de Montfort speaks to being in that number, "Be one of the small number who find the way to life, and enter by the narrow gate into Heaven. Take care not to follow the majority and the common herd, so many of whom are lost. Do not be deceived; there are only two roads: one that leads to life and is narrow; the other that leads to death and is wide. There is no middle way."

If *Against The Grain* resonates with the person you are in this moment, know that it does not define who you will be in the future. Who you decide to be tomorrow is entirely up to you. If you desire to be a saint, it is more achievable than you realize. Keep in mind that only when you decide to do something new, will you have the opportunity to become someone new. Decide to do what it takes to be a saint today, tomorrow and for all eternity.

Saint Philip Neri, featured in the epic hagiographical movie, *Preferisco il Paradiso* (I prefer heaven), tells us, "The best way to prepare for death is to live every day as though it were the last." So how will you live your day with faith today? How will you evidence eternal hope? How will you exude Christlike charity? Be not the Debbie Downer, the rusty arrow, a poison around the souls of others, and the one that puts all virtue to flight in others. May all your actions be conducive to your salvation and that of others close to you. God has given us all the graces we need to be faithful to Him and merit our eternal salvation. Go forth, march, be in that number, and stay the course as a faithful son or daughter of the Catholic Church. May your eternal reward be great in heaven! As Catholic author and podcaster Patrick Coffin says, "Be a saint; what else is there?"

U2 (Passengers) in their profoundly understated, yet achingly, beautiful song "Your Blue Room" has several lyrics that connect with me in a substantial *Against the Grain* sort of way. Described by Bono as a conversation with God, the song was first performed live at Soldier Field in Chicago on September 13, 2009. It featured pre-recorded ethereal vocals from Sinéad O'Conner, a former (for a time) fellow Wilmette, IL resident. For the highest quality version, however, I suggest checking out the version performed ten days later at Giants Stadium, East Rutherford, NJ.[510] Be sure to marinate in guitarist The Edge's dulcet ostinato near the end of the song.

> *"It's a different kind of conversation, in your blue room.*
> *See the future just hanging there, in your blue room.*
> *And you crave a new perspective, looking down on my objectives.*
> *Your instructions, whatever the direction, in your blue room.*
> *Soldier, soldier, light inside your love, you harbor love.*
> *You don't belong, you don't belong.*
> *You really want inside a song, soldier boy, won't you fall in line."*[511]

How can the confused and twisted direction of our church, nation and culture leave faithful Catholics not craving a different kind of conversation, a new perspective and a new objective? My God, my God, to be saints, to be with You in heaven, we know we must fall in line and follow Your instructions, whatever the direction, whatever the cost(s). We don't belong to this world. We belong to You. As such, when called upon to be discordant notes serving You and Christ's Bride, we know deep down in our souls we must go against the grain. We know there's absolutely nothing wrong with being different from the crowd. In fact, it's the ideal path forward. Fellow soldier boys (and

---

510 U2, "Your Blue Room," YouTube posted February 9, 2013.
https://www.youtube.com/watch?v=Jj0v54bGHNs&list=PLbeGV9LVm_PExydFXYyFmwQl2VKaDhqoz&index=7

girls), members of the Church Militant; it's time. God, love, invites us each day to fall in line. Will we? Our eternal future is just hanging there.

Be a saint; why not me?
Pax tibi cum sanctis (Peace for you with the saints).
We few. We children of the light. We blessed warriors for Christ.
Be who you are meant to be. Be Catholic.
What more can you do? What else is inside you?
What can you draw out of others?
Our home is not here, our home is in heaven.
Life is short, eternity isn't.
Evil is powerless if the good are unafraid.
There will be blood. There will be martyrdom (wet and dry).
Your faith is a hill worthy of dying on. Come and take it.
Always forward, never back.
Nolite timere (Fear Not!)
Oh, I still believe.
Be a sustainer of virtue.
Be a saint; why not you?
Deus vult! (God wills it!)

Saint Josemaría Escrivá provided the opening line of our Introduction, "A Saint is a sinner that keeps trying." Sir Winston Churchill helps us close our Afterword defining success as, "the ability to move from failure to failure with no loss of enthusiasm." So, after you fail and sin, get up, confess, try again, with no loss of enthusiasm. Saint Camillus adds, "Commitment is doing what you said you would do, after the feeling you said it in has passed." So, when you put this book down, and the fervor of your feeling passes, that is precisely the time to commit. Your family, your nation, and your church need you.

Be a sign of contraction in the world. You have heroism in you. How soon is now? It's time. Let it out.

Go against the grain.

"Go forward bravely. Fear nothing. Trust in God; all will be well."
- Saint Joan of Arc

ACKNOWLEDGEMENTS

My sincere gratitude to Italian Archbishop Carlo Maria Viganò, a spiritual General, for writing the Foreword. Viganò's episcopal motto, fittingly, is *"Scio Cui credidi"* (I know whom I have believed.) Of all the bishops in the world at this time (2018-2021), he is a leading, pivotal figure in our fight for integrity in our church and world. Viganò has not shirked his responsibility to speak the truth as he sees it. In his role now as the "truth-telling bishop," he is a foremost cleric evincing heroic virtue speaking out against the error, confusion, irreverence, and heresy among the bishopric ranks. While today many scoff at his methods and message, in time others will appreciate how prescient his comments were. He also seeks to defend those defending freedom and patriotism in the United States.

In some ways the archbishop reminds me a bit of Saint Paul. Saul (his Jewish name before conversion) of Tarsus, was struck by God with lightning, made blind, sent to visit Ananias "and immediately there fell from his eyes as it were scales, and he received his sight; and rising up, he was baptized." (Acts 9:18) Filled with the Holy Ghost, Paul, from that point forward, was on fire boldly saying what needed to be said promoting and defending the Christian faith. In much the same way, that is how I see Abp. Viganò's role since he released his eleven page "Testimony" on August 25, 2018. The triggering event for Abp. Viganò was the then-Cardinal Theodore McCarrick sexual abuse scandal.

In speaking out publicly, and forcefully, against his brother bishops and their culture of silence, Abp. Viganò chose to go against the grain and stand with the vulnerable (the abused), for the Church, and for the faith, and call for those who covered up McCarrick's abuse to resign, including Pope Francis. In essence, Abp. Viganò was stepping up to be a ray of sunlight being the best disinfectant. In response, many of the bishops considered Archbishop Viganò to be a Judas. If only holy Mother Church had a few dozen Viganòs ready, willing and able to fight for her, and for Christ. Alas, it is not so.

Instead, the twenty-first century church appears to be led by a legion of milquetoast apostolic successors. Thank you, Abp. Viganò, for writing the Foreword, but more importantly for your integrity, your anti-corruption agenda, your strong support for the forces of good in the United States of America, and for your recent zeal these past couple years in being a true shepherd as a witness to the truth. "We all have the duty to speak up," writes the archbishop, "We all have the duty to witness to the truth without fear. Dishonorably rebellious are those who presume to break or change the perennial tradition of the Church."[512] Amen. We hear your voice, Archbishop.

Thank you to all who wrote endorsements for the book: Bishop Athanasius Schneider, Bishop Thomas J. Paprocki, Fr. James Altman, Rev. C. Frank Phillips, C.R., Jesse Romero, Rev. Anthony J. Brankin, Mike Church, Fr. Dwight Campbell, John Zmirak, Sr. Deidre "Dede" Byrne, POSC, and Jason Jones.

Thank you to my children, Gabi, Nathan, Alex and Charlie. I am forever grateful for the opportunity to be your dad. You four were the primary motivation for this book. Know that wherever you go, whatever you do, your dad believes in you. Know that my prayers for you will always petition God for his love, grace, and mercy for you such that you will live as saints, and one day a little place in heaven will be set aside for all of you. Always remember: "Do Great. Have fun. Be Catholic."

Thanks to Mary, my wife, who accepts all my serendipitous professional pursuits with the patience of a saint. Funny story, when I told Mary that I was going to write a book, she said "Oh great, another distraction." Priceless. A thousand thank yous, Mary, for being an unbelievable wife, mom, and a beacon of love and friendship to all.

To my parents, Fred and Mary Ellen. I was blessed to have won the birthday lottery with you as my parents. Your heroic example as parents is appreciated more than you know. Thanks, Dad, for your strong example of how to lead a Catholic family, how to work hard, and be ethical in business, and all you do. Thanks, Mom, for being the heart of our home growing up, and for all you did, and continue to do, nurturing my love for God, the Catholic Faith, and the Saints. Thank you both for modeling the faith, and for believing in me.

---

[512] "Archbishop Carlo Maria Viganò gives his first extended interview since calling on the pope to resign,"
Washington Post, June 10, 2019.

To my sister Kelly, and brother Bryan. Kelly, thanks for all the good times we have and continue to share. Your tender, heart of gold models service to God, your kids, our family, (and your cats) in innumerable and countless ways. *Muchos abrazos.* (P.S. Don't start crying.) Bryan, thanks for always bringing your big heart, wicked smarts, sense of humility, and screwy sense of humor to our family. You're an outstanding brother, husband, dad, hockey afficionado, and dog whisperer. Thanks both, for letting me be your big bro.

The Grane Clan, circa 1984.
Pictured left to right, Mom, Dad, Doug, Kelly and Bryan.

Thanks to Dr. Paul Kengor, Grove City College, for his encouragement to write this book. Paul and I are classmates from grad school at the School of International Service at The American University in Washington, D.C. Paul and I reconnected in Chicago a few years ago at a talk he gave on Marxism. In follow up emails, Paul assuaged my concerns of hesitancy to write prodding me stating, "It's a badge of honor to suffer humiliation and carry the cross for Christ and His Church, especially against evil. You have the mind and the skills. You've been blessed with gifts." Thanks, Paul, for the "kick in the pants" to buckle down and enter the fray as a published Catholic author. Last, but not least, I appreciate Paul's introduction to John Moorehouse, to whom a special debt of gratitude is owed as mentioned in the *"In Memoriam"* at the front of this book.

Thanks to John Zmirak who put me in contact with John Vella, who valiantly stepped in as an interim editor to work on the completed first draft. While John readily admitted the format for *Against the Grain* was outside his usual approach to editing books, he nonetheless admirably rose to the challenge and tapped into the spirit of my voice to edit about half the book before I signed a contract with Defiance Press. Many thanks John!

A Texas-sized thank you to Heather Siler, General Manager, Quata Diann Merit, editor, and the entire team at Defiance Press. They are an incredible group of individuals whose love of authors is matched only by their love of country. For an undertaking with a theme of going against the grain, Defiance Press was the ideal publishing partner. Great job Defiance Press! Texas forever, ya'll!

An atypical thank you "3 Mikes and a Taylor," my 'Mt. Rushmore of Catholic Political Commentary,' who provide a lion's share of information and entertain me, and many others, from a traditional Catholic perspective. Mike Church, Michael Matt, Michael Voris and Dr. Taylor Marshall. Gentleman, keep up the great work all. Hammer down.

I'd like to ask you all to say a prayer for a unique mentor of mine (and tens of millions of other Americans), Rush Limbaugh. Rush passed away on Feb. 17, 2021, the time when I was finishing up the first draft of this book. The "Doctor of Democracy" was an American Original. Listening to Rush for thirty years, I received a Doctorate in love of country, American Exceptionalism, conservatism and having ultimate faith in people. From Rush, a voice of reason in the darkness, I learned right is still right. It might seem odd to say, but Rush was a friend I never met. I never spoke with him, but I did, however, email him a couple times to ask him to convert to Catholicism. Sadly, I do not believe he did.

Rush shaped the soul of a nation. He helped shape my political soul. Rush once said, "Freedom will never go out of style." Freedom and free will comes from God. Rush fought for what he believed in, and he believed in America. His love of country was boundless and palpable. Rush would want us to carry on his legacy and to fight for liberty with all we have. Rush loved the founding fathers who put in place a system of government that allowed America to become the greatest country God ever gave man. Rush was an anchor of conservatism who defended conservative values and rugged individualism like no one else. Rush was a cultural touchstone who believed in God, faith, family, country, goodness, strength and the virtue of America. He was a brilliant and irreplaceable trailblazer, pioneer, and patriot. He encouraged so many of us to learn, and then lead. Rush, the GOAT of talk radio, was America's spokesman. He gave us hope. Most importantly, Rush cared. A good portion of what I believe about the goodness of America, I owe to Rush. Rush, you truly were a talent on loan from God. Godspeed. Mega-dittos. *Requiescat in Pace.*

Thank you to the many Catholic priests and nuns who have contributed to my faith over the years. Special prayers for Fr. Phillip Hahn who baptized me; Fr. Kevin Farrell who gave me First Confession and First Communion; Bishop Raymond Vonesh who confirmed me; Fr. C. Frank Phillips who married Mary and me; Fr. Joshua Caswell, my current pastor; and for all the other traditional priests who have celebrated Mass, heard confessions, and given Holy Communion to me. Through the goodness of God the Father, he has provided you to me. Thank you for ministering to my soul, and that of my family. Thank you for the encouragement to always increase in holiness. I thank the Holy Trinity for you all! *Deo gratias!* (Thanks be to God!)

In gratitude, we thank God for the gift of all the saints who were martyred, who sacrificed, who persisted often times under extremely difficult circumstances, and who lived their lives going against the grain with the singular desire to serve God and his holy will. In conjunction with the holy saints, we consecrate our service, and everything we have to you, Almighty God, our benign benefactor. We offer thanks to the Holy Trinity in our hearts this moment of this day. Let us all practice and build up the virtue of gratefulness. "Ingratitude is a scorching wind," Saint Bernard writes, "that dries up the source of goodness. Ingratitude obstructs grace." Fr. Dennis Koliński, SJC at St. John Cantius in Chicago, IL, has said on a couple occasions, "Nothing is as pleasing to God as a grateful soul." Gratitude and thanksgiving combat the deadly sin of envy. We are grateful to you O God, and we thank you, for all your holy saints. Blessed be God in his saints.

I am grateful for the saints who serve as an example and inspiration for us all in general, and for me in particular. My "go to" favorites include: Saint Michael the archangel, Saint Joan of Arc, Saint Catherine of Siena, and Saint Thérèse of Lisieux. I thank all those saints in heaven who inspired me, and helped me, to tell their stories in the pages of this book.

For all of you who have read *Against the Grain*, and embrace its urgings to lead a more virtuous life, I ask all the heavenly saints to intercede for you and assist you in your daily fight for Holy Mother Church, to stand firm for the Catholic faith, and for an increase in your personal holiness. May God bless you all your days. Should we all make it to heaven, perhaps we can visit and you can tell me what part of *Against the Grain* most resonated with you.

Thanks for accompanying me on this journey through the centuries visiting with some of the Catholic Churches finest saints. In closing, it is with grateful appreciation that I say to you, my friends in Jesus and Mary, *aujourd'hui nous conclure* (today we conclude). Or, better yet, *aujourd'hui nous commençons* (today we begin)!

Me on the Tee Box at the Par-4, 405-Yard, 15ᵗʰ Hole, "Purgatory" at Royal Portrush in Northern Ireland.

Upon expiration, I'm fairly certain that, unless I'm martyred in the state of grace, I most likely will not be taking the express train to heaven. I'm hoping, and praying, for heaven as my goal. If I happen to fall short of the ideal, however, through God's mercy I'll spend time in purgatory perfectly satisfying God's justice to one day truly merit heaven. My Jesus, mercy. Please remember to pray each day for our dear, dear friends in the Church Suffering, the holy souls in purgatory. Much obliged!

APPENDIX I

Twenty-one Habits of Holy Apostolic People

"Let us begin in earnest to work out our salvation, for no one will do it for us, since even He Himself, who made us without ourselves, will not save us without ourselves."
- *Saint Margaret Mary Alacoque*

In researching *Against the Grain*, I came across Fr. John McCloskey's "Seven Daily Habits of Holy Apostolic People." The seven daily habits are: morning offering, spiritual reading, the Holy Rosary, Holy Mass and Communion, at least fifteen minutes of mental prayer, the Angelus, and the examination of conscience. I liked the list, but having devotion to several other Catholic practices, I had the idea to add a few additional items. As this book had twenty-one chapters for twenty-one centuries, when I thought about adding helpful habits, the number twenty-one was top of mind.

With life for Catholics appearing to be heading into further turbulent times, how do we prepare ourselves for whatever comes? The obvious answer: Imitate the saints by becoming more holy. Saint Francis of Assisi encourages training in holiness as the primary starting point: "Sanctify yourself and you will sanctify society." And not just holy, but, "be perfect as your Heavenly Father is perfect." How do we increase holiness and virtue? We need to tap further into "the light" (i.e., the truth). To fight as children of the light. To exercise our option to call upon God Almighty to "give us this day our daily bread" (the graces we need in battle). To petition Him to sustain us in all engagements with the spiritual and temporal enemies who perpetually advocate and scheme for our defeat and damnation.

Our enemies desire to crush our spirits. They want us to be afraid and to not engage in the holy war for salvation. As we walk with God, we know that God can use our enemies and their trials and tribulations to sharpen our resolve and help make us stronger. Not just marginally stronger, but Catholic strong. A strength that, with God, will be victorious.

How many souls will make it to heaven? Only God knows the answer to that question. For us humans, we can contemplate the odds of how many Catholics will make it to heaven. To be candid, we know it's not many. Rather than Hans Urs von Balthasar's position that hell is essentially empty of souls, or certain other bishops (i.e., Robert Baron), who believe that "all men having a reasonable hope of being saved," Jesus, the scriptures, and church tradition, tell us the percentage that actually make it to heaven are relatively few. Jesus himself said, "Many are called, few are chosen." I forget where I read this, but two saints from France were speaking about how many souls made it to heaven in a Catholic town of 30,000. The answer? Three. To be sure, the odds are long.

You have to want to go to heaven. Those who don't, choose hell by choosing mortal sin. As we know not the day or the hour, we should all strive to perpetually be in the state of grace. We all need to cultivate a better moral sense and view of this world with our focus set on God. How do we grow in personal holiness? How do we get our souls, and all those we love, to heaven? We do so by imitating the saints, their heroic virtue, and by cultivating holier habits. By developing holy habits to direct our daily thoughts, actions and desires in service of God alone.

If you feel called to focus on holiness for yourself, those in your immediate family, and in your circle of friends, then cooperate with those promptings and graces. If you feel called to *Duc En Altum* (Go out into the deep.) and let down your nets in the larger community, then cooperate with those promptings and graces. In other words, if for the faith you feel called to be a lion, be a lion. Cooperate with God wherever he leads you.

As we grow in holiness and fight the spiritual battle, there are many 'weapons' to deploy to fortify our souls. As there have been twenty-one centuries since the birth of Christ, there were twenty-one chapters in this book. Accordingly, assembled below are "Twenty One Habits of Holy Apostolic People." I suppose it's one thing to encourage people to be saints with lives of heroic virtue, and leave it at that. But I imagine several people will ask. "What other armaments are available in the church arsenal to help us become holier?" And that is the reason for this section. Below you will see a list, in descending order of importance, of what I have found to be the most efficacious holy habits available to Catholics.

PLEASE NOTE: Although I did sleep at a Holiday Inn Express last night (joke), I'm not a spiritual advisor, authority, or theologian by any stretch of the imagination; the list that follows is just that—a list. Please do your own research and speak with a trusted priest as to the value of the habits below, come up with your own list, and then pursue your holiness accordingly. Each of us have similar, yet distinct, paths to salvation. Find your path, and chart your course.

On final point, while twenty-one habits made the list, I believe the first seven are the most essential. They are what some would refer to as the "need to haves." The other items on the list, while important, are the "nice/wise to haves." The list is presented first in outline form, then followed with further explanations of the habit as appropriate. Without further ado, my list:

Habits of Holy Apostolic People:

1. Attend the Most Holy Sacrifice of the Mass
   - ⊙ Attend Mass more often than weekly, and on holy days of obligation.
   - ⊙ Attend Mass on first Fridays and first Saturdays, with corresponding devotions to the Sacred Heart of Jesus and the Immaculate Heart of Mary (as instructed at Fatima).
2. Frequent the Sacraments
   - ⊙ Communion only in the state of grace.
   - ⊙ Confession monthly.
3. Daily Prayer. *Oremus* (Let Us Pray)
   - ⊙ The Morning Offering
   - ⊙ The Angelus (Morning, Noon, Night)
   - ⊙ The Evening Examination of Conscience/Act of Contrition
   - ⊙ The Sign of the Cross
4. Say a Daily Rosary
5. Wear the Brown Scapular
6. Frequent Eucharistic Adoration
7. Penance, Penance, Penance
   - ⊙ Acts of Reparation

⊙ For the Conversion of Sinners
8. Practice Faith, Hope and Charity
    Spiritual Works of Mercy.
    ⊙ Corporal Works of Mercy.
9. Spiritual Reading (at least fifteen minutes a day)
    ⊙ Read the Bible, or other spiritual books and materials.
10. Ask for the assistance and grace of the Holy Ghost
    ⊙ Deploy the Seven Gifts of the Holy Ghost
11. Fast regularly
12. Speak the Holy Name of Jesus often
13. Cultivate a devotion to the Sacred Heart of Jesus
14. Cultivate a devotion to the Immaculate Heart of Mary
15. Make a Total Consecration to Jesus Through Mary. Renew
    frequently.
16. Wear a Miraculous Medal
17. Use holy water
18. Acknowledge the presence of your holy guardian angel
19. Go Weapons HOT (Humility, Obedience, Trust)
20. Say binding prayers
21. Say the heroic act of charity

1. Attend the Most Holy Sacrifice of the Mass

⊙ Attend Mass more often than weekly, and on holy days
   of obligation.

⊙ Attend Mass on first Fridays and first Saturdays, with
   corresponding devotions to the Sacred Heart of Jesus
   and the Immaculate Heart of Mary (as instructed at
   Fatima).

The single Mass is far more valuable than you are able to
comprehend. The Holy Mass is the most powerful prayer in
the church. The concelebrated Mass is the greatest invention
in the history of man. The Eucharistic Sacrifice "is the source
and summit of all Christian worship and life."[513] Consider the
following commentary from a few great saints:

"A single Mass gives more honor to God than can ever be
given to Him by all the prayers and austerities of the saints, all
the labors and fatigues of the Apostles, all the torments of the

---

[513] Code of Canon Law, Canon 897.

martyrs, and all the adoration's of the Seraphim, and of the Mother of God."

- Saint Alphonsus Ligouri

"You cannot do anything to glorify God more, nor profit your soul more, than by devoutly assisting at Mass, and assisting as often as possible."

- Saint Eymard

"The celebration of Holy Mass has the same value as the death of Jesus on the Cross."

- Saint Thomas Aquinas

"It would be easier for the world to survive without the sun than to do so without the Holy Mass."

- Saint Padre Pio

Recent estimates are that roughly 70 percent of baptized Catholics no longer attend Mass on a weekly basis. In some European nations that number is 80-90 percent. If the Mass is the source of summit of Catholic life, why are so many forsaking it? The reason is our spiritual and temporal adversaries know the value of the Mass and do all they can to dissuade us from receiving the many graces so as to make us weaker and easier to manipulate living lives of sin. Push back. Resist. Attend Mass, the unbloody sacrifice of our Lord, Jesus Christ, more frequently and with greater devotion.

A final thought on the Mass, consider the Irish aphorism: "Ní luach go h-Aifrionn De eisteachd." (There is no reward like hearing God's Mass.)

2. Frequent the Sacraments
  ⊙ Communion only in the state of grace.
  ⊙ Confession monthly.

Let us look to the martyr Saint Tarcisius who died while transporting the blessed communion and protecting it from sacrilege. He knew the value of the Holy Eucharist and was most willing to die for protecting it. Do we respect the Holy Eucharist as much as we should?

"Man should tremble, the world should quake, all Heaven should be deeply moved when the Son of God appears on the altar in the hands of the priest."

- Saint Francis of Assisi

"Of thy Mystic Supper, O Son of God, accept me today as a communicant; for I will not speak of thy Mystery to thine enemies, neither will I give thee a kiss as did Judas; but like the thief will I confess thee: Remember me, O Lord, in thy Kingdom. Not unto judgement nor unto condemnation be my partaking of thy Holy Mysteries, O Lord, but unto the healing of soul and body."

- Saint John Chrysostom (prayer prescribed to be said on the way to receiving Holy Communion)

"Upon receiving Holy Communion, the Adorable Blood of Jesus Christ really flows in our veins and His Flesh is really blended with ours."

- Saint John Vianney

"If you ate only one meal a week would you survive? It is the same for your soul. Nourish it with the Blessed Sacrament."

- Saint André Bessette

"If angels could be jealous of men, they would be so for one reason: Holy Communion."

- Saint Maximilian Kolbe

"God removes the sin of the one who makes humble confession, and thereby the devil loses the sovereignty he had gained over the human heart."

- Saint Bernard

"We receive grace from the sacraments. And when we fumble due to sin - and it's gonna happen - confession puts us back on the field."

- Lou Holtz, Catholic and National Championship (1988) Football Coach with Notre Dame

3. Daily Prayer. *Oremus* ("Let Us Pray")
- The Morning Offering
- The Angelus (Morning, Noon, Night)

- The Evening Examination of Conscience/ Act of Contrition
- The Sign of the Cross

"Prayer is the best weapon we possess. It is the key that opens the heart of God."

- Saint Padre Pio of Pietrelcina

"When we pray, the voice of the heart must be heard more than the proceedings from the mouth."

- Saint Bonaventure

"Know, dearest daughter, how, by humble, continual, and faithful prayer, the soul acquires, with time and perseverance, every virtue. Wherefore should she persevere and never abandon prayer... The soul should advance by degrees, and I know well that, just as the soul is at first imperfect and afterwards perfect, so also is it with her prayer. She should nevertheless continue in vocal prayer, while she is yet imperfect, so as not to fall into idleness. But she should not say her vocal prayers without joining them to mental prayer, that is to say, that while she is reciting, she should endeavor to elevate her mind in My love, with the consideration of her own defects and of the Blood of My only-begotten Son, wherein she finds the breadth of My charity and the remission of her sins."[514]

- God the Father to Saint Catherine Of Siena

"If, then, we wish to persevere and to be saved—for no one can be saved without perseverance—we must pray continually. Our perseverance depends, not on one grace, but on a thousand helps which we hope to obtain from God during our whole lives, that we may be preserved in his grace. Now, to this chain of graces a chain of prayers on our part must correspond: without these prayers, God ordinarily does not grant his graces. If we neglect to pray, and thus break the chain of prayers, the chain of graces shall also be broken, and we shall lose the grace of perseverance."[515]

- Saint Alphonsus Liguori,

---

[514] "The Dialogues of Saint Catherine of Siena," 92.
[515] "Sermons of Saint Alphonsus Liguori," 201.

"Those who pray will be saved; those who do not pray will be condemned."

- Saint Alphonsus Liguori

"Prayer is, beyond doubt, the most powerful weapon the Lord gives us to conquer evil ... but we must really put ourselves into the prayer, it is not enough just to say the words, it must come from the heart. And also prayer needs to be continuous, we must pray no matter what kind of situation we find ourselves in: the warfare we are engaged in is ongoing, so our prayer must be on-going also."

- Saint Alphonsus Liguori

"We must pray literally without ceasing— without ceasing—in every occurrence and employment of our lives . . . that prayer of the heart which is independent of place or situation, or which is rather a habit of lifting up the heart to God as in a constant communication with Him."

- Saint Elizabeth Ann Seton

"If you would suffer with patience the adversities and miseries of this life, be a man of prayer. If you would obtain courage and strength to conquer the temptations of the enemy, be a man of prayer. If you would mortify your own will with all its inclinations and appetites, be a man of prayer. If you would know the wiles of Satan and unmask his deceits, be a man of prayer. If you would live in joy and walk pleasantly in the ways of penance, be a man of prayer. If you would banish from you soul the troublesome flies of vain thoughts and cares, be a man of prayer. If you would nourish your soul with the very sap of devotion, and keep it always full of good thoughts and good desires, be a man of prayer. If you would strengthen and keep up your courage in the ways of God, be a man of prayer. In fine, if you would uproot all vices from your soul and plant all virtues in their place, be a man of prayer. It is in prayer that we receive the unction and grace of the Holy Ghost, who teaches all things."[516]

- Saint Bonaventure

---

[516] Lehodey, Rt. Rev. Dom Vitalis, "The Ways of Mental Prayer," 25-26,

Begin each morning with this most simple, yet highly efficacious, prayer: "In the name of our Lord, Jesus Christ, Crucified, I offer this day in service of you, and of others."

Prayer begets prayer begets prayer. Stay on the prayer path. Prayer is a continuous battle to live a life dedicated to God. Have self-discipline and pray every day. Meditate on the eternal truths for the sake of your eternal salvation.

Most of the above has been referencing private prayer. What about public prayer? When you go out to eat, do you say grace before meals? A friend told me that after 9/11, he made it a point when eating a meal in public to start and end grace with the sign of the cross. That's going against the grain. How often do you notice someone blessing himself and saying grace before a meal? Anyone? Bueller? Be a rebel and reclaim a bit of the public sphere for Christ. You never know who may be watching and will be inspired to do the same from that point forward. The same about making the sign of the cross in public. Given our secular, anti-God culture, it could be considered revolutionary.

Finally, how often do you make the sign of the cross? You should do it several times a day. It's more important than you know. Saint Basil the Great tells us that the apostles themselves taught the sign of the cross. Some people may nag you about drinking water throughout the day. It's good to do as it helps your body. Think more about making the sign of the cross throughout the day, especially when tempted, as it helps your soul. Demons truly dislike it when you make the sign of the cross; they flee. And when you do make the sign of the cross, do so reverently. Realize that you are calling upon Holy Trinity to bless you, and that you are not performing a gesture akin to swatting flies. Be intentional.

4. Say a Daily Rosary

The Blessed Virgin Mary appeared to Saint Dominic in 1214, and instructed him how to say the Rosary. Saint Dominic, pray for us.

> "Never be afraid of loving the Blessed Virgin too much. You can never love her more than Jesus did."
>
> - Saint Maximilian Kolbe

"Love the Madonna and pray the rosary, for her Rosary is the weapon against the evils of the world today. All graces given by God pass through the Blessed Mother,'"

- Saint Padre Pio

"Give me an army saying the Rosary and I will conquer the world."

- Pope Pius IX

For additional reasons to say the Rosary, you may want to independently look of the Fifteen Promises of Mary granted to those who recite the Rosary. Here is one site to check out: https://americaneedsfatima.org/The-Holy-Rosary/15-promises-to-those-who-pray-the-rosary.html

Personally, I'm a fan of:

1) Whosoever shall faithfully serve me by the recitation of the Rosary shall receive signal graces.

3) The Rosary shall be a powerful armor against Hell; it will destroy vice, decrease sin, and defeat heresies.

4) It will cause virtue and good works to flourish; it will obtain for souls the abundant Mercy of God; ...

5) The soul which recommends itself to me by the recitation of the Rosary shall not perish.

15) Devotion to my Rosary is a great sign of predestination.

5. Wear the Brown Scapular

Blessed Mother appeared to Saint Simon Stock at Cambridge, England on Sunday, July 16, 1251, and instructed him to create a sacramental for people to wear saying, "Take, beloved son, this scapular of thy order as a badge of my confraternity and for thee and all Carmelites a special sign of grace; whoever dies in this garment, will not suffer everlasting fire. It is the sign of salvation, a safeguard in dangers, a pledge of peace and of the covenant." If you die in the state of grace, this is Our Lady's promise. Have confidence in her promise. Trust in her. As you do, your Blessed Mother will help guide you to heaven.

"One day through the rosary and the brown scapular, Our Lady will save the world."

- Saint Dominic

6. Frequent Eucharistic Adoration

"Do you realize that Jesus is there in the tabernacle expressly for you - for you alone?
He burns with the desire to come into your heart."
- Saint Thérèse of Lisieux

Over the centuries, Eucharistic Miracles, where a host begins to bleed, and upon further scientific analysis is determined to be human myocardial (human) tissue with the same proteins as normal human blood, have happened in several places, foremost among them in Italy at Lanciano (about 700) and Orvieto (1263).[517]

As Catholics, we believe Transubstantiation during Mass changes the host to the actual body and blood of Christ. It's a miracle that happens the world over every day. While the physical miracle of a bloody host is uncommon, the unbloody miracle of a changed host it not. We can make pilgrimages to Lanciano or Orvieto; we can also visit Jesus in the tabernacle in our own church every day. Sometimes a parish will place a consecrated host in a monstrance and leave it displayed for public veneration. When that happens, we can go to our church where Christ is present in the Holy Eucharist and adore him. We bring prayers of thanksgiving, wonder, atonement, and petition. Alternatively we may choose to be with Jesus asking nothing, but waiting in silence, listening for his voice.

Fr. Richard Heilman writes about the Blessed Sacrament as follows, "Saint Clare of Assisi would work to carry on the deep devotion of Saint Francis. We may not have realized it, but as we brought our Eucharistic Lord out into the streets, we had been doing the "Saint Clare of Assisi thing." This is in regard to the famous story of the invasion of the Saracens in 1240. As the invading forces surrounded and attacked Assisi, they made their way to the city they first encountered San Damiano - the convent where Saint Clare and her sisters lived - because it was outside the city walls. As the warriors approached, Saint Clare's sisters panicked and roused Saint Clare from her sick bed. She in turn lead them in prayer and as the invaders began to show themselves over the convent walls, "Does it please you, O God, to deliver into the hands of these beasts the defenseless children I have nourished with your love? I beseech you, dear Lord, protect

---

517 "The Divine Logic Behind Eucharistic Adoration," *Word Among Us*,
https://wau.org/resources/article/the_divine_logic_behind_eucharistic_adoration/

these whom I am now unable to protect." To her sisters she said, "Don't be afraid. Trust in Jesus." Then Saint Clare took the monstrance from the chapel with the consecrated Host and showed it to the Saracens. Upon seeing Saint Clare holding the Blessed Sacrament, the enemy first froze in their tracks and then gripped with a feeling of terror began to retreat. The power of the Holy Eucharist to turn back invading evil!!"[518]

When facing evil and temptation in your life, spend time with our Lord in the Blessed Sacrament in Eucharistic Adoration. He waits for you! Go to Him!

7. Penance, Penance, Penance
⊙ Acts of Reparation
⊙ For the Conversion of Sinners

As the Angel that appeared to the children of Fatima in 1916, preparing the way for Our Lady's appearances in 1917, exhorting the children (and us) to, "Penance. Penance. Penance."

We would do well to heed that message of penance, self-denial and prayers offered for reparation of sins committed that offend the Sacred Heart of Jesus and Immaculate Heart of Mary. Especially sins of the flesh.

Also, we practice penance for the benefit of all souls that they may convert to the true faith and serve the true God. As Jesus instructed us with the Great Commission, "Go and make disciples of all nations."

8. Faith, Hope and Charity
⊙ Spiritual Works of Mercy.
⊙ Corporal Works of Mercy.

"If you wish to go to extremes, let it be in sweetness, patience, humility and charity."

- Saint Philip Neri

"You know well enough that Our Lord does not look so much at the greatness of our actions, nor even at their difficulty, but at the love with which we do them."

- Saint Thérèse of Lisieux

---

[518] Heilman, Fr. Richard, email to U.S. Grace Force members, December 26, 2020.

Even if you keep all of the aforementioned Habits of Holy Apostolic People, if you have not charity in your heart, that is not enough. Faith, Hope, Charity are key.

Jesus gave us the two great commandments, "Love the Lord your God with your whole heart, mind and soul" and "Love one another as you love yourself." Then on Holy Thursday at the Last Supper he upped the mandate, "Love one another as I have loved you." In other words, if you are not like Jesus and show charity to all, you will not be admitted to heaven.

So how are we to be charitable? By Faith, Hope and Acts of Charity. By the Spiritual and Corporal Works of Mercy. And by being joyful while we carry our crosses.

Faith. 'The most beautiful thing on this sinful earth is the Faith."
Hope. "Hope has two beautiful daughters; their names are Anger and Courage.
Anger at the way things are, and Courage to see that they do not remain as they are."
- Saint Augustine
Charity. "God is charity." (1John 4:8)

The Spiritual Works of Mercy: Admonish the sinner, instruct the ignorant, council the doubtful, comfort the afflicted, bear wrongs patiently, forgive offenses willingly, pray for the living and the dead.

The Corporal Works of Mercy: Feed the hungry, give drink to the thirsty, cloth the naked, shelter the homeless, visit the sick, ransom the captive (visit the imprisoned), bury the dead.

Be joyful as you are charitable. All of the saints are marked with an uncompromisable joy in times of trial, difficulty and pain. Every saint carried a heavy cross, but each was joyful. One of the hallmarks, something truly different, of the true Catholic is that they possess joy in all they do. Joy exists only where there is the presence of God. Followers of Christ, carry your cross with joy. Be Catholic.

9. Spiritual Reading (at least fifteen minutes a day)
⊙ Read the Bible, or other spiritual books and materials.

"Saint Jerome says that when we pray we speak to God, but when we read God speaks to us."[519]

"Saint Alphonus wrote that without good books and spiritual reading, it is morally impossible to save our souls."[520]

"Saint John Bosco said that only God knows the good that can come about by reading one good Catholic book."[521]

"Saint Augustine, Saint Ignatius of Loyola, and Saint John Colombino, all left the world and dedicated their lives completely to God, after reading a good spiritual book."[522]

10. Ask for the assistance and grace of the Holy Ghost
⊙ Deploy the Seven Gifts of the Holy Ghost

Wisdom, Understanding, Counsel, Fortitude, Knowledge, Piety, and Fear of the Lord

As the Holy Ghost infused those present at Pentecost with fire to spread the faith, we too through our confirmation have been commissioned as the *Milites Christi* (Soldiers of Christ) to convert all nations and bring souls to Christ through the Holy Catholic Church. Allow the Holy Ghost to use you as a means to make Christ and His Mother more known and more loved. The doctrine of the Seven Gifts of the Holy Ghost has a hallowed antiquity, yet they are subject to much benign neglect. Reverse that trend.

Saint Augustine's Prayer to the Holy Ghost
Breathe in me O Holy Spirit that my thoughts may all be holy;
Act in me O Holy Spirit that my works, too, may be holy;
Draw my heart O Holy Spirit that I love but what is holy;
Strengthen me O Holy Spirit to defend all that is holy;
Guard me then O Holy Spirit that I always may be holy.

Act of Consecration to the Holy Ghost
On my knees before the great multitude of heavenly witnesses I offer myself, soul and body to You, Eternal Spirit of God. I adore the brightness of Your purity, the unerring keenness of Your justice, and

---

[519] Saint Alphonsus de Liguori, *"Preparation for Death,"* 2.
[520] Ibid.
[521] Ibid.
[522] Ibid.

the might of Your love. You are the Strength and Light of my soul. In You I live and move and am. I desire never to grieve You by unfaithfulness to grace and I pray with all my heart to be kept from the smallest sin against You. Mercifully guard my every thought and grant that I may always watch for Your light, and listen to Your voice, and follow Your gracious inspirations. I cling to You and give myself to You and ask You, by Your compassion to watch over me in my weakness. Holding the pierced Feet of Jesus and looking at His Five Wounds, and trusting in His Precious Blood and adoring His opened Side and stricken Heart, I implore You, Adorable Spirit, Helper of my infirmity, to keep me in Your grace that I may never sin against You. Give me grace O Holy Spirit, Spirit of the Father and the Son to say to You always and everywhere, "Speak Lord for Your servant heareth." Amen.

Prayer for the Seven Gifts of the Holy Ghost

O Lord Jesus Christ Who, before ascending into heaven did promise to send the Holy Spirit to finish Your work in the souls of Your Apostles and Disciples, deign to grant the same Holy Spirit to me that He may perfect in my soul, the work of Your grace and Your love. Grant me the Spirit of Wisdom that I may despise the perishable things of this world and aspire only after the things that are eternal, the Spirit of Understanding to enlighten my mind with the light of Your divine truth, the Spirit on Counsel that I may ever choose the surest way of pleasing God and gaining heaven, the Spirit of Fortitude that I may bear my cross with You and that I may overcome with courage all the obstacles that oppose my salvation, the Spirit of Knowledge that I may know God and know myself and grow perfect in the science of the Saints, the Spirit of Piety that I may find the service of God sweet and amiable, and the Spirit of Fear that I may be filled with a loving reverence towards God and may dread in any way to displease Him. Mark me, dear Lord with the sign of Your true disciples, and animate me in all things with Your Spirit. Amen.

11. Fast regularly

While many understand the need for a Catholic to pray, most underestimate the value of Catholic fasting. Fasting is a way to unite your self-denial more closely to serving our Lord. One clear example of the need for fasting was when Jesus was attempting to drive a particularly intransigent demon from a soul; he remarked, "This kind cannot be driven out but by prayer and fasting." Fasting is one of the lesser known practices available to Catholics. We would do well to fast every Friday, and/or Wednesday, to further unite us to our Lord. More fasting, less feasting.

12. Speak the Holy Name of Jesus often

Recite often the holy name of "Jesus." When you do so, slightly bow your head as the angels and saints in heaven do at the utterance of his holy name. Many saints, including Saint Joan of Arc, died with one name on their lips, "Jesus." When we face temptation, call upon Jesus and say his holy name with love and confidence. Similarly, saying the names of the holy family is also a formidable practice, "Jesus, Mary, Joseph." Repeat this holy practice throughout your day, and even throughout the night should you have difficulty sleeping.

According to the Catholic Company, "The Feast of the Holy Name of Jesus is historically associated with the Feast of the Circumcision of Jesus. According to Jewish law, on the 8th day after his birth, a male child was circumcised and received his name, thus becoming a full member of God's covenant people. The name 'Jesus' means 'God Saves' and is the name that Saint Joseph was instructed by an angel to name the Divine Child, the sacred name before which "every knee should bend, in heaven and on earth and under the earth, and every tongue should confess that Jesus Christ is Lord, to the glory of God the Father" (Phil. 2:10-11). Devotion to the Most Holy Name of Jesus was popularized by Saint Bernardine of Siena in the 15th century, often symbolized by the monogram IHS (denoting the first three letters of the Greek spelling of Jesus' name)."[523]

13. Cultivate a devotion to the Sacred Heart of Jesus

One of the more popular Catholic devotions is to the Sacred Heart of Jesus. Although it was beloved in previous centuries, Jesus appeared to Saint Margaret Mary Alacoque in 1673, showing her a vision of the now-famous image of His Sacred Heart, surrounded by flames. He said to her: "My Heart is so full of love for men that It can no longer contain the flames of Its burning love. I must discover to men the treasures of My Heart and save them from perdition."

According to The Catholic Company, "Jesus gave St. Margaret Mary many promises associated with this devotion, and requested that a feast day in honor of His Sacred Heart be instituted on the Friday

---

[523] The Catholic Company, email, "Morning Offering," January 3, 2021.

after the Octave of Corpus Christi. In 1856, the Feast of the Sacred Heart was spread to the Universal Church, and in 1899 Pope Leo XIII solemnly consecrated all mankind to the Sacred Heart of Jesus, calling it "the great act" of his pontificate."[524]

Throughout history the great Catholic counter-revolutionaries placed themselves under the protection of the Sacred Heart: the Carlists in Spain, the Vendéens in France, and the Cristeros in Mexico. Let us do the same in our day.

Act of Consecration of the Human Race to the Sacred Heart of Jesus

Most Sweet Jesus, Redeemer of the human race, look down upon us humbly prostrate before Thine altar. We are Thine, and Thine we wish to be; but to be more surely united to Thee, behold each one of us freely consecrates ourselves today to Thy Most Sacred Heart.

Many indeed have never known Thee; Many too, despising Thy precepts, have rejected Thee. Have mercy on them all, most merciful Jesus, and draw them to Thy Sacred Heart. Be Thou King, O Lord, not only of the faithful children, who have never forsaken Thee, but also of the prodigal children, who have abandoned Thee; Grant that they may quickly return to their Father's house lest they die of wretchedness and hunger.

Be Thou King of those who are deceived by erroneous opinions, or whom discord keeps aloof, and call them back to the harbor of truth and unity of faith, so that there may be but one flock and one Shepherd.

Be Thou King of all those who are still involved in the darkness of idolatry or of Islamism, and refuse not to draw them into the light and kingdom of God. Turn Thine eyes of mercy towards the children of the race, once Thy chosen people: of old they called down upon themselves the Blood of the Savior; may it now descend upon them a laver of redemption and of life.

Grant, O Lord, to Thy Church assurance of freedom and immunity from harm; give peace and order to all nations, and make the earth resound from pole to pole with one cry; praise to the Divine

---

[524] The Catholic Company, email "Morning Offering," June 4, 2021.

Heart that wrought our salvation; To it be glory and honor forever. Amen.

14. Cultivate a devotion to the Immaculate Heart of Mary

Mary, venerated under the title "God-bearer," is also the Mother of all Christians.

> "As mariners are guided into port by the shining of a star, so Christians are guided to heaven by Mary."
>
> — Saint Thomas Aquinas

> "Men do not fear a powerful hostile army as the powers of hell fear the name and protection of Mary."
>
> — Saint Bonaventure

Sr. Lucia commented, "[Our Lady of Fatima] told me, as well as my cousins, that God is giving two last remedies to the world [for its salvation]: the Holy Rosary and devotion to the Immaculate Heart of Mary. And, being the last remedies, that is to say, they are the final ones, means that there will be no others."[525]

Archbishop Viganò on Dec. 15, 2020 wrote, "Blessed Mother will not deny us Her holy assistance; She will not leave us alone in the battle; She will not abandon those who have recourse to Her with trusting prayer in the moment in which the conflict is decisive and the confrontation is nearing an end. And to those who dare to challenge Heaven in the name of "Nothing will be the same again," we respond by invoking God with renewed fervor: "As it was in beginning, is now and ever shall be, world without end."[526]

Let us consider a story from the life of Saint John Bosco. A boy he knew was one day struck by a carriage and died. That night in a dream, Saint John Bosco saw the boy standing before the judgment seat of God. The sins of his life were placed on a scale and they outweighed the merits of his life. But then the saint saw three drops of water placed on the scale and the balance turned in the boy's favor. The three drops of water were the tears of Blessed Mother. She placed her tears to save the boy as throughout his life he had prayed Hail Mary three times every night. Let us all say our Rosaries, wear our scapulars,

---

[525] Sr Lucia, "Conversation with Fr. Augustin Fuentes," *Tradition in Action,* December 26, 1957. https://www.traditioninaction.org/HotTopics/g23ht_Interview.html

[526] Viganò, *Archbishop Carlo Maria,* "'We are not alone': A 2020 recap by Archbishop Viganò," *LifeSite News,* December 15, 2020.

and have increased devotion to our Blessed Mother. Let us humbly place ourselves at her feet, at her service, so that one day through her intercession we may be with her son in heaven for all eternity.

15. Make a Total Consecration to Jesus Through Mary. Renew frequently.

"He who does not have Mary as Mother, does not have God as Father."

- Saint Louis de Montfort

The "Total Consecration to Jesus Through Mary" was written by Saint Louis Marie de Montfort as a personal devotion in which a person prepares oneself spiritually to become consecrated to Jesus through Mary. Participants spend thirty-three days prior to the Consecration preparing themselves interiorly through spiritual readings from the Bible and other Catholic resources (such as True Devotion, Imitation of Christ, etc.) and praying a series of prayers.
Saint Louis de Montfort, pray for us.

16. Wear the Miraculous Medal.
Signal graces are available to all those who wear the miraculous medal.

From The Catholic Company, "On November 27, 1830, the Blessed Virgin Mary appeared to Saint Catherine Laboure in Paris, France and gave her a vision of an image, with instructions to strike the image, front and back, onto a medal. With this medal Our Lady promised that, "All those who wear it will receive great graces; these graces will be abundant for those who wear it with faith." The medal bears an image of Our Lady standing on the world, the serpent crushed under her feet, with arms extended and graces pouring forth from her hands. On the reverse is a cross surmounted by the letter 'M', and beneath it the side-by-side symbols of the Sacred Heart of Jesus and Immaculate Heart of Mary, all encircled by twelve stars. The medal symbolizes Mary's perfect spiritual union with Jesus' redemptive mission, and, consequently, her intercessory role in salvation history as the mediatrix of God's graces to mankind through her Son. The medal spread widely and became a source of many graces and miracles for its wearers, earning the name "Miraculous Medal." It is traditionally worn around the neck and has become a treasured sacramental of the

Catholic Church. Our Lady of the Miraculous Medal's feast day is November 27th."[527]

Fr. Rick Heilman wrote to his U.S. Grace Force, "As World War II raged around him in Poland, Saint Maximilian Kolbe fought for souls using a printing press and another "weapon" - the Miraculous Medal. Kolbe formed the Militia Immaculata in 1917 to "lead every individual with Mary to the most Sacred Heart of Jesus." He asked all Militia Immaculata members to wear the Miraculous Medal as a sign of their total consecration to Mary."[528]

Saints Catherine Laboure and Maximilian Kolbe, pray for us.

17. Use Holy Water

Holy water is a sacramental. It reminds us of our baptisms and is used in exorcisms. The *Catechism of the Catholic Church* teaches that sacramentals operate by means of the Church's intercession. We are told that, through the prayers of the Church, by the pious use of holy water, the intellect is enlightened, and the will moved from evil while being prompted to do good; and both body and mind are thereby strengthened and healed. Great to use holy water every day.

'I was once in an oratory, and [the devil] appeared to me in an abominable form at my left side. Because he spoke to me, I looked particularly at his mouth — which was most frightening. It seemed that a great flame, all bright without shadow, came forth from his body. He told me in a terrifying way that I had really freed myself from his hands but that he would catch me with them again. I was struck with great fear and blessed myself as best I could; he disappeared, but returned right away. This happened to me twice. I didn't know what to do. There was some holy water there, and I threw it in that direction; he never returned again … I often experience that there is nothing the devils flee from more - without returning - than holy water'."

- Saint Teresa of Avila, Doctor of the Church

18. Acknowledge the presence of your Holy Guardian Angel

From the moment of your conception, God assigned to you a Holy Guardian Angel. Your "bodyguard" has been with you all your days, and will be so until you stand before God in judgment. Saint Thomas

---

[527] *The Catholic Company,* email, November 27, 2020
[528] Heilman, Fr. Richard, email to U.S. Grace Force members, November 27, 2020.

Aquinas teaches us that "your Guardian Angel fights off demons for you." (*Summa Theologica*, Part 1, Question 113, Articles 2-6).[529]

According to Paul Thigpen in the *Manual for Spiritual Warfare*, "Christians long ago concluded that each individual human being has his or her own particular guardian angel. Though the Church has never defined the teaching about individual guardian angels, the "Catechism of the Catholic Church" sums up the matter this way, quoting Saint Basil: 'From infancy to death human life is surrounded by [the angels'] watchful care and intercession. Beside each believer stands an angel as protector and shepherd leading him to life.' In this light, we can turn to our guardian angels for help in spiritual warfare, especially to resist the temptations of the Enemy. Yet angels are more than guardians; they are also warriors."[530]

19. Go Weapons HOT (Humility, Obedience, Trust)

The following is an excerpt from the *Church Militant Field Manual: Special Forces Training for the Life in Christ* composed by Fr. Richard M. Heilman, "Go Weapons Hot" is a military command that means to make whatever preparations are necessary so that when you pull the trigger, something happens. In spiritual terms, are we using live ammunition or are we firing blanks? In other words, are we making the preparations necessary to ensure that our efforts to combat evil and rescue souls are ignited by the fire of the Holy Spirit? What are the preparations necessary so that "something (effective) happens" as we exercise the three offices of Christ in the war "against the principalities and powers, the rulers of this world of darkness, the evil spirits in regions above" (Eph 6:10-12)? The word "hot" ("Go Weapons Hot") gives us an excellent acronym for understanding how we are best positioned to receive the free offer of God's supernatural grace: H.O.T. = Humility, Obedience, Trust.

Humility: One of Blessed Mother's greatest virtues was her humility. The devil is proud. He hates humility. God loves humility. Saint Ignatius of Loyola said, "There is no doubt that God will never be wanting to us, provided that he finds in us that humility which makes us worthy of his gifts, the desire of possessing them, and the promptitude to co-operate industriously with the graces he gives us." Saint Vincent

[529] Beale, Stephen, "The 20 Things Guardian Angels Do For Us," *Catholic Exchange*, June 22, 2020.
[530] Thigpen, Paul, *"Manual For Spiritual Warfare,"* 30.

DePaul said, "The most powerful weapon to conquer the devil is humility."

Obedience: Saint Josemaría Escrivá wrote, "The power of obedience! The lake of Gennesareth had denied its fishes to Peter's nets. A whole night in vain. Then, obedient, he lowered his net again to the water and they caught 'a huge number of fish.' Believe me: the miracle is repeated each day."

Trust: Saint Alphonsus Liguori taught: "He who trusts himself is lost. He who trusts in God can do all things." The most important aspect of the Devotion of Divine Mercy is the need to trust in God's goodness. Jesus revealed to Saint Faustina that "the vessel with which souls receive abundant graces, and special favors, is confidence!" The confident, trusting soul is like a lightning rod for God's mercy and grace.[531]

20. Binding Prayers.

Binding prayers are particularly useful for breaking various forms of oppression by demons. By relinquishing what belongs to us into the hands of the Blessed Virgin, Satan cannot touch them. This is a strong prayer of protection on you and yours:

Consecration of One's Exterior Goods to the Blessed Virgin Mary

I; (Name), a faithless sinner, renew and ratify today in thy hands the vows of my Baptism; I renounce forever Satan, his pomps and works; and I give myself entirely to Jesus Christ, the Incarnate Wisdom, to carry my cross after Him all the days of my life, and to be more faithful to Him than I have ever been before. In the presence of all the heavenly court, I choose thee, O Mary, this day for my Mother and Mistress. Knowing that I have received rights over all my exterior goods by the promulgation of the Natural Law by the Divine Author, I deliver and consecrate to thee, as thy slave, all of my exterior goods, past, present and future; I relinquish into thy hands, my Heavenly Mother, all rights over my exterior goods, including our President, the fairness, honesty and accuracy of the outcome of the election, and our country and I retain for myself no right of disposing the goods that come to me but leave to thee the entire and full right of disposing of all that belongs to me, without exception, according to thy good pleasure, for the greater glory of God in time and in eternity. As I now interiorly relinquish what belongs to me exteriorly into thy hands, I entrust to thee the protection of those exterior goods against the evil one, so that, knowing that they now belong to thee, he cannot touch them. Receive, O good and pious Virgin, this little offering of what little is, in honor of, and in union with, that subjection which the

---

[531] Heilman, Fr. Richard, *Church Militant Field Manual*, n.p.

511

Eternal Wisdom deigned to have to Thy maternity; in homage to the power which both of You have over this poor sinner, and in thanksgiving for the privileges with which the Holy Trinity has favored thee. Trusting in the providential care of God the Father and thy maternal care, I have full confidence that thou wilst take care of me as to the necessities of this life and will not leave me forsaken. God the Father, increase my trust in Thy Son's Mother; Our Lady of Fair Love, give me perfect confidence in the providence of Thy Son. Amen.

21. The Heroic Act of Charity

The Heroic Act of Charity consists in offering to the Divine Majesty for the souls of purgatory all the satisfactions of our works and indulgences throughout life, as well as all the suffrages that shall be offered after our death. It is a laudable custom to make this offering through the hands of the Blessed Virgin, that she may apply our satisfactions as she may elect.

The Heroic Act is not a giving over of our merits; nor does it deprive us of the benefit of our prayers; but only a surrender of the remission of temporal punishment due to sin which would otherwise belong to us. On the contrary, those who make this act gain for themselves special merits and the particular blessing of God. It is well to renew it frequently. No special words are required, but the following words may be used:

> O Heavenly Father, in union with the merits of Jesus and Mary, I offer Thee, for the poor souls of Purgatory, all the works of satisfaction of my entire life, as well as all the satisfactory works that will be offered for me after my death. These works I surrender into the most-pure hands of the Immaculate Virgin Mary, that she may apply them to those souls which, according to her wisdom and motherly love, should be first delivered from Purgatory. Graciously accept, O my God, this offering, and may it win for me thy constant favor.*

* A plenary indulgence for the souls in purgatory is gained by those who make this act (1) whenever they go to Holy Communion, (2) whenever, for the souls in purgatory, they assist at Mass on a Monday, or, if this is not possible, on a Sunday. Condition: Visit a church and prayer therein for the pope. – Pius X, Feb. 20, 1907.

APPENDIX II

Messages to Various Denominations

Gertrude Elizabeth Margaret (G.E.M. or Elizabeth) Anscombe, an important twentieth century British analytic philosopher, was one of the most important women logicians of all time.

As an influential and committed Catholic, Miss Anscombe was an original thinker in the Catholic tradition; yet she held conservative views on sexual ethics including promoting chastity and traditional marriage. Miss Anscombe is perhaps best known for her statement, "Corrupt minds cannot be reasoned with." Her statement follows in the tradition of Saint Thomas Aquinas who said, "To one who has faith, no explanation is necessary. To one without faith, no explanation is possible."

If indeed it is futile to try to influence those with malformed or corrupted minds, or those who have no faith, why do Catholics make the effort? What's the point? Because Jesus told us to. He said, "Go, and make disciples of all nations." Note, Jesus did not say, "Go, and make disciples of all nations, except those who have corrupted minds or have little, or no, faith." We must not be indifferent. We must try. We must have zeal. We must succeed.

If this section appears harsh, please note that the moral law of the Catholic Church instructs the faithful to be candid when the salvation of souls is at stake.

People rationalize and justify their belonging to different factions/parishes within the Catholic Church (modernist to traditional, and everything in between) and different faiths other than Catholicism, or with some no faith at all. As Catholics, however, we believe that salvation is only possible to those who live, and die, as Catholics in good standing.

Fr. Richard Heilman has written, "When our loved ones are 'dead in sin,' they are not only separated from God, but they lose their desire to seek God. Some become so far removed from God that they find repulsive all things spiritual. So prayer, Holy Mass, spiritual reading, etc. all become boring and, to some, even detestable when they are dead inside: no Divine Life. Spiritually speaking, many have crossed into the dry and lifeless valley of the dry bones prophesied in Ezekiel 37. Dead in their sins, with the rigor mortis of indifference hardening their hearts, they are without the breath of the Spirit, destined for eternal damnation, unless some campaign of search and rescue is launched. They are, quite literally, caught behind enemy lines (imprisoned in their worldliness). Does our love, care, and concerns for them extend to their eternal salvation? Remember the Warrior Ethos: "I will never leave a fallen comrade!"[532]

Saint John Vianney wrote, "I can't stop praying for poor sinners who are on the road to hell. If they come to die in that state, they will be lost for all eternity. What a pity! We have to pray for sinners! Praying for sinners is the most beautiful and useful of prayers because the just are on the way to heaven, the souls of purgatory are sure to enter there, but the poor sinners will be lost forever."

If we attempt to convert others resting on our own intellect, strengths and powers of persuasion, we may meet with some successes here and there but most of us will be largely unsuccessful. If, however, we humble ourselves and reach out to others in conjunction with the Holy Ghost, then we are setting ourselves up for maximum success as is in accordance with the will of God. With God all things are possible. After the Holy Ghost descended on the twelve apostles who took Jesus's message to the four corners of the Earth, they had success with many persons and in many lands. We too must unite our efforts more fully with the Holy Ghost if we wish to have proper impact in this regard.

As our mad world is massively corrupted and evidence abounds that it lacks faith, what's the strategy? One strategy could be for those who are faithful Catholics, to kick it up a notch and live as Saints. For Catholics in the state of grace, Appendix I was a set of excellent tactics (i.e., spiritual practices) that should be further deployed/maximized without delay.

What about unfaithful Catholics, lapsed Catholics, non-Catholic Christians, non-Christians or those with no religious beliefs and moorings at all? Well, Appendix II is largely for you as it speaks to the

---

[532] Heilman, Fr. Richard, "Novena for Our Nation- Day 31," Church Militant Field Manual, n.p.

spectrum of religious positions held by people the world over. Before each particular group is addressed, let's briefly examine a few facts about American Catholics compiled by the Pew Research Center:

"The Catholic Church is larger than any other single religious institution in the United States, with over 17,000 parishes that serve a large and diverse population. In spite of its size and influence, the church in recent decades has faced a number of significant challenges, from a decline in membership to a shortage of priests to continuing revelations that some Catholic clergy sexually abused minors and (in many cases) that their superiors covered up these actions. There are roughly 51 million Catholic adults in the U.S., accounting for about one-fifth of the total U.S. adult population, according to Pew Research Center's "2014 Religious Landscape Study." That study found that the share of Americans who are Catholic declined from 24% in 2007 to 21% in 2014.

Catholicism has experienced a greater net loss due to religious switching than has any other religious tradition in the U.S. Overall, 13% of all U.S. adults are former Catholics – people who say they were raised in the faith, but now identify as religious "nones," as Protestants, or with another religion. By contrast, 2% of U.S. adults are converts to Catholicism – people who now identify as Catholic after having been raised in another religion (or no religion). This means that there are 6.5 former Catholics in the U.S. for every convert to the faith. No other religious group analyzed in the "2014 Religious Landscape Study" has experienced anything close to this ratio of losses to gains via religious switching."[533]

To say the least, it is clear that being a faithful Catholic in the U.S. is challenging these days. Of course, the same could be said for being Catholic in most likely every other nation in the world as well. Why has the Catholic Church been hemorrhaging not just membership but those who believe in the morals, teachings and Magisterium of our faith? If the Catholic Church is in decline, why would anyone want to join, or rejoin, what appears to be a failing entity? To take a step back, why is there so much confusion and division in not just the church, but the world? The demonic agenda has been ascendant for several decades, if not centuries (and, actually, since the Garden of Eden). The

---

[533] "2014 Religious Landscape Study," *Pew Research Center,* May 12, 2015.
https://www.pewforum.org/2015/05/12/americas-changing-religious-landscape/

moral state of our nation(s) confirms this. As Jesus instructed us to make disciples of all nations, we must do all we can to edify the faithful and instruct the ignorant.

Wherever you are among the following seven categories, may you be blessed with an illumination of conscience to repent, sin no more, and enter into the fullness of the Catholic faith. If you are participating in a non-Catholic faith, there may never be a better time than now to convert. Maybe those promptings to explore becoming Catholic will grow fainter and perhaps dissipate altogether for you. Act now. We are told that we will not know the day or the hour (of Christ's return).

Please accept what is offered in these pages in the spirit in which it was intended—solely out of concern for your soul and the desire for you to live your remaining days in communion with Our Lord, Jesus Christ and His bride the One, Holy, Apostolic, Roman Catholic Church, to live as a saint, and to one day be in heaven with God the Father, his heavenly court, and all the angels and saints, for all eternity.

To which group do you belong? Choose one, then skip ahead to read that section below:

1. To the faithful inside the Catholic Church
2. To the unfaithful inside the Catholic Church
3. To the lapsed Catholics
4. To the former Catholics who have converted to a non-Catholic faith
5. To the practicing Christians (who have never been Catholic)
6. To the non-Christians
7. To the atheists, paganists and satanists

1. To the faithful inside the Catholic Church

To those who believe in the true teachings of the Catholic Church and who could generally be considered to be living in conjunction with the dictates of the faith, when Jesus says to you, "I gave you the faith and you stayed true." Imagine that day and that time. Keep serving the Lord. Keep fighting.

To those who are lukewarm. Do not be complacent. Saint Philip Neri said when observing a murderer going to execution, "but for the grace of god, there goes I." Do what is necessary to increase in grace, holiness and charity.

Continue to stand with Blessed Mother and Saint John the Beloved at the foot of the cross. Know that if you are not being persecuted, be it large or small, you are not living the faith but being part of this secular world. Withstand the spiritual exhaustion. Stay close to our Lord and His Blessed Mother. Keep the commandments. Proclaim the truth, for God is Truth.

With God's grace to sustain us, and His mercy to forgive us, one day all faithful Catholics will be together in heaven. Speak up and defend our Savior, Our Divine Lord Jesus Christ. Rise up and enter deeper into the field of battle. Remember, short term pain for everlasting gain.

2. To the unfaithful inside the Catholic Church

To the Judas's inside the church. Repent. Make reparations. Go and sin no more. Put aside your pride. Be humble. Do not continue to be a lost soul doing evil while you think you are doing good. Jesus instructs us on this matter through the parable of the vine. A good tree will bear good fruit. A rotten tree will bear rotten fruit. What are the fruits of Vatican II? What are the fruits of modernism? What are the fruits of false Catholicism?

To those imposter Catholics who support positions that are contrary to the faith, those who do not believe in the true presence of Christ in the Eucharist, those who are Catholics-in-name-only (CINO), cultural Catholics, and those Catholics whose primary goal is to confuse others. Stop. Repent.

To the Modernist, Masonic, and Marxist (Liberation Theology/ Social Justice Warriors) influenced individuals inside the Church, the time to make things right is right now. To those who support abortion, contraception or other objectionable 'unions' or practices, and to those who do not correct Catholic elected officials from supporting abortion, penance. It's one thing to fall from grace; it's another thing to continue in manifest error. Enough. Repent.

To the cowardly bishops and priests, stop persecuting the faithful inside the church by actively working to distort and destroy church teachings. Start preaching the authentic gospel that brings souls to Christ, not the weak, wispy version you trot out on Sundays that only drive many away from the church. And stop advancing your personal and worldly agendas—those that are contrary to the faith. Your spiritual damage is unfathomable. As Our Blessed Lord said to the Pharisees, "How can any of you escape damnation?" Penance and repent.

Saint Bernadette Soubirous, in response to asking if she was afraid of the advancing Prussian army, said "no." When asked "well, what are you afraid of?" She replied, "I only fear bad Catholics." To the unfaithful Catholics inside the Church, stop being bad Catholics! You know who you are. God has given you so many internal locutions, stop neglecting His voice. Stop the scandalous sacrilege. Amend your ways. Seek only that which pleases God, not man. Shun earthly praise. There is still time. Have the humility of heart to amend your faith! No imposter Catholics! No bad Catholics!

This is made crystal clear for us in Matthew 7:21, "Not everyone who says to me, 'Lord, Lord,' will enter the kingdom of heaven, but only the one who does the will of my Father in heaven." Do God's will. Not your own. Not that of the Agenda. Many bishops and priests need to repent. If they do anything short of recommitting themselves to the full service of God, they should resign. For the sake of your immortal souls, get right with God.

3. To the Lapsed Catholics

Jesus tells us the parable of the vineyard. Those who stay attached to him will bear fruit. Those who do not stay attached to him will bear no fruit, will be cut down, and get thrown into the fire and burned. There are only two paths to choose, the narrow road or the broad road. We know that Jesus is literally talking about heaven and hell.

To those fallen away Catholics, it is time to reconnect to the vine. It is time to shake off the dust and come home. Get back on the team. We want you to reconnect with your spiritual brethren. The hardest part for you may be that first step. Take it. We will cheer on every step of your reconnecting with Christ and the Catholic Church. Please also know that your enemy will place obstacles large and small in your way. Ask Blessed Mother to help you crush the head of Satan and walk over, around and through any barriers put in your way. Call out to her and say, "Immaculate Conception, I wish to come home, intercede for me!" She will most assuredly hear you and assist you. Until such time as you are fully reunited with the Catholic Church, in humility, say the Angelus three times a day upon waking, at noon, and at night.

"Let us pray for those who have left the flock and rejected their faith. Jesus said that there will be great rejoicing in Heaven when one who was lost returns to Him." - Immaculate Conception Novena.

Saint Padre Pio exclaimed, "Keep close to the Catholic Church at all times, for the Church alone can give you true peace, since she alone possesses Jesus, the true Prince of Peace, in the Blessed Sacrament."

Imagine that shining moment when after you have made a contrite confession, attended your first valid Catholic Mass after who knows how long, and returned to your pew after having received Christ in the Most Blessed Eucharist, you kneel down and pray, "Thank you God the Father. Thank you, Blessed Mother. I am home. The prodigal son has returned home. Bless me all my days to remain true to you and to keep your commandments. My Jesus, mercy. My Jesus, thank you. My Jesus, please send me all the graces necessary to remain in a state of grace and never be separated from you again. I ask this through the Sacred Heart of Jesus and through the Immaculate Heart of Mary. My Father, may your will be done."

You can do it. You know you can. You know what must be done. Take the first step. We're praying for you.

4. To the former Catholics who have converted to a non-Catholic faith

Come back to the Catholic Church. If by chance you picked up this book and made it to this point, God's favor is upon you. Now you know. What you choose to do from this point forward is up to you. It's time to come home.

As with #3 (the Lapsed Catholics), Satan, the adversary, will tell you through his lies, guiles and deceits that, "As long as I am a good person, Jesus loves me, and I love him, it doesn't matter what Christian denomination I am. My place in heaven is secured given that I have accepted Jesus Christ as my Lord and Savior." Um, nope. It doesn't work like that. And deep down in your core you know that it doesn't work that way either. You know the Catholic Church teaches that unless you have Christ in you, you have no life in you, but that also means that to be in full union with God, you must also partake of valid Sacraments receiving ongoing valid confession and communion. Listen to your core, the silent voice of truth within you, and your guardian angel.

When Martin Luther issued his 95 Theses in 1517 and sparked the Protestant Reformation, he, with Satan's assistance, unleased untold chaos and calamity in the lives of billions of souls. Accordingly, Luther has a most notorious place in hell. The rationalization and spiritual contortion necessary to justify separating oneself from Holy Mother Church he foisted on malformed Christians the world over is lengthy and infamous. It is generally reported that there are 40,000 non-Catholic Christian churches in existence. Hundreds of millions of people have created a sophisticated theological, mental and physical infrastructure to justify living as Christians outside the Catholic Church. All do so at their own peril.

Many great saints have offered spiritual, intellectual, and philosophical arguments to point out the errors beginning with the Counter Reformation. If interested, research them. You know the information is there. Do not fear what you will learn. Seek only the truth.

Through a combination of pride and many other factors, non-Catholic Christians perpetuate their false notion that that are among the just. They are not. As Catholics we believe that there is no salvation outside the Catholic Church.

If you are a non-Catholic Christian reading these words, the devil is no doubt telling you right now to stop reading and put this book down. But for some reason you read on. Deep down in your soul, at this moment, know that your guardian angel has led you to precisely this moment to read this section. You know that in the near future when you wake up in the silence of the middle of the night and you speak with Jesus about converting back to the Catholic faith, his one true church, you already know what Jesus will tell you. Do not deny the grace he wishes to infuse into your soul to be strong. Revert to Catholicism.

Please know that good Catholics the world over pray each day, make sacrifices each day, for your conversion. Come home.

5. To the practicing Christians (who have never been Catholic)

To my many friends who live as good Protestants, please, for the sake of your eternal soul, convert to Catholicism. Know that your dedication to Christianity is admirable in numerous ways. Your zeal for Christ, your kindness, and love for God and country is without question.

I know you are trying to do His will, and I know Jesus loves you. In my soul I believe that you will have an easier time at your judgment than many modernist Catholics. Many of you have been abundantly blessed with good will and much natural virtue. In charity please know that as a faithful Catholic, I am obliged to state that your Protestant faith, however, in the most important regard is incomplete.

Luther erroneously said we are justified by faith alone. That the righteousness of Christ is imputed to us. It is an alien and external righteousness. No. Catholics believe that God desires to turn sinners into saints through His grace and mercy found in His church. End your protest against Catholicism. As Catholics, we only want the best for you. To obtain salvation, do so in full communion inside the Catholic Church.

Consider the case of the most famous convert in the history of England, and one of the most iconic in the world, the exemplar Anglican convert Saint Cardinal John Henry Newman, the patron saint of converts. On the day he was received into the Catholic Church, October 9, 1845, he sent out thirty letters to his closest friends, calling the Catholic Church, "the one true Fold of the Redeemer."534 He prayed for his Protestant friends to have their prejudices removed and, drawn by God's grace, the desire and will to become Catholic. After his conversion, he prayed that England would return to the Faith, and he worried seriously about the salvation of those outside the fold (as do I, hence this section and plea). In a letter of 1850, Newman states that he "considered other Christians to possess individual truths, but that these truths find their normal, natural, and complete form and home in the Catholic Church." In a letter to Francis William Newman on January 18, 1860, he wrote: "I think many a Protestant has principles in him which ought to make him a Catholic, if he followed them out."535

Follow out your Christian principles and let them lead you, too, to Catholicism. My comments to you are not those that most Catholics will share with you. Why? There are probably many reasons, but two are most likely. First, they themselves may not believe in the Catholic dogma that there is no salvation outside the Catholic Church. Second, they fear offending you. In Christian charity, both are deficient. Please note, the sole reason for my candor here is that I desire to not only be friends with you in this life, but also, God willing, in the next.

As it says in Colossians 4:2-6, "Let your speech always be gracious, seasoned with salt, so that you know how you should respond to each one." Pardon in advance if my message is a bit too salty for your taste, but read on, please.

If by chance you picked up this book and made it to this point, God's favor is upon you. Justification alone is insufficient to merit heaven. Grace, the sacraments, and charity are required for entrance to heaven and they are available through the one, true bride of Christ— Catholicism. To state this as charitably as possible, if Roman Catholicism is refused, so too may be heaven. Have you ever heard "outside the Church there is no salvation"?

---

534 "Saint of the Day- St. John Naumann," The Catholic Company, July 1, 2020.
535 Ibid.

The Catholic, and Eastern Orthodox, dogma of *"extra Ecclesiam nulla salus"* which means "outside the Church there is no salvation" was first introduced by Saint Cyprian of Carthage in the third century. This held true into the nineteenth century when the Church recognized "extraordinary means" of salvation (i.e., baptism by blood or baptism of desire).536 Post Vatican II, the Church's teaching on this dogma splintered into various factions and depending on whom one would query (modernist or traditionalist), you would receive varying degrees of adherence or rejection of the principle.537

The 1992 Catechism of the Catholic Church sought to address this dogmatic principle by commenting "all salvation comes from Christ the Head through the Church which is His Body."538 The Catholic Church also teaches that the doctrine does not mean that everyone who is not visibly within the Church is necessarily damned in case of inculpable ignorance.539

Which brings us to the distinction between invincible and vincible ignorance. Although the concept of ignorance (not knowing Christianity) goes back to the third century, and Saint Thomas Aquinas addressed it in his Summa Theologica, it was not as well known until Pope Pius IX published his allocution *Singulari Quadam* (December 9, 1854) and his encyclicals *Singulari Quidem* (March 17, 1856) and *Quanto Conficiamur Moerore* (August 10, 1863). Invincible refers to persons (such as pagans and infants) who are ignorant because they have not yet had an opportunity to hear the Catholic message. Or to state it another way, "Invincible ignorance excuses from all culpability. An action committed in ignorance of the law prohibiting it, or of the facts of the case, is not a voluntary act."540 On the other hand, "it is culpable to remain willfully ignorant of matters that one is obligated to

---

536 Eric Sammons, "The Ongoing Debate Over Extra *Ecclesiam Nulla Salus*," Crisis Magazine, May 21, 2021.
https://www.crisismagazine.com/2021/the-ongoing-debate-over-extra-ecclesiam-nulla-salus
537 Ibid.
538 Catechism of the Catholic Church, 846-848, 851.
539 *"Extra Ecclesiam nulla salus,"* Wikipedia.
https://en.wikipedia.org/wiki/Extra_Ecclesiam_nulla_salus
540 George Hayward Joyce, "Invincible Ignorance," ed. James Hastings, John A. Selbie, and Louis H. Gray, Encyclopædia of Religion and Ethics (Edinburgh; New York: T. & T. Clark; Charles Scribner's Sons, 1908–1926), 403.

know (vincible ignorance). In this case the individual is morally responsible for their ignorance, and for the acts resulting from it."541

Whether one is able to claim invincible or vincible ignorance, God, of course, can make exceptions for the soul who lives a most unique life, and perhaps lays down their life for another, or some other circumstance, but faithful, traditional Catholics believe that it is exceedingly rare, and it is the exception and not the rule.

The division between Catholic and Protestant was, and still is, of the devil. Rest assured he is at the root of your separation from the one, true faith. In Psalm 119:2 it says, "O Lord deliver my soul from wicked lips, and a deceived tongue." From this day forth, be not deceived.

Psalm 126:1 "Unless the Lord built the house, they labor in vain that built it." Jesus built the Catholic Church. Jesus did not build a single Protestant Church. Not one. Each Protestant denomination was started by a person corrupted by original sin. Saint Elizabeth Ann Seton said, "I will go peaceably and firmly to the Catholic Church: for if Faith is so important to our salvation, I will seek it where true Faith first began, seek it among those who received it from God Himself."

Dr. Taylor Marshall, a former Anglican priest and convert to Catholicism, spoke about the Catholic Church being "the way." "The Catholic Church, or any of its representatives, is in error when it says Catholicism is just one of many good choices in the buffet line of religions in the world. Up until a few generations ago the Church was unequivocal in its position that outside of the Catholic Church there is no salvation. It is not a holy desire to tell all worshipers that their non-Catholic religion will help them gain eternal life. Indifferentism and ecumenism is wrong. Being Catholic is special. Being Catholic is the way. John 3 and 4. The Church is the vessel of salvation. The church is Noah's ark. If you stay in the boat you have a chance of salvation. If you jump out of the boat, you will drown (damnation). I Peter and II Peter. If God would have wanted diversity of religions, why would Jesus pray that all may be one? Catholic means universal."542

---

541 Ibid.
542 Marshall, Taylor. Episode 418.

If after reading this you remain a non-Catholic Christian, what will Jesus say to you at your particular judgment? For the sake of argument, let's say the Catholic Church is dead wrong about *extra Ecclesiam nulla salus* ("outside the Church there is no salvation.") If that's the case, then your immortal soul could be OK. What if the Catholic Church is right? Is that gamble, proposition, possibility something you are willing to accept, and to risk?

What you choose to do from this point forward is up to you. God has blessed your life to have been introduced to Jesus and the Bible. Time to take it one step further, and become Catholic. Discover the fullness of the faith. Enter into the true fold of the Redeemer. And do not seek out a phony, faux, liberal, social justice syrup that is predominant in the mainstream Catholic church these days. Seek out a Mass and parish that embraces the authentic, timeless, truth of Catholic tradition.

Do not be deterred by the perceived, and actual mess the church hierarchy makes of things at times. Do not let this twig trip you up. The scandals they are aware of and do not address on their watch are immoral and criminal. God will judge them most severely. Despite the weaknesses and shortcomings of the church leadership on Earth, they are our only conduit to the leadership in heaven, The Holy Trinity. The Church Militant, the faithful Catholics here on Earth, must struggle through all the bad along with the good. It's part of carrying the cross in this life that we are not blessed with the best men to lead us through this vale of tears. So be it. No matter what we remain in the barque of Peter, the Catholic Church.

If this speaks to you in the least, there is still time! Step into the fulness of the light. Come to The Truth. Seek The Truth. Embrace The Truth. Experience what it is to live in a state of sanctifying grace. Come home to the Catholic Church. Convert! Do not delay. You know not the day or the hour.

Know that your conversion will require great humility. Being a saint, being heroic, requires great humility. Your conversion to Catholicism may very well feel like an act of heroism to you given the degree of difficulty, perceived and actual, it would entail. Do it anyway.

Keep your eye on the goal—eternal life with God. Give yourself wholly to God. To say "I am weak," is an opportunity to appeal to God for grace and strength to convert. Know that a combination of God's grace and your humility will conquer the fears, apprehension, excuses, and evil, that stands in your way. Jesus said Saint Maria Faustina Kowalska, "Know that a pure soul is humble." God's grace will be there. Will your humility?

Saint Cardinal John Henry Newman became a Catholic at immense personal cost. Should you convert, the cost of conversion among family members, friends, business opportunities, etc., will also likely be quite high. There is a simple answer, not an easy answer. In faithful courage Saint Newman said, "I put away reputation and honor, and influence, and power, for my praise and strength shall be in you. Enable me to carry out what I profess."543 What will you profess? The devil, most assuredly, will not make it easy. Can there be any valid temporary inconveniences or disruptions of this life when weighed against eternity?

6. To Non-Christians

If by chance you picked up this book and made it to this point. God's favor is upon you. Now you know. What you choose to do from this point forward is up to you.

Jesus said to him, "I am the way, and the truth, and the life. No one comes to the Father except through me." John 14:6

In Mark 16:16 Christ stated, "He who believes and is baptized shall be saved, but he who does not believe shall be condemned."

Again, we turn to Pius IX's writing on "invincible ignorance" (see also #5 "To the practicing Christians (who have never been Catholic.") That doctrine stated that someone may be permitted into heaven without being Catholic. There were extremely rare instances when this would apply, but Pius IX did say it was possible.

If you have made it to this point in the book, you have heard the Catholic message and are familiar enough with Catholicism. If you

---

543 Newman, John Henry, *Everyday Meditations*, 135.

choose to remain against Christ in this life, you will most likely have no chance of remaining with him in heaven in the next life. If you do not desire him, he does not force you to, but know that there will be damnable consequences.

Jesus and His Catholic Church are necessary for eternal salvation. Convert. The gospel tells us that there will be "weeping and gnashing of teeth." Other quotes to consider:

"And this is the testimony: God gave us eternal life, and this life is in his Son. Whoever has the Son has life; whoever does not have the Son of God does not have life." 1 John 5:11

"Blessed are they who hear the word of God and keep it." - Jesus

C.S. Lewis in Mere Christianity "If you are thinking of becoming a Christian, I warn you, you are embarking on something which is going to take the whole of you, brains and all. But, fortunately, it works the other way around. Anyone who is honestly trying to be a Christian will soon find his intelligence being sharpened: one of the reasons why it needs no special education to be a Christian is that Christianity is an education itself."[544]

7. To Atheists, Pagans, Satanists
If by chance you picked up this book and made it to this point. God's favor is upon you. Now you know. What you choose to do from this point forward is up to you.

"And this is the testimony: God gave us eternal life, and this life is in his Son. Whoever has the Son has life; whoever does not have the Son of God does not have life." - 1 John 5:11

"Saint Paul writes, "The unspiritual man does not receive the gifts of the Spirit of God, for they are foolishness to him, and he is not able to understand them because they are spiritually discerned" (1 Cor 2:14). This is the person who acts only by using his or her human faculties (intelligence and will) and who therefore can be wise only in

---

[544] C. S. Lewis, p. 78

the things of the world. He remains superficial and worldly. This is a heart that has hardened to the presence of God."

Jesus and His Catholic Church are necessary for eternal salvation. Convert.

SELECT BIBLIOGRAPHY

de Bergamo, Padre Gaetano Maria. *Humility of Heart.* Founding Fathers Films Publishing, Mandeville, LA, 2017.

Butler, Rev. Alban. *The Lives of the Fathers, Martyrs and Other Principal Saints.* The Catholic Press, Inc. Chicago, IL 1959.

Carroll, Warren. *The Guillotine and the Cross.* Trinity Communications. Manassas, VA. 1986.

Catechism of the Catholic Church. Doubleday. New York, NY. 1994.

Cruz, Joan Carrol. *Secular Saints: 250 Canonized and Beatified Lay Men, Women and Children.* TAN Books and Publishers, Inc. Rockford, IL. 1989.

Davies, Michael. *The Second Vatican Council and Religious Liberty.* The Neumann Press. Long Prairie, MN. 1992.

Delaney, John. *Dictionary of Saints.* Doubleday. New York, NY. 1980.

Laux, Fr. John. *Church History: A Complete History of the Catholic Church to the Present Day.* TAN Books and Publishers, Inc. Rockford, IL. 1989.

Liguori, St. Alphonsus. *The 12 Steps to Holiness and Salvation.* TAN Books and Publishers, Inc. Rockford, IL. 1986.

Loido, J. Urteaga. *Man, The Saint.* Roman Catholic Books. Fort Collins, CO. 1959.

Lord, Bob and Penny. *Saints and Other Powerful Women in the Church.* Journeys of Faith. Westlake Village, CA. 1989.

Marshall, Taylor R. *Infiltration: The Plot to Destroy the Church From Within.* Crisis Publications (imprint of Sophia Institute Press) Manchester, NH. 2019.

Mioni, Jr., Anthony J., Editor *The Popes Against Modern Errors: 16 Papal Documents.* TAN Books, Charlotte, NC 2012.

Neill, Thomas P. and Schmandt, Raymond H. *History of the Catholic Church.* The Bruce Publishing Company, Milwaukee, WI. 1957

Radecki, Fr. Francisco. *Vatican II Exposed as Counterfeit Catholicism,* St. Joseph's Media, 2019.

Sandefer, Jeff and Sirico, Rev. Robert. *A Field Guide for the Hero's Journey.* Acton Institute. Grand Rapids, MI. 2012.

Trese, Leo. *You Are Called To Greatness.* Fides Publishers, Inc. Notre Dame, IN. 1964.

Made in the USA
Coppell, TX
26 July 2022

80442246R00299